Summary of FORTRAN 77 Statements

STATEMENT	DESCRIPTION (Page in Text)	EXAMPLE OF USAGE
ENTRY	Specifies entry point in a subprogram (784)	ENTRY POLY (X)
EQUIVALENCE	Establishes sharing of memory locations by different variables in same program unit (779)	EQUIVALENCE(X,Y), (ALPHA,A,T(3))
EXTERNAL	Specifies externally defined subprograms that may be used as arguments (369)	EXTERNAL F, QUAD
FORMAT	Defines a list of descriptors (257)	20 FORMAT (1X, 'ROOTS ARE', 2F8.3)
FUNCTION	Heading for a function subprogram (318)	FUNCTION AVE(X, N)
GO TO	Unconditionally transfers control to a specified statement (201)	GO TO 100
IMPLICIT	Used to establish a naming convention (771)	IMPLICIT REAL (L, N-Z), INTEGER (A-K)
INQUIRE	Determines properties of a file or of its connection to a unit number (722)	INQUIRE (EXIST = FLAG, NAME = FNAME)
INTEGER	Specifies integer type (46)	INTEGER X, CLASS, TABLE(10,20)
INTRINSIC	Specifies intrinsic functions that may be used as arguments (373)	INTRINSIC SIN, DSQRT
LOGICAL	Specifies logical type (160)	LOGICAL P, Q, TABLE(4,6)
Logical IF	Executes or bypasses a statement, depending on the truth or falsity of a logical expression (129)	IF (DISC .GT. 0) DISC = SQRT(DISC)
OPEN	Opens a file (287, 718)	OPEN(UNIT = 12, FILE = FNAME, STATUS = 'OLD')
PARAMETER	Defines parameters (48)	PARAMETER (LIM = 100, RATE = 1.5)
PAUSE	Interrupts program execution, program may be restarted (771)	PAUSE PAUSE 'PROGRAM PAUSE'
PRINT	Output statement (67–68, 256)	PRINT *, 'X = ',X PRINT * PRINT '(1X, 3I7)', M, N, M + N
PROGRAM	Program heading (72)	PROGRAM WAGES
READ	Input statement (68, 271, 284, 724)	READ *, ALPHA, BETA READ '(15, F7.2)', NUM, Z READ (12, *, END = 20) HOURS, RATE
REAL	Specifies real type (46)	REAL NUM, GAMMA, MAT(10,10)
RETURN	Returns control from subprogram to calling program unit (319, 786)	RETURN RETURN 2
REWIND	Positions file at initial point (290, 728)	REWIND 12
SAVE	Saves values of local variables in a subprogram for later references (421)	SAVE X, Y, NUM SAVE
Statement function	Function defined within a program unit by a single statement (330)	F(X,Y) = X**2 + Y**2
STOP	Terminates execution (770)	STOP STOP 'PROGRAM HALTS'
SUBROUTINE	Heading for subroutine subprogram (394)	SUBROUTINE CONVER (U, V, RHO, PHI)

WHILE, DO WHILE	First statement of a WHILE loop; not in standard FORTRAN 77 (204)	WHILE X > 0 DO DO WHILE X > 0
		   PRINT *, X PRINT *, X
		   X = X − .1 X = X − .1
		END WHILE END DO

WRITE	Output statement (67–68, 282, 729)	WRITE (*,*) A, B, C WRITE (12, '(1X, 316)') N1, N2, N3

FORTRAN 77
for Engineers and Scientists

with an Introduction to Fortran 90

FOURTH EDITION

Larry Nyhoff
CALVIN COLLEGE

Sanford Leestma
CALVIN COLLEGE

Prentice Hall, Upper Saddle River, New Jersey 07458

Library of Congress Cataloging-in-Publication Data

NYHOFF, LARRY R.
   FORTRAN 77 for engineers and scientists with an introduction to
  FORTRAN 90 / Larry Nyhoff, Sanford Leestma.—4th ed.
     p. cm.
   Includes index.
   ISBN 0-13-363003-X
    1. FORTRAN 77 (Computer program language) I. Leestma, Sanford.
  II. Title.
  QA76.73.F25N9 1996
  005.13'3—dc20   95-35426
                                      CIP

Acquisitions Editor: Alan Apt
Developmental Editor: Sondra Chavez
Managing Editor: Laura Steele
Creative Director: Paula Maylahn
Art Director: Amy Rosen
Assistant to Art Director: Rod Hernandez
Production Manager: Judy Winthrop
Interior Designer: Sheree Goodman
Cover Designer: Heather Scott
Cover Photo: Science Museum/Science and Society Picture Library
Manufacturing Buyer: Donna Sullivan
Copy Editor: Kristen Cassereau

Printed in the United States of America

10 9 8 7 6 5 4 3 2 1

ISBN 0-13-363003-X

PRENTICE HALL INTERNATIONAL (UK) LIMITED, *London*
PRENTICE HALL OF AUSTRALIA PTY. LIMITED, *Sydney*
PRENTICE HALL CANADA INC., *Toronto*
PRENTICE HALL HISPANOAMERICANA, S.A., *Mexico*
PRENTICE HALL OF INDIA PRIVATE LIMITED, *New Delhi*
PRENTICE HALL OF JAPAN, INC., *Tokyo*
SIMON & SCHUSTER ASIA PTE., LTD., *Singapore*
EDITORA PRENTICE HALL DO BRASIL, LTDA., *Rio de Janeiro*

Brief Table
of Contents

Preface   xxiii

1   Introduction to Computing   1

2   Basic Fortran   40

3   Selective Execution   118

4   Repetitive Execution   176

5   Input/Output   252

6   Programming with Functions   314

7   Programming with Subroutines   394

8   One-Dimensional Arrays   472

9   MultiDimensional Arrays   562

10   Other Data Types   628

11   File Processing   718

12   Additional FORTRAN Features   764

13   New Directions in Fortran 90   790

Appendixes   816

Index of Programming Problems   868

Index   874

Contents

Preface   xxiii

| 1 | INTRODUCTION TO COMPUTING | 2 |

1.1 Computing Systems   3

Early Computing Devices   3
Electronic Computers   6
System Software   8
Applications   10

1.2 Computer Organization   10

Computing Systems   10
Memory Organization   12
Quick Quiz 1.2   14
Exercises 1.2   15

1.3 Programming and Problem Solving — An Example   16

PROBLEM: Radioactive Decay   16
Step 1: Problem Analysis and Specification   16
Step 2: Data Organization and Algorithm Design   17
Step 3: Program Coding   20
Step 4: Execution and Testing   22

1.4 Programming and Problem Solving — An Overview   23

Step 1: Problem Analysis and Specification   23
Step 2: Data Organization and Algorithm Design   24
Step 3: Program Coding   28
Step 4: Execution and Testing   32
Step 5: Maintenance   34

Quick Quiz 1.4   34
Exercises 1.4   35
Chapter Review   36
Summary   36
FORTRAN Summary   37

2   BASIC FORTRAN   40

2.1   Data Types + Algorithms = Programs   42

2.2   Data Types, Constants, and Variables   43

Integers   43
Reals   43
Character Strings   44
Identifiers   45
Variables   46
Named Constants: The PARAMETER Statement   48
Variable Initialization: The DATA Statement   50
Quick Quiz 2.2   51
Exercises 2.2   52

2.3   Arithmetic Operations and Functions   54

Operations   54
Functions   57
Quick Quiz 2.3   59
Exercises 2.3   59

2.4   The Assignment Statement   60

Quick Quiz 2.4   64
Exercises 2.4   65

2.5   Input/Output   66

List-Directed Output   67
List-Directed Input   68

2.6   Program Composition and Format   72

Program Composition   72
Program Format   74
Quick Quiz 2.6   75

2.7   Application: Temperature Conversion   76
PROBLEM   76
Solution   76

2.8   Application: Circuits with Parallel Resistors   82
PROBLEM: Radioactive Decay   82
Solution   82

2.9   Application: Concentration of an Acid Bath   85
PROBLEM   85
Solution   86

*2.10   Introduction to File Input/Output   91
Opening Files   92
File I/O   92
Example: The Projectile Problem Revisited   93

*2.11   Arithmetic Errors   94
Overflow/Underflow Errors   94
Roundoff Errors   95
Chapter Review   96
Summary   96
FORTRAN Summary   97
Programming Pointers   101
Program Style and Design   102
Potential Problems   103
Programming Problems   106
Fortran 90   112
New Features   112
Examples   115

3   SELECTIVE EXECUTION   118

3.1   Logical Expressions   121
Simple Logical Expressions   121
Compound Logical Expressions   123
Quick Quiz 3.1   126
Exercises 3.1   126

3.2   Simple Selection Structures: The IF Statement   128

Simple IF Statement   128
General Form of the IF Construct   129
Example: Quadratic Equations   131
The Effect of Roundoff Error   134

3.3   Application: Pollution Index   136

PROBLEM   136
Solution   136

3.4   Compound Selection Structures: Nested IFs and IF-ELSE IF Constructs   141

Nested IF Constructs   141
Example: Pay Calculation   142
IF-ELSE IF Construct   146
Example: Modified Pollution Index Problem   148

3.5   Application: Fluid Flow in a Pipe   151

PROBLEM   151
Solution   153
Quick Quiz 3.5   156
Exercises 3.5   158

3.6   The LOGICAL Data Type   160

3.7   Application: Logical Circuits   161

PROBLEM   161
Solution   162
Quick Quiz 3.7   165
Exercises 3.7   166
Chapter Review   168
Summary   168
FORTRAN Summary   168
Programming Pointers   171
Program Style and Design   171
Potential Problems   172
Programming Problems   173
Fortran 90   176
Features   176
Example   178

4   REPETITIVE EXECUTION   180

4.1   Repetition Structure: DO Loops   182
Example: A Table of Points on a Curve   185
Example: A Multiplication Table   187
Quick Quiz 4.1   189
Exercises 4.1   190

4.2   Application: Depreciation Tables   191
PROBLEM   191
Solution   192

4.3   The While Repetition Structure   197
Example: Summation   197
Sentinel-Controlled While Loops   200

4.4   Implementing While Loops   200
In Standard FORTRAN   201
*The DO WHILE Statement   204

4.5   Application: Mean Time to Failure   205
PROBLEM   205
Solution   206

4.6   A Posttest Repetition Structure   213
Example: Temperature Conversions   213

4.7   Program Testing and Debugging Techniques   216
An Example: Range of Noise Levels   216
Trace Tables   219
Debugging   220
Modifying and Testing the Program   220
Summary   223
Quick Quiz 4.7   224
Exercises 4.7   225

4.8   Application: Least-Squares Line   230
PROBLEM   230
Solution   231

Exercises 4.8   235
Chapter Review   236
Summary   236
FORTRAN Summary   237
Programming Pointers   239
Program Style and Design   239
Potential Problems   240
Programming Problems   243
Fortran 90   250
Features   250
Example   252

5   INPUT/OUTPUT   254

5.1   Formatted Output   256
Control Characters   258
Integer Output — The I Descriptor   259
Real Output — The F Descriptor   261
Real Output — The E Descriptor   262
Character Output   263
Positional Descriptors — X and T   264
Repeating Groups of Format Descriptors   265
The Slash (/) Descriptor   266
Scanning the Format   267

5.2   Example: Printing Tables of Computed Values   269

5.3   Formatted Input   271
Integer Input   272
Real Input   273
Character Input   275
Skipping Input Characters   276
Multiple Input Lines   277
Quick Quiz 5.3   278
Exercises 5.3   279

5.4   The WRITE Statement and the General READ Statement   282
The WRITE Statement   282
The General READ Statement   284

5.5   File Processing   285
Opening Files   286
Closing Files   288
File Input/Output   288
The IOSTAT = Clause   289
The END = Clause   290
File-Positioning Statements   290
Quick Quiz 5.5   291

5.6   Application: Temperature and Volume Readings   292
PROBLEM   292
Solution   292
A Refinement Using Run-Time Formatting   297
Chapter Review   300
Summary   300
FORTRAN Summary   301
Programming Pointers   306
Program Style and Design   306
Potential Problems   306
Programming Problems   308
Fortran 90   311
Features   311
Example   312

6   PROGRAMMING WITH FUNCTIONS   314

6.1   Functions   315
Library Functions   315
Function Subprograms   317
Example: Voltage Across a Capacitor   319
Argument Association   321
Example: Function of Several Variables   322
Example: Pollution Index   323
Local Identifiers — The Factorial Function   324
Example: Poisson Probability Function   325
Statement Functions   330
Quick Quiz 6.1   332
Exercises 6.1   333

6.2   **Application: Beam Deflection   334**
Modular Programming   334
PROBLEM   334
Solution   335

6.3   **Application: Root Finding, Integration, and Differential Equations   344**
Root Finding   344
Numerical Integration   348
Numerical Solutions of Differential Equations   352

6.4   **Application: Road Construction   357**
PROBLEM   357
Solution   357
Exercises 6.4   361

6.5   **Functions as Arguments   369**
The `EXTERNAL` Statement   369
The `INTRINSIC` Statement   372
Chapter Review   374
Summary   374
FORTRAN Summary   374
Programming Pointers   375
Program Style and Design   375
Potential Problems   376
Programming Problems   377
Fortran 90   385
Features   385
Examples   388

7   PROGRAMMING WITH SUBROUTINES   392

7.1   **Subroutine Subprograms   393**
Example: Displaying an Angle in Degrees   395
Example: Displaying an Angle in Degrees-Minutes-Seconds Format   398
Example of a Subroutine that Returns Values: Converting Coordinates   402

Argument Association   406
Subprograms as Arguments   408
Quick Quiz 7.1   408
Exercises 7.1   409

7.2   Application: Designing a Coin Dispenser   410
PROBLEM   410
Soluton   410

7.3   Random Numbers and Simulation   416
Random Number Generators   417
Example: Dice Tossing   417
The SAVE Statement   421
Normal Distributions   421

7.4   Application: Shielding a Nuclear Reactor   422
PROBLEM   422
Solution   422

7.5   Application: Checking Academic Standing   428
Top-Down Design   428
PROBLEM   428
Solution   428

7.6   The COMMON Statement   450
Blank Common   451
Named Common   454
Chapter Review   456
Summary   456
FORTRAN Summary   456
Programming Pointers   458
Program Style and Design   458
Potential Problems   459
Programming Problems   460
Fortran 90   466
Features   466
Example   468

8   ONE-DIMENSIONAL ARRAYS   470

8.1   Introduction to Arrays and Subscripted Variables   472
PROBLEM   472
Arrays   475
Array Declarations   479

8.2   Input/Output of Arrays   481
Input/Output Using a DO Loop   481
Input/Output Using the Array Name   485
Input/Output Using Implied DO Loops   487
Quick Quiz 8.2   490
Exercises 8.2   490

8.3   Example: Processing a List of Failure Times   492

8.4   Application: Average Corn Yields   495
PROBLEM   495
Solution   496

8.5   Array Processing   499
Assigning Values to Arrays   500
Arrays as Arguments   501
Arrays in Common   505
Quick Quiz 8.5   505
Exercises 8.5   507

8.6   Application: Quality Control   509
PROBLEM   509
Solution   509
A Graphical Solution   513

8.7   Example: Vector Processing   516
Exercises 8.7   519

8.8   Sorting   520
Simple Selection Sort   520
Bubble Sort   523

8.9   Application: Analyzing Construction Costs   525

PROBLEM   525
Solution   525
Exercises 8.9   529

8.10   Searching   530

Linear Search   530
Binary Search   531

8.11   Application: Searching a Chemistry Database   534

PROBLEM   534
Solution   535
Chapter Review   541
Summary   541
FORTRAN Summary   541
Programming Pointers   542
Program Style and Design   542
Potential Problems   542
Programming Problems   545
Fortran 90   553
Features   553
Examples   557

9   MULTIDIMENSIONAL ARRAYS   560

9.1   Introduction to Multidimensional Arrays and Multiply Subscripted Variables   561

9.2   Processing Multidimensional Arrays   564

Input/Output Using DO Loops   566
Input/Output Using the Array Name   569
Input/Output Using Implied DO Loops   570
Multidimensional Arrays as Arguments   575
Multidimensional Arrays in Common   576
Quick Quiz 9.2   577
Exercises 9.2   578

9.3   Application: Pollution Table   581
PROBLEM   581
Solution   582

**9.4   Application: Oceanographic
Data Analysis   586**
PROBLEM   586
Solution   587

9.5   Example: Matrix Processing   593
Exercises 9.5   595

9.6   Application: Electrical Networks   597
PROBLEM   597
Solution   597
Exercises 9.6   605
Chapter Review   608
Summary   608
FORTRAN Summary   609
Programming Pointers   609
Program Style and Design   609
Potential Problems   610
Programming Problems   613
Fortran 90   619
Features   619
Examples   623

10   OTHER DATA TYPES   626

10.1 The DOUBLE PRECISION **Data Type   628**
The DOUBLE PRECISION Type Statement   629
Double-Precision Values   630
Double-Precision I/O — The D Descriptor   631
Double-Precision Functions   632

**10.2 Application: Ill-Conditioned
Linear Systems   633**
PROBLEM   633
Solution   633

10.3 The COMPLEX Data Type   638
Representation of Complex Numbers   638
The COMPLEX Type Statement   639
Operations on Complex Numbers   639
Complex Functions   642
Complex I/O   643
Example: Solving Equations   644

10.4 Application: A-C Circuits   646
PROBLEM   646
Solution   646
Quick Quiz 10.4   649
Exercises 10.4   650

10.5 The CHARACTER Data Type   651
Character Operations   655
Character Input/Output   655

10.6 Application: Finite-State Machines   658
Exercises 10.6   664

10.7 Character Functions   665
The INDEX and LEN Functions   665
Example: Text Editing   667
Character Comparison   673
The LLT, LLE, LGT, and LGE Functions   674
The ICHAR and CHAR Functions   674
Quick Quiz 10.7   675
Exercises 10.7   676

10.8 Application: Data Security   678
PROBLEM   678
Solutions   679
Exercises 10.8   686

10.9 Application: Computer Graphics   686
Example 1: Scatter Plots   688
Example 2: Density Plots and Level Curves   693
Chapter Review   700

Summary   700
FORTRAN Summary   700
Programming Pointers   702
Program Style and Design   702
Potential Problems   702
Programming Problems   705
Fortran 90   711
Features   711
Examples   713

11   FILE PROCESSING   716

11.1 The OPEN, CLOSE, and INQUIRE Statements   718
Opening Files   718
Closing Files   721
The INQUIRE Statement   722

11.2 File Input/Output and Positioning   724
File Input   724
Example 1: Direct-Access Inventory File   726
File-Positioning Statements   728
File Output   729
Example 2: Merging Files   729
Example 3: External Sorting: Mergesort   734
Unformatted Files   736
Internal Files   736

11.3 Application: Pharmacy Inventory   738
PROBLEM   738
Solution   738
Quick Quiz 11.3   750
Exercises 11.3   751
Chapter Review   751
Summary   751
FORTRAN Summary   751
Programming Problems   757
Fortran 90   759

Features   759
Example   760

12   ADDITIONAL FORTRAN FEATURES   766

12.1 Miscellaneous Input/Output Topics   763
The G Descriptor   763
The L Descriptor   764
Scale Factors   765
The BN and BZ Descriptors   767
The S, SP, and SS Descriptors   768
The H Descriptor   768
The TL and TR Descriptors   769
List-Directed Input   769

12.2 The STOP and PAUSE Statements   770

12.3 The IMPLICIT Statement   771

12.4 Other Control Statements: Arithmetic IF, Computed GO TO, Assigned GO TO   772
The Arithmetic IF Statement   772
The Computed GO TO Statement   774
The Assigned GO TO Statement   774

12.5 More About COMMON and Block Data Subprograms   775
Other COMMON Features   775
Block Data Subprograms   778

12.6 The EQUIVALENCE Statement   779

12.7 Alternate Entries and Returns   784
The ENTRY Statement   784
Alternate Returns   785
Fortran 90   786

13   NEW DIRECTIONS IN FORTRAN 90   788

13.1 Modules   789

13.2 Derived Data Types   796

13.3 Pointers and Linked Structures   803

APPENDIXES

A	ASCII and EBCDIC	814
B	Sample Files	822
C	Program Composition	835
D	Generic and Specific Names of Functions	837
E	Internal Representation	841
F	Answers to Quick Quizzes	851

Index of Programming Problems   868

Index   874

Preface

*F*ORTRAN, now nearly forty years old, is a language that is used throughout the world to write programs for solving problems in science and engineering. Since its creation in the late 1950s, it has undergone a number of modifications that have made it a very powerful yet easy-to-use language. These modifications, however, led to a proliferation of different dialects of FORTRAN, which hindered program portability. Since some uniformity was desirable, the American National Standards Institute (ANSI) published the first FORTRAN standard in 1966. In the years following, extensions to this standard version of FORTRAN were developed, some of which came into common use. It became apparent that many of these features should be incorporated into a new standard. This updated ANSI FORTRAN standard (ANSI X3.9-1978), popularly known as FORTRAN 77, is the basis for this text. A new standard has recently been finalized and the version of Fortran—Fortran 90—specified by it has many new features. In special Fortran 90 sections at the chapter ends and in Chapter 13 we describe some of these additions to the Fortran language.

Key Features

This book gives a complete and accurate presentation of FORTRAN 77 and also strives to be more than a programming manual. It reflects the fact that the main reason for learning a programming language is to use the computer to solve problems. A key emphasis of this text is problem-solving. It contains:

- 50 complete programming examples
- 28 are special applications that illustrate problem solving methodolgy

Examples of these applications include the following:

- Beam deflection
- Quality control
- Computer graphics
- Electrical networks
- Road construction
- Searching a chemistry database

In addition, we have concentrated on making this the most effective FORTRAN 77 and Fortran 90 learning tool. We include:

- 300 Quick quizzes
- 500 Written exercises
- 230 Programming problems relevant to engineering and science
- Fortan 90 sections at the end of each chapter that teach the important new features of the Fortran 90 language and include programming examples

The text also emphasizes the importance of good structure and style in programs. In addition to describing these concepts in general, each of the examples and applications is intended to demonstrate good algorithm design and programming style. At the end of each chapter a Programming Pointers section summarizes the main points regarding structure and style. These sections also emphasize language features presented and warn against some problems that beginning programmers may experience.

Like the first three editions, this text is intended for a first course in computing and assumes no previous experience with computers. It provides a comprehensive description of FORTRAN 77 and an introduction to Fortran 90, and most of the material presented can be covered in a one-semester course. Each chapter progresses from the simpler features to the more complex ones; the more difficult material thus appears in the last sections of the chapters. More advanced and/or esoteric features are described in starred sections near the end of each chapter or in Chapter 12 and may be omitted without loss of continuity.

New to the Fourth Edition

Since publication of the first three editions, we have received a number of constructive comments and suggestions for improvements from instructors and students and we have incorporated many of these into the fourth edition. The significant changes in the new edition include the following:

- Topics have been rearranged and some introductory material has been condensed or moved so that the study of FORTRAN begins earlier.
- New Application sections illustrate problem-solving methodology.
- The presentation of subprograms has been expanded and improved.
- More examples and exercises of an engineering and/or scientific nature have been added.
- Sample programs have been added to the descriptions of Fortran 90 features.
- Chapter summaries have been added at the end of each chapter. These include summaries of the FORTRAN features described in that chapter.
- A new design makes the text more attractive and readable.
- Boxed displays make it easy to find descriptions of the basic FORTRAN statements and constructs.

Supplementary Materials

A number of supplementary materials are available from the publisher. These include the following:

- An instructor's manual containing solutions to exercises and many of the programming problems and sample test questions.
- Disks containing solutions to programming exercises.
- Sample programs and data files referenced in the text can be downloaded from
    ftp to ftp.prenhall.com
    login as anonymous
    use your e-mail address as the password
    cd to pub/esm/nyhoff/fortran77

Acknowledgments

We express our sincere appreciation to all who helped in any way in the preparation of this text, especially our editor Alan Apt, managing editor Laura Steele, development editor Sondra Chavez, and production editor Judy Winthrop. We also thank Larry Genalo for reviewing the material and suggesting several new examples and exercises. And, of course, we must once again thank our wives Shar and Marge, whose love and understanding have kept us going through another year of textbook writing, and to our kids and grandkids, Jeff and Dawn, Jim, Greg and Julie, Tom and Joan, Rebecca and Megan, Michelle, Sandy and Lori, and Michael, for not complaining about the times that their needs and wants were slighted because of our busyness. Above all, we give thanks to God for giving us the opportunity, ability, and stamina to prepare this text.

LARRY NYHOFF
SANFORD LEESTMA

FORTRAN 77
for Engineers
and Scientists

with an **Introduction to Fortran 90**

1

Introduction to Computing

I wish these calculations had been executed by steam.

CHARLES BABBAGE

One machine can do the work of fifty ordinary men. No machine can do the work of one extraordinary man.

ELBERT HUBBARD

If we really understand the problem, the answer will come out of it, because the answer is not separate from the problem.

KRISHNAMURTI

It's the only job I can think of where I get to be both an engineer and an artist. There's an incredible, rigorous, technical element to it, which I like because you have to do very precise thinking. On the other hand, it has a wildly creative side where the boundaries of imagination are the only real limitation.

ANDY HERTZFELD

C H A P T E R   C O N T E N T S

1.1   Computing Systems

1.2   Computer Organization

1.3   Programming and Problem Solving — An Example

1.4   Programming and Problem Solving — An Overview

Chapter Review

*T*he modern electronic computer is one of the most important products of the twentieth century. It is an essential tool in many areas, including business, industry, government, science, and education; indeed, it has touched nearly every aspect of our lives. The impact of the twentieth-century information revolution brought about by the development of high-speed computing systems has been nearly as widespread as the impact of the nineteenth-century industrial revolution.

In this chapter we describe computing systems, their main components, and how information is stored in them. We also begin our study of programming and problem solving by developing a FORTRAN program to solve a simple problem.

1.1 COMPUTING SYSTEMS

There are two important concepts that led to computers as we know them today: the **mechanization of arithmetic** and the **stored program** for the automatic control of computations. We will briefly describe some devices that have implemented these concepts.

Early Computing Devices

One of the earliest mechanical devices used in ancient civilizations to assist in computation is the abacus. Although its exact origin is unknown, it was used by the Chinese perhaps 3000 to 4000 years ago. In the early 1600s, the English mathematician William Oughtred invented the slide rule (Figure 1.1 a), which used logarithms for rapid approximate computations. In 1642, the young French mathematician Blaise Pascal invented one of the first mechanical adding machines, a device that used a series of ten-toothed wheels connected so that numbers could be added or subtracted by moving the wheels. In the 1670s, the German mathematician Gottfried Wilhelm von Leibniz improved on the design of Pascal's machine so that it could also perform multiplication

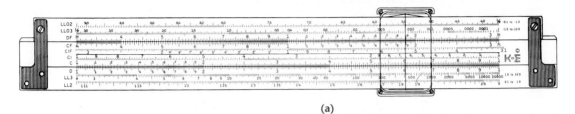

(a)

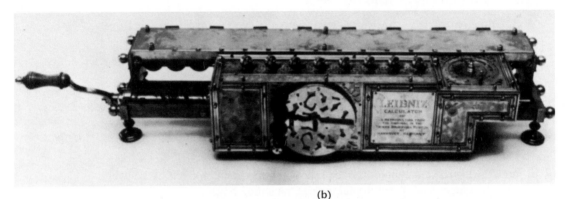

(b)

Figure 1.1

(a) A slide rule. (b) Leibniz's calculator. (Courtesy of IBM)

and division (Figure 1.1 b). A number of other mechanical calculators followed that further refined Pascal's and Leibniz's designs. By the end of the nineteenth century, these calculators had become important tools in science, business, and commerce.

The second fundamental idea in the development of computers is that of a stored program to control the calculations. One early example of an automatically controlled device is the weaving loom invented by the Frenchman Joseph Marie Jacquard. This automatic loom used punched cards to position threads for the weaving process. A collection of these cards made up a program that directed the loom.

The two fundamental concepts of mechanical calculation and stored program control were combined by the English mathematician Charles Babbage, who began work in 1822 on a machine called the Difference Engine (Figure 1.2 a). This machine was designed to compute polynomials for the preparation of mathematical tables. With the assistance of his associate Ada Augusta, considered by some to be the first programmer, Babbage later designed a more sophisticated machine called the Analytical Engine (Figure 1.2 b). This machine had several special-purpose components that were intended to work together: a "mill" to carry out the arithmetic computations; a "store" for storing data and intermediate results; and other components for input and output of information. The operation of this machine was to be fully automatic, controlled by programs stored on punched cards, an idea based on Jacquard's earlier work. Although Babbage's machines could not be built during his lifetime because technology was not sufficiently advanced, they are considered by many to be the forerunners of the modern computer.

(a)

(b)

Figure 1.2

(a) Babbage's
Difference
Engine.
(b) Babbage's
Analytical
Engine.
(Courtesy of
IBM)

A related development in the United States was the census bureau's use of punched-card systems designed by Herman Hollerith to help compile the 1890 census. These systems used electrical sensors to interpret the information stored on the punched cards. In 1896, Hollerith left the census bureau and formed his own tabulating company, which in 1924 became the International Business Machines Corporation (IBM).

The development of computing devices continued at a rapid pace in the United States. Some of the pioneers in this effort were Howard Aiken, John Atanasoff, J. P. Eckert, J. W. Mauchly, and John von Neumann. Repeating much of the work of Babbage, Aiken designed a system consisting of several mechanical calculators working together. This work, which was supported by IBM, led to the invention in 1944 of the electromechanical Mark I computer. This machine is the best-known computer built before 1945 and may be regarded as the first realization of Babbage's Analytical Engine.

Electronic Computers

The first fully electronic computer was developed by John Atanasoff at Iowa State University. With the help of his assistant, Clifford Berry, he built a prototype in 1939 and completed the first working model in 1942. The best known of the early electronic computers was the ENIAC (Electronic Numerical Integrator and Computer), constructed in 1946 by J. P. Eckert and J. W. Mauchly at the Moore School of Electrical Engineering of the University of Pennsylvania (Figure 1.3). This extremely large machine contained over 18,000 vacuum tubes and 1500 relays and nearly filled a room 20 feet by 40 feet in size. It could multiply numbers approximately one thousand times faster than the Mark I could, but it was quite limited in its applications and was used primarily by the Army Ordnance Department to calculate firing tables and trajectories for various types of shells. Eckert and Mauchly later left the University of Pennsylvania to form the Eckert-Mauchly Computer Corporation, which built the UNIVAC (Universal Automatic Computer), the first commercially available computer designed for both scientific and business applications.

The instructions, or program, that controlled the ENIAC's operation were entered into the machine by rewiring some parts of the computer's circuits. This complicated process was very time-consuming, sometimes taking several people several days, and during this time, the computer was idle. In other early computers, the instructions were stored outside the machine on punched cards or some other medium and were transferred into the machine one at a time for interpretation and execution. A new scheme, developed by Princeton mathematician John von Neumann and others, used internally stored commands. The advantages of this stored program concept are that internally stored instructions can be processed more rapidly and, more important, that they can be modified by the computer itself while computations are taking place.

The actual physical components used in constructing a computer system are its **hardware.** Several generations of computers can be identified by the type of hardware used. The ENIAC and UNIVAC are examples of **first-generation** computers, which are characterized by their extensive use of vacuum tubes (Figure 1.4 (a)). Advances in electronics brought changes in computing systems, and in 1958, IBM introduced the first of the **second-generation** computers, the IBM 7090. These computers were built between

Figure 1.3

ENIAC.
(Courtesy of
Sperry
Corporation)

1959 and 1965 and used transistors in place of vacuum tubes (Figure 1.4 (b)). Consequently, these computers were smaller, required less power, generated far less heat, and were more reliable than their predecessors. They were also less expensive, as illustrated by the introduction of the first **minicomputer** in 1963, the PDP-8, which sold for $18,000, in contrast with earlier computers whose six-digit price tags limited their sales to large companies. The **third-generation** computers that followed used integrated circuits and introduced new techniques for better system utilization, such as multiprogramming and time-sharing. The IBM System/360 introduced in 1964 is commonly accepted as the first of this generation of computers. Computers of the 1980s and 1990s, called **fourth-generation** computers, use very large-scale integrated circuits (VLSI) on silicon chips and other microelectronic advances to shrink their size and cost still more while enlarging their capability (Figure 1.4 (c)). One of the pioneers in the development of transistors was Robert Noyce, a cofounder of the Intel Corporation, which introduced the 4004 microprocessor in 1971.

Microprocessors like the Intel 4004 made possible the development of the personal computers that are so common today. One of the most popular personal computers was the Apple II constructed in a makeshift facility in a garage and introduced in 1977 by Steven Jobs and Steve Wozniak, then 21 and 26 years old, respectively. They founded the Apple Computer Company, one of the major manufacturers of microcomputers today. This was followed in 1981 by the first of IBM's PCs, which have become the microcomputer standard in business and industry.

Continued advances in technology have produced a wide array of computer systems, ranging from portable palmtop and notebook computers to powerful desktop machines such as workstations, to supercomputers capable of performing billions of

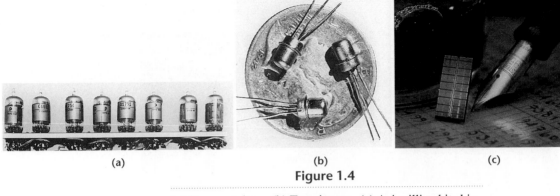

(a)   (b)   (c)

Figure 1.4

(a) Vacuum tubes.   (b) Transistors.   (c) A 4 million bit chip.
(Photos courtesy of (a) IBM, (b) Bettmann, (c) IBM.)

operations each second, and to massively parallel computers that use a large number of microprocessors working together in parallel to solve large problems (Figure 1.5). Someone once noted that if progress in the automotive industry had been as rapid as in computer technology since 1960, today's automobile would have an engine that is less than 0.1 inch in length, would get 120,000 miles to a gallon of gas, would have a top speed of 240,000 miles per hour, and would cost $4.00.

System Software

The stored-program concept was a significant improvement over manual programming methods, but early computers still were difficult to use because of the complex coding schemes required for the representation of programs and data. Consequently, in addition to improved hardware, computer manufacturers began to develop collections of programs known as **system software,** which make computers easier to use. One of the more important advances in this area was the development of **operating systems,** which allocate storage for programs and data and carry out many other supervisory functions. In particular, it acts as an interface between the user and the machine. The operating system interprets commands given by the user and then directs the appropriate system software and hardware to carry them out. One of the most commonly used operating systems is UNIX, developed in 1971 by Ken Thompson and Dennis Ritchie at AT&T's Bell Laboratories. It is the only operating system that has been implemented on computers ranging from microcomputers to supercomputers. The most popular operating system for personal computers has for many years been MS-DOS, which was developed in 1981 by Bill Gates, founder of the Microsoft Corporation. More recently, **graphical user interfaces (GUI)**, such as MIT's X Window System for UNIX-based machines, Microsoft's Windows for personal computers, and Apple's Macintosh interface, have been devised to provide a simpler and more intuitive interface between humans and computers.

Another important advance in system software was the development of **high-level languages,** which allow users to write programs in a language similar to natural language. A program written in a high-level language is known as a **source program.** For most high-level languages, the instructions that make up a source program must be translated into **machine language,** that is, the language used directly by a particular computer for all its calculations and processing. This machine language program is

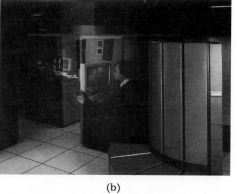

Figure 1.5

(a) A Sun workstation. (b) A Cray supercomputer. (Photos courtesy of (a) Sun Microsystems Inc. (b) Boeing Corporation.)

(a)   (b)

called an **object program.** The programs that translate source programs into object programs are called **compilers.**

One of the first high-level languages to gain widespread acceptance was **FORTRAN** (**FOR**mula **TRAN**slation), which was developed for the IBM 704 computer by **John Backus** and a team of 13 other programmers at IBM over a 3-year period (1954–1957). The group's first report on the completed language included the following comments:

> The programmer attended a one-day course on FORTRAN and spent some more time referring to the manual. He then programmed the job in four hours, using 47 FORTRAN statements. These were compiled by the 704 in six minutes, producing about 1000 instructions. He ran the program and found the output incorrect. He studied the output and was able to localize his error in a FORTRAN statement he had written. He rewrote the offending statement, recompiled, and found that the resulting program was correct. He estimated that it might have taken three days to code the job by hand, plus an unknown time to debug it, and that no appreciable increase in speed of execution would have been achieved thereby.

As computer hardware improved, the FORTRAN language also was refined and extended. By 1962 it had undergone its fourth revision, and in 1977 the fifth revision appeared, known as FORTRAN 77. More recently, an extensive revision known as Fortran 90 was prepared and approved, and compilers to support this new version of FORTRAN have been developed.[1] The American National Standards Institute (ANSI), which establishes standards for programming languages, decided that during the transition period there should be two American standards for FORTRAN, FORTRAN 77 and Fortran 90, while International Standards Organization (ISO) groups decided that Fortran 90 will be the only international FORTRAN standard. Many other high-level languages have also been developed—BASIC, COBOL, Pascal, Modula-2, C, C++, and Ada, to name a few. As with FORTRAN, there has been a considerable effort to standardize several of these languages so that programs written in these higher-level languages are **portable**, which means they can be processed on several different machines with little or no alteration.

---

[1] "FORTRAN" has traditionally been written in all upper case. The new ANSI standard, however, specifies "Fortran" as the official spelling for Fortran 90.

Applications

As the development of system software made computers increasingly easier to use, applications were developed in many areas, and in particular, in science and engineering. These applications are far too many to enumerate, and those pictured in Figure 1.6 are intended only to show their diversity. In this text we will describe problems in many such areas and develop computer programs to solve these problems.

1.2 COMPUTER ORGANIZATION

In the preceding section, we noted that Babbage designed his Analytical Engine as a system of several separate components, each with its own particular function. This general scheme was incorporated in many later computers and is, in fact, a common feature of most modern computers. In this section we briefly describe the major components of a modern computing system and how program instructions and data are stored and processed.

Computing Systems

The heart of any computing system is its **central processing unit,** or **CPU.** The CPU controls the operation of the entire system, performs the arithmetic and logic operations, and stores and retrieves instructions and data. The instructions and data are stored in a high-speed **memory unit**, and the **control unit** fetches these instructions from memory, decodes them, and directs the system to execute the operations indicated by the instructions. Those operations that are arithmetical or logical in nature are carried out using the circuits of the **arithmetic-logic unit (ALU)** of the CPU.

The memory unit typically consists of several components. One of these components is used to store the instructions and data of the programs being executed and has many names, including **internal**, **main**, **primary**, and **random access memory (RAM)**. A second component is a set of special high-speed memory locations within the CPU, called **registers**. Values that are stored in registers can typically be accessed thousands of times faster than can values stored in RAM.

One problem with both RAM and registers is that they are **volatile** memory components, that is, information stored in these components is lost if the power to the computing system is shut off (either intentionally or accidentally). **Read-only memory (ROM)** is **nonvolatile** memory used to store critical information such as start-up instructions which is too important to lose.

To provide long-term storage of programs and data, most computing systems also

Figure 1.6 (see next page)   (a) CAD design of an automobile. (b) Automated insertion of components on electronic engine control modules. (c) Robot-controlled Chrysler automobile assembly plant. (d) National Weather Service satellite imagery. (e) Oil drilling computerized tracking model. (f) Northern Arizona University observatory. (g) Flight deck of the space shuttle Columbia. (Photos courtesy of (a) (b) Ford Motor Company, (c) Cincinnati Milacron, (d) Tony Stone Images, (e)(f) Uniphoto Picture Agency, (g) The Stock Market.)

(a)

(b)

(c)

(d)

(e)

(f)

(g)

11

include memory components called **external** or **auxiliary** or **secondary memory.** Common forms of this type of memory are magnetic disks (such as hard disks and floppy disks) and magnetic tapes. These **peripheral devices** provide long-term storage for large collections of data, even if power is lost. However, the time required to access data stored on such devices can be thousands of times greater than the access time for data stored in RAM.

Other peripherals are used to transmit instructions, data, and computed results between the user and the CPU. These are the **input/output devices**, which have a variety of forms, such as terminals, scanners, voice input devices, printers, and plotters. Their function is to convert information from an external form understandable to the user to a form that can be processed by the computer system, and vice versa.

Figure 1.7 shows the relationship between the components in a computer system.

Memory Organization

The devices that comprise the memory unit of a computer are two-state devices. If one of the states is interpreted as 0 and the other as 1, then it is natural to use a **binary scheme,** using only the two binary digits (**bits**) 0 and 1 to represent information in a computer. These two-state devices are organized into groups of eight called **bytes.** Memory is commonly measured in bytes, and a block of $2^{10} = 1024$ bytes is called **1 K** of memory. Thus, one **megabyte** ($= 1024$ K) of memory consists of $1024 \times 2^{10} = 2^{10} \times 2^{10} = 2^{20} = 1,048,576$ bytes, or, equivalently, $2^{20} \times 2^3 = 2^{23} = 8,384,608$ bits.

Bytes are typically grouped together into **words**. The number of bits in a word is equal to the number of bits in a CPU register. The word size thus varies from one computer to another, but common word sizes are 16 bits ($= 2$ bytes) and 32 bits ($= 4$ bytes). Associated with each word or byte is an **address** that can be used to directly access that word or byte. This makes it possible for the control unit to store information in a specific memory location and then to retrieve it later. The details of how various types of data are represented in a binary form and stored in a computer's memory are described in Appendix E.

Program instructions for processing data must also be stored in memory. They must be instructions that the machine can execute and they must be expressed in a form that the machine can understand, that is, they must be written in the machine language for that machine. These instructions consists of two parts: (1) a numeric **opcode**, which represents a basic machine operation such as load, multiply, add, and store; and (2) the address of the **operand.** Like all information stored in memory, these instructions must be represented in a binary form.

As an example, suppose that values have been stored in three memory locations with addresses 1024, 1025, and 1026, and that we want to multiply the first two values, add the third, and store the result in a fourth memory location 1027. To perform this computation, the following instructions must be executed:

1. Fetch the contents of memory location 1024 and load it into a register in the ALU.
2. Fetch the contents of memory location 1025 and compute the product of this value and the value in the register.
3. Fetch the contents of memory location 1026 and add this value to the value in the register.

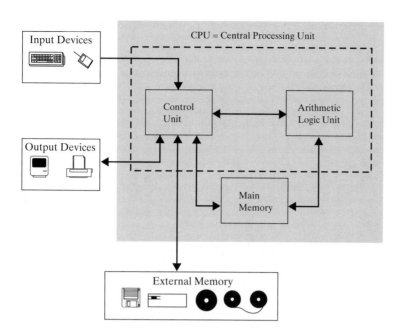

Figure 1.7

Major
components of
a computing
system.

4. Store the contents of the register in memory location 1027.

If the opcodes for load, store, add, and multiply are 16, 17, 35, and 36, respectively, these four instructions might be written in machine language as follows:

1. 00010000000000000000010000000000
2. 00100100000000000000010000000001
3. 00100011000000000000010000000010
4. 00010001000000000000010000000011

    opcode   operand

These instructions can then be stored in four (consecutive) memory locations. When the program is executed, the control unit will fetch each of these instructions, decode it to determine the operation and the address of the operand, fetch the operand, and then perform the required operation, using the ALU if necessary.

Programs for early computers had to be written in such machine language. Later it became possible to write programs in **assembly language,** which uses mnemonics (names) in place of numeric opcodes and variable names in place of numeric addresses. For example, the preceding sequence of instructions might be written in assembly language as

1. LOAD A
2. MULT B
3. ADD C
4. STORE X

An **assembler,** which is part of the system software, translates such assembly language instructions into machine language.

Today, most programs are written in a high-level language such as FORTRAN, and a **compiler** translates each statement in a program into a sequence of basic machine (or assembly) language instructions.

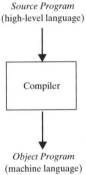

Source Program
(high-level language)

Compiler

Object Program
(machine language)

For example, for the preceding problem, the programmer could write the FORTRAN statement

$$X = A * B + C$$

which instructs the computer to multiply the values of A and B, add the value of C, and assign the resulting value to X. The compiler then translates this statement into the sequence of four machine (or assembly) language instructions considered earlier.

Quick Quiz 1.2

1. What are two important concepts in the early history of computation?

2. Match each item in the first column with the associated item in the second column.

_____ John von Neumann	A. early high-level language
_____ Charles Babbage	B. first commercially available computer
_____ Blaise Pascal	C. graphical user interface
_____ Herman Hollerith	D. stored program concept
_____ input/output device	E. Difference Engine
_____ first generation	F. designer of FORTRAN language
_____ bit	G. central processing unit
_____ compiler	H. language translator
_____ object program	I. binary digit
_____ Joseph Jacquard	J. electronic computer
_____ Ada Augusta	K. 1024
_____ source program	L. random access memory
_____ John Backus	M. written in high-level language

_____ byte	N. read-only memory
_____ UNIVAC	O. punched card
_____ UNIX	P. automatic loom
_____ CPU	Q. vacuum tubes
_____ FORTRAN	R. adding machine
_____ ENIAC	S. operating system
_____ K	T. written in machine language
_____ GUI	U. group of binary digits
_____ RAM	V. terminals, readers, printers
_____ ROM	W. first programmer

Exercises 1.2

For Exercises 1–12, describe the importance of the person to the history of computing:

1. Charles Babbage
2. Blaise Pascal
3. John von Neumann
4. Herman Hollerith
5. Joseph Jacquard
6. Gottfried Wilhelm von Leibniz
7. John Atanasoff
8. Steven Jobs
9. Robert Noyce
10. J. P. Eckert
11. John Backus
12. Steve Wozniak

For Exercises 13–17, describe the importance of the device to the history of computing:

13. ENIAC
14. Analytical Engine
15. Jacquard loom
16. UNIVAC
17. Mark I
18. Distinguish the four different generations of computers.

Briefly define each of the terms in Exercises 19–31:

19. stored-program concept
20. FORTRAN
21. UNIX
22. MS-DOS
23. source program
24. object program
25. machine language
26. assembly language
27. bit
28. byte
29. word
30. K

31. megabyte

32. What are the main functions of an operating system?

33. What are the main functions of a compiler?

34. What are the main functions of an assembler?

1.3 PROGRAMMING AND PROBLEM SOLVING— AN EXAMPLE

A computer **program** is a sequence of instructions that must be followed to solve a particular problem, and the main reason that people learn programming is so that they can use the computer as a problem-solving tool. At least four steps or stages can be identified in the program-development process:

1. Problem analysis and specification

2. Data organization and algorithm design

3. Program coding

4. Execution and testing

In this section we illustrate these steps with an example. This is a very simple example so that we can emphasize the main ideas at each stage without getting lost in a maze of details.

PROBLEM: RADIOACTIVE DECAY

Problem:
Radioactive Decay

Nick Nuke is a nuclear physicist at Dispatch University and is conducting research with the radioactive element polonium. The half-life of polonium is 140 days, which means that because of radioactive decay the amount of polonium that remains after 140 days is one-half of the original amount. Nick would like to know how much polonium will remain after running his experiment for 180 days if 10 milligrams are present initially.

Step 1:
Problem Analysis and Specification

The first stage in solving this problem is to analyze the problem and formulate a precise **specification** of it. This specification must include a description of the problem's **input**—what information is given and which items are important in solving the problem—and its **output**—what information must be produced to solve the problem. Input and output are two major parts of the problem's specification. Formulating the specification for this problem is easy:

Input	Output
Initial amount: 10 mg Half-life: 140 days Time period: 180 days	Amount remaining

The other given items of information—the physicist's name, the name of the university, the name of the particular radioactive element—are not relevant (at least not to this problem) and can be ignored.

Determining the amount of polonium remaining can be done by hand or by using a calculator and does not warrant the development of a computer program for its solution. A program written to solve this particular problem would probably be used just once; because if the experiment runs longer, or if there is a different initial amount of polonium, or if a radioactive element with a different half-life is used, we have a new problem requiring the development of a new program. This is obviously a waste of effort, since it is clear that each such problem is a special case of the more general problem of finding the residual amount of a radioactive element at any time, given any initial amount and the half-life for that element. Thus a program that solves the general problem can be used in a variety of situations and is consequently more useful than one designed for solving only the original special problem.

Generalization is therefore an important aspect of problem analysis**.** The effort involved in later phases of the problem-solving process demands that the program eventually developed be sufficiently flexible, that it solve not only the given specific problem but also related problems of the same kind with little, if any, modification required. In this example, therefore, the specification of the problem would be better formulated in general terms:

Input	Output
Initial amount Half-life Time period	Amount remaining

Step 2:
Data Organization and Algorithm Design

Now that we have a precise specification of the problem, we are ready to begin designing a plan for its solution. This plan has two parts:

1. Determine how to organize and store the data in the problem.

2. Develop procedures to process the data and produce the required output. These procedures are called **algorithms.**

Data Organization. As we noted, the input for this problem consists of the initial amount of some radioactive element, its half-life, and a time period. The output to be produced is the amount of the substance that remains at the end of the specified time period. We will use the variables INIT, HFLIFE, TIME, and RESID to represent these quantities.

Algorithm Design. The first step in an algorithm for solving this problem is to obtain the values for the input items—initial amount, half-life, and time period. Next we must determine how to use this information to calculate the amount of the substance remaining after the given time period. Finally, the amount remaining must be displayed. Thus, our initial description of an algorithm for solving the problem is

1. Get values for INIT, HFLIFE, and TIME.
2. Compute the value of RESID for the given TIME.
3. Display RESID.

Algorithm Refinement. The next step in developing an algorithm to solve the problem is the **refinement** of any steps in the algorithm that require additional details. For example, in step 2 of the preceding algorithm, a formula is needed to compute the amount of polonium that remains after a given time period. The half-life of polonium is 140 days, and if we assume that the initial amount of polonium is 10 mg, then after 140 days, or one half-life,

$$10 \times 0.5$$

milligrams remain. At the end of 280 days, or two half-lives, the amount of polonium remaining is one-half of this amount,

$$(10 \times 0.5) \times 0.5$$

which can also be written

$$10 \times (0.5)^2$$

Similarly, the amount of polonium at the end of 420 days, or three half-lives, is

$$10 \times (0.5)^3$$

The general formula for the amount of the substance remaining is

$$\text{amount remaining} = \text{initial amount} \times (0.5)^{\text{time}/\text{half-life}}$$

Thus, the second step in our algorithm is to perform this calculation for the data entered in step 1.

This rather lengthy description of the algorithm can be expressed more concisely as follows:

ALGORITHM FOR RADIOACTIVE DECAY PROBLEM

* This algorithm calculates the amount RESID of a radioactive substance that remains *
* after a specified time for a given initial amount and a given half-life. *
* *
* Input: An initial amount INIT of a radioactive substance, its half-life HFLIFE, and *
*   a TIME period in days. *
* Output: The amount remaining. *

1. Enter INIT, HFLIFE, and TIME.
2. Calculate
       RESID = INIT * (0.5) ** (TIME / HFLIFE)
3. Display RESID.

Note that the symbols *, / , and ** indicate multiplication, division, and exponentiation, respectively. Note also that we have included a brief specification of the problem that the algorithm solves at the beginning of the algorithm (the part enclosed in asterisks). Such **documentation** is important and should be included in every algorithm.

The steps in this algorithm might also be displayed graphically:

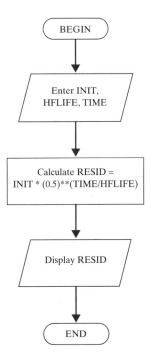

Here, parallelograms are used to indicate input/output operations, and rectangles represent assignments of values to variables.

Once we have finished the algorithm, we are ready to proceed to the coding stage.

Step 3:
Program Coding

The third step in developing a program to solve a problem is to implement the algorithm for solving the problem in some programming language. Figure 1.8 shows a FORTRAN program for this example.

Figure 1.8 Radioactive decay

```
      PROGRAM DECAY
*********************************************************************
* This program calculates the amount of a radioactive substance that *
* remains after a specified time, given an initial amount and its    *
* half-life.  Variables used are:                                    *
*      INIT    :  initial amount of substance                        *
*      HFLIFE  :  half-life of substance                             *
*      TIME    :  time at which the amount remaining is calculated    *
*      RESID   :  amount remaining                                   *
*                                                                    *
* Input:   INIT, HFLIFE, TIME                                        *
* Output:  RESID                                                     *
*********************************************************************

      REAL INIT, HFLIFE, TIME, RESID

* Get values for INIT, HFLIFE, and TIME.
      PRINT *, 'ENTER INITIAL AMOUNT, HALF-LIFE, AND TIME'
      READ *, INIT, HFLIFE, TIME

* Compute the residual amount for the given time.
      RESID = INIT * 0.5 ** (TIME / HFLIFE)
                              ↳ Power

* Display RESID.
      PRINT *, 'AMOUNT REMAINING =', RESID

      END
```

The program begins with the PROGRAM statement

```
      PROGRAM DECAY
```

which marks the beginning of the program and associates the name DECAY with it. In standard FORTRAN, this statement and all FORTRAN statements must begin in position 7 or after of a line and may not extend beyond position 72.

The PROGRAM statement is followed by **opening documentation** in the form of comments that describe the program. These comments summarize the purpose of the program and give the specification of the problem the program is to solve. An asterisk (*) in the first position of a line indicates a comment line.

The statement

```
REAL INIT, HFLIFE, TIME, RESID
```

that follows the opening documentation declares that INIT, HFLIFE, TIME, and RESID are variables that will be used in the program and that their values will be real numbers.

The first step in the algorithm is an input instruction to enter values for the variables INIT, HFLIFE, and TIME:

1. Enter INIT, HFLIFE, and TIME.

This is translated into two statements in the program:

```
PRINT *, 'ENTER INITIAL AMOUNT, HALF-LIFE, AND TIME'
READ *, INIT, HFLIFE, TIME
```

The PRINT statement is used to prompt the user that the input values are to be entered. The READ statement actually assigns the three values entered by the user to the three variables INIT, HFLIFE, and TIME. Thus, if the user enters

```
2, 140, 180
```

the value 2 is assigned to INIT, 140 to HFLIFE, and 180 to TIME.

The next step in the algorithm

2. Calculate RESID = INIT * 0.5 ** (TIME / HFLIFE).

translates into the FORTRAN assignment statement

```
RESID = INIT * 0.5 ** (TIME / HFLIFE)
```

The output instruction

3. Display RESID.

is translated into the FORTRAN statement

```
PRINT *, 'AMOUNT REMAINING =', RESID
```

The end of the program is indicated by the FORTRAN statement

```
END
```

This statement terminates execution of the program.

Step 4:
Execution and Testing

Once an algorithm has been coded, the fourth step in the development process is to check that the algorithm and program are *correct*. One way to do this is to execute the program with input values for which the correct output values are already known (or are easily calculated). The procedure for submitting a program to a computer and executing it varies from one system to another; the details regarding your particular system can be obtained from your instructor, computer center personnel, or user manuals supplied by the manufacturer.

First you must gain access to the computer system. In the case of a personal computer, this may only mean turning on the machine and inserting the appropriate diskette in the disk drive. For a larger system, some **login** procedure may be required to establish contact between a remote terminal and the computer. When you have gained access, you must enter the program, often by using an **editor** provided as part of the system software.

Once the FORTRAN source program has been entered, it must be compiled to produce an object file by giving appropriate system commands.[2] The resulting object file can then be executed with test data to check its correctness. For example, the program in Figure 1.8 might be compiled on a UNIX system with the command

```
f77 fig1-8.f -o fig1-8
```

Giving the command

```
fig1-8
```

then causes the program to execute:

```
ENTER INITIAL AMOUNT, HALF-LIFE, AND TIME
2, 140, 140
AMOUNT REMAINING = 1.00000
```

The program displays a message prompting the user for three input values, and after these values (highlighted in color) are entered, the desired output value is calculated and displayed.

Here we have entered the values 2, 140, and 140 since it is easy to check that the correct answer for these inputs is 1.0. Similarly, the correct results for simple input values like 4, 140, 280 and 4, 140, 420 are easily calculated and can be used as a quick check of the answers produced by the program.

---

[2] On some systems it may also be necessary to link the object file with certain system files.

Once we are confident that the program is correct, we can use it to solve the original problem of finding the amount of polonium remaining after 180 days if there are 10 mg present initially:

```
ENTER INITIAL AMOUNT, HALF-LIFE, AND TIME
10, 140, 180
AMOUNT REMAINING = 4.10168
```

This example illustrates the **interactive mode** of processing, in which the user enters data values during program execution (from the keyboard), and the output produced by the program is displayed directly to the user (usually on a video screen). Another mode of operation is **batch processing**, in which the user prepares a file containing the program, the data, and certain command lines and submits it to the system. Execution then proceeds without any user interaction.

1.4 PROGRAMMING AND PROBLEM SOLVING— AN OVERVIEW

Programming and problem solving is an art in that it requires a good deal of imagination, ingenuity, and creativity. But it is also a science in that it uses certain techniques and methodologies. The term **software engineering** has come to be applied to the study and use of these techniques.

In the preceding section, we identified four steps in the program-development process:

1. Problem analysis and specification
2. Data organization and algorithm design
3. Program coding
4. Execution and testing

We illustrated these steps using the simple radioactive-decay problem. It must be realized, however, that in more substantial problems, these stages will be considerably more complex. In this section we will describe some of the additional questions and complications that arise, together with some of the software engineering techniques used to deal with them. We will also briefly describe an additional step that is particularly important in the **life cycle** of programs developed in real-world applications:

5. Program maintenance

Step 1:
Problem Analysis and Specification

As we have seen, the first step in developing a program to solve a problem is to analyze the problem and specify precisely what a solution to the problem requires. This specification must include

- A description of the problem's **input**: what information is given and which items are important in solving the problem

- A description of the problem's **output**: what information must be produced to solve the problem

Input and output are the two major parts of the problem's specification, and for a problem that appears in a programming text, they are usually not too difficult to identify.

The specifications of more complex problems often include other items, and considerable effort may be required to formulate them completely. These problems are sometimes stated vaguely and imprecisely, because even the person posing the problem may not fully understand it. For example, the manager of a large engineering firm might request a programmer to "develop a program to estimate costs for constructing a new engineering lab."

In these situations, many questions must be answered to formulate the problem's specification. Some of these answers are required to describe more completely the problem's input and output. What information is available regarding the construction project? How is the program to access this data? Has the information been validated, or must the program provide error checking? In what format should the output be displayed? Must reports be generated for company executives, zoning boards, environmental agencies, and/or other governmental agencies?

Other questions deal more directly with the required processing. What materials are required? What equipment will be needed? Are employees paid on an hourly or a salaried basis, or are there some of each? What premium, if any, is paid for overtime? What items must be withheld—for federal, state, and city income taxes, retirement plans, insurance, and the like—and how are they to be computed?

In some situations, still other questions concern how the program will be used. Will the users of the program be technically sophisticated, or must the program be made very user-friendly to accommodate novice users? How often will the program be used? What are the response time requirements? What is the expected life of the program; that is, how long will it be used, and what changes can be expected in the future? What hardware and software are available?

Although this list is by no means exhaustive, it does indicate the wide range of information that may be required in analyzing and specifying a problem.

Step 2:
Data Organization and Algorithm Design

Once the specification of a problem is complete, the next step is to select appropriate structures to organize and store the problem's data and design algorithms to process the data. For the problems considered in the first several chapters of this text, the data items will be processed and stored using simple variables much like those used in mathematics to name quantities in algebraic formulas and equations; more complex structures will be discussed in later chapters.

Because the computer is a machine possessing no inherent problem-solving capabilities, the algorithms developed to solve a problem must be expressed as a sequence of simple steps. Programs to implement algorithms must be written in a language that the computer can understand. It is natural, therefore, to describe algorithms in a language that resembles those used to write computer programs, that is, in a "pseudoprogramming language" or, as it is more commonly called, **pseudocode.**

Unlike the definitions of high-level programming languages such as FORTRAN, there is no set of rules that precisely define pseudocode. It varies from one programmer to another. Pseudocode is a mixture of natural language and symbols, terms, and other features commonly used in high-level programming languages. Typically one finds the following features in various pseudocodes:

1. The usual computer symbols are used for arithmetic operations: + for addition, − for subtraction, * for multiplication, / for division, and ** for exponentiation.

2. Symbolic names (variables) are used to represent the quantities being processed by the algorithm.

3. Some provision is made for including comments. This is often done by enclosing each comment line between special symbols such as asterisks (*).

4. Certain key words that are common in high-level languages may be used: for example, *Read* or *Enter* to indicate input operations, and *Display, Print,* or *Write* for output operations.

5. Indentation is used to indicate key blocks of instructions.

Some programmers use graphical representations of algorithms in addition to or in place of pseudocode descriptions. A number of such representations have been developed over the years, but probably the most common one is the **flowchart**, a diagram that uses symbols like those shown in Figure 1.9. Each step of the algorithm is placed in a box of the appropriate shape, and the order in which these steps are to be carried out is indicated by connecting them with arrows called **flow lines.** Although the use of flowcharts has diminished considerably, their two-dimensional nature, as opposed to the one-dimensional nature of a pseudocode description, makes it easier to visualize and understand the structure of some algorithms. For this reason, although most of the algorithms in this book will be given in pseudocode, we will use flowcharts for a few algorithms or parts of algorithms.

The steps that comprise an algorithm must be organized in a logical and clear manner so that the program that implements the algorithm will be similarly well structured. **Structured algorithms** and **programs** are designed using three basic methods of control:

1. *Sequential:* Steps are performed in a strictly sequential manner, each step being executed exactly once.

2. *Selection:* One of a number of alternative actions is selected and executed.

3. *Repetition:* One or more steps are performed repeatedly.

These three control structures are individually quite simple, but in fact they are sufficiently powerful that any algorithm can be constructed using combinations of these structures.

Sequential execution is the default control mechanism—if the programmer does not stipulate selection or repetition, the statements in a program are executed in sequence from beginning to end. Our solution to the radioactive-decay problem used only sequential control; the steps are simply executed in order, from beginning to end, with

Figure 1.9

Flowchart symbols.

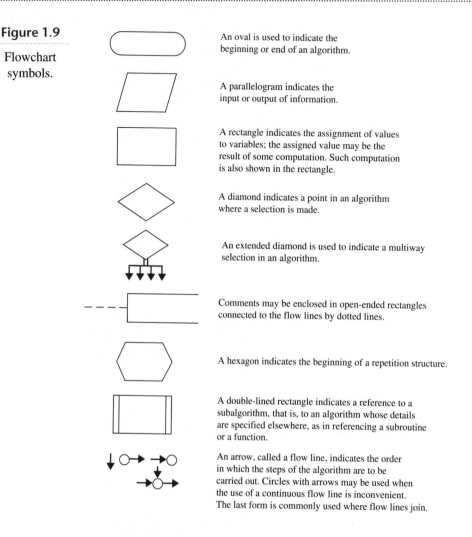

An oval is used to indicate the beginning or end of an algorithm.

A parallelogram indicates the input or output of information.

A rectangle indicates the assignment of values to variables; the assigned value may be the result of some computation. Such computation is also shown in the rectangle.

A diamond indicates a point in an algorithm where a selection is made.

An extended diamond is used to indicate a multiway selection in an algorithm.

Comments may be enclosed in open-ended rectangles connected to the flow lines by dotted lines.

A hexagon indicates the beginning of a repetition structure.

A double-lined rectangle indicates a reference to a subalgorithm, that is, to an algorithm whose details are specified elsewhere, as in referencing a subroutine or a function.

An arrow, called a flow line, indicates the order in which the steps of the algorithm are to be carried out. Circles with arrows may be used when the use of a continuous flow line is inconvenient. The last form is commonly used where flow lines join.

each step being performed exactly once. The flowchart representation of the algorithm clearly displays its sequential nature.

For other problems, however, the solution may require that some of the steps be performed in some situations and bypassed in others. Such problems are considered in Chapter 3. Still other problems require that a step or a collection of steps be repeated; such problems are considered in Chapter 4.

As we have noted, two important parts of the plan for solving a problem are choosing structures to organize and store the data and designing algorithms to process the data. For example, in the construction problem we considered earlier, a file of personnel records containing names, social security numbers, number of dependents, and so on contains permanent information that must be stored in some structure so that it can be accessed and processed. Other information such as hours worked will be entered during program execution and can perhaps be stored in simple variables, as in the example we considered in the preceding section.

A problem may be so complex that it is difficult to visualize or anticipate at the out-set all the details of a complete solution to the problem. To solve such problems, a **di-vide-and-conquer** strategy is used, in which the original problem is partitioned into simpler subproblems, each of which can be considered independently. We begin by identifying the major tasks to be performed to solve the problem and arranging them in the order in which they are to be carried out. These tasks and their relation to one another can be displayed in a **structure diagram.** For example, a first structure diagram for the problem might be

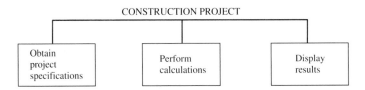

Usually one or more of these first-level tasks is still quite complex and must be di-vided into subtasks. For example, in the construction problem, some of the input data pertains to personnel requirements. Other data items refer to material requirements, and still others to equipment needs. Consequently, the task "Obtain project specifications" can be subdivided into three subtasks:

1. Obtain personnel requirements.
2. Obtain equipment requirements.
3. Obtain materials requirements.

Similarly, the task "Perform calculations" may be split into three subtasks:

1. Calculate personnel cost.
2. Calculate equipment cost.
3. Calculate materials cost.

In a structure diagram, these subtasks are placed on a second level below the corre-sponding main task, as pictured in Figure 1.10. These subtasks may require further di-vision into still smaller subtasks, resulting in additional levels, as illustrated in Figure 1.11. This **successive refinement** continues until each subtask is sufficiently simple that the design of an algorithm for that subtask is straightforward.

This **top-down** approach to software development allows the programmer to de-sign and test an algorithm and the corresponding program **module** for each subproblem independently of the others. For very large projects, a team approach might be used in which the low-level subtasks are assigned to different programmers. The individual program modules they develop are eventually combined into one complete program that solves the original problem.

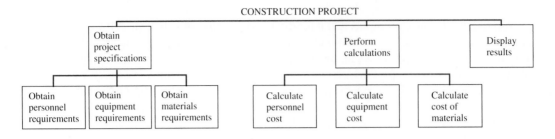

Figure 1.10

Second structure diagram.

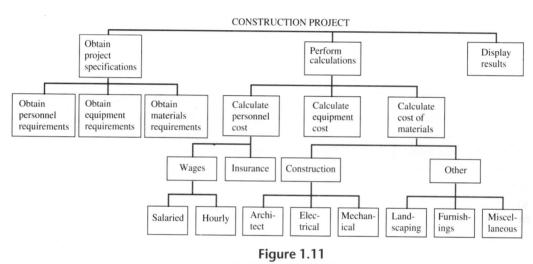

Figure 1.11

Third structure diagram.

Step 3:
Program Coding

The first two steps of the program-development process are extremely important, be-cause the remaining phases will be much more difficult if the first two steps are skipped or are not done carefully. On the other hand, if the problem has been carefully analyzed and specified and if an effective plan has been designed, the program-coding step is usu-ally straightforward.

Coding is the process of implementing data objects and algorithms in some pro-gramming language. In the second step of the problem-solving process, algorithms may be described in a natural language or pseudocode, but a program that implements an al-gorithm must be written in the vocabulary of a programming language and must con-form to the **syntax**, or grammatical rules, of that language. This text is concerned with the vocabulary and syntax of FORTRAN, some features of which we now describe in the context of the example in the preceding section.

Variables. **Variables** are names used to identify various quantities. In the radioactive-decay problem, the variables INIT, HFLIFE, and TIME represent the initial amount of a radioactive substance, its half-life, and time, respectively. The output in this example is the amount of the substance remaining after the specified time and is represented by the variable RESID.

In standard FORTRAN, variable names must begin with a letter, which may be followed by up to five letters or digits. Thus, `INIT`, `HFLIFE`, `TIME`, and `RESID` are valid FORTRAN variable names, and each name suggests what the variable represents. *Meaningful variable names should always be used because they make programs easier to read and understand.*

Types. The types of values that each variable may have must be declared. Variables whose values are real numbers — numbers that have a fractional part — are declared by placing a statement of the form

```
REAL list
```

at the beginning of the program, where `list` is a list of the variable names of real type. Thus, the statement

```
REAL INIT, HFLIFE, TIME, RESID
```

in the program in Figure 1.8 declares that the variables `INIT`, `HFLIFE`, `TIME`, and `RESID` are real variables. Variables whose values are integers are declared using a statement of the form

```
INTEGER list
```

Other types will be considered later.

Operations. Addition and subtraction are denoted in FORTRAN by the usual + and − symbols. Multiplication is denoted by * and division by / . Exponentiation is denoted by * * .

Assignment. Assignment of a value to a variable is denoted by = in FORTRAN programs. For example, the assignment statement

```
RESID = INIT * 0.5 ** (TIME / HFLIFE)
```

assigns the value of the expression

```
INIT * 0.5 ** (TIME / HFLIFE)
```

to the variable `RESID`.

Input/Output. In the pseudocode description of an algorithm, the words *Read* and *Enter* are used for input operations, and *Display*, *Print*, and *Write* are used for output operations. The FORTRAN statement used for input is the READ statement. A simple form of this statement is

```
READ *, list
```

where `list` is a list of variables for which values are to be read. For example, the statement

```
READ *, INIT, HFLIFE, TIME
```

reads values for the variables INIT, HFLIFE, and TIME.

Simple output statements in FORTRAN are the PRINT statement of the form

```
PRINT *, list
```

and the WRITE statement of the form

```
WRITE (*, *) list
```

where `list` is a list of items to be displayed. For example, the statement

```
PRINT *, 'AMOUNT REMAINING = ', RESID
```

displays the label

```
AMOUNT REMAINING =
```

followed by the value of the variable RESID.

Comments. Comment lines can also be incorporated into FORTRAN programs. Any line that is completely blank or that contains the letter C or an asterisk (*) in the first position of the line is a comment line.

Programming Style. Programs must be *correct, readable, and understandable*, and there are three principles for developing such programs We conclude this section with a brief discussion of these principles.

1. *Programs should be well structured.* Two helpful guidelines in this regard are as follows:

   - *Use a top-down approach when developing a program for a complex problem.* Divide the problem into simpler and simpler subproblems until the solution of these subproblems is clear.

- *Strive for simplicity and clarity*   Avoid clever programming tricks intended only to demonstrate the programmer's ingenuity or to produce code that executes only slightly faster.

2. The second principle is that *each program unit should be documented.* In particular:

- *Each program should include opening documentation.* Comments should be included to explain what the program does, how it works, any special algorithms it uses, a summary of the problem's specification, assumptions, and so on; they may also include such items of information as the name of the programmer, the date the program was written and when it was last modified, and references to books and manuals that give additional information about the program. In addition, it is good practice to explain the variables that are being used in the program.

- *Comments should also be used to explain key program segments and/or segments whose purpose or design is not obvious.* However, too many detailed or unnecessary comments clutter the program and only make it more difficult to read and understand.

- *Meaningful identifiers should be used.* For example, the statement

```
Dist = Rate * Time
```

is more meaningful than

```
D = R * T
```

or

```
X7 = R * ZEKE
```

Don't use "skimpy" abbreviations just to save a few keystrokes. Also, avoid "cute" identifiers, as in

```
HOWFAR = GOGO * SQUEAL
```

3. *A program should be formatted in a style that enhances its readability.* The following are some guidelines for good program style:

- *Use spaces between the items in a statement to make it more readable,* for example, before and after each operator $(+, -, =,$ etc.).

- *Insert a blank line between sections of a program and wherever appropriate in a sequence of statements to set off blocks of statements.*

- *Adhere rigorously to alignment and indentation guidelines to emphasize the relationship between various parts of the program.*

It is often difficult for beginning programmers to appreciate the importance of learning good programming habits that lead to the design of readable and understandable programs. The reason is that programs written in an academic environment are often quite different from those developed in real-world situations, in which program style and form are critical. Student programs are usually quite small (usually less than a few hundred lines of code); are executed and modified only a few times (almost never, once they have been handed in); are rarely examined in detail by anyone other than the student and the instructor; and are not developed within the context of budget constraints. Real-world programs, on the other hand, may be very large (several thousand lines of code); may be developed by teams of programmers; are commonly used for long periods of time and thus require maintenance if they are to be kept current and correct; and are often maintained by someone other than the original programmer.

As we discuss features of the FORTRAN language in the following chapters, additional principles for program design will be given. It is important for beginning programmers to follow these guidelines, even in early simple programs, so that good habits are established and carried on into the design of more complex programs.

Step 4:
Execution and Testing

Obviously, the most important characteristic of any program is that it be *correct*. No matter how well structured, how well documented, or how nice the program looks, if it does not produce correct results, it is worthless. The fact that a program executes without producing any error messages is no guarantee that it is correct. The results produced may be erroneous because of logic errors that the computer system cannot detect. It is the responsibility of the programmer to test each program in order to ensure that it is correct. (See Section 4.7 for more about program testing.)

Errors may occur in any of the phases of the program-development process. For example, the specifications may not accurately reflect information given in the problem; the algorithms may contain logic errors; and the program may not be coded correctly. The detection and correction of errors is an important part of software development and is known as validation and verification. **Validation** is concerned with checking that the algorithms and the program meet the problem's specification. **Verification** refers to checking that they are correct and complete. Validation is sometimes described as answering the question, Are we solving the correct problem? and verification as answering the question, Are we solving the problem correctly?

The program in Figure 1.8 was entered, compiled, and executed without error. Usually, however, a programmer will make some errors when designing the program or when attempting to enter and execute it. Errors may be detected at various stages of program processing and may cause the processing to be terminated. For example, an incorrect system command will be detected early in the processing and will usually prevent compilation and execution of the program. Errors in the program's syntax, such as incorrect punctuation or misspelled key words, will be detected during compilation. (On some systems, syntax errors may be detected while the program is being entered.) Such errors are called **syntax errors** or **compile-time errors** and usually make it impossible to complete the compilation and execution of the program. For example, if the output statement that displays the residual amount of radioactive substance were mistakenly written as

```
PRINT *, 'AMOUNT REMAINING =, RESID
```

without a quotation mark after the equal sign, an attempt to compile and execute the program might result in a message like the following, signaling a "fatal" error:

```
MAIN decay: "error.f", line 21: Error: unbalanced quotes
```

Less severe errors may generate "warning" messages but the compilation will continue.

Other errors, such as an attempt to divide by zero in an arithmetic expression, may not be detected until execution of the program has begun. Such errors are called **run-time errors.** Explanations of the error messages displayed by your particular system can be found in the user manuals supplied by the manufacturer. In any case, the errors must be corrected by replacing the erroneous statements with correct ones, and the modified program must be recompiled and reexecuted.

Errors that are detected by the computer system are relatively easy to identify and correct. There are, however, other errors that are more subtle and difficult to identify. These are **logic errors** that arise in the design of the algorithm or in the coding of the program that implements the algorithm. For example, if the statement

```
RESID = INIT * 0.5 ** (TIME / HFLIFE)
```

in the program of Figure 1.8 were mistakenly entered as

```
RESID = INIT * 0.5 * (TIME / HFLIFE)
```

with the exponentiation symbol (* *) replaced by the symbol for multiplication (*), the program would still be syntactically correct. No error would occur during the compilation or execution of the program. But the results produced by the program would be incorrect because an incorrect formula would have been used to calculate the residual amount of the substance. If the values 2, 140, and 140 were entered for the variables INIT, HFLIFE, and TIME, respectively, the output produced by the program would be

```
AMOUNT REMAINING = 1.00000
```

which is correct, even though the formula is not. However, for the test data 4, 140, 280, the output is

```
AMOUNT REMAINING = 4.00000
```

which is obviously incorrect (since the initial and residual amounts cannot be the same).

As this example demonstrates, *it is important that the user run a program several times with input data for which the correct results are known in advance.* This process of **program testing** is extremely important, as a *program cannot be considered to be correct until it has been checked with several sets of test data.* The test data should be carefully selected so that each part of the program is tested.

Step 5:
Maintenance

The life cycle of a program written by a student programmer normally ends with the fourth step; that is, once the program has been written, executed, and tested, the assignment is complete. Programs in real-world applications, however, are often used for several years and are likely to require some modification. Software systems, especially large ones developed for complex projects, may have obscure bugs that were not detected during testing and that surface after the software has been placed in use. One important aspect of software maintenance is fixing such flaws in the software.

It may also be necessary to modify software to improve its performance, to add new features, and so on. Other modifications may be required because of changes in the computer hardware and/or the system software such as the operating system. External factors may also force program modification; for example, changes in building codes may mean revising part of a construction cost program. It is easier to make such changes in a well-structured program than in one that is poorly designed.

Quick Quiz 1.4

1. Name the five steps in the program-development process.
2. What are two important parts of a problem's specification?
3. What are the three basic methods of control used in designing structured algorithms?
4. Pseudocode is a high-level programming language (true or false).
5. A _____ is a graphical display of an algorithm.
6. The grammatical rules of a language are called its _____.
7. The approach to a problem of identifying the major tasks to be performed, arranging them in the order in which they are to be carried out, and refining them into simpler subtasks, perhaps several times, until they are simple enough to be solved is called _____ .
8. What are the three types of errors that can occur in developing a program?
9. For the following temperature-conversion problem:
   (a) Identify both the information that must be produced to solve the problem and the given information that will be useful in obtaining the solution. Then design an algorithm to solve the problem.
   (b) Using the program in Figure 1.8 as a guide, write a FORTRAN program to solve the problem.
   Problem: The boiling point of water is 212° on the Fahrenheit scale and 100° on the Celsius scale. The freezing point of water is 32° on the Fahrenheit scale and 0° on the Celsius scale. Assuming a linear relationship ($F = a \cdot C + b$) between these two temperature scales, convert a temperature of $C°$ on the Celsius scale to the corresponding Fahrenheit temperature, and display the Fahrenheit temperature.

Exercises 1.4

For each of the problems described in Exercises 1 and 2, identify both the information that must be produced to solve the problem and the given information that will be useful in obtaining the solution. Then design an algorithm to solve the problem.

1. Calculate and display the radius, circumference, and area of a circle with a given diameter.

2. Three resistors are arranged in parallel in the following circuit:

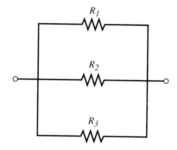

Calculate and display the combined resistance

$$\frac{1}{\dfrac{1}{R_1} + \dfrac{1}{R_2} + \dfrac{1}{R_3}}$$

for given values of R_1, R_2, and R_3.

3. Enter and execute the following FORTRAN program on your computer system, but with the name, course name, and date replaced with your name and course name and the current date.

```
      PROGRAM ARITH
*******************************************************************
*  John Doe              CPSC 141C              September 1, 1995  *
*                      ASSIGNMENT #1                              *
*                                                                *
*  Program to add two real numbers.  Variables used are:         *
*      X, Y :   the two real numbers                             *
*      SUM  :   the sum of X and Y                               *
*                                                                *
*  Output:  X, Y, and SUM                                        *
*******************************************************************

      REAL X, Y, SUM
```

```
X = 3.14
Y = 2.057
SUM = X + Y
PRINT *, 'SUM OF', X, ' AND', Y, ' IS', SUM
END
```

4. For the program in Exercise 3, make the following changes and execute the modified program:

   (a) Change 3.14 to 17.2375 in the statement that assigns a value to X.

   (b) Change the variable names X and Y to ALPHA and BETA throughout.

   (c) Insert the comment

   ```
   *** Calculate the sum
   ```

   before the statement that assigns a value to SUM.

   (d) Insert the following comment and statement before the PRINT statement

   ```
   *** Now calculate the difference
            DIFF = ALPHA - BETA
   ```

   add the variable DIFF to the list of variables in the REAL statement, and add another PRINT statement to display the value of DIFF. Also, change the comments in the opening documentation appropriately.

5. Using the program in Figure 1.8 as a guide, write a FORTRAN program for the circle problem in Exercise 1.

6. Proceed as in Exercise 5, but for the resistance problem in Exercise 2.

CHAPTER REVIEW

Summary

In this chapter we have discussed the fundamental concepts of computing systems. We began with a brief history, focusing on the mechanization of arithmetic and the stored-program concept and on how these were implemented in various machines. We described the four generations of computers developed since the 1940s. We also reviewed the development of system software including operating systems and compilers. The main components of computing systems were described in Section 1.2, which included a description of machine-language and assembly-language programming and the compilation process. Section 1.3 contains an example that illustrates the four steps of the programming and problem-solving process:

1. Problem analysis and specification
2. Data organization and algorithm design

3. Program coding
4. Execution and testing

These steps are described more generally in the overview of the program-development process given in the last section of the chapter. These sections also contain a brief introduction to the FORTRAN programming language.

FORTRAN SUMMARY

Identifiers

Identifiers such as program names and variable names must begin with a letter, which may be followed by up to five letters or digits.

Program Format

In standard FORTRAN, each statement must be placed in positions 7 through 72 of a line.

Comments

A blank or a line that contains the letter C or an asterisk (*) in the first position of the line is a comment line.

PROGRAM Statement

```
PROGRAM program-name
```

Example:

```
PROGRAM DECAY
```

Purpose:
The PROGRAM statement names the program.

Types

```
REAL list-of-variable-names
INTEGER list-of-variable-names
```

Example:

```
REAL INIT, HFLIFE, TIME, RESID
INTEGER COUNT
```

Purpose:
Type statements declare the type of values that variables will have.

Operations

Operator	Operation
+	addition
−	subtraction
*	multiplication
/	division
**	exponentiation

Assignment Statement

```
variable = expression
```

Example:

```
RESID = INIT * 0.5 ** (TIME / HFLIFE)
COUNT = 0
```

Purpose:
Assign the value of the `expression` to the specified `variable`.

Input Statement

```
READ *, input-list-of-variables
```

Example:

```
READ *, INIT, HFLIFE, TIME
READ *, COUNT
```

Purpose:
The READ statement reads values for the variables in the input list.

Output Statements

```
PRINT *, output-list-of-expressions
WRITE (*, *) output-list-of-expressions
```

Examples:

```
PRINT *, 'AMOUNT REMAINING = ', RESID
WRITE (*, *) 'NUMBER OF ITEMS = ', COUNT - 1
```

Purpose:

The `PRINT` and `WRITE` statements display the values of the expressions in the output list.

END **Statement**

```
END
```

Purpose:

The `END` statement marks the end of a program and stops execution.

2

Basic FORTRAN

In language, clarity is everything.

CONFUCIUS

Kindly enter them in your note-book. And, in order to refer to them conveniently, let's call them A, B, and Z.

THE TORTOISE IN LEWIS CARROLL'S
WHAT THE TORTOISE SAID TO ACHILLES.

Arithmetic is being able to count up to twenty without taking off your shoes.

MICKEY MOUSE

All the news that's fit to print.

ADOLPH S. OCHS

C H A P T E R   C O N T E N T S

2.1 Data Types + Algorithms = Programs

2.2 Data Types, Constants, and Variables

2.3 Arithmetic Operations and Functions

2.4 The Assignment Statement

2.5 Input / Output

2.6 Program Composition and Format

2.7 Application: Temperature Conversion

2.8 Application: Circuits with Parallel Resistors

2.9 Application: Concentration of an Acid Bath

*2.10 Introduction to File Input / Output

*2.11 Arithmetic Errors

Chapter Review

Programming Pointers

Programming Problems

Fortran 90

*O*ne important part of using the computer to solve a problem is implementing the algorithm for solving that problem as a program. We noted in the preceding chapter that while algorithms can be described somewhat informally in a pseudoprogramming language, the corresponding program must be written in strict compliance with the rules of some programming language. The program we wrote to solve the radioactive-decay problem introduced several features of the FORTRAN language. In this chapter we consider these and other features in more detail.

As we noted in Chapter 1, FORTRAN, one of the first high-level languages, was developed at IBM in the mid 1950s by a team of programmers led by John Backus. In the years that followed, a number of versions of FORTRAN were developed by different computer companies. In an attempt to minimize the differences among these versions, the American National Standards Institute (ANSI) established standards for the FORTRAN language. The first of these standards was called FORTRAN 66. It was revised in the 1970s to produce FORTRAN 77, which has been the most commonly used version of FORTRAN for the past several years. However, the FORTRAN standard was revised again more recently to produce Fortran 90. Both FORTRAN 77 and Fortran 90 have been retained as American standards, but Fortran 90 is the only international standard. This text is based on FORTRAN 77, but the new features of Fortran 90 are described and illustrated in special sections at the end of each chapter.

2.1 DATA TYPES + ALGORITHMS = PROGRAMS

We have seen in the preceding chapter that organizing a problem's data is an important part of developing a program to solve that problem. This may be numeric data representing times or temperatures, or character data representing names, or logical data used in designing a circuit, and so on. Consequently, a program for solving a problem must be written in a language that can store and process various types of data.

FORTRAN is designed to handle six types of data:

integer

real or single precision

double precision

complex

character

logical

The first four are numeric types used to store and process various kinds of numbers; the character type is used to store and process strings of characters; and the logical type is used to store and process logical data values (.FALSE. and .TRUE.). In this chapter we will restrict our attention to integer, real, and character types; we will consider the logical data type in Chapter 3 and the double-precision and complex types in Chapter 10.

Another important aspect of solving a problem is the development of algorithms to process the input data and produce the required output. A program for solving a problem must be written in a language that provides operations for processing data and instructions that carry out the steps of the algorithm. For example, FORTRAN provides basic arithmetic operations for numeric computations, input and output instructions for entering and displaying data, instructions for implementing the basic control structures, and so on.

Since these two basic aspects of problem solving—data types and algorithms—cannot be separated, a program for solving a problem must incorporate both; that is, some part of the program must specify the data to be processed, and another part must contain the instructions to do the processing. A FORTRAN program contains a **specification part** in which the names and types of constants and variables used to store input and output values as well as intermediate results are declared. This is followed by an **execution part,** which contains the statements that carry out the steps of the algorithm.

The general form of a program in FORTRAN is

FORTRAN Program

heading
specification part
execution part

The first statement of a FORTRAN program is its **heading.** This statement marks the beginning of the program and gives it a name. The heading is normally followed by **opening documentation** in the form of comments about the program's input, output, and purpose and may include other relevant information such as special algorithms that it implements, the date the program was written, when it was last modified, the name of the programmer, and so on. Each of the parts of a program is described in detail in the following sections.

2.2   DATA TYPES, CONSTANTS, AND VARIABLES

We noted in the preceding section that organizing the data in a problem is an important part of program development and that a problem may involve several different types of data. In this section we describe the FORTRAN integer, real, and character data types and how to declare constants and variables of these types.

Integers

An **integer constant** is a string of digits *that does not contain commas or a decimal point;* negative integer constants must be preceded by a minus sign, but a plus sign is optional for nonnegative integers. Thus

```
0
137
−2516
+17745
```

are valid integer constants, whereas the following are invalid for the reasons indicated:

`5,280`	(Commas are not allowed in numeric constants.)
`16.0`	(Integer constants may not contain decimal points.)
`−−5`	(Only one algebraic sign is allowed.)
`7−`	(The algebraic sign must precede the string of digits.)

Reals

Another numeric data type is the **real** type, also known as **single-precision** data. Constants of this type may be represented as ordinary decimal numbers or in exponential notation. *In the decimal representation of real constants, a decimal point must be* *present, but no commas are allowed.* Negative real constants must be preceded by a minus sign, but the plus sign is optional for nonnegative reals. Thus

```
1.234
-0.01536
+56473.
```

are valid real constants, whereas the following are invalid for the reasons indicated:

```
12,345      (Commas are not allowed in numeric constants.)
   63       (Real constants must contain a decimal point.)
```

The scientific representation of a real constant consists of an integer or decimal number, representing the mantissa or fractional part, followed by an exponent written as the letter E *with an integer constant following.* For example, the real constant `337.456` may also be written as

```
3.37456E2
```

which means 3.37456×10^2, or it may be written in a variety of other forms, such as

```
0.337456E3
337.456E0
33745.6E-2
337456E-3
```

Character Strings

Character constants, also called **strings,** are sequences of symbols from the FORTRAN character set. The ANSI standard character set for FORTRAN is given in Table 2.1. Many versions of FORTRAN also include lowercase letters and other special symbols in their character sets. *The sequence of characters that comprise a character constant must be enclosed in apostrophes* (single quotes), and the number of such characters is the **length** of the constant. For example,

```
'PDQ123-A'
```

is a character constant of length 8;

```
'JOHN Q. DOE'
```

is a character constant of length 11, because blanks are characters and are included in the character count. *If an apostrophe is to be one of the characters in a constant, it must be entered as a pair of apostrophes.*

Table 2.1   FORTRAN Character Set

Character	Meaning
blank	blank or space
$0, \ldots, 9$	digits
$A, \ldots, Z$	uppercase letters
$	dollar sign
'	apostrophe (single quote)
(	left parenthesis
)	right parenthesis
*	asterisk
+	plus sign
−	minus sign
/	slash
,	comma
.	period
:	colon
=	equal sign

```
'DON''T'
```

is thus a character constant consisting of the five characters D, O, N, ', and T.

Identifiers

Identifiers are names used to identify programs, constants, variables, and other entities in a program. In standard FORTRAN, *identifiers must begin with a letter, which may be followed by up to five letters or digits.* Thus

```
MASS
RATE
VELOC
ALPHA1
```

are valid FORTRAN identifiers, but the following are invalid for the reasons indicated:

```
TOOLONG  (Identifiers must consist of at most six characters.)
R2-D2    (Only letters and digits are allowed in identifiers.)
6FEET    (Identifiers must begin with a letter.)
```

One should always use identifiers that are as meaningful as possible so that the name suggests what the identifier represents.

Variables

In mathematics, a symbolic name is often used to refer to a quantity. For example, the formula

$$A = l \cdot w$$

is used to calculate the area (denoted by A) of a rectangle with a given length (denoted by l) and a given width (denoted by w). These symbolic names, A, l, and w, are called **variables.** If values are assigned to l and w, this formula can be used to calculate the value of A, which is then the area of a particular rectangle.

Variables were used in Chapter 1 in the discussion of algorithms and programs. When a variable is used in a FORTRAN program, the compiler associates it with a memory location. The value of a variable at any time is the value stored in the associated memory location at that time. Variable names are identifiers and thus must follow the rules for forming valid identifiers.

The type of a FORTRAN variable must be one of the six FORTRAN data types, and the type of each variable determines the type of value that may be assigned to that variable. It is therefore necessary to declare the type of each variable in a FORTRAN program. This can be done using **type statements** of the form

---

Type Statement

Form:

```
type-specifier list
```

where
    `type-specifier` is one of the following:
    `INTEGER`
    `REAL`
    `DOUBLE PRECISION`
    `COMPLEX`
    `CHARACTER*`n (n is an integer constant)
    `LOGICAL`
and `list` is a list of identifiers, separated by commas.

Purpose:
Declares that the identifiers in `list` have the specified type. *Type statements must appear in the specification part of the program.*

The type statements used to declare integer variables and real variables have the forms

```
REAL list
INTEGER list
```

respectively. Thus, the statements

```
INTEGER COUNT, FACTOR, SUM
REAL MASS, VELOC
```

declare COUNT, FACTOR, and SUM to be integer variables and MASS and VELOC to be real variables.

The type statement used to declare character variables has the form

```
CHARACTER*n list
```

where n is an integer constant specifying the length of character constants to be assigned to the variables in this list. The names in the list must be separated by commas; a comma may also be used to separate the length specifier $*n$ from the list. The length specifier $*n$ may be omitted, in which case the length of the values for the variables in the list is 1. For example, the type statement

```
CHARACTER*15 FNAME, LNAME
```

declares FNAME and LNAME to be character variables and specifies that the length of any character value assigned to any of these variables is 15. The statement

```
CHARACTER INIT
```

declares INIT to be a character variable with values of length 1.

A length specifier may also be attached to any of the individual variables in the list of a CHARACTER statement. In this case, this length specification for that variable overrides the length specification given for the list. The statement

```
CHARACTER*15 FNAME, LNAME*20, INIT*1, STREET, CITY
```

declares that FNAME, LNAME, INIT, STREET, and CITY are character variables and that the length of values for FNAME, STREET, and CITY is 15, the length of values for LNAME is 20, and the length of values for INIT is 1.

For any variable whose type is not *explicitly* specified in a type statement, FOR-TRAN will *implicitly* assign it a type according to its **naming convention:** All variables whose names begin with I, J, K, L, M, or N are integer variables, whereas all those whose names begin with any other letter are real variables. (This naming convention may be modified using the IMPLICIT statement described in Chapter 12.)

Variables of a given type must be used in a manner that is appropriate to that data type, since the program may fail to execute correctly otherwise. *It is therefore important to declare explicitly the type of each variable used in a program.* This practice encourages one to think carefully about each variable, what it represents, what type of values it will have, what operations will be performed on it, and so on.[1] It also avoids (or at least lessens) the mixed-mode errors described in Potential Problem 12 of the Programming Pointers at the end of this chapter.

Named Constants: The PARAMETER Statement

Certain constants occur so often that they are given names. For example, the name "pi" is commonly given to the constant 3.14159 . . . and the name "e" to the base 2.71828 . . . of natural logarithms. FORTRAN allows the programmer to assign identifiers to constants in a PARAMETER **statement** in the program's specification part. This statement has the form

---

PARAMETER *Statement*

Form:

$$PARAMETER\ (param_1\ =\ const_1,\ \ldots,\ param_n\ =\ const_n)$$

where
  $param_1, \ldots, param_n$ are identifiers, and
  $const_1, \ldots, const_n$ are constants or expressions involving only constants and previously defined parameters.

Purpose:
Associates each parameter name $param_i$ with the specified constant value $const_i$. The value of a parameter cannot be changed; any attempt to do so will cause a compile-time error. PARAMETER statements must be preceded by type statements that specify the types of the parameters.

For example, the statements

```
INTEGER LIM
PARAMETER (LIM = 50)

REAL PI, TWOPI
PARAMETER (PI = 3.14159, TWOPI = 2.0 * PI)

CHARACTER*2 UNITS
PARAMETER (UNITS = 'CM')
```

---

[1] Fortran 90 and several other versions of FORTRAN provide a modified form of the IMPLICIT statement, IMPLICIT NONE, which cancels the naming convention, with the result that the types of all named constants and variables (and functions) *must be* specified explicitly in type statements.

or equivalently,

```
INTEGER LIM
REAL PI, TWOPI
CHARACTER*2 UNITS

PARAMETER (LIM = 50, PI = 3.14159, TWOPI = 2.0 * PI, UNITS = 'CM')
```

associate the names LIM with the integer 50, PI and TWOPI with the real constants 3.14159 and 6.28318, respectively, and UNITS with the character string 'CM'. These names can be used anywhere in the program that the corresponding constant value can be used (except as noted later in the text). For example, a statement such as

```
XCOORD = RATE * COS(TWOPI * TIME)
```

is equivalent to

```
XCOORD = RATE * COS(6.28318 * TIME)
```

but the first form is preferable because it is more readable and does not require modification if a different value with more or fewer significant digits is required for PI.

Another way that named constants can make programs easier to read and to modify is by using them to avoid "magic numbers." To illustrate, suppose that the statements

```
CHANGE = (0.1758 − 0.1257) * POPUL
POPUL = POPUL + CHANGE
```

appear at one point in a program and that the statements

```
POPINC = 0.1758 * POPUL
POPDEC = 0.1257 * POPUL
```

appear later. In these statements, the constants 0.1758 and 0.1257 magically appear, without explanation. If they must be changed, it will be necessary for someone to search through the program to locate all the places where they appear and to determine what they represent and which are the appropriate ones to change. To make the program more understandable and to minimize the number of statements that must be changed when other values are required, it is better to associate these constants with names, as in

```
REAL BIRTH, DEATH
PARAMETER (BIRTH = 0.1758, DEATH = 0.1257)
```

(or to assign them to variables) and then use these names in place of the magic numbers:

```
CHANGE = (BIRTH - DEATH) * POPUL
POPUL = POPUL + CHANGE
   .
   .
   .
POPINC = BIRTH * POPUL
POPDEC = DEATH * POPUL
```

Readability is improved and the flexibility of the program is increased, because if these constants must be changed, one need only change the PARAMETER statement.

Variable Initialization: The DATA Statement

It is important to note that in standard FORTRAN, *all variables are initially undefined.* Although some compilers may initialize a variable with a particular value (e.g., 0 for numeric variables), this is not always true. It should be assumed that all variables are initially undefined, and they therefore should be initialized in the program.

This initialization can be done at compile time using a DATA **statement** of the form

---

DATA *Statement*

Form:

DATA $list_1/data_1/$, $list_2/data_2/$, . . . , $list_n/data_n/$

where
each $list_i$ is a list of variables separated by commas, and
each $data_i$ is a list of constants, separated by commas, used to initialize the variables in $list_i$.

Purpose:
Initializes each variable in $list_i$ with the corresponding constants in $data_i$ at compile time. DATA statements may appear in the execution part of a program, but it is standard practice to place them after the PARAMETER and type statements in the specification part.

For example, to initialize the values of variables W, X, Y, and Z to $1.0, 2.5, 7.73$, and -2.956, respectively, we could use the statements

```
REAL W, X, Y, Z
DATA W, X, Y, Z /1.0, 2.5, 7.73, -2.956/
```

The DATA statement could also be written as

```
DATA W /1.0/, X, Y /2.5, 7.73/, Z /-2.956/
```

or in a variety of other forms.

A list of n variables may all be initialized with the same value by preceding the value with $n*$, where n is an integer constant or parameter. For example, the following statements

```
INTEGER M, N
REAL A, B, C, D
DATA ZETA, M, N, A, B, C, D /1.23578E-10, 2*3, 4*3.14/
```

initialize ZETA to 1.23578E-10, M and N to 3, and each of A, B, C, and D to 3.14.

Quick Quiz 2.2

1. Name the six FORTRAN data types.

2. Name the three parts of a FORTRAN program.

3. Character constants must be enclosed in _____ .

4. Identifiers must begin with _____.

5. The maximum number of characters in an identifier (in standard FORTRAN) is

   _____ .

For Questions 6–11, tell whether the string of characters forms a legal identifier (in standard FORTRAN). If it is not legal, indicate the reason.

6. CALORIE	7. TYPE-A	8. 55MPH
9. PS.175	10. N/4	11. M$

For Questions 12–26, tell whether the string of characters forms an integer, real, or character constant. If it is none of these, indicate the reason.

12. 1234	13. 1,234	14. -1.234
15. -1.	16. 0.123E+04	17. 'ONE'
18. ONE	19. 'OHM'S LAW'	20. '1234'
21. $12.34	22. 123E4	23. E4
24. +1234	25. 12+34	26. '12+34'

27. Write a type statement to declare MU to be of real type.

28. Write a type statement to declare TIME and DIST to be of real type.

29. Write a type statement to declare NAME1 and NAME2 to be of character type with values of length 20 and NAME3 to be of character type with values of length 10.

For Questions 30–37, tell whether, according to the standard FORTRAN naming convention, the identifier is an integer variable, a real variable, or neither.

30. GAUSS   31. FORTRAN   32. H   33. I

34. LIST   35. TABLE   36. COUNT   37. INT

For Questions 38–40, write type statements and PARAMETER statements to name the constants with the specified names.

38. 32 with GRAV   39. 1.2E12 with MARS and 1.5E10 with EARTH

40. 'CPSC 141' with COURSE and 141 with CNUMB

For Questions 41–43, write type statements and DATA statements to declare each variable to have the specified type and initial value.

41. RATE1 and RATE2 to be real variables with initial values 1.25 and 2.33, respectively

42. DEPT to be a character variable with initial value 'CPSC' and COURS1, COURS2 to be integer variables with initial values 141 and 142, respectively

43. LIM1, LIM2, LIM3, LIM4, LIM5, and LIM6 to be integer variables with initial values 10, 10, 10, 20, 20, and 30, respectively

Exercises 2.2

For Exercises 1–16, tell whether the string of characters forms a legal identifier (in standard FORTRAN). If it is not legal, indicate the reason.

1. X AXIS   2. X-AXIS   3. XAXIS   4. CARBON14

5. CARB14   6. 3M   7. ANGLE   8. AGNLE

9. ANGEL   10. R2D2   11. R2-D2   12. R2 D2

13. TWO   14. A+   15. Z0000Z   16. ZZZZZZ

For Exercises 17–34, tell whether the string of characters forms an integer constant or a real constant. If it is neither of these, indicate the reason.

17. 5,280   18. 5280   19. '5280'   20. 528.0

21. 5280E0   22. −5280   23. − −5280   24. +5280

25. 52+80   26. $52.80   27. 52E80   28. E5280

29. EIGHTY   30. 0.528E0   31. .00005280   32. 5280−

33. −52.80   34. +52E+80

For Exercises 35–42, tell whether the string of characters forms a legal character constant. If it is not legal, indicate the reason.

35. `'RESULTANT FORCE:'`   36. `'ISN''T'`

37. `'$5,280.00'`   38. `'ABC`

39. `'E = M * C ** 2'`   40. `'A''B''C'`

41. `'PRINT *, '`   42. `'''S LAW'`

43. Write a type statement to declare TEMP, PRESS, and VOLUME to be of real type.

44. Write type statements to declare CODE and COUNT to be of integer type, XCOORD and YCOORD to be of real type.

45. Write type statements to declare FORMUL and NAME to be of character type with values of length 10 and AMOUNT to be of real type.

46. Write a type statement to declare NAME, STREET, CITY, and STATE to be of character type with values of length 20, 30, 15, and 2, respectively.

For Exercises 47–61, tell whether, according to the standard FORTRAN naming convention, the identifier is an integer variable, a real variable, or neither.

47. ENIAC   48. MARK1   49. BABBAGE

50. JOB   51. LAMBDA   52. GAMMA

53. D3   54. 3D   55. DISTANCE

56. DISTNCE   57. H2O   58. CHAR

59. LOGIC   60. DIGIT   61. TWO

For Exercises 62–66, write type statements and PARAMETER statements to name the constants with the specified names.

62. 1.25 with RATE

63. 100 with CBOIL and 212 with FBOIL

64. 1.0E−5 with EPSIL, 0.001 with DELTAX, 500 with NUMINT

65. `'FE2O3'` with FORMUL, `'FERRIC OXIDE'` with NAME, and .182 with SPHEAT

66. 12713 with IDNUMB, `'J. SMITH'` with IDNAME, and 12.75 with RATE

For Exercises 67–71, write type statements and DATA statements to declare each variable to have the specified type and initial value.

67. NUM1 and NUM2 to be integer variables with initial values 10 and 20, respectively

68. DIST1, DIST2, DIST3, and DIST4 to be real variables, each with the initial value of 0.0

69. SUM1 and SUM2 to be real variables, each with an initial value of 0.0; and SIZE1, SIZE2, SIZE3, and SIZE4 to be integer variables with initial values 100, 100, 100, and 500, respectively

70. CH1, CH2, CH3, CH4, and CH5 to be character variables of length 1, each with the initial value 'X'

71. UNITS1, UNITS2, UNITS3, and UNITS4 to be character variables with initial values 'FEET', 'FEET', 'INCHES', and 'CENTIMETERS', respectively; NUM1, NUM2, NUM3, NUM4, NUM5, and NUM6 to be integer variables with initial values 0, 0, 0, 0, 1, and 1, respectively; and RATE1, RATE2, RATE3, and RATE4 to be real variables with initial values 0.25, 1.5, 1.5, and 2.0, respectively

2.3 ARITHMETIC OPERATIONS AND FUNCTIONS

In the preceding section we considered variables and constants of various types. These variables and constants can be processed by using operations and functions appropriate to their types. In this section we discuss the arithmetic operations and functions that are used with numeric data.

Operations

In FORTRAN, addition and subtraction are denoted by the usual plus (+) and minus (−) signs. Multiplication is denoted by an asterisk (*). This symbol must be used to denote every multiplication; thus, to multiply N by 2, we must use 2 * N or N * 2, not 2N. Division is denoted by a slash (/), and exponentiation is denoted by a pair of asterisks (**). For example, the quantity $B^2 - 4AC$ is written as

```
B ** 2 - 4 * A * C
```

in a FORTRAN program. Table 2.2 summarizes these arithmetic operations.

Table 2.2   Operations

Operator	Operation
+	addition, unary plus
−	subtraction, unary minus
*	multiplication
/	division
**	exponentiation

When two constants or variables of the same type are combined using one of the four basic arithmetic operations (+, −, *, /), the result has the same type as the operands. For example, the sum of the integers 3 and 4 is the integer 7, whereas the sum of the real numbers 3.0 and 4.0 is the real number 7.0. This distinction may seem unimportant until one considers the division operation. Division of the real constant 9.0 by the real constant 4.0,

$$9.0 / 4.0$$

produces the real quotient 2.25, whereas dividing the integer 9 by the integer 4,

$$9 / 4$$

produces the integer quotient 2, which is equal to the integer part of the real quotient 2.25. Similarly, if the integer variable N has the value 2 and the real variable X has the value 2.0, the real division

$$1.0 / X$$

yields 0.5, whereas the integer division

$$1 / N$$

yields 0.

Mixed-Mode Expressions. It is possible to combine integer and real quantities using these arithmetic operations. Expressions involving different types of numeric operands are called **mixed-mode expressions.** When an integer quantity is combined with a real one, the integer quantity is converted to its real equivalent, and the result is of real type.

The following examples illustrate the evaluation of some mixed-mode expressions; note that type conversion does not take place until necessary:

```
1.0 / 4 → 1.0 / 4.0 → 0.25
3.0 + 8 / 5 → 3.0 + 1 → 3.0 + 1.0 → 4.0
3 + 8.0 / 5 → 3 + 8.0 / 5.0 → 3 + 1.6 → 3.0 + 1.6 → 4.6
```

The last two examples show why *using mixed-mode expressions is usually considered poor programming practice.* The two expressions 3.0 + 8 / 5 and 3 + 8.0 / 5 are algebraically equal but are in fact not equal because of the differences in real and integer arithmetic.

The only expressions in which operands of different types should be used are those in which a real value is raised to an integer power. For such expressions, exponentiation is carried out using repeated multiplication, as the following examples illustrate:

```
2.0 ** 3 → 2.0 * 2.0 * 2.0 → 8.0
(−4.0) ** 2 → (−4.0) * (−4.0) → 16.0
```

If, however, the exponent is a real quantity, exponentiation is performed using logarithms. For example,

$$2.0 \;**\; 3.0$$

is evaluated as

$$e^{3.0 \; \ln(2.0)}$$

which will not be exactly 8.0 because of roundoff errors that arise in storing real numbers and because the exponentiation and logarithm functions produce only approximate values. Another consequence of this method of performing exponentiation is that a negative quantity raised to a real power is undefined because the logarithms of negative values are not defined. Consequently, $(-4.0) \;**\; 2.0$ is undefined, even though $(-4.0) \;**\; 2$ is evaluated as $(-4.0) \;*\; (-4.0) = 16.0$. These examples show why *a real exponent should never be used in place of an integer exponent.*

There are, however, computations in which real exponents are appropriate. For example, in mathematics, $7^{1/2}$ denotes $\sqrt{7}$, the square root of 7. In FORTRAN, this operation of extracting roots can be performed using exponentiation with real exponents. Thus, to compute the square root of 7.0, we could write $7.0 \;**\; 0.5$ or $7.0 \;**\; (1.0 \;/\; 2.0)$. (Note, however, that $7.0 \;**\; (1 \;/\; 2)$ yields $7.0 \;**\; 0 = 1.0$.) Similarly, the cube root of a real variable X can be computed using $X \;**\; (1.0 \;/\; 3.0)$.

Priority Rules. Arithmetic expressions are evaluated in accordance with the following **priority rules:**

1. *All exponentiations are performed first; consecutive exponentiations are performed from right to left.*

2. *All multiplication and divisions are performed next, in the order in which they appear from left to right.*

3. *The additions and subtractions are performed last, in the order in which they appear from left to right.*

The following examples illustrate this order of evaluation:

$$2 \;**\; 3 \;**\; 2 = 2 \;**\; 9 = 512$$
$$10 - 8 - 2 = 2 - 2 = 0$$
$$10 \;/\; 5 \;*\; 2 = 2 \;*\; 2 = 4$$
$$2 + 4 \;/\; 2 = 2 + 2 = 4$$
$$2 + 4 \;**\; 2 \;/\; 2 = 2 + 16 \;/\; 2 = 2 + 8 = 10$$

The standard order of evaluation can be modified by using parentheses to enclose subexpressions within an expression. These subexpressions are evaluated first in the standard manner, and the results are then combined to evaluate the complete expression.

If the parentheses are "nested," that is, if one set of parentheses is contained within another, the computations in the innermost parentheses are performed first.

For example, consider the expression

```
(5 * (11 - 5) ** 2) * 4 + 9
```

The subexpression `11 - 5` is evaluated first, producing

```
(5 * 6 ** 2) * 4 + 9
```

Next, the subexpression `5 * 6 ** 2` is evaluated in the standard order, giving

```
180 * 4 + 9
```

Now the multiplication is performed, giving

```
720 + 9
```

and the addition produces the final result

```
729
```

Expressions containing two or more operations must be written carefully to ensure that they will be evaluated in the order intended. Even though parentheses may not be necessary, they should be used freely to clarify the intended order of evaluation and to write complicated expressions in terms of simpler subexpressions. However, parentheses must balance (i.e., each left parenthesis must match a right parenthesis that appears later in the expression), since an unpaired parenthesis will result in an error.

The symbols + and − can also be used as **unary operators;** for example, +X and −(A + B) are allowed. But unary operators must be used carefully, because standard *FORTRAN does not allow two operators to follow in succession.* (Note that `* *` is interpreted as a single operator rather than two operators in succession.) For example, the expression `N * −2` is not allowed; rather, it must be written as `N * (−2)`. The unary operations have the same low priority as the corresponding binary operations.

Functions

FORTRAN provides functions for many of the common mathematical operations and functions. For example, many computations involve the square root of a quantity, and consequently, FORTRAN provides a special **function** to implement this operation. This function is denoted by `SQRT` and is used by writing

```
SQRT(argument)
```

where `argument` is a real-valued constant, variable, or expression. For example, to calculate the square root of 7, we would write

```
SQRT(7.0)
```

but not SQRT(7). If B ** 2 − 4.0 * A * C is a nonnegative real-valued expression, its square root can be calculated by writing

    SQRT(B ** 2 − 4.0 * A * C)

If the value of the expression B ** 2 − 4.0 * A * C is negative, an error will result because the square root of a negative number is not defined. To calculate the square root of an integer variable NUM, it is necessary first to convert its value to a real value using the type conversion function REAL before using SQRT:

    SQRT(REAL(NUM))

The Nth root of a real variable X can be computed by using

    X ** (1.0 / REAL(N))

and the Nth root of an integer variable NUM by using

    REAL(NUM) ** (1.0 / REAL(N))

There are several other functions provided in FORTRAN; some of the more commonly used functions are listed in Table 2.3. Other functions including the inverse trigonometric functions (ACOS, ASIN, ATAN, ATAN2) and the hyperbolic functions (COSH, SINH, TANH) are described in Table 6.1 and in Appendix D. To use any of

Table 2.3   Some FORTRAN Functions

Function	Description	Type of Argument(s)*	Type of Value
ABS(x)	Absolute value of x	Integer or real	Same as argument
COS(x)	Cosine of x radians	Real	Real
EXP(x)	Exponential function e^x	Real	Real
INT(x)	Integer part of x	Real	Integer
LOG(x)	Natural logarithm of x	Real	Real
MAX($x_1, \ldots, x_n$)	Maximum of $x_1, \ldots, x_n$	Integer or real	Same as arguments
MIN($x_1, \ldots, x_n$)	Minimum of $x_1, \ldots, x_n$	Integer or real	Same as arguments
MOD(x, y)	$x \pmod y$; $x - \text{INT}(x/y) * y$	Integer or real	Same as arguments
NINT(x)	x rounded to nearest integer	Real	Integer
REAL(x)	Conversion of x to real type	Integer	Real
SIN(x)	Sine of x radians	Real	Real
SQRT(x)	Square root of x	Real	Real
TAN(x)	Tangent of x radians	Real	Real

* In several cases, the arguments (and values) may be of double-precision or complex types. See Table 6.1.

these functions, we simply give the function name followed by the argument(s) enclosed in parentheses. In each case, the argument(s) must be of the type specified for that function in the table.

Quick Quiz 2.3

Find the value of each of the expressions in Questions 1–10.

1. `9 - 5 - 3`   2. `2.0 + 3.0 / 5.0`

3. `2 + 3 / 5`   4. `5 / 2 + 3`

5. `2 + 3 ** 2`   6. `(2 + 3) ** 2`

7. `25.0 ** 1 / 2`   8. `12.0 / 1.0 * 3.0`

9. `(2 + 3 * 4) / (8 - 2 + 1)`   10. `SQRT(6.0 + 3.0)`

Given that `TWO = 2.0`, `TRI = 3.0`, `FOUR = 4.0`, `IJK = 8`, and `INK = 5`, find the value of each of the expressions in Questions 11–17.

11. `TWO + TRI * TRI`   12. `INK / 3`

13. `(TRI + TWO / FOUR) ** 2`   14. `IJK / INK * 5.1`

15. `FOUR ** 2 / TWO ** 2`   16. `INK ** 2 / TWO ** 2`

17. `SQRT(TWO + TRI + FOUR)`

18. Write a FORTRAN expression equivalent to $10 + 5B - 4AC$.

19. Write a FORTRAN expression equivalent to the square root of $A + 3B^2$.

Exercises 2.3

Find the value of each of the expressions in Exercises 1–17.

1. `12 - 5 + 3`   2. `2 ** 3 + 3 / 5`

3. `2.0 / 4`   4. `3 + 4 ** 2`

5. `(3 + 4) ** 2`   6. `3 ** 2 ** 3`

7. `(3 ** 2) ** 3`   8. `3 ** (2 ** 3)`

9. `(3 ** 2 ** 3)`   10. `25 ** 1 / 2`

11. `-3.0 ** 2`   12. `ABS(1 - 2 - 3)`

13. `EXP(3.0 - 2.0 - 1.0)`   14. `INT(5.0 + 4.0 / 3.0)`

15. `((2 + 3) ** 2) / (8 - (2 + 1))`

16. `(2 + 3 ** 2) / (8 - 2 + 1)`

17. `(2.0 + 3 ** 2) / (8 - 2 + 1)`

18. Write a FORTRAN expression equivalent to three times the difference $4 - N$ divided by twice the quantity $M^2 + N^2$.

19. Write a FORTRAN expression equivalent to the cube root of X (calculated as X to the one-third power).

20. Write a FORTRAN expression equivalent to $A^2 + B^2 - 2AB \cos T$.

21. Write a FORTRAN expression equivalent to the natural logarithm of the absolute value of $\dfrac{X - Y}{X + Y}$.

2.4 THE ASSIGNMENT STATEMENT

The **assignment statement** is used to assign values to variables and has the form

Assignment Statement

Form:

```
variable = expression
```

where

variable is a valid **FORTRAN** identifier and

expression may be a constant, another variable to which a value has previously been assigned, or a formula to be evaluated.

Purpose:
Assigns the value of *expression* to *variable*.

For example, suppose that `XCOORD` and `YCOORD` are real variables and `NUMBER` and `TERM` are integer variables, as declared by the following statements:

```
REAL XCOORD, YCOORD
INTEGER NUMBER, TERM
```

These declarations associate memory locations with these variables. This might be pictured as follows, with the question marks indicating that these variables are initially undefined.

XCOORD	?
YCOORD	?
NUMBER	?
TERM	?

Now consider the following assignment statements:

```
XCOORD = 5.23
YCOORD = SQRT(25.0)
NUMBER = 17
TERM = NUMBER / 3 + 2
XCOORD = 2.0 * XCOORD
```

The first assignment statement assigns the real constant 5.23 to the real variable XCOORD, and the second assigns the real constant 5.0 to the real variable YCOORD. The next assignment statement assigns the integer constant 17 to the integer variable NUMBER; the variable TERM is still undefined, and the content of the memory location associated with it is uncertain.

XCOORD	5.23
YCOORD	5.0
NUMBER	17
TERM	?

This means that until the contents of these memory locations are changed, these values are substituted for the variable names in any subsequent expression containing these variables. Thus, in the fourth assignment statement, the value 17 is substituted for the variable NUMBER; the expression NUMBER / 3 + 2 is evaluated, yielding 7; and this value is then assigned to the integer variable TERM; the value of NUMBER is unchanged.

XCOORD	5.23
YCOORD	5.0
NUMBER	17
TERM	7

In the last assignment statement, the variable XCOORD appears on both sides of the assignment operator (=). In this case, the current value 5.23 for XCOORD is used in evaluating the expression 2.0 * XCOORD, yielding the value 10.46; this value is then assigned to XCOORD. The old value 5.23 is lost because it has been replaced with the new value 10.46.

XCOORD	10.46
YCOORD	5.0
NUMBER	17
TERM	7

Because there are different types of numeric variables and constants, it is possible to have not only mixed-mode arithmetic, as described in the preceding section, but also mixed-mode assignment. This occurs when the type of the value being assigned to a variable is different from the type of the variable.

If an integer-valued expression is assigned to a real variable, the integer value is converted to a real constant and then assigned to the variable. Thus, if the integer variable N has the value 9, and ALPHA and BETA are real variables, the statements

```
ALPHA = 3
BETA = (N + 3) / 5
```

assign the real value 3.0 to ALPHA and the real value 2.0 to BETA.

In the case of a real-valued expression assigned to an integer variable, the fractional part of the real value is truncated, and the integer part is assigned to the variable. For example, if the real variable X has the value 5.75, and I, KAPPA, and MU are integer variables, the statements

```
I = 3.14159
KAPPA = X / 2.0
MU = 1.0 / X
```

assign the integer values 3, 2, and 0 to the variables I, KAPPA, and MU, respectively. As this example shows, *using mixed-mode assignments is dangerous and should usually be avoided.* If it is necessary to truncate the fractional part of a real-valued expression and assign only the integer part, it would be better to indicate this explicitly by writing, for example,

```
KAPPA = INT(X / 2.0)
```

An assignment statement may also be used to assign a value to a character variable. To illustrate, suppose that the character variables STR, TRUN, and PAD are declared by the type statement

```
CHARACTER*5 STR, TRUN, PAD*10
```

The assignment statement

```
STR = 'ALPHA'
```

assigns the value 'ALPHA' to STR. In this example, the declared length of the variable is equal to the length of the corresponding value assigned to this variable. *If, however, the lengths do not match, the values are padded with blanks or truncated as necessary.* If the declared length of the variable is greater than the length of the value being assigned, trailing blanks are added to the value; thus the statement

```
PAD = 'PARTICLE'
```

assigns the value 'PARTICLEƀƀ' to the variable PAD (where ƀ denotes a blank character). If the declared length of the variable is less than the length of the value being assigned, the value is truncated to the size of the variable, and the leftmost characters are assigned; thus the statement

```
TRUN = 'TEMPERATURE'
```

assigns the value 'TEMPE' to the variable TRUN.

It is important to remember that *the assignment statement is not a statement of algebraic equality; rather, it is a* replacement *statement.* Some beginning programmers forget this and write the assignment statement

```
A = B
```

when the statement

```
B = A
```

is intended. These two statements produce very different results, as the first assigns the value of B to A, leaving B unchanged,

$$
\begin{array}{cc} A & 8.5 \\ B & 9.37 \end{array} \quad \xrightarrow{A = B} \quad \begin{array}{cc} A & 9.37 \\ B & 9.37 \end{array}
$$

and the second assigns the value of A to B, leaving A unchanged.

$$
\begin{array}{cc} A & 8.5 \\ B & 9.37 \end{array} \quad \xrightarrow{B = A} \quad \begin{array}{cc} A & 8.5 \\ B & 8.5 \end{array}
$$

To illustrate further that an assignment statement is a replacement statement, suppose that DELTA and RHO are integer variables with the values 357 and 59, respectively. The following statements interchange the values of DELTA and RHO, using the auxiliary variable TEMP:

```
INTEGER DELTA, RHO, TEMP
       .
       .
       .
TEMP = DELTA
DELTA = RHO
RHO = TEMP
```

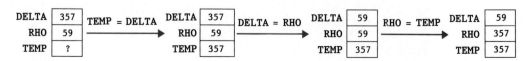

As another example, consider the statement

```
SUM = SUM + X
```

Such a statement, in which the same variable appears on both sides of the assignment operator, often confuses beginning programmers. Execution of this statement causes the values of SUM and X to be substituted for these variables to evaluate the expression SUM + X, and the resulting value is then assigned to SUM. The following diagram illustrates this statement for the case in which the real variables SUM and X have the values 132.5 and 8.4, respectively.

Note that the old value of the variable SUM is lost because it was replaced with a new value.

Quick Quiz 2.4

For Questions 1–8, assume the following declarations

```
INTEGER M, N
REAL PI, ALPHA
```

and determine if the given string is a valid FORTRAN assignment statement. If it is not valid, explain why it is not.

1. PI = 3.141592
2. 3 = N
3. N   = N+ 1
4. N+1 = N
5. ALPHA = 1
6. ALPHA = '1'
7. ALPHA = ALPHA
8. M = N = 1

For Questions 9–14, assume that NUM and MIX are integer variables with values 8 and 5, respectively; TWO, TRI, and FOUR are real variables with values 2.0, 3.0, and 4.0, respectively; JOB is an integer variable; and XVAL is a real variable. Find the value assigned to the given variable or indicate why the statement is not valid.

9. XVAL = (TRI + TWO / FOUR) ** 2
10. XVAL = NUM / MIX + 5.1
11. JOB = NUM / MIX + 5.1
12. NUM = NUM + 2
13. XVAL = SQRT(TRI ** 2 + FOUR ** 2)
14. NUM = ABS(TRI - 4.5)

For Questions 15–18, assume that the following declarations have been made:

```
CHARACTER*4 ALPHA, BETA*1
```

Find the value assigned to the given variable, or indicate why the statement is not valid.

15. BETA = 1
16. BETA = '1'
17. ALPHA = 'ONETWO'
18. ALPHA = '12'

For each of Questions 19–21, write a FORTRAN assignment statement that calculates the given expression and assigns the result to the specified variable.

19. RATE times TIME to DIST
20. $\sqrt{A^2 + B^2}$ to C
21. Increments COUNT by 1

Exercises 2.4

For Exercises 1–10, assume that the following declarations have been made,

```
INTEGER NUM, MIX, JOB, LIMIT
REAL TWO, TRI, FOUR, XVAL
PARAMETER (LIMIT = 10, TWO = 2.0)
```

and that NUM = 2, MIX = 5, TRI = 3.0, and FOUR = 4.0. Describe what the assignment statement does, or indicate why it is not valid.

1. XVAL = (TRI + 5.0 / FOUR) ** 2
2. JOB = MIX ** 2 / LIM ** 2
3. LIM = MIX ** 2 / NUM ** 2
4. XVAL = MIX ** 2 / LIM ** 2
5. XVAL = MIX ** 2 / NUM ** 2
6. XVAL = MIX ** 2 / FOUR ** 2 + TWO
7. JOB = MIX ** 2 / FOUR ** 2 + LIMIT
8. MIX = MIX + MIX
9. XVAL = SQRT(ABS(TWO - INT(TRI)))
10. JOB = MAX(INT(FOUR / 3), MIX)

For Exercises 11–20, assume that the following declarations have been made,

```
CHARACTER*10 ALPHA, BETA*5, GAMMA*1, DELTA*4
```

and that `DELTA = 'FOUR'`. Find the value assigned to the given variable, or indicate why the statement is not valid.

11. `GAMMA = 17`

12. `GAMMA = '17'`

13. `ALPHA = 'ONETWOTHREEFOUR'`

14. `ALPHA = '1234'`

15. `BETA = 'DON'T'`

16. `BETA = 'DON''T'`

17. `BETA = 'ABCDEFGHIJKLMNOPQRSTUVWXYZ'`

18. `BETA = '123,456,789'`

19. `ALPHA = DELTA`

20. `GAMMA = DELTA`

For each of Exercises 21–25, write a FORTRAN assignment statement that calculates the given expression and assigns the result to the specified variable.

21. $\dfrac{1}{\dfrac{1}{R1} + \dfrac{1}{R2} + \dfrac{1}{R3}}$ to RESIST

22. P times $(1 + R)^N$ to VALUE

23. Area of triangle (one-half base times height) of base B and height H to AREA

24. 5/9 of the difference $F - 32$ to C (conversion of Fahrenheit to Celsius)

25. $\dfrac{2V^2 \sin A \cos A}{G}$ to RANGE

For Exercises 26–28, give values for the integer variables I, J, and K and the real variable X for which the two expressions are not equal.

26. `I * (J / K)` and `I * J / K`

27. `X * I / J` and `X * (I / J)`

28. `(I + J) / K` and `I / K + J / K`

2.5 INPUT/OUTPUT

In the preceding section we considered the assignment statement, which enables us to calculate the values of expressions and store the results of these computations by assigning them to variables. For example, if a projectile is launched from an initial height of HGHT0 with an initial vertical velocity of VELOC0 and a vertical acceleration of ACCEL, then the equations

$$HGHT = 0.5 \cdot ACCEL \cdot TIME^2 + VELOC0 \cdot TIME + HGHT0$$

and

$$VELOC = ACCEL \cdot TIME + VELOC0$$

give the height (HGHT) and the vertical velocity (VELOC) at any TIME after launch. Assignment statements to implement these equations are easy to write:

```
HGHT = 0.5 * ACCEL * TIME ** 2 + VELOC0 * TIME + HGHT0
VELOC = ACCEL * TIME + VELOC0
```

Values must be assigned to the variables ACCEL, TIME, VELOC0, and HGHT0, however, before these statements can be used to compute values for HGHT and VELOC. The input statement that we consider in this section provides a convenient way to assign such values. Moreover, these assignment statements store the values of HGHT and VELOC, but they do not display them. The output statement also described in this section provides a method for easily displaying such information.

FORTRAN provides two types of input/output statements. In the first type, the programmer must explicitly specify the format in which the data is presented for input or, in the case of output, the precise format in which it is to be displayed. In the second type of input/output, certain predetermined standard formats that match the types of items in the input/output list are automatically provided by the compiler. It is this second type, known as **list-directed input/output,** that we consider in this section.

List-Directed Output

The simplest list-directed output statement has the following form:

List-Directed Output Statement

Forms:

```
PRINT *, output-list
```

or

```
WRITE (*, *) output-list
```

where

output-list is a single expression or a list of expressions separated by commas. Each of these expressions is a constant, a variable, or a formula.

These statements may also be used with no output list:

```
PRINT *
```

or

```
WRITE (*, *)
```

Purpose:
Displays the values of the items in the output list. Each output statement produces a new line of output. If the output list is omitted, a blank line is displayed.

For example, the PRINT statements

```
PRINT *, 'AT TIME ', TIME, ' THE VERTICAL VELOCITY IS ', VELOC
PRINT *, 'AND THE HEIGHT IS ', HGHT
```

could be used to display values of TIME, HGHT, and VELOC. Execution of these statements will produce output similar to the following:

```
AT TIME     4.30000 THE VERTICAL VELOCITY IS     47.8299
AND THE HEIGHT IS     396.334
```

Note that each PRINT statement produces a new line of output. The exact format and spacing used to display these values are compiler-dependent, however; for example, in some systems, real values might be displayed in exponential notation, and the number of spaces in an output line might be different from that shown.

List-Directed Input

The simplest form of the list-directed input statement is

List-Directed Input Statement

Form:

```
READ *, input-list
```

or

```
READ (*, *) input-list
```

where

> *input-list* is a single variable or a list of variables separated by commas.

Purpose:
Obtains values (usually from the keyboard) and assigns them to the variables in the input list. The following rules apply:

1. A new line of data is processed each time a READ statement is executed.
2. If there are fewer entries in a line of input data than there are variables in the input list, successive lines of input are processed until values for all variables in the list have been obtained.
3. If there are more entries in a line of input data than there are variables in the input list, the first data values are used, and all remaining values are ignored.
4. The entries in each line of input data must be constants and of the same type as the variables to which they are assigned. (However, an integer value may be assigned to a real variable, with automatic conversion taking place.)
5. Consecutive entries in a line of input data must be separated by a comma or by one or more spaces.

For example, the statement

```
READ *, HGHT0, VELOC0, TIME
```

can be used to obtain and assign values to the variables HGHT0, VELOC0, and TIME. These values will be entered during program execution. For example, to assign the values 100.0, 90.0, and 4.3 to the variables HGHT0, VELOC0, and TIME, respectively, the following line of input data could be used:

```
100.0, 90.0, 4.3
```

Spaces could be used as separators in place of the commas,

```
100.0 90.0 4.3
```

or more than one line of data could be used:

```
100.0 90.0
4.3
```

Character values can also be read using list-directed input, but they must be enclosed in single quotes. Truncation or blank padding is done when necessary, as described earlier for assignment statements. For example, if UNITS1 and UNITS2 have been declared by

```
CHARACTER*8 UNITS1, UNITS2
```

then entering the values

```
'METER', 'CENTIMETER'
```

in response to the statement

```
READ *, UNITS1, UNITS2
```

assigns the value 'METER₿₿₿' to UNITS1 (where ₿ denotes a blank) and the value 'CENTIMET' to UNITS2.

In an interactive mode of operation, the values assigned to variables in an input list are entered during program execution. In this case, when a READ statement is encountered, program execution is suspended while the user enters values for all the variables in the input list. Program execution then automatically resumes. Because execution is interrupted by a READ statement, and because the correct number and types of values must be entered before execution can resume, *it is good practice to provide some message to prompt the user when it is necessary to enter data values.* This is done by preceding each READ statement with a PRINT statement that displays the appropriate prompts. The program in Figure 2.1 illustrates this by prompting the user when values for HGHT0, VELOC0, and TIME are to be entered.

Figure 2.1 Projectile problem.

```
    PROGRAM PROJEC
*****************************************************************************
* This program calculates the velocity and height of a projectile         *
* given its initial height, initial velocity, and constant                *
* acceleration.  Variables used are:                                      *
*    HGHT0   :  initial height of projectile                              *
*    HGHT    :  height at any time                                        *
*    VELOC0  :  initial vertical velocity                                 *
*    VELOC   :  vertical velocity at any time                             *
*    ACCEL   :  vertical acceleration                                     *
*    TIME    :  time elapsed since projectile was launched                *
*                                                                         *
* Input : HGHT0, VELOC0, TIME                                             *
* Output: VELOC, HGHT                                                     *
*****************************************************************************
```

Figure 2.1 *(cont.)*

```
        REAL HGHT0, HGHT, VELOC0, VELOC, ACCEL, TIME
        DATA ACCEL / -9.807 /

* Obtain values for HGHT0, VELOC0, and TIME
        PRINT *, 'ENTER THE INITIAL HEIGHT AND VELOCITY:'
        READ *, HGHT0, VELOC0
        PRINT *, 'ENTER TIME AT WHICH TO CALCULATE HEIGHT AND VELOCITY:'
        READ *, TIME

* Calculate the height and velocity
        HGHT = 0.5 * ACCEL * TIME ** 2  +  VELOC0 * TIME  +  HGHT0
        VELOC = ACCEL * TIME + VELOC0

* Display VELOC and HGHT
        PRINT *, 'AT TIME ', TIME, ' THE VERTICAL VELOCITY IS ', VELOC
        PRINT *, 'AND THE HEIGHT IS ', HGHT

        END
```

Sample runs:

```
ENTER THE INITIAL HEIGHT AND VELOCITY:
100.0 90.0
ENTER TIME AT WHICH TO CALCULATE HEIGHT AND VELOCITY:
4.3
AT TIME     4.30000 THE VERTICAL VELOCITY IS     47.8299
AND THE HEIGHT IS     396.334


ENTER THE INITIAL HEIGHT AND VELOCITY:
150.0 100.0
ENTER TIME AT WHICH TO CALCULATE HEIGHT AND VELOCITY:
5.0
AT TIME     5.00000 THE VERTICAL VELOCITY IS     50.9650
AND THE HEIGHT IS     527.412


ENTER THE INITIAL HEIGHT AND VELOCITY:
150.0 100.0
ENTER TIME AT WHICH TO CALCULATE HEIGHT AND VELOCITY:
0
AT TIME    0. THE VERTICAL VELOCITY IS    100.0000
AND THE HEIGHT IS     150.000
```

Figure 9.4 *(cont.)*

```
ENTER THE INITIAL HEIGHT AND VELOCITY:
150.0 100.0
ENTER TIME AT WHICH TO CALCULATE HEIGHT AND VELOCITY:
21.79
AT TIME      21.7900 THE VERTICAL VELOCITY IS      −113.695
AND THE HEIGHT IS     0.797852
```

2.6 PROGRAM COMPOSITION AND FORMAT

Program Composition

In Section 2.1 we noted that a FORTRAN program has the form

heading
specification part
execution part

The **program heading** has the form

```
PROGRAM name
```

where *name* is a legal FORTRAN identifier. This name must be distinct from all other names in the program and should be chosen to indicate the purpose of the program. Thus, the first statement in the program of Figure 2.1 to calculate the height and velocity of a projectile is

```
PROGRAM PROJEC
```

Although the PROGRAM statement is optional, it should be used to identify the program and to distinguish it from other program units such as function subprograms, subroutine subprograms, and block data subprograms, which are described later.

Following the PROGRAM statement, there should be **opening documentation** that explains the purpose of the program, clarifies the choice of variable names, and provides other pertinent information about the program. This documentation consists of comment lines, which are blank lines or lines having the letter C or an asterisk (*) in the first position of the line. Comment lines are not considered to be program statements and may be placed anywhere in the program. Such comment lines can be used to clarify the purpose and structure of key parts of the program. Program documentation is invaluable when revisions and modifications are made in the future, especially when they are made by persons other than the original programmer.

The **specification part** of a program must appear next. This part contains type statements such as

```
REAL HGHTO, HGHT, VELOCO, VELOC, ACCEL, TIME
```

whose purpose is to specify the type of each of the variables used in the program. The type statements we have considered thus far have the form

```
REAL list
```

for declaring real variables,

```
INTEGER list
```

for declaring integer variables, and

```
CHARACTER*n list
```

for declaring character variables. Others will be considered in later chapters.

The specification part may also contain PARAMETER statements that may be used to associate names with constants to be used in the program. These statements have the form

```
PARAMETER (param₁ = const₁,..., paramₙ = constₙ)
```

Data statements of the form

```
DATA list₁/data₁/, list₂/data₂/,..., listₙ/dataₙ/
```

may be included to initialize the values of variables at compile time. They must appear after all PARAMETER and type statements.

FORTRAN statements are classified as either executable or nonexecutable. **Nonexecutable statements** provide information that is used during compilation of a program, but they do not cause any specific action to be performed during execution. For example, the PROGRAM statement, PARAMETER statements, DATA statements, and type statements are nonexecutable statements.

Executable statements do specify actions to be performed during execution of the program. Assignment statements and input/output statements are examples. Executable statements are placed in the last part of a FORTRAN program, its **execution part,** which has the form

```
statement₁
statement₂
      .
      .
      .
END
```

Note that the last statement in this part and thus the last statement of every program must be the END **statement.** This statement indicates to the compiler the end of the program; it also halts execution of the program and thus is an executable statement.

Program Format

Although some versions of FORTRAN allow considerable flexibility in the program format, standard FORTRAN has rather strict rules that dictate where statements and comments are to be placed. These rules are summarized in the following diagram:

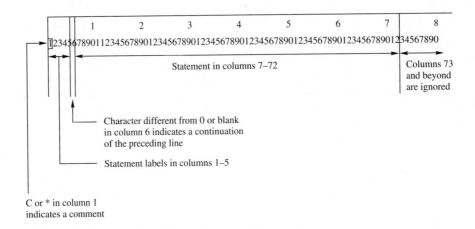

The positions within a line are called **columns** and are numbered 1, 2, 3, ... All FORTRAN statements must be positioned in columns 7 through 72; characters that appear in columns 73 and beyond are ignored. If a statement requires a **statement label,** this label must appear in columns 1 through 5. Statement labels must be integers in the range 1 through 99999.

Occasionally it may not be possible to write a complete FORTRAN statement using only columns 7 through 72 of a line. In this case, the statement may be continued on another line or lines (up to a maximum of 19), provided that a **continuation indicator** is placed in column 6 of the line(s) on which the statement is continued. This continuation indicator may be any alphabetic or numeric character other than a zero or a space. A zero or a space in column 6 indicates the first line of a statement.

Lines that contain only blanks or that have the letter C or an asterisk (*) in column 1 represent **comment lines.** Comments are not executed; in fact, they are ignored by the compiler. In standard FORTRAN, comments may not be continued from one line to another by using a continuation indicator in column 6; instead, all comments must begin with a C or * in column 1.

Quick Quiz 2.6

1. What are two ways to indicate a comment line?
2. Distinguish between executable and nonexecutable statements.
3. (True or False)   Each execution of a PRINT statement produces output on a new line.
4. (True or False)   Data values for a READ statement must be entered on the same line.
5. (True or False)   Entries in a line of input data must be separated by commas.
6. (True or False)   Every program must have a heading.
7. (True or False)   Execution of an END statement halts program execution.
8. What output is produced by the statement PRINT *?
9. What output (if any) will be produced by the following program?

```
PROGRAM DEMO
INTEGER I, J
REAL X, Y

X = 37
I = INT(X / 5)
PRINT *, X, I
READ *, X, I
PRINT *, 'X = ', X, ' I = ', I
READ *, Y
READ *, J
PRINT *, Y
PRINT *, J
END
```

Assume that the data values are entered as follows:

```
1.74 29
4.23 10
15
```

10. The following column numbers refer to columns used in preparing a FORTRAN program. For each of them, fill in the blank with the letter of the phrase from the list at the right which best describes how the columns are used:

   column 1   ___   A. Used to indicate that a program statement is a continuation of the previous statement.

columns 1–5	___	B. Used for statement numbers.
column 6	___	C. Used for the FORTRAN statement.
columns 7–72	___	D. Could be used to number the program statements, but will be ignored by the compiler.
column 73	___	E. Used to indicate a comment.

2.7 APPLICATION: TEMPERATURE CONVERSION

Problem

The boiling point of water is 212° on the Fahrenheit scale and 100° on the Celsius scale. The freezing point of water is 32° on the Fahrenheit scale and 0° on the Celsius scale. A program is to be developed that will convert a temperature on the Celsius scale to the corresponding Fahrenheit temperature.

Solution

Specification. Since the purpose of the program is to convert a Celsius temperature to the corresponding Fahrenheit temperature, it is clear that the input for this problem is a temperature on the Celsius scale and the output is a temperature on the Fahrenheit scale:

Input: A Celsius temperature

Output: A Fahrenheit temperature

Design. An initial description of an algorithm for solving this problem is straightforward:

1. Obtain the Celsius temperature.
2. Calculate the corresponding Fahrenheit temperature.
3. Display the Fahrenheit temperature.

Here, steps 1 and 3 are easy to implement using input and output statements. Step 2, however, requires some refinement, because we need a formula for converting a Celsius temperature into the equivalent Fahrenheit temperature. There is a linear relationship between the Celsius and Fahrenheit temperature scales; that is, $C°$ Celsius corresponds to $F°$ Fahrenheit, where

$$F = aC + b$$

for some constants a and b. We must first find the constants a and b. Because $0°$ Celsius corresponds to $32°$ Fahrenheit, we must have

$$32 = a \cdot 0 + b$$

so that $b = 32$. This means that

$$F = aC + 32$$

Because $100°$ Celsius corresponds to $212°$ Fahrenheit, we must have

$$212 = a \cdot 100 + 32$$

which gives $a = 9/5$, so that our equation becomes

$$F = \frac{9}{5}C + 32$$

In a program to solve this problem, variables must be used to store two temperatures. Selecting names that are self-documenting, we will use the following:

VARIABLES FOR TEMPERATURE PROBLEM

CELS   Temperature on the Celsius scale

FAHREN   Temperature on the Fahrenheit scale

A final version of the algorithm in pseudocode can now be given:

ALGORITHM FOR TEMPERATURE PROBLEM

```
* This algorithm converts a temperature of CELS degrees on the Celsius scale to the   *
* corresponding FAHREN degrees on the Fahrenheit scale.                               *
* Input:      A temperature in degrees Celsius                                        *
* Output:     A temperature in degrees Fahrenheit                                     *
```

1. Enter CELS.
2. Calculate the Fahrenheit temperature: $\text{FAHREN} = \frac{9}{5}\,\text{CELS} + 32$
3. Display FAHREN.

Expressed in flowchart form, the algorithm is

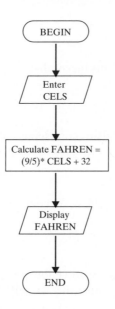

Program Coding. The program in Figure 2.2 is a first attempt to implement this algorithm. Note that the opening documentation contains a brief description of the program, a variable directory that explains what each variable represents, and the input/output specifications. Such documentation is important because it provides a brief summary of what the program does and makes it easier to read and understand the program itself.

Figure 2.2 Temperature conversion—a first attempt.

```
      PROGRAM TEMPS
*******************************************************************
* Program to convert a temperature of CELS degrees on the Celsius   *
* scale to the corresponding temperature on the Fahrenheit scale.   *
* Variables used are:                                               *
*     CELS   :   temperature on the Celsius scale                   *
*     FAHREN :   temperature on the Fahrenheit scale                *
*                                                                   *
* Input : CELS                                                      *
* Output: FAHREN                                                    *
*******************************************************************

      REAL CELS, FAHREN
```

Figure 2.2 *(cont.)*

```
* Obtain Celsius temperature
      PRINT *, 'ENTER TEMPERATURE IN DEGREES CELSIUS:'
      READ *, CELS

* Calculate corresponding Fahrenheit temperature
      FAHREN = (9/5) * CELS + 32.0

* Display FAHREN
      PRINT *, 'FAHRENHEIT TEMPERATURE IS', FAHREN

      END
```

Execution and Testing. Beginning programmers are sometimes tempted to skip the testing phase of program development. Once a program has compiled without errors, they are content simply to execute the program using the input data given in the assignment and then hand in the output. For example, if the program is to be used to convert the three Celsius temperatures 11.193, −17.728, and 49.1, a student might simply execute the program three times and hand in the output produced:

```
ENTER TEMPERATURE IN DEGREES CELSIUS:
11.193
FAHRENHEIT TEMPERATURE IS    43.1930

ENTER TEMPERATURE IN DEGREES CELSIUS:
−17.728
FAHRENHEIT TEMPERATURE IS    14.2720

ENTER TEMPERATURE IN DEGREES CELSIUS
49.1
FAHRENHEIT TEMPERATURE IS    81.1000
```

The fact that the program compiled without errors is no guarantee that it is correct, however, because it may contain logic errors. As we noted in Chapter 1, program testing is extremely important. Programs should be executed with test data for which the output produced can be verified by hand. For this program, we might first use an input value of 0 since it is easy to check that 0°C corresponds to 32°F.

Test run #1:
```
ENTER TEMPERATURE IN DEGREES CELSIUS:
0
FAHRENHEIT TEMPERATURE IS    32.0000
```

We see that the program has indeed produced the correct answer. However, we cannot be confident that a program is correct simply because it executes correctly for one set of test data.

Another natural test value to use for the temperature conversion program is 100°C, which corresponds to 212°F.

Test run #2:
```
ENTER TEMPERATURE IN DEGREES CELSIUS:
100.0
FAHRENHEIT TEMPERATURE IS    132.000
```

From this test run we see that the program is not correct. In fact, additional test runs will show that each output value is simply 32 plus the input value.

A review of the algorithm indicates that it is correct; thus the error apparently did not occur in the design stage. The error therefore must have occurred in the coding step. The statement that is suspect is the one that carries out the conversion:

```
FAHREN = (9/5) * CELS + 32
```

The fact that each output value is simply 32 plus the input value suggests that the Celsius temperature CELS is being multiplied by 1 instead of by 1.8 (= 9/5). This is indeed the case since the integer division $9/5$ in this expression produces the value 1.

Making this correction gives the program in Figure 2.3. (A version that uses repetition to process several temperatures is given in Section 4.1.)

Figure 2.3 Temperature conversion — final version.

```
      PROGRAM TEMPS
*************************************************************************
* Program to convert a temperature of CELS degrees on the Celsius      *
* scale to the corresponding temperature on the Fahrenheit scale.      *
* Variables used are:                                                  *
*     CELS   :  temperature on the Celsius scale                       *
*     FAHREN :  temperature on the Fahrenheit scale                    *
*                                                                      *
* Input:  CELS                                                         *
* Output: FAHREN                                                       *
*************************************************************************

      REAL CELS, FAHREN
```

Figure 2.3 *(cont.)*

```
* Obtain Celsius temperature
      PRINT *, 'ENTER TEMPERATURE IN DEGREES CELSIUS:'
      READ *, CELS

* Calculate corresponding Fahrenheit temperature
      FAHREN = 1.8 * CELS + 32.0

* Display FAHREN
      PRINT *, 'FAHRENHEIT TEMPERATURE IS', FAHREN

      END
```

The following test runs suggest that the program is correct:

Test run #1:
```
ENTER TEMPERATURE IN DEGREES CELSIUS:
0
FAHRENHEIT TEMPERATURE IS    32.0000
```

Test run #2:
```
ENTER TEMPERATURE IN DEGREES CELSIUS:
100.0
FAHRENHEIT TEMPERATURE IS    212.0000
```

After several more test runs have been made so that we are confident the program is correct, we can execute the program with the given input values and be quite sure that the output values produced are correct:

```
ENTER TEMPERATURE IN DEGREES CELSIUS:
11.193
FAHRENHEIT TEMPERATURE IS    52.1474

ENTER TEMPERATURE IN DEGREES CELSIUS:
-17.728
FAHRENHEIT TEMPERATURE IS    8.95996E-02

ENTER TEMPERATURE IN DEGREES CELSIUS:
49.1
FAHRENHEIT TEMPERATURE IS    120.380
```

2.8 APPLICATION: CIRCUITS WITH PARALLEL RESISTORS

Problem

In an electrical circuit, a current is generated if a voltage is applied across one or more resistances. Suppose that a circuit contains three resistors arranged in parallel:

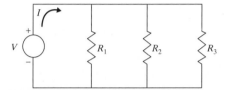

For such a circuit, the current depends on the voltage and the combined resistance of the three resistors. A program is needed to compute the current I in the circuit for a given voltage V and three given resistances R_1, R_2, and R_3.

Solution

Specification. The input and the output for this problem are easy to identify:

Input: Voltage
          Three resistances
Output: Current

Design. An initial description of an algorithm for solving this problem is

1. Obtain the voltage and the three resistances.
2. Calculate the current.
3. Display the current.

Here the second step requires refinement, since a formula is needed to calculate the current. By Ohm's law, the current I in a circuit is given by

$$I = \frac{V}{R}$$

where I is in amperes, the voltage V is in volts, and R is the total resistance in ohms. For three resistors connected in parallel, the total resistance is given by

$$R = \frac{1}{\dfrac{1}{R_1} + \dfrac{1}{R_2} + \dfrac{1}{R_3}}$$

It seems natural, therefore, to refine step 2 as follows:

2.1. Calculate the total resistance using the preceding formula.

2.2. Use Ohm's law to calculate the current.

Once again, variables must be used to store the values in this problem. We will use the following self-documenting names:

VARIABLES FOR CIRCUIT PROBLEM

VOLTS	Voltage
RESIS1, RESIS2, RESIS3	Three resistances
TOTRES	Total resistance
CURR	Current

A pseudocode description of the final algorithm is

ALGORITHM FOR CIRCUIT PROBLEM

* This algorithm determines the current CURR in a circuit containing three resistors *
* RESIS1, RESIS2, and RESIS3 in parallel and in which a voltage VOLTS is applied.   *
*   *
* Input: RESIS1, RESIS2, RESIS3, VOLTS   *
* Output: CURR   *

1. Enter RESIS1, RESIS2, RESIS3, VOLTS.

2.1. Calculate total resistance:

$$TOTRES = \frac{1}{\dfrac{1}{RESIS1} + \dfrac{1}{RESIS2} + \dfrac{1}{RESIS3}}$$

2.2. Calculate the current:

$$CURR = \frac{VOLTS}{TOTRES}$$

3. Display CURR.

Program Coding. The program in Figure 2.4 implements this algorithm. Note again the brief description of the program, the variable directory explaining what each variable represents, and the input/output specifications in the opening documentation.

Figure 2.4 Circuit problem.

```
      PROGRAM CIRC
***********************************************************************
* Program to determine the current in a circuit containing three     *
* resistors in parallel and in which a given voltage is applied.     *
* Variables used are:                                                *
*     VOLTS   :  voltage applied (volts)                             *
*     RESIS1,                                                        *
*     RESIS2,                                                        *
*     RESIS3  :  three resistances (ohms)                            *
*     TOTRES  :  total resistance                                    *
*     CURR    :  current (amperes)                                   *
*                                                                    *
* Input:   RESIS1, RESIS2, RESIS3, VOLTS*       RESIS1,              *
* Output:  CURR*       RESIS1,                                       *
***********************************************************************

      REAL RESIS1, RESIS2, RESIS3, TOTRES, VOLTS, CURR

* Obtain three resistances and voltage
      PRINT *, 'ENTER THREE RESISTANCES:'
      READ *, RESIS1, RESIS2, RESIS3
      PRINT *, 'ENTER THE VOLTAGE APPLIED:'
      READ *, VOLTS

* Calculate total resistance and current
      TOTRES = 1.0 / (1.0 / RESIS1 + 1.0 / RESIS2 + 1.0 / RESIS3)
      CURR = VOLTS / TOTRES

* Display the current
      PRINT *, 'THE CURRENT IS', CURR, ' AMPS'

      END
```

Execution and Testing. As we saw in the preceding section, testing a program is extremely important. In the following sample runs, simple test data was selected so that the output can be verified by hand.

Test run #1:

```
ENTER THREE RESISTANCES:
1.0, 1.0, 1.0
ENTER THE VOLTAGE APPLIED:
6.0
THE CURRENT IS    18.0000 AMPS
```

Test run #2:

```
ENTER THREE RESISTANCES:
0.5, 0.5, 0.5
ENTER THE VOLTAGE APPLIED:
4.0
THE CURRENT IS    24.0000 AMPS
```

Test run #3:

```
ENTER THREE RESISTANCES:
0.3, 0.4, 0.5
ENTER THE VOLTAGE APPLIED:
5.0
THE CURRENT IS    39.1667 AMPS
```

2.9 APPLICATION: CONCENTRATION OF AN ACID BATH

Problem

Suppose that the manufacturing process for castings at a certain plant includes cooling each casting in a water bath, followed by cleaning it by immersion in an acid. When the casting is transferred from the water bath to the acid bath, a certain amount of water accompanies it, thereby diluting the acid. When the casting is removed from the acid bath, the same amount of this diluted mixture is also removed; thus the volume of the liquid in the acid bath remains constant, but the acidity decreases each time a casting is immersed. We wish to design a program to (1) determine when the acidity falls below some lower limit at which the mixture becomes too diluted to clean castings; and (2) determine the acidity of the liquid in the acid bath after a given number of castings have been immersed.

Solution

Specification. From the preceding description of the problem, we can easily determine the problem's input and output.

Input: Initial amount of acid in the acid bath

Amount of water that is mixed with the acid when a casting is transferred from the water bath

Lower limit on the acidity

Number of castings immersed

Output: Maximum number of castings that may be immersed before the acidity falls below the specified lower limit

Measure of the acidity after the specified number of castings have been immersed

Design. A first version of an algorithm for solving this problem is as follows:

1. Get the initial amount of acid in the acid bath, the amount of water transferred with each casting, and the lower limit on the acidity.
2. Calculate the maximum number of castings that may be immersed before acidity falls below this limit.
3. Display this number of castings.
4. Enter the number of castings to be cleaned.
5. Calculate the acidity of the mixture after cleaning the castings.
6. Display this acidity.

Here steps 2 and 5 must be refined. We observe that if A is the original amount of acid and W is the amount of water that is mixed in at each stage, the concentration of acid in the mixture when the first casting is immersed is

$$\frac{A}{A + W}$$

When this casting is removed from the acid bath, the amount of acid in the diluted mixture is

$$\left(\frac{A}{A + W}\right) \cdot A$$

This means that when the second casting is immersed, the concentration of the mixture becomes

$$\frac{\left(\dfrac{A}{A + W}\right) \cdot A}{A + W}$$

Cast aluminum block for a V-8 engine at Ford's Romeo, MI Engine Plant. (Photo courtesy of Ford Motor Company.)

which can be written as

$$\left(\frac{A}{A + W}\right)^2$$

In general, the concentration of acid in the diluted mixture after n castings have been immersed is given by

$$\left(\frac{A}{A + W}\right)^n$$

This is the formula needed in step 5 of the problem.

For step 2, if L denotes the lower limit on acidity, we must determine the least value of n for which

$$\left(\frac{A}{A + W}\right)^n < L$$

Taking logarithms, we find that this inequality is equivalent to

$$n > \frac{\log L}{\log A - \log(A + W)}$$

so that the desired value of n is the least integer greater than the expression on the right side.

We will use the following variables to store the quantities involved:

VARIABLES FOR ACID DILUTION PROBLEM

ACID	Amount of acid in the mixture
WATER	Amount of water added with each immersion
LIMIT	Lower limit on acidity
MAXNUM	Maximum number of castings that can be cleaned
NCASTS	Number of castings to be cleaned
CONCEN	Proportion of acid in the mixture

With the preceding refinements and using these variables, we can write the following pseudocode description of the final algorithm for solving the problem.

ALGORITHM FOR ACID DILUTION PROBLEM

```
*  This algorithm determines how often a mixture of acid and water can be used before   *
*  acidity falls below some lower limit. It also determines the acidity of the mixture after   *
*  a given number of castings have been immersed in it.                                   *
*                                                                                          *
*  Input:    ACID, WATER, LIMIT, NCASTS                                                    *
*  Output:   MAXNUM, CONCEN                                                                *
```

1. Enter ACID, WATER, and LIMIT.

2. Calculate $\text{MAXNUM} = 1 + \dfrac{\log(\text{LIMIT})}{\log(\text{ACID}) - \log(\text{ACID} + \text{WATER})}$.

3. Display MAXNUM.
4. Enter NCAST.
5. Calculate CONCEN = (ACID/(ACID + WATER)) ** NCASTS.
6. Display CONCEN.

Program Coding. The program in Figure 2.5 implements the preceding algorithm.

Figure 2.5 Acid dilution problem.

```
      PROGRAM DILUTE
************************************************************************
* Program to determine how often a mixture of acid and water can be   *
* used before its acidity falls below some specified lower limit, and *
* to determine the acidity of the diluted mixture after a given number*
* of castings have been immersed in it. Variables used are:           *
*      ACID    :  amount of acid in the mixture                       *
*      WATER   :  amount of water added with each casting immersion    *
*      LIMIT   :  lower limit on acidity                              *
*      MAXNUM  :  maximum number of castings that can be cleaned      *
*      NCASTS  :  number of castings to be cleaned                    *
*      CONCEN  :  proportion of acid in the mixture                   *
*                                                                     *
* Input:   ACID, WATER, LIMIT, NCASTS                                 *
* Output:  MAXNUM, CONCEN                                             *
************************************************************************

      INTEGER MAXNUM, NCASTS
      REAL ACID, WATER, LIMIT, CONCEN

* Enter original amount of acid, amount of water transferred,
* and lower limit on acidity
      PRINT *, 'ENTER ORIGINAL AMOUNT OF ACID, AMOUNT OF WATER ADDED,'
      PRINT *, 'AND THE LOWER LIMIT ON THE ACIDITY:'
      READ *, ACID, WATER, LIMIT

* Calculate and display the maximum number of castings that can
* be cleaned
      MAXNUM = 1 + INT(LOG(LIMIT) / (LOG(ACID) − LOG(ACID + WATER)))
      PRINT *, 'AT MOST', MAXNUM, ' CASTINGS CAN BE IMMERSED BEFORE'
      PRINT *, 'ACIDITY FALLS BELOW', LIMIT
```

Figure 2.5 *(cont.)*

```
* Enter number of castings to be cleaned
      PRINT *
      PRINT *, 'HOW MANY CASTINGS ARE TO BE CLEANED (AT MOST',
     +          MAXNUM, ')?'
      READ *,  NCASTS

* Calculate and display the acidity after this many castings have
* been immersed
      CONCEN = (ACID / (ACID + WATER)) ** NCASTS
      PRINT *, 'THE PROPORTION OF ACID IN THE MIXTURE AFTER'
      PRINT *, NCASTS, ' IMMERSIONS IS ', CONCEN

      END
```

Execution and Testing. The following sample runs use test data to verify that the program is correct.

Test run #1:

```
ENTER ORIGINAL AMOUNT OF ACID, AMOUNT OF WATER ADDED,
AND THE LOWER LIMIT ON THE ACIDITY:
100, 100, 1
AT MOST  1 CASTINGS CAN BE IMMERSED BEFORE
ACIDITY FALLS BELOW    1.00000

HOW MANY CASTINGS ARE TO BE CLEANED (AT MOST 1)?
1
THE PROPORTION OF ACID IN THE MIXTURE AFTER
   1 IMMERSIONS IS    0.500000
```

Test run #2:

```
ENTER ORIGINAL AMOUNT OF ACID, AMOUNT OF WATER ADDED,
AND THE LOWER LIMIT ON THE ACIDITY:
100, 100, 0.1
AT MOST  4 CASTINGS CAN BE IMMERSED BEFORE
ACIDITY FALLS BELOW    1.00000E-01

HOW MANY CASTINGS ARE TO BE CLEANED (AT MOST 4)?
2
THE PROPORTION OF ACID IN THE MIXTURE AFTER
   2 IMMERSIONS IS    0.250000
```

Test run #3:

```
ENTER ORIGINAL AMOUNT OF ACID, AMOUNT OF WATER ADDED,
AND THE LOWER LIMIT ON THE ACIDITY:
90, 10, 0.7
AT MOST  4 CASTINGS CAN BE IMMERSED BEFORE
ACIDITY FALLS BELOW   0.700000

HOW MANY CASTINGS ARE TO BE CLEANED (AT MOST 4)?
2
THE PROPORTION OF ACID IN THE MIXTURE AFTER
  2 IMMERSIONS IS   0.810000
```

Test run #4:

```
ENTER ORIGINAL AMOUNT OF ACID, AMOUNT OF WATER ADDED,
AND THE LOWER LIMIT ON THE ACIDITY:
400, 0.05, 0.75
AT MOST  2303 CASTINGS CAN BE IMMERSED BEFORE
ACIDITY FALLS BELOW   0.750000

HOW MANY CASTINGS ARE TO BE CLEANED (AT MOST 2303)?
190
THE PROPORTION OF ACID IN THE MIXTURE AFTER
   190 IMMERSIONS IS   0.976541
```

*2.10 INTRODUCTION TO FILE INPUT/OUTPUT

Up to this point we have assumed that the data for the sample programs was entered from the keyboard during program execution and that the output was displayed on the screen. For some computer systems, such interactive input/output is not possible or may be clumsy. For these systems it may be necessary or convenient to store input data in a disk file and design the program so that it reads data from this file; it may also be necessary or convenient to store a program's output in a disk file for later processing. In this section we briefly describe how such input and output using files can be carried out in FORTRAN. (A more detailed description is given in Section 5.5 and in Chapter 11.)

To illustrate these file-processing features, we will rewrite the projectile program in Figure 2.1 so that input values are read from a file named fig2-6.dat:

Listing of fig2-6.dat:

```
100.0, 90.0
4.3
```

The first line contains the initial height and the initial velocity, and the second line contains the time at which the height and velocity are to be calculated. We will also design the program so that the output will be written to a file named `fig2-6.out`:

Listing of `fig2-6.out`:

```
AT TIME    4.30000 THE VERTICAL VELOCITY IS
47.8299 AND THE HEIGHT IS    396.334
```

Opening Files

Before a file can be used for input or output in a FORTRAN program, it must be "opened." This can be accomplished using an `OPEN` **statement** of the form

```
OPEN (UNIT = unit-number, FILE = file-name, STATUS = status)
```

where `unit-number` is an integer that will be used to reference this file in a `READ` or `WRITE` statement, `file-name` is the name of the disk file, and `status` is the character string `'OLD'` if the file already exists, or the string `'NEW'` otherwise. Thus we might use the statement

```
OPEN(UNIT = 12, FILE = 'fig2-6.dat', STATUS = 'OLD')
```

to open the input file, and the statement

```
OPEN(UNIT = 13, FILE = 'fig2-6.out', STATUS = 'NEW')
```

to create and open an output file.

File I/O

Once a file has been given a unit number, data can be read from or written to that file using special forms of the `READ` and `WRITE` statements:

```
READ (unit-number, *) input-list

WRITE (unit-number, *) output-list
```

For example, the statement

```
READ (12, *) HGHT0, VELOC0, TIME
```

can be used to read values for `HGHT0`, `VELOC0`, and `TIME` from the file `fig2-6.dat`. The statements

```
WRITE (13, *) 'AT TIME ', TIME, ' THE VERTICAL VELOCITY IS '
WRITE (13, *) VELOC, ' AND THE HEIGHT IS ', HGHT
```

can be used to produce output to the file `fig2-6.out`.

Example: The Projectile Program Revisited

Figure 2.6 shows the complete program for the projectile problem. It reads the initial height, the initial velocity, and the time from the disk file `fig2-6.dat` described earlier and writes output to the disk file `fig2-6.out`. Note that no output statements are used to prompt for input since all values are read from a file, but a `PRINT` statement is used to display a message indicating that program execution is complete.

Figure 2.6 Projectile program with file I/O.

```
      PROGRAM PROJEC
*********************************************************************
* This program calculates the velocity and height of a projectile  *
* given its initial height, initial velocity, and constant         *
* acceleration. Variables used are:                                *
*     HGHT0    : initial height                                    *
*     HGHT     : height at any time                                *
*     VELOC0   : initial vertical velocity                         *
*     VELOC    : vertical velocity at any time                     *
*     ACCEL    : vertical acceleration                             *
*     TIME     : time elapsed since projectile was launched        *
*                                                                  *
* Input (file):  HGHT0, VELOC0, TIME                               *
* Output (file): VELOC, HGHT                                       *
*********************************************************************

      REAL HGHT0, HGHT, VELOC0, VELOC, ACCEL, TIME
      DATA ACCEL / -9.807 /

* Open disk files fig2-6.dat and fig2-6.out
      OPEN(UNIT = 12, FILE = 'fig2-6.dat', STATUS = 'OLD')
      OPEN(UNIT = 13, FILE = 'fig2-6.out', STATUS = 'NEW')

* Read values for HGHT0, VELOC0, and TIME from fig2-6.dat
      READ (12, *) HGHT0, VELOC0, TIME

* Calculate the height and velocity
      HGHT = 0.5 * ACCEL * TIME ** 2 + VELOC0 * TIME + HGHT0
      VELOC = ACCEL * TIME + VELOC0

* Write values of VELOC and HGHT to fig2-6.out
      WRITE(13, *) 'AT TIME ', TIME, ' THE VERTICAL VELOCITY IS ',
      WRITE(13, *) VELOC, ' AND THE HEIGHT IS ', HGHT

* Signal user that program is finished
      PRINT *, '*** PROGRAM IS FINISHED ***'

      END
```

*2.11 ARITHMETIC ERRORS

In Chapter 1 we learned that all information stored in a computer must be represented in a binary form. One common representation of a real number is to express it in scientific binary form

$$f \times 2^e$$

with a mantissa (fractional part) f and an exponent e, and then use one part of a memory word or words to store the mantissa and another part to store the exponent (see Appendix E):

On many systems, real numbers are stored using twenty-four bits for the mantissa and eight for the exponent. It should be clear that

1. Because of the limited number of bits allotted to the exponent, only a finite range of real numbers can be stored.
2. Because of the limited number of bits allotted to the mantissa, most real numbers in this range cannot be stored exactly.

The limited range of reals that can be stored gives rise to two kinds of errors: **overflow errors** and **underflow errors,** and the limited number of bits allotted to the mantissa gives rise to **roundoff errors.**

Overflow/Underflow Errors

Overflow occurs when an exponent for a real value is too large to be stored. For single-precision values, an 8-bit exponent restricts the range of reals to approximately -10^{38} to 10^{38}, and overflow occurs for values outside this range:

Underflow occurs when an exponent for a real value is too small to be stored. For single-precision values, an 8-bit exponent requires values to be greater than approximately 10^{-38} or less than -10^{-38}, and underflow occurs between these values:

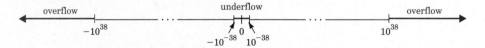

On some systems, execution of a program is terminated when an underflow or overflow error occurs and an appropriate error message is displayed. On others, execution may continue with the largest or smallest representable value used in the computation.

Roundoff Errors

Real numbers like $\pi = 3.141592653589\ldots$ and $1/3 = 0.33333333\ldots$, which do not have terminating decimal representations, do not have terminating binary representations either and thus cannot be stored exactly using a finite number of bits. Even such "nice" terminating decimals as 0.1 do not have terminating binary representations (see Appendix E). In fact, of all reals of the form $0.d$, where d is a digit, only 0.0 and 0.5 can be represented exactly; 0.1, 0.2, 0.3, 0.4, 0.6, 0.7, 0.8, and 0.9 cannot. Only 4 two-digit reals of the form $0.d_1d_2$ can be represented exactly, namely, 0.00, 0.25, 0.50, and 0.75; the remaining 96 two-digit reals cannot. In general, the only real numbers that can be represented exactly in the computer's memory are those that can be written in the form $m/2^k$, where m and k are integers.

Roundoff errors may be compounded when real numbers are combined in arithmetic expressions. To illustrate, consider adding the three real numbers 0.4104, 1.0, and 0.2204; for simplicity, assume that the computations are done using decimal representation with four-digit precision. The scientific representations of these values are 0.4104×10^0, 0.1000×10^1, and 0.2204×10^0. The first step in the addition of two values is to "align the decimal point" by increasing the smaller of the two exponents and shifting the mantissa. Thus, the sum of the first two values is obtained by adding 0.0410×10^1 and 0.1000×10^1, which gives 0.1410×10^1. Adding the third number again requires adjusting the exponent and shifting the mantissa, 0.0220×10^1, and the final result is 0.1630×10^1, or 1.630. On the other hand, if the two smaller values are added first, giving 0.6308×10^0, and then the larger number is added, the result is 0.1631×10^1, or 1.631 (assuming rounding). In a long chain of such calculations, these small errors can accumulate so that the error in the final result may be very large. This example also illustrates that two real quantities that are algebraically equal, such as $(A + B) + C$ and $(A + C) + B$, may have computed values that are not equal. Consequently, care must be taken when comparing two real values to see whether they are equal.

Many other familiar algebraic equalities fail to hold for real data values; for example, values of the real variables A, B, and C can be found for which the values of the following real expressions are not equal:

$$(A + B) + C \quad \text{and} \quad A + (B + C)$$

$$(A * B) * C \quad \text{and} \quad A * (B * C)$$

$$A * (B + C) \quad \text{and} \quad (A * B) + (A * C)$$

As another example of the effect of roundoff error, consider the following short program:

```
PROGRAM DEMO1

REAL A, B, C
READ *, A, B
C = ((A + B) ** 2 - 2 * A * B - B ** 2) / A ** 2
PRINT *, C
END
```

The following table shows the output produced by one computer system for various values of A and B:

A	B	C
0.5	888.0	1.00000
0.1	888.0	-12.5000
0.05	888.0	-50.0000
0.003	888.0	-13888.9
0.001	888.0	-125000.0

These results are rather startling, since the algebraic expression

$$\frac{(A + B)^2 - 2AB - B^2}{A^2}$$

can be written as

$$\frac{A^2 + 2AB + B^2 - 2AB - B^2}{A^2}$$

which simplifies to

$$\frac{A^2}{A^2}$$

and thus is identically 1 (provided $A \neq 0$).

CHAPTER REVIEW

Summary

This chapter begins a systematic study of the FORTRAN language. We started by considering the six FORTRAN data types,

integer
real or single precision
double precision
complex
character
logical

and we described how variables and constants are formed and declared using the INTEGER, REAL, and CHARACTER type statements and how values can be assigned to them using PARAMETER and DATA statements. Sections 2.3 and 2.4 described how expressions are formed and how the assignment statement can be used to assign values of expressions to variables. Input and output were discussed in Section 2.5. Section 2.6 described the overall composition of a program and the format in which it must be written. The three examples in the next sections illustrated the program-development process and the FORTRAN features considered in this chapter. The chapter ends with two optional sections. The first gives a brief introduction to file input/output and the second describes some of the arithmetic errors that may occur in computing with real numbers.

FORTRAN SUMMARY

Identifiers

Identifiers such as program names and variable names must begin with a letter, which may be followed by up to five letters or digits.

Program Structure

program heading   (PROGRAM statement)
specification part   (type declarations, PARAMETER statements,
                     and DATA statements)
execution part   (executable statements)

Comments

A blank line or a line that contains the letter C or an asterisk (*) in the first position of the line is a comment line.

PROGRAM Statement

```
PROGRAM program-name
```

Example:

```
PROGRAM PROJEC
```

Purpose:

The PROGRAM statement names the program.

Type Statements

```
REAL list-of-variable-names
INTEGER list-of-variable-names
CHARACTER*n list-of-variable-names
```

Example:

```
REAL HGHT0, HGHT, VELOC0, VELOC, ACCEL, TIME
INTEGER MAXNUM, NCASTS
CHARACTER *10 FNAME, LNAME, INIT*1
```

Purpose:
Type statements declare the type of values that variables will have.

PARAMETER Statement

$$\text{PARAMETER } (param_1 = const_1, \ldots, param_n = const_n)$$

where each $param_i$ is an identifier and each $const_i$ is a constant expression.

Example:

```
INTEGER LIMIT
REAL PI
PARAMETER (LIMIT = 100, PI = 3.14159)
```

Purpose:
The PARAMETER statement associates each $param_i$ with the constant $const_i$.

DATA Statement

$$\text{DATA } list_1/data_1/, \ list_2/data_2/, \ldots, \ list_n/data_n/$$

where each $list_i$ is a list of variables and each $data_i$ is a list of constants.

Example:

```
INTEGER COUNT
REAL SUMX, SUMY
CHARACTER*20 NAME
DATA COUNT, SUMX, SUMY / 1, 2*0.0 /, NAME /'JOHN Q. DOE'/
```

Purpose:
The DATA statement initializes each variable name in $list_i$ with the corresponding constant value in $data_i$ at compile time.

Operations

Operator	Operation
+	addition
−	subtraction
*	multiplication
/	division
**	exponentiation

Functions

Function	Description
ABS(x)	Absolute value of x
COS(x)	Cosine of x radians
EXP(x)	Exponential function e^x
INT(x)	Integer part of x
LOG(x)	Natural logarithm of x
MAX$(x_1, \ldots, x_n)$	Maximum of $x_1, \ldots, x_n$
MIN$(x_1, \ldots, x_n)$	Minimum of $x_1, \ldots, x_n$
MOD(x, y)	$x \pmod y$; $x - INT(x/y)$ * y
NINT(x)	x rounded to nearest integer
REAL(x)	Conversion of x to real type
SIN(x)	Sine of x radians
SQRT(x)	Square root of x
TAN(x)	Tangent of x radians

See Tables 2.3 and 6.1 and Appendix D for additional information about these and other functions provided in FORTRAN.

Assignment Statement

```
variable = expression
```

Examples:

```
COUNT = 0
HGHT = 0.5 * ACCEL * TIME ** 2 + VELOCO * TIME + HGHTO
VELOC = ACCEL * TIME + VELOCO
NAME = 'JOHN Q. DOE'
```

Purpose:
Assigns the value of the *expression* to the specified *variable*.

Input Statement
For interactive input:

```
READ *, input-list-of-variables
```

or

```
READ (*, *) input-list-of-variables
```

For input from a file:

```
READ (unit-number, *) input-list-of-variables
```

Example:

```
READ *, HGHTO, VELOCO
READ *, NCASTS
READ (12, *) HGHTO, VELOCO, TIME
```

Purpose:
The READ statement reads values for the variables in the input list.

Output Statements
For interactive output:

```
PRINT *, output-list-of-expressions
WRITE (*, *) output-list-of-expressions
```

For output to a file:

```
WRITE (unit-number, *) output-list-of-expressions
```

Examples:

```
PRINT *, 'ENTER THE INITIAL HEIGHT AND VELOCITY:'

PRINT *, 'AT TIME ', TIME, ' VERTICAL VELOCITY IS ', VELOC
PRINT *, 'AND THE HEIGHT IS ', HGHT
PRINT *

WRITE(13, *) 'AT TIME ', TIME, ' VERTICAL VELOCITY IS ', VELOC,
WRITE(13, *) 'AND THE HEIGHT IS ', HGHT
```

Purpose:
The `PRINT` and `WRITE` statements display the values of the expressions in the output list.

OPEN **Statement**

```
OPEN (UNIT = unit-number, FILE = file-name, STATUS = status)
```

Examples:

```
OPEN(UNIT = 12, FILE = 'fig2-6.dat', STATUS = 'OLD')
OPEN(UNIT = 13, FILE = 'fig2-6.out', STATUS = 'NEW')
```

Purpose:
The `OPEN` statement assigns a unit number to a disk file, which may already exist (status is `OLD`) or which will be created (status is `NEW`), and makes it accessible for input/output.

END **Statement**

```
END
```

Purpose:
The `END` statement marks the end of a program and stops execution.

Program Format

Line Position (Column)	Description
1	C or * indicates a comment line
1–5	Used for statement labels
6	Character different from a blank or 0 indicates continuation of preceding line
7–72	FORTRAN statement
73–	Ignored by the compiler

PROGRAMMING POINTERS

In this section we consider some aspects of program design and suggest guidelines for good programming style. We also point out some errors that may occur when writing FORTRAN programs.

Program Style and Design

1. In the examples in this text, we adopt certain style guidelines for FORTRAN programs, and you should write your programs in a similar style. The following standards are used (others are described in the Programming Pointers of subsequent chapters).

- *When a statement is continued from one line to another, indent the continuation line(s).*

- *Document each program with comment lines at the beginning of the program to explain the purpose of the program and what the variables represent. You should also include in this documentation your name, date, course number, assignment number, and so on.*

- *Break up long expressions into simpler subexpressions.*

- *Insert a blank comment line between the opening documentation and the specification statements at the beginning of the program and between these statements and the rest of the program.*

- *To improve readability, insert a blank space between items in a FORTRAN statement such as before and after assignment operators and arithmetic operators.*

2. *Programs cannot be considered correct until they have been validated using test data.* Test all programs with data for which the results are known or can be checked by hand calculation.

3. *Programs should be readable and understandable.*

- *Use meaningful identifiers that suggest what each identifier represents.* For example,

```
DIST = RATE * TIME
```

is more meaningful than

```
D = R * T
```

or

```
Z7 = ALPHA * X
```

Also, avoid "cute" identifiers, as in

```
HOWFAR = GOGO * SQUEAL
```

- *Do not use "magic numbers" that suddenly appear without explanation,* as in the statement

```
OUTPUT = 0.1237 * AMOUNT + 1.34E-5
```

If these numbers must be changed, someone must search through the program to determine what they represent and which ones should be changed and to locate all their occurrences. It is thus better to associate them with named constants, as in

```
REAL RATE, ERROR
PARAMETER (RATE = 0.1758, ERROR = 1.34E-5)
```

or assign them to variables, as in

```
REAL RATE, ERROR
DATA RATE, ERROR /0.1758, 1.34E-5/
```

- *Use comments to describe the purpose of a program, the meaning of variables, and the purpose of key program segments.* However, do not clutter the program with needless comments; for example, the comment in

```
* ADD 1 TO COUNT
      COUNT = COUNT + 1
```

is not helpful in explaining the statement that follows it and so should be omitted.
- *Label all output produced by a program.* For example,

```
PRINT *, 'RATE = ', RATE, ' TIME = ', TIME
```

produces more informative output than does

```
PRINT *, RATE, TIME
```

4. *Programs should be general and flexible.* They should solve a class of problems rather than one specific problem. It should be relatively easy to modify a program to solve a related problem without changing much of the program. Avoiding the use of magic numbers, as described in 3, is important in this regard.

Potential Problems

1. *Do not confuse* I *or* l *(lowercase "ell") and* 1 *or* 0 *(zero) and* O *(the letter "oh").* For example, the statement

```
PROGRAM DILUTE
```

produces an error, because the numeral 0 is used in place of the letter O. Many programmers distinguish between these in handwritten programs by writing the numeral 0 as ∅.

2. *When preparing a FORTRAN program, do not let any statement extend past column 72.* Most FORTRAN compilers ignore any characters beyond column 72, which can easily lead to errors caused by incomplete statements. For example, if one uses

```
PRINT *, 'FOR THE X-VALUE ', X, ' THE CORRESPONDING Y-VALUE IS ', Y
```

in a program where the last character (Y) is in column 73, an error message such as the following may result:

```
PRINT *, 'FOR THE X-VALUE ', X, ' THE CORRESPONDING Y-VALUE IS ',
   *** Input/output list is incomplete
```

3. *String constants must be enclosed in single quotes.* If either the beginning or the ending quote is missing, an error will result. An apostrophe is represented in a string constant as a pair of apostrophes, for example,

```
'ISN''T'
```

4. *String constants should not be broken at the end of a line.* All character positions through column 72 of a line are read, and so unintended blanks may be produced in a string constant. For example, the statement

```
    PRINT *, 'ENTER THE VALUES ON SEPARATE LINES. SEPARATE
   + THEM BY COMMAS'
```

produces the output

```
ENTER THE VALUES ON SEPARATE LINES. SEPARATE          THEM BY COMMAS.
```

5. *All multiplications must be indicated by* `*`. For example, `2*N` is valid, but `2N` is not.

6. *Division of integers produces an integer.* For example `1/2` has the value 0. Similarly, if N is an integer variable greater than 1, `1/N` will have the value 0.

7. *Parentheses in expressions must be paired.* For each left parenthesis there must be a matching right parenthesis that appears later in the expression.

8. *The values of parameters may not be changed.* Any attempt to do so produces a compile-time error.

9. *All variables are initially undefined.* Although some compilers may initialize variables to specific values (e.g., 0 for numeric variables), it should be assumed that all variables are initially undefined. For example, the statement Y = X + 1 usually produces a "garbage" value for Y if X has not previously been assigned a value.

10. *Initialization by means of* DATA *statements is done only once, during compilation, before execution of the program begins.* In particular, this means that the variables

are not reinitialized while the program is being executed. Potential Problem 6 in the Programming Pointers section of Chapter 4 explains this problem in detail.

11. *A value assigned to a variable must be of a type that is appropriate to the type of the variable.* Thus, entering the value 2.7 for an integer variable NUMBER in the statement

```
READ *, NUMBER
```

may generate an error message. However, an integer value read for a real variable is automatically converted to real type.

12. *Mixed-mode assignment must be used with care.* For example, if A, B, and C are real variables but NUMBER is an integer variable, the statement

```
NUMBER = -B + SQRT(B ** 2 - 4.0 * A * C)
```

calculates the real value of the expression on the right side correctly but then assigns only the integer part to NUMBER. This happens, for example, when the types of these variables are determined by FORTRAN's naming convention.

13. *In assignment statements and in list-directed input, if a character value being assigned or read has a length greater than that specified for the character variable, the rightmost characters are truncated. If the value has a length less than that specified for the variable, blanks are added at the right.* Thus, if STRING is declared by

```
CHARACTER*10 STRING
```

the statement

```
STRING = 'ABCDEFGHIJKLMNO'
```

will assign the string 'ABCDEFGHIJ' to STRING, and

```
STRING = 'ABC'
```

will assign the string 'ABCḃḃḃḃḃḃḃ' to STRING. An acronym sometimes used to remember this is

- **APT:** For **A**ssignment (and list-directed input), both blank-**P**adding and **T**runcation occur on the right.

14. *The types of all variables should be declared in type statements.* Any variable whose type is not explicitly specified will have its type determined by the FORTRAN naming convention. Thus, if the variable NUMBER has not been declared to be of real type, the function reference SQRT(NUMBER) causes an error, since SQRT requires a real argument and NUMBER is of integer type according to the naming convention. If A, B, C, and NUMBER have not been declared, execution of the statement

```
NUMBER = -B + SQRT(B ** 2 - 4.0 * A * C)
```

produces the result described in Potential Problem 12. According to FORTRAN's naming conventions, A, B, and C are real variables, so the real value of the expression on the right side is calculated correctly, but only its integer part is assigned to NUMBER because the naming convention specifies that it is an integer variable.

15. *A comma must precede the input/output list in input/output statements of the form*

```
READ *, input-list
PRINT *, output-list
```

PROGRAMMING PROBLEMS

1. For three resistors connected in series as in the following circuit,

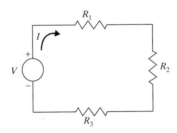

the total resistance is the sum of the individual resistances. Modify the program in Figure 2.4 so that it calculates and displays the current in a circuit in which the three resistors are connected in series.

2. For a circuit like that in Problem 1, the voltage across one of resistors R_1, R_2, R_3 is given by R_i*I, $i = 1, 2, 3$, where I is the current in the circuit. Modify the program of Problem 1 to calculate and display the voltages across each of the resistors for a given current.

3. Write a program to read the lengths of the two legs of a right triangle and calculate and display the area of the triangle (one-half the product of the legs) and the length of the hypotenuse (square root of the sum of the squares of the legs).

4. The Pythagorean theorem states that the sum of the squares of the sides of a right triangle is equal to the square of the hypotenuse. Thus, for a right triangle with sides 3 and 4, the length of the hypotenuse is 5. Similarly, a right triangle with sides 5 and 12 has a hypotenuse of 13, and a right triangle with sides 8 and 15 has a hypotenuse of 17. Triples of integers such as 3, 4, 5, or 5, 12, 13, or 8, 15, 17, which represent the two sides and the hypotenuse of a right triangle, are called *Pythagorean triples*. There are infinitely many such triples, and they all can be generated by the formulas

$$side1 = m^2 - n^2$$

$$\text{side2} = 2mn$$

$$\text{hypotenuse} = m^2 + n^2$$

where m and n are positive integers and $m > n$. Write a program that reads values for m and n and then calculates and displays the Pythagorean triple generated by these formulas.

5. Write a program to read values for the three sides a, b, and c of a triangle and then calculate its perimeter and its area. These should be displayed together with the values of a, b, and c using appropriate labels. (For the area, you might use Hero's formula for the area of a triangle:

$$\text{area} = \sqrt{s(s - a)(s - b)(s - c)}$$

where s is one-half the perimeter.)

6. The current in an alternating current circuit that contains resistance, capacitance, and inductance in series is given by

$$I = \frac{E}{\sqrt{R^2 + (2\pi fL - 1/(2\pi fC))^2}}$$

where I = current (amperes), E = voltage (volts), R = resistance (ohms), L = inductance (henrys), C = capacitance (farads), and f = frequency (hertz). Write a program that reads values for the voltage, resistance, capacitance, and frequency and then calculates and displays the current.

7. At t seconds after firing, the horizontal displacement x and the vertical displacement y (in feet) of a rocket are given by

$$x = v_0 t \cos \theta$$

$$y = v_0 t \sin \theta - 16t^2$$

where v_0 is the initial velocity (ft/sec) and θ is the angle at which the rocket is fired. Write a program that reads values for x_0, θ, and t, calculates x and y using these formulas, and displays these values.

8. The speed in miles per hour of a satellite moving in a circular orbit about a celestial body is given approximately by

$$\text{speed} = \sqrt{\frac{C}{D}}$$

where C is a constant depending on the celestial body and D is the distance from the center of the celestial body to the satellite (in miles). Write a program that reads the value of the constant C for a celestial body and a value for D and then calculates and displays the speed of the satellite. Run the program with the following values: (Earth) $C = 1.2E12$; (moon) $C = 1.5E10$; (Mars) $C = 1.3E11$.

9. One set of *polar coordinates* of a point in a place is given by (r, θ), where r is the length of the ray from the origin to the point and θ is the measure of an angle from the positive x-axis to this ray.

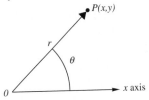

Write a program that reads polar coordinates for a point and calculates and displays its rectangular coordinates (x, y) obtained by using the formulas

$$x = r \cos \theta$$

$$y = r \sin \theta$$

10. The equation of the curve formed by a hanging cable weighing w pounds per foot of length can be described by

$$y = a \cosh \frac{x}{a}$$

where $a = H/w$, with H representing the horizontal tension pulling on the cable at its low point, and cosh is the hyperbolic cosine function defined by

$$\cosh u = \frac{e^u + e^{-u}}{2}$$

Write a program that reads values of w, H, and x and calculates and displays the corresponding value of y.

11. Write a program to convert a measurement given in feet to the equivalent number of **(a)** yards, **(b)** inches, **(c)** centimeters, and **(d)** meters (1 foot = 12 inches; 1 yard = 3 feet; 1 inch = 2.54 centimeters; 1 meter = 100 centimeters). Read the number of feet, and display, with appropriate labels, the number of yards, the number of feet, the number of inches, the number of centimeters, and the number of meters.

12. The formula for the volume of an oblate spheroid, such as the Earth, is

$$V = \frac{4}{3} \pi a^2 b$$

where a and b are the half-lengths of the major and minor axes, respectively. Write a program that reads values for a and b and then calculates and displays the volume. Use your program to find the volume of the Earth for which the values of a and b are 3963 miles and 3950 miles, respectively.

13. In order for a shaft with an allowable shear strength of S lb/in² to transmit a torque of T in-lbs, it must have a diameter of at least D inches, where D is given by

$$D = \sqrt[3]{\frac{16T}{S}}$$

If P horsepower is applied to the shaft at a rotational speed of N rpm, the torque is given by

$$T = 63000\,\frac{P}{N}$$

Write a program that reads values for P, N, and S and then calculates and displays the torque developed and the required diameter to transmit that torque. Run your program with the following inputs:

P (HP)	N (rpm)	S (psi)
20	1500	5000
20	50	5000
270	40	6500

14. The period of a pendulum is given by the formula

$$P = 2\pi\sqrt{\frac{L}{g}}\left(1 + \frac{1}{4}\sin^2\left(\frac{\alpha}{2}\right)\right)$$

where

$g = 980$ cm/sec²
$L =$ pendulum length (cm)
$\alpha =$ angle of displacement

Write a program to read values for L and α and then calculate and display the period of a pendulum having this length and angle of displacement. Run your program with the following inputs:

L (cm)	α (degrees)
120	15
90	20
60	5
74.6	10
83.6	12

15. A containing tank is to be constructed that will hold 500 cubic meters of oil when filled. The shape of the tank is to be a cylinder (including a base) surmounted by a cone, whose height is equal to its radius. The material and labor costs to construct the cylindrical portion of the tank are $300 per square meter, and the costs for the conical top are $400 per square meter. Write a program that calculates and displays the heights of the cylinder and the cone for a given radius that is input and that also calculates and displays the total cost of constructing the tank. Starting with a radius of 4.0 meters and incrementing by various (small) step sizes, run your program several times to determine the dimensions of the tank that will cost the least.

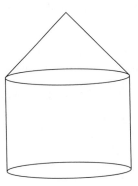

16. Write a program to read the thickness, density, and outside radius of a hollow ball and to calculate and display its volume and the mass. Starting with a value of 0.2 cm, run your program several times to find the largest wall thickness of a copper ball (density = 0.0089 kg/cm^3) with an outside radius of 50.0 cm that will float in water. (For the ball to float, its volume must be at least 1000 times its mass.)

17. The declining-balance formula for calculating depreciation is

$$V_N = V_0(1 - R)^N$$

where

V_N = the value after N years
V_0 = the initial value
R = the rate of depreciation
N = the number of years

Write a program to read values for V_0, R, and N and then calculate and display the depreciated value. Run the program several times to find the depreciated value of a new machine just purchased by Dispatch Die-Casting for $50,000 at the end of each year of its useful life. Assume that the rate of depreciation is 12 percent and that the useful life of the machine is 5 years.

18. The castings produced at Dispatch Die-Casting must be shipped in special contain-ers that are available in four sizes — huge, large, medium, and small — that can hold 50, 20, 5, and 1 castings, respectively. Write a program that reads the number of castings to be shipped and displays the number of containers needed to send the shipment most efficiently. The output for input value 598 should be similar to the following:

```
CONTAINER      NUMBER
=====================
   HUGE           11
   LARGE           2
   MEDIUM          1
   SMALL           3
```

19. The length of the line segment joining two points $P_1(x_1, y_1)$ and $P_2(x_2, y_2)$ is given by

$$\sqrt{(x_2 - x_1)^2 + (y_2 - y_1)^2}$$

and the midpoint of the segment has the coordinates

$$\left(\frac{x_1 + x_2}{2}, \frac{y_1 + y_2}{2}\right)$$

The slope of the line through P_1 and P_2 is given by

$$\frac{y_2 - y_1}{x_2 - x_1}$$

(provided $x_1 \neq x_2$), and the slope-intercept equation of this line is

$$y = mx + b$$

where m is the slope and b is the y-intercept; b can be calculated by

$$b = y_1 - mx_1$$

The perpendicular bisector of the line segment joining P_1 and P_2 is the line through the midpoint of this segment and having slope $-1/m$ (provided $m \neq 0$). Write a program that reads the coordinates of two points, P_1 and P_2, with distinct x-coordinates and distinct y-coordinates, and calculates and displays the length of the segment $\overline{P_1 P_2}$, the midpoint of the segment, the slope of the line through P_1 and P_2, its y-intercept, its slope-intercept equation, and the equation of the perpendicular bisector of $\overline{P_1 P_2}$.

20. Write a program that will read a student's number, his or her old grade point average (GPA), and old number of course credits (e.g., 30179, 3.29, 19) and then display these with appropriate labels. Then read the course credit and grade for each of four courses; for example, C1 = 1.0, G1 = 3.7, C2 = 0.5, G2 = 4.0, and so on. Calculate

$$\text{number of old honor points} = (\text{old \# of course credits}) * (\text{old GPA})$$

$$\text{number of new honor points} = C1 * G1 + \cdots + C4 * G4$$

$$\text{total \# of new course credits} = C1 + C2 + C3 + C4$$

$$\text{current GPA} = \frac{\text{\# of new honor points}}{\text{\# of new course credits}}$$

Display the current GPA with an appropriate label. Then calculate

$$\text{cumulative GPA} = \frac{(\text{\# of old honor points}) + (\text{\# of new honor points})}{(\text{\# of old course credits}) + (\text{\# of new course credits})}$$

and display this with a label.

Fortran 90

Several variations of and extensions to the features of FORTRAN 77 described in this chapter have been provided in Fortran 90. This section briefly describes and illustrates the most important ones.

New Features
Program Format

- Free-form source code is allowed. There is no special significance attached to the various columns of a line. Statements may begin in any column.
- Lower case is equivalent to upper case except in character strings.
- Lines may extend up to 132 characters.
- More than one statement may be placed on a line. A semicolon is used to separate such statements.

- In-line comments are allowed. Such comments begin with an exclamation point (!) and extend to the end of the line; for example,

```
Fahren = 1.8 * Cels + 32.0    ! Convert to Fahrenheit
```

- Continuation of a statement is indicated by using an ampersand (&) as the last non-blank character in the line being continued or the last nonblank character before the exclamation mark that marks the beginning of a comment. Up to 39 continuation lines are allowed.

Constants and Variables

- Modified forms of type specification statements can be used to initialize variables; for example, the type statement

```
REAL :: Rate = 7.25
```

declares RATE to be a real variable with initial value 7.25.

- Parameters can be declared and defined in a single type statement. For example, the type statement

```
REAL, PARAMETER :: Pi = 3.14159
```

declares Pi to be a real parameter associated with the constant 3.14159.

- The separator : : is required in a type specification statement whenever it is used to initialize variables or to declare that an identifier has a special attribute (e.g., PARAMETER). It may be omitted in other type specification statements, although it is standard practice always to include it. Thus, for example,

```
INTEGER X, Y
```

and

```
INTEGER :: X, Y
```

are equivalent, but we will use the latter form in our examples.

- The precision of a real (or double-precision or complex) constant or variable may be specified by using kind type parameters. Every processor must provide at least two kinds of precision, one corresponding to single-precision real type and one cor-responding to double-precision type. A KIND = clause is used in the declaration of parameters and variables to specify their precision:

```
REAL (KIND = kind-type-parameter) :: list-of-identifiers
```

Two intrinsic functions, SELECTED_REAL_KIND and KIND, are used to determine the kind type parameters. A reference to SELECTED_REAL_KIND has the form

```
SELECTED_REAL_KIND(N)
```

where N is an integer, and returns the kind type parameter that will provide at least N decimal digits of precision. For example, the statements

```
REAL (KIND = SELECTED_REAL_KIND(10)) :: V, W
```

or

```
INTEGER, PARAMETER :: PREC10 = SELECTED_REAL_KIND(10)
REAL (KIND = PREC10) :: V, W
```

declare that V and W are real variables whose values are to have at least 10 decimal digits of precision. A reference to the KIND function has the form

```
KIND(X)
```

and returns the kind type parameter of X. For example, the declaration

```
REAL (KIND = KIND(0.0123456789)) :: V, W
```

is equivalent to the preceding declarations of V and W.

- The intrinsic function PRECISION can be used to determine the precision of a real (or complex) value; for example, for the preceding variable X, the function reference PRECISION(X) returns the value 10.

- The REAL function can be referenced with a second argument,

```
REAL(x, kind-type-parameter)
```

to convert x of type integer or real (or complex) to a real value whose precision is specified by the kind type parameter.

- Integer values may have binary, octal, or hexadecimal representation in DATA statements. Such representations consist of the binary, octal, or hexadecimal digits enclosed in quotes (single or double) and preceded by B, O, or Z, respectively; for example, the binary representation B'1001' of the integer 9 may be used in a DATA statement.

- Strings may be enclosed in either single (') or double (") quotes.

- Identifiers may consist of up to 31 letters, digits, or underscores (_); the first character must be a letter. For example, `Area_of_Circle` is a valid Fortran 90 identifier.

- A modified form of the `IMPLICIT` statement, `IMPLICIT NONE`, cancels the naming convention, with the result that the types of all named constants and variables (and functions) *must be* specified explicitly in type statements.

Arithmetic Operations and Functions

- Several new arithmetic functions have been added.

Program Composition

- A Fortran program may have a subprogram section that immediately precedes the `END` statement.

Examples

The following programs in Figures 2.7 and 2.8 illustrate several of the preceding new features. They are Fortran 90 versions of the projectile program in Figure 2.1 and the temperature conversion program in Figure 2.3.

Figure 2.7 Projectile—Fortran 90 version.

```
PROGRAM Projectile
!-------------------------------------------------------------------
! This program calculates the velocity and height of a projectile
! given its initial height, initial velocity, and constant
! acceleration. Identifiers used are:
!   InitialHeight    : initial height of projectile
!   Height           : height at any time
!   InitialVelocity  : initial vertical velocity
!   Velocity         : vertical velocity at any time
!   Acceleration     : vertical acceleration
!   Time             : time since launch
!
! Input:  InitialHeight, InitialVelocity, Time
! Output: Velocity, Height
!-------------------------------------------------------------------
```

Figure 2.7 *(cont.)*

```
  IMPLICIT NONE
  REAL :: InitialHeight, Height, InitialVelocity, Velocity, &
          Acceleration = -9.807,  Time

! Obtain values for InitialHeight, InitialVeloc, and Time
  PRINT *, "Enter the initial height and velocity:"
  READ *, InitialHeight, InitialVelocity
  PRINT *, "Enter time at which to calculate height and velocity:"
  READ *, Time

! Calculate the height and velocity
  Height = 0.5 * Acceleration * Time ** 2 &
           + InitialVelocity * Time + InitialHeight
  Velocity = Acceleration * Time + InitialVelocity

! Display Velocity and Height
  PRINT *, "At time ", Time, "the vertical velocity is ", Velocity
  PRINT *, "and the height is ", Height

END PROGRAM Projectile
```

Figure 2.8 Temperature conversion—Fortran 90 version.

```
  PROGRAM Temperature_Conversion
!-----------------------------------------------------------------------
! Program to convert a temperature on the Celsius scale to the
! corresponding temperature on the Fahrenheit scale.
! Variables used are:
!   Celsius   : temperature on the Celsius scale
!   Fahrenheit: temperature on the Fahrenheit scale
!
! Input:   Celsius
! Output:  Fahrenheit
!-----------------------------------------------------------------------

  IMPLICIT NONE
  REAL :: Celsius, Fahrenheit

! Obtain Celsius temperature
  PRINT *, "Enter temperature in degrees Celsius:"
  READ *, Celsius
```

Figure 2.8 *(cont.)*

```
! Calculate corresponding Fahrenheit temperature
  Fahrenheit = 1.8 * Celsius + 32.0

! Display Fahrenheit
  PRINT *, "Fahrenheit temperature is ", Fahrenheit

END PROGRAM Temperature_Conversion
```

3

Selective
Execution

When you get to the fork in the road, take it.

YOGI BERRA

If you can keep your head, when all about are losing theirs . . .

RUDYARD KIPLING

"Would you tell me, please, which way I ought to go from here?"
"That depends a great deal on where you want to get to," said the Cat.

ALICE AND THE CAT IN LEWIS CARROLL'S ALICE'S ADVENTURES IN
WONDERLAND

Then Logic would take you by the throat, and force you to do it!

ACHILLES IN LEWIS CARROLL'S
WHAT THE TORTOISE SAID TO ACHILLES

CHAPTER CONTENTS

3.1 Logical Expressions

3.2 Simple Selection Structures: The `IF` Statement

3.3 Application: Pollution Index

3.4 Compound Selection Structures: Nested `IF`s and `IF-ELSE IF` Constructs

3.5 Application: Fluid Flow in a Pipe

3.6 The `LOGICAL` Data Type

3.7 Application: Logical Circuits

Chapter Review

Programming Pointers

Programming Problems

Fortran 90

In Chapter 2 we described several software engineering techniques that assist in the design of programs that are easy to understand and whose logical flow is easy to follow. Such programs are more likely to be correct when first written than poorly structured programs; and if they are not correct, the errors are easier to find and correct. Such programs are also easier to modify, which is especially important since such modifications may be required long after the program was originally written and are often made by someone other than the original programmer.

We noted that one important software engineering principle is that algorithms and programs should be structured. In a **structured program**, the logical flow is governed by three basic control structures: **sequence, selection, and repetition.** Sequential control, as illustrated in the diagram on page 120, simply refers to the execution of a sequence of statements in the order in which they appear so that each statement is executed exactly once. All the sample programs in Chapter 2 are "straight-line" programs in which the only control used is sequential.

Sequence is a fundamental control mechanism, but it is not powerful enough to solve all problems. For some problems, the solution requires selecting one of several alternative actions. Two such problems will be described in detail and solved in this chapter.

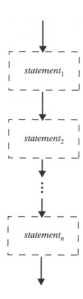

Problem 1: Classifying a Pollution Index.   The pollution-index problem described in Section 3.3 requires calculating and classifying a pollution index. A value of 50 or greater for the index indicates a hazardous condition, whereas a value less than 50 indicates a safe condition:

> If the pollution index is greater than 50
>> Display a "hazardous condition" message
>
> Else
>> Display a "safe condition" message

In this problem, one of two possible actions is selected, but in other problems there may be several alternative actions. The fluid-flow problem described and solved in Section 3.5 is such a problem.

Problem 2: Determining the Type of Fluid Flow in a Pipe.   Flow of a fluid through a pipe may be one of three types—laminar, turbulent, or unstable (switches between turbulent and laminar). The problem is to determine the type of flow for a particular pipe and fluid.

To solve this problem, the *Reynold's number* must be computed and compared with two cutoff values:

> If the Reynold's number is less than the first cutoff value, the flow is laminar.
>
> If the Reynold's number is greater than or equal to the first cutoff value but less than a second cutoff value, the flow is turbulent.
>
> If the Reynold's number is greater than or equal to the second cutoff value, the flow is unstable.

There are thus three alternatives and exactly one of them must be selected.

In this chapter we show how the selection structures needed to solve such problems are implemented in FORTRAN.

3.1 LOGICAL EXPRESSIONS

Several of the FORTRAN statements that are used to implement selection and repetition structures involve logical expressions. Consequently, before we can describe these control structures, we must examine logical expressions in more detail.

Simple Logical Expressions

Logical expressions may be either **simple** or **compound**. Simple logical expressions are logical constants (.TRUE. and .FALSE.) or logical variables (see Section 3.6) or **relational expressions** of the form

```
expression₁ relational-operator expression₂
```

where both $expression_1$ and $expression_2$ are numeric or character (or logical) expressions, and the $relational\text{-}operator$ may be any of the following:

Symbol	Meaning
.LT.	Is less than
.GT.	Is greater than
.EQ.	Is equal to
.LE.	Is less than or equal to
.GE.	Is greater than or equal to
.NE.	Is not equal to

The periods must appear as parts of these relational symbols because they serve to distinguish a logical expression such as X.EQ.Y from the variable XEQY.

The following are examples of simple logical expressions:

```
.TRUE.
X .LT. 5.2
NUMBER .EQ. -999
```

If X has the value 4.5, the logical expression X .LT. 5.2 is true. If NUMBER has the value 400, the logical expression NUMBER .EQ. -999 is false. In logical expressions such as

```
B ** 2 .GE. 4.0 * A * C
```

which contain both arithmetic operators and relational operators, the arithmetic operators are evaluated first; that is, this logical expression is equivalent to

```
(B ** 2) .GE. (4.0 * A * C)
```

Thus, if A, B, and C have the values 2.0, 1.0, and 3.0, respectively, this logical expression is evaluated as

```
1.0 .GE. 24.0
```

which is clearly false.

When using the relational operators .EQ. and .NE., it is important to remember that *many real values cannot be stored exactly* (see Section 2.11). *Consequently, logical expressions formed by comparing real quantities with .EQ. are often evaluated as false, even though these quantities are algebraically equal.* This is illustrated by the program in Figure 3.3.

For character data, numeric codes are used to establish an ordering for the character set. Two standard coding schemes are ASCII and EBCDIC (see Appendix A). They differ in the codes assigned to characters, but in both schemes the letters are in alphabetical order, and the digits are in numerical order. Thus

```
'A' .LT. 'F'
'6' .GT. '4'
```

are true logical expressions. Two strings are compared character by character using these numeric codes. For example, for a logical expression of the form

```
string₁ .LT. string₂
```

if the first character of $string_1$ is less than the first character of $string_2$ (that is, precedes it in the coding sequence), then $string_1$ is less than $string_2$. Thus,

```
'CAT' .LT. 'DOG'
```

is true, since C is less than D. If the first characters of $string_1$ and $string_2$ are the same, the second characters are compared; if these characters are the same, the third characters are compared, and so on. Thus,

```
'CAT' .LT. 'COW'
```

is true, since A is less than O. Similarly,

```
'JUNE' .GT. 'JULY'
```

is true, since N is greater than L. Two strings with different lengths are compared as though blanks are appended to the shorter string, resulting in two strings of equal length to be compared. For example, the logical expression

```
'CAT' .LT. 'CATTLE'
```

is evaluated in the same manner as

```
'CATbbb' .LT. 'CATTLE'
```

(where b denotes a blank) which is true because a blank character precedes all letters.

Compound Logical Expressions

Compound logical expressions are formed by combining logical expressions by using the **logical operators**

```
.NOT.
.AND.
.OR.
.EQV.
.NEQV.
```

These operators are defined in the following table, where P and Q represent logical expressions.

Logical Operator	Logical Expression	Definition
.NOT.	.NOT. P	.NOT. P is true if P is false and is false if P is true.
.AND.	P .AND. Q	*Conjunction* of P and Q: P .AND. Q is true if both P and Q are true; it is false otherwise.
.OR.	P .OR. Q	*Disjunction* of P and Q: P .OR. Q is true if P or Q or both are true; it is false otherwise.
.EQV.	P .EQV. Q	*Equivalence* of P and Q: P .EQV. Q is true if both P and Q are true or both are false; it is false otherwise.
.NEQV.	P .NEQV. Q	*Nonequivalence* of P and Q: P .NEQV. Q is the negation of P .EQV. Q; it is true if one of P or Q is true and the other is false; it is false otherwise.

These definitions are summarized in the following **truth tables**, which display all the possible values for the logical expressions P and Q and the corresponding values of the compound logical expression:

P	.NOT. P
.TRUE.	.FALSE.
.FALSE.	.TRUE.

P	Q	P .AND. Q	P .OR. Q	P .EQV. Q	P .NEQV. Q
.TRUE.	.TRUE.	.TRUE.	.TRUE.	.TRUE.	.FALSE.
.TRUE.	.FALSE.	.FALSE.	.TRUE.	.FALSE.	.TRUE.
.FALSE.	.TRUE.	.FALSE.	.TRUE.	.FALSE.	.TRUE.
.FALSE.	.FALSE.	.FALSE.	.FALSE.	.TRUE.	.FALSE.

In a logical expression containing several of these operators, the operations are performed in the order .NOT., .AND., .OR., .EQV. (or .NEQV.). Parentheses may be used to indicate those subexpressions that should be evaluated first. For example, consider logical expressions of the form

```
.NOT. P .AND. Q
P .AND. (Q .OR. R)
```

In the first expression, the subexpression .NOT. P is evaluated first, and this result is then combined with the value of Q, using the operator .AND.. The entire expression is therefore true only in the case that P is false and Q is true. In the second example, the subexpression Q .OR. R is evaluated first; the possible values it may have are displayed in the following truth table:

P	Q	R	P .AND. (Q .OR. R)
.TRUE.	.TRUE.	.TRUE.	.TRUE.
.TRUE.	.TRUE.	.FALSE.	.TRUE.
.TRUE.	.FALSE.	.TRUE.	.TRUE.
.TRUE.	.FALSE.	.FALSE.	.FALSE.
.FALSE.	.TRUE.	.TRUE.	.TRUE.
.FALSE.	.TRUE.	.FALSE.	.TRUE.
.FALSE.	.FALSE.	.TRUE.	.TRUE.
.FALSE.	.FALSE.	.FALSE.	.FALSE.

These values are then combined with the values of P using the operator .AND.:

P	Q	R	P .AND. (Q .OR. R)	
.TRUE.	.TRUE.	.TRUE.	.TRUE.	.TRUE.
.TRUE.	.TRUE.	.FALSE.	.TRUE.	.TRUE.
.TRUE.	.FALSE.	.TRUE.	.TRUE.	.TRUE.
.TRUE.	.FALSE.	.FALSE.	.FALSE.	.FALSE.
.FALSE.	.TRUE.	.TRUE.	.FALSE.	.TRUE.
.FALSE.	.TRUE.	.FALSE.	.FALSE.	.TRUE.
.FALSE.	.FALSE.	.TRUE.	.FALSE.	.TRUE.
.FALSE.	.FALSE.	.FALSE.	.FALSE.	.FALSE.

When a logical expression contains arithmetic operators, relational operators, and logical operators, they are performed in the following order:

1. Arithmetic operations (and functions)
2. Relational operations
3. Logical operations in the order .NOT., .AND., .OR., .EQV. (or .NEQV.)

For example, if the integer variable N has the value 4, the logical expression

```
N**2 + 1 .GT. 10 .AND. .NOT. N .LT. 3
```

or with parentheses inserted to improve readability,

```
(N**2 + 1 .GT. 10) .AND. .NOT. (N .LT. 3)
```

is true. The logical expression

```
N .EQ. 3 .OR. N .EQ. 4
```

is valid and is true, whereas

```
N .EQ. 1 .OR. 2
```

is not, since this would be evaluated as

```
(N .EQ. 1) .OR. 2
```

and 2 is not a logical expression to which .OR. can be applied.

Quick Quiz 3.1

1. The two logical constants are _____ and _____ .

2. List the six relational operators.

3. List the five logical operators.

For Questions 4–8, assume that P, Q, and R are logical expressions with the values .TRUE., .TRUE., and .FALSE., respectively. Find the value of each logical expression.

4. P .AND. .NOT. Q

5. P .AND. Q .OR. .NOT. R

6. P .AND. .NOT. (Q .OR. R)

7. .NOT. P .AND. Q

8. P .OR. Q .AND. R

For Questions 9–13, assume that NUM, COUNT, and SUM are integer variables with values 3, 4, and 5, respectively. Find the value of each logical expression or indicate why it is not valid.

9. SUM − NUM .LE. 4

10. NUM**2 + COUNT**2 .EQ. SUM**2

11. NUM .LT. COUNT .OR. COUNT .LT. SUM

12. 0 .LE. COUNT .LE. 5

13. (NUM + 1 .LT. SUM) .AND. .NOT. (COUNT + 1 .LT. SUM)

14. Write a logical expression to express that X is nonzero.

15. Write a logical expression to express that X is strictly between −10 and 10.

16. Write a logical expression to express that both X and Y are positive or both X and Y are negative.

Exercises 3.1

For Exercises 1–10, assume that M and N are integer variables with the values −5 and 8, respectively, and that X, Y, and Z are real variables with the values −3.56, 0.0, and 44.7, respectively. Find the value of the logical expression.

1. M .LE. N

2. 2 * ABS(M) .LE. 8

3. X * X .LT. SQRT(Z)

4. NINT(Z) .EQ. (6 * N − 3)

5. (X .LE. Y) .AND. (Y .LE. Z)

6. .NOT. (X .LT. Y)

7. .NOT. ((M .LE. N) .AND. (X + Z .GT. Y))

8. .NOT. (M .LE. N) .OR. .NOT. (X + Z .GT. Y))

9. .NOT. ((M .GT. N) .OR. (X .LT. Z)) .EQV. ((M .LE. N) .AND. (X .GE. Z))

10. .NOT. ((M .GT. N) .AND. (X .LT. Z)) .NEQV. ((M .LE. N).AND. (X .GE. Z))

For Exercises 11–16, assume that A, B, and C are logical variables. Use truth tables to display the value of the logical expression for all possible values of A, B, and C.

11. A .OR. .NOT. B

12. .NOT. (A .AND. B)

13. .NOT. A .OR. .NOT. B

14. A .AND. .TRUE. .OR. (1 + 2 .EQ. 4)

15. A .AND. (B .OR. C)

16. (A .AND. B) .OR. (A .AND. C)

For Exercises 17–25, write a logical expression to express the given condition.

17. X is greater than 3.

18. Y is strictly between 2 and 5.

19. R is negative and Z is positive.

20. ALPHA and BETA are both positive.

21. ALPHA and BETA have the same sign (both are negative or both are positive).

22. $-5 < X < 5$.

23. A is less than 6 or is greater than 10.

24. $P = Q = R$.

25. X is less than 3, or Y is less than 3, but not both.

For Exercises 26–28, assume that A, B, and C are logical variables.

26. Write a logical expression that is true if and only if A and B are true and C is false.

27. Write a logical expression that is true if and only if A is true and at least one of B or C is true.

28. Write a logical expression that is true if and only if exactly one of A and B is true.

3.2 SIMPLE SELECTION STRUCTURES: THE IF STATEMENT

A selection structure selects one of several alternative sets of statements for execution. This selection is based on the value of a logical expression.

Simple IF Statement

In the simplest selection structure, a sequence of statements (also called a *block* of statements) is executed or bypassed depending on whether a given logical expression is true or false. This is pictured in the following diagram:

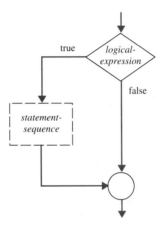

This selection structure is implemented in FORTRAN by using an IF **construct** (also called a **block IF statement**) of the form

IF *Construct (Simple Form)*

Form:

```
IF (logical-expression) THEN
    statement-sequence
END IF
```

where
    `statement-sequence` is a sequence of FORTRAN statements.
Note that the logical expression must be enclosed in parentheses.

Purpose:
If the logical expression is true, the specified sequence of statements is executed; otherwise it is bypassed. In either case, execution continues with the statement in the program following the END IF.

For example, in the IF construct

```
IF (X .GE. 0) THEN
   Y = X * X
   Z = SQRT(X)
END IF
```

the logical expression X .GE. 0 is evaluated, and if it is true, Y is set equal to the square of X and Z is set equal to the square root of X; otherwise, these assignment statements are not executed.

FORTRAN also provides a simplified IF construct that can be used if the statement sequence consists of a single statement. This short form is called a **logical IF statement** and has the following form:

Logical I F Statement

Form:

```
IF (logical-expression) statement
```

where
    statement is a FORTRAN statement.
Note that the logical expression must be enclosed in parentheses.

Purpose:
If the logical expression is true, the specified statement is executed; otherwise it is bypassed. In either case, execution continues with the next statement in the program.

For example, in the logical IF statement

```
IF (1.5 .LE. X .AND. X .LE. 2.5) PRINT *, X
```

if $1.5 \leq X \leq 2.5$, the value of X is displayed; otherwise, the PRINT statement is bypassed. In either case, execution continues with the next statement in the program.

General Form of the IF Construct

In the preceding selection structure, the selection is made between (1) executing a given sequence of statements and (2) bypassing these statements. In the two-way selection pictured in the diagram on page 130, the selection is made between (1) executing one sequence (block) of statements and (2) executing a different sequence (block) of statements.

This selection structure is implemented in FORTRAN by an IF construct that allows the programmer not only to specify the sequence of statements to be executed

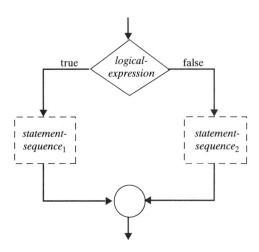

when the logical expression is true but also to indicate an alternative statement sequence to be executed when it is false. This IF construct has the form

---

IF *Construct (General Form)*

Form:

```
IF (logical-expression) THEN
    statement-sequence₁
ELSE
    statement-sequence₂
END IF
```

where
    statement-sequence₁ and *statement-sequence₂* are sequences
       of FORTRAN statements; and
    the ELSE part is optional.
Note that the logical expression must be enclosed in parentheses.

Purpose:
If the logical expression is true:
    statement-sequence₁ is executed and
    statement-sequence₂ is bypassed.
If the logical expression is false:
    statement-sequence₁ is bypassed;
    if there is an ELSE part, *statement-sequence₂* is executed;
    otherwise, execution will simply continue with the next statement following
    the END IF statement that terminates the IF construct.
In either case, execution continues with the next statement in the program (unless, of course, execution is terminated or control is transferred elsewhere by one of the statements in the statement sequence selected).

As an example of this form of an IF construct, consider the problem of calculating the values of the following piecewise continuous function:

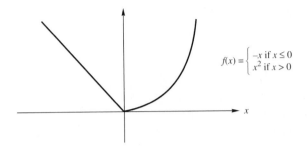

$$f(x) = \begin{cases} -x \text{ if } x \le 0 \\ x^2 \text{ if } x > 0 \end{cases}$$

An IF construct containing an ELSE clause makes this easy:

```
IF (X .LE. 0) THEN
    FVAL = -X
ELSE
    FVAL = X ** 2
END IF
```

Example: Quadratic Equations

As another illustration of using an IF construct to implement a two-alternative selection structure, consider the problem of solving the quadratic equation

$$Ax^2 + Bx + C = 0$$

by using the quadratic formula to obtain the roots

$$\frac{-B \pm \sqrt{B^2 - 4AC}}{2A}$$

In this problem, the input values are the coefficients A, B, and C of the quadratic equation, and the output is the pair of real roots or a message indicating that there are no real roots (in case $B^2 - 4AC$ is negative). An algorithm for solving a quadratic equation is as follows:

ALGORITHM FOR SOLVING QUADRATIC EQUATIONS

```
*   This algorithm solves a quadratic equation Ax² + Bx + C = 0 using the quadratic for-  *
*   mula. If the discriminant DISC = B² − 4AC is nonnegative, the pair of real roots  *
*   ROOT1 and ROOT2 is calculated; otherwise, a message is displayed indicating that  *
*   there are no real roots.                                                          *
*                                                                                     *
*   Input:    The coefficients A, B, and C                                            *
```

*   Output: The roots of the equation or the (negative) discriminant and a no-real-roots *
*   message   *

1. Enter A, B, and C.
2. Calculate DISC = B ** 2 − 4 * A * C.
3. If DISC ≥ 0 then do the following:
   a. Calculate DISC = $\sqrt{\text{DISC}}$.
   b. Calculate ROOT1 = (−B + DISC) / (2 * A).
   c. Calculate ROOT2 = (−B − DISC) / (2 * A).
   d. Display ROOT1 and ROOT2.
   Else do the following:
   a. Display DISC.
   b. Display a message that there are no real roots.

Figure 3.1 displays the structure of this algorithm in flowchart form.

Figure 3.1

Flowchart for
quadratic
equation
algorithm.

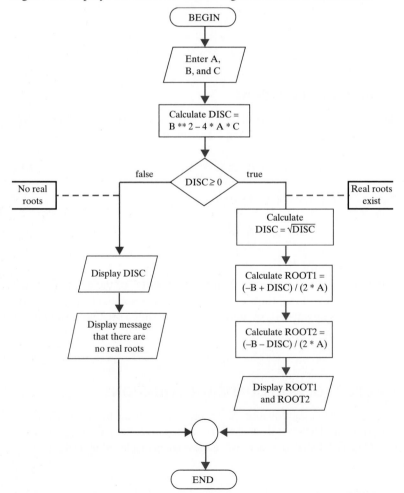

The program in Figure 3.2 implements this algorithm. Note the indentation of the statements in the IF construct. Although not required, it is good programming style to set off these statements in this manner to emphasize that they constitute a single block.

Figure 3.2 Quadratic equations.

```
      PROGRAM QUAD1
****************************************************************************
* Program to solve a quadratic equation using the quadratic formula.  *
* Variables used are:                                                 *
*     A, B, C      : the coefficients of the quadratic equation       *
*     DISC         : the discriminant, B ** 2 - 4 * A * C             *
*     ROOT1, ROOT2 : the two roots of the equation                    *
*                                                                     *
* Input:  The coefficients A, B, and C                                *
* Output: The two roots of the equation or the (negative) discriminant*
*         and a message indicating that there are no real roots       *
****************************************************************************

      REAL A, B, C, DISC, ROOT1, ROOT2

* Get the coefficients
      PRINT *, 'ENTER THE COEFFICIENTS OF THE QUADRATIC EQUATION'
      READ *, A, B, C

* Calculate the discriminant
      DISC = B ** 2 - 4.0 * A * C

* Check if discriminant is nonnegative.  If it is, calculate and
* display the roots.  Otherwise display the value of the discriminant
* and a no-real-roots message.
      IF (DISC .GE. 0) THEN
         DISC = SQRT(DISC)
         ROOT1 = (-B + DISC) / (2.0 * A)
         ROOT2 = (-B - DISC) / (2.0 * A)
         PRINT *, 'THE ROOTS ARE', ROOT1, ROOT2
      ELSE
         PRINT *, 'DISCRIMINANT IS', DISC
         PRINT *, 'THERE ARE NO REAL ROOTS'
      END IF

      END
```

Figure 3.2 (*cont.*)

Sample runs:

```
ENTER THE COEFFICIENTS OF QUADRATIC EQUATION
1, -5, 6
THE ROOTS ARE    3.00000    2.00000
ENTER THE COEFFICIENTS OF THE QUADRATIC EQUATION
1, 0, -4
THE ROOTS ARE    2.00000   -2.00000

ENTER THE COEFFICIENTS OF THE QUADRATIC EQUATION
1, 0, 4
DISCRIMINANT IS    -16.0000
THERE ARE NO REAL ROOTS

ENTER THE COEFFICIENTS OF THE QUADRATIC EQUATION
3.7, 16.5, 1.7
THE ROOTS ARE  -0.105528  -4.35393
```

The Effect of Roundoff Error

As we noted in Section 3.1, it is important to remember that because real values cannot be stored exactly, logical expressions formed by comparing real quantities with .EQ. are often evaluated as false, even though these quantities are algebraically equal. The program in Figure 3.3 demonstrates this by showing that for some real values X, the value of Y computed by

```
Y = X * (1.0 / X)
```

is not 1. In this program, an IF construct uses the logical expression

```
Y .EQ. 1.0
```

to check if the value of Y is equal to 1 and selects an appropriate message to be displayed based on the value of this logical expression.

Figure 3.3 The effect of roundoff error.

```
      PROGRAM APPROX
*************************************************************************
* Program to show inexact representation of reals by showing that      *
* for some real values X, X * (1.0 / X) is not equal to 1. Variables    *
* used are:                                                             *
*     X        : a real number entered by the user                     *
*     Y        : X * (1.0 / X)                                          *
* Input:  X                                                             *
* Output: The value of X, the value of Y = X * (1.0 / X), and a         *
*         message indicating whether Y is equal to 1                    *
*************************************************************************

      REAL X, Y

* Get an arbitrary nonzero real number X
      PRINT *, 'ENTER NONZERO REAL NUMBER'
      READ *, X

* Calculate product of X and 1/X, display it and difference
* between it and 1
      Y = X * (1.0 / X)
      PRINT *, 'X = ', X, '     Y = X *  (1 / X) = ', Y
      PRINT *, '1.0 - Y = ', 1.0 - Y

* Check if product is 1 and display appropriate message
      IF (Y .EQ. 1.0) THEN
          PRINT *, 'Y EQUALS 1'
      ELSE
          PRINT *, 'DUE TO ROUNDOFF ERROR, Y DOES NOT EQUAL 1'
      END IF

      END
```

Sample runs:

```
ENTER NONZERO REAL NUMBER
0.5
X =    0.500000     Y = X * (1 / X) =     1.00000
1.0 - Y = 0.
Y EQUALS 1
```

Figure 3.3 *(cont.)*

```
ENTER NONZERO REAL NUMBER
6.39631
X =      6.39631     Y = X * (1 / X) =     1.000000
1.0 - Y =     5.96046E-08
DUE TO ROUNDOFF ERROR, Y DOES NOT EQUAL 1

ENTER NONZERO REAL NUMBER
15.7981
X =      15.7981     Y = X * (1 / X) =     1.000000
1.0 - Y =     5.96046E-08
DUE TO ROUNDOFF ERROR, Y DOES NOT EQUAL 1
```

As this program demonstrates, if two real values are subject to the roundoff error caused by inexact representation, it is usually not advisable to check whether they are equal. Rather, one should check whether the absolute value of their difference is small:

```
IF (ABS(real-value₁ - real-value₂) .LT. ERRTOL) THEN
    ⋮
    ⋮
```

where ERRTOL is some small positive real value such as $1E-6$.

3.3 APPLICATION: POLLUTION INDEX

Problem

The level of air pollution in the city of Dogpatch is measured by a pollution index. Readings are made at 12:00 P.M. at three locations: at the Abner Coal Plant, downtown at the corner of Daisy Avenue and 5th Street, and at a randomly selected location in a residential area. The integer average of these three readings is the pollution index, and a value of 50 or greater for this index indicates a hazardous condition, whereas values less than 50 indicate a safe condition. Because this index must be calculated daily, the Dogpatch environmental statistician would like a program that calculates the pollution index and then determines the appropriate condition, safe or hazardous.

Solution

Specification. The relevant given information consists of three pollution readings and the cutoff value used to distinguish between safe and hazardous conditions. A solution to the problem consists of the pollution index and a message indicating the con-

Smog over Los Angeles, California. (Photo courtesy of Uniphoto Picture Agency.)

dition. Generalizing so that any cutoff value, not just 50, can be used, we can specify the problem as follows:

Input: Three pollution readings
Constant: Cutoff value to distinguish between safe and hazardous conditions
Output: Pollution index = integer average of the pollution readings
                Condition: safe or hazardous

Design.   The first step in an algorithm to solve this problem is to obtain values for the input items—the three pollution readings. The next step is to calculate the pollution index by averaging the three readings. An appropriate air-quality message must then be displayed. Thus, an initial description of an algorithm is

1. Obtain the three pollution readings.
2. Calculate the pollution index.
3. Display an appropriate air-quality message.

Coding step 1 is straightforward, but steps 2 and 3 require some refinement. For step 2, once the three pollution readings have been entered, we need only add them and divide the sum by 3 to obtain their average. We will use the following identifiers to store the input values, the cutoff value, and the pollution index:

▼

IDENTIFIERS FOR POLLUTION INDEX PROBLEM

LEVEL1, LEVEL2, LEVEL3	Three pollution readings
CUTOFF	Cutoff value
INDEX	Pollution index

▲

In step 3, one of two possible actions must be selected. Either a message indicating a safe condition or a message indicating a hazardous condition must be displayed. The appropriate action is selected by comparing the pollution index with the cutoff value. A refined version of step 3 might thus be written in pseudocode as

> If INDEX < CUTOFF then
>   Display 'Safe condition'
> Else
>   Display 'Hazardous condition'

A final version of the algorithm can now be given.

▼

ALGORITHM FOR POLLUTION INDEX PROBLEM

```
*  This algorithm reads three pollution levels and then calculates a pollution index,   *
*  which is the integer average of these three readings. If this index is less than a speci-  *
*  fied cutoff value, a message indicating a safe condition is displayed; otherwise, a mes-   *
*  sage indicating a hazardous condition is displayed.                                   *
*                                                                                         *
*  Input:      LEVEL1, LEVEL2, LEVEL3                                                      *
*  Constant:   CUTOFF                                                                      *
*  Output:     The pollution INDEX and a message indicating the air quality               *
```

1. Enter LEVEL1, LEVEL2, and LEVEL3.
2. Calculate
$$INDEX = \frac{LEVEL1 + LEVEL2 + LEVEL3}{3}$$
3. If INDEX < CUTOFF then
    Display 'Safe condition'
Else
    Display 'Hazardous condition'

▲

The following flowchart representation of this algorithm shows that its basic overall structure is sequential but that one of the steps in this sequential execution is a selection. The highlighted region of the diagram clearly shows the two alternatives, one of which must be selected according to the truth or falsity of the condition INDEX < CUTOFF; a diamond-shaped box like that shown is commonly used to indicate that a selection must be made.

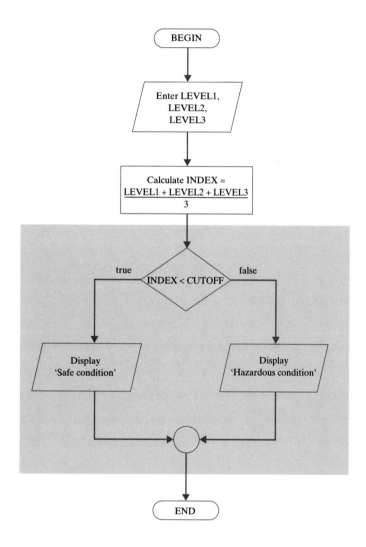

Coding.   The FORTRAN program in Figure 3.4 implements the preceding algorithm. A PARAMETER statement is used to set the value of CUTOFF so that it can be easily modified later if necessary. The selection structure

If INDEX < CUTOFF then
   Display 'Safe condition'
Else
   Display 'Hazardous condition'

in the algorithm is implemented in the FORTRAN program by the following IF construct:

```
IF (INDEX .LT. CUTOFF) THEN
    PRINT *, 'SAFE CONDITION'
ELSE
    PRINT *, 'HAZARDOUS CONDITION'
END IF
```

Figure 3.4 Pollution index.

```
      PROGRAM POLLUT
*************************************************************************
* Program that reads 3 pollution levels, calculates a pollution        *
* index as their integer average, and then displays an appropriate     *
* air-quality message.   Identifiers used are:                         *
*     LEVEL1, LEVEL2, LEVEL3: the three pollution levels               *
*     CUTOFF: a cutoff value that distinguishes between hazardous      *
*             and safe conditions (parameter)                          *
*     INDEX:  the integer average of the pollution levels              *
*                                                                      *
* Input:  The three pollution levels and the cutoff value             *
* Output: The pollution index and a "safe condition" message if       *
*         this index is less than the cutoff value, otherwise a        *
*         "hazardous condition" message                                *
*************************************************************************

      INTEGER LEVEL1, LEVEL2, LEVEL3, CUTOFF, INDEX
      PARAMETER (CUTOFF = 50)

* Get the 3 pollution readings
      PRINT *, 'ENTER 3 POLLUTION READINGS:'
      READ *, LEVEL1, LEVEL2, LEVEL3

* Calculate the pollution index
      INDEX = (LEVEL1 + LEVEL2 + LEVEL3) / 3
```

Figure 3.4 *(cont.)*

```
* Check if the pollution index is less than the cutoff and
* display an appropriate air-quality message
      IF (INDEX .LT. CUTOFF) THEN
         PRINT *, 'SAFE CONDITION'
      ELSE
         PRINT *, 'HAZARDOUS CONDITION'
      END IF

      END
```

Execution and Testing.   Test runs with input data like the following indicate that the program is correct:

```
ENTER 3 POLLUTION READINGS:
1 2 3
SAFE CONDITION

ENTER 3 POLLUTION READINGS:
50 60 70
HAZARDOUS CONDITION
```

It can then be used to calculate pollution indices and conditions for other inputs such as

```
ENTER 3 POLLUTION READINGS:
55, 39, 48
SAFE CONDITION

ENTER 3 POLLUTION READINGS:
68, 49, 57
HAZARDOUS CONDITION
```

3.4 COMPOUND SELECTION STRUCTURES: NESTED IFS AND IF-ELSE IF CONSTRUCTS

Nested IF Constructs

The sequence(s) of statements in an IF construct may themselves contain other IF constructs. In this case, the second IF construct is said to be **nested** within the first. For example, suppose the right branch of the earlier piecewise continuous function is modified so that the function becomes constant for $x \geq 1$:

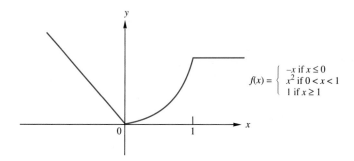

$$f(x) = \begin{cases} -x \text{ if } x \leq 0 \\ x^2 \text{ if } 0 < x < 1 \\ 1 \text{ if } x \geq 1 \end{cases}$$

The earlier `IF` construct for evaluating this function can be modified by inserting another `IF` construct within the `ELSE` block:

```
IF (X .LE. 0) THEN
    FVAL = -X
ELSE
    IF (X .LT. 1.0) THEN
        FVAL = X ** 2
    ELSE
        FVAL = 1.0
    END IF
END IF
```

Example: Pay Calculation

As another example of a nested `IF` construct, consider the following problem of calculating wages. Suppose that some employees of a company are paid weekly an amount equal to their annual salaries divided by 52, whereas all other employees are paid on an hourly basis with all hours over 40 paid at one-and-a-half times the regular hourly rate. A program is to be written to calculate wages for either type of employee.

A first version of an algorithm for solving this problem is

1. Enter the employee type: S (salaried) or H (hourly).

2. Enter the appropriate pay information, annual salary or hourly rate and hours worked, and calculate the employee's pay.

3. Display the employee's pay.

Here, step 2 obviously needs refinement. If the employee is salaried, the annual salary must be entered and the pay calculated. Otherwise, the hourly rate and hours worked must be entered and the employee's pay calculated. We will use the following variables to store the input values and the employee's pay:

VARIABLES FOR PAY CALCULATION PROBLEM

EMTYPE   Type of employee ('S' or 'H')

SALARY   Annual salary for a salaried employee

HOURS   Hours worked for an hourly employee

RATE   Hourly rate for an hourly employee

PAY   Employee's pay

The following algorithm solves this problem.

ALGORITHM FOR PAY CALCULATION PROBLEM

```
*   This algorithm calculates weekly pay for an employee. Some are salaried and others   *
*   are paid on an hourly basis. For hourly employees, time and a half is paid for overtime.   *
*   Input:     EMTYPE, the employee type                                                 *
*              SALARY for salaried employees                                             *
*              HOURS and RATE for hourly employees                                       *
*   Output:    PAY                                                                       *
```

1. Enter EMTYPE (S or H).
2. If EMTYPE = 'S' (salaried) do the following:
   a. Enter SALARY.
   b. Calculate PAY = SALARY / 52.

   Else do the following:
   a. Enter HOURS and RATE.
   b. IF (HOURS > 40)

      Calculate PAY = 40 * RATE + 1.5 * RATE * (HOURS − 40)

      Else

      Calculate PAY = HOURS * RATE
3. Display PAY.

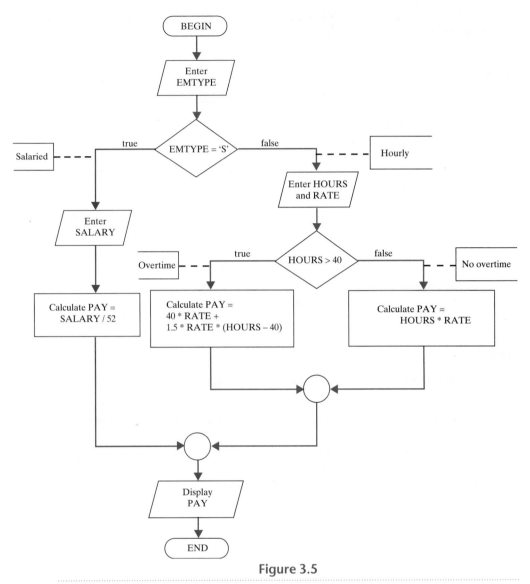

Figure 3.5

Flowchart for pay calculation algorithm.

The nesting of the IF construct based on the condition HOURS > 40 within the outer construct based on the condition EMTYPE = 'S' is clearly seen in the flowchart in Figure 3.5, which shows the structure of this algorithm.

The program in Figure 3.6 implements this algorithm. Note again the indentation used to indicate the blocks in the IF constructs and the nesting of the IF construct for calculating hourly wages within the ELSE part of the IF construct that checks the employee's type.

Figure 3.6 Pay calculation.

```
      PROGRAM WAGES
***********************************************************************
* Program to calculate weekly pay for an employee.  Salaried employees *
* receive 1/52 of their annual salaries.  Other employees are paid on  *
* an hourly basis with overtime hours paid at 1.5 times the regular    *
* hourly rate.  Identifiers used are:                                  *
*     EMTYPE       : employee type (S or H)                            *
*     SALARY       : annual salary (for salaried employees)            *
*     HOURS, RATE  : hours worked and hourly rate (for hourly employees)*
*     OVMULT       : multiplier for overtime pay                       *
*     PAY          : employee's pay                                    *
*                                                                      *
* Input:  EMTYPE                                                       *
*         SALARY for salaried employees, or                            *
*         HOURS and RATE for hourly employees                          *
* Output: PAY                                                          *
***********************************************************************

      CHARACTER EMTYPE
      REAL OVMULT, SALARY, HOURS, RATE, PAY
      PARAMETER (OVMULT = 1.5)

* Get employee type (S or H)
      PRINT *, 'ENTER THE TYPE OF EMPLOYEE (''S'' OR ''H''):'
      READ *, EMTYPE

* Select appropriate method of calculating pay:
      IF (EMTYPE .EQ. 'S') THEN

*         Salaried employee
          PRINT *, 'ENTER EMPLOYEE''S ANNUAL SALARY:'
          READ *, SALARY
          PAY = SALARY / 52
```

Figure 3.6 *(cont.)*

```
        ELSE

*           Hourly employee
            PRINT *, 'ENTER HOURS WORKED AND HOURLY RATE:'
            READ *, HOURS, RATE
            IF (HOURS .GT. 40.0) THEN
                PAY = 40.0 * RATE + OVMULT * RATE * (HOURS - 40.0)
            ELSE
                PAY = HOURS * RATE
            END IF
        END IF

* Display employee's pay
        PRINT *, 'EMPLOYEE''S PAY IS ', PAY

        END
```

Sample runs:

```
ENTER THE TYPE OF EMPLOYEE ('S' OR 'H'):
'S'
ENTER EMPLOYEE'S ANNUAL SALARY:
55000
EMPLOYEE'S PAY IS      1057.69

ENTER THE TYPE OF EMPLOYEE ('S' OR 'H'):
'H'
ENTER HOURS WORKED AND HOURLY RATE:
35.0 9.50
EMPLOYEE'S PAY IS      332.500

ENTER THE TYPE OF EMPLOYEE ('S' OR 'H'):
'H'
ENTER HOURS WORKED AND HOURLY RATE:
50.0 11.25
EMPLOYEE'S PAY IS      618.750
```

`IF-ELSE IF` Construct

The selection structures considered thus far have involved selecting one of two alternatives. It is also possible to use the `IF` construct to design selection structures that contain more than two alternatives. For example, consider again the piecewise continuous function defined by

$$f(x) = \begin{cases} -x & \text{if } x \le 0 \\ x^2 & \text{if } 0 < x < 1 \\ 1 & \text{if } x \ge 1 \end{cases}$$

This definition really consists of three alternatives and was implemented earlier using an IF construct of the form

```
IF (logical-expression₁) THEN
    statement-sequence₁
ELSE
    IF (logical-expression₂) THEN
        statement-sequence₂
    ELSE
        statement-sequence₃
        END IF
END IF
```

But compound IF constructs that implement selection structures with many alternatives can become quite complex, and the correspondence among the IFs, ELSEs, and END IFs may not be clear, especially if the statements are not indented properly. A better format that clarifies the correspondence between IFs and ELSEs and also emphasizes that the statement implements a **multialternative selection structure** is an IF-ELSE IF **construct:**

IF-ELSE IF *Construct*

Form:
```
IF (logical-expression₁) THEN
    statement-sequence₁
ELSE IF (logical-expression₂) THEN
    statement-sequence₂
ELSE IF (logical-expression₃) THEN
    statement-sequence₃
        ⋮
ELSE
    statement-sequenceₙ
END IF
```

where
    each *statement-sequence*$_i$ is a sequence of FORTRAN statements; and the ELSE clause is optional.

Purpose:

When an IF-ELSE IF construct is executed, the logical expressions are evaluated to determine the first expression that is true; the associated sequence of statements is executed, and execution then continues with the next statement following the construct (unless one of these statements transfers control elsewhere or terminates execution). If none of the logical expressions is true, the statement sequence associated with the ELSE statement is executed, and execution then continues with the statement following the construct (unless it is terminated or transferred to some other point by a statement in this block). This IF construct thus implements an *n*-way selection structure in which exactly one of *statement-sequence*$_1$, *statement-sequence*$_2$, . . . , *statement-sequence*$_n$ is executed.

Example: Modified Pollution Index Problem

As an example of an IF-ELSE IF construct, suppose that in the pollution index problem of the preceding section, three air-quality conditions—good, fair, and poor—are to be used instead of two — safe and hazardous. Two cutoff values will be used, LOWCUT and HICUT; a pollution index less than LOWCUT indicates a good condition, an index between LOWCUT and HICUT a fair condition, and an index greater than HICUT a poor condition. The following algorithm solves this problem.

ALGORITHM FOR MODIFIED POLLUTION INDEX PROBLEM

```
* This algorithm reads three pollution levels and then calculates a pollution index,  *
* which is the integer average of these three readings. If this index is less than a speci-  *
* fied cutoff value, a message indicating a good condition is displayed; if it is between  *
* this cutoff value and a larger one, a message indicating a fair condition is displayed;  *
* and if the index is greater than the larger cutoff value, a message indicating a poor con-  *
* dition is displayed.                                                                      *
* Input:       LEVEL1, LEVEL2, LEVEL3                                                        *
* Constants:   LOWCUT and HICUT                                                              *
* Output:      The pollution INDEX and a message indicating the air quality                  *
```

1. Enter LEVEL1, LEVEL2, and LEVEL3.

2. Calculate

$$\text{INDEX} = \frac{\text{LEVEL1} + \text{LEVEL2} + \text{LEVEL3}}{3}.$$

3. If INDEX < LOWCUT then

  Display 'Good condition'

  Else if INDEX < HICUT then

  Display 'Fair condition'

  Else

  Display 'Poor condition'

The flowchart in Figure 3.7 that displays the structure of this algorithm clearly shows the three-way selection structure in step 3. The program in Figure 3.8 uses an IF-ELSE IF construct to implement this three-way selection structure.

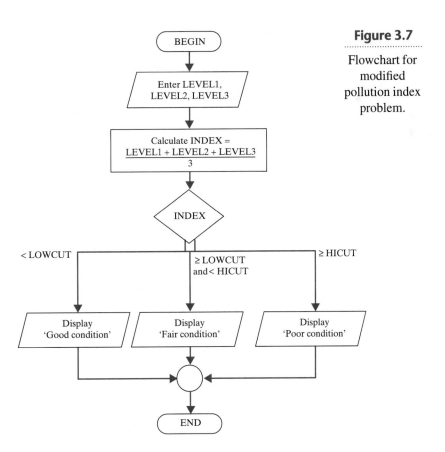

Figure 3.7

Flowchart for modified pollution index problem.

Figure 3.8 Pollution index—modified.

```
      PROGRAM POLUT2
***************************************************************
* Program that reads 3 pollution levels, calculates a pollution   *
* index as their integer average, and then displays an appropriate *
* air-quality message.   Identifiers used are:                    *
*     LEVEL1, LEVEL2, LEVEL3 : the three pollution levels          *
*     LOWCUT, HICUT          : cutoff values that distinguish      *
*                              between good/fair, and fair/poor    *
*                              conditions, respectively            *
*     INDEX:  the integer average of the pollution levels          *
*                                                                  *
* Input:     The three pollution levels                            *
* Constants: The two cutoff values                                 *
* Output:    The pollution index and a "good condition" message if *
*            this index is less than LOWCUT, a "fair condition"    *
*            message if it is between LOWCUT and HICUT, and a       *
*            "poor condition" message otherwise                    *
***************************************************************

      INTEGER LEVEL1, LEVEL2, LEVEL3, LOWCUT, HICUT, INDEX
      PARAMETER (LOWCUT = 25, HICUT = 50)

* Get the 3 pollution readings
      PRINT *, 'ENTER 3 POLLUTION READINGS:'
      READ *, LEVEL1, LEVEL2, LEVEL3

* Calculate the pollution index
      INDEX = (LEVEL1 + LEVEL2 + LEVEL3) / 3

* Classify the pollution index and display an appropriate
* air-quality message
      IF (INDEX .LT. LOWCUT) THEN
         PRINT *, 'GOOD CONDITION'
      ELSE IF (INDEX .LT. HICUT) THEN
         PRINT *, 'FAIR CONDITION'
      ELSE
         PRINT *, 'POOR CONDITION'
      END IF

      END
```

Figure 3.8 (*cont.*)

Sample runs:

```
ENTER 3 POLLUTION READINGS:
30 40 50
FAIR CONDITION

ENTER 3 POLLUTION READINGS:
50 60 70
POOR CONDITION

ENTER 3 POLLUTION READINGS:
20 21 24
GOOD CONDITION
```

There are three other statements in FORTRAN that may be used to form multialternative selection structures: the arithmetic IF statement, the computed GO TO statement, and the assigned GO TO statement. These statements are not used as commonly as the other control statements and are described in Chapter 12.

3.5 APPLICATION: FLUID FLOW IN A PIPE

Problem

The flow of fluid through a pipe is either laminar, turbulent, or unstable (switches between turbulent and laminar), depending on certain characteristics of the flow and the pipe. In laminar flow, the fluid travels the pipe in concentric layers, called *laminae*, with little mixing between the layers. Turbulent flow is much less structured, with considerable mixing.

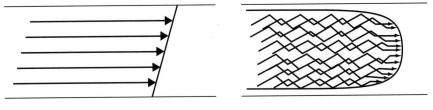

Laminar   Turbulent

The Great Alaska Pipeline near Delta, Alaska. (Photo courtesy of Photo Researchers, Inc.)

Experiments have shown that a combination of four factors determines which type of flow exists. This dimensionless combination is referred to as the *Reynold's number*, N_R, and is given by

$$N_R = \frac{\rho \cdot V \cdot D}{\eta}$$

where

> ρ is the density of the fluid
> V is the average forward velocity for the fluid across the pipe
> D is the diameter of the pipe
> η is the viscosity

N_R is dimensionless and is therefore the same value in any consistent set of units. Since it is a ratio of density $\times$ velocity $\times$ diameter to viscosity, the less viscous the material (all other things being equal), the higher the Reynold's number and, therefore, the more turbulent the flow.

A program is needed to compute the Reynold's number and to determine whether the flow for a given fluid is laminar, turbulent, or unstable.

Solution

Specification. To solve the problem, we must know the density of the fluid, its average forward velocity, its viscosity, and the diameter of the pipe. The Reynold's number N_R can then be calculated. We must also know what cutoff values for N_R determine the type of flow; we will assume that these are constants for the problem. A solution to the problem consists of the Reynold's number and a message indicating the type of flow. This gives the following specification for the problem:

Input: The fluid's density, average forward velocity, and viscosity

           The diameter of the pipe

Constant: Cutoff values to distinguish between laminar, turbulent, and unstable flows

Output: Reynold's number

           Type of flow

Design. An algorithm for this problem is very similar to that for the modified pollution index problem in the preceding section. We will use the following identifiers:

IDENTIFIERS FOR FLOW PROBLEM

DENS, VELOC, VISC	Density, average forward velocity, and viscosity of the fluid
DIAM	Diameter of the pipe
NR	Reynold's number
LOWCUT, HICUT	Cutoff values

ALGORITHM FOR FLOW PROBLEM

* This algorithm reads the density, average forward velocity, and viscosity of a fluid and   *
* the diameter of the pipe through which it is flowing. The Reynold's number is calcu-   *
* lated and the type of flow—turbulent, laminar, unstable—is then determined accord-   *
* ing to whether the Reynold's number is less than a lower cutoff value, is between two   *
* cutoff values, or is greater than the larger cutoff value.   *
*   *
*   Input: DENS, VELOC, VISC, DIAM   *
*   Constants: LOWCUT, HICUT   *
*   Output: The Reynold's number NR and the type of flow   *

1. Enter DENS, VELOC, VISC, and DIAM.
2. Calculate

$$NR = \frac{DENS \times VELOC \times DIAM}{VISC}$$

3. Display NR.
4. If NR < LOWCUT then

      Display 'Flow is laminar'

    Else if NR < HICUT

      Display 'Flow is turbulent'

    Else

      Display 'Flow is unstable'

Coding, Execution, and Testing. The program in Figure 3.9 implements the preceding algorithm. It was tested with several input values for which the results were easy to check. The sample run shown is for water at 20°C where density is 1 g/cm^3 and viscosity is 0.01 dyne/cm^2.

Figure 3.9 Flow through a pipe.

```
    PROGRAM FLOW
* * * * * * * * * * * * * * * * * * * * * * * * * * * * * * * * * * * * * * * * * * * * * * * * * * * * * *
* Program that reads the density, average forward velocity, and        *
* viscosity of a fluid and the diameter of the pipe through which      *
* it is flowing.  The Reynold's number is calculated and the type     *
* of flow -- laminar, turbulent, unstable -- is then determined       *
* according to whether the Reynold's number is less than a lower      *
* cutoff value, is between two cutoff values, or is greater than      *
* the larger cutoff value. Identifiers used are:                      *
*     DENS, VISC   : density and viscosity of the fluid               *
*     VELOC        : average forward flow of the fluid                *
*     DIAM         : diameter of the pipe                             *
```

Figure 3.9 (*cont.*)

```
*     LOWCUT, HICUT : cutoff values that distinguish between           *
*                    turbulent/laminar and laminar/unstable types     *
*                    of flow                                           *
*     NR             : the Reynold's number                           *
*                                                                     *
* Input:    DENS, VELOC, VISC, and DIAM                               *
* Constants: LOWCUT and HICUT                                         *
* Output:    NR and a message indicating the type of flow            *
***********************************************************************

      REAL DENS, VELOC, VISC, DIAM, LOWCUT, HICUT, NR
      PARAMETER (LOWCUT = 2000.0, HICUT = 3000.0)

* Get the density, velocity, viscosity, and diameter
      PRINT *, 'ENTER THE DENSITY OF THE FLUID:'
      READ *, DENS
      PRINT *, 'ENTER THE VISCOSITY OF THE FLUID:'
      READ *, VISC
      PRINT *, 'ENTER THE AVERAGE FORWARD VELOCITY OF THE FLUID:'
      READ *, VELOC
      PRINT *, 'ENTER THE DIAMETER OF THE PIPE:'
      READ *, DIAM

* Calculate the Reynold's number
      NR = (DENS * VELOC * DIAM) / VISC

* Display the input data, the Reynold's number, and a message
* indicating the type of flow
      PRINT *, 'FOR A FLUID WITH DENSITY ', DENS, ', VISCOSITY ', VISC
      PRINT *, 'AND AVERAGE FORWARD VELOCITY ', VELOC
      PRINT *, 'FLOWING THROUGH A PIPE OF DIAMETER ', DIAM
      PRINT *, 'THE REYNOLD''S NUMBER IS ', NR
      PRINT *
      IF (NR .LT. LOWCUT) THEN
         PRINT *, 'FLOW IS LAMINAR'
      ELSE IF (NR .LT. HICUT) THEN
         PRINT *, 'FLOW IS TURBULENT'
      ELSE
         PRINT *, 'FLOW IS UNSTABLE'
      END IF

      END
```

Figure 3.9 *(cont.)*

Sample run:

```
ENTER THE DENSITY OF THE FLUID:
1.0
ENTER THE VISCOSITY OF THE FLUID:
0.01
ENTER THE AVERAGE FORWARD VELOCITY OF THE FLUID:
10.0
ENTER THE DIAMETER OF THE PIPE:
1.0
FOR A FLUID WITH DENSITY     1.00000, VISCOSITY     1.00000E-02
AND AVERAGE FORWARD VELOCITY    10.00000
FLOWING THROUGH A PIPE OF DIAMETER     1.00000
THE REYNOLD'S NUMBER IS    1000.000


FLOW IS LAMINAR
```

Quick Quiz 3.5

For Questions 1–6, determine if each is a legal `IF` statement.

1. `IF (A .GT. B) PRINT *, A`   2. `IF B .LT. C  N = N + 1`

3. `IF (X .LE. Y) END`   4. `IF (A = X) READ *, Y`

5. `IF (N .GE. 1 .AND. .LE. 10) N = 10`

6. `IF (N .OR. 1) PRINT *, '*'`

Questions 7–9 refer to the following `IF` construct:

```
IF (X .GE. Y) THEN
   PRINT *, X
ELSE
   PRINT *, Y
END IF
```

7. Describe the output produced if X = 5 and Y = 6.

8. Describe the output produced if X = 5 and Y = 5.

9. Describe the output produced if X = 6 and Y = 5.

Questions 10–12 refer to the following IF construct:

```
IF (X .GE. 0) THEN
    IF (Y .GE. 0) THEN
        PRINT *, X + Y
    ELSE
        PRINT *, X - Y
    END IF
    ELSE
        PRINT *, Y - X
END IF
```

10. Describe the output produced if X = 5 and Y = 5.

11. Describe the output produced if X = 5 and Y = −5.

12. Describe the output produced if X = −5 and Y = 5.

Questions 13–17 refer to the following IF construct:

```
IF (N .GE. 90) THEN
    PRINT *, 'EXCELLENT'
ELSE IF (N .GE. 80)
    PRINT *, 'GOOD'
ELSE IF (N .GE. 70)
    PRINT *, 'FAIR'
ELSE
    PRINT *, 'BAD'
END IF
```

13. Describe the output produced if N = 100.

14. Describe the output produced if N = 90.

15. Describe the output produced if N = 89.

16. Describe the output produced if N = 70.

17. Describe the output produced if N = 0.

18. Write a statement that displays 'OUT OF RANGE' if NUMBER is negative or greater than 100.

19. Write an efficient IF statement to assign N the value 1 if X < 1.5, 2 if $1.5 \leq X < 2.5$, and 3 otherwise.

Exercises 3.5

Exercises 1–4 refer to the following IF statement:

```
IF (X * Y .GE. 0) THEN
    PRINT *, 'YES'
ELSE
    PRINT *, 'NO'
END IF
```

1. Describe the output produced if X = 5 and Y = 6.
2. Describe the output produced if X = 5 and Y = −6.
3. Describe the output produced if X = −5 and Y = 6.
4. Describe the output produced if X = −5 and Y = −6.

Exercises 5–7 refer to the following IF statement:

```
IF (ABS(N) .LE. 4) THEN
    IF (N .GT. 0) THEN
        PRINT *, 2*N + 1
    ELSE
        PRINT *, 2*N
    END IF
ELSE
    PRINT *, N, 'OUT OF RANGE'
END IF
```

5. Describe the output produced if N = 2.
6. Describe the output produced if N = −7.
7. Describe the output produced if N = 0.

For Exercises 8–11, write FORTRAN statements that will do what is required.

8. If CODE = 1, read X and Y and calculate and print the sum of X and Y.
9. If A is strictly between 0 and 5, set B equal to $1/A^2$; otherwise set B equal to A^2.
10. Display the message 'LEAP YEAR' if the integer variable YEAR is the number of a leap year. (A leap year is a multiple of 4; and if it is a multiple of 100, it must also be a multiple of 400.)

11. Assign a value to COST corresponding to the value of DIST given in the following table:

DIST	COST
0 through 100	5.00
More than 100 but not more than 500	8.00
More than 500 but less than 1000	10.00
1000 or more	12.00

For Exercises 12–15, write an IF construct to evaluate the given function.

12. The output of a simple d-c generator; the shape of the curve is the absolute value of the sine function. (100 V is the maximum voltage.)

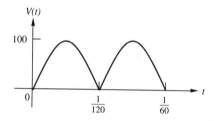

13. A rectified half-wave; the curve is a sine function for half the cycle and zero for the other half. (Maximum current is 5 amp.)

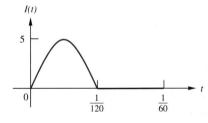

14. Sawtooth; the graph consists of two straight lines. The maximum voltage of 100 V occurs at the middle of the cycle.

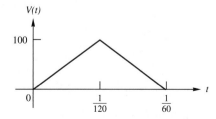

15. The excess pressure *p(t)* in a sound wave whose graph is as follows:

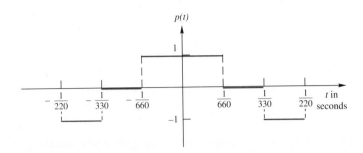

3.6 THE LOGICAL DATA TYPE

Recall that there are two **logical constants** in FORTRAN:

    .TRUE.

and

    .FALSE.

and logical variables may have only these values. (Note the periods that must appear as part of these logical constants.) A **logical variable** is declared using a `LOGICAL` type statement of the form

    LOGICAL *list*

where `list` is a list of variables being typed as logical. Like all type statements, this type statement must appear in the specification part of the program. For example,

    LOGICAL EXISTS, ENDATA

declares that `EXISTS` and `ENDATA` are logical variables.

An assignment statement of the form

    logical-variable = logical-expression

can be used to assign a value to a logical variable. Thus,

    ENDATA = .TRUE.

is a valid assignment statement; it assigns the value true to `ENDATA`. Likewise,

    EXISTS = DISC .GE. 0

is a valid assignment statement and assigns `.TRUE.` to `EXISTS` if `DISC` is non-negative and assigns `.FALSE.` otherwise.

Logical values can be displayed using list-directed output. A logical value is displayed as only a T or an F, usually preceded by a space. For example, if A, B, and C are logical variables with the values true, false, and false, respectively, the statement

```
PRINT *, A, B, C, .TRUE., .FALSE.
```

produces

```
 T F F T F
```

as output.

Logical values can also be read using list-directed input. In this case, the input values consist of optional blanks followed by an optional period followed by T or F, which may be followed by other characters. The value true or false is assigned to the corresponding variable according to whether the first letter encountered is T or F. For example, for the statements

```
LOGICAL A, B, C

READ *, A, B, C
```

the following data could be entered:

```
.T., F, .FALSE
```

The values assigned to A, B, and C would be true, false, and false, respectively. This would also be the case if the following data were entered:

```
.T., FALL, .FLASE
```

In the next section we consider the design of logical circuits. The program in Figure 3.10 that models a circuit for a binary half-adder uses logical variables A and B to represent inputs to the circuit and logical variables SUM and CARRY to represent the outputs produced by the circuit.

3.7 APPLICATION: LOGICAL CIRCUITS

Problem

Addition of binary digits is defined by the following table:

+	0	1
0	0	1
1	1	10

We wish to design a program to model a logical circuit, called a **binary half-adder**, that implements this operation.

Solution

Specification. The input in this problem consists of two binary digits. Adding two bits produces a sum bit and a carry bit whose values are given by

Inputs	Carry bit	Sum bit
0 0	0	0
0 1	0	1
1 0	0	1
1 1	1	0

Thus the input/output specification for this problem is as follows:

Input: Two binary digits to be added

Output: A sum bit and a carry bit that result from adding the inputs

Design. Arithmetic operations are implemented in computer hardware by logical circuits. The following circuit is a binary half-adder that adds two binary digits:

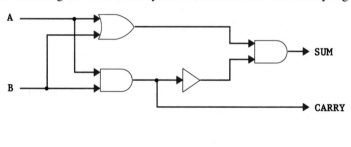

It contains four basic electronic components called **gates:** two AND gates, one OR gate, and one NOT gate (also called an *inverter*). The inputs to these gates are pulses of current applied to the lines leading into the gates, and the outputs are pulses of current on the lines emanating from the gates. In the case of an AND gate, an output pulse is produced only if there are pulses on both input lines. An OR gate produces an output pulse only if there is an input pulse on at least one of the input lines. A NOT gate is designed to produce an output pulse only when there is no incoming pulse.

If we associate the logical expression "a pulse is present" with each line, that is, if we interpret true as the presence of a pulse and false as the absence of a pulse, then logical expressions can be used to represent the outputs produced by a logical circuit. In circuit design, + is used to denote OR, · to denote AND, and an overbar to denote NOT.

Using this notation, we can represent the output SUM in the circuit for a binary half-adder by

$$SUM = (A + B) \cdot \overline{(A \cdot B)}$$

and the output CARRY by

$$CARRY = A \cdot B$$

The values of these logical expressions are displayed in the following truth table:

A	B	CARRY	SUM
true	true	true	false
true	false	false	true
false	true	false	true
false	false	false	false

If we interpret false as the binary digit 0 and true as the binary digit 1, we see that this truth table corresponds to the table for the sum and carry bits given earlier in the problem's specification.

For this problem we will use the following variable names.

VARIABLES FOR THE LOGICAL CIRCUIT PROBLEM

A, B   Input bits

SUM, CARRY   The sum and carry bits produced when A and B are added

An algorithm for solving the problem is simple:

ALGORITHM FOR LOGICAL CIRCUIT PROBLEM

* This algorithm determines the sum and carry bits produced by a binary half-adder.   *
* Input: A, B   *
* Output: SUM, CARRY   *

1. Enter A and B.
2. Calculate SUM $= (A + B) \cdot \overline{(A \cdot B)}$.
3. Calculate CARRY $= A \cdot B$.
4. Display SUM and CARRY.

Coding.   The program in Figure 3.10 implements the preceding algorithm, using logical variables A, B, SUM, and CARRY. The logical expressions for SUM and CARRY,

$$SUM = (A + B) \cdot \overline{(A \cdot B)}$$

$$CARRY = A \cdot B$$

are implemented by the FORTRAN logical expressions

```
SUM = (A .OR. B) .AND. .NOT. (A .AND. B)
CARRY = A .AND. B
```

Figure 3.10   A binary half-adder.

```
PROGRAM HADDER
***********************************************************************
* Program to calculate the outputs from a logical circuit that        *
* represents a binary half-adder.  Variables used are:                *
*    A, B       : the two logical inputs to the circuit               *
*    SUM, CARRY : the two logical outputs                             *
*                                                                     *
* Input:   The two logical inputs A and B                             *
* Output:  The two logical outputs SUM and CARRY, which represent the *
*          sum and carry that result when the input values are added  *
***********************************************************************

      LOGICAL A, B, SUM, CARRY

      PRINT *, 'ENTER LOGICAL INPUTS A AND B:'
      READ *, A, B
      SUM = (A .OR. B) .AND. .NOT. (A .AND. B)
      CARRY = A .AND. B
      PRINT *, 'CARRY, SUM = ', CARRY, SUM

      END
```

Execution and Testing.   The following sample runs show the outputs produced for each possible combination of logical values for the two inputs:

```
ENTER LOGICAL INPUTS A AND B:
T T
CARRY, SUM = T F
```

```
                ENTER LOGICAL INPUTS A AND B:
                T F
                CARRY, SUM = F T

                ENTER LOGICAL INPUTS A AND B:
                F T
                CARRY, SUM = F T

                ENTER LOGICAL INPUTS A AND B:
                F F
                CARRY, SUM = F F
```

Note that if we identify the binary digits 0 and 1 with false and true, respectively, the program's output can be interpreted as a demonstration that $1 + 1 = 10$ (SUM = 0, CARRY = 1), $1 + 0 = 01$, $0 + 1 = 01$, and $0 + 0 = 00$. This program, therefore, correctly implements binary addition of one-bit numbers.

Quick Quiz 3.7

For Questions 1–4, determine whether each statement is true or false:

1. If OKAY is a logical variable, the statement OKAY = FALSE will set it to false.
2. If OKAY is a logical variable and CODE has the value 6128, then the statement OKAY = (CODE = 6128) will set OKAY to true.
3. If OKAY is a logical variable and ALPHA has the value 5, then the statement OKAY = ALPHA .LT. 7 .AND. .GT. 1 will set OKAY to true.
4. If OKAY is a logical variable and the character variable LOGIC has the value '.TRUE.', then the statement OKAY = LOGIC will set OKAY to true.

For Questions 5–7, assume that OKAY, HERE, and THERE are logical variables and that HERE and THERE have been set to true.

5. OKAY = .NOT. HERE .AND. .NOT. THERE will set OKAY to true.
6. OKAY = .NOT. (HERE .OR. THERE) will set OKAY to true.
7. OKAY = HERE .AND. .NOT. .NOT. THERE will set OKAY to true.
8. If the logical variable OKAY has been set to true, then the statement PRINT *, OKAY will display .TRUE..
9. FALSE, .FALSE., and FALLS, are all legal input values for a logical variable in a READ statement.
10. If Fred T. Tarantula is input for the statement READ *, P, Q, R, the logical variables P, Q, and R will become false, true, and true, respectively.

11. Write statements to declare LARGER to be a logical variable and to set it to true if the value of A is greater than the value of B and to false otherwise.

12. Write statements to declare logical variables FRESH and UPPER, to set FRESH to true if the value of CLASS is 1 and to false otherwise, and to set UPPER to false if the value of CLASS is 1 and to true otherwise.

Exercises 3.7

In Exercises 1–9, assume that M and N are integer variables with the values −2 and 5, respectively, and that X, Y, and Z are real variables with the values −1.99, 5.5, and 9.99, respectively. Find the value assigned to the logical variable OKAY or indicate why an error occurs.

1. OKAY = M .LE. N
2. OKAY = 2 * ABS(M) .LE. 8
3. OKAY = X * X .LT. SQRT(Z)
4. OKAY = NINT(Z) .EQ. (6 * N − 3)
5. OKAY = OKAY .AND. (N .EQ. 6)
6. OKAY = .NOT. (X .LT. Y)
7. OKAY = .NOT. ((M .LE. N) .AND. (X + Z .GT. Y))
8. OKAY = .NOT. (M .LE. N) .OR. .NOT. (X + Z .GT. Y)
9. OKAY = .NOT. ((M .GT. N) .OR. (X .LT. Z)) .EQV.
          ((M .LE. N) .AND. (X .GE. Z))

For Exercises 10–17, write an assignment statement that will set the logical variable OKAY to true if the condition is true and to false otherwise.

10. X is strictly between 0 and 10.
11. X and Y are both positive.
12. X and Y are both negative, or both are positive.
13. $-1 \leq X < 1$.
14. X is neither less than 0 nor greater than 100.
15. W, X, Y, and Z are all equal to each other.
16. W, X, Y, and Z are in increasing order.
17. X is greater than 10, or Y is greater than 10, but not both.
18. A *binary full-adder* has three inputs: the two bits A and B being added and a "carry-in" bit CIN (representing the carry bit that results from adding the bits to the right

of A and B in two binary numbers). It can be constructed from two binary half-adders and an OR gate:

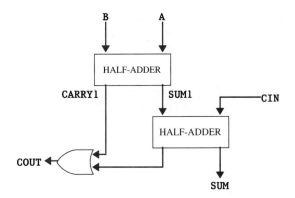

Assuming that SUM1, CARRY1, SUM, and COUT have been declared to be logical variables, and that values have been assigned to the inputs A, B, and CIN, write assignment statements to assign values to

(a) SUM1 and CARRY1

(b) SUM and COUT (assuming that values have already been assigned to SUM1 and CARRY1)

19. An *adder* to calculate binary sums of two-bit numbers

```
         A2  A1
     +   B2  B1
    ───────────
    COUT S2  S1
```

where S1 and S2 are the sum bits and COUT is the carry-out bit can be constructed from a binary half-adder and a binary full-adder:

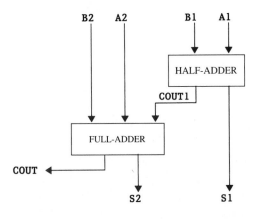

Assuming that S1, S2, COUT1, and COUT have been declared to be logical variables, and that values have been assigned to the inputs A1, A2, B1, and B2, write statements to assign values to

(a) S1 and COUT1

(b) S2 and COUT (assuming that values have already been assigned to S1 and COUT1)

CHAPTER REVIEW

Summary

This focus of this chapter was selective execution, the second of the three basic control structures used in writing programs. In selective execution, the action selected is determined by the value of a logical expression; thus the chapter began with a study of logical expressions, both simple and compound. Simple logical expressions are formed using the relational operators .LT., .GT., .EQ., .NE., .LE., and .GE., and compound expressions are formed by using the logical operators .NOT., .AND., .OR., .EQV., and .NEQV.. Selective execution is implemented in FORTRAN using an IF statement, the various forms of which are described in detail and illustrated in this chapter. In the last two sections we described the LOGICAL data type and illustrated its use in the design of logical circuits.

FORTRAN SUMMARY

Relational Operators

Symbol	Meaning
.LT.	Is less than
.GT.	Is greater than
.EQ.	Is equal to
.LE.	Is less than or equal to
.GE.	Is greater than or equal to
.NE.	Is not equal to

Logical Operators

.NOT.

.AND.

.OR.

.EQV.

.NEQV.

Logical Expressions

Logical constants (.TRUE. and .FALSE.)
Logical variables
Simple logical expressions of the form

```
expression₁ relational-operator expression₂
```

where the expressions are both numeric or character (or logical) expressions.
Compound logical expressions of the form

```
NOT logical-expr
```

or

```
logical-expr₁ logical-operator logical-expr₂
```

where $logical-expr_1$ and $logical-expr_2$ are logical expressions and the $logical-operator$ is a binary logical operator (.AND., .OR., .EQV., .NEQV.)

Block IF Statement

```
IF (logical-expression) THEN
    statement-sequence₁
ELSE
    statement-sequence₂
END IF
```

where the ELSE part is optional.

Examples:

```
IF (X .GT. 0) THEN
    PRINT *, X
    Y = SQRT(X)
    PRINT *, Y
ELSE
    PRINT *, 'X IS NEGATIVE'
END IF


IF (COUNT .EQ. 0) THEN
    PRINT *, 'NO DATA VALUES WERE PROCESSED'
END IF
```

Purpose:

If the logical expression is true, $statement\text{-}sequence_1$ is executed and $statement\text{-}sequence_2$ is bypassed; otherwise $statement\text{-}sequence_1$ is bypassed and $statement\text{-}sequence_2$ is executed, unless the ELSE part is omitted. In either case, execution continues with the next statement in the program (unless it is terminated or control is transferred elsewhere by one of the statements in the statement sequence selected).

Logical IF Statement

```
IF (logical-expression) statement
```

Example:

```
IF (COUNT .EQ. 0) PRINT *, 'NO DATA VALUES WERE PROCESSED'
```

Purpose:

If the logical expression is true, $statement$ is executed; otherwise, it is bypassed.

IF-ELSE IF Construct

```
IF (logical-expression₁) THEN
    statement-sequence₁
ELSE IF (logical-expression₂) THEN
    statement-sequence₂
ELSE IF (logical-expression₃) THEN
    statement-sequence₃
        ⋮
ELSE
    statement-sequenceₙ
END IF
```

Example:

```
IF (INDEX .LT. LOWCUT) THEN
    PRINT *, 'GOOD CONDITION'
ELSE IF (INDEX .LT. HICUT)
    PRINT *, 'FAIR CONDITION'
ELSE
    PRINT *, 'POOR CONDITION'
END IF
```

Purpose:

The logical expressions are evaluated to determine the first expression that is true; the associated sequence of statements is executed; if none of the logical expressions is true, the statement sequence in the ELSE statement is executed. Execution then continues with the next statement following the construct (unless one of these statements transfers control elsewhere or terminates execution).

LOGICAL Type Statement

```
LOGICAL list-of-variable-names
```

Example:

```
LOGICAL ENDATA, SORTED
```

Purpose:
Declares identifiers to be of LOGICAL type.

PROGRAMMING POINTERS

Program Style and Design

1. *The statement sequence(s) within an* IF *construct should be indented.*

```
IF (logical-expression)
    statement₁
       ⋮
    statementₙ
ELSE
    statementₙ₊₁
       ⋮
    statementₘ
END IF
```

2. *All programs can be written using the three basic control structures: sequential, selection, and repetition.*

3. *Multialternative selection structures can be implemented more efficiently with an* IF-ELSE IF *construct than with a sequence of* IF *statements.* For example, using the statements

```
IF (SCORE .LT. 60) GRADE = 'F'
IF ((SCORE .GE. 60) .AND. (SCORE .LT. 70)) GRADE = 'D'
IF ((SCORE .GE. 70) .AND. (SCORE .LT. 80)) GRADE = 'C'
IF ((SCORE .GE. 80) .AND. (SCORE .LT. 90)) GRADE = 'B'
IF (SCORE .GE. 90) GRADE = 'A'
```

is less efficient than using

```
IF (SCORE .LT. 60) THEN
   GRADE = 'F'
ELSE IF (SCORE .LT. 70) THEN
   GRADE = 'D'
ELSE IF (SCORE .LT. 80) THEN
   GRADE = 'C'
ELSE IF (SCORE .LT. 90) THEN
   GRADE = 'B'
ELSE
   GRADE = 'A'
END IF
```

In the first case, all of the IF statements are executed for each score processed, and three of the logical expressions are compound expressions. In the second case, each logical expression is simple, and not all of the expressions are evaluated for each score; for example, for a score of 65, only the logical expressions SCORE .LT. 60 and SCORE .LT. 70 are evaluated.

Potential Problems

1. *Periods must be used in the relational operators* .LT., .GT., .EQ., .LE., .GE., *and* .NE. *and in the logical operators* .NOT., .AND., .OR., .EQV., *and* .NEQV..

2. *Parentheses must enclose the logical expression in an* IF *construct or* IF *statement.*

3. *Real quantities that are algebraically equal may yield a false logical expression when compared with* .EQ. *because most real values are not stored exactly.* For example, even though the two real expressions X * (1.0 / X) and 1.0 are algebraically equal, the logical expression X * (1.0 / X) .EQ. 1.0 is usually false. Thus, if two real values RNUM1 and RNUM2 are subject to the roundoff error caused by inexact representation, it is usually not advisable to check whether they are equal. Rather, one should check whether the absolute value of their difference is small:

```
IF (ABS(RNUM1 - RNUM2) .LT. ERRTOL) THEN
   ⋮
```

where ERRTOL is some small positive real value such as 1E-6.

4. *Each* IF *construct must be closed with an* END IF *statement.*

5. *It should be assumed that all subexpressions are evaluated when determining the*

value of a compound logical expression. Suppose, for example, that we write an IF construct of the form

```
IF ((X .GE. 0) .AND. (SQRT(X) .LT. 5.0)) THEN
   PRINT *, 'SQUARE ROOT IS LESS THAN 5'
      ⋮
END IF
```

in which the subexpression X .GE. 0 is intended to prevent an attempt to calculate the square root of a negative number when X is negative. Some compilers may evaluate the subexpression X. GE. 0 and, if it is false, then not evaluate the second subexpression, SQRT(X) .LT. 5.0. Other compilers evaluate both parts, and thus an error results when X is negative. This error can be avoided by rewriting the constructs as

```
IF (X .GE. 0) THEN
   IF (SQRT(X) .LT. 5.0) THEN
      PRINT *, 'SQUARE ROOT IS LESS THAN 5'
         ⋮
   END IF
END IF
```

PROGRAMMING PROBLEMS

Section 3.4

1. Write a program to read one of the codes 1 for circle, 2 for square, or 3 for equilateral triangle, and a number representing the radius of the circle, the side of the square, or the side of the triangle, respectively. Then calculate and display the area and the perimeter of that geometric figure with appropriate labels. (See Programming Problems 3 and 5 in Chapter 2.)

2. Modify the program in Figure 3.2 for solving quadratic equations so that when the discriminant is negative, the complex roots of the equation are displayed. If the discriminant D is negative, these roots are given by

$$\frac{-B \pm \sqrt{-D}i}{2A}$$

where $i^2 = -1$.

3. Write a program that reads values for the coefficients $A, B, C, D, E,$ and F of the equations

$$Ax + By = C$$
$$Dx + Ey = F$$

of two straight lines. Then determine whether the lines are parallel (their slopes are equal) or the lines intersect and, if they intersect, whether the lines are perpendicular (the product of their slopes is equal to -1).

4. Write a program that reads the coordinates of three points and then determines whether they are collinear.

5. Suppose the following formulas give the safe loading L in pounds per square inch for a column with slimness ratio S:

$$L = \begin{cases} 16500 - .475S^2 & \text{if } S < 100 \\ \dfrac{17900}{2 + (S^2/17900)} & \text{if } S \geq 100 \end{cases}$$

Write a program that reads a slimness ratio and then calculates the safe loading.

6. Suppose that charges by a gas company are based on consumption according to the following table:

Gas Used	Rate
First 70 cubic meters	$5.00 minimum cost
Next 100 cubic meters	5.0¢ per cubic meter
Next 230 cubic meters	2.5¢ per cubic meter
Above 400 cubic meters	1.5¢ per cubic meter

Write a program in which the meter reading for the previous month and the current meter reading are entered, each a four-digit number and each representing cubic meters, and that then calculates the amount of the bill. *Note:* The current reading may be less than the previous one; for example, the previous reading may have been 9897, and the current one is 0103.

Section 3.5

7. Write a program that reads a cutoff value and then finds the average forward velocity for water at 20°C (density $= 1$ g/cm^3 and viscosity $= 0.01$ dyne/cm^2) flowing in a 1 cm pipe so that N_R is equal to this cutoff value. Execute the program with the following values:

    (a) 2000.0, the cutoff between laminar and turbulent flow in Figure 3.9

    (b) 3000.0, the cutoff between turbulent and unstable flow in Figure 3.9

Section 3.7

8. In a certain region, pesticide can be sprayed from an airplane only if the temperature is at least 70° F, the relative humidity is between 15 and 35 percent, and the wind speed is at most 10 miles per hour. Write a program that accepts three numbers representing temperature, relative humidity, and wind speed; assigns the value true

or false to the logical variable PESTOK according to these criteria; and displays this value.

9. Write a program that reads triples of real numbers and assigns the appropriate value true or false to the following logical variables:

TRIANG:	True if the real numbers can represent lengths of the sides of a triangle and false otherwise (the sum of any two of the numbers must be greater than the third)
EQUIL:	True if TRIANG is true and the triangle is equilateral (the three sides are equal)
ISOS:	True if TRIANG is true and the triangle is isosceles (at least two sides are equal)
SCAL:	True if TRIANG is true and the triangle is scalene (no two sides are equal)

The output from your program should have a format similar to the following:

```
ENTER 3 LENGTHS:
2, 3, 3
TRIANG IS:     T
EQUIL IS:      F
ISOS IS:       T
SCAL IS:       F
```

10. Write a program to implement a binary full-adder as described in Exercise 18 of Section 3.7 and use it to verify the results shown in the following table:

A	B	CIN	SUM	COUT
0	0	0	0	0
0	0	1	1	0
0	1	0	1	0
0	1	1	0	1
1	0	0	1	0
1	0	1	0	1
1	1	0	0	1
1	1	1	1	1

11. Write a program to implement an adder as described in Exercise 19 of Section 3.7 and use it to demonstrate that $00 + 00 = 000$, $01 + 00 = 001$, $01 + 01 = 010$, $10 + 01 = 011$, $10 + 10 = 100$, $11 + 10 = 101$, and $11 + 11 = 110$.

Fortran 90

Features

The selection structures described in this chapter have been carried over into Fortran 90 with a few extensions:

- Symbolic forms of the relational operators are allowed:

Relational Operator	Symbol
.LT.	<
.GT.	>
.EQ.	==
.LE.	<=
.GE.	>=
.NE.	/=

- IF and IF-ELSE IF constructs may be named by attaching a label at the beginning and end of the construct so that it has the form

```
name: IF (logical-expression) THEN
         ⋮
      END IF name
```

For example,

```
Update: IF (X > Largest) THEN
           Largest = X
           Position = N
        END IF Update
```

The name may also be attached to any ELSE IF and ELSE statements appearing in the construct; for example,

```
Test: IF (Discriminant > 0) THEN
         PRINT *, "Distinct real roots"
      ELSE IF (Discriminant == 0) THEN Test
         PRINT *, "One (repeated) real root"
      ELSE Test
         PRINT *, "Complex roots"
      END IF Test
```

- A CASE construct can be used to implement certain multialternative selection structures. It has the form

```
SELECT CASE (selector)
   CASE (label-list₁)
      statement-sequence₁
   CASE (label-list₂)
      statement-sequence₂
         ⋮
   CASE (label-listₙ)
      statement-sequenceₙ
END SELECT
```

where the `selector` is an integer, character, or logical expression, and each of the `label-listᵢ` is a list of one or more possible values of the selector, and is enclosed in parentheses, or is the word DEFAULT. The values in this list may have any of the forms

```
value
value₁ : value₂
value :
: value
```

to denote a single `value`, the range of values from `value₁` through `value₂`, the set of all values greater than or equal to `value`, or the set of all values less than or equal to `value`, respectively. When this CASE construct is executed, the selector is evaluated; if this value is in `label-listᵢ`, `statement-sequenceᵢ` is executed, and execution continues with the statement following the END SELECT statement. If the value is not in any of the lists of values, the sequence of statements associated with DEFAULT is executed, if there is such a statement sequence, and continues with the statement following the CASE construct otherwise. A name may also be attached to a CASE construct:

```
SELECT CASE (selector) name
         ⋮
END SELECT name
```

An example of a CASE construct is the following:

```
SELECT CASE (Distance)
   CASE (0:99)
      Fare = 5
   CASE (100:300)
      Fare = 10
   CASE DEFAULT
      PRINT *, "Distance", Distance, " out of range"
END SELECT
```

It assigns the value 5 to `Fare` if the value of the integer variable `Distance` is in the range 0 through 99, the value 10 if `Distance` is in the range 100 through 300, and displays an out-of-range message otherwise.

Example

The Fortran 90 program in Figure 3.11 illustrates several of the preceding new features. It is a modification of the pollution index program in Figure 3.8 that uses a `CASE` construct to classify pollution indices into one of three categories.

 Figure 3.11 Pollution indices—Fortran 90 version

```
PROGRAM Pollution_Indices
!-----------------------------------------------------------------------
! Program that reads 3 pollution levels, calculates a pollution
! index as their integer average, and then displays an appropriate
! air-quality message. Identifiers used are:
!   Level_1, Level_2, Level_3 : the three pollution levels
!   LowCutoff, HighCutoff     : cutoff values that distinguish
!                               between good/fair, and fair/poor
!                               conditions, respectively
!   Index  : the integer average of the pollution levels
!
! Input     : The three pollution levels and the cutoff value
! Constants : The two cutoff values
! Output    : The pollution index and a "good condition" message if
!             this index is less than LowCutoff, a "fair condition"
!             message if it is between LowCutoff and HighCutoff,
!             and a "poor condition" message otherwise
!-----------------------------------------------------------------------

  IMPLICIT NONE
  INTEGER :: Level_1, Level_2, Level_3, Index
  INTEGER, PARAMETER :: LowCutoff = 25, HighCutoff = 50

! Get the 3 pollution readings
  PRINT *, "Enter 3 pollution readings:"
  READ *, Level_1, Level_2, Level_3

! Calculate the pollution index
  Index = (Level_1 + Level_2 + Level_3) / 3
```

Figure 9.4 *(cont.)*

```
! Classify the pollution index and display an appropriate
! air-quality message
  SELECT CASE (Index )
     CASE (:LowCutoff - 1)
        PRINT *, "Good condition"
     CASE (LowCutoff : HighCutoff - 1)
        PRINT *, "Fair condition"
     CASE (HighCutoff:)
        PRINT *, "Poor condition"
  END SELECT

END PROGRAM Pollution_Indices
```

4

Repetitive Execution

*P*rogress might be a circle, rather than a straight line.

EBERHARD ZEIDLER

*B*ut what has been said once can always be repeated.

ZENO OF ELEA

*I*t's deja vu all over again.

YOGI BERRA

A rose is a rose is a rose.

GERTRUDE STEIN

CHAPTER CONTENTS

4.1   Repetition Structure: DO Loops

4.2   Application: Depreciation Tables

4.3   The While Repetition Structure

4.4   Implementing While Loops

4.5   Application: Mean Time to Failure

4.6   A Posttest Repetition Structure

4.7   Program Testing and Debugging Techniques

4.8   Application: Least-Squares Line

Chapter Review

Programming Pointers

Programming Problems

Fortran 90

*W*e have noted that programs can be designed using three basic control structures: sequence, selection, and repetition. In the preceding chapters we described sequence and selection, and in this chapter we consider the third basic control structure, repetition. A **repetition structure** or **loop** makes possible the repeated execution of one or more statements, called the **body of the loop**. There are two basic types of repetition:

1. *Repetition controlled by a counter* in which the body of the loop is executed once for each value of some control variable in a specified range of values.

2. *Repetition controlled by a logical expression* in which the decision to continue or to terminate repetition is determined by the value of some logical expression.

We will consider both types of loops in this chapter and illustrate how they are used in solving several problems, including the following:

Problem 1: Calculating Depreciation Tables. The depreciation-table problem described in Section 4.2 requires calculating and displaying a table showing how much a product has depreciated in each year of its useful life.

Displaying a depreciation table requires a loop that varies a year counter over the specified number of years:

For each year ranging from 1 to the useful life of the product do the following:
1. Calculate the depreciation for that year.
2. Display the year and the amount of depreciation.

In this problem the number of times that steps 1 and 2 must be repeated is known before repetition begins. In other problems like the following, the number of repetitions is not known in advance.

Problem 2: Calculating Mean Time to Failure. In the mean-time-to-failure problem described in Section 4.5, a collection of data values must be read and processed. The number of data values is not known in advance and must be determined as the program executes.

In the solution of this problem, repetition continues until a special end-of-data value is entered:

Repeat the following:
1. Read the next data value.
2. If the end-of-data value was read, terminate repetition.
   Else process the data value.

In this chapter we will show how DO loops can be used in FORTRAN to implement counter-controlled loops and also show how other kinds of loops can be constructed.

4.1 REPETITION STRUCTURE: DO LOOPS

In FORTRAN a counter-controlled loop is called a DO **loop** and is implemented using the DO and CONTINUE **statements:**

DO *Loop*

Form:

```
    DO n control-var = initial-value, limit, step-size
        statement-sequence
    n CONTINUE
```

where
   n is a statement number that is a positive integer of up to five digits; it may be followed by a comma;
   initial-value, *limit*, and *step-size* are integer or real (or double-precision) expressions; *step-size* must be nonzero;

step-size (and the comma preceding it) may be omitted; in this case, the value of *step-size* is taken to be 1.

Purpose:
Implements the repetition structures shown in Figure 4.1. When a DO loop is executed:

1. The control variable is assigned the initial value.
2. The control variable is compared with the limit to see if it is
   - less than or equal to the limit, for a positive step size.
   - greater than or equal to the limit, for a negative step size.
3. If so, the sequence of statements, called the **body of the loop**, is executed, the step size is added to the control variable, and step 2 is repeated. Otherwise, repetition terminates.

Note that if the termination test in 2 is satisfied initially, the body of the loop is never executed.

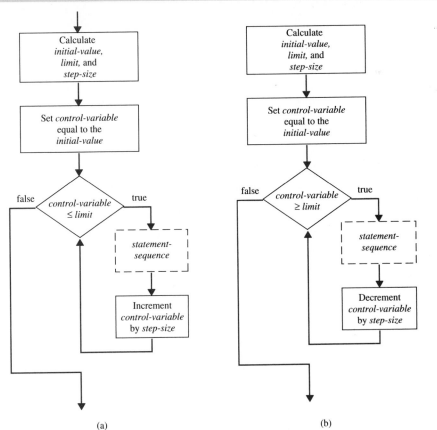

Figure 4.1

DO loop with
(a) positive
step size
(b) negative
step size.

(a)   (b)

DO loops will be represented in flowcharts as shown in Figure 4.2 to emphasize that they are repetition structures. The hexagon at the beginning of the loop is intended to include the initialization, testing, and incrementing, which are shown explicitly in Figure 4.1.

Figure 4.2

DO loops in flowcharts.

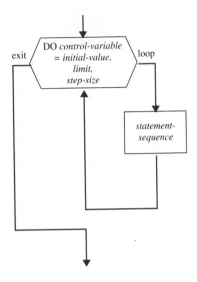

To illustrate, consider the DO loop

```
DO 10 NUMBER = 1, 9
    PRINT *, NUMBER, NUMBER**2
10 CONTINUE
```

where NUMBER is an integer variable. In this example, NUMBER is the control variable, the initial value is 1, the limit is 9, and the step size is 1. When this DO loop is executed, the initial value 1 is assigned to NUMBER, and the PRINT statement is executed. The value of NUMBER is then increased by 1, and because this new value 2 is less than the limit 9, the PRINT statement is executed again. This repetition continues as long as the value of the control variable NUMBER is less than or equal to the limit 9. Thus, the output produced by this DO loop is

```
1   1
2   4
3   9
4   16
5   25
6   36
7   49
8   64
9   81
```

If the step size in a DO loop is negative, the control variable is decremented rather than incremented, and repetition continues as long as the value of the control variable is greater than or equal to the limit. This is illustrated in Figure 4.1b. Note that if the initial value is less than the limit, the body of the loop is never executed.

For example, consider the DO loop

```
    DO 10 NUMBER = 9, 1, -1
        PRINT *, NUMBER, NUMBER **2
10 CONTINUE
```

The control variable NUMBER is assigned the initial value 9, and because this value is greater than the limit 1, the PRINT statement is executed. The value of NUMBER is then decreased to 8, and because this new value is greater than the limit, the PRINT statement is executed again. This process continues as long as the value of NUMBER is greater than or equal to the limit 1. Thus the output produced is

```
9   81
8   64
7   49
6   36
5   25
4   16
3   9
2   4
1   1
```

The initial values of the control variable, the limit, and the step size are determined before repetition begins and cannot be changed during execution of the DO *loop.* Within the body of the DO loop, the values of variables that specify the initial value, the limit, and the step size may change, but this does not affect the number of repetitions.[1] Also, the statements within a DO loop may use the value of the control variable, but *they must not modify the value of the control variable.* (See Potential Problem 4 in the Programming Pointers at the end of this chapter.) Upon exit from a DO loop, the control variable retains its value, and so this value may be used later in the program.

Example: A Table of Points on a Curve

The initial value, the limit, and the step size in a DO loop may be variables or expressions. To illustrate, consider the declarations

```
REAL FIRSTX, LASTX, DELTAX, X, Y
```

---

[1] The number of repetitions is calculated as the larger of the value 0 and the integer part of

$$\frac{limit - initial\text{-}value + step\text{-}size}{step\text{-}size}$$

and the statements

```
      READ *, FIRSTX, LASTX, DELTAX
      DO 10 X = FIRSTX, LASTX, DELTAX
         Y = EXP(-X) * SIN(X)
         PRINT *, X, Y
   10 CONTINUE
```

The values read for FIRSTX, LASTX, and DELTAX are the initial value, limit, and step size, respectively, for the DO loop. The program in Figure 4.3 uses these statements to print a table of points on the damped vibration curve

$$y = e^{-x} \sin x$$

Figure 4.3 Table of points on a curve.

```
      PROGRAM VIBRAT
*******************************************************************************
* Program to print a table of points on the curve                            *
*                -x                                                           *
*         y = e  *  sin x                                                     *
* Variables used are:                                                         *
*     X, Y          : coordinates of the point                               *
*     FIRSTX, LASTX : lower and upper limits on X                            *
*     DELTAX        : step size                                              *
*                                                                             *
* Input:  FIRSTX, LASTX, and DELTAX                                           *
* Output: Table of values of X and Y                                          *
*******************************************************************************

      REAL X, Y, FIRSTX, LASTX, DELTAX

      PRINT *, 'ENTER LOWER AND UPPER LIMITS ON X AND STEP SIZE'
      READ *, FIRSTX, LASTX, DELTAX
      PRINT *, '        X               Y'
      PRINT *, ' ============================='

      DO 10 X = FIRSTX, LASTX, DELTAX
         Y = EXP(-X) * SIN(X)
         PRINT *, X, Y
   10    CONTINUE

      END
```

Sample run:

```
ENTER LOWER AND UPPER LIMITS ON X AND STEP SIZE
1, 3, .25
```

Figure 4.3 *(cont.)*

```
      X                Y
============================
   1.00000    0.309560
   1.25000    0.271889
   1.50000    0.222571
   1.75000    0.170991
   2.00000    0.123060
   2.25000     8.20083E-02
   2.50000     4.91256E-02
   2.75000     2.43988E-02
   3.00000     7.02595E-03
```

Example: A Multiplication Table

The body of a DO loop may contain another DO loop. In this case, the second DO loop is said to be **nested** within the first DO loop. As an example, consider the program in Figure 4.4 that calculates and displays products of the form M * N for M ranging from 1 through LASTM and N ranging from 1 through LASTN for integer variables M, N, LASTM, and LASTN. The table of products is generated by the DO loop

```
      DO 20 M = 1, LASTM
         DO 10 N = 1, LASTN
            PROD = M * N
            PRINT *, M, N, PROD
10       CONTINUE
20 CONTINUE
```

In the sample run, both LASTM and LASTN are assigned the value 4. The control variable M is assigned its initial value 1, and the DO loop

```
      DO 10 N = 1, LASTN
         PROD = M * N
         PRINT *, M, N, PROD
10 CONTINUE
```

is executed. This calculates and displays the first four products, 1 * 1, 1 * 2, 1 * 3, and 1 * 4. The value of M is then incremented by 1, and the preceding DO loop is executed again. This calculates and displays the next four products, 2 * 1, 2 * 2, 2 * 3, and 2 * 4. The control variable M is then incremented to 3, producing the next four products, 3 * 1, 3 * 2, 3 * 3, and 3 * 4. Finally, M is incremented to 4, giving the last four products, 4 * 1, 4 * 2, 4 * 3, and 4 * 4.

Figure 4.4 Printing a multiplication table.

```
      PROGRAM MULT
*******************************************************************
* Program to calculate and display a list of products of two numbers.  *
* Variables used are:                                                   *
*     M, N           : the two numbers being multiplied                 *
*     PROD           : their product                                    *
*     LASTM, LASTN : the last values of M and N                         *
*                                                                       *
* Input:  LASTM and LASTN, the largest numbers to be multiplied         *
* Output: List of products M * N                                        *
*******************************************************************

      INTEGER M, N, LASTM, LASTN, PROD

      PRINT *, 'ENTER THE LAST VALUES OF THE TWO NUMBERS'
      READ *, LASTM, LASTN
      PRINT *, '  M  N  M * N'
      PRINT *, '=============='

      DO 20 M = 1, LASTM
         DO 10 N = 1, LASTN
            PROD = M * N
            PRINT *, M, N, PROD
10       CONTINUE
20    CONTINUE

      END
```

Sample run:

```
ENTER THE LAST VALUES OF THE TWO NUMBERS
4, 4

  M  N  M * N
==============
  1  1  1
  1  2  2
  1  3  3
  1  4  4
  2  1  2
  2  2  4
  2  3  6
  2  4  8
```

Figure 4.4 *(cont.)*

```
3  1  3
3  2  6
3  3  9
3  4  12
4  1  4
4  2  8
4  3  12
4  4  16
```

Quick Quiz 4.1

1. Name and briefly describe the two basic types of repetition structures.

For Questions 2–7, describe the output produced.

```
2.     DO 10 I = 1, 5
           PRINT *, 'HELLO'
       10 CONTINUE
```

```
3.     DO 10 I = 1, 5, 2
           PRINT *, 'HELLO'
       10 CONTINUE
```

```
4.     DO 10 I = 1, 6
           PRINT *, I, I + 1
       10 CONTINUE
```

```
5.     DO 10 I = 6, 1, -1
           PRINT *, I
           PRINT *
           PRINT *, I**2
       10 CONTINUE
```

```
6.     DO 10 I = 6, 6
           PRINT *, 'HELLO'
       10 CONTINUE
```

```
7.     DO 10 I = 6, 5
           PRINT *, 'HELLO'
       10 CONTINUE
```

8. What, if anything, is wrong with the following DO loop?
```
       DO 10 I = 1, 10
           PRINT *, I
           I = I + 1
       10 CONTINUE
```

9. How many lines of output are produced by the following DO loop?
```
       DO 10 I = 1, 5
           PRINT *, I
           DO 5 J = 1, 4
               PRINT *, I + J
        5      CONTINUE
       10 CONTINUE
```

Exercises 4.1

For Exercises 1–5, assume that I, J, and K are integer variables. Describe the output produced by the given program segment.

1.
```
    DO 10 I = -2, 3
        PRINT *, I, ' SQUARED = ', I * I
 10 CONTINUE
```

2.
```
    DO 30 I = 1, 5
        PRINT *, I
        DO 20 J = I, 1, -1
            PRINT *, J
 20     CONTINUE
 30 CONTINUE
```

3.
```
    K = 5
    DO 40 I = -2, 3
        PRINT *, I + K
        K = 1
 40 CONTINUE
```

4.
```
    DO 70 I = 1, 3
        DO 60 J = 1, 3
            DO 50 K = 1, J
                PRINT *, I, J, K
 50         CONTINUE
 60     CONTINUE
 70 CONTINUE
```

5.
```
     DO 100 I = 1, 3
         DO 90 J = 1, 3
             DO 80 K = I, J
                 PRINT *, I + J + K
 80          CONTINUE
 90      CONTINUE
100 CONTINUE
```

In Exercises 6–10, assume that I, J, and LIMIT are integer variables and that ALPHA and XINC are real variables. Describe the output produced, or explain why an error occurs.

6.
```
    DO 10 ALPHA = 2.25, 4.75
        PRINT *, 3.0 * ALPHA
 10 CONTINUE
```

7.
```
    ALPHA = -5
    XINC = 0.5
    DO 20 I = 1, 5
        PRINT *, ALPHA
        ALPHA = ALPHA + XINC
 20 CONTINUE
```

8.
```
    PRINT *, 'VALUES:'
    DO 50 I = 0, 2
       DO 40 J = 1, I
          PRINT *, I, J
40     CONTINUE
50 CONTINUE
    PRINT *, 'THE END'
```

9.
```
    LIMIT = 3
    DO 60 I = 1, LIMIT
       LIMIT = 1
       PRINT *, I, LIMIT
60 CONTINUE
```

10.
```
    DO 70 I = 1, 3
       PRINT *, I
70 CONTINUE
    PRINT *, I
```

11. Write statements to print the first 100 positive integers.

12. Write statements to print the first 100 even positive integers.

13. Write statements to read a value for the integer variable N and then print the first N positive even integers.

14. Write statements to print all positive integers having at most three digits, the last of which is 0.

15. Write statements to read a value for the integer variable N and then print all integers from 1 through 1000 that are multiples of N.

16. Write statements to read a value for the integer variable N, and then read and find the sum of N real numbers.

17. Write statements to print the square roots of the first 25 odd positive integers.

18. Write statements to print a list of points (x, y) on the graph of the equation $y = x^3 - 3x + 1$ for x ranging from -2 to 2 in increments of 0.1.

4.2 APPLICATION: DEPRECIATION TABLES

Problem

Depreciation is a decrease in the value over time of some asset due to wear and tear, decay, declining price, and so on. For example, suppose that a company purchases a new robot for $20,000 that will be used on its assembly line for 5 years. After that time, called the *useful life* of the robot, it can be sold at an estimated price of $5,000, which is the robot's *salvage value*. Thus, the value of the robot will have depreciated $15,000 over the 5-year period. A program is needed to calculate depreciation tables that display the depreciation in each year of an item's useful life.

Solution

Specification. The input for this problem is the purchase price of an item, its useful life, and its salvage value. The output is a depreciation table. However, there are several ways to calculate depreciation, and thus another input is an indicator of which method to use. A specification for this problem is therefore as follows:

Input: The purchase price of an item

The item's useful life (in years)

The item's salvage value

An indicator of which method of depreciation to use

Output: A depreciation table

Design. A first version of an algorithm for solving this problem is:

1. Get the purchase price, useful life, and salvage value of the item.
2. Calculate the amount to depreciate: purchase price − salvage value.

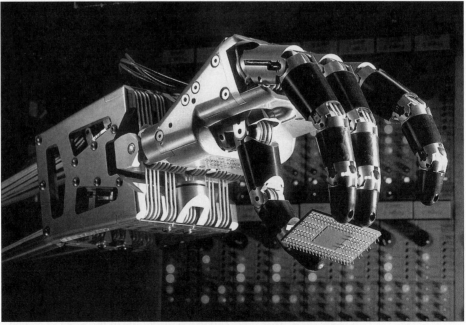

A robotic arm. (Photo courtesy of The Stock Market.)

3. Determine which method of depreciation is to be used.

4. Generate a depreciation table.

Coding steps 1 and 2 is straightforward as is coding step 3, once we know how many different methods of calculating depreciation to provide. There are many methods, but we will consider only two here: the *straight-line* method and the *sum-of-the-years'-digits* method. Thus we might refine step 3 as:

3. Enter an indicator to select the method of depreciation to be used: 1 for the straight-line method and 2 for the sum-of-the-years'-digits method.

Step 4 also obviously needs refinement. Generating a table requires a loop, and a do loop is appropriate here. We can rewrite step 4 as

4. Do the following for each year from 1 to the end of the useful life:

   Display the year number and the depreciation for that year, calculated using the method selected in step 3.

To complete the algorithm, we must describe the two methods of calculating depreciation. We will use the following variables:

VARIABLES FOR DEPRECIATION PROBLEM

PRICE   Purchase price of item

SALVAG   Its salvage value

AMOUNT Amount to be depreciated

LIFE   Useful life in years

METHOD Method of depreciation to use

YEAR   Year in which depreciation is being calculated

DEPREC   Depreciation for that year

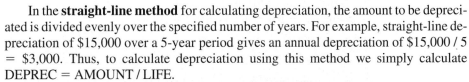

In the **straight-line method** for calculating depreciation, the amount to be depreciated is divided evenly over the specified number of years. For example, straight-line depreciation of $15,000 over a 5-year period gives an annual depreciation of $15,000 / 5 = $3,000. Thus, to calculate depreciation using this method we simply calculate DEPREC = AMOUNT / LIFE.

To illustrate the **sum-of-the-years'-digits method** of calculating depreciation, consider again depreciating $15,000 over a 5-year period. To use this method, we first calculate the "sum of the years," 1 + 2 + 3 + 4 + 5 = 15. In the first year, 5/15 of

$15,000 ($5,000) is depreciated; in the second year, 4/15 of $15,000 ($4,000) is depreciated; and so on, giving the following depreciation table:

Year	Depreciation
1	$5,000
2	$4,000
3	$3,000
4	$2,000
5	$1,000

Thus, to use this method we must add another variable to our list of identifiers:

ANOTHER VARIABLE FOR DEPRECIATION PROBLEM

SUM: $1 + 2 + \cdots + LIFE$

Once this sum has been calculated, we can calculate depreciation for a given YEAR as DEPREC = (LIFE − YEAR + 1) * AMOUNT / SUM.

We are now ready to give a complete algorithm for solving this problem. We must add statements to calculate SUM. These should be placed before the do loop for generating the depreciation table, since it would be inefficient to calculate this sum over and over again for each year. Our final algorithm is as follows:

ALGORITHM FOR DEPRECIATION PROBLEM

```
*  Algorithm to generate depreciation tables using either the straight-line method or  *
*  the sum-of-the-years'-digits method.                                                 *
*  Input:     PRICE, LIFE, SALVAG, and METHOD                                           *
*  Output:    A depreciation table showing the year number and the amount to be de-     *
*             preciated in that year                                                    *
```

1. Enter PRICE, LIFE, and SALVAG.

2. Calculate AMOUNT = PRICE − SALVAG.

3. Enter METHOD.

4. If METHOD = 1

   Calculate DEPREC = AMOUNT / LIFE

   Else:

   a. Set SUM to 0.

b. Do the following for YEAR ranging from 1 to LIFE:

Add YEAR to SUM.

5. Do the following for YEAR ranging from 1 to LIFE:

a. If METHOD = 2, calculate

DEPREC = (LIFE − YEAR + 1) * AMOUNT / SUM

b. Display YEAR and DEPREC.

Coding. The program in Figure 4.5 implements this algorithm. It uses DO loops to carry out the repetitions required in steps 4 and 5.

Figure 4.5 Calculating depreciation.

```
      PROGRAM DTABLE
* * * * * * * * * * * * * * * * * * * * * * * * * * * * * * * * * * * * * * * * * * * * * * * * * * * * * * * * * * * * * * * * *
* Program to calculate and display a depreciation table using one of   *
* two methods of depreciation:                                         *
*      (1) straight-line                                               *
*      (2) sum-of-the-years'-digits                                    *
* Variables used are:                                                  *
*      PRICE  :  purchase price of item                                *
*      SALVAG :  and its salvage value                                 *
*      AMOUNT :  amount to be depreciated (PRICE - SALVAG)             *
*      LIFE   :  its useful life                                       *
*      METHOD :  method of depreciation (1 or 2)                       *
*      YEAR   :  number of year in depreciation table                  *
*      SUM    :  1 + 2 + ... + LIFE (for sum-of-years'-digits method)  *
*                                                                      *
* Input:  PRICE, SALVAG, LIFE, and METHOD                              *
* Output: Table showing year number and depreciation for that year    *
* * * * * * * * * * * * * * * * * * * * * * * * * * * * * * * * * * * * * * * * * * * * * * * * * * * * * * * * * * * * * * * * *

      REAL PRICE, SALVAG, AMOUNT
      INTEGER LIFE, METHOD, YEAR, SUM
* Get the information about the item

      PRINT *, 'ENTER PURCHASE PRICE, USEFUL LIFE, AND SALVAGE VALUE:'
      READ *, PRICE, LIFE, SALVAG


* Calculate amount to be depreciated

      AMOUNT = PRICE - SALVAG
```

Figure 4.5 *(cont.)*

```
* Get method of depreciation to be used

      PRINT *, 'ENTER:'
      PRINT *, '   1 FOR STRAIGHT-LINE DEPRECIATION'
      PRINT *, '   2 FOR SUM-OF-THE-YEARS''-DIGITS METHOD'
      READ *, METHOD
* If straight-line selected, calculate annual depreciation
* Else calculate SUM for sum-of-the-years'-digits method

      IF (METHOD .EQ. 1) THEN
         DEPREC = AMOUNT / LIFE
      ELSE
         SUM = 0
         DO 10 YEAR = 1, LIFE
            SUM = SUM + YEAR
10       CONTINUE
      END IF

* Generate the depreciation table

      PRINT *
      PRINT *, 'YEAR    DEPRECIATION'
      PRINT *, '===================='
      DO 20 YEAR = 1, LIFE
         IF (METHOD .EQ. 2) THEN
            DEPREC = (LIFE - YEAR + 1) * AMOUNT / REAL(SUM)
         END IF
         PRINT *, YEAR, '    ', DEPREC
20    CONTINUE

      END
```

Execution and Testing. This program was executed several times using test data for which the results were easy to check. It was then run with the data given in the problem.

Run #1 of program:

```
ENTER PURCHASE PRICE, USEFUL LIFE, AND SALVAGE VALUE:
20000, 5, 5000
ENTER:
   1 FOR STRAIGHT-LINE DEPRECIATION
   2 FOR SUM-OF-THE-YEARS'-DIGITS METHOD
1
```

```
YEAR    DEPRECIATION
====================
  1          3000.00
  2          3000.00
  3          3000.00
  4          3000.00
  5          3000.00
```

Run #2 of program:

```
ENTER PURCHASE PRICE, USEFUL LIFE, AND SALVAGE VALUE:
20000, 5, 5000
ENTER:
   1 FOR STRAIGHT-LINE DEPRECIATION
   2 FOR SUM-OF-THE-YEARS'-DIGITS METHOD
2

YEAR    DEPRECIATION
====================
  1          5000.00
  2          4000.00
  3          3000.00
  4          2000.00
  5          1000.00
```

4.3   THE WHILE REPETITION STRUCTURE

The DO loop described in Section 4.1 can be used to implement a repetition structure in which the number of iterations is determined before execution of the loop begins. In some cases, however, a repetition structure is required in which repetition is controlled by some logical expression and continues while this logical expression remains true, terminating when it becomes false. Such a repetition structure is called a **while loop** and is pictured in Figure 4.6 a. It will be represented in flowcharts as shown in Figure 4.6 b, to emphasize that it is a repetition structure.

Example: Summation

To illustrate the use of a while loop, consider the following problem:

For a given value of LIMIT, what is the smallest positive integer NUMBER for which the sum

$$1 + 2 + \cdots + \text{NUMBER}$$

is greater than LIMIT, and what is the value of this sum?

Figure 4.6

The while
repetition
structure.

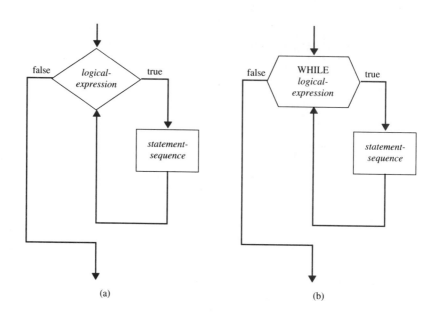

(a)   (b)

To solve this problem we use three variables:

> NUMBER: A positive integer added to the sum
>
> SUM: $1 + 2 + \cdots + $ NUMBER
>
> LIMIT: The specified limit for the sum

We begin with NUMBER and SUM initialized to 0. If this value of SUM exceeds the
value of LIMIT, the problem is solved. Otherwise we increment NUMBER by 1, add it
to SUM, and then check to see if this value of SUM exceeds LIMIT. Once again, if it
does, the problem is solved; and if not, NUMBER must again be incremented and added
to SUM. This process is continued as long as the value of SUM is less than or equal to
LIMIT. Eventually the value of SUM will exceed LIMIT and the problem is solved.
This leads to the following algorithm. Figure 4.7 displays the structure of this algorithm
in flowchart form.

ALGORITHM FOR SUMMATION PROBLEM

```
*  Algorithm to find the smallest positive NUMBER for which the sum  *
*  1 + 2 + ··· + NUMBER is greater than some specified value LIMIT.   *
*  Input:    An integer LIMIT                                         *
*  Output:   NUMBER and SUM                                          *
```

  1. Enter LIMIT.
  2. Set NUMBER equal to 0.

3. Set SUM equal to 0.
4. While SUM ≤ LIMIT, do the following:
    a. Increment NUMBER by 1.
    b. Add NUMBER to SUM.
5. Display NUMBER and SUM.

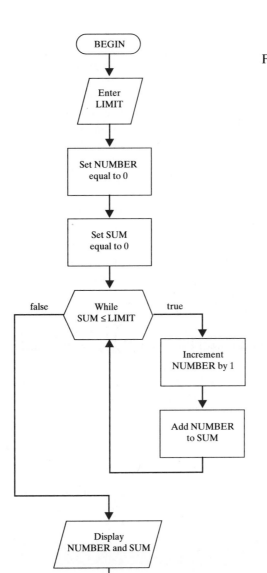

Figure 4.7

Flowchart for summation algorithm.

As the diagrams in Figure 4.6 indicate, the logical expression in a while loop is evaluated *before* repetition, and thus this loop is sometimes called a **pretest loop** or a "test-at-the-top" loop. If the logical expression that controls repetition is false initially, the body of the loop is not executed. Thus, in the preceding summation algorithm, if the value −1 is entered for LIMIT, the body of the while loop is bypassed, and execution continues with the display instruction that follows the while loop; the value 0 will be displayed for both NUMBER and SUM.

Sentinel-Controlled While Loops

One common use of while loops is reading and processing a set of data values. Because it may not be possible or practical to determine beforehand how many data values must be processed, a general loop such as a while loop should be used rather than a DO loop.

One commonly used method is to use a **sentinel-controlled loop** and to append to the data set an artificial data value called an **end-of-data flag** or **sentinel** , which is distinct from any possible data item. As each data item is read, it is checked to determine whether it is this end-of-data flag. If it is not, the value is processed. When the end-of-data flag is read, it is not processed as a regular data value. It serves only to terminate repetition.

One way to implement this scheme is by using a sentinel-controlled while loop of the form:

1. Read the first data value.
2. While the data value is not the end-of-data flag, do the following:
    a. Process the data value.
    b. Read the next data value.

Note the presence of two input instructions, one before the while loop and one at the bottom of the while loop. The first data value must be read before the while loop is entered for the first time; otherwise the logical expression that controls repetition cannot be checked. If this data value is not the end-of-data flag, the body of the while loop is entered, and the value is processed. Within the while loop, after the current data value has been processed, a new value must be read before the next pass through the loop. This value is then checked to determine whether it is the end-of-data flag, and if it is not, the value is processed. When the end-of-data flag is eventually read, the while loop will be exited without processing this artificial data value. This standard technique for reading and processing data values is illustrated in the mean-time-to-failure problem in Section 4.5.

4.4 IMPLEMENTING WHILE LOOPS

A while statement that implements a while loop is not included in standard FORTRAN, but it is a common extension that is available in many versions of FORTRAN and is included in Fortran 90. In this section we show how while loops can be implemented in standard FORTRAN and then how they can be implemented using a DO WHILE statement provided in many versions of FORTRAN. We will illustrate each method by showing how it can be used to implement the summation algorithm of the preceding section. In later programs in this text, all while loops will be implemented in standard FORTRAN, but each will be clearly marked with a comment to indicate where a DO WHILE statement could be used.

In Standard FORTRAN

While loops can be implemented in standard FORTRAN by using a GO TO **statement** within an IF construct. The GO TO statement is a branching statement and has the form

---

GO TO *Statement*

Form:

```
GO TO statement-number
```

where
  statement-number is the number of an executable statement.

Purpose:
Alters the usual sequential execution so that the statement with the specified number is executed next.

A while loop can be implemented by a program segment of the form

```
n IF (logical-expression) THEN
     statement-sequence
  GO TO n
  END IF
```

Repeated execution of the statements in the body of the while loop must eventually cause the logical expression to become false, because an **infinite loop** results otherwise.

The program in Figure 4.8 illustrates this implementation of while loops. It uses the summation algorithm of the preceding section to find the smallest positive integer NUMBER for which the sum $1 + 2 + \cdots + \text{NUMBER}$ is greater than some specified value LIMIT. The statements

```
10 IF (SUM .LE. LIMIT) THEN
      NUMBER = NUMBER + 1
      SUM = SUM + NUMBER
   GO TO 10
   END IF
```

implement the while loop

> While SUM ≤ LIMIT, do the following:
> a. Increment NUMBER by 1.
> b. Add NUMBER to SUM.

in this algorithm.

Because the logical expression in a while loop is evaluated before the repetition begins, the statements that comprise the body of the while loop are not executed if this expression is initially false. This is demonstrated in the last sample run, where the value −1 is entered for LIMIT. The while loop causes an immediate transfer of control to the last PRINT statement that displays the value 0 for both NUMBER and SUM.

Figure 4.8 Calculating sums.

```
      PROGRAM ADDER2
* * * * * * * * * * * * * * * * * * * * * * * * * * * * * * * * * * * * * * * * * * * * * * * * * * * * * * * * * * * * * * * *
* Program to find the smallest positive integer NUMBER for which the     *
* sum 1 + 2 + ... + NUMBER is greater than some specified value LIMIT.    *
* Variables used are:                                                     *
*     NUMBER : the current number being added                             *
*     SUM    : the sum 1 + 2 + ... + NUMBER                               *
*     LIMIT  : the value which SUM is to exceed                           *
*                                                                         *
* Input:  An integer LIMIT                                                *
* Output: NUMBER and the value of SUM                                     *
* * * * * * * * * * * * * * * * * * * * * * * * * * * * * * * * * * * * * * * * * * * * * * * * * * * * * * * * * * * * * * * *

      INTEGER NUMBER, SUM, LIMIT

* Read LIMIT and initialize NUMBER and SUM

      PRINT *, 'ENTER VALUE 1 + 2 + ... + ? IS TO EXCEED'
      READ *, LIMIT
      NUMBER = 0
      SUM = 0


* While SUM does not exceed LIMIT, increment NUMBER and add to SUM

10    IF (SUM .LE. LIMIT) THEN
         NUMBER = NUMBER + 1
         SUM = SUM + NUMBER
      GO TO 10
      END IF
```

Figure 4.8 *(cont.)*

```
* Print the results

      PRINT *, '1 + ... +', NUMBER, ' = ', SUM, ' >', LIMIT
      END
```

Sample runs:

```
ENTER VALUE 1 + ... + ? IS TO EXCEED
10
1 + ... + 5 = 15 > 10

ENTER VALUE 1 + ... + ? IS TO EXCEED
10000
1 + ... + 141 = 10011 > 10000

ENTER VALUE 1 + ... + ? IS TO EXCEED
−1
1 + ... + 0 = 0 > −1
```

In the first sample run of Figure 4.8 in which the value 10 is entered for LIMIT, the body of the while loop is executed five times, as indicated in the following table, which traces its execution:

NUMBER	SUM	SUM .LE. LIMIT	Action
0	0	.TRUE.	Execute body of while loop
1	1	.TRUE.	Execute body of while loop
2	3	.TRUE.	Execute body of while loop
3	6	.TRUE.	Execute body of while loop
4	10	.TRUE.	Execute body of while loop
5	15	.FALSE.	Terminate repetition

A similar trace table for the second sample run would show that the loop body is executed 141 times. A trace table for the third sample run shows that the loop body is not executed because the logical expression SUM .LE. LIMIT that controls repetition is initially false:

NUMBER	SUM	SUM .LE. LIMIT	Action
0	0	.FALSE.	Terminate repetition; that is, bypass loop body.

*The DO WHILE Statement

Many versions of FORTRAN provide a DO WHILE statement for implementing while loops. This statement usually has one of the following forms:

```
DO WHILE (logical-expression)    WHILE (logical-expression) DO
    statement-sequence                statement-sequence
END DO                           END WHILE
```

When this statement is executed, the logical expression is evaluated, and if it is true, the sequence of statements that comprise the *body* of the while loop is executed. The logical expression is then reevaluated, and if it is still true, these statements are executed again. This process of evaluating the logical expression and executing the specified statements is repeated as long as the logical expression is true. When it becomes false, repetition is terminated.

The program in Figure 4.9 is a modification of that in Figure 4.8 for solving the summation problem of the preceding section. It uses the DO WHILE statement

```
DO WHILE (SUM .LE. LIMIT)
    NUMBER = NUMBER + 1
    SUM = SUM + NUMBER
END DO
```

to implement the while loop.

Figure 4.9 Calculating sums.

```
      PROGRAM ADDER1
*****************************************************************************
* Program that uses a DO WHILE statement to find the smallest positive    *
* integer NUMBER for which the sum 1 + 2 + ... + NUMBER is greater        *
* than some specified LIMIT.  Variables used are:                         *
*     NUMBER : the current number being added                             *
*     SUM    : the sum 1 + 2 + ... + NUMBER                               *
*     LIMIT  : the value which SUM is to exceed                           *
*                                                                         *
* Input:  An integer LIMIT                                                *
* Output: NUMBER and the value of SUM                                     *
*****************************************************************************

      INTEGER NUMBER, SUM, LIMIT

* Read LIMIT and initialize NUMBER and SUM
      PRINT *, 'ENTER VALUE 1 + 2 + ... + ? IS TO EXCEED'
      READ *, LIMIT
      NUMBER = 0
      SUM = 0
```

Figure 4.9 *(cont.)*

```
* While SUM does not exceed LIMIT, increment NUMBER and add to SUM

      DO WHILE (SUM .LE. LIMIT)
         NUMBER = NUMBER + 1
         SUM = SUM + NUMBER
      END DO

* Print the results

      PRINT *, '1 + ... +', NUMBER, ' =', SUM, ' >', LIMIT
      END
```

Sample runs:

```
ENTER VALUE 1 + ... + ? IS TO EXCEED
10
1 + ... + 5 = 15 > 10

ENTER VALUE 1 + ... + ? IS TO EXCEED
10000
1 + ... + 141 = 10011 > 10000

ENTER VALUE 1 + ... + ? IS TO EXCEED
-1
1 + ... + 0 = 0 > -1
```

4.5 APPLICATION: MEAN TIME TO FAILURE

Problem

One important statistic used in measuring the reliability of a component in a circuit is the *mean time to failure*, which can be used to predict the circuit's lifetime. This is especially important in situations in which repair is difficult or even impossible, such as for a computer circuit in a space satellite. Suppose that NASA has awarded an engineering laboratory a contract to evaluate the reliability of a particular component for a future space probe to Mars. As part of this evaluation, an engineer at this laboratory has tested several of these circuits and recorded the time at which each failed; now she would like a program to process this data and determine the mean time to failure.

Solution

Specification. The input for this problem is obviously a collection of failure times for the component being tested, and the output is clearly the average or mean of these times. To calculate this mean, we must know how many tests were conducted, but this information is not given in the statement of the problem. We cannot assume, therefore, that it is part of the input, and so the program will have to be flexible enough to process any number of data values. A specification of the input and output for this problem thus might be

Input: A collection of numeric values (number unknown)

Output: The number of values

         The mean of the values

Design. In developing algorithms to solve problems like this, one useful method is to begin by considering how the problem could be solved without using a computer, perhaps instead using pencil and paper and/or a calculator. To solve the problem in this manner, we enter the values one at a time, counting each value as it is entered and adding it to the sum of the preceding values. This procedure involves two quantities:

1. A counter that is incremented by 1 each time a data value is entered.
2. A running sum of the data values.

Data Value	Counter	Sum
	0	0.0
3.4	1	3.4
4.2	2	7.6
6.0	3	13.6
5.5	4	19.1
⋮	⋮	⋮

The procedure begins with 0 as the value of the counter and 0.0 as the initial value of the sum. At each stage, a data value is entered, the value of the counter is incremented by 1, and the data value is added to the sum, producing a new sum. These steps are repeated until eventually all the data values have been processed, and the sum is then divided by the counter to obtain the mean value. An initial algorithm for solving the problem thus is

1. Initialize a counter and a running sum to zero.
2. Repeatedly read a new data value, count it, and add it to the running sum.
3. After all the data has been processed, calculate the mean value and display the counter and the mean value.

Space probe. (Photo courtesy of The Stock Market.)

Here, coding step 1 is straightforward and only steps 2 and 3 require some refinement. Clearly, step 2 requires a repetition structure like the sentinel-controlled while loop described in Section 4.3:

2.1. Read the first failure time.

2.2. While the failure time is not the data sentinel, do the following:

    a. Increment the counter by 1.

    b. Add the failure time to the running sum.

    c. Read the next failure time.

After the data sentinel has been entered, signaling that all the failure times have been processed, the mean failure time is computed by dividing the final sum by the counter. If, however, the data sentinel were entered immediately, the while loop would be bypassed and both the counter and the sum would be 0. The division operation required in step 3 to compute the mean failure time cannot be performed because division by zero is not permitted. To guard against this error, we will check that the counter is nonzero before performing this division:

3. If the counter is nonzero do the following:

    a. Divide the sum by the count to obtain the mean failure time.

    b. Display the count and the mean failure time.

Else

Display a "no data" message.

We can now write a complete algorithm for solving this problem. We will use the following variables:

VARIABLES FOR MEAN-TIME-TO-FAILURE PROBLEM

FAILTM   Current failure time read
COUNT   Number of failure-time readings
SUM   Sum of failure times
MEAN   Mean time to failure

A pseudocode description of this algorithm then is

ALGORITHM FOR MEAN-TIME-TO-FAILURE PROBLEM

```
* Algorithm to read failure times, count them, and find the mean time to failure *
* (MEAN). FAILTM represents the current failure time entered, COUNT is the        *
* number of failure times, and SUM is their sum. Values are read until an         *
* end-of-data flag is encountered.                                                *
* Input:    A collection of failure times                                         *
* Output:   The mean time to failure and the number of failure times              *
```

1.   Initialize COUNT to 0 and SUM to 0.0.
2.1. Enter first value for FAILTM.
2.2. While FAILTM is not the end-of-data flag, do the following:

a. Increment COUNT by 1.

b. Add FAILTM to SUM.

c. Enter next value for FAILTM.

3.   If COUNT $\neq$ 0 do the following:

a. Calculate MEAN = SUM / COUNT.

b. Display COUNT and MEAN.

Else

Display a 'no data' message.

The flowchart in Figure 4.10 gives a graphical representation of the structure of this algorithm. Note that all three control structures — sequence, selection, and repetition — are used in this algorithm. The highlighted region shows the sentinel-controlled loop used to read and process failure times.

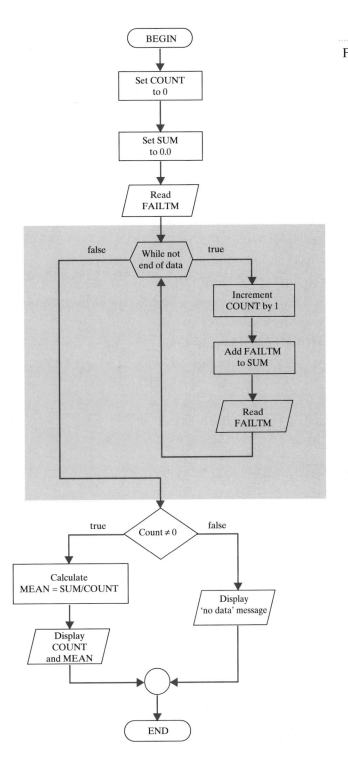

Figure 4.10

Flowchart for mean-time-to-failure algorithm.

Coding. The program in Figure 4.11 implements the algorithm for solving this problem. It uses the statements

```
PRINT *, 'ENTER FAILURE TIME OF', ENDATA, ' OR LESS TO STOP'
PRINT *, 'ENTER FAILURE TIME'
READ *, FAILTM

10 IF (FAILTM .GT. ENDATA) THEN
      COUNT = COUNT + 1
      SUM = SUM + FAILTM
      PRINT *, 'ENTER FAILURE TIME'
      READ *, FAILTM
   GO TO 10
   END IF
```

to implement the following instructions in the algorithm:

2.1. Enter first value for FAILTM.

2.2. While FAILTM is not the end-of-data flag, do the following:

    a. Increment COUNT by 1.

    b. Add FAILTM to SUM.

    c. Enter next value for FAILTM.

Figure 4.11 Mean time to failure.

```
PROGRAM FAIL
**************************************************************
* Program to read a list of failure times, count them, and find the  *
* mean time to failure.  Values are read until an end-of-data flag    *
* is read.  Identifiers used are:                                     *
*    FAILTM  :  the current failure time read                         *
*    ENDATA  :  a parameter -- the end-of-data flag                   *
*    COUNT   :  the number of failure time readings                   *
*    SUM     :  sum of failure times                                  *
*    MEAN    :  the mean time to failure                              *
*                                                                     *
* Input:  A list of failure times                                     *
* Output: Number of failure times read and their mean or a message    *
*         indicating that no failure times were entered               *
**************************************************************

      INTEGER COUNT
      REAL FAILTM, ENDATA, SUM, MEAN
      PARAMETER (ENDATA = -1.0)
```

Figure 4.11 *(cont.)*

```
* Initialize SUM and COUNT, and read first failure time

      SUM = 0.0
      COUNT = 0
      PRINT *, 'ENTER FAILURE TIME OF ', ENDATA, ' OR LESS TO STOP'
      PRINT *, 'ENTER FAILURE TIME'
      READ *, FAILTM

* While not end-of-data, count, sum, and read failure times

10    IF (FAILTM .GT. ENDATA) THEN
          COUNT = COUNT + 1
          SUM = SUM + FAILTM
          PRINT *, 'ENTER FAILURE TIME'
          READ *, FAILTM
      GO TO 10
      END IF

* Calculate and display mean time to failure
      IF (COUNT .NE. 0) THEN
          MEAN = SUM / COUNT
          PRINT *
          PRINT *, 'NUMBER OF FAILURE TIME READINGS:', COUNT
          PRINT *, 'MEAN TIME TO FAILURE:', MEAN
      ELSE
          PRINT *, 'NO FAILURE TIMES WERE ENTERED.'
      END IF

      END
```

In those versions of FORTRAN that provide a DO-WHILE statement, the while loop in the preceding program might be implemented as follows:

```
* While not end-of-data, count, sum, and read fail times

      DO WHILE (FAILTM .GT. ENDATA)
          COUNT = COUNT + 1
          SUM = SUM + FAILTM
          PRINT *, 'ENTER FAILURE TIME'
          READ *, FAILTM
      END DO
```

Execution and Testing. Test runs with input data like the following indicate that the program is correct:

Test run #1:

```
ENTER FAILURE TIME OF   -1.00000 OR LESS TO STOP
ENTER FAILURE TIME
-1.0
NO FAILURE TIMES WERE ENTERED.
```

Test run #2:

```
ENTER FAILURE TIME OF   -1.00000 OR LESS TO STOP
ENTER FAILURE TIME
25.5
ENTER FAILURE TIME
-2.0

NUMBER OF FAILURE TIME READINGS:   1
MEAN TIME TO FAILURE:    25.5000
```

Test run #3:

```
ENTER FAILURE TIME OF   -1.00000 OR LESS TO STOP
ENTER FAILURE TIME
3.0
ENTER FAILURE TIME
4.0
ENTER FAILURE TIME
5.0
ENTER FAILURE TIME
-1.0

NUMBER OF FAILURE TIME READINGS:   3
MEAN TIME TO FAILURE:    4.00000
```

It can then be used to calculate mean failure times for other data sets such as

```
ENTER FAILURE TIME OF   -1.00000 OR LESS TO STOP
ENTER FAILURE TIME
127
ENTER FAILURE TIME
123.5
ENTER FAILURE TIME
155.4
ENTER FAILURE TIME
99
```

```
ENTER FAILURE TIME
117.3
ENTER FAILURE TIME
201.5
ENTER FAILURE TIME
−999

NUMBER OF FAILURE TIME READINGS:   6
MEAN TIME TO FAILURE:     137.283
```

4.6 A POSTTEST REPETITION STRUCTURE

A while loop is a **pretest** loop in which the logical expression that controls the repetition is evaluated *before* the body of the loop is executed. Sometimes, however, it is appropriate to use a **posttest** or "test-at-the-bottom" loop in which the termination test is made *after* the body of the loop is executed. Such a structure is pictured in Figure 4.12 and can be implemented in FORTRAN with a program segment of the form

```
n CONTINUE
     statement-sequence
  IF (logical-expression) GO TO n
```

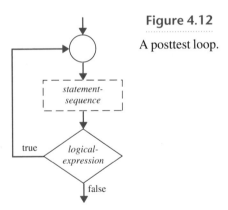

Figure 4.12

A posttest loop.

Example: Temperature Conversions

To illustrate a posttest loop, we reconsider the problem described in Section 2.7 of converting Centigrade temperatures to Fahrenheit temperatures. The program developed there to solve this problem was designed to process only one temperature at a time. To process several temperatures, the program must be executed for each one.

This program can be easily modified to process several temperatures by "wrapping" the executable statements within a loop. This might be a sentinel-controlled while loop, but for this problem there is really no good value to use as a data flag. A better alternative is to *query* the user after each temperature has been processed and ask if there is more data to be processed. Using such a **query-controlled input loop**, we can modify the algorithm given earlier as follows:

ALGORITHM FOR TEMPERATURE CONVERSION PROBLEM

```
*   This algorithm converts temperatures on the Celsius scale to the corresponding tem-    *
*   peratures on the Fahrenheit scale. Values are processed until the user indicates that   *
*   there is no more data.                                                                  *
*   Input:     temperatures in degrees Celsius                                              *
*              user responses                                                               *
*   Output:   temperatures in degrees Fahrenheit                                            *
```

Repeat the following until RESPON = 0:

1. Enter CELS.

2. Calculate

$$FAHREN = 1.8 * CELS + 32$$

3. Display FAHREN.

4. Enter RESPON (0 to stop, 1 to continue).

The posttest loop in this algorithm can be implemented with the statements

```
10 CONTINUE
      PRINT *, 'ENTER TEMPERATURE IN DEGREES CELSIUS:'
      READ *, CELS
      FAHREN = 1.8 * CELS + 32.0
      PRINT *, 'FAHRENHEIT TEMPERATURE IS', FAHREN
      PRINT *
      PRINT *, 'MORE (0 = NO, 1 = YES)?'
      READ *, RESPON
   IF (RESPON .NE. 0) GO TO 10
```

as shown in the program of Figure 4.13.

Figure 4.13 Temperature conversion—repetitive version.

```
        PROGRAM TEMPS2
**************************************************************************
* Program to convert temperatures on the Celsius scale to the corres-  *
* ponding temperatures on the Fahrenheit scale.  Variables used are:   *
*     CELS   :  Celsius temperature                                    *
*     FAHREN :  Fahrenheit temperature                                 *
*     RESPON :  user response                                          *
*                                                                      *
* Input:  CELS, RESPON                                                 *
* Output: FAHREN                                                       *
**************************************************************************

        REAL CELS, FAHREN
        INTEGER RESPON

10      CONTINUE
            PRINT *, 'ENTER TEMPERATURE IN DEGREES CELSIUS:'
            READ *, CELS
            FAHREN = 1.8 * CELS + 32.0
            PRINT *, 'FAHRENHEIT TEMPERATURE IS', FAHREN
            PRINT *
            PRINT *, 'MORE (0 = NO, 1 = YES)?'
            READ *, RESPON
        IF (RESPON .NE. 0) GO TO 10

        END
```

Sample run:

```
ENTER TEMPERATURE IN DEGREES CELSIUS:
0
FAHRENHEIT TEMPERATURE IS     32.0000

MORE (0 = NO, 1 = YES)
1
ENTER TEMPERATURE IN DEGREES CELSIUS:
100.0
FAHRENHEIT TEMPERATURE IS    212.0000

MORE (0 = NO, 1 = YES)
1
ENTER TEMPERATURE IN DEGREES CELSIUS:
11.193
FAHRENHEIT TEMPERATURE IS     52.1474
```

Figure 4.13 *(cont.)*

```
MORE (0 = NO, 1 = YES)
1
ENTER TEMPERATURE IN DEGREES CELSIUS:
-17.728
FAHRENHEIT TEMPERATURE IS    8.95996E-02

MORE (0 = NO, 1 = YES)
1
ENTER TEMPERATURE IN DEGREES CELSIUS:
49.1
FAHRENHEIT TEMPERATURE IS    120.380

MORE (0 = NO, 1 = YES)
0
```

4.7 PROGRAM TESTING AND DEBUGGING TECHNIQUES

In Section 1.4 we noted that three types of errors may occur when developing a program to solve a problem: syntax or compile-time errors, run-time errors, and logic errors. **Syntax errors** such as incorrect punctuation, unbalanced parentheses, and misspelled key words are detected during the program's compilation, and an appropriate error message is usually displayed. **Run-time errors** such as division by zero and integer overflow are detected during the program's execution, and again, a suitable error message is often displayed. These two types of errors are, for the most part, relatively easy to correct, since the system error messages often indicate the type of error and where it occurred. **Logic errors,** on the other hand, are usually more difficult to detect, since they arise in the design of the algorithm or in coding the algorithm as a program, and in most cases, no error messages are displayed to assist the programmer in identifying such errors.

The Programming Pointers at the ends of the chapters in this book include warnings about some of the more common errors. As programs become increasingly complex, however, the logic errors that may occur are more subtle and consequently more difficult to identify and correct. In this section we consider an example of a program that contains logic errors and describe techniques that are useful in detecting them.

An Example: Range of Noise Levels

Suppose that as a programming exercise, students were asked to write a program to read a list of positive integers representing noise levels (in decibels) in an automobile under various conditions and to determine the range, that is, the difference between the largest and the smallest values. The following program heading, opening documentation, and variable declarations were given, and the students were asked to write the rest of the program:

```
        PROGRAM RANGE
* * * * * * * * * * * * * * * * * * * * * * * * * * * * * * * * * * * * * * * * * * * * * * * * * * * * * * * * *
* Program to read a list of noise levels in decibels and determine *
* the range of values.  A negative noise level is used to signal  *
* the end of data.  Variables used are:                           *
*    NOISE  :  the current noise level being processed             *
*    LARGE  :  the largest value read so far                       *
*    SMALL  :  "  smallest  "     "   "  "                         *
*                                                                  *
* Input:  A list of noise levels in decibels                       *
* Output: The range of noise levels                                *
* * * * * * * * * * * * * * * * * * * * * * * * * * * * * * * * * * * * * * * * * * * * * * * * * * * * * * * * *

        INTEGER NOISE, LARGE, SMALL
```

One attempted solution was the following (in which the statements have been numbered for easy reference):

```
(1)        PRINT *, 'ENTER NOISE LEVELS IN DECIBELS (INTEGERS).'
(2)        PRINT *, 'ENTER ZERO OR A NEGATIVE VALUE TO STOP.'

    * Initialize largest noise level with a small value
    * and smallest with a very large value

(3)        LARGE = 0
(4)        SMALL = 999

    * While NOISE is not the end-of-data flag do:

(5) 10     IF (NOISE .GT. 0) THEN
(6)            PRINT *, 'NOISE LEVEL?'
(7)            READ *, NOISE
(8)            IF (NOISE .GT. LARGE) THEN
(9)                LARGE = NOISE
(10)           ELSE IF (NOISE .LT. SMALL) THEN
(11)               SMALL = NOISE
(12)           END IF
(13)        GO TO 10
(14)        END IF

(15)        PRINT *, 'RANGE OF NOISE LEVELS =', LARGE - SMALL, ' DECIBELS'
(16)        END
```

Execution of the program produced

```
ENTER NOISE LEVELS IN DECIBELS (INTEGERS).
ENTER ZERO OR A NEGATIVE VALUE TO STOP.
RANGE OF NOISE LEVELS =  -999 DECIBELS
```

Since the user was not allowed to enter any data, it is clear that the body of the while loop was not entered. This suggests that the logical expression NOISE .GT. 0 that controls repetition was initially false, thus causing immediate termination.

This is in fact what happened. Because the student did not ensure that NOISE had been assigned a value before the beginning of the while loop in line 5 was encountered, NOISE had an undefined value when the logical expression NOISE .GT. 0 was evaluated. (The student did not heed the warning in Potential Problem 9 in the Programming Pointers of Chapter 2!) The particular system on which the program was executed used a value of 0 for NOISE, making this logical expression false and causing the while loop to terminate immediately.

To remedy the situation, the student inserted the assignment statement NOISE = 1 ahead of the IF construct to force an entrance into the while loop:

```
(1)        PRINT *, 'ENTER NOISE LEVELS IN DECIBELS (INTEGERS).'
(2)        PRINT *, 'ENTER ZERO OR A NEGATIVE VALUE TO STOP.'

   * Initialize largest noise level with a small value
   * and smallest with a very large value

(3)        LARGE = 0
(4)        SMALL = 999
(5)        NOISE = 1

     * While NOISE is not the end-of-data flag do:

(6) 10    IF (NOISE .GT. 0) THEN
(7)           PRINT *, 'NOISE LEVEL?'
(8)           READ *, NOISE
(9)           IF (NOISE .GT. LARGE) THEN
(10)              LARGE = NOISE
(11)          ELSE IF (NOISE .LT. SMALL) THEN
(12)              SMALL = NOISE
(13)          END IF
(14)       GO TO 10
(15)       END IF
(16)       PRINT *, 'RANGE OF NOISE LEVELS = ', LARGE - SMALL, ' DECIBELS'
(17)       END
```

This "quick and dirty patch" fixed the problem of premature termination of the while loop, and execution of this revised program produced

```
ENTER NOISE LEVELS IN DECIBELS (INTEGERS).
ENTER ZERO OR A NEGATIVE VALUE TO STOP.
NOISE LEVEL?
94
NOISE LEVEL?
102
NOISE LEVEL?
88
NOISE LEVEL?
−1
RANGE OF NOISE LEVELS =   103 DECIBELS
```

Data values were read and processed, terminating when the end-of-data flag −1 was read. The correct range for this set of noise levels is 14, however, and not 103 as computed by the program.

Trace Tables

One common approach to finding logic errors in a program is manually constructing a **trace table** of the segment of the program that is suspect. This technique, also known as **desk checking,** consists of recording in a table, step by step, the values of all or certain key variables in the program segment. In this example, the following trace table for the loop in statements 6 through 15 might be obtained:

Statements	NOISE	LARGE	SMALL	
	1	0	999	← Initial values
6	1	0	999	First pass through the loop
7–8	94	94	999	
9–10	94	94	999	
6	94	94	999	Second pass through the loop
7–8	102	94	999	
9–10	102	94	999	
6	102	102	999	Third pass through the loop
7–8	88	102	88	
11–12	88	102	88	
6	102	102	999	Fourth pass through the loop
7–8	−1	102	88	
11–12	−1	102	−1	

The last line in this trace table shows why the range is incorrect: the value of SMALL became −1 on the last pass through the loop because the value −1 used to signal the end of data was read and processed as a noise level.

Debugging

The execution of a program segment can also be traced automatically by inserting temporary output statements or by using special system-debugging software to display the values of key variables at selected stages of program execution. For example, we might insert the statement

```
PRINT *, 'NOISE LEVEL', NOISE
```

after the READ statement to echo the data values as they are entered, and the statement

```
PRINT *, 'LARGEST', LARGE, ' SMALLEST', SMALL
```

at the bottom of the loop to display the values of these variables at the end of each pass through the loop. The resulting output then is

```
ENTER NOISE LEVELS IN DECIBELS (INTEGERS).
ENTER ZERO OR A NEGATIVE VALUE TO STOP.
NOISE LEVEL?
94
NOISE LEVEL   94
LARGEST   94   SMALLEST   999
NOISE LEVEL?
102
NOISE LEVEL   102
LARGEST   102   SMALLEST   999
NOISE LEVEL?
88
NOISE LEVEL   88
LARGEST   102 SMALLEST   88
NOISE LEVEL?
-1
NOISE LEVEL   -1
LARGEST   102   SMALLEST   -1
RANGE OF NOISE LEVELS =   103 DECIBELS
```

This technique must not be used indiscriminately, however, since incorrect placement of such temporary debugging statements may display output that is not helpful in locating the source of the error. Also, if too many such statements are used, so much output may be produced that it will be difficult to isolate the error.

Modifying and Testing the Program

Either manual or automatic tracing of this program reveals that the error is that the value −1 used to signal the end of data was processed as an actual noise level. A first reaction might be to fix this error by using an IF statement to keep this from happening:

```
IF (NOISE .GT. 0) THEN
   IF (NOISE .GT. LARGE) THEN
      LARGE = NOISE
   ELSE IF (NOISE .LT.SMALL) THEN
      SMALL = NOISE
   END IF
END IF
```

Patches like this one and the one used earlier are not recommended, however, because they often fail to address the real source of the problem and make the program unnecessarily complicated and messy.

The real source of difficulty in the preceding example is that the student did not use the correct technique for reading and processing data. As we noted in Section 4.3, when an end-of-data flag is used to signal the end of data, the correct approach is to read the first data value before the while loop is entered, to ensure that the logical expression that controls repetition is evaluated correctly the first time. This would solve the problem in the student's first version of the program. Also, as we noted, subsequent data values should be read at the "bottom" of the while loop so that they are compared with the end-of-data flag *before* they are processed in the next pass through the loop.

Using this standard technique for reading and processing data, the student rewrote his program as follows:

```
(1)       PRINT *, 'ENTER NOISE LEVELS IN DECIBELS (INTEGERS).'
(2)       PRINT *, 'ENTER ZERO OR A NEGATIVE VALUE TO STOP.'

   * Initialize largest noise level with a small value
   * and smallest with a very large value

(3)       LARGE = 0
(4)       SMALL = 999

(5)       PRINT *, 'NOISE LEVEL?'
(6)       READ *, NOISE

   * While NOISE is not the end-of-data flag do:

(7) 10    IF (NOISE .GT. 0)  THEN
(8)          IF (NOISE .GT. LARGE)  THEN
(9)             LARGE = NOISE
(10)         ELSE IF (NOISE .LT. SMALL)  THEN
(11)            SMALL = NOISE
(12)         END IF
(13)         PRINT *, 'NOISE LEVEL?'
(14)         READ *, NOISE
(15)         GO TO 10
(16)      END IF
```

```
(17)      PRINT *, 'RANGE OF NOISE LEVELS =', LARGE − SMALL, ' DECIBELS'
(18)      END
```

A sample run with the same data values now produces the correct output:

```
ENTER NOISE LEVELS IN DECIBELS (INTEGERS).
ENTER ZERO OR A NEGATIVE VALUE TO STOP.
NOISE LEVEL?
94
NOISE LEVEL?
102
NOISE LEVEL?
88
NOISE LEVEL?
−1
RANGE OF NOISE LEVELS = 14 DECIBELS
```

The student may now be tempted to conclude that the program is correct. However, to establish confidence in the correctness of a program, it is necessary to test it with several sets of data. For example, the following sample run reveals that the program still contains a logic error:

```
ENTER NOISE LEVELS IN DECIBELS (INTEGERS).
ENTER ZERO OR A NEGATIVE VALUE TO STOP.
NOISE LEVEL?
88
NOISE LEVEL?
94
NOISE LEVEL?
102
NOISE LEVEL?
−1
RANGE OF NOISE LEVELS − −897 DECIBELS
```

Tracing the execution of the while loop produces the following:

Statements	NOISE	LARGE	SMALL	
	88	0	999	← Initial values
7–9	88	88	999	First pass through the loop
12–15	94	88	999	
7–9	94	94	999	Second pass through the loop
12–15	102	94	999	
7–9	102	102	999	Third pass through the loop
12–15	−1	102	999	

This trace table reveals that the value of SMALL never changes, suggesting that the statement

```
SMALL = NOISE
```

is never executed. The reason is that the logical expression NOISE .GT. LARGE is true for each data value because these values are entered in increasing order; consequently, the ELSE IF statement is never executed. This error can be corrected by using two IF constructs in place of the single IF-ELSE IF construct,

```
IF  (NOISE .GT. LARGE) THEN
    LARGE = NOISE
END IF
IF  (NOISE .LT. SMALL) THEN
    SMALL = NOISE
END IF
```

or using logical IF statements,

```
IF (NOISE .GT. LARGE) LARGE = NOISE
IF (NOISE .LT. SMALL) SMALL = NOISE
```

The resulting program is then correct but is not as efficient as it could be, because the logical expressions in both of these IF statements must be evaluated on each pass through the loop. A more efficient alternative is described in the exercises.

Summary

Logic errors may be very difficult to detect, especially in more complex programs, and it is very important that test data be carefully selected so that each part of the program is thoroughly tested. The program should be executed with data values entered in several different orders, with large data sets and small data sets, with extreme values, and with "bad" data. For example, entering the noise levels in increasing order revealed the existence of a logic error in the program considered earlier. Also, even though the last version of the program will produce correct output if legitimate data values are read, the output

```
RANGE OF NOISE LEVELS = -999 DECIBELS
```

would be produced if a negative value were entered immediately. Although it may not be necessary to guard against invalid input data in student programs, those written for the public domain—especially programs used by computer novices—should be as **robust** as possible and should not "crash" or produce "garbage" results when unexpected data values are read.

When a logic error is detected, a trace table is an effective tool for locating the source of the error. Once it has been found, the program must be corrected and then tested again. It may be necessary to repeat this cycle of testing, tracing, and correcting many times before the program produces correct results for a wide range of test data, thereby allowing us to be reasonably confident that it is correct. It is not possible, however, to check a program with every possible set of data, and thus obscure bugs may still remain. In some applications, this may not be critical, but in others, for example, in programs used to guide a space shuttle, errors cannot be tolerated. Certain formal techniques have been developed for proving that a program is correct and will always execute correctly (assuming no system malfunction), but a study of these techniques is beyond the scope of this introductory text.

Quick Quiz 4.7

1. What is the difference between a pretest and a posttest loop?

2. Is a while loop a pretest loop or a posttest loop?

3. (True or false) A while loop is always executed at least once.

4. (True or false) A posttest loop is always executed at least once.

5. Name the three types of errors that may occur in developing a program to solve a problem.

6. Division by zero is an example of a _____ error.

7. A missing quote is an example of a _____ error.

8. Omitting a step in the design of an algorithm is an example of a _____ error.

9. Assuming that NUM is an integer variable, describe the output produced by the following while loop:

```
      NUM = 1                        NUM = 1
   10 IF (NUM .LE. 100) THEN   or  DO WHILE (NUM .LE. 100)
         PRINT *, NUM                  PRINT *, NUM
         NUM = 2 * NUM                 NUM = 2 * NUM
      GO TO 10                      END DO
      END IF
```

10. Assume that NUM and LIMIT are integer variables, and consider the following program segment:

```
      READ *, LIMIT                  READ *, LIMIT
      NUM = 0                        NUM = 0
   10 IF (NUM .LE. LIMIT) THEN or  DO WHILE (NUM .LE. LIMIT)
         PRINT *, NUM                  PRINT *, NUM
         NUM = NUM + 1                 NUM = NUM + 1
      GO TO 10                      END DO
      END IF
```

Describe the output produced for the following inputs:

(a) 4   (b) −2

11. Assume that `I` and `LIMIT` are integer variables, and consider the following program segment:

```
    READ *, LIMIT
    NUM = 0
10 CONTINUE
       PRINT *, NUM
       NUM = NUM + 1
    IF (NUM .GT. LIMIT) GO TO 10
```

Describe the output produced for the following inputs:

(a) 4   (b) −2

Exercises 4.7

1. Consider the following algorithm:
   1. Initialize X to 0, Y to 5, Z to 25.
   2. While X ≤ 4 do the following:
        a. Set Y = Z − Y, A = X + 1, and then increment X by 1.
        b. If A > 1 then
             Set Z = Z − 5, A = A^2, and then set B = Z − Y.
   3. Display A, B, X, Y, and Z.

   Complete the following trace table for this algorithm, which displays the labels of the statements in the order in which they are executed and the values of the variables at each stage:

Statement	A	B	X	Y	Z
1	?	?	0	5	25
2	"	"	"	"	"
2-a	1	"	1	20	"
2-b	"	"	"	"	"
2-a	2	"	2	5	"
.	.	.	.	.	.
.	.	.	.	.	.
.	.	.	.	.	.
3	"	"	"	"	"

(? = undefined)

Exercises 2–4 use the following algorithm:

1. Enter A.
2. While A ≤ 0.3 do the following:
     a. Increment A by 0.1.

    b. If A ≠ 0.3 then do the following:
       i. Set S and X to 0, T to 1.
      ii. While T ≤ 6 do the following:
          (a) Add T to X and then increment T by 2.
    c. Else do the following:
       i. Set T to 0, X to 1, and S = 3 + S.
      ii. While T ≤ 5 do the following:
          (a) Increment T by 1 and then set X = X * T.
    d. Display A, S, and X.

Construct a trace table similar to that in Exercise 1 for the given algorithm, assuming that the given value is entered for A.

   2. 0.   3. 0.3   4. 1.0

5. Given the following algorithm:
   1. Initialize I, A, and X to 0.
   2. While I < 4 do the following:
      a. Increment I by 1.
      b. Enter b, h, k.
      c. If k ≥ 1 then do the following:
         i. Set A = (bh/2).
        ii. If k ≥ 2 then do the following:

$$(a)\ \text{Set } X = \frac{bh^3}{36}$$

      d. Display I, b, h, A, and X.

Construct a trace table similar to that in Exercise 1 for the given algorithm, assuming that the given values are entered for b, h, and k.

     3, 6, 1;   4, 3, 2;   5, 2, 0;   2, 6, 2

6. Write a while loop to print the first 100 positive integers.

7. Write a while loop to print the value of X and decrease X by 0.5 as long as X is positive.

8. Write a while loop to read values for A, B, and C and print their sum, repeating this procedure while none of A, B, or C is negative.

9. Write a while loop to print the square roots of the first 25 odd positive integers.

10. Write a while loop to calculate and print the squares of consecutive positive integers until the difference between a square and the preceding one is greater than 50.

11. Write a while loop to print a list of points (X, Y) on the graph of the equation $Y = X^3 - 3X + 1$ for X ranging from -2 to 2 in steps of .1.

12. Write a posttest loop for the problem in Exercise 6.

13. Write a posttest loop for the problem in Exercise 7.

14. Write a posttest loop for the problem in Exercise 8.

15. Write a posttest loop for the problem in Exercise 9.

16. Write a posttest loop for the problem in Exercise 10.

17. Write a posttest loop for the problem in Exercise 11.

18. Suppose that the pretest loop in the summation algorithm in Section 4.3 is replaced by a posttest loop so that the statements in the program of Figure 4.8 that implements this algorithm are replaced by

```
      PRINT *, 'ENTER VALUE 1 + ... + ? IS TO EXCEED'
      READ *, LIMIT
      NUMBER = 0
      SUM = 0

*     Increment NUMBER and add it to SUM until SUM
*     exceeds LIMIT

10    CONTINUE
          NUMBER = NUMBER + 1
          SUM = SUM + NUMBER
      IF (SUM .LE. LIMIT) GO TO 10

*     Print the results

      PRINT *, '1 + ... + ', NUMBER, ' = ', SUM, ' >', LIMIT
      END
```

Would the resulting program produce the same results as those in Figure 4.8?

19. Design an algorithm that uses a posttest loop to count the number of digits in a given integer.

20. Write FORTRAN statements to implement the algorithm in Exercise 19.

21. Rewrite the algorithm in Exercise 19 so that it uses a pretest loop.

22. Write FORTRAN statements to implement the algorithm in Exercise 21.

23. Which of the repetition structures in Exercises 19–22 seems the most natural, and why?

24. Develop an algorithm to approximate the value of e^x using the infinite series

$$e^x = \sum_{n=0}^{\infty} \frac{x^n}{n!}$$

25. Construct a trace table for the algorithm in Exercise 24, and trace the value of n, x^n, $n!$, each term $x^n / n!$, and the value of the sum of all terms up through the current one for $n = 0, 1, \ldots, 10$, and $x = 0.8$.

For each of the problems described in Exercises 26–29, specify the input and output for the problem, make a list of variables you will use in describing a solution to the problem, and then design an algorithm to solve the problem.

26. Suppose that a professor gave a quiz to her class and compiled a list of scores ranging from 50 through 100. She intends to use only three grades: A if the score is 90 or above, B if it is below 90 but above or equal to 75, and C if it is below 75. She would like a program to assign the appropriate letter grades to the numeric scores.

27. A car manufacturer wants to determine average noise levels for the ten different models of cars the company produces. Each can be purchased with one of five different engines. Design an algorithm to enter the noise levels (in decibels) that were recorded for each possible model and engine configuration and to calculate the average noise level for each model as well as the average noise level over all models and engines.

28. The "divide-and-average" method for approximating the square root of any positive number A is as follows: for any initial approximation X that is positive, find a new approximation by calculating the average of X and A/X, that is,

$$\frac{X + A/X}{2}$$

Repeat this procedure with X replaced by this new approximation, stopping when X and A/X differ in absolute value by some specified error allowance, such as .00001.

29. Dispatch Die-Casting currently produces 200 castings per month and realizes a profit of $300 per casting. The company now spends $2000 per month on research and development and has a fixed operating cost of $20,000 per month that does not depend on the amount of production. If the company doubles the amount spent on research and development, it is estimated that production will increase by 20 percent. The company president would like to know, beginning with the current status and successively doubling the amount spent on research and development, at what point the net profit will begin to decline.

30. Consider a cylindrical reservoir with a radius of 10.0 feet and a height of 40.0 feet that is filled and emptied by a 12-inch diameter pipe. The pipe has a 1000.0-foot-long run and discharges at an elevation 20.0 feet lower than the bottom of the reservoir. The pipe has been tested and has a roughness factor of 0.0130.

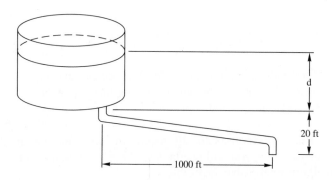

Several formulas have been developed experimentally to determine the veloc-ity at which fluids flow through such pipes. One of these, the *Manning formula*, is

$$V = \frac{1.486}{N} R^{2/3} S^{1/2}$$

where

V = velocity in feet per second

N = roughness coefficient

R = hydraulic radius = $\dfrac{\text{cross-sectional area}}{\text{wetted perimeter}}$

S = slope of the energy gradient $\left(= \dfrac{d + 20}{1000} \text{ for this problem} \right)$

The rate of fluid flow is equal to the cross-sectional area of the pipe multiplied by the velocity.

Design an algorithm to estimate the time required to empty the reservoir, given the reservoir's height, roughness coefficient, hydraulic radius, and pipe radius. Do this by assuming a constant flow rate for 5-minute segments.

31. A 100.0-pound sign is hung from the end of a horizontal pole of negligible mass. The pole is attached to the building by a pin and is supported by a cable, as shown. The pole and cable are each 6.0 feet long.

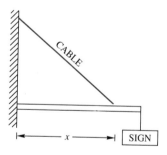

Design an algorithm to find the appropriate place (indicated by x in the diagram) to attach the cable to the pole so that the tension in the cable will be minimized. The equation governing static equilibrium tells us that

$$\text{tension} = \frac{100 \cdot 6 \cdot 6}{x\sqrt{36 - x^2}}$$

Calculate the tension for x starting at 1.0 and incrementing it by 0.1 until the ap-proximate minimum value is located.

4.8 APPLICATION: LEAST-SQUARES LINE

Problem

Suppose the following data was collected in an experiment to measure the effect of temperature on resistance:

Temperature (°C)	Resistance (ohms)
20.0	761
31.5	817
50.0	874
71.8	917
91.3	1018

The plot of this data in Figure 4.14 indicates a linear relationship between temperature and resistance.

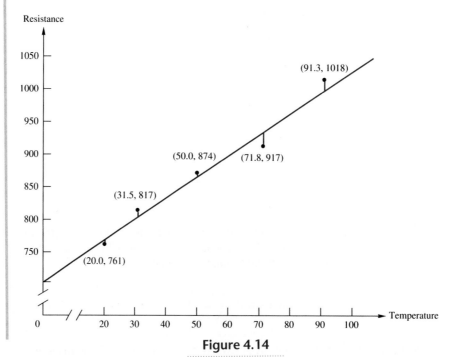

Figure 4.14

Least-squares line.

In general, whenever the relation between two quantities x and y appears to be roughly linear, that is, when a plot of the points (x, y) indicates that they tend to fall along a straight line, one can ask for the equation

$$y = mx + b$$

of a best-fitting line for these points. We wish to develop a program that finds the equation of the line that "best fits" such a data set. This equation (called a **regression equation**) can then be used to predict the value of y by evaluating the equation for a given value of x.

Solution

Specification:

Input: A set of data points

Output: Equation of a line that best fits the data

Design. A standard method for finding the **regression coefficients** m and b of the line that best fits a given data set is the **method of least squares**, so named because it produces the line $y = mx + b$, for which the sum of the squares of the deviations of the observed y-values from the predicted y-values (using the equation) is as small as possible (see Figure 4.14); that is, values of m and b are found to minimize the sum

$$\sum_{i=1}^{n}[y_i - (mx_i + b)]^2 = [y_1 - (mx_1 + b)]^2 + [y_2 - (mx_2 + b)]^2 + \cdots + [y_n - (mx_n + b)]^2$$

Using the methods of calculus for minimizing a function of two variables, one obtains the following formulas for the slope m and the y-intercept b:

$$\text{slope} = m = \frac{(\sum xy) - (\sum x)\bar{y}}{(\sum x^2) - (\sum x)\bar{x}}$$

$$y\text{-intercept} = b = \bar{y} - m\bar{x}$$

where

$\sum x$ is the sum of the x-values

$\sum x^2$ is the sum of the squares of the x-values

$\sum xy$ is the sum of the products xy of corresponding x- and y-values

$\bar{x}$ and $\bar{y}$ are the means of the x- and y-values, respectively

From these formulas we see that a program to find a least-squares line must count the data points and compute several sums. The variables we will use are:SUMX

VARIABLES FOR LEAST-SQUARES LINE PROBLEM

X, Y   Coordinates of data point

ENDATA   End-of-data flag

COUNT   Number of data points

SUMX	Sum of the X values
SUMY	Sum of the Y values
SUMX2	Sum of the squares of the X values
SUMXY	Sum of the products X * Y
XMEAN, YMEAN	Mean of the Xs and mean of the Ys
SLOPE, YINT	Slope and y-intercept of least-squares line

ALGORITHM FOR LEAST-SQUARES LINE PROBLEM

* Algorithm to find the equation of the least-squares line for a set of data points   *
* (X, Y).   *
*   *
* Input: A collection of data points   *
* Output: The equation of the least-squares line   *

1. Initialize COUNT, SUMX, SUMY, SUMX2, AND SUMXY all to 0.
2. Read the first data point X, Y.
   * End-of-data values are entered to terminate input *
3. While X and Y are not the end-of-data values, do the following:
   a. Increment COUNT by 1.
   b. Add X to SUMX.
   c. Add X^2 to SUMX2.
   d. Add Y to SUMY.
   e. Add X*Y to SUMXY.
   f. Read next data point X, Y.
4. Calculate

$$XMEAN = \frac{SUMX}{COUNT}$$

and

$$YMEAN = \frac{SUMY}{COUNT}$$

5. Calculate

$$SLOPE = \frac{SUMXY - SUMX*YMEAN}{SUMX2 - SUMX*XMEAN}$$

and

$$YINT = YMEAN - SLOPE * XMEAN$$

6. Display SLOPE and YINT.

Coding. The program in Figure 4.15 implements the preceding algorithm for finding the equation of the least-squares line for a given set of data points.

Figure 4.15 Least-squares line.

```
      PROGRAM LSQUAR
*********************************************************************
* Program to find the equation of the least-squares line for a set  *
* of data points.   Identifiers used are:                           *
*     X, Y    : (X,Y) is the observed data point                    *
*     ENDATA  : end-of-data flag (parameter)                        *
*     COUNT   : number of data points                               *
*     SUMX    : sum of the Xs                                        *
*     SUMX2   : sum of the squares of the Xs                        *
*     SUMY    : sum of the Ys                                        *
*     SUMXY   : sum of the products X*Y                              *
*     XMEAN   : mean of the Xs                                       *
*     YMEAN   : mean of the Ys                                       *
*     SLOPE   : slope of least-squares line                         *
*     YINT    : y-intercept of the line                             *
*                                                                   *
* Input:  A collection of data points                               *
* Output: The equation of the least-squares line                    *
*********************************************************************

      INTEGER COUNT
      REAL X, Y, ENDATA, SUMX, SUMX2, SUMY, SUMXY, XMEAN, YMEAN,
     +     SLOPE, YINT
      PARAMETER (ENDATA = -999.0)

* Initialize counter and the sums to 0 and read first data point

      COUNT = 0
      SUMX = 0
      SUMX2 = 0
      SUMY = 0
      SUMXY = 0
      PRINT *, 'TO STOP, ENTER', ENDATA, ' FOR COORDINATES OF POINT.'
      PRINT *, 'ENTER POINT:'
      READ *, X, Y
* While there is more data, calculate the necessary sums
* and read the next data point (X, Y)
```

Figure 4.15 *(cont.)*

```
10     IF ((X .NE. ENDATA) .AND. (Y .NE. ENDATA)) THEN
          COUNT = COUNT + 1
          SUMX = SUMX + X
          SUMX2 = SUMX2 + X ** 2
          SUMY = SUMY + Y
          SUMXY = SUMXY + X * Y
          PRINT *, 'ENTER NEXT POINT:'
          READ *, X, Y
       GO TO 10
       END IF

* Find equation of least-squares line

       XMEAN = SUMX / COUNT
       YMEAN = SUMY / COUNT
       SLOPE = (SUMXY - SUMX * YMEAN) / (SUMX2 - SUMX * XMEAN)
       YINT = YMEAN - SLOPE * XMEAN
       PRINT *
       PRINT *, 'EQUATION OF LEAST-SQUARES LINE IS Y = MX + B, WHERE'
       PRINT *, 'SLOPE = M =       ', SLOPE
       PRINT *, 'Y-INTERCEPT = B= ', YINT

       END
```

Execution and Testing. After the program has been tested with several simple data sets to check its correctness, it can be run with the given data to find the equation of the least-squares line:

Sample run:

```
TO STOP, ENTER  -999.000 FOR COORDINATES OF POINT.
ENTER POINT:
20.0, 761
ENTER NEXT POINT:
31.5, 817
ENTER NEXT POINT:
50.0, 874
ENTER NEXT POINT:
71.8, 917
```

```
ENTER NEXT POINT:
91.3, 1018
ENTER NEXT POINT:
-999, -999

EQUATION OF LEAST-SQUARES LINE IS Y = MX + B, WHERE
SLOPE = M =            3.33658
Y-INTERCEPT = B =      700.828
```

Exercises 4.8

1. Display in a flowchart the structure of the algorithm for calculating a least-squares line.

2. The density ρ (g/ml) of water is given in the following table for various temperatures $T(C°)$:

T	$\rho(T)$
0	0.99987
10	0.99973
20	0.99823
30	0.99568
40	0.99225
50	0.98807
60	0.98324

Find the least-squares line for this data, and use it to estimate the density at 5, 15, 25, 35, 45, and 55. Compare the computed values with the actual values given in the following table:

T	$\rho(T)$
5	0.99999
15	0.99913
25	0.99707
35	0.99406
45	0.99024
55	0.98573

3. An oxyacetylene torch was used to cut a 1-inch piece of metal. The relationship between the metal thickness and cutting time is shown in the following table:

Thickness (in)	Cutting Time (min)
0.25	0.036
0.375	0.037
0.5	0.039
0.75	0.042
1.0	0.046
1.25	0.050
1.5	0.053
2.0	0.058
2.5	0.065
3.0	0.073
3.5	0.078
4.0	0.085
4.5	0.093
5.0	0.102

Find the least-squares line for this data, and use it to estimate the cutting time for thicknesses of 1.75 inches, 3.25 inches, and 4.75 inches.

CHAPTER REVIEW

Summary

The focus of this chapter was repetitive execution, the third of the three basic control structures used in writing programs. There are two basic types of repetition structures: loops controlled by a counter and loops controlled by a logical expression. Counter-controlled loops are implemented in FORTRAN as DO loops, and the chapter began with a detailed study of these loops. Loops controlled by logical expressions can be while loops (also called pretest loops) or posttest loops. Sections 4.3 and 4.4 describe while loops and how they can be implemented in standard FORTRAN using block IF and GO TO statements. Many versions of FORTRAN provide a special looping statement for implementing while loops, and one such statement (DO-WHILE) is also described here. One important use of while loops is to read and process a collection of data values, and a standard method of using such sentinel-controlled loops is described and illustrated:

1. Read the first data value.
2. While the data value is not the end-of-data flag, do the following:

    a. Process the data value.

    b. Read the next data value.

Posttest loops and their implementation using logical IF and GO TO statements are also described. One important use of these is in constructing query-controlled input loops.

Section 4.7 describes the three types of errors that can occur in program development: syntax or compile-time errors, run-time errors, and logic errors. In general, logical errors are more difficult to find and correct than are syntax and run-time errors, and this section thus illustrates several program testing and debugging techniques.

FORTRAN SUMMARY

DO Loop

```
DO n control-var = initial-value, limit, step-size
    statement-sequence
n CONTINUE
```

where *n* is a statement number.

Examples:

```
DO 10 NUMBER = 1, 10
    PRINT *, NUMBER, NUMBER ** 2
10 CONTINUE

DO 20 X = 5.0, 0.0, -0.5
    PRINT *, X, SQRT(X)
20 CONTINUE
```

Purpose:
When a DO loop is executed:

1. The control variable is assigned the initial value.
2. The control variable is compared with the limit to see if it is:
   - less than or equal to the limit, for a positive step size
   - greater than or equal to the limit, for a negative step size
3. If so, the sequence of statements, called the *body of the loop*, is executed, the step size is added to the control variable, and step 2 is repeated. Otherwise, repetition terminates.

GO TO Statement

```
GO TO statement-number
```

Purpose:
Alters the usual sequential execution so that the statement with the specified number is executed next.

Implementation of a `While` Loop

In Standard FORTRAN:

```
n IF (logical-expression) THEN
     statement-sequence
   GO TO n
   END IF
```

Using a `DO-WHILE` Statement:

```
DO WHILE (logical-expression)
   statement-sequence
END DO
```

Examples:

```
10 IF (SUM .LE. LIMIT) THEN
       NUMBER = NUMBER + 1
       SUM = SUM + NUMBER
   GO TO 10
   END IF

   DO WHILE (SUM .LE. LIMIT)
      NUMBER = NUMBER + 1
      SUM = SUM + NUMBER
   END DO
```

Purpose:
Implement a while loop.

Implementation of a Posttest Loop

```
n CONTINUE
     statement-sequence
   IF (logical-expression) GO TO n
```

Examples:

```
10 CONTINUE
       PRINT *, 'ENTER DATA VALUE:'
       READ *, VALUE
       SUM = SUM + VALUE
       PRINT *, 'MORE (0 = NO, 1 = YES)?'
       READ *, RESPON
   IF (RESPON .NE. 0) GO TO 10
```

Purpose:
Implement a posttest loop.

PROGRAMMING POINTERS

Program Style and Design

1. *The body of a loop should be indented.*

   a. DO loops:

   ```
   DO ## variable = init, limit, step
       statement₁
         .
         .
       statementₙ
   ## CONTINUE
   ```

   b. While loops:

   ```
   ## IF (logical-expression) THEN
       statement₁
         .
         .
       statementₙ
       GO TO ##
       END IF

   DO WHILE (logical-expression)
       statement₁
         .
         .
       statementₙ
       END DO
   ```

   c. Posttest loops:

   ```
   ## CONTINUE
       statement₁
         .
         .
       statementₙ
       IF (logical-expression) GO TO ##
   ```

2. *All programs can be written using the three control structures considered in this chapter: sequence, selection, and repetition.*

3. *The* GO TO *statement should ordinarily be used only in standard repetition structures (while loops and posttest loops). Indiscriminate use of* GO TO *makes the logic of the program difficult to follow and is symptomatic of a poorly designed program.*

Potential Problems

1. *Periods must be used in the relational operators* `.LT.`, `.GT.`, `.EQ.`, `.LE.`, `.GE.`, *and* `.NE.` *and in the logical operators* `.NOT.`, `.AND.`, `.OR.`, `.EQV.`, *and* `.NEQV.`.

2. *Parentheses must enclose the logical expression in* `IF` *statements.*

3. *Real quantities that are algebraically equal may yield a false logical expression when compared with* `.EQ.` *because most real values are not stored exactly.*

4. *The control variable in a* DO *loop may not be modified within the loop. Modifying the initial value, limit, or step size does not affect the number of repetitions.* **For example, the statements**

```
K = 5
DO 10  = 1, K
    PRINT *, K
    K = K - 1
10 CONTINUE
```

produce the output

```
5
4
3
2
1
```

Modifying the control variable I, as in the following DO loop,

```
DO 10 = 1, 5I
    PRINT *, I
    I = I - 1
10 CONTINUE
```

is an error and produces a message such as

```
A CONTROL VARIABLE MAY NOT BE ALTERED IN A DO LOOP
```

One consequence is that nested DO loops must have different control variables.

5. *The statements within a while loop controlled by a logical expression must eventually cause the logical expression to become false, because otherwise an infinite loop will result.* **For example, if X is a real variable, the statements**

```
    X = 0.0
* While X is not equal to 1, print its value and
* increment it
```

```
10 IF (X .NE. 1.0) THEN
      PRINT *, X
      X = X + 0.3
   GO TO 10
   END IF
```

will produce an infinite loop.

Output:
```
0.000000
0.300000
0.600000
0.900000
1.200000
1.500000
1.800000
   .
   .
   .
```

Since the value of X is never equal to 1.0, repetition is not terminated. In view of Potential Problem 3, the statements

```
      X = 0.0

*    While X is not equal to 1, print its value and
*    increment it

 10   IF (X .NE. 1.0) THEN
          PRINT *, X
          X = X + 0.2
      GO TO 10
      END IF
```

may also produce an infinite loop.

Output:
```
0.000000
0.200000
0.400000
0.600000
0.800000
1.000000
1.200000
1.400000
1.600000
   .
   .
   .
```

Since X is initialized to 0 and 0.2 is added to X five times, X should have the value 1. However, the logical expression X .NE. 1.0 may remain true because most real values are not stored exactly.

6. DATA *statements initialize variables at compile time, not during execution.* This is important to remember when a program processes several sets of data and uses variables that must be initialized to certain values before processing each data set. To illustrate, consider the following program:

```
      INTEGER NUMBER, SUM
      DATA SUM /0/

      READ *, NUMBER

******While there is more data, do the following:

10    IF (NUMBER .NE. -8888) THEN

**********While NUMBER is not -999, do the following:

20         IF (NUMBER .NE. -999) THEN
               SUM = SUM + NUMBER
               READ *, NUMBER
           GO TO 20
           END IF
           PRINT *, 'SUM = ', SUM
       GO TO 10
       END IF
       END
```

If the following data is entered,

```
10
20
30
-999
0
15
25
-999
-8888
```

the output produced will be

```
SUM = 60
SUM = 100
```

When the second set of numbers is processed, SUM is not reset to 0, because the DATA statement does this at compile time, not during execution. This problem cannot be solved by simply attaching a label to the DATA statement and then branching to it, because DATA statements are not executable. The obvious solution is to insert the statement

```
SUM = 0
```

after statement 10 and delete the DATA statement.

PROGRAMMING PROBLEMS

Sections 4.1 and 4.2

1. A certain product is to sell for PRICE dollars per item. Write a program that reads values for PRICE and the NUMBER of items sold and then produces a table showing the total price of from 1 through NUMBER units.

2. A ship with a total displacement of M metric tons starts from rest in still water under a constant propeller thrust of T kilonewtons. The ship develops a total resistance to motion through water that is given by $R = 4.50V^2$, where R is in kilonewtons and V is in meters per second. The acceleration of the ship is $A = (T - R) / M$. From these equations, an equation for the velocity of the ship can be derived:

$$V = \sqrt{\frac{T}{4.50}} \, (1 - e^{-9.00S/M})$$

where S is the distance in meters. Write a program that will read values for M, T, and S and will display a table of values of V in knots for S ranging from 0 to 20 nautical miles in steps of 0.5 nautical miles (1 nautical mile = 1.852 km, 1 knot = 1 nautical mile per hour). Deduce from your table the maximum possible speed for the ship.

3. The mechanism shown is part of a machine that a company is designing:

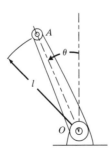

During operation, the rod OA will oscillate according to $\theta = \theta_0 \sin(2\pi t/\tau)$, where θ is measured in radians, θ_0 is the maximum angular displacement, τ is the period of motion, t = time in seconds measured from $t = 0$ when OA is vertical. If l is the length OA, the magnitude of the acceleration of point A is given by

$$|a_A| = \frac{4\pi^2 l\,\theta_0}{\tau^2}\sqrt{\theta_0^2\,\cos^4\left(\frac{2\pi t}{\tau}\right) + \sin^2\left(\frac{2\pi t}{\tau}\right)}$$

Write a program that will read values for θ_0, l, and τ, and that will then calculate a table of values of t, θ, and $|a_A|$ for $t = 0.0$ to 0.5 in steps of 0.05 (in seconds). Execute the program with $\tau = 2$ s, $\theta_0 = \pi/2$, and $l = 0.1$ m.

4. Suppose that at a given time, genotypes AA, AB, and BB appear in the proportions x, y, and z, respectively, where $x = 0.25$, $y = 0.5$, and $z = 0.25$. If individuals of type AA cannot reproduce, the probability that one parent will donate gene A to an offspring is

$$p = \frac{1}{2}\left(\frac{y}{y + z}\right)$$

since $y/(y + z)$ is the probability that the parent is of type AB and $1/2$ is the probability that such a parent will donate gene A. Then the proportions x', y', and z' of AA, AB, and BB, respectively, in each succeeding generation are given by

$$x' = p^2, \qquad y' = 2p(1 - p), \qquad z' = (1 - p)^2$$

and the new probability is given by

$$p' = \frac{1}{2}\left(\frac{y'}{y' + z'}\right)$$

Write a program to calculate and print the generation number and the proportions of AA, AB, and BB under appropriate headings until the proportions of both AA and AB are less than some small positive value.

5. The sequence of **Fibonacci numbers** begins with the integers

$$1, 1, 2, 3, 5, 8, 13, 21, \ldots$$

where each number after the first two is the sum of the two preceding numbers. Write a program that reads a positive integer n and then displays the first n Fibonacci numbers.

6. One property of the Fibonacci sequence (see Problem 5) is that the ratios of consecutive Fibonacci numbers ($1/1$, $1/2$, $2/3$, $3/5$, $\ldots$) approach the "golden ratio"

$$\frac{\sqrt{5} - 1}{2}$$

Modify the program in Problem 5 to display Fibonacci numbers and the decimal values of the ratios of consecutive Fibonacci numbers.

7. The infinite series

$$\sum_{k=0}^{\infty} \frac{1}{k!}$$

converges to the number *e*. (For a positive integer *k*, *k*!, read "*k* factorial," is the product of the integers from 1 through *k*; 0! is defined to be 1.) The *n*th *partial sum* of such a series is the sum of the first *n* terms of the series; for example,

$$\frac{1}{0!} + \frac{1}{1!} + \frac{1}{2!} + \frac{1}{3!}$$

is the fourth partial sum. Write a program to calculate and print the first 10 partial sums of this series.

8. If a loan of *A* dollars, which carries a monthly interest rate of *R* (expressed as a decimal), is to be paid off in *N* months, then the monthly payment *P* will be

$$P = A\left[\frac{R(1 + R)^N}{(1 + R)^N - 1}\right]$$

During this time period, some of each monthly payment will be used to repay that month's accrued interest, and the rest will be used to reduce the balance owed.

Write a program to print an *amortization table* that displays the payment number, the amount of the monthly payment, the interest for that month, the amount of the payment applied to the principal, and the new balance. Use your program to produce an amorization table for a loan of $50,000 to be repaid in 36 months at 1 percent per month.

9. Another method of calculating depreciation is the **double-declining balance method**. In this method, if an amount is to be depreciated over *n* years, 2/*n* times the undepreciated balance is depreciated annually. For example, using this method to depreciate $150,000 over a 5-year period, we would depreciate 2/5 of $150,000 ($60,000) the first year, leaving an undepreciated balance of $90,000. In the second year, 2/5 of $90,000 ($36,000) would be depreciated, leaving an undepreciated balance of $54,000. Since only a fraction of the remaining balance is depreciated in each year, the entire amount will never be depreciated. Consequently, it is permissible to switch to the straight-line method at any time.

(**a**) Develop an algorithm for this method of calculating depreciation.

(**b**) Modify the program in Figure 4.5 so that it includes this third method of calculating depreciation as one of the options. Also, modify the output so that the year numbers in depreciation tables begin with the current year rather than with year number 1.

Section 4.6 or 4.7

10. (a) Write a program that solves the noise-level range problem discussed in Section 4.7 but is more efficient than those described in the text. (*Hint:* Initialize LARGE and SMALL to the first data value.)

    (b) For each of the following data sets, construct a trace table for the repetition structure used in your program and determine the range of noise levels that will be computed by your program:

    (i)   88, 102, 94, −1
    (ii) 88, 94, 102, −1
    (iii) 102, 94, 88, −1
    (iv) 88, −1
    (v)   −1

11. Write a program to implement the algorithm displayed in the flowchart of Figure 4.16.

12. Write a program to calculate all the Fibonacci numbers less than 5000 and the decimal values of the ratios of consecutive Fibonacci numbers (see Problem 5).

13. Write a program to read the data values shown in the following table, calculate the miles per gallon in each case, and print the values with appropriate labels:

Miles Traveled	Gallons of Gasoline Used
231	14.8
248	15.1
302	12.8
147	9.25
88	7
265	13.3

14. Write a program to read a set of numbers, count them, and find and print the largest and smallest numbers in the list and their positions in the list.

15. Suppose that a ball dropped from a building bounces off the pavement and that on each bounce it returns to a certain constant percentage of its previous height. Write a program to read the height from which the ball was dropped and the percentage of rebound. Then let the ball bounce repeatedly, and print the height of the ball at the top of each bounce, the distance traveled during that bounce, and the total distance traveled thus far, terminating when the height of the ball is almost zero (less than some small positive value).

16. Write a program to implement the divide-and-average algorithm in Exercise 28 of Section 4.7. Execute the program with $A = 3$, error allowance $= 0.00001$, and use the following initial approximations: 1, 10, 0.01, and 100. Also execute the program with $A = 4$, error allowance $= 0.00001$, and initial approximations 1 and 2.

17. Write a program to read a set of numbers, count them, and calculate the mean, vari-

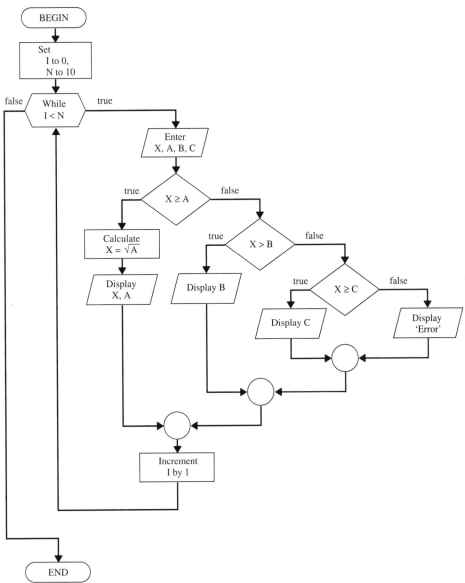

Figure 4.16

ance, and standard deviation of the set of numbers. The *mean* and *variance* of numbers $x_1, x_2, \ldots, x_n$ can be calculated using the following formulas:

$$\text{mean} = \frac{1}{n}\sum_{i=1}^{n} x_i, \qquad \text{variance} = \frac{1}{n}\sum_{i=1}^{n} x_i^2 - \frac{1}{n^2}\left(\sum_{i=1}^{n} x_i\right)^2$$

The *standard deviation* is the square root of the variance.

18. Two measures of central tendency other than the (arithmetic) mean (defined in Exercise 17) are the geometric mean and the harmonic mean defined for a list of positive numbers $x_1, x_2, \ldots, x_n$ as follows:

$$\text{geometric mean} = \sqrt[n]{x_1 \cdot x_2 \cdots \cdot x_n}$$

$$= \text{the } n\text{th root of the product of the numbers}$$

$$\text{harmonic mean} = \frac{n}{\dfrac{1}{x_1} + \dfrac{1}{x_2} + \cdots + \dfrac{1}{x_n}}$$

Write a program that reads a list of numbers, counts them, and calculates their arithmetic mean, geometric mean, and harmonic mean. These values should be printed with appropriate labels.

19. Write a program to implement the algorithm for estimating the time required to empty the reservoir described in Exercise 30 of Section 4.7.

20. Suppose that two hallways, one 8 feet wide and the other 10 feet wide, meet at a right angle and that a ladder is to be carried around the corner from the narrower hallway into the wider one. Using the similar triangles in the following diagram, we see that

$$L = x + \frac{10x}{\sqrt{x^2 - 64}}$$

Write a program that initializes x to 8.1 and then increments it by 0.1 to find to the nearest 0.1 foot the length of the longest ladder that can be carried around the corner. (*Note:* This length is the same as the minimum value of the distance L.)

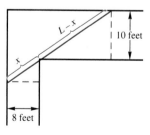

Section 4.8

21. In some situations, an exponential function

$$y = ae^{bx}$$

gives a better fit to a set of data points than does a straight line. To determine the constants a and b, one common method is to take logarithms

$$\ln y = \ln a + bx$$

and then use the method of least squares to find values of the constants b and $\ln a$. Write a program that uses this method to fit an exponential curve to a set of data points. Run it for the values in the following table, which gives the barometric pressure readings, in millimeters of mercury, at various altitudes.

Altitude (meters) x	Barometric Pressure (millimeters) y
0	760
500	714
1000	673
1500	631
2000	594
2500	563

22. Related to the least-squares method is the problem of determining whether there is a linear relationship between two quantities x and y. One statistical measure used in this connection is the *correlation coefficient.* It is equal to 1 if there is a perfect positive linear relationship between x and y, that is, if y increases linearly as x increases. If there is a perfect negative linear relationship between x and y, that is, if y decreases linearly as x increases, then the correlation coefficient has the value -1. A value of 0 for the correlation coefficient indicates that there is no linear relationship between x and y, and nonzero values between -1 and 1 indicate a partial linear relationship between the two quantities. The correlation coefficient for a set of n pairs of x- and y- values is calculated by

$$\frac{n(\Sigma xy) - (\Sigma x)(\Sigma y)}{\sqrt{n\Sigma x^2 - (\Sigma x)^2)(n\Sigma y^2 - (\Sigma y)^2)}}$$

where

Σx is the sum of the x-values
Σy is the sum of the y-values
Σx^2 is the sum of the squares of the x-values
Σy^2 is the sum of the squares of the y-values
Σxy is the sum of the products xy of corresponding x- and y-values

Write a program to calculate the correlation coefficient of a set of data points. Run it for the data points used in the sample run for Figure 4.15 and for several data sets of your own.

Fortran 90

Features

The DO loop from FORTRAN 77 has been carried over into Fortran 90 and extended so that it can implement several kinds of loops. The new features are described here:

- DO loops may have either of the forms

```
DO control-variable = initial-value, limit, step-size
   statement-sequence
END DO
```

or

```
DO n, control-variable = initial-value, limit, step-size
   statement-sequence
n CONTINUE
```

where in both cases, the step-size is optional, and the comma after n in the second form is optional.

- Like IF constructs, DO constructs may have names attached; for example,

```
OUTER: DO = 1, 10
        .
        .
        .
   INNER: DO J = 1, 20
           .
           .
           .
   END DO INNER
        .
        .
        .
END DO OUTER
```

- While loops are implemented with DO constructs of the form

```
DO WHILE (logical-expression)
   statement-sequence
END DO
```

which are executed in the manner described in Section 4.3. This form of the DO construct may also have a name attached.

- Loop-forever repetition structures can be implemented with `DO` constructs of the form

```
DO
    statement-sequence
END DO
```

or

```
DO n
    statement-sequence
n CONTINUE
```

In this case, one of the statements within the body of the loop must cause termination, or an infinite loop will result. An `EXIT` statement of the form

```
EXIT
```

or

```
EXIT name
```

is provided for this purpose; in the second form, *name* is a name attached to the `DO` construct containing the `EXIT` statement. For example,

```
DO
    .
    .
    .
    IF (N .EQ. 0) EXIT
    .
    .
    .
END DO
```

- A `CYCLE` statement of the form

```
CYCLE
```

or

```
CYCLE name
```

can be used to terminate the current pass through a loop and proceed to the next iteration. In the second form, *name* is the name attached to the `DO` construct in which the `CYCLE` statement appears.

Example

The program in Figure 4.17 illustrates several of the preceding new features. It is a Fortran 90 version of the mean-time-to-failure program in Figure 4.10. Note the use of a loop-forever structure in this program. It is used to construct a test-in-the-middle loop to repeatedly read and process data values.

Figure 4.17 Mean time to failure — Fortran 90 version.

```
PROGRAM Mean_Time_to_Failure
!-----------------------------------------------------------------
! Program to read a list of failure times, count them, and find the
! mean time to failure.  Values are read until an end-of-data flag
! is read.  Identifiers used are:
!   FailureTime      : the current failure time read
!   EndDataFlag      : a constant -- the end-of-data flag
!   NumTimes         : the number of failure time readings
!   Sum              : sum of failure times
!   MeanFailureTime  : the mean time to failure
!
! Input:  A list of failure times
! Output: Number of failure times read and their mean or a message
!         indicating that no failure times were entered
!-----------------------------------------------------------------

  INTEGER :: NumTimes
  REAL :: FailureTime, Sum, MeanFailureTime
  REAL, PARAMETER :: EndDataFlag = -1.0

! Initialize Sum and NumTimes and give instructions to user

  Sum = 0.0
  NumTimes = 0
  PRINT *, "Enter failure time of", EndDataFlag, "or less to stop."

! Repeat the following
  DO
     PRINT *, "Enter failure time:"
     READ *, FailureTime

     ! If end-of-data, terminate repetition
     IF (FailureTime <= EndDataFlag) EXIT
```

Figure 4.17 *(cont.)*

```
     ! Otherwise, continue with the following:
     NumTimes = NumTimes + 1
     Sum = Sum + FailureTime
  END DO

! Calculate and display mean time to failure
  IF (NumTimes /= 0) THEN
     MeanFailureTime = Sum / NumTimes
     PRINT *
     PRINT *, "Number of failure time readings:", NumTimes
     PRINT *, "Mean time to failure:", MeanFailureTime
  ELSE
     PRINT *, "No failure times were entered."
  END IF

END PROGRAM Mean_Time_to_Failure
```

5

Input/Output

*The moving finger writes; and having writ
Moves on; not all your piety nor wit
Shall lure it back to cancel half a line,
Nor all your tears wash out a word of it.*

THE RUBAIYAT

*When I read some of the rules for speaking and writing the English
language correctly . . . I think
Any fool can make a rule
And every fool will mind it.*

H. THOREAU

*I can only assume that a "Do Not File" document is filed in a "Do Not
File" file.*

SENATOR FRANK CHURCH

C H A P T E R   C O N T E N T S

5.1 Formatted Output

5.2 Example: Printing Tables of Computed Values

5.3 Formatted Input

5.4 The WRITE Statement and the General READ Statement

5.5 File Processing

5.6 Application: Temperature and Volume Readings

Chapter Review

Programming Pointers

Programming Problems

Fortran 90

*I*n Chapter 2 we noted that there are two types of input/output statements in FOR-TRAN, **list directed** and **formatted** (or more precisely, user-formatted). In our discussion thus far, we have restricted our attention to list-directed input/output. This method is particularly easy to use because the format for the input or output of data is automatically supplied by the compiler. It does not, however, permit the user to control the precise format of the output. For example, using list-directed output, one cannot specify that real values are to be displayed with only two digits to the right of the decimal point, even though this might be appropriate in some applications. The precise form of the output can be specified, however, using the formatted output statement introduced in this chapter.

Sometimes input data has a predetermined form, and the programmer must design the program to read this data. This can be accomplished by using the formatted input statement, which is also introduced in this chapter.

Finally, if the volume of input data is large, a data file is usually prepared, and during program execution, data is read from it rather than entered from the keyboard. In this chapter we consider some of the statements provided in FORTRAN for processing files.

5.1 FORMATTED OUTPUT

There are two output statements in FORTRAN, the `PRINT` statement and the `WRITE` statement. The `PRINT` **statement** is the simpler of the two and has the following form:

PRINT *Statement*

Form:

```
PRINT format-specifier, output-list
```

where
  format-specifier is one of the following:
  1. * (an asterisk);
  2. a character constant or a character variable (or expression or array) whose value specifies the format for the output;
  3. the label of a `FORMAT` statement.

  output-list is a single expression or a list of expressions separated by commas; it may also be empty, in which case the comma preceding the list is omitted.

Purpose:
Displays the values of the items in the *output-list*. Each execution of a `PRINT` statement produces a new line of output. If the output list is omitted, a blank line is displayed. The *format-specifier* specifies the format in which the values of the expressions in the output list are to be displayed.

As we saw in Chapter 2, an asterisk (*) indicates list-directed output whose format is determined by the types of expressions in the output list. This is adequate when the precise form of the output is not important. However, for reports and other kinds of output in which results must appear in a precise form, list-directed formatting is not adequate, and format specifiers of type 2 or 3 must be used. A large part of this section is devoted to the design of these format specifiers.

In the second type of format specifier, the formatting information is given as a character string of the form

```
'(list of format descriptors)'
```

that is, a character string that consists of format descriptors, separated by commas and enclosed in parentheses.

In the third type of format specifier, the formatting information is supplied by a FORMAT **statement** whose label is specified. This statement has the form

FORMAT *Statement*

Form:

```
FORMAT(list of format descriptors)
```

Purpose:
Specifies output format.

The format descriptors specify precisely the format in which the items in the output list are to be displayed. For example, any of the following output statements

```
PRINT *, NUMBER, TEMP
PRINT '(1X, I5, F8.2)', NUMBER, TEMP
PRINT 20, NUMBER, TEMP
```

where statement 20 is the statement

```
20 FORMAT(1X, I5, F8.2)
```

could be used to display the values of the integer variable NUMBER and the real variable TEMP. In these statements, 1X, I5, and F8.2 are format descriptors that specify the format in which the values of NUMBER and TEMP are to be displayed. If NUMBER and TEMP have the values 17 and 10.25, respectively, then we know that list-directed output produced by the first statement is compiler-dependent but might appear as follows:

```
   17   10.25000
```

The output produced by the second and third forms is not compiler-dependent and appears as follows:

```
    17   10.25
```

(If control characters are not in effect, there will be one additional space at the beginning of this output line.)

There are many format descriptors that may be used in format specifiers. A complete list of these descriptors is given in Table 5.1. In this section we consider those most commonly used: I, F, E, character strings, A, T, X, and /, deferring the others until Section 12.1.

Table 5.1   Format Descriptors

Forms			Use
Iw	I$w.m$		Integer data
F$w.d$			Real data in decimal notation
E$w.d$	E$w.d$Ee		Real data in scientific notation
D$w.d$			Double precision data
G$w.d$			F or E input/output, depending on the value of the item
A	Aw		Character data
'x . . . x'	nHx . . . x		Character strings
Lw			Logical data
Tc	TLn	TRn	Tab descriptors
nX			Horizontal spacing
/			Vertical spacing
:			Format scanning control
S	SP	SS	Sign descriptors
kP			Scale factor
BN		BZ	Blank interpretation

w: a positive integer constant specifying the field width
m: a nonnegative integer constant specifying the minimum number of digits to be read/displayed
d: a nonnegative integer constant specifying the number of digits to the right of the decimal point
e: a nonnegative integer constant specifying the number of digits in an exponent
x: a character
c: a positive integer constant representing a character position
n: a positive integer constant specifying the number of character positions
k: a nonnegative integer constant specifying a scale factor

Control Characters

In some computer systems, the first character of each line of output directed to a printer is used to control the vertical spacing. If this character is a **control character**, it is used only to effect the appropriate printer control and is not printed. The standard control characters with their effects are as follows:

Control Characters

Control Character	Effect
blank	Normal spacing: Advance to the next line before printing
0	Double spacing: Skip one line before printing
1	Advance to top of next page before printing
+	Overprint the last line printed

Some systems may implement other control characters and may also use such characters to control output to devices other than the printer. Consequently, if some character other than a standard control character appears in the first position of a line, the resulting output will depend on the computer system being used. The details regarding how your particular system uses control characters can be obtained from the system manuals, your instructor, or computer center personnel.

In the case of list-directed output, a blank is automatically inserted at the beginning of each output line as a control character. This blank then produces normal spacing and in some systems is not printed.

In the case of formatted output, some attention must be paid to printer control, because otherwise the output may not be what the user intended. To illustrate, suppose that control characters are in effect, and consider the following statements:

```
     PRINT 20, N
  20 FORMAT(I3)
```

The format descriptor I3 specifies that the value to be printed is an integer and is to be printed in the first three positions of a line. If the value of N is 15, the three positions are filled with ƀ15 (where ƀ denotes a blank). Because the blank appears in the first position, it is interpreted as a control character. This produces normal spacing and displays the value 15 in the first two positions of a new line, as follows:

15

If, however, the value of N is 150, the first three positions are filled with 150. The character 1 in the first position is again interpreted as a control character. It is not printed, but instead the value 50 is printed at the top of a new page:

50

When control characters are in effect, it is a good practice to use the first print position of each output line to indicate explicitly what printer control is desired. This can be done by making the first descriptor of each format specifier one of the following:

1X or ' ' for normal spacing

'0' for double spacing

'1' for advancing to a new page

'+' for overprinting

We follow this practice in the examples in this text.

Integer Output—The I Descriptor

The I descriptor used to describe the format in which integer data is to be displayed has the form

rIw **or** *rIw.m*

where

    I denotes integer data

    w is an integer constant indicating the width of the field in which the data is to be displayed, that is, the number of spaces to be used in displaying it

    r is an integer constant called a *repetition indicator,* indicating the number of such fields; for example, 4I3 is the same as I3, I3, I3, I3; if there is only one such field, the number 1 need not be given

    m is the minimum number of digits to be displayed

Integer values are *right justified* in fields of the specified sizes; that is, each value is displayed so that its last digit appears in the rightmost position of the field. For example, if the values of the integer variables NUM, L, and KAPPA are

```
NUM = 3
L = 5378
KAPPA = -12345
```

then the statements

```
PRINT '(1X, 2I5, I7, I10)', NUM, NUM - 3, L, KAPPA
```

or

```
    PRINT 30, NUM, NUM - 3, L, KAPPA
30 FORMAT(1X, 2I5, I7, I10)
```

produce the following output:

```
    3    0   5378      -12345
```

The statements

```
PRINT '(1X, 2I5.2, I7, I10.7)', NUM, NUM - 3, L, KAPPA
PRINT '(1X, 2I5.0, I7, I10)', NUM, NUM - 3, L, KAPPA
```

or

```
    PRINT 31, NUM, NUM - 3, L, KAPPA
    PRINT 32, NUM, NUM - 3, L, KAPPA
31 FORMAT(1X, 2I5.2, I7, I10.7)
32 FORMAT(1X, 2I5.0, I7, I10)
```

produce

```
   03   00   5378   -0012345
    3         5378      -12345
```

If an integer value (including a minus sign if the number is negative) requires more spaces than are allowed by the field width specified by a descriptor, the field is filled with asterisks. Thus, the statement

```
    PRINT 40, NUM, NUM - 3, L, KAPPA
40 FORMAT(1X, 4I3)
```

will produce

```
  3  0******
```

Real Output—The F Descriptor

One of the descriptors used to describe the format of real (floating-point) data has the form

```
rFw.d
```

where

F denotes real (floating-point) data

w is an integer constant indicating the *total width of the field* in which the data is to be displayed

d is an integer constant indicating the number of digits to the right of the decimal point

r is the repetition indicator, an integer constant indicating the number of such fields; again, if there is to be only one such field, the number 1 is not required

Real values are *right justified* in the specified fields. For a descriptor F$w.d$, if the corresponding real value has more than d digits to the right of the decimal point, it is *rounded* to d digits. If it has fewer than d digits, the remaining positions are filled with zeros. In most systems, values less than 1 in magnitude are displayed with a zero to the left of the decimal point (for example, 0.123 rather than .123).

For example, to display the values of the integer variables IN and OUT and the values of the real variables A, B, and C as given by

```
IN = 625
OUT = -19
A = 7.5
B = .182
C = 625.327
```

we can use the statements

```
    PRINT '(1X, 2I4, 2F6.3, F8.3)', IN, OUT, A, B, C
```

or

```
    PRINT 50, IN, OUT, A, B, C
50 FORMAT(1X, 2I4, 2F6.3, F8.3)
```

The resulting output is

```
_625_−19_7.500_0.182_625.327
```

To provide more space between the numbers and to round each of the real values to two decimal places, we can use the format specification

```
(1X, 2I10, 3F10.2)
```

This displays the numbers right justified in fields containing ten spaces, as follows:

```
        625        −19       7.50       0.18     625.33
```

As with the I descriptor, if the real number being output requires more spaces than are allowed by the field width specified in the descriptor, the entire field is *filled with asterisks.* For example,

```
      REAL BETA

      BETA = −567.89
      PRINT 55, 123.4
      PRINT 55, BETA
55 FORMAT(1X, F5.2)
```

produces

```
*****

*****
```

It should be noted that for a descriptor Fw. d, one should have

$$w \geq d + 3$$

to allow for the sign of the number, the first digit, and the decimal point.

Real Output—The E Descriptor

Real data may also be output in scientific notation using a descriptor of the form

```
rEw.d    or    rEw.dEe
```

where

E indicates that the data is to be output in scientific notation

w is an integer constant that indicates the total width of the field in which the data is to be displayed

d is an integer constant indicating the number of decimal digits to be displayed

r is the repetition indicator, an integer constant indicating the number of such fields; it need not be used if there is only one field

e is the number of positions to be used in displaying the exponent

Although some details of the output are compiler-dependent, real values are usually displayed in *normalized form*—a minus sign, if necessary, followed by one leading zero, then a decimal point followed by d significant digits, and E with an appropriate exponent in the next four spaces for the first form or e spaces for the second form. For example, if values of real variables A, B, C, and D are given by

```
REAL A, B, C, D
A = .12345E8
B = .0237
C = 4.6E-12
D = -76.1684E12
```

the statements

```
    PRINT 60, A, B, C, D
60 FORMAT(1X, 2E15.5, E15.4, E14.4)
```

produce output like the following:

```
   0.12345E+08    0.23700E-01    0.4600E-11   -0.7617E+14
```

As with the F descriptor, a field is *asterisk filled* if it is not large enough for the value. It should also be noted that for a descriptor E$w.d$ one should have

$$w \geq d + 7$$

or for the second form E$w.dEe$,

$$w \geq d + e + 5$$

to allow space for the sign of the number, a leading zero, a decimal point, and E with the exponent.

Character Output

Character constants may be displayed by including them in the list of descriptors of a format specifier. For example, if X and Y have the values 0.3 and 7.9, respectively, the statements

```
    PRINT 70, X, Y
70 FORMAT(1X, 'X =', F6.2, ' Y =', F6.2)
```

or

```
PRINT '(1X, ''X ='', F6.2, '' Y ='', F6.2)', X, Y
```

produce as output

```
X =  0.30 Y =  7.90
```

Character data may also be displayed by using an A format descriptor of the form

*r*A   or   *r*A*w*

where

w (if used) is an integer constant specifying the field width

r is the repetition indicator, an integer constant indicating the number of such fields; it may be omitted if there is only one field

In the first form, the field width is determined by the length of the character value being displayed. In the second form, if the field width exceeds the length of the character value, that value is *right justified* in the field. In contrast with numeric output, however, if the length of the character value exceeds the specified field width, the output consists of the *leftmost* w characters. For example, the preceding output would also be produced if the labels were included in the output list, as follows:

```
   PRINT 71, 'X =', X, ' Y =', Y
71 FORMAT(1X, A, F6.2, A, F6.2)
```

or

```
PRINT '(1X, A, F6.2, A, F6.2)', 'X =', X, ' Y =', Y
```

Placing labels in the output list rather than in the format specifier allows the format specifier to be reused to print other labels and values, as in

```
PRINT 71, 'MEAN IS', XMEAN, 'WITH STANDARD DEVIATION', STDEV
```

Positional Descriptors—X and T

Two format descriptors can be used to provide spacing in an output line. An X descriptor can be used to insert blanks in an output line. It has the form

*n*X

where *n* is a positive integer constant that specifies the number of blanks to be inserted. The T descriptor has the form

T*c*

where c is an integer constant denoting the number of the space on a line at which a field is to begin. This descriptor functions much like a tab key and causes the next output field to begin at the specified position on the current line. One difference is that the value of c may be less than the current position; that is, "tabbing backward" is possible.[1]

As an illustration of these descriptors, suppose that NUMBER is an integer variable, and consider the output statement

```
PRINT 75, 'JOHN Q. DOE', 'CPSC', NUMBER
```

together with either of the following FORMAT statements:

```
75 FORMAT(1X, A11, 3X, A4, 2X, I3)
```

or

```
75 FORMAT(1X, A11, T16, A4, 2X, I3)
```

If NUMBER has the value 141, the output produced is

```
JOHN Q. DOE   CPSC  141
```

Note that the descriptor 2X in either FORMAT statement can be replaced by T22 or that the pair of descriptors 2X, I3 can be replaced by the single descriptor I5. This same output is produced by the statements

```
    PRINT 75, 'JOHN Q. DOE', NUMBER, 'CPSC'
75 FORMAT(1X, A11, T22, I3, T16, A4)
```

which use the backward-tabbing feature of the T descriptor.

Repeating Groups of Format Descriptors

As we have seen, it is possible to repeat some format descriptors by preceding them with a *repetition indicator.* For example,

```
3F10.2
```

is the same as

```
F10.2, F10.2, F10.2
```

It is also possible to repeat a group of descriptors by enclosing the group in parentheses and then placing a repetition indicator before the left parenthesis. For example, the FORMAT statement

```
80 FORMAT(1X, A, F6.2, A, F6.2)
```

---

[1] In some systems, a run-time error will occur if c is less than the current position.

can be written more compactly as

```
80 FORMAT(1X, 2(A, F6.2))
```

Similarly, the `format` statement

```
81 FORMAT(1X, I10, F10.2, I10, F10.2, I10, F10.2, E15.8)
```

can be shortened to

```
81 FORMAT(1X, 3(I10, F10.2), E15.8)
```

Additional levels of groups are permitted. For example, the FORMAT statement

```
82 FORMAT(1X, E18.2, I3, A, I3, A, E18.2, I3, A, I3, A, F8.4)
```

can be written more compactly as

```
82 FORMAT(1X, 2(E18.2, 2(I3, A)), F8.4)
```

The Slash (/) Descriptor

A single output statement can be used to display values on more than one line, with different formats, by using a slash (/) descriptor. The slash causes output to begin on a new line. It can also be used repeatedly to skip several lines. It is not necessary to use a comma to separate a slash descriptor from other descriptors. For example, the statements

```
      PRINT 85, 'VALUES'
      PRINT *
      PRINT *
      PRINT 86, N, A, M, B
      PRINT 87, C, D
   85 FORMAT(1X, A)
   86 FORMAT(1X, 2(I10, F10.2))
   87 FORMAT(1X, 2E15.7)
```

can be combined in the pair of statements

```
      PRINT 88, 'VALUES', N, A, M, B, C, D
   88 FORMAT(1X, A /// 1X, 2(I10, F10.2) / 1X, 2E15.7)
```

(Note the 1X descriptors following the slashes to indicate the control characters for the new output lines.) If the values of N, A, M, B, C, and D are given by

```
      N = 5173
      A = 617.2
      M = 7623
      B = 29.25
      C = 37.555
      D = 5.2813
```

then in both cases the resulting output is

```
VALUES



     5173      617.20        7623      29.25
  0.3755500E+02  0.5281300E+01
```

Scanning the Format

When a formatted output statement is executed, the corresponding format specifier is scanned from left to right in parallel with the output list to locate the appropriate descriptors for the output items. The type of the descriptors should match the type of the values being displayed; for example, a real value should not be displayed with an I descriptor. If the values of all the items in the output list have been displayed before all the descriptors have been used, scanning of the format specifier continues. Values of character constants are displayed, and the positioning specified by slash, X, and T descriptors continues until one of the following is encountered:

1. The right parenthesis signaling the end of the list of format descriptors
2. An I, F, E, A, D, L, or G descriptor
3. A colon

In cases 2 and 3, all remaining descriptors in the format specifier are ignored.
    To illustrate, consider the statements

```
      PRINT 100, I, J
100 FORMAT(1X, I5, 3I6)
      PRINT 105, X, Y
105 FORMAT(1X, F5.1, F7.0, F10.5)
      PRINT 110, 'BUMPER', 'HEADLIGHT'
110 FORMAT(1X, 5('  ITEM IS ', A10))
      PRINT 115, 'BUMPER', 'HEADLIGHT'
115 FORMAT(1X, 5(: '  ITEM IS ', A10))
```

If I and J are integer variables with values I = 1 and J = 2 and X and Y are real variables with values given by X = 5.6 and Y = 7.8, these statements produce the output

```
    1     2
  5.6     8.
  ITEM IS      BUMPER   ITEM IS   HEADLIGHT   ITEM IS
  ITEM IS      BUMPER   ITEM IS   HEADLIGHT
```

Note that like the slash, the colon descriptor need not be separated from other descriptors by a comma.

If the list of descriptors is exhausted before the output list is, a new line of output is begun, and the format specifier or part of it is rescanned. If there are no internal parentheses within the format specifier, the rescanning begins with the first descriptor. For example, the statements

```
      INTEGER M1, M2, M3, M4, M5

      M1 = 1
      M2 = 2
      M3 = 3
      M4 = 4
      M5 = 5
      PRINT 120, M1, M2, M3, M4, M5
  120 FORMAT(1X, 2I3)
```

produce the output

```
  1   2
  3   4
  5
```

If the format specifier does contain internal parentheses, rescanning begins at the left parenthesis that matches the next-to-last right parenthesis; any repetition counter preceding this format group is in effect. Thus, if integer variables K, L1, L2, and L3 have values

```
      K = 3
      L1 = 21
      L2 = 22
      L3 = 23
```

and real variables X, Y1, Y2, and Y3 have values

```
      X = 4.0
      Y1 = 5.5
      Y2 = 6.66
      Y3 = 7.77
```

the statements

```
      PRINT 125, K, X, L1, Y1, L2, Y2, L3, Y3
  125 FORMAT(1X, I5, F10.3 / (1X, I10, F12.2))
```

produce the output

```
    3     4.000
   21        5.50
   22        6.66
   23        7.77
```

Thus, it is possible to specify a special format for the first output items and a different format for subsequent items by enclosing the last format descriptors in parentheses. In this example, when the right parenthesis of the FORMAT statement is encountered after printing the value of Y1, a new line is begun, and the descriptors following the second left parenthesis are reused to print the values of L2 and Y2 and then again on a new line for L3 and Y3.

5.2 EXAMPLE: PRINTING TABLES OF COMPUTED VALUES

In some of the sample programs of Chapter 4, the output was displayed in a table format. For example, the output produced in the sample run of the program in Figure 4.3 was

```
     X              Y
================================
  1.00000     0.309560
  1.25000     0.271889
  1.50000     0.222571
  1.75000     0.170991
  2.00000     0.123060
  2.25000      8.20083E−02
  2.50000      4.91256E−02
  2.75000      2.43988E−02
  3.00000      7.02595E−03
```

One unpleasant feature of this table is that the last four values in the second column are printed in scientific notation, whereas all the others are printed in decimal format. Note also that all the values are displayed with five or six digits to the right of the decimal point, even though two or three might be sufficient for our purposes. With list-directed output, however, the format of the output cannot be controlled by the user.

Positioning headings for the columns of a table above the values in the columns can also be rather difficult, as the user cannot control the format or the spacing of these values. It may be necessary to change the output statements and reexecute the modified program several times before the appearance of the output is satisfactory.

The format descriptors in this section make it quite easy to control the format of the output, and correct placement of items such as table headings is also considerably easier than with list-directed output. The program in Figure 5.1 demonstrates this. It reads a value for an integer LAST and then prints a table of values of N, the square and the cube of N, and its square root for N = 1, 2, . . . , LAST.

Figure 5.1 Table of squares, cubes, and square roots—version 1.

```
      PROGRAM TABLE
*********************************************************************
* Program demonstrating the use of formatted output to print a table  *
* of values of N, the square and cube of N, and the square root of N  *
* for N = 1, 2, ..., LAST, where the value of LAST is read during     *
* execution.  Variables used are:                                     *
*      N    :   counter                                               *
*      LAST :   last value of N                                       *
*                                                                     *
* Input:  LAST                                                        *
* Output: Table of values of N, N**2, N**3, and square root of N      *
*********************************************************************

      INTEGER N, LAST

      PRINT *, 'ENTER LAST NUMBER TO BE USED'
      READ *, LAST

*     Print headings

      PRINT 100, 'NUMBER', 'SQUARE', ' CUBE', 'SQ. ROOT'
100   FORMAT(// 1X, A8, T11, A8, T21, A8, T31, A10 / 1X, 40('='))

*     Print the table

      DO 10 N = 1, LAST
         PRINT 110, N, N**2, N**3, SQRT(REAL(N))
110      FORMAT(1X, I6, 2I10, 2X, F10.4)
10    CONTINUE

      END
```

Sample run:

```
ENTER LAST NUMBER TO BE USED
10
```

Figure 5.1 *(cont.)*

```
  NUMBER    SQUARE      CUBE    SQ. ROOT
==========================================
     1         1          1      1.0000
     2         4          8      1.4142
     3         9         27      1.7321
     4        16         64      2.0000
     5        25        125      2.2361
     6        36        216      2.4495
     7        49        343      2.6458
     8        64        512      2.8284
     9        81        729      3.0000
    10       100       1000      3.1623
```

5.3 FORMATTED INPUT

We have seen that input is accomplished in FORTRAN by a READ **statement**. This statement has two forms, the simpler of which is

READ *Statement*

Form:

    READ *format-specifier, input-list*

where
   input-list is a single variable or a list of variables separated by commas; and
   format-specifier specifies the format in which the values for the items in the input list are to be entered. As in the case of output, the format specifier may be

1. * (an asterisk)
2. a character constant or a character variable (or expression or array) whose value specifies the format for the output
3. the label of a FORMAT statement

Effect:
Reads values for the variables in the *input-list* using the formats given in the *format-specifier*.

The most commonly used form of the READ statement is the one in which the format specifier is an asterisk. As we saw in Chapter 2, this form indicates list-directed input in which the format is determined by the types of variables in the input list. In all situations except those in which the data has a specific predetermined form, list-directed input should be adequate. When the data items are of a predetermined form, it may be necessary to use a format specifier of type 2 or 3 to read them.

As in the case of output, the format specifier may be a character constant or variable (or expression or array) whose value has the form

```
'(list of format descriptors)'
```

or the label of a FORMAT statement of the form

```
FORMAT(list of format descriptors)
```

The format descriptors are essentially the same as those discussed for output in the preceding section. Character constants, however, may not appear in the list of format descriptors, and the colon separator is not relevant to input.

Integer Input

Integer data can be read using the I descriptor of the form

```
rIw
```

where w indicates the width of the field, that is, the number of characters to be read, and r is the repetition indicator specifying the number of such fields. To illustrate, consider the following example:

```
INTEGER I, J, K
READ '(I6, I4, I7)', I, J, K
```

or

```
     READ 5, I, J, K
5 FORMAT(I6, I4, I7)
```

For the values of I, J, and K to be read correctly, the numbers should be entered as follows: the value for I in the first six positions, the value for J in the next four positions, and the value for K in the next seven positions, with each value right justified within its field. Thus, if the values to be read are

```
I:    -123
J:    45
K:    6789
```

the data may be entered as follows:

```
  -123  45   6789
```

Blanks within a field read with an I descriptor can be interpreted as zeros or they can be ignored. If they are interpreted as zeros, integer values must be right justified within their fields if they are to be read correctly. Had they been entered as

```
-123 45 6789
```

I would have been assigned the value −1230, J the value 4506, and K the value 7890000. If blanks are ignored, the location of an integer value within its field is irrelevant. We assume in the examples of this text that *blanks within numeric fields are ignored,* since this agrees with the ANSI standard. (The BZ and BN descriptors described in Section 12.1 can be used to specify which of the two interpretations is to apply.)

If the format specification were changed to

```
(I4, I2, I4)
```

the data should be entered as

```
-123456789
```

with no intervening blanks. Here the first four characters are read for I, the next two characters for J, and the next four characters for K.

Real Input

One of the descriptors used to input real data is the F descriptor of the form

```
rFw.d
```

where w indicates the width of the field to be read, d is the number of digits to the right of the decimal point, and r is the repetition counter.

There are two ways that real data may be entered:

1. The numbers may be entered without decimal points.
2. The decimal point may be entered as part of the input value.

In the first case, the d specification in the format descriptor $Fw.d$ automatically positions the decimal point so that there are d digits to its right. For example, if we wish to enter the following values for real variables A, B, C, D, and E,

A:	6.25
B:	−1.9
C:	75.0
D:	.182
E:	625.327

we can use the statements

```
    READ 10, A, B, C, D, E
10 FORMAT(F3.2, 2F3.1, F3.3, F6.3)
```

or

```
        READ '(F3.2, 2F3.1, F3.3, F6.3)', A, B, C, D, E
```

and enter the data in the following form:

```
 625-19750182625327
```

Of course, we can use wider fields, for example,

```
 (F4.2, 2F4.1, 2F8.3)
```

and enter the data in the form

```
 625 -19 750      182  625327
```

with the values right justified within their fields.

In the second method of entering real data, the position of the decimal point in the value entered overrides the position specified by the descriptor. Thus, if the number to be read is 9423.68, an appropriate descriptor is F6.2 if the number is entered without a decimal point and F7.2, or F7.1, or F7.0, and so on, if the number is entered with a decimal point. For example, the preceding values for A, B, C, D, and E can be read using the statements

```
        READ 15, A, B, C, D, E
     15 FORMAT(4F5.0, F8.0)
```

with the data entered in the following form:

```
 6.25 -1.9  75. .182 625.327
```

Note that each field width must be large enough to accommodate the number entered, including the decimal point and the sign.

Real values entered in E notation can also be read using an F descriptor. Thus for the format specification

```
 (5F10.0)
```

the data of the preceding example could also have been entered as

```
      .625E1      -1.9     75.0   18.2E-2 6.25327E2
```

In this case, the E need not be entered if the exponent is preceded by a sign. The following would therefore be an alternative method for entering the preceding data:

```
      .625+1      -1.9     75.0   18.2-2 6.25327+2
```

The E descriptor may also be used in a manner similar to that for the F descriptor.

Character Input

Character data can be read using an A descriptor of the form

```
rA   or   rAw
```

where r is a repetition indicator, and in the second form w is the width of the field to be read. In the first form, the width of the field read for a particular variable in the input list is the length specified for that variable in the CHARACTER statement.

When a READ statement whose input list contains a character variable is executed, *all* characters in the field associated with the corresponding A descriptor are read. For example, if the line of data

```
FOURSCORE AND SEVEN YEARS AGO
```

is read by the statements

```
      CHARACTER*6 STRA, STRB

      READ 20, STRA, STRB
20 FORMAT(2A)
```

the value

```
FOURSC
```

is assigned to STRA and

```
ORE AN
```

to STRB.

Note that six characters were read for each of STRA and STRB, because this is their declared length. If the following line of data

```
AB1''34'AN,APPLE A DAY
```

is entered, the values assigned to STRA and STRB would be

```
AB1''3
```

and

```
4'AN,A
```

respectively.

If the FORMAT statement

```
20 FORMAT(2A6)
```

were used, the same values would be assigned to STRA and STRB. If, however, the FORMAT statement

```
20 FORMAT(A2, A12)
```

were used, the value assigned to STRA would be

```
ABȠȠȠȠ
```

(where ȡ denotes a blank) and the value assigned to STRB would be

```
AN,APP
```

Note that in the case of STRB, a field of size 12 was read but the *rightmost* six characters were assigned. (See Potential Problem 3 in the programming pointers at the end of this chapter.)

Skipping Input Characters

The positional descriptors X and T may be used in the format specifier of a READ statement to skip over certain input characters. For example, if we wish to assign the following values to the integer variables I, J, and K:

```
I:    4
J:    56
K:    137
```

by entering data in the form

```
I = 4   J = 56  K = 137
```

the following statements may be used:

```
    READ 20, I, J, K
20 FORMAT(3X, I2, 6X, I3, 5X, I4)
```

or

```
20 FORMAT(T4, I2, T12, I3, T20, I4)
```

Input characters are also skipped if the end of the input list is encountered before the end of the data line has been reached. To illustrate, if the statements

```
    READ 25, NUM1, X
    READ 25, NUM2, Y
25 FORMAT(I5, F7.0)
```

are used to read values for the integer variables NUM1 and NUM2 and real variables X and Y from the following data lines:

```
   17   3.56   34   13.4
 9064 570550 3199 47
```

the values assigned to NUM1 and X are

```
NUM1:   17
   X:   3.56
```

and the values assigned to NUM2 and Y are

```
NUM2:    9064
   Y:    570550.
```

All other information on these two lines is ignored.

Multiple Input Lines

Recall that a new line of data is required each time a READ statement is executed. A new line of data is also required whenever a slash (/) is encountered in the format specifier for the READ statement. This may be used in case some of the data entries are separated by blank lines, remarks, and the like, which are to be skipped over by the READ statement. For example, the following data

```
AMOUNT TO BE PRODUCED
585.00
REACTION RATE
(THIS ASSUMES CONSTANT TEMPERATURE)
5.75
```

can be read by a single READ statement, and the values 585.00 and 5.75 assigned to AMOUNT and RATE, respectively, as follows:

```
   REAL AMOUNT, RATE

   READ 30, AMOUNT, RATE
30 FORMAT(/ F6.0 /// F4.0)
```

or

```
   READ '(/ F6.0 /// F4.0)', AMOUNT, RATE
```

The first slash causes the first line to be skipped, so that the value 585.00 is read for AMOUNT; the three slashes then cause an advance of three lines, so that 5.75 is read for RATE.

A new line is also required if all descriptors have been used and there are still variables remaining in the input list for which values must be read. In this case, the format specifier is rescanned, as in the case of output. Thus, the statements

```
INTEGER I, J, K, L, M

READ 35, I, J, K, L, M
35 FORMAT(3I8)
```

require two lines of input, the first containing the values of I, J, and K and the second, the values of L and M.

Quick Quiz 5.3

1. (True or false) The control character 0 causes the printer to advance to a new page.

2. (True or false) The format descriptor 3I2 is the same as I2,I2,I2.

3. (True or false) In the format descriptor F10.3, 10 refers to the number of digits to the left of the decimal point, and 3 refers to the number of digits to the right of the decimal point.

4. (True or false) For the format descriptor I2, if the integer to be output requires more than 2 spaces, the entire field will be blank.

5. (True or false) The format descriptor T is used to truncate values.

6. (True or false) If there are fewer descriptors than values in the output list, then the remaining values will be output using the last descriptor in the format identifier.

7. (True or false) For an F descriptor, real values are rounded to the number of decimal places specified.

8. The _____ descriptor causes output to begin on a new line.

9. Integers are _____ (left or right) justified in the fields specified in an I descriptor.

10. If NUM has the value 100, the statement PRINT '(1X, 4I3)', NUM will print the value 100 _____ times.

For Questions 11–13, assume the following declarations and assignments:

```
REAL X, Y
INTEGER I, J

X = 234.56
Y = -1.0
I = 987
J = -44
```

Describe the output produced by each statement. Indicate clearly the spacing of characters within each line as well as the spacing between lines. (Assume that printer control characters are in effect.)

```
11.    PRINT 5, I, X
     5 FORMAT (1X, 'I =', I3, 2X, 'X =', F8.3, 'THE END')
12.    PRINT 6, I, X, J, Y
     6 FORMAT (1X, I5, F10.1)
13.    PRINT '(1X, F10.0 / ''0'', I3, T11, I5)', X, I, J
```

For each of the READ statements in Questions 14–18, show how the data must be entered so that X is assigned the value 123.45, Y the value 6.0, I the value 99 and J the value 876.

```
14.    READ *, I, J, X, Y
15.    READ '(2I3, 2F6.0)', I, J, X, Y
16.    READ 7, I, X, J, Y
     7 FORMAT (I3, F7.0, 2X, I5, T20, F5.0)
17.    READ 8, I, J, X, Y
     8 FORMAT (2I3, F5.2, F1.0)
18.    READ 9, I, X, J, Y
     9 FORMAT (I2, F5.2 / I3, F2.1)
```

Exercises 5.3

Assuming that the declarations and assignments

```
INTEGER NUMBER
REAL ALPHA
CHARACTER*8 TITLE
NUMBER = 12345
ALPHA = 87.6543
TITLE = 'EXERCISE'
```

have been made, describe the output that will be produced by the statements in Exercises 1–20. (Assume that control characters are in effect):

```
1.    PRINT *, 'COMPUTER SCIENCE -- ', TITLE, ' 5.3'
2.    PRINT *, NUMBER, NUMBER + 1
3.    PRINT *, 'ALPHA = ', ALPHA, ' NUMBER =', NUMBER
4.    PRINT *
5.    PRINT '('' COMPUTER SCIENCE -- EXERCISE'', F4.1)',
    +       3 * 2.1 - 1
```

6.   PRINT 10, TITLE, 5.3
      10 FORMAT(' COMPUTER SCIENCE -- ', A, F5.2)

7.   PRINT 20, 'COMPUTER SCIENCE', 5.3
      20 FORMAT(1X, A, F4.1)

8.   PRINT 30, TITLE, 5.3
      30 FORMAT('1COMPUTER SCIENCE --', A10, F6.3)

9.   PRINT 40, TITLE, 5.3
      40 FORMAT('COMPUTER SCIENCE --', A2, F3.1)

10.   PRINT 50, NUMBER, NUMBER + 1, ALPHA, ALPHA + 1,
      +   ALPHA + 2
      50 FORMAT('0', 2I7, F10.5, F10.3, F10.0)

11.   PRINT '(1X, I5, 4X, I4, T20, I6)', NUMBER,
      +   NUMBER + 1, NUMBER + 2

12.   PRINT 60, NUMBER, ALPHA, NUMBER + 1, ALPHA + 1
      60 FORMAT(1X, I5, F7.4 / I5, E12.5)

13.   PRINT 70, NUMBER, ALPHA, NUMBER + 1, ALPHA + 1
      70 FORMAT(1X, I10, F10.3)

14.   PRINT 80, NUMBER, ALPHA, NUMBER + 1, ALPHA + 1
      80 FORMAT(1X, I10, F10.2, '---')

15.   PRINT 90, NUMBER, ALPHA, NUMBER + 1, ALPHA + 1
      90 FORMAT(1X, I10, F10.2 : '---')

16.   PRINT 100, NUMBER, '=', 12345
     100 FORMAT(1X, I5, A2, I6, / 1X, 13('='))

17.   PRINT 110, NUMBER, ALPHA, NUMBER, ALPHA
     110 FORMAT(/// 2(1X, I6 // 1X, F6.2) /// ' ******')

18.   PRINT 120, NUMBER, ALPHA, NUMBER, ALPHA, NUMBER, ALPHA
     120 FORMAT(1X, I6, F7.2, (1X, I5, F6.1))

19.   PRINT 130, NUMBER, ALPHA, NUMBER, ALPHA, NUMBER, ALPHA
     130 FORMAT(1X, I6, F7.2, (1X, I5, F6.1))

20.   PRINT 140, 'THE END'
     140 FORMAT(1X, 10 ('*'), A, 10 ('*'))

For the READ statements in Exercises 21–33, assuming the declarations

```
INTEGER I, J
REAL X, Y
CHARACTER*8 C
```

show how the data should be entered so that X, Y, I, J and C are assigned the values 123.77, 6.0, 77, 550, and 'FORTRAN', respectively:

21.   READ *, I, J, X, Y
22.   READ 5, I, J, X, Y
      5 FORMAT(2I3, 2F6.0)

23.
```
      READ 6, I, J, X, Y
    6 FORMAT(I3, F7.0, 2X, I5, T20, F5.0)
```

24.
```
      READ 7, I, J, X, Y
    7 FORMAT(2I3, F5.2, F1.0)
```

25.
```
      READ 8, I, X, J, Y
    8 FORMAT(I5, F6.0)
```

26.
```
      READ 9, I, X, J, Y
    9 FORMAT(I2, F5.2 / I3, F2.1)
```

27.
```
      READ 10, X, Y, I, J
   10 FORMAT(F5.2, 1X, F1.0, T4, I2, T9, I3)
```

28.
```
      READ 11, X, I, Y, J
   11 FORMAT(2(F5.2, I3))
```

29.
```
      READ 12, X, I, Y, J, C
   12 FORMAT(F6.2 / I5 // F6.0, I6 / A)
```

30.
```
      READ *, C, J
```

31.
```
      READ '(A, I2, F5.2)', C, I, X
```

32.
```
      READ 13, C, I, X
   13 FORMAT(A7, I3, F6.2)
```

33.
```
      READ 14, C, I, X
   14 FORMAT(A10, I10, F10.0)
```

34. Describe the output that will be produced if the following program is executed with the specified input data:

```
      PROGRAM COLUMN

      INTEGER N, I
      REAL R, DELTAR, R1, S1

      READ (5, 100) N, R, DELTAR
      PRINT 110

      DO 10 I = 1, N
         R1 = R + DELTAR*(I - 1)
         IF (R1 .LT. 120.0) THEN
             S1 = 17000.0 - 0.485*R1**2
         ELSE
             S1 = 18000.0 / (1.0 + R1**2/18000.0)
         END IF

         IF (MOD(I, 2) .EQ. 0) THEN
             PRINT 120, I, R1, S1
         END IF
   10 CONTINUE
```

```
100 FORMAT(/ I5, 2F10.4)
110 FORMAT('1', T3, 'INDEX', T14, 'S RATIO', T30,
   +        'LOAD')
120 FORMAT('0', 2X, I2, 2(5X, F10.3))

    END
```

Input data:

```
12345678901234567890123456789 0  ←  Character positions
    4      100.0      100000
```

5.4 THE WRITE STATEMENT AND THE GENERAL READ STATEMENT

The PRINT and READ statements used thus far are simple FORTRAN input/output statements. However, in Sections 2.5 and 2.10 we saw that there is a more general output statement, the WRITE statement, and a more general form of the READ statement. In this section we will describe these more general forms, and in the next section we will show how they are used for file input/output.

The WRITE Statement

The WRITE **statement** has a more complicated syntax than the PRINT statement, but it is a more general output statement. It has the following form:

WRITE *Statement*

Form:

```
WRITE (control-list) output-list
```

where
   output-list has the same syntax as in the PRINT statement; and
   control-list may include items selected from the following:
   1. a unit specifier indicating the output device
   2. a format specifier
   3. other items that are especially useful in file processing (These are considered in Chapter 11.)

Purpose:
Displays the values of the items in the *output-list* as directed by the specifications in the *control-list*, which must include a unit specifier and (except for the more advanced applications described in Chapter 11) a format specifier as well.

The **unit specifier** is an integer expression whose value designates the output device, or it may be an asterisk, indicating the standard output device (usually a monitor screen or a printer). The unit specifier may be given in the form

```
UNIT = unit-specifier
```

or simply

```
unit-specifier
```

If the UNIT = clause is not used, the unit specifier must be the first item in the control list.

The **format specifier** may be given in the form

```
FMT = format-specifier
```

or simply

```
format-specifier
```

where *format-specifier* may be of any of the forms allowed in the PRINT statement. If the format specifier without the FMT = clause is used, then it must be the second item in the control list, and the UNIT = clause must also be omitted for the unit specifier.

To illustrate the WRITE statement, suppose that the values of GRAV and WEIGHT are to be displayed on an output device having unit number 6. The statement

```
WRITE (6, *) GRAV, WEIGHT
```

or any of the following equivalent forms

```
WRITE (6, FMT = *) GRAV, WEIGHT

WRITE (UNIT = 6, FMT = *) GRAV, WEIGHT

WRITE (NOUT, *) GRAV, WEIGHT

WRITE (UNIT = NOUT, FMT = *) GRAV, WEIGHT
```

where NOUT is an integer variable with value 6, produce list-directed output to this device. If this device is the system's standard output device, the unit number 6 may be replaced by an asterisk in any of the preceding statements; for example,

```
WRITE (*, *) GRAV, WEIGHT
```

and each of these is equivalent to the short form

```
PRINT *, GRAV, WEIGHT
```

Formatted output of these values can be produced by statements like the following:

```
WRITE (6, '(1X, 2F10.2)') GRAV, WEIGHT

WRITE (6, FMT = '(1X, 2F10.2)') GRAV, WEIGHT

WRITE (6, 30) GRAV, WEIGHT
30 FORMAT(1X, 2F10.2)

WRITE (UNIT = 6, FMT = 30) GRAV, WEIGHT
30 FORMAT(1X, 2F10.2)
```

The General READ Statement

The general form of the READ statement is

READ *Statement*

Form:

```
READ (control-list) input-list
```

where
     input-list is a variable or a list of variables separated by commas; and
     control-list may include items selected from the following:
     1. a unit specifier indicating the input device
     2. a format specifier
     3. an IOSTAT = clause or an END = clause to detect an input error or an
        end-of-file condition, as described in the next section
     4. other items that are particularly useful in processing files (These are con-
        sidered in Chapter 11.)

Purpose:
Reads values for the variables in the *input-list* as directed by the specifications in the *control-list*. The unit specifier and the format specifier have the
same forms as described for the WRITE statement.

As an illustration of the general form of the READ statement, suppose that values
for CODE, TIME, and RATE are to be read using the input device 5. The statement

```
READ (5, *) CODE, TIME, RATE
```

or any of the following equivalent forms

```
READ (5, FMT = *) CODE, TIME, RATE

READ (UNIT = 5, FMT = *) CODE, TIME, RATE

READ (IN, *) CODE, TIME, RATE

READ (UNIT = IN, FMT = *) CODE, TIME, RATE
```

where IN has the value 5, can be used. If this device is the system's standard input device, an asterisk may be used in place of the device number in any of the preceding unit specifications; for example,

```
READ (*, *) CODE, TIME, RATE
```

Formatted input is also possible with the general READ statement; for example,

```
READ (5, '(I6, 2F6.2)') CODE, TIME, RATE
```

or

```
READ (UNIT = 5, FMT = '(I6, 2F6.2)') CODE, TIME, RATE
```

or

```
READ (UNIT = 5, FMT = 10) CODE, TIME, RATE
```

or

```
READ (5, 10) CODE, TIME, RATE
```

where 10 is the number of the following FORMAT statement:

```
10 FORMAT(I6, 2F6.2)
```

5.5 FILE PROCESSING

Up to this point we have assumed that the data for the sample programs was entered from the keyboard during program execution and that the output was displayed on the screen. This is usually adequate if the amounts of input/output data are relatively small. However, applications involving large data sets can be processed more conveniently if the data is stored in a file for later processing, for example, by a program as it reads input data from this file or by a printer as it produces a hard copy of the output. Files are usually stored on disks or on some other form of external (secondary) memory. In this section we consider the characteristics of files and some of the FORTRAN statements used in processing them. (Others are described in Chapter 11.)

The data values in a file to be used as an input file must be arranged in a form suitable for reading by a READ statement. These values are read during program execution, just like data entered by the user from the keyboard. For example, if the variables CODE, TEMP, and PRESS are declared by

```
INTEGER CODE
REAL TEMP, PRESS
```

and the values for these variables are to be read from a file using a list-directed READ statement, this data file might have the following form:

```
37, 77.5, 30.39
22, 85.3, 30.72
1, 100.0, 29.95
78, 99.5, 29.01
        .
        .
        .
```

If the values are to be read using the format specifier

```
(I2, 2F8.0)
```

the file might have the form

```
37      77.5    30.39
22      85.3    30.72
 1     100.0    29.95
78      99.5    29.01

        .
        .
        .
```

whereas the format specifier

```
(I2, F4.1, F4.2)
```

would be appropriate for the file

```
37 7753039
22 8533072
 110002995
78 9952901

        .
        .
        .
```

Opening Files

Before a file can be used in a FORTRAN program, a number, called a *unit number*, must be connected to it and several items of information about the file must be supplied.

This process is called *opening* the file and is accomplished using an OPEN **statement** of the following form:

OPEN *Statement*

Form:

    OPEN (*open-list*)

where
   open-list includes
   1. a unit specifier indicating a unit number connected to the file being opened
   2. a FILE = clause giving the name of the file being opened
   3. a STATUS = clause specifying whether the file is a new or an old file
      (Other items that may be included are described in Chapter 11.)

Purpose:
Opens the file associated with the specified unit number so that input/output can take place. The unit specifier has the form described for the WRITE statement. Reference to this file by a READ or WRITE statement is by means of this unit number.
   The FILE = clause has the form

    FILE = *character-expression*

where the value of *character-expression* (ignoring trailing blanks) is the name of the file to be connected to the specified unit number.
   The STATUS = clause has the form

    STATUS = *character-expression*

where the value of *character-expression* (ignoring trailing blanks) is

    'OLD'

or

    'NEW'

OLD means that the file already exists in the system; NEW means that the file does not yet exist and is being created by the program; execution of the OPEN statement creates an empty file with the specified name and changes its status to OLD.

Closing Files

The CLOSE **statement** has a function opposite that of the OPEN statement and is used to disconnect a file from its unit number. This statement has the form

---

CLOSE *Statement*

Form:

    CLOSE (*close-list*)

where
  close-list must include a unit specifier and may include other items as described in Chapter 11.

Purpose:
Closes the file associated with the specifed unit number.

After a CLOSE statement is executed, the closed file may be reopened by using an OPEN statement; the same unit number may be connected to it or a different one may be used. All files that are not explicitly closed by means of a CLOSE statement are automatically closed when an END statement or a STOP statement is executed.

File Input/Output

Once a file has been connected to a unit number, data can be read from or written to that file using the general forms of the READ and WRITE statements in which the unit number appearing in the control list is the same as the unit number connected to the file. For example, to read values for CODE, TEMP, and PRESS from a file named INFO, the statement

    OPEN (UNIT = 12, FILE = 'INFO', STATUS = 'OLD')

opens the file, and the statement

    READ (12, *) CODE, TEMP, PRESS

reads the values.

Similarly, a file named REPORT to which values of CODE, TEMP, and PRESS are to be written can be created by

    OPEN (UNIT = 13, FILE = 'REPORT', STATUS = 'NEW')

Values can then be written to this file with a statement like

    WRITE (13, '(1X, I3, F7.0, F10.2)') CODE, TEMP, PRESS

or

    WRITE (13, 30) CODE, TEMP, PRESS
    30 FORMAT(1X, I3, F7.0, F10.2)

Each execution of a READ statement causes an entire line in the file to be read and then positions the file so that the next execution of a READ (WRITE) statement will cause values to be read from (written to) the next line in the file. Similarly, execution of a WRITE statement writes an entire line into the file and then positions the file so that the next execution of a WRITE (READ) statement will produce output to (input from) the next line in the file.

The IOSTAT = Clause

In the preceding section, we noted that the control list of a general READ statement may contain an IOSTAT = **clause** to detect an end-of-file condition or an input error. This clause has the following form:

IOSTAT = *Clause*

Form:

```
IOSTAT = status-variable
```

where
    status-variable is an integer variable.

Purpose:
When a READ statement containing an IOSTAT = clause is executed, the status-variable is assigned:
1. a positive value if an input error occurs
2. a negative value if the end of data is encountered but no input error occurs
3. zero if neither an input error nor the end of data occurs

In the first case, the value assigned to the status variable is usually the number of an error message in a list found in the system manuals. For example, if EOF is an integer variable, a while loop of the following form can be used to read and process values for CODE, TEMP, and PRESS from a file, terminating repetition when the end of the file is reached:

```
* While there is more data
      READ (12, *, IOSTAT = EOF) CODE, TEMP, PRESS
10    IF (EOF .GE. 0) THEN
         COUNT = COUNT + 1
            .
            .
            .
         SUMP = SUMP + PRESS
         READ (12, *, IOSTAT = EOF) CODE, TEMP, PRESS
      GO TO 10
      END IF
```

The END = Clause

An alternative method of detecting an end-of-file condition is to use an END = **clause** in the control list of a general READ statement. This clause has the form

---

END = *Clause*

Form:

```
END = statement-number
```

where
statement-number is the number of an executable statement.

Purpose:
When a READ statement containing an END = clause is executed, if the end of data is encountered, the statement with the specified *statement-number* is the next statement to be executed.

For example, the statement

```
READ (12, *, END = 20) CODE, TEMP, PRESS
```

can be used within a loop to read values for CODE, TEMP, and PRESS from a file. When the end of this file is reached, control transfers to statement 20, which marks the end of the loop:

```
*  Read and process data until the end of the file
*  is encountered

10      CONTINUE
            READ (12, *, END = 20), CODE, TEMP, PRESS
            COUNT = COUNT + 1
                      .
                      .
                      .
            SUMP = SUMP + PRESS
        GO TO 10
20      CONTINUE
```

File-Positioning Statements

There are several FORTRAN statements that may be used to position a file. One of these is the REWIND **statement** of the form

---

REWIND *Statement*

Form:

```
REWIND unit
```

where
>   *unit* is the unit number connected to a file.

Purpose:
Positions the file at its beginning.

Another file-position statement is the BACKSPACE **statement,** which has the following form:

BACKSPACE *Statement*

Form:

>   BACKSPACE *unit*

where
>   *unit* is the unit number connected to a file.

Purpose:
Causes the file to be positioned at the beginning of the preceding line.

For each statement, if the file is at its initial point, these statements have no effect.

Quick Quiz 5.5

1. In the statement WRITE (10, 20) X, Y, 10 is the _____ of some output device.
2. In the statement WRITE (10, 20) X, Y, 20 is the number of a _____ statement.
3. Write a WRITE statement that is equivalent to the statement PRINT *, ANSWER.
4. (True or false) The clause FILE = 'NEW' in an OPEN statement indicates that the file does not yet exist and is being created by the program.
5. Write a statement to open an existing file QUIZ with unit number 15.
6. Write a statement to read an integer value SCORE from columns 6–8 of the file in Question 5.
7. (True or false) The clause IOSTAT = VAR will assign a negative value to VAR if the end of data is encountered but no input error occurs.
8. In the statement READ (5, 10, END = 15) SCORE, program execution will continue at statement 15 when there are no more values to be read.
9. (True or false) The BACKSPACE statement can be used to print a value to the left of the current position.
10. The _____ statement can be used to position a file at its beginning.

5.6 APPLICATION: TEMPERATURE AND VOLUME READINGS

Problem

Suppose that a device monitoring a process records time, temperature, pressure, and volume and stores this data in a file. Each record in this file contains

    Time in positions 1–4
    Temperature in positions 5–8
    Pressure in positions 9–12
    Volume in positions 13–16

The value for time is an integer representing the time at which the measurements were taken. The values for temperature, pressure, and volume are real numbers but are recorded with no decimal point. Each must be interpreted as a real value having a decimal point between the third and fourth digits.

A program is to be designed to read the values for the temperature and volume, print these values in tabular form, and display the equation of the least-squares line determined by these values (see Section 4.8).

Solution

Specification

Input (entered by the user):	Name of the data file
Input (from the data file):	Temperature and volume readings
Output (to the screen):	Table of temperature and volume readings
	Equation of least-squares line

Design. The main part of an algorithm for solving this problem is calculating the least-squares line that best fits the given data. Using the algorithm given in Section 4.8 for finding this least-squares line, we can easily design an algorithm for solving this problem.

ALGORITHM FOR TEMPERATURE–VOLUME PROBLEM

1. Get the name of the file and open the file for input.
2. Display headings for the table.
3. Read the first pair of temperature and volume readings from the file.
4. While there are data values in the file, do the following:
    a. Display the temperature and volume in the table.

Monitoring temperature with a digital thermometer. (Photo courtesy of Photo Researchers, Inc.)

    b.   Compute the quantities needed to calculate the least-squares line as described in the algorithm of Section 4.8.
    c.   Read the next pair of temperature and volume readings from the file.
5. Compute and display the equation of the least-squares line.

Coding.   The program in Figure 5.2 implements the preceding algorithm.

Figure 5.2 Temperature and volume readings.

```
      PROGRAM TEMVOL
***********************************************************************
* Program to read temperatures and volumes from a file containing    *
* time, temperature, pressure, and volume readings made by some      *
* monitoring device.  The temperature and volume measurements are    *
* displayed in tabular form, and the equation of the least-squares   *
* line y = mx + b (x = temperature, y = volume) is calculated.       *
* Variables used are:                                                *
*                                                                    *
*      FNAME   : name of data file                                   *
*      EOF     : end-of-file indicator                               *
*      TEMP    : temperature recorded                                *
*      VOLUME  : volume recorded                                     *
*      COUNT   : count of (TEMP, VOLUME) pairs                       *
*      SUMT    : sum of temperatures                                 *
*      SUMT2   : sum of squares of temperatures                      *
*      SUMV    : sum of volumes                                      *
*      SUMTV   : sum of the products TEMP * VOLUME                   *
*      TMEAN   : mean temperature                                    *
*      VMEAN   : mean volume                                         *
*      SLOPE   : slope of the least-squares line                     *
*      YINT    : y-intercept of the line                            *
*                                                                    *
* Input (file):    Collection of temperature and volume readings     *
* Output (screen): Table of readings and equation of least-squares   *
*                  line                                              *
***********************************************************************

      INTEGER COUNT, EOF
      CHARACTER*20 FNAME
      REAL TEMP, VOLUME, SUMT, SUMT2, SUMV, SUMTV, TMEAN, VMEAN,
     +     SLOPE, YINT
      DATA COUNT, SUMT, SUMT2, SUMV, SUMTV /0, 4*0.0/

* Open the file as unit 15, set up the input and output
* formats, and print the table heading

      PRINT *, 'ENTER NAME OF DATA FILE:'
      READ '(A)', FNAME
      OPEN (UNIT = 15, FILE = FNAME, STATUS = 'OLD')
```

Figure 5.2 *(cont.)*

```
100    FORMAT(4X, F4.1, T13, F4.1)
110    FORMAT(1X, A11, A10)
120    FORMAT(1X, F8.1, F12.1)
       PRINT *
       PRINT 110, 'TEMPERATURE', 'VOLUME'
       PRINT 110, '===========', '======'

* While there is more data, read temperatures and volumes,
* display each in the table, and calculate the necessary sums

       READ (UNIT = 15, FMT = 100, IOSTAT = EOF) TEMP, VOLUME
10     IF (EOF .GE. 0) THEN
          PRINT 120, TEMP, VOLUME
          COUNT = COUNT + 1
          SUMT = SUMT + TEMP
          SUMT2 = SUMT2 + TEMP ** 2
          SUMV = SUMV + VOLUME
          SUMTV = SUMTV + TEMP * VOLUME
          READ (UNIT = 15, FMT = 100, IOSTAT = EOF) TEMP, VOLUME
       GO TO 10
       END IF

* Find equation of least-squares line

       TMEAN = SUMT / COUNT
       VMEAN = SUMV / COUNT
       SLOPE = (SUMTV - SUMT * VMEAN) / (SUMT2 - SUMT * TMEAN)
       YINT = VMEAN - SLOPE * TMEAN
       PRINT 130, SLOPE, YINT
130    FORMAT(//1X, 'EQUATION OF LEAST-SQUARES LINE IS'
      +          /1X, '     Y =', F5.1, 'X + ', F5.1,
      +          /1X, 'WHERE X IS TEMPERATURE AND Y IS VOLUME')

       CLOSE (15)
       END
```

Execution and Testing. This program should be tested with several small data files to check its correctness. It can then be run with the data file described in the statement of the problem:

Listing of file `FIL5-2.DAT`:

```
1200034203221015
1300038803221121
1400044803241425
1500051303201520
1600055503181665
1700061303191865
1800067503232080
1900072103282262
2000076803252564
2100083503272869
2200088903303186
```

Execution of the program using this file produced the following output:

Sample run:

```
ENTER NAME OF DATA FILE:
FIL5-2.DAT
   TEMPERATURE      VOLUME
   ============     ======
         34.2        101.5
         38.8        112.1
         44.8        142.5
         51.3        152.0
         55.5        166.5
         61.3        186.5
         67.5        208.0
         72.1        226.2
         76.8        256.4
         83.5        286.9
         88.9        318.6

   EQUATION OF LEAST-SQUARES LINE IS
         Y = 3.8X + -39.8
   WHERE X IS TEMPERATURE AND Y IS VOLUME
```

A Refinement Using Run-Time Formatting

In most of our examples of formatted input/output we used a FORMAT statement. As we noted, however, a format specifier may also be a character expression whose value is the list of format descriptors. For example, the statement

```
PRINT '(1X, F8.1, F12.1)', TEMP, VOLUME
```

is equivalent to the pair of statements

```
    PRINT 120, TEMP, VOLUME
120 FORMAT(1X, F8.1, F12.1)
```

A character variable could also be used:

```
CHARACTER*40 FORM
      .
      .
      .
FORM = '(1X, F8.1, F12.1)'
PRINT FORM, TEMP, VOLUME
```

A list of format descriptors can also be read at run time and assigned to a character variable like FORM which can then be used as a format specifier. This makes it possible to change the format used for input or output each time a program is run without having to modify the program itself. This is illustrated in the program in Figure 5.3, which is like that in Figure 5.2 except that the input format is entered by the user during execution.

Two sample runs are shown. The first uses the data file given earlier,

```
1200034203221015
1300038803221121
1400044803241425
1500051303201520
1600055503181665
1700061303191865
1800067503232080
1900072103282262
2000076803252564
2100083503272869
2200088903303186
```

in which the fifth through eighth digits constitute the temperatures and the last four digits are the volumes. A decimal point must be positioned in each value so there is one digit to its right. Thus, an appropriate format specifier is

```
(4X, F4.1, T13, F4.1)
```

The second data file is

```
12:00PM
34.2 32.2 101.5
1:00PM
33.8 32.2 112.1
2:00PM
44.8 32.4 142.5
3:00PM
51.3 32.0 152.0
4:00PM
55.5 31.8 166.5
5:00PM
61.3 31.9 186.5
6:00PM
67.5 32.3 208.0
7:00PM
72.1 32.8 226.2
8:00PM
76.8 32.5 256.4
9:00PM
83.5 32.7 286.9
10:00PM
88.9 33.0 318.6
```

for which an appropriate format specifier is

```
(/F4.0, 5X, F6.0)
```

When the program is executed, the user enters the name of the file (FNAME) and the appropriate format specifier (FORM) for that file.

Figure 5.3 Temperature and volume readings—version 2.

```
     PROGRAM TEMVOL
*******************************************************************
* Program to read temperatures and volumes from two different files  *
* containing time, temperature, pressure, and volume readings made by *
* some monitoring device and display the temperature and volume       *
* measurements in tabular form.  Format specifiers for these files    *
* are entered during execution.  Variables used are:                  *
*     FNAME   : name of data file                                     *
*     EOF     : end-of-file indicator                                 *
*     FORM    : input format specifier                                *
*     TEMP    : temperature recorded                                  *
*     VOLUME  : volume recorded                                       *
```

Figure 5.3 *(cont.)*

```
*                                                                      *
* Input (files):    Collection of temperature and volume readings      *
* Input (keyboard): Format specifiers               .                  *
* Output (screen):  Table of readings                                  *
***********************************************************************

      CHARACTER*50 FORM, FNAME*20
      INTEGER EOF
      REAL TEMP, VOLUME

* Open the file as unit 15, read the input format,
* and print the table heading

      PRINT *, 'ENTER NAME OF DATA FILE:'
      READ '(A)', FNAME
      OPEN (UNIT = 15, FILE = FNAME, STATUS = 'OLD')

      PRINT*, 'ENTER INPUT FORMAT FOR ', FNAME
      READ '(A)', FORM
110   FORMAT(1X, A11, A10)
120   FORMAT(1X, F8.1, F12.1)
      PRINT *
      PRINT 110, 'TEMPERATURE', 'VOLUME'
      PRINT 110, '===========', '======'

* While there is more data, read temperatures and volumes,
* displaying each in the table

      READ (UNIT = 15, FMT = FORM, IOSTAT = EOF) TEMP, VOLUME
10    IF (EOF .GE. 0) THEN
         PRINT 120, TEMP, VOLUME
         READ (UNIT = 15, FMT = FORM, IOSTAT = EOF) TEMP, VOLUME
      GO TO 10
      END IF

      CLOSE (15)
      END
```

Sample runs:

```
ENTER NAME OF DATA FILE:
FIL5-3A.DAT
ENTER INPUT FORMAT FOR FIL5-3A.DAT
(4X, F4.1, T13, F4.1)
```

Figure 5.3 *(cont.)*

```
TEMPERATURE     VOLUME
============     ======
   34.2         101.5
   38.8         112.1
   44.8         142.5
   51.3         152.0
   55.5         166.5
   61.3         186.5
   67.5         208.0
   72.1         226.2
   76.8         256.4
   83.5         286.9
   88.9         318.6


ENTER NAME OF DATA FILE:
FIL5-3B.DAT
ENTER INPUT FORMAT FOR FIL5-3B.DAT
(/F4.0, 5X, F6.0)
TEMPERATURE     VOLUME
============     ======
   34.2         101.5
   38.8         112.1
   44.8         142.5
   51.3         152.0
   55.5         166.5
   61.3         186.5
   67.5         208.0
   72.1         226.2
   76.8         256.4
   83.5         286.9
   88.9         318.6
```

CHAPTER REVIEW

Summary

This chapter gives a detailed look at input/output. The first two sections deal with formatted input/output of integer, real, and character values together with format descriptors that control spacing. Section 5.3 describes the WRITE statement and the general form of the READ statement, both of which are used for file input/output. The last sections describe and illustrate the most commonly used file-processing features of FORTRAN.

FORTRAN SUMMARY

PRINT Statement

```
PRINT format-specifier, output-list
```

where *format-specifier* is one of the following:

1. * (an asterisk) for list-directed output
2. a character constant or a character variable (or expression or array) whose value specifies the format for the output
3. the label of a FORMAT statement

Examples:

```
    PRINT *, 'AT TIME', TIME,' VELOCITY IS ', VELOC

    PRINT 10, TIME, VELOC
10 FORMAT(1X, 'AT TIME', F6.2, ' VELOCITY IS', F6.3)

    PRINT '(A, F6.2, A, F6.3)',
  +      'AT TIME', TIME, ' VELOCITY IS', VELOC
```

Purpose:
The PRINT statement displays the values of the expressions in the output list in the format specified by the format specifier.

FORMAT Statement

```
FORMAT(list of format descriptors)
```

where each *format descriptor* has one of the following forms:

Iw or Iw.m	for integer data
Fw.d	for real data in decimal notation
Ew.d or Ew.dEe	for real data in scientific notation
Dw.d	for double-precision data
Gw.d	for F or E input/output, depending on the value of the item
A or Aw	for character data
'x . . . x' or nHx . . . x	for character strings

Lw	for logical data
Tc, TLn, or TRn	tab descriptors
nX	for horizontal spacing
/	for vertical spacing
:	for format scanning control
S, SP, or SS	sign descriptors
kP	scale factor
BN or BZ	blank interpretation

Example:

```
10 FORMAT(1X, 'AT TIME', F6.2, ' VELOCITY IS ', F6.3)
```

Purpose:
Specify input or output format.

WRITE Statement

```
WRITE (control-list) output-list
```

where *output-list* has the same syntax as in the PRINT statement; and *control-list* may include items selected from the following:

1. a unit specifier indicating the output device:

```
UNIT = unit-specifier
```

or simply

```
unit-specifier
```

2. a format specifier:

```
FMT = format-specifier
```

or simply

```
format-specifier
```

3. other items that are especially useful in file processing

Examples:

```
    WRITE (*, *) 'AT TIME ', TIME, ' VELOCITY IS', VELOC


    WRITE (*, 10), TIME, VELOC
    WRITE (6, 10), TIME, VELOC
 10 FORMAT(1X, 'AT TIME', F6.2, ' VELOCITY IS', F6.3)


    WRITE (6, '(A, F6.2, A, F6.3)')
   +      'AT TIME', TIME, ' VELOCITY IS', VELOC
```

Purpose:

The WRITE statement displays the values of the expressions in the output list on the specified output device, using the format determined by the format specifier.

Control Characters

In some systems, the first character of each line of output is used to control vertical spacing:

Control Character	Effect
blank	Normal spacing: Advance to the next line before printing
0	Double spacing: Skip one line before printing
1	Advance to top of next page before printing
+	Overprint the last line printed

READ Statement

```
READ format-specifier, input-list
```

or

```
READ (control-list) input-list
```

where *input-list* is a list of variables; and *control-list* may include items selected from the following:

1. a unit specifier (as described earlier for the WRITE statement) indicating the input device
2. a format specifier (as described earlier for the WRITE statement)
3. an IOSTAT = clause or an END = clause
4. other items that are especially useful in file processing

Example:

```
      READ *, CODE, TIME, RATE
      READ (*, *) CODE, TIME, RATE
      READ (5, *) CODE, TIME, RATE
      READ (UNIT = 5, FMT = *) CODE, TIME, RATE
      READ (UNIT = 5, FMT = '(I6, 2F6.2)') CODE, TIME, RATE
      READ (UNIT = 5, FMT = 10) CODE, TIME, RATE
   10 FORMAT(I6, 2F6.2)
```

Purpose:

The READ statement reads values for the variables in the input list from the specified input device, using the format specified by the format specifier.

IOSTAT = Clause

```
IOSTAT = integer-variable
```

Example:

```
      READ (12, *, IOSTAT = EOF) CODE, TEMP, PRESS
```

Purpose:

When used in a READ statement, this clause assigns a value to the specified integer variable, indicating the following:

A positive value:	An input error has occurred
A negative value:	End of data was encountered, but no input error occurred
Zero:	No input error nor the end of data occurred

END = Clause

```
END = statement-number
```

Example:

```
      READ (12, *, END = 20) CODE, TEMP, PRESS
```

Purpose:

When used in a READ statement, this clause causes the statement with the specified number to be executed next if the end of data is encountered.

OPEN Statement

```
OPEN (open-list)
```

where *open-list* includes (among other things):

1. a unit specifier (as described earlier for the WRITE statement) indicating the input/output device
2. a clause of the form FILE = *name-of-file-being-opened*
3. a STATUS = clause specifying whether the file is 'NEW' or 'OLD'

Examples:

```
OPEN(UNIT = 12, FILE = 'fig5-2.dat', STATUS = 'OLD')
OPEN(UNIT = 13, FILE = 'fig5-2.out', STATUS = 'NEW')
```

Purpose:
The OPEN statement assigns a unit number to a disk file, which may already exist (status is OLD) or will be created (status is NEW), and makes it accessible for input/output.

CLOSE Statement

```
CLOSE (close-list)
```

where *close-list* must include a unit specifier (and may include other items).

Examples:

```
CLOSE(UNIT = 12)
CLOSE(13)
```

Purpose:
The CLOSE statement closes the file associated with the specifed unit number.

REWIND Statement

```
REWIND unit
```

where *unit* is the unit number connected to a file.

Example:

```
REWIND 12
```

Purpose:
The REWIND statement positions the file at its beginning.

BACKSPACE Statement

```
BACKSPACE unit
```

where *unit* is the unit number connected to a file.

Example:

```
BACKSPACE 12
```

Purpose:
The BACKSPACE statement positions the file at the beginning of the preceding line.

PROGRAMMING POINTERS

Program Style and Design

1. *Label all output produced by a program.* For example,

```
       PRINT 10, RATE, TIME
   10  FORMAT(1X, 'RATE =', 8.2, ' TIME =', F8.2)
```

produces more informative output than does

```
       PRINT 10, RATE, TIME
   10  FORMAT(1X, 2F8.2)
```

2. *To ensure portability, use the first print position of each output line to indicate explicitly what printer control is desired.* In some computer systems, control characters are always in effect; in others, they are not in effect unless a specific system command or compiler option is used.

3. *Echo input values.* Input values, especially those read from a file, should be echoed; that is, they should be displayed as they are read (at least during program testing).

Potential Problems

1. *Formatted output of a numeric value produces a field filled with asterisks if the output requires more spaces than allowed by the specified field width.* For formatted output of real numbers with a descriptor of the form F$w.d$, one should always have

$$w \geq d + 3$$

for an E descriptor of the form E$w.d$, one should have

$$w \geq d + 7$$

and for an E descriptor of the form $Ew.dEe$

$$w \geq d + e + 5$$

2. *For formatted input, blanks within a numeric field may be interpreted as zeros by some systems and ignored by others.* (The BZ and BN descriptors described in Section 12.1 may be used to specify explicitly which interpretation is to be used.)

3. *For formatted input/output, characters are truncated or blanks are added, depending on whether the field width is too small or too large. For input, truncation occurs on the left, and blank padding on the right; for output, truncation occurs on the right, and blank padding on the left.* The acronyms sometimes used to remember this are

- **POT: P**adding on the left with blanks occurs for formatted **O**utput, or **T**runcation of rightmost characters occurs.
- **TIP: T**runcation of leftmost characters occurs for formatted **I**nput, or **P**adding with blanks on the right occurs.

These are analogous to that given in Potential Problem 13 in the Programming Pointers of Chapter 2 for assignment of character values:

- **APT:** For **A**ssignment (and list-directed input), both blank **P**adding and **T**runcation occur on the right.

To illustrate, suppose STRING is declared by

```
CHARACTER*10 STRING
```

If STRING = 'ABCDEFGHIJ', then the output produced by the statements

```
      PRINT 10, STRING
      PRINT 20, STRING
10    FORMAT(1X, A5)
20    FORMAT(1X, A15)
```

is

```
ABCDE
ƀƀƀƀƀABCDEFGHIJ
```

For the formatted input statement

```
READ '(A5)', STRING
```

if the value entered is

```
ABCDE
```

(which might be followed by any other characters), the value assigned to STRING is ABCDE𝖻𝖻𝖻𝖻𝖻. For the statement

```
READ '(A5)', STRING
```

entering the data

```
ABCDEFGHIJKLMNO
```

assigns the value FGHIJKLMNO to STRING.

PROGRAMMING PROBLEMS

Section 5.1

1. Write a program that reads two three-digit integers and then calculates and prints their sum and their difference. The output should be formatted to appear as follows:

```
    456              456
+ 123            - 123
- - - - -        - - - - -
    579              333
```

2. Write a program that reads two three-digit integers and then calculates and prints their product, and the quotient and the remainder that result when the first is divided by the second. The output should be formatted to appear as follows:

```
    739                    61  R  7
X   12                   - - - -
- - - - - -        12 ) 739
    8868
```

3. Write a program that reads two three-digit integers and then prints their product in the following format:

```
    749
X   381
- - - - - -
    749
  5992
2247
- - - - - -
285369
```

Execute the program with the following values: 749 and 381; −749 and 381; 749 and −381; −749 and −381; 999 and 999.

4. Suppose that a certain culture of bacteria has a constant growth rate r, so that if there are n bacteria present, the next generation will have $n + r \cdot n$ bacteria. Write a program that reads the original number of bacteria, the growth rate, and an upper limit on the number of bacteria and then prints a table with appropriate headings that shows the generation number, the increase in the number of bacteria from the previous generation, and the total number of bacteria in that generation, for the initial generation number through the first generation for which the number of bacteria exceeds the specified upper limit.

Section 5.2

5. Angles are commonly measured in degrees, minutes ('), and seconds ("). There are 360 degrees in one complete revolution, 60 minutes in 1 degree, and 60 seconds in 1 minute. Write a program that reads two angular measurements, each in the form

$$dddDmm'ss"$$

where ddd, mm, and sss are the number of degrees, minutes, and seconds, respectively, and then calculates and displays their sum. Use this program to verify each of the following:

```
74D29'13"  +  105D8'16"  =  179D37'29"

7D14'55"  +  5D24'55"  =  12D39'50"

20D31'19"  +  0D31'30"  =  21D2'49"

122D17'48"  +  237D42'12"  =  0D0'0"
```

6. Write a program that will read a student's number, his or her old GPA, and old number of course credits, followed by the course credit and grade for each of four courses. Calculate and print the current and cumulative GPAs with appropriate labels. (See Programing Problem 20 of Chapter 2 for details of the calculations.) Design the program so that it will accept data entered in the form

```
SNUMB 24179 GPA 3.25 CREDITS 19.0
- - - - - - - - - - - - - - - - - - - - - - - - - - - - - - - - - - - - -
CREDITS/GRADES 1.0 3.7 0.5 4.0 1.0 2.7 1.0 3.3
- - - - - - - - - - - - - - - - - - - - - - - - - - - - - - - - - - - - -
```

Section 5.6

7. Write a program that reads the time, temperature, pressure, and volume measurements from a data file like that described in Section 5.6; converts the time from military to ordinary time (e.g., 0900 is 9:00 A.M., 1500 is 3:00 P.M.); calculates the

average temperature, average pressure, and average volume; and displays a table like the following:

```
   TIME        TEMPERATURE        PRESSURE        VOLUME
============================================================
12:00 PM          34.2             32.2           101.5
   .               .                .               .
   .               .                .               .
   .               .                .               .
10:00 PM          88.9             33.0           318.6
============================================================
AVERAGES           ?                ?               ?
```

(with the ?s replaced by the appropriate averages).

For the following exercises, see Appendix B for a description of the files USERS.DAT, STUDENT.DAT, and INVENTOR.DAT.

8. Write a program to search the file USERS.DAT to find and display the resource limit for a specified user's identification number.

9. Write a program to read the file STUDENT.DAT and produce a report for all freshmen with GPAs below 2.0. This report should include the student's number and cumulative GPA, with appropriate headings.

10. Write a program to search the file INVENTOR.DAT to find an item with a specified stock number. If a match is found, display the unit price, the item name, and the number currently in stock; otherwise, display a message indicating that the item was not found.

11. At the end of each month, a report is produced that shows the status of each user's account in the file USERS.DAT. Write a program to accept the current date and produce a report of the following form, in which the three asterisks (***) indicate that the user has already used 90 percent or more of the resources available to him or her and xx is the current year.

```
        USER ACCOUNTS--06/30/xx

                RESOURCE    RESOURCES
    USER-ID      LIMIT        USED
    -------      -----        ----
     10101       $750        $380.81
     10102       $650        $598.84***
                   .
                   .
                   .
```

12. Write a program to read the file STUDENT.DAT and calculate
   (a) the average cumulative GPA for all male students
   (b) the average cumulative GPA for all female students

Fortran 90

Features

- Additional format descriptors have been added. For example, integer descriptors of the form Bw, $Bw.m$, Ow, $Ow.m$, Zw, and $Zw.m$ can be used to display integers in binary, octal, and hexadecimal form, respectively. An *engineering* descriptor EN is used in the same manner as the E descriptor, except that the exponent is constrained to be a multiple of 3 so that a nonzero mantissa is greater than or equal to 1 and less than 1000. The G descriptor can also be used with integer, logical, and character types, and in these cases, it follows the rules of the I, L, and A descriptors.

- A repetition indicator may be used with the slash descriptor; for example, 3/ is equivalent to /// in a format specifier.

- An ADVANCE = clause may appear in the control list of a general formatted READ or WRITE statement; ADVANCE = 'NO' causes nonadvancing input/output, whereas ADVANCE = 'YES' is the default condition and causes an advance to a new line of input or output after the input/output statement has been executed. Nonadvancing output is useful in displaying prompts for interactive input, as illustrated in the program in Figure 5.4.

- A NAMELIST feature can be used to read or display an annotated list of values. This is acccomplished by grouping the items together in a NAMELIST declaration of the form

```
NAMELIST /group-name/ variable-list
```

in the specification part of a program unit, for example,

```
NAMELIST /Point/ XCoord, YCoord
```

To read or display the variables in a namelist group, a general READ or WRITE statement is used that contains no input/ouput list and in which the format specifer is replaced by the namelist *group-name* or by a clause of the form NML = *group-name*; for example,

```
READ (*, NML = Point)
WRITE (*, NML = Point)
```

Data for namelist input has the form

$$\&group\text{-}name\ variable_1 = value_1,\ variable_2 = value_2,\ \ldots\ /$$

for example,

```
&POINT XCoord = 1.5, YCoord = 3.78 /
```

Data for namelist output has this same form; for example, the statement

```
WRITE (*, Point)
```

might produce as output

```
&POINT XCoord = 1.50000, YCoord = 3.78000 /
```

Example

The program in Figure 5.4 illustrates the use of the ADVANCE = clause. It is a modification of the programs in Figures 5.1.

Figure 5.4 Table of squares, cubes, and square roots—Fortran 90 version.

```
    PROGRAM Table_of_Values
!-------------------------------------------------------------------
! Program demonstrating the use of formatted output to print a table
! of values of N, the square and cube of N, and the square root of N
! for N = 1, 2, ..., LastNumber where the value of LastNumber is read
! during execution.  Variables used are:
!   N           : counter
!   LastNumber : last value of N
! Input:  LastNumber
! Output: Table of values of N, N**2, N**3, and square root of N
!-------------------------------------------------------------------
    INTEGER :: N, LastNumber

    WRITE (*, '(A)', ADVANCE = "NO") "Enter last number to be used: "
    READ *, LastNumber

! Print headings

    PRINT '(// 1X, A8, T11, A8, T21, A8, T31, A10 / 1X, 40("="))', &
          "Number", "Square", " Cube", "Sq. root"

! Print the table

    DO N = 1, LastNumber
       PRINT '(1X, I6, 2I10, 2X, F10.4)', &
             N, N**2, N**3, SQRT(REAL(N))
    END DO
END PROGRAM Table_of_Values
```

Figure 5.4 *(cont.)*

Sample run:

```
Enter last number to be used:  10

   Number    Square      Cube    Sq. root
========================================
      1         1          1     1.0000
      2         4          8     1.4142
      3         9         27     1.7321
      4        16         64     2.0000
      5        25        125     2.2361
      6        36        216     2.4495
      7        49        343     2.6458
      8        64        512     2.8284
      9        81        729     3.0000
     10       100       1000     3.1623
```

6

Programming with Functions

On two occasions I have been asked [by members of Parliament], 'Pray, Mr. Babbage, if you put into the machine wrong figures, will the right answers come out?' I am not able rightly to apprehend the kind of confusion of ideas that could provoke such a question.

CHARLES BABBAGE

Fudd's Law states: 'What goes in must come out.' Aside from being patently untrue, Fudd's Law neglects to mention that what comes out need not bear any resemblance to what went in.

V. OREHICK III (FICTITIOUS)

All the best work is done the way ants do things—by tiny but untiring and regular additions.

LAFCADIO HEARN

C H A P T E R   C O N T E N T S

6.1   Functions

6.2   Application: Beam Deflection

6.3   Application: Root Finding, Integration, and Differential Equations

6.4   Application: Road Construction

6.5   Functions as Arguments

      Chapter Review

      Programming Pointers

      Programming Problems

      Fortran 90

*T*he problems we have considered thus far have been simple enough that algorithms for their complete solution are quite straightforward. For a more complex problem, it may not be possible to anticipate at the outset all the steps needed to solve the problem. In this case, it is helpful to divide the problem into a number of simpler problems. Each of these subproblems is then considered individually and algorithms are designed to solve them. The complete algorithm for the original problem is then described in terms of these subalgorithms. **Subprograms** can be written to implement each of these subalgorithms, and these subprograms can be combined to give a complete program that solves the original problem. In FORTRAN these subprograms are **functions** and **subroutines** whose execution is controlled by some other program unit, either the main program or some other subprogram. In this chapter we will consider how functions are written and used in this modular style of programming. In the next chapter, subroutines will be considered.

6.1 FUNCTIONS

Library Functions

The FORTRAN language provides many **library,** or **intrinsic, functions.** These library functions include not only the numeric functions introduced in Chapter 2 but also a number of other numeric functions, as well as character and logical functions. Table 6.1 gives a complete list of the standard FORTRAN numeric library functions.

Table 6.1   Standard FORTRAN Numeric Library Functions

FORTRAN Function	Description	Type of Arguments*	Type of Value
ABS(x)	Absolute value of x	I, R, DP C	Same as argument R
ACOS(x)	Arccosine (in radians) of x	R, DP	Same as argument
AIMAG(x)	Imaginary part of x	C	R
AINT(x)	Value resulting from truncation of fractional part of x	R, DP	Same as argument
ANINT(x)	x rounded to the nearest integer INT(x + .5) if x ≥ 0 INT(x − .5) if x < 0	R, DP	Same as argument
ASIN(x)	Arcsine (in radians) of x	R, DP	Same as argument
ATAN(x)	Arctangent (in radians) of x	R, DP	Same as argument
ATAN2(x, y)	Arctangent (in radians) of x / y	R, DP	Same as argument
COS(x)	Cosine of x (in radians)	R, DP, C	Same as argument
COSH(x)	Hyperbolic cosine of x	R, DP	Same as argument
CMPLX(x)	Conversion of x to complex type (x + 0i)	I, R, DP, C	C
CMPLX(x, y)	Conversion of x, y to complex type (x + yi)	I, R, DP, C	C
CONJG(x)	Conjugate of x	C	C
DBLE(x)	Conversion of x to double-precision type	I, R	D
DIM(x, y)	x − y if x ≥ y 0 if x ≤ y	I, R, DP	Same as argument
DPROD(x, y)	Double- precision product of x and y	I, R	DP
EXP(x)	Exponential function e^x	R, DP, C	Same as argument
INT(x)	Conversion of x to integer type; sign of x or real part of x times the greatest integer ≤ ABS(x)	I, R, DP, C	I
LOG(x)	Natural logarithm of x	R, DP, C	Same as argument
LOG10(x)	Common (base 10) logarithm of x	R, DP	Same as argument
MAX(x_1, ..., x_n)	Maximum of $x_1, ..., x_n$	I, R, DP	Same as argument
MIN(x_1, ..., x_n)	Minimum of $x_1, ..., x_n$	I, R, DP	Same as argument
MOD(x,y)	x (mod y); x − INT(x /y) * y	I, R, DP	Same as argument
NINT(x)	x rounded to the nearest integer [see ANINT(x)]	R, DP	I
REAL(x)	Conversion of x to real type	I, R, DP, C	R

Table 6.1 *(cont.)*

FORTRAN Function	Description	Type of Arguments*	Type of Value
SIGN(x,y)	Transfer of sign: ABS(x) if $y \geq 0$ $-$ABS(x) if $y \leq 0$	I, R, DP	Same as argument
SIN(x)	Sine of x (in radians)	R, DP, C	Same as argument
SINH(x)	Hyperbolic sine of x	R, DP	Same as argument
SQRT(x)	Square root of x	R, DP, C	Same as argument
TAN(x)	Tangent of x (in radians)	R, DP	Same as argument
TANH(x)	Hyperbolic tangent of x	R, DP	Same as argument

*I = integer, R = real, DP = double precision, C = complex. Types of arguments in a given function reference must be the same.

As we have seen, any of these functions may be used in an expression by giving its name followed by the actual arguments, enclosed in parentheses. For example, if NUM1, NUM2, SMALL, ALPHA, BETA, and X are declared by

```
INTEGER NUM1, NUM2, SMALL
REAL ALPHA, BETA, X
```

then the statements

```
PRINT *, ABS(X)
ALPHA = ANINT(100.0 * BETA) / 100.0
SMALL = MIN(0, NUM1, NUM2)
```

display the absolute value of X, assign to ALPHA the value of BETA rounded to the nearest hundredth, and assign to SMALL the smallest of the three integers 0, NUM1, and NUM2.

Function Subprograms

In some programs it is convenient for the user to define additional functions. Such **programmer-defined functions** are possible in FORTRAN, and once defined, they are used in the same way as the library functions. The most common way to do this is to use **function subprograms** which are separate program units external to any other program unit (main program or other subprogram) that references them. Thus, once a subprogram has been prepared and saved, it may be used in any program, simply by attaching it to that program.

The syntax of a function subprogram is similar to that of a FORTRAN (main) program:

Function Subprogram

function heading
specification part
execution part

The **function heading** is a FUNCTION **statement** of the following form:

Function Heading

Form:

```
type-identifier FUNCTION name(formal-argument-list)
```

where
  `name` is the name of the function and may be any legal FORTRAN identifier;
  `formal-argument-list` is an identifier or a list (possibly empty) of
    identifiers separated by commas;
  `type-identifier` is an optional type identifier (INTEGER, REAL,
    DOUBLE PRECISION, COMPLEX, LOGICAL, CHARACTER*n).

Purpose:
Names the function and declares its arguments and the type of the value returned
by the function. If the `type-identifier` is omitted, the type of the function
value must be specified in the specification part of the function. The variables in the
`formal-argument-list` are called **formal** or **dummy arguments** and are
used to pass information to the function subprogram.

The specification part of a function subprogram has the same form as the specification part of a FORTRAN program with the additional stipulation that it must include a specification of the type of the function value if this has not been included in the function heading. Similarly, the execution part of a function subprogram has the same form as the execution part of a FORTRAN program with the additional stipulation that it must include at least one statement that assigns a value to the identifier that names the function. Normally, this is done with an assignment statement of the form

```
name = expression
```

where *expression* may be any expression involving constants, the formal arguments of the function, other variables already assigned values in this subprogram, as well as references to other functions. The last statement of the execution part must be

```
END
```

The value of the function is returned to the program unit that references the function when this END statement or a RETURN **statement** of the form

```
RETURN
```

is executed.

Example: Voltage Across a Capacitor

Suppose we wish to use the function

$$v(t) = (t + 0.1)e^{\sqrt{t}}$$

which measures the voltage across a certain capacitor, where t is a real number representing time. A function subprogram to implement this function will have one formal argument T, and so an appropriate heading is

```
REAL FUNCTION V(T)
```
result function — formal
type name argument

Since T must be of type REAL, the specification part of this function subprogram is

```
REAL T
```

The complete function subprogram is

```
** V(T) *************************************
* Accepts:  Time T                          *
* Returns:  The voltage across a certain    *
*           capacitor at time T             *
*********************************************

      REAL FUNCTION V(T)
      REAL T

      V = (T + 0.1) * EXP(SQRT(T))

      END
```

If this subprogram is attached to a program, called the **main program,** it can be referenced like any other function, provided

1. it is placed after the END statement of the main program; and
2. its type is specified in the main program.

Figure 6.1 illustrates. In this example, program CAPAC is the main program (because its heading contains the keyword PROGRAM), and the function subprogram is named V. *Note the declaration of the type of the function subprogram both in the subprogram itself and in the main program.*

Figure 6.1 Table of voltages across a capacitor—version 1.

```
      PROGRAM CAPAC
*******************************************************************
* Program to display a table of values of voltages across a capacitor. *
* A function subprogram is used to compute these values.  Identifiers  *
* used are:                                                            *
*      V               : function subprogram that computes voltages    *
*      START, FINISH : the first and last times                        *
*      STEP            : step size for times in the table              *
*      TIME            : DO loop control variable                      *
*      VOLTS           : voltage across the capacitor at time TIME     *
*                                                                      *
* Input:    START, FINISH, STEP                                        *
* Output:   VOLTS                                                      *
*******************************************************************

      REAL V, START, FINISH, STEP, TIME, VOLTS

      PRINT *, 'ENTER THE STARTING AND ENDING TIMES AND'
      PRINT *, 'THE STEP SIZE TO USE FOR TIMES IN THE TABLE:'
      READ *, START, FINISH, STEP

      PRINT 10
10    FORMAT (/ 1X, '  TIME     VOLTAGE' / 1X,' ================')
      DO 30 TIME = START, FINISH, STEP
         VOLTS = V(TIME)
         PRINT 20, TIME, VOLTS
20       FORMAT (1X, F5.2, F12.4)
30    CONTINUE

      END
```

Figure 6.1 *(cont.)*

```
** V(T) ***********************************************************
* Accepts:   Time T                                              *
* Returns:   The voltage across a certain capacitor at time T *
******************************************************************

      REAL FUNCTION V(T)
      REAL T

      V = (T + 0.1)* EXP(SQRT(T))

      END
```

Sample run:

```
ENTER THE STARTING AND ENDING TIMES AND
THE STEP SIZE TO USE FOR TIMES IN THE TABLE:
0  4  0.5

   TIME     VOLTAGE
   ================
 0.00       1.0000
 0.50       1.2169
 1.00       2.9901
 1.50       5.4453
 2.00       8.6378
 2.50      12.6373
 3.00      17.5219
 3.50      23.3772
 4.00      30.2951
```

Argument Association

The arguments in a function reference are called **actual arguments.** When a function is referenced, the values of these actual arguments become the values of the corresponding formal arguments and are used in computing the value of the function. For example, in the statement

```
VOLTS = V(2.5)
```

the actual argument 2.5 becomes the value of the formal argument T. The value of the expression

```
(2.5 + 0.1) * EXP(SQRT(2.5))
```

is then computed and assigned to VOLTS. Similarly, when the value of the real variable TIME is 4.0 and the statement

```
VOLTS = V(TIME)
```

is executed, the value 4.0 of the actual argument TIME becomes the value of the formal argument T and the value of the expression

```
(4.0 + 0.1) * EXP(SQRT(4.0))
```

is computed and assigned to VOLTS.

It is important to note that an actual argument that is a variable and the corresponding formal argument are associated with the same memory location. This means that *if the value of the formal argument is changed in the subprogram, the value of the corresponding actual argument also changes.* For example, if the function subprogram V with formal argument T contained the statement

```
T = 0.0
```

a function reference such as

```
VOLTS = V(TIME)
```

would change the value of the actual argument TIME to zero.

Another consequence of this association between actual arguments and formal arguments is that *the number and types of the actual arguments must agree with the number and types of the formal arguments.* For example, the function reference in

```
VOLTS = V(2)
```

is not allowed because the type of the actual argument (integer) does not match the type of the formal argument T (real).

Example: Function of Several Variables

In the preceding example, the function subprogram V had a single argument. Functions may, however, have any number of arguments, and they need not all be of the same type. To illustrate, suppose we wish to use the function

$$f(x, y, n) = \begin{cases} x^n + y^n & \text{if } x \geq y \\ 0 & \text{otherwise} \end{cases}$$

where x and y are real numbers and n is an integer. A function subprogram to implement this function will have three formal arguments, X, Y, and N, and so an appropriate function heading is

```
REAL FUNCTION F(X, Y, N)
```

Since X and Y must be of type REAL and N is of type INTEGER, the specification part of this function subprogram is

```
REAL X, Y
INTEGER N
```

The complete function subprogram is

```
REAL FUNCTION F(X, Y, N)

REAL X, Y
INTEGER N

IF (X .GE. Y) THEN
   F = X ** N + Y ** N
ELSE
   F = 0
END IF
END
```

If I is an integer variable and A, B, C, and D are real variables, then the function reference in the statement

```
PRINT *, F(A, B + C, I)
```

is legal, but those in the statements

```
C = F(A, 2)
D = F(A, B, C)
```

are not, because the first function reference has an incorrect number of arguments, and in the second the argument C is not the correct type.

Example: Pollution Index

In the preceding example, the argument types and the result types of the functions all were numeric. This need not be the case, however. The arguments and the function values may be of any type. To illustrate, consider again the pollution index problem described in Section 3.3 in which air quality is determined by the value of a pollution index. The air quality is judged to be safe if this index is less than some cutoff value and is considered hazardous otherwise. A function that accepts this pollution index and returns the appropriate air-quality indicator will have an integer argument, and the function values will be character strings.

```
** AIR ***********************************************
* Determines the air quality for a given pollution    *
* index.  It is 'SAFE' if the index is less than some  *
* CUTOFF value and is 'HAZARDOUS' otherwise.           *
*                                                      *
* Accepts: An integer pollution INDEX                  *
* Returns: Character string AIR describing air quality *
*                                                      *
* Note:  CUTOFF is a local parameter                   *
******************************************************


      CHARACTER*9 FUNCTION AIR(INDEX)

      INTEGER INDEX, CUTOFF
      PARAMETER (CUTOFF = 50)

      IF (INDEX .LT. CUTOFF) THEN
         AIR = 'SAFE'
      ELSE
         AIR = 'HAZARDOUS'
      END IF

      END
```

We could also specify the type and length of values of function AIR using the **assumed length specifier (*)** in the function heading:

```
CHARACTER*(*) FUNCTION AIR(INDEX)
```

The length of the function values would then be taken to be the same as the length declared for AIR in the program unit (main program or subprogram) that references AIR. The assumed length specifer may also be used in the specification part of a subprogram to declare the types of formal character arguments.

Local Identifiers—The Factorial Function

Some function subprograms like that in the preceding example require the use of constants and/or variables in addition to the formal arguments. As illustrated in function subprogram AIR, these **local identifiers** are declared in the specification part of the subprogram.

As an example of a function subprogram that uses local variables, we consider the *factorial function*. The factorial of a nonnegative integer n is denoted by $n!$ and is defined by

$$n! = \begin{cases} 1 \text{ if } n = 0 \\ 1 \times 2 \times 3 \times \cdots \times n \text{ if } n > 0 \end{cases}$$

A function subprogram to define this integer-valued function will have one integer argument N, but it will also use a local variable I as a control variable in a DO loop that computes N!. The complete function subprogram is

```
** FACTOR ********************************************************
* Function to calculate the factorial N! of N which is 1    *
* if N = 0, 1 * 2 * · · · · * N if N > 0.                    *
*                                                            *
* Accepts:  Integer N                                        *
* Returns:  The integer N!                                   *
*                                                            *
* Note:  I is a local integer variable used as a counter.  *
****************************************************************

      FUNCTION FACTOR(N)

      INTEGER FACTOR, N, I

      FACTOR = 1
      DO 10 I = 2, N
         FACTOR = FACTOR * I
10    CONTINUE
      END
```

Example: Poisson Probability Function

The program in Figure 6.3 uses the function subprogram FACTOR in calculating values of the **Poisson probability function,** which is the probability function of a random variable, such as the number of radioactive particles striking a target in a given period of time, the number of flaws in a given length of magnetic tape, or the number of failures in an electronic device during a given time period. This function is defined by

$$P(n) = \frac{\lambda^n \cdot e^{-\lambda}}{n!}$$

where

λ = the average number of occurrences of the phenomenon per time period

n = the number of occurrences in that time period

For example, if the average number of particles passing through a counter during 1 millisecond in a laboratory experiment is 3 ($\lambda = 3$), then the probability that exactly five particles enter the counter ($n = 5$) in a given millisecond will be

$$P(5) = \frac{3^5 \cdot e^{-3}}{5!} = 0.1008$$

The program in Figure 6.3 reads values for N and LAMBDA, references the function POISS, which calculates the Poisson probability, and displays this probability. The value of N! is obtained by the function POISS from the function subprogram FACTOR. This program implements the algorithm whose structure is shown in Figure 6.2. Note the use of double-lined rectangles to indicate references to subprograms.

Figure 6.2

Flowcharts for Poisson probability problem.

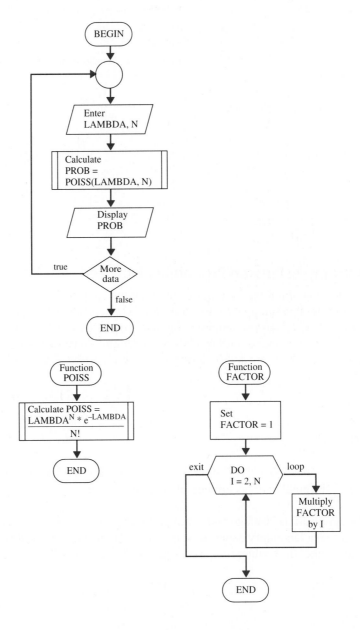

Figure 6.3 Poisson probability distribution.

```
      PROGRAM PROBAB
***********************************************************************
* Program to calculate the Poisson probability function using the      *
* function subprogram POISS. Identifiers used are:                     *
*      LAMBDA : average # of occurrences of phenomenon per time period *
*      N      : number of occurrences in a time period                 *
*      PROB   : Poisson probability                                    *
*      POISS  : function subprogram to calculate Poisson probability   *
*                                                                      *
* Input:   LAMBDA and N                                                *
* Output:  The Poisson probability PROB                                *
***********************************************************************

      REAL LAMBDA, POISS, PROB
      INTEGER N

      PRINT *, 'THIS PROGRAM CALCULATES THE POISSON PROBABILITY FOR'
      PRINT *, 'LAMBDA = AVERAGE # OF OCCURRENCES PER TIME PERIOD'
      PRINT *, 'N = # OF OCCURRENCES FOR WHICH PROBABILITY TO BE FOUND'
      PRINT *, 'ENTER LAMBDA AND N (NEGATIVE VALUES TO STOP)'
      READ *, LAMBDA, N

* While LAMBDA >= 0 do the following

10    IF (LAMBDA .GE. 0) THEN
         PROB = POISS(LAMBDA, N)
         PRINT 20, PROB
20       FORMAT (1X, 'POISSON PROBABILITY = ', F6.4 /)
         PRINT *, 'ENTER LAMBDA AND N (NEGATIVE VALUES TO STOP)'
         READ *, LAMBDA, N
      GO TO 10
      END IF

      END
```

Figure 6.3 *(cont.)*

```
**POISS*****************************************************************
* Function to calculate the Poisson probability                       *
*                           N    -LAMBDA                              *
*                   LAMBDA * e                                        *
*          POISS(N) =  - - - - - - - - - - - - - - - - -               *
*                              N!                                     *
* Function FACTOR is called to calculate N!                           *
*                                                                     *
* Accepts:  Real number LAMBDA and integer N                          *
* Returns:  The poisson probability given by the formula above        *
***********************************************************************

      FUNCTION POISS(LAMBDA, N)

      INTEGER N, FACTOR
      REAL POISS, LAMBDA

      POISS = (LAMBDA ** N * EXP(-LAMBDA)) / FACTOR(N)

      END


**FACTOR***************************************************************
* Function to calculate the factorial N! of N which is 1 if N = 0,    *
* 1 * 2 * ... * N for N > 0. It uses variable I as a counter.         *
*                                                                     *
* Accepts:  Integer N                                                 *
* Returns:  The integer N!                                            *
***********************************************************************

      FUNCTION FACTOR(N)

      INTEGER FACTOR, N, I

      FACTOR = 1
      DO 10 I = 2, N
         FACTOR = FACTOR * I
10    CONTINUE

      END
```

Figure 6.3 *(cont.)*

Sample run:

```
THIS PROGRAM CALCULATES THE POISSON PROBABILITY FOR
LAMBDA = AVERAGE # OF OCCURRENCES PER TIME PERIOD
N = # OF OCCURRENCES FOR WHICH PROBABILITY TO BE FOUND
ENTER LAMBDA AND N (NEGATIVE VALUES TO STOP)
3, 5
POISSON PROBABILITY = 0.1008

ENTER LAMBDA AND N (NEGATIVE VALUES TO STOP)
4, 6
POISSON PROBABILITY = 0.1042

ENTER LAMBDA AND N (NEGATIVE VALUES TO STOP)
-1, -1
```

The order in which subprograms are arranged following the main program is not important. Thus, in Figure 6.3, the subprogram FACTOR could just as well precede the subprogram POISS. Notice that there is no conflict between statement numbers and identifiers in different program units; for example, both the main program and the subprogram FACTOR have a statement numbered 10. Similarly, if the main program or the subprogram POISS declared and used the identifier I, used as a control variable in FACTOR, no conflict would result, because these are independent program units connected only via the function names and the arguments.

Declaring a Function's Type. As illustrated in the examples, *the type of a function must be declared both in the subprogram defining the function and in each program unit that references the function.* The declaration in the subprogram can be made in two ways. The first method is to declare the function's result type in the function heading itself as illustrated in the following examples.

```
INTEGER FUNCTION PHI(X, Y)
REAL X, Y

CHARACTER*10 FUNCTION TRUN(STRING, N)
CHARACTER*15 STRING
INTEGER N
```

In the last example, we could specify the type and length of the function TRUN and/or the formal argument STRING using the assumed length specifier (*) as follows:

```
CHARACTER*(*) FUNCTION TRUN(STRING, N)
CHARACTER*(*) STRING
INTEGER N
```

In this case, the length of TRUN is the length specified in the program unit referencing the function, and the length of STRING is the length of the corresponding actual argument.

The second method of declaring a function's type is to declare it in the specification part of the subprogram. Thus, the preceding examples could also be written as follows:

```
FUNCTION PHI(X, Y)
INTEGER PHI
REAL X, Y
      .
      .
      .
END

FUNCTION TRUN(STRING, N)
CHARACTER*15 STRING, TRUN*10
INTEGER N
      .
      .
      .
END
```

or using the assumed length specifier in the last example,

```
FUNCTION TRUN(STRING, N)
CHARACTER*(*) STRING, TRUN
INTEGER N
```

Statement Functions

In addition to function subprograms, FORTRAN also provides **statement functions**. A statement function is appropriate when the function can be defined by means of a single expression that does not change from one execution of the program to another. A statement function is defined by a single statement:

Statement Function

Form:

```
name(formal-argument-list) = expression
```

where

  name is the name of the function and may be any legal FORTRAN identifier;

  formal-argument-list is an identifier or a list (possibly empty) of identifiers separated by commas;

  expression may contain constants, variables, formulas, or references to library functions, to previously defined statement functions, or to functions defined by subprograms, but not references to the function being defined.

> **Purpose:**
> Defines the function with the specified name and arguments. The variables in the
> *formal-argument-list* are called **formal** or **dummy arguments** and are
> used to pass information to the function.
>
> *Note: Statement functions must appear in the program unit in which the functions
> are referenced, and they must be placed at the end of the specification part.*

To illustrate, a program that requires the logical *exclusive or* operation XOR might
include the following type specification statement and statement function at the end of
the specification part,

```
LOGICAL P, Q, XOR
XOR(P, Q) = (P .OR. Q) .AND. .NOT. (P. AND. Q)
```

and the function XOR can then be used in the same manner as any other function. A program that computes voltages might define the voltage function as a statement function:

```
REAL T, V
V(T) = (T + 0.1) * EXP(SQRT(T))
```

The program in Figure 6.4, which is a modification of the program in Figure 6.1, uses
this statement function to calculate voltages across a capacitor.

Figure 6.4 Table of voltages across a capacitor—version 2.

```
      PROGRAM CAPAC
**************************************************************************
* Program to display a table of values of voltages across a capacitor. *
* A statement function is used to compute these values.  Identifiers    *
* used are:                                                             *
*      V              : statement function that computes voltages       *
*      T              : argument for function V                         *
*      START, FINISH  : the first and last times                        *
*      STEP           : step size for times in the table                *
*      TIME           : DO loop control variable                        *
*      VOLTS          : voltage across the capacitor at time TIME       *
*                                                                       *
* Input:    START, FINISH, STEP                                         *
* Output:   VOLTS                                                       *
**************************************************************************
```

Figure 6.4 *(cont.)*

```
REAL T, V, START, FINISH, STEP, TIME, VOLTS
V(T) = (T + 0.1) * EXP(SQRT(T))

PRINT *, 'ENTER THE STARTING AND ENDING TIMES AND'
PRINT *, 'THE STEP SIZE TO USE FOR TIMES IN THE TABLE:'
READ *, START, FINISH, STEP

DO 10 TIME = START, FINISH, STEP
   VOLTS = V(TIME)
   PRINT *, 'AT TIME', TIME, ' VOLTAGE = ', VOLTS
10    CONTINUE

END
```

Quick Quiz 6.1

1. What are the two kinds of FORTRAN subprograms?
2. List the three parts of a function subprogram.
3. In the function heading REAL FUNCTION SUM(A, B), A and B are called _____ .
4. For a function whose heading is REAL FUNCTION SUM(A, B), the type of the values returned by the function is _____ .
5. The type of a function subprogram must be declared both in the _____ and in the _____ .
6. (True or false) Function subprograms must always be placed after the main program.
7. (True or false) Function subprograms and the main program may use the same identifiers.

Questions 8–10 deal with the following function subprogram:

```
INTEGER FUNCTION WHAT(N)

INTEGER N
WHAT = (N * (N + 1)) / 2
END
```

8. If the statement NUM1 = WHAT(NUM2) appears in the main program, NUM2 is called a(n) _____ argument in this function reference.
9. If the statement NUM = WHAT(3) appears in the main program, the value assigned to NUM will be _____ .
10. (True or false) The value assigned to NUM by the statement NUM = WHAT(1.2) in the main program will be 1.32.

11. (True or false) A statement function consists of a single statement.

12. Write a function subprogram that calculates values of $x^2 \sin x$.

13. Write a statement function that calculates values of $x^2 \sin x$.

Exercises 6.1

1. Write a function RANGE that calculates the range between two integers, that is, the result of subtracting the smaller integer from the larger one.

2. Write a real-valued function ROUND that has a real argument AMOUNT and an integer argument N and that returns the value of AMOUNT rounded to N places. For example, the function references ROUND(10.536, 0), ROUND(10.536, 1), and ROUND(10.536, 2) should give the values 11.0, 10.5, and 10.54, respectively.

3. The number of bacteria in a culture can be estimated by

$$N \cdot e^{kt}$$

where N is the initial population, k is a rate constant, and t is time. Write a function to calculate the number of bacteria present at time t for given values of k and N.

4. Write functions to define the logical functions

$$\sim p \wedge \sim q \qquad (\text{not } p \text{ and not } q)$$

and

$$\sim(p \vee q) \qquad (\text{not } (p \text{ or } q))$$

5. Write a function that has as arguments the coordinates of two points $P_1(x_1, y_1)$ and $P_2(x_2, y_2)$ and returns the distance $\sqrt{(x_2 - x_1)^2 + (y_2 - y_1)^2}$ between P_1 and P_2.

6. Write a real-valued function NGRADE that accepts a letter grade and returns the corresponding numeric value (A = 4.0, B = 3.0, C = 2.0, D = 1.0, F = 0.0).

7. Write a character-valued function LGRADE that assigns a letter grade to an integer score using the following grading scale:

90–100 :	A
80–89 :	B
70–79 :	C
60–69 :	D
Below 60 :	F

8. Write a function that calculates the sum $m + (m + 1) + \cdots + n$, for two given integers m and n.

9. Write a function `DAYSIN` that returns the number of days in a given month and year. (See Exercise 10 of Section 3.5, which describes which years are leap years.)

10. Write a logical-valued function that determines if an integer is a perfect square.

11. The *greatest common divisor* (GCD) of two integers a and b, not both of which are zero, is the largest positive integer that divides both a and b. The *Euclidean algorithm* for finding the greatest common divisor of a and b, GCD(a, b), is as follows: if $b = 0$, GCD(a, b) is a. Otherwise, divide a by b to obtain quotient q and remainder r, so that $a = bq + r$. Then GCD(a, b) = GCD(b, r). Replace a by b and b by r and repeat this procedure. Because the remainders are decreasing, a remainder of 0 will eventually result. The last nonzero remainder is then GCD(a, b). For example:

$$
\begin{aligned}
1260 &= 198 \cdot 6 + 72 & \text{GCD}(1260, 198) &= \text{GCD}(198, 72) \\
198 &= 72 \cdot 2 + 54 & &= \text{GCD}(72, 54) \\
72 &= 54 \cdot 1 + 18 & &= \text{GCD}(54, 18) \\
54 &= 18 \cdot 3 + 0 & &= 18
\end{aligned}
$$

Note: If either a or b is negative, replace it with its absolute value.

Write a function subprogram to calculate the GCD of two integers.

12. A *prime number* is an integer $n \geq 1$ whose only positive divisors are 1 and n itself. Write a logical-valued function that determines whether n is a prime number.

6.2 APPLICATION: BEAM DEFLECTION

Modular Programming

In the introduction to this chapter, we claimed that one of the advantages of subprograms is that they enable a programmer to develop programs in a **modular** fashion. This means that the major tasks to be performed by the program can be identified and individual subprograms for these tasks can then be designed and tested. Programs written in this manner are not only easier to develop and test and easier to understand, but they are also easier to modify, since individual modules can be added, deleted, or altered. In this section we illustrate this technique of modular programming by developing a *menu-driven* program for calculating beam deflections.

Problem

The analysis of beams is an important part of the structural analysis carried out before the construction of a building begins. One frequently used type of beam is a *cantilever beam*, which has one end fixed and the other end free. The deflection at the free end of the beam depends on the beam's loading conditions. Three of the many possible loading cases are shown in the following diagrams.

In these diagrams, W is the total load, δ is the deflection caused by the load, x is the distance from the free end of the beam, l is the length of the beam, a and b are the lengths as shown, and w is the unit load in the uniform loading cases.

1. end load, W

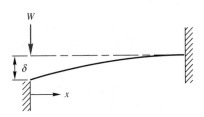

2. intermediate load, W

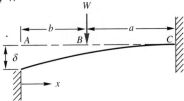

3. uniform load, $W = wl$

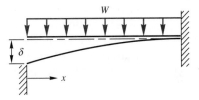

We wish to develop a program that will calculate the deflection of a cantilever beam for each of these three loading cases.

Solution

Specification. We assume that all forces are coplanar, that the beam is in static equilibrium, and that the mass of the beam may be neglected. With these assumptions, the following equations can be used to calculate the deflections for the three load cases:

1. $\delta = [-W/(6EI)][x^3 - 3l^2x + 2l^3]$
2. $\delta = [-W/(6EI)][-a^3 + 3a^2l - 3a^2x]$ from A to B
   $\delta = [-W/(6EI)][(x - b)^3 - 3a^2(x - b) + 2a^3]$ from B to C
3. $\delta = [-W/(24EIl\,)][x^4 - 4l^3x + 3l^4]$

Here E is the modulus of elasticity, which depends on the material the beam is made of, and I is the moment of inertia, which depends on the cross section of the beam. In this example we consider an I beam made of steel, where $I = 4.15 \times 10^{-8}$ and $E = 2.05 \times 10^{11}$.

We see from the description of the problem and the preceding equations that the problem's input and output include the following:

Input: Modulus of elasticity

Moment of inertia

Length of the beam

Type of loading condition

Distance from end of beam for an intermediate load

Output: Deflection of the beam

Design. The program will read the beam information, including the modulus of elasticity, the moment of inertia, and the length of the beam, and also the number of points along the beam at which the deflection is to be calculated. The user will then indicate which types of loading conditions are to be used, and the deflection at the number of equally spaced points specified by the user will be calculated. A first version of an algorithm for solving this problem thus is:

1. Read the beam information.

2. Repeat the following until user is ready to stop:
   a. Get an option from the user (0, 1, 2, or 3).
   b. If the option is not between 0 and 3
        Display an illegal option message.
       Else if option is 0
        Display a termination message.
       Else
        Output a table of deflections for a load type corresponding to the user-selected option.

Here, the else part of step 2b clearly requires refinement. We must specify the number of points at which the deflection is to be calculated. A loop is needed to range over these points, calculate the deflection at each point, using the formula appropriate for the case selected, and then display the deflection. We can now give a complete algorithm for solving this problem. We will use the following variables:

▼

VARIABLES FOR BEAM DEFLECTION PROBLEM

ELAST	Modulus of elasticity
INERT	Moment of inertia
LENG	Length of the beam
NUMPTS	Number of points at which deflections are to be found
DELTAX	Distance between points
OPTION	Option selected by the user
LOAD	Load on the beam

X	Distance from the free end of the beam
A	Distance along the beam (needed in Case 2)
I	Counts points along the beam
DEFLEC	Deflection at distance X

ALGORITHM FOR BEAM DEFLECTION PROBLEM

```
* Algorithm to calculate deflections in a cantilever beam under a given load at equally  *
* spaced points along the beam. There are three types of load conditions:                 *
*       1. single point load at the free end                                              *
*       2. single point load at an interior point                                         *
*       3. uniformly distributed load                                                     *
* Input:    ELAST, INERT, LENG, OPTION, LOAD, NUMPTS                                      *
* Output:   Table of deflections at points along the beam                                 *
```

1. Read ELAST, INERT, LENG.
2. Repeat the following until OPTION = 0:

   a. Enter OPTION.

   b. If OPTION is not between 0 and 3
       Display an illegal option message.

   Else if OPTION = 0
       Display a termination message.

   Else do the following:
      i. Enter LOAD.

     ii. If OPTION = 2, enter A.

    iii. Enter NUMPTS.

     iv. Calculate DELTAX = LENG / NUMPTS.

      v. Set X to 0.

     vi. Do the following for I ranging from 1 to NUMPTS:

         (1) Calculate DEFLEC at distance X using the appropriate formula as
             determined by OPTION.

         (2) Display X and DEFLEC.

         (3) Increment X by DELTAX.

Coding. The fact that the method of calculating the deflection is different in the three cases suggests that separate subprograms be used to do the calculations in each of the cases. Figure 6.5 shows three such function subprograms CASE1, CASE2, and CASE3. The main program is **menu-driven:** it displays a menu of options; the user selects one of these options; and the appropriate function CASE1, CASE2, or CASE3 is called to calculate the deflection.

Although the final program is given here, it could well be developed in a piecewise manner by writing and testing only some of the subprograms before writing the others. For example, we might develop and test function CASE1 before working on the other two functions. The undeveloped functions could simply have empty execution parts that consist only of the END statement. Usually, however, they are **program stubs** that at least signal execution of these subprograms; for example,

```
PRINT *, 'EXECUTING CASE2'
CASE2 = 0
END
```

In some cases they might also produce temporary printouts to assist in checking other subprograms. The example in Section 7.5 illustrates the use of such program stubs.

Figure 6.5 Beam deflection.

```
      PROGRAM BEAM
*******************************************************************
* This program calculates deflections in a cantilever beam       *
* under a given load. Three different loading conditions are     *
* analyzed:                                                      *
*    Case #1 : a single point load at the free end of the beam   *
*    Case #2 : a single point load at an interior point          *
*    Case #3 : load uniformly distributed along the beam         *
*                                                                *
* Variables used are:                                            *
*      ELAST   : modulus of elasticity                           *
*      INERT   : moment of inertia                               *
*      LENG    : length of the beam                              *
*      NUMPTS  : number of divisions at which deflections are found*
*      DELTAX  : distance between points                         *
*      OPTION  : option selected by the user                     *
*      LOAD    : load on the beam                                *
*      X       : distance from the free end of the beam          *
*      A       : distances along the beam                        *
*      I       : control variable used in DO loop                *
*      DEFLEC  : deflection at distance X                        *
*                                                                *
*      CASE1   : function to compute deflection in Case #1       *
*      CASE2   :      "    "      "        "      " Case #2       *
*      CASE3   :      "    "      "        "      " Case #3       *
*                                                                *
* Input:  ELAST, INERT, LENG, NUMPTS, OPTION, LOAD               *
* Output: A table of deflections at points along the beam        *
*******************************************************************
```

Figure 6.5 *(cont.)*

```
      INTEGER NUMPTS, OPTION
      REAL ELAST, INERT, LENG, DELTAX, DEFLEC, CASE1, CASE2, CASE3,
     +     LOAD

* Get beam information

      PRINT *, 'ENTER MODULUS OF ELASTICITY, MOMENT OF INERTIA,',
     +         ' LENGTH OF THE BEAM:'
      READ *, ELAST, INERT, LENG

* Repeat the following until user selects option 0 to stop

10    CONTINUE
          PRINT *
          PRINT *, 'SELECT ONE OF THE FOLLOWING OPTIONS:'
          PRINT *, '0 : STOP'
          PRINT *, '1 : END LOAD'
          PRINT *, '2 : INTERMEDIATE LOAD'
          PRINT *, '3 : UNIFORM LOAD'
          READ *, OPTION

          IF (OPTION .LT. 0 .OR. OPTION .GT. 3) THEN
              PRINT *, 'NOT A VALID OPTION'
          ELSE IF (OPTION .EQ. 0) THEN
              PRINT *, 'DONE PROCESSING FOR THIS BEAM'
          ELSE
              PRINT *, 'ENTER LOAD (TOTAL LOAD FOR CASES 1 AND 2, ',
     +                 'UNIT LOAD FOR CASE 3): '
              READ *, LOAD
              IF (OPTION .EQ. 2) THEN
                  PRINT *, 'ENTER THE DISTANCE A:'
                  READ *, A
              END IF
              PRINT *, 'ENTER NUMBER OF POINTS TO USE:'
              READ *, NUMPTS
              DELTAX = LENG / REAL(NUMPTS)
              PRINT *
              PRINT *, 'DISTANCE    DEFLECTION'
              PRINT *, '========================'
```

Figure 6.5 *(cont.)*

```
            X = 0.0
            DO 30 I = 1, NUMPTS
               IF (OPTION .EQ. 1) THEN
                  DEFLEC = CASE1(ELAST, INERT, LENG, LOAD, X)
               ELSE IF (OPTION .EQ. 2) THEN
                  DEFLEC = CASE2(ELAST, INERT, LENG, LOAD, A, X)
               ELSE
                  DEFLEC = CASE3(ELAST, INERT, LENG, LOAD, X)
               END IF

               PRINT 20, X, DEFLEC
20             FORMAT (1X, F5.2, E16.6)

               X = X + DELTAX

30          CONTINUE
         END IF
      IF (OPTION .NE. 0) GO TO 10

      END

** CASE1 ****************************************************
* Computes deflections for a single point load at the free end  *
* of the beam. Local variable used:                             *
*    TEMP    : temporary variable used in calculation of DEFLEC *
* Accepts: ELAST, INERT, LENG, LOAD (see main program)          *
* Returns: Deflection                                           *
* ************************************************************

      FUNCTION CASE1(ELAST, INERT, LENG, LOAD, X)

      REAL CASE1, ELAST, INERT, LENG, LOAD, TEMP

      TEMP = X**3 - 3.0 * LENG**2 * X + 2.0 * LENG**3
      CASE1 = (-LOAD / (6.0 * ELAST * INERT)) * TEMP

      END
```

Figure 6.5   *(cont.)*

```
**CASE2********************************************************
* Computes deflections for a single point load at an interior  *
* point of the beam. Local variables used:                     *
*     B     : distance along the beam                          *
*     TEMP  : temporary variable used in calculation of DEFLEC *
* Accepts: ELAST, INERT, LENG, LOAD, A, X (see main program)   *
* Returns: Deflection                                          *
***************************************************************

      FUNCTION CASE2(ELAST, INERT, LENG, LOAD, A, X)

      REAL CASE2, ELAST, INERT, LENG, LOAD, A, B, X, TEMP

      B = LENG - A
      IF (X .LT. B) THEN
         TEMP = -A**3 + 3.0 * A**2 * LENG - 3.0 * A**2 * X
      ELSE
         TEMP = (X - B)**3 - 3.0 * A**2 * (X - B) + 2.0 * A**3
      END IF
      CASE2 = (-LOAD / (6.0 * ELAST * INERT)) * TEMP

      END


**CASE3********************************************************
* Computes deflections for a load uniformly distributed along  *
* the beam.  Local variables used:                             *
*     TLOAD  : total load                                      *
*     TEMP   : temporary variable used in calculation of DEFLEC*
* Accepts: ELAST, INERT, LENG, LOAD (see main program)         *
* Returns: Deflection                                          *
***************************************************************

      FUNCTION CASE3(ELAST, INERT, LENG, LOAD, X)

      REAL CASE3, ELAST, INERT, LENG, LOAD, TLOAD, TEMP

      TLOAD = LOAD * LENG
      TEMP = X**4 - 4.0 * LENG**3 * X + 3.0 * LENG**4
      CASE3 = (-TLOAD / (24.0 * ELAST * INERT * LENG)) * TEMP

      END
```

Execution and Testing. The program was tested with several sets of test data to verify its correctness. The following sample run shows the deflection tables obtained using the modulus of elasticity and moment of inertia given in the statement of the problem.

Sample run:

```
ENTER MODULUS OF ELASTICITY, MOMENT OF INERTIA, LENGTH OF THE BEAM:
2.05E11, 4.15E-8, 1.0

SELECT ONE OF THE FOLLOWING OPTIONS:
0 : STOP
1 : END LOAD
2 : INTERMEDIATE LOAD
3 : UNIFORM LOAD
1
ENTER LOAD (TOTAL LOAD FOR CASES 1 AND 2, UNIT LOAD FOR CASE 3):
125.0
ENTER NUMBER OF POINTS TO USE:
10

DISTANCE     DEFLECTION
========================
   0.00    -0.489764E-02
   0.10    -0.416544E-02
   0.20    -0.344794E-02
   0.30    -0.275982E-02
   0.40    -0.211578E-02
   0.50    -0.153051E-02
   0.60    -0.101871E-02
   0.70    -0.595063E-03
   0.80    -0.274268E-03
   0.90    -0.710156E-04

SELECT ONE OF THE FOLLOWING OPTIONS:
0 : STOP
1 : END LOAD
2 : INTERMEDIATE LOAD
3 : UNIFORM LOAD
2
```

```
ENTER LOAD (TOTAL LOAD FOR CASES 1 AND 2, UNIT LOAD FOR CASE 3):
125.0
ENTER THE DISTANCE A:
0.5
ENTER NUMBER OF POINTS TO USE:
10

DISTANCE    DEFLECTION
========================
  0.00    -0.153051E-02
  0.10    -0.134685E-02
  0.20    -0.116319E-02
  0.30    -0.979528E-03
  0.40    -0.795866E-03
  0.50    -0.612205E-03
  0.60    -0.430992E-03
  0.70    -0.264472E-03
  0.80    -0.127339E-03
  0.90    -0.342834E-04

SELECT ONE OF THE FOLLOWING OPTIONS:
0 : STOP
1 : END LOAD
2 : INTERMEDIATE LOAD
3 : UNIFORM LOAD
3
ENTER LOAD (TOTAL LOAD FOR CASES 1 AND 2, UNIT LOAD FOR CASE 3):
125.0
ENTER NUMBER OF POINTS TO USE:
10

DISTANCE    DEFLECTION
========================
  0.00    -0.183661E-02
  0.10    -0.159179E-02
  0.20    -0.134783E-02
  0.30    -0.110693E-02
  0.40    -0.872759E-03
  0.50    -0.650468E-03
  0.60    -0.446665E-03
  0.70    -0.269431E-03
  0.80    -0.128318E-03
  0.90    -0.343446E-04
```

```
SELECT ONE OF THE FOLLOWING OPTIONS:
0 : STOP
1 : END LOAD
2 : INTERMEDIATE LOAD
3 : UNIFORM LOAD
0

DONE PROCESSING FOR THIS BEAM
```

6.3 APPLICATION: ROOT FINDING, INTEGRATION, AND DIFFERENTIAL EQUATIONS

Mathematical models are used to solve problems in a wide variety of areas including science, engineering, business, and the social sciences. Many of these models consist of ordinary algebraic equations, differential equations, systems of equations, and so on, and the solution of the problem is obtained by finding solutions of these equations. Methods for solving such equations that can be implemented in a computer program are called **numerical methods,** and the analysis and application of such numerical methods is an important area of scientific computing. In this section we consider three types of problems in which numerical methods are routinely used: root finding, integration, and solving differential equations.

Root Finding

In many applications, it is necessary to find a **zero** or **root** of a function f, that is, to solve the equation

$$f(x) = 0$$

For some functions f, it may be very difficult or even impossible to find this solution exactly. Examples include the function

$$f(v) = 50 \cdot 10^{-9}(e^{40v} - 1) + v - 20$$

which may arise in a problem of determining the DC operating point in an electrical circuit, or the function

$$f(x) = x \tan x - a$$

for which a zero must be found to solve some heat conduction problems.

For such functions, an iterative numerical method may be used to find an approximate zero. One method that is often used for differentiable functions is **Newton's method.** This method consists of taking an initial approximation x_1 to the root and constructing the tangent line to the graph of f at point $P_1(x_1, f(x_1))$. The point x_2 at which this tangent line crosses the x-axis is the second approximation to the root. Another tangent line may be constructed at point $P_2(x_2, f(x_2))$, and the point x_3 where this tangent line crosses the x-axis is the third approximation. For many functions, this sequence of approximations $x_1, x_2, x_3, \ldots$ converges to the root, provided that the first approximation is sufficiently close to the root. The following diagram illustrates Newton's method:

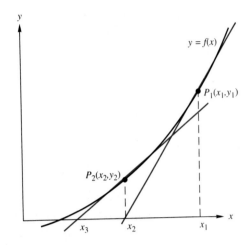

If x_n is an approximation to the zero of f, then the formula for obtaining the next approximation x_{n+1} by Newton's method is

$$x_{n+1} = x_n - \frac{f(x_n)}{f'(x_n)}$$

where f' is the derivative of f.

The following algorithm uses Newton's method to find a root of a function F. An initial approximation to a zero of F is read, and successive approximations using Newton's method are then generated and displayed as long as

$$|F(X)| \geq \text{EPSIL}$$

for some small positive number EPSIL. If the number of iterations exceeds an upper limit NUMITS (in case of divergence), execution is terminated.

ALGORITHM FOR NEWTON'S METHOD

```
* Algorithm to find an approximate root of a given function F. FPRIME is the deriva-   *
* tive of F.                                                                           *
* Input:   An error tolerance EPSIL, limit (NUMITS) on the number of iterations,       *
*          and an initial approximation XOLD to the root                               *
* Output: Iteration number N, the Nth approximation XNEW, and F(XNEW)                  *
```

1. Read EPSIL, NUMITS, and XOLD.

2. Set FVALUE equal to F(XOLD).

3. Initialize N to 0.

4. Display N, XOLD, and FVALUE.

5. While $|\text{FVALUE}| \geq \text{EPSIL}$ and $N \leq \text{NUMITS}$, do the following:

    a. Increment N by 1.

    b. Set FPOLD equal to FPRIME(XOLD).

    c   If FPOLD = 0 then do the following:

        i. Display a message that Newton's method fails.

        ii. Set N = NUMITS to force termination.

    Else do the following:

        i. Calculate

$$\text{XNEW} = \text{XOLD} - \frac{\text{FVALUE}}{\text{FPOLD}}$$

        ii. Set FVALUE equal to F(XNEW).

        iii. Display N, XNEW, and FVALUE.

        iv. Set XOLD equal to XNEW.

The program in Figure 6.6 implements this algorithm and uses it to find an approximate root of the function

$$f(x) = x^3 + x - 5$$

Function subprograms are used to define this function and its derivative:

$$f'(x) = 3x^2 + 1$$

Figure 6.6 Newton's method.

```
      PROGRAM NEWTON
*********************************************************************
*  Program to find an approximate root of a function F using Newton's  *
*  method.   Variables used are:                                    *
*      XOLD   : previous approximation (initially the first one)    *
*      FPOLD  : value of the derivative of F at XOLD                 *
*      XNEW   : the new approximation                               *
*      FVALUE : value of F at an approximation                      *
*      EPSIL  : repetition stops when ABS(FVALUE) is less than EPSIL *
*      NUMITS : limit on number of iterations                       *
*      N      : number of iterations                                *
*                                                                   *
*  Input:   EPSIL, NUMITS, and XOLD                                 *
*  Output: A sequence of approximations to the root or an error message *
*          indicating that the method fails                         *
*********************************************************************
```

Figure 6.6   *(cont.)*

```
      INTEGER NUMITS, N
      REAL XOLD, FPOLD, XNEW, EPSIL, F, FPRIME, FVALUE

* Get termination values EPSIL & NUMITS and initial approximation

      PRINT *, 'ENTER EPSILON, LIMIT ON # OF ITERATIONS, AND'
      PRINT *, 'THE INITIAL APPROXIMATION'
      READ *, EPSIL, NUMITS, XOLD

* Initialize FVALUE and N; print headings and initial values

      FVALUE = F(XOLD)
      N = 0
      PRINT *, ' N     X(N)    (F(X(N))'
      PRINT *, '========================='
      PRINT 10, 0, XOLD, FVALUE
10    FORMAT (1X, I3, F11.5, E14.5)

* Iterate using Newton's method while ABS(FVALUE) is greater
* than or equal to EPSIL and N has not reached NUMITS
* Terminate if the derivative is 0 at some approximation

20    IF ((ABS(FVALUE) .GE. EPSIL) .AND. (N .LT. NUMITS)) THEN
         N = N + 1
         FPOLD = FPRIME(XOLD)
         IF (FPOLD .EQ. 0) THEN
            PRINT *, 'NEWTON''S METHOD FAILS -- DERIVATIVE = 0'
*           Force repetition to terminate
            N = NUMITS
         ELSE
            XNEW = XOLD - (FVALUE / FPOLD)
            FVALUE = F(XNEW)
            PRINT 10, N, XNEW, FVALUE
            XOLD = XNEW
         END IF
      GO TO 20
      END IF


      END
```

Figure 6.6   *(cont.)*

```
**F(X)*************************************
*  Function for which a root is being found  *
*******************************************

      FUNCTION F(X)

      REAL X, F

      F = X**3 + X - 5
      END


**FPRIME(X)*************************
*  The derivative of the function f  *
***********************************

      FUNCTION FPRIME(X)

      REAL X, FPRIME

      FPRIME = 3*X**2 + 1
      END
```

Sample run:

```
ENTER EPSILON, LIMIT ON # OF ITERATIONS, AND
THE INITIAL APPROXIMATION
1E-4 20 1.0
   N        X(N)        (F(X(N)))
==============================
   0      1.00000     -0.30000E+01
   1      1.75000      0.21094E+01
   2      1.54294      0.21620E+00
   3      1.51639      0.32449E-03
   4      1.51598      0.95367E-07
```

Numerical Integration

Another problem in which numerical methods are often used is that of approximating the area under the graph of a nonnegative function $y = f(x)$ from $x = a$ to $x = b$, thus obtaining an approximate value for the integral

$$\int_a^b f(x)dx$$

One common method is to divide the interval $[a, b]$ into n subintervals each of length $\Delta x = (b - a)/n$ using $n - 1$ equally spaced points $x_1, x_2, \ldots, x_{n-1}$. Locating the corresponding points on the curve and connecting consecutive points using line segments forms n trapezoids:

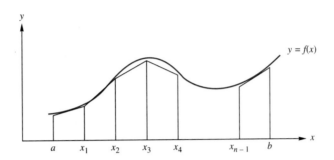

The sum of the areas of these trapezoids is approximately the area under the graph of f. The bases of the first trapezoid are $y_0 = f(a)$ and $y_1 = f(x_1)$ and thus its area is

$$\frac{1}{2}\Delta x (y_0 + y_1)$$

Similarly, the area of the second trapezoid is

$$\frac{1}{2}\Delta x (y_1 + y_2)$$

where $y_2 = f(x_2)$, and so on. The sum of the areas of the n trapezoids is

$$\frac{1}{2}\Delta x(y_0 + y_1) + \frac{1}{2}\Delta x(y_1 + y_2) + \frac{1}{2}\Delta x(y_2 + y_3) + \cdots + \frac{1}{2}\Delta x(y_{n-1} + y_n)$$

where $y_0, y_1, \ldots, y_{n-1}, y_n$ are the values of the function f at $a, x_0, \ldots, x_{n-1}, b$, respectively. Combining terms, we can write this sum more simply as

$$\Delta x\left(\frac{y_0 + y_n}{2} + y_1 + y_2 + \cdots + y_{n-1}\right)$$

or, written more concisely using Σ (sigma) notation,

$$\Delta x\left(\frac{y_0 + y_n}{2} + \sum_{i=1}^{n-1} y_i\right)$$

which is then an approximation of the area under the curve.

The following algorithm uses this **trapezoidal method** to approximate the integral of some given function F.

ALGORITHM FOR TRAPEZOIDAL APPROXIMATION OF AN INTEGRAL

* Algorithm to approximate the integral of a function F over an interval [A, B] using the   *
* trapezoidal method.   *
* Input: The endpoints A, B of the interval and the number N of subintervals to use   *
* Output: Approximate value of the integral of F from A to B   *

1. Read A, B, and N.

2. Calculate

$$\text{DELX} = \frac{B - A}{N}$$

3. Set X equal to A.

4. Set SUM equal to 0.

5. Do the following for I ranging from 1 to N $-$ 1:
   a. Add DELX to X.
   b. Calculate Y = F(X).
   c. Add Y to SUM.

6. Calculate

$$\text{SUM} = \text{DELX} \cdot \left(\frac{F(A) + F(B)}{2} + \text{SUM} \right)$$

7. Display N and SUM.

The program in Figure 6.7 implements the preceding algorithm and uses it to approximate

$$\int_0^1 (x^2 + 1)dx$$

A function subprogram is used to define the integrand

$$f(x) = x^2 + 1$$

Figure 6.7 Trapezoidal approximation of an integral—version 1.

```
      PROGRAM AREA
*****************************************************************************
* Program to approximate the integral of a function over the interval   *
* [A,B] using the trapezoidal method.  Identifiers used are:            *
*     A, B : the endpoints of the interval of integration               *
*     N    : the number of subintervals used                            *
*     I    : counter                                                    *
*     DELX : the length of the subintervals                             *
*     X    : a point of subdivision                                     *
*     Y    : the value of the function at X                             *
*     SUM  : the approximating sum                                      *
*     F    : the integrand                                              *
*                                                                       *
* Input:  A, B, and N                                                   *
* Output: Approximation to integral of F on [A, B]                      *
*****************************************************************************

      REAL F, A, B, DELX, X, Y, SUM
      INTEGER N, I

      PRINT *, 'ENTER THE INTERVAL ENDPOINTS AND THE # OF SUBINTERVALS'
      READ *, A, B, N

* Calculate subinterval length
* and initialize the approximating SUM and X

      DELX = (B - A) / REAL(N)
      X = A
      SUM = 0.0

* Now calculate and display the sum

      DO 10 I = 1, N - 1
         X = X + DELX
         Y = F(X)
         SUM = SUM + Y
10    CONTINUE
      SUM = DELX * ((F(A) + F(B)) / 2.0 + SUM)
```

Figure 6.7 *(cont.)*

```
      PRINT 20, N, SUM
20    FORMAT (1X, 'APPROXIMATE VALUE USING', I4,
     +            ' SUBINTERVALS IS', F10.5)

      END

** F(X) *********
* The integrand *
* * * * * * * * * * * * * * * *

      FUNCTION F(X)
      REAL F, X

      F = X**2 + 1

      END
```

Sample runs:

```
ENTER THE INTERVAL ENDPOINTS AND THE # OF SUBINTERVALS
0, 1, 10
APPROXIMATE VALUE USING 10 SUBINTERVALS IS    1.33500

ENTER THE INTERVAL ENDPOINTS AND THE # OF SUBINTERVALS
0, 1, 50
APPROXIMATE VALUE USING 50 SUBINTERVALS IS    1.33340

ENTER THE INTERVAL ENDPOINTS AND THE # OF SUBINTERVALS
0, 1, 100
APPROXIMATE VALUE USING 100 SUBINTERVALS IS    1.33335
```

Numerical Solutions of Differential Equations

Equations that involve derivatives or differentials are called **differential equations.** These equations arise in a large number of problems in science and engineering. It is very difficult or even impossible to solve many differential equations exactly, but it may be possible to find an approximate solution using a numerical method. There are many such methods, and in this example we describe two of the simpler ones. We will assume that we wish to find an approximate solution to a **first-order differential equation**

$$y' = f(x, y)$$

that satisfies a given **initial condition**

$$y(x_0) = y_0$$

Euler's Method. **Euler's method** for obtaining an approximation solution over some interval $[a, b]$ where $a = x_0$ is as follows:

EULER'S METHOD

1. Select an x increment Δx.
2. For $n = 0, 1, 2, \ldots$, do the following:
   - a. Set $x_{n+1} = x_n + \Delta x$.
   - b. Find the point $P_{n+1}(x_{n+1}, y_{n+1})$ on the line through $P_n(x_n, y_n)$ with slope $f(x_n, y_n)$.
   - c. Display y_{n+1}, which is the approximate value of y at x_{n+1}.

The following diagram illustrates Euler's method:

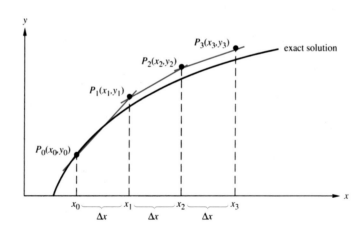

The program in Figure 6.8 uses Euler's method to obtain an approximate solution for

$$y' = 2xy$$

$$y(0) = 1$$

Sample runs with $a = 0, b = 0.5, \Delta x = 0.2$ and $a = 0, b = 0.5, \Delta x = 0.05$ are shown.

Figure 6.8 Euler's method.

```
      PROGRAM EULER
*****************************************************************************
* Program that uses Euler's method to obtain an approximate solution    *
* to a first-order differential equation of the form:                   *
*                         Y' = F(X, Y)                                   *
* Variables used are:                                                    *
*       X       : current X-value                                        *
*       XNEXT   : next X-value (X + DELTAX)                              *
*       Y       : approximate Y-value corresponding to X                 *
*       DELTAX  : X-increment used                                       *
*       NVALS   : number of iterations                                   *
*       N       : counts iterations                                      *
*                                                                        *
* Input:   Initial values for X and Y, DELTAX, and NVALS                *
* Output: A sequence of points (X, Y) that approximate the solution     *
*         curve                                                          *
*****************************************************************************

      REAL X, Y, XNEXT, DELTAX, F
      INTEGER N, NVALS

* Get given information; print table headings and initial values

      PRINT *, 'ENTER X0 AND Y0, X-INCREMENT TO USE, AND'
      PRINT *, 'THE NUMBER OF VALUES TO CALCULATE.'
      READ *, X, Y, DELTAX, NVALS
      PRINT *
      PRINT *, '       X          Y'
      PRINT *, '===================='
      PRINT 10, X, Y
10    FORMAT (1X, 2F10.5)


* Iterate with Euler's method

      DO 20 N = 1, NVALS
         XNEXT = X + DELTAX
         Y = Y + F(X,Y) * DELTAX
         X = XNEXT
         PRINT 10, X, Y
20    CONTINUE
      END
```

Figure 6.8 *(cont.)*

```
** F(X, Y) ************************************************
* The function F in differential equation Y' = F(X, Y) *
********************************************************

      FUNCTION F(X, Y)

      REAL X, Y, F

      F = 2.0 * X * Y
      END
```

Sample runs:

```
ENTER X0 AND Y0, X-INCREMENT TO USE, AND
THE NUMBER OF VALUES TO CALCULATE.
0, 1, .2, 5

        X            Y
======================
   0.00000    1.00000
   0.20000    1.00000
   0.400000   1.08000
   0.600000   1.25280
   0.800000   1.55347
   1.00000    2.05058


ENTER X0 AND Y0, X-INCREMENT TO USE, AND
THE NUMBER OF VALUES TO CALCULATE.
0, 1, .05, 10

        X            Y
======================
   0.00000    1.00000
   0.05000    1.00000
   0.10000    1.00500
   0.150000   1.01505
   0.200000   1.03028
   0.250000   1.05088
   0.300000   1.07715
   0.350000   1.10947
   0.400000   1.14830
   0.450000   1.19423
   0.500000   1.24797
```

For the differential equation and initial condition considered in the preceding example, the exact solution is

$$y = e^{x^2}$$

In this case, therefore, we can compare the approximate y-values with the exact values to see how well Euler's method does.

x	$y = e^{x^2}$
0.0	1.00000
0.1	1.01005
0.2	1.04081
0.3	1.09417
0.4	1.17351
0.5	1.28401

Comparing these values with the approximate y-values in the sample runs of Figure 6.7, we note that the accuracy of Euler's method did improve when a smaller x increment was used. However, if Euler's method is used over a larger range of x-values, the error in the y-values can grow rapidly; for example, if we had used 40 iterations in the second sample run, the approximate y-value for $x = 2$ would have been 39.0929, but the exact y-value is 54.5982.

Runge-Kutta Method. One of the most popular and most accurate numerical methods for solving a first-order differential equation is the following **Runge-Kutta method:**

RUNGE-KUTTA METHOD

1. Select an x increment Δx.

2. The approximate solution y_{n+1} at $x_{n+1} = x_0 + (n+1)\Delta x$ for $n = 0, 1, 2, \ldots$ is given by

$$y_{n+1} = y_n + \tfrac{1}{6}(K_1 + 2K_2 + 2K_3 + K_4)$$

where

$$K_1 = \Delta x \cdot f(x_n, y_n)$$
$$K_2 = \Delta x \cdot f\left(x_n + \frac{\Delta x}{2}, y_n + \frac{K_1}{2}\right)$$
$$K_3 = \Delta x \cdot f\left(x_n + \frac{\Delta x}{2}, y_n + \frac{K_2}{2}\right)$$
$$K_4 = \Delta x \cdot f(x_n + \Delta x, y_n + K_3)$$

A program implementing the Runge-Kutta method is left as an exercise.

6.4 APPLICATION: ROAD CONSTRUCTION

Problem

The Cawker City Construction Company has contracted to build a highway for the state highway commission. Several sections of this highway must pass through hills from which large amounts of dirt must be excavated to provide a flat and level roadbed. For example, one section that is 1000 feet in length must pass through a hill whose height above the roadbed has been measured at equally spaced distances and tabulated as follows:

Distance	Height
0	0
100	6
200	10
300	13
400	17
500	22
600	25
700	20
800	13
900	5
1000	0

1000 ft

75 ft

In estimating the construction costs, the company needs to know the volume of dirt that must be excavated from the hill.

Solution

Specification. The input to this problem consists of the length of the section of road to be constructed, the width of the road, and the estimates of the hill's height at equally spaced points along this section. The output is the volume of dirt that must be removed. Thus, we have the following specification for the problem:

Input: The length of a section of road
          The width of the road
          A list of heights at equally spaced points along this section

Output: The volume of dirt to be removed

Freeway construction (F3 Freeway, Oahu, HI). (Photo courtesy of Tony Stone Images.)

Design. To estimate the volume of dirt to be removed, we will assume that the height of the hill does not vary from one side of the road to the other. The volume can then be calculated as

Volume = (cross-sectional area of the hill) × (width of the road)

The cross-sectional area of the hill is given by an integral,

$$\text{Cross-sectional area of the hill} = \int_0^{1000} h(x)dx$$

where $h(x)$ is the height of the hill at a distance x along the section of road. Since the value of $h(x)$ is known at equally spaced points along the road, the trapezoidal method can be used to approximate this integral.

An algorithm for solving the problem is then straightforward.

ALGORITHM FOR HIGHWAY CONSTRUCTION PROBLEM

```
*   Algorithm to approximate the volume of dirt to be removed in constructing a section   *
*   of highway through a hill.                                                            *
```

```
*  Input:     Length and width of the road section and heights of the hill at equally  *
*             spaced points                                                            *
*  Output:    Volume of dirt to be removed                                             *
```

1. Obtain the length and width of the section of highway.

2. Use the trapezoidal method to approximate the integral for the cross-sectional area of the hill.

3. Compute the volume of dirt to be removed:

$$\text{Volume} = (\text{cross-sectional area of the hill}) \times (\text{width of the road})$$

Coding. The program in Figure 6.9 implements this algorithm. The number of equally spaced points at which height measurements have been made and the heights themselves are read from a data file. The length and width of the section of highway are entered from the keyboard. Note that the coding of the trapezoidal method from Figure 6.7 has been modified so that function values are read from a file rather than computed using a function subprogram.

Figure 6.9 Road construction.

```
      PROGRAM ROAD
************************************************************************
* Program to approximate the volume of dirt to be removed in          *
* constructing a section of highway through a hill.  Identifiers       *
* used are:                                                            *
*     LENGTH : length of the section of road                           *
*     WIDTH  : width of the road                                       *
*     FNAME  : name of data file containing hill information           *
*     NUMPTS : the number of points where height of hill was measured  *
*     DELX   : distance between points                                 *
*     I      : counter                                                 *
*     Y      : the height of the hill                                  *
*     SUM    : sum approximating the integral for cross-sectional area *
*              of the hill                                             *
*                                                                      *
* Input (keyboard): LENGTH, WIDTH                                      *
* Input (file)    : NUMPTS and values of Y (heights of hill)          *
* Output:          : Volume of dirt to be removed                      *
************************************************************************

      REAL LENGTH, WIDTH, DELX, Y, SUM
      INTEGER NUMPTS, I
      CHARACTER*20 FNAME
```

Figure 6.9 *(cont.)*

```
* Get road information and name of data file containing hill information

      PRINT *, 'ENTER LENGTH AND WIDTH OF SECTION OF ROAD (IN FEET):'
      READ *, LENGTH, WIDTH
      PRINT *, 'ENTER NAME OF FILE CONTAINING HILL INFORMATION:'
      READ '(A)', FNAME

* Open the data file, read the number of points at which height of hill
* was measured, and compute the distance between these points

      OPEN (UNIT = 10, FILE = FNAME, STATUS = 'OLD')
      READ (10, *) NUMPTS
      DELX = LENGTH / REAL(NUMPTS - )

* Initialize the approximating SUM
      READ (10, *) Y
      SUM = Y / 2.0

* Now calculate SUM, which approximates cross-sectional area of hill

      DO 10 I = 1, NUMPTS - 2
         READ (10, *) Y
         SUM = SUM + Y
10       CONTINUE

      READ (10, *) Y
      SUM = SUM + Y/2.0
      SUM = DELX * SUM

      PRINT *, 'VOLUME OF DIRT TO BE REMOVED IS APPROXIMATELY '
      PRINT *,  SUM * WIDTH, ' CUBIC FEET.'

      END
```

Execution and Testing. The program was executed with several simple data files to verify its correctness. It was then executed using a file containing the data given in the statement of the problem:

Listing of file `fil6-9.dat`

```
11
0
6
10
13
17
22
25
20
13
5
0
```

Run of program:

```
ENTER LENGTH AND WIDTH OF SECTION OF ROAD (IN FEET):
1000.0, 75.0
ENTER NAME OF FILE CONTAINING HILL INFORMATION:
fil6-9.dat
VOLUME OF DIRT TO BE REMOVED IS APPROXIMATELY
     982500. CUBIC FEET.
```

Exercises 6.4

Root Finding

1. The steady state of a certain circuit with a coil wound around an iron core is obtained by solving the equation $f(\Phi) = 0$ for the flux Φ, where

$$f(\Phi) = 20 - 2.5\Phi - 0.015\Phi^3$$

It is easy to check that the function f changes sign in the interval [6, 7]. Use Newton's method to find a solution to the equation in this interval.

2. The state of an imperfect gas is given by van der Waal's equation:

$$\left(p + \frac{\alpha}{v^2}\right)(v - \beta) = RT$$

where

p = pressure (atm)

v = molar volume (l/mole)

T = absolute temperature (°K)

R = gas constant (0.0820541 atm/mole °K)

For carbon dioxide, $\alpha = 3.592$ and $\beta = 0.04267$. Assume that $p = 0.9$ atm and $T = 300$°K. Use Newton's method to solve the equivalent cubic equation

$$pv^3 - (\beta p + RT)v^2 + \alpha v - \alpha\beta = 0$$

for v.

3. The Cawker City Construction Company can purchase a new microcomputer for $4440 or by paying $141.19 per month for the next 36 months. You are to determine what annual interest rate is being charged in the monthly payment plan.

The equation that governs this calculation is the *annuity formula*

$$A = P \cdot \left(\frac{(1 + R)^N - 1}{R(1 + R)^N} \right)$$

where A is the amount borrowed, P is the monthly payment, R is the monthly interest rate (annual rate / 12), and N is the number of payments. Use Newton's method to solve this equation for R.

4. In level flight, the total drag on the Cawker City Construction Company jet is equal to the sum of parasite drag (D_P) and the drag due to lift (D_L), which are given by

$$D_P = \frac{\sigma f V^2}{391} \quad \text{and} \quad D_L = \frac{1245}{\sigma e}\left(\frac{W}{b}\right)^2 \frac{1}{V^2}$$

where V is velocity (mph), W is weight (15,000 lb), b is the span (40 ft), e is the wing efficiency rating (0.800), f = parasite drag area (4 ft²), and σ = (air density at altitude)/(air density at sea level) = 0.533 at 20,000 ft (for standard atmosphere). Use Newton's method to find the constant velocity V needed to fly at minimum drag (level flight), which occurs when $D_P = D_L$.

5. The following figure shows a mass M attached to a slender steel rod of mass m:

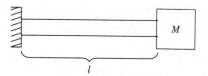

The frequency equation for the free undamped longitudinal vibration is

$$\beta \tan \beta = \frac{m}{M}$$

where

$$\beta = \frac{wl}{c}$$

Here

$$c = \sqrt{\frac{E}{\rho}}$$

l = length of the rod (115 in)

E = Young's modulus (= 3×10^7 psi)

ρ = mass per unit volume (= 7.2×10^{-4} lb $\times$ sec^2 / in^4)

Use Newton's method to find the smallest positive root of the frequency equation if $m / M = 0.40$.

6. Flexible cables have many applications in engineering, such as suspension bridges and transmission lines. Cables used as transmission lines carry their own uniformly distributed weight and assume the shape of a catenary shown in the following figure. These curves have equations of the form

$$y = a \cosh\left(\frac{x}{a}\right)$$

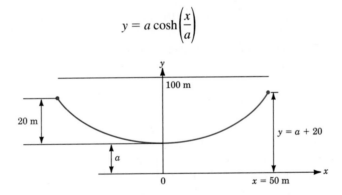

Assume that the cable has a span of 100 m and maximum deflection of 20 m and that the weight of the cable per unit length is $w = 50$ N/m. The minimum and maximum tensions occur in the middle (when $y = a$) and at the ends (when $y = a + 20$) and can be computed as

$$T_{min} = w \cdot a \text{ and } T_{max} = w \cdot (a + 20)$$

Find these extreme tension values by first using Newton's method to solve the equation

$$a + 20 = a \cosh\left(\frac{50}{a}\right)$$

to find the value of a and then substituting this value into the equations for T_{min} and T_{max}.

7. The cross section of a trough with length L is a semicircle with radius $r = 1$ m. Assume that the trough is filled with water to within a distance h from the top. The volume V of the water is given by

$$V = L\left(\frac{1}{2}\pi r^2 - r^2 \arcsin\left(\frac{h}{r}\right) - h\sqrt{r^2 - h^2}\right)$$

where the three terms represent the area of the semicircle and areas $2A_1$ and $2A_2$, respectively, as pictured in the following figure:

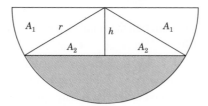

Assume that $L = 10$ m and $V = 10$ m³. Find the depth of the water (which is $r - h = 1 - h$). Note that $V(0) = \pi L / 2 \approx 15.7$, that $V(r) = 0$, and that V decreases as h increases; thus, there is a unique solution for h. Use Newton's method to find this solution.

Numerical Integration

8. The current i passing through a capacitor is given by

$$i(t) = 10 \sin^2\left(\frac{t}{\pi}\right) \quad \text{(amps)}$$

where t denotes time in seconds. Assume that the capacitance C is 5 F (farads). The voltage across the capacitor is given by

$$v(T) = \frac{1}{C}\int_0^T i(t)\,dt \quad \text{(volts)}$$

Find the value of $v(T)$ for $T = 1, 2, 3, 4$, and 5 seconds.

9. The circumference C of an ellipse with major axis $2a$ and minor axis $2b$ is given by

$$C = 4a\int_0^{\pi/2}\sqrt{1 - \left(\frac{a^2 - b^2}{a^2}\right)\sin^2\Phi}\,d\Phi$$

Assume that a room has the shape of an ellipse with $a = 20$ m, $b = 10$ m, and height $h = 5$ m. Find the total area $A = hC$ of the wall.

10. The fraction f of certain fission neutrons having energies above a certain threshold energy E^* can be determined by the formula

$$f = 1 - 0.484 \int_0^{E^*} e^{-E} \sin(h\sqrt{2E})dE$$

Find the value of f for $E^* = 0.5, 1.0, 1.5, 2.0, 2.5,$ and 3.0.

11. A particle with mass $m = 20$ kg is moving through a fluid and is subjected to a viscous resistance

$$R(v) = -v^{3/2}$$

where v is its velocity. The relation between time t, velocity v, and resistance R is given by

$$t = \int_{v_0}^{v(t)} \frac{m}{R(v)}dv \qquad \text{(seconds)}$$

where v_0 is the initial velocity. Assuming that $v_0 = 15$ m/sec, find the time T required for the particle to slow down to $v(T) = 7.5$ m/sec.

12. Suppose that a spring has been compressed a distance x_c:

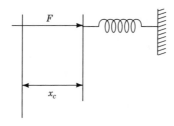

If $F(x)$ is the external force, then the absorbed energy can be expressed as

$$E = \int_0^{x_c} F(x)dx$$

Assume that

$$F(x) = \frac{1}{2} e^{x^2}\sin^2(3x^2) \qquad \text{(Newtons)}$$

and $x_c = 1$ cm. Compute the absorbed energy.

Numerical Solutions of Differential Equations

13. The linear-lag behavior of the components of control systems usually is modeled by the differential equation

$$y' + \frac{1}{\tau}y = \frac{Au(t)}{\tau}$$

where

y = time-dependent output of the component

A = gain factor

u = time-dependent input of the component

τ = time constant

Select $\tau = 1, A = 8$, and assume that $y(0) = 0$ and that the input is given by

$$u(t) = e^{t/2} \sin t$$

Use Euler's method with step size $\Delta t = 0.1$ to obtain an approximate solution to this initial-value problem for $y(t)$ in the interval $[0, 10]$.

14. Consider a spherical water tank with radius R drained through a circular orifice with radius r at the bottom of the tank:

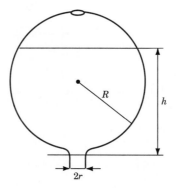

Since there is an air hole at the top of the tank, an atmospheric pressure can be found in the empty portion of the tank. In order to determine the time when the tank should be drained from any level to any other level, the water height h as a function of time should be determined. For any height, the volume of the tank is known to be

$$V = \frac{1}{3}\pi h^2(3R - h)$$

If the area of the orifice is A and the velocity of the water flowing through the orifice is V, then

$$\frac{dv}{dt} = -\pi r^2 \sqrt{2gh}$$

where $g = 115.8$ ft/min^2 is the gravitation constant. Differentiation of the equation for V leads to the following:

$$\frac{dV}{dt} = (2\pi hR - \pi h^2)\frac{dh}{dt}$$

so

$$\frac{dh}{dt} = \frac{-r^2\sqrt{2gh}}{2hR - h^2}$$

Assume that $R = 15$ ft and $r = 0.2$ ft and that the initial condition is $h(0) = 28$ ft. Use Euler's method to solve the initial-value problem for h. Select the step size $\Delta t = 1$ min, and continue the calculations until the water height becomes less than 0.2 ft.

15. A new gas well was discovered that is estimated to contain 9000 tons of natural gas at a pressure of $p_0 = 900$ psia. The distribution system is connected to the well at the discharge pressure $p^* = 400$ psia. The discharge Q in tons per day through the outlet pipe from the well is approximated by the equation

$$Q = \alpha(p^2 - p^{*2})^\beta$$

where

$\alpha = 1.115 \times 10^{-4}$

$\beta = 0.8$

p = initial pressure of gas in the well in psia

It is also assumed that the gas pressure is directly proportional to the discharge Q, which is modeled by the differential equation

$$\frac{dp}{dt} = -kQ$$

with

$$k = \frac{900 \ \text{psia}}{9000 \ \text{tons}} = 0.1 \ \frac{\text{psia}}{\text{tons}}$$

Combining the two equations leads to the initial-value problem

$$\frac{dp}{dt} = -k\alpha(p^2 - p^{*2})^\beta$$

$$p(0) = p_0$$

Use Euler's method with step size $\Delta t = 0.01$ to solve this initial-value problem. Perform 10 steps.

16. The following figure shows a circuit consisting of a coil wound around an iron core, a resistance, a switch, and a voltage source:

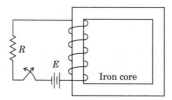

The magnetization curve is given by the equation

$$Ni = \frac{1}{2}\Phi + \frac{3}{1000}\Phi^3$$

where

N = number of turns of coil

i = current (amperes)

Φ = flux in core (kilolines)

Kirchoff's law gives the differential equation

$$E = Ri + L\frac{di}{dt} = Ri + 10^{-5}\frac{d\Phi}{dt}$$

where

L = self-inductance (henrys),

R = resistance (ohms),

t = time (sec)

Assume $N = 100$ and $R = 500$. Then

$$\frac{d\Phi}{dt} = E - 2.5\Phi - 0.015\Phi^3, \qquad \Phi(0) = 0$$

where T is now measured in milliseconds. Assume that $E = 20$ V. Use Euler's method with step size $\Delta t = 0.01$ to obtain a solution of this initial-value problem in the interval $[0, 2]$.

17. The number of individuals in a population is measured in each year. Let $P(t)$ denote the population at year t. Let α denote the birthrate, and assume that the death rate is proportional to the size of the population, that is, the death rate is $\beta = \gamma P(t)$, where γ is a constant. Hence the growth rate of the population is given by the logistic equation

$$P'(t) = \alpha P(t) - \gamma [P(t)]^2$$

Assume that $P(0) = 50,000$, $\alpha = 3 \times 10^{-2}$, and $\gamma = 1.5 \times 10^{-7}$. Use Euler's method with step size $\Delta t = 0.01$ to find the population after 5 years.

6.5 FUNCTIONS AS ARGUMENTS

In our examples of subprograms thus far, the actual arguments have been constants, variables, or expressions, but FORTRAN also permits function names (and subroutine names) as arguments for other subprograms. In this case, the name of the subprogram being used as an actual argument must be listed in an EXTERNAL or INTRINSIC statement in the program unit in which it is used as an actual argument.

The EXTERNAL Statement

The EXTERNAL **statement** has the form

EXTERNAL *Statement*

Form:

```
EXTERNAL name₁, name₂, . . .
```

where
> $name_1$, $name_2$, . . . are the names of *programmer-written* subprograms (not statement functions).

Purpose:
Specifies that programmer-written subprograms $name_1$, $name_2$, . . . may be used as arguments to other subprograms. This statement must appear in the specification part of the program unit in which $name_1$, $name_2$, . . . are being used as actual arguments.

Example: Numerical Integration. To illustrate the use of a user-defined function as an argument, consider a function subprogram DEFINT that approximates an integral

$$\int_a^b f(x)dx$$

using the trapezoidal method of Section 6.3. We wish to use this subprogram in another program to calculate the integral of the function POLY(x), defined by POLY(x) = $x^2 + 1$, for $0 \le x \le 1$. We indicate that POLY will be an argument by using an EXTERNAL statement, and we define POLY in a function subprogram (*not* as a statement function), as shown in Figure 6.10.

Figure 6.10 Trapezoidal approximation of an integral—version 2.

```
      PROGRAM AREA
* * * * * * * * * * * * * * * * * * * * * * * * * * * * * * * * * * * * * * * * * * * * * * * * * * * * * * * * *
* Program to approximate the integral of a function over the interval  *
* [A,B] using the trapezoidal method. This approximation is calculated *
* by the function subprogram DEFINT; the integrand, the interval of    *
* integration, and the # of subintervals are passed as arguments to    *
* DEFINT.   Identifiers used are:                                       *
*     A, B   : the endpoints of the interval of integration            *
*     POLY   : the integrand                                           *
*     NSUBS  : the number of subintervals used                         *
*                                                                       *
* Input:  A, B, and NSUBS                                               *
* Output: Approximation to integral of F on [A, B]                      *
* * * * * * * * * * * * * * * * * * * * * * * * * * * * * * * * * * * * * * * * * * * * * * * * * * * * * * * * *

      REAL A, B, DEFINT, POLY
      INTEGER NSUBS
      EXTERNAL POLY

      PRINT *, 'ENTER THE INTERVAL ENDPOINTS AND THE # OF SUBINTERVALS'
      READ *, A, B, NSUBS

      PRINT 10, NSUBS, DEFINT(POLY, A, B, NSUBS)
10    FORMAT (1X, 'APPROXIMATE VALUE USING', I4,
     +               ' SUBINTERVALS IS', F10.5)

      END
```

Figure 6.10 *(cont.)*

```
**  DEFINT ****************************************************************
* Function to calculate the trapezoidal approximation of the integral   *
* of the function F over the interval [A,B] using N subintervals.       *
* Local variables used are:                                             *
*      I    : counter                                                   *
*      DELX : the length of the subintervals                            *
*      X    : a point of subdivision                                    *
*      Y    : the value of the function at X                            *
* Accepts: Function F, endpoints A and B, and number N of subintervals  *
* Returns: Approximate value of integral of F over [A, B]               *
* ***********************************************************************

      FUNCTION DEFINT(F, A, B, N)

      INTEGER N, I
      REAL DELX, X, DEFINT, F, A, B

* Calculate subinterval length
* and initialize the approximating sum and X

      DELX = (B - A) / REAL(N)
      X = A
      DEFINT = 0.0

* Now calculate the approximating sum

      DO 10 I = 1, N - 1
         X = X + DELX
         Y = F(X)
         DEFINT = DEFINT + Y
10    CONTINUE
      DEFINT = DELX * ((F(A) + F(B)) / 2.0 + DEFINT)

      END


**POLY***********************************************************************
*                         The integrand                                  *
* ***********************************************************************

      FUNCTION POLY(X)

      REAL X, POLY

      POLY = X ** 2 + 1.0
      END
```

Figure 6.10 *(cont.)*

Sample run:

```
ENTER THE INTERVAL ENDPOINTS AND THE # OF SUBINTERVALS
0, 1, 10
APPROXIMATE VALUE USING 10 SUBINTERVALS IS    1.33500
```

The INTRINSIC Statement

To approximate the integral of the sine function from 0 to 0.5, we can simply change the definition of POLY to

```
POLY = SIN(X)
```

and reexecute the program. An alternative is to delete the function subprogram POLY and pass the library function SIN as an argument to DEFINT, provided that we indicate that it is to be an argument by listing it in an INTRINSIC statement, as shown in the program of Figure 6.11.

Figure 6.11 Trapezoidal approximation of an integral—version 3.

```
      PROGRAM AREA
*************************************************************
* Program to approximate the integral of a function over the interval  *
* [A,B] using the trapezoidal method. This approximation is calculated  *
* by the function subprogram DEFINT; the integrand, the interval of     *
* integration, and the # of subintervals are passed as arguments to     *
* DEFINT.  Identifiers used are:                                        *
*     A, B   : the endpoints of the interval of integration            *
*     SIN    : the integrand (library function)                        *
*     NSUBS  : the number of subintervals used                         *
*                                                                       *
* Input:  A, B, and NSUBS                                               *
* Output: Approximation to integral of F on [A, B]                      *
*************************************************************

      REAL A, B, DEFINT
      INTEGER NSUBS
      INTRINSIC SIN

      PRINT *, 'ENTER THE INTERVAL ENDPOINTS AND THE # OF SUBINTERVALS'
      READ *, A, B, NSUBS
```

Figure 6.11 *(cont.)*

```
      PRINT 10, NSUBS, DEFINT(SIN, A, B, NSUBS)
10    FORMAT (1X, 'APPROXIMATE VALUE USING', I4,
     +            ' SUBINTERVALS IS', F10.5)

      END

*************************************************************
*          Insert function DEFINT (see Figure 6.10) here   *
*************************************************************
```

Sample run:

```
ENTER THE INTERVAL ENDPOINTS AND THE # OF SUBINTERVALS
0, 0.5, 50
APPROXIMATE VALUE USING 50 SUBINTERVALS IS    0.12242
```

In our discussion of the FORTRAN intrinisic functions, we have in most cases used the *generic* names of these functions. These generic names simplify references to the functions, because the same function may be used with more than one type of argument. Intrinsic functions may, however, also be referenced by *specific* names, as indicated in the table in Appendix D. These specific names—but not the generic names—of the FORTRAN intrinsic functions may be used as arguments in a subprogram reference, provided that they have been listed in an INTRINSIC **statement.** This statement has the form

INTRINSIC *Statement*

Form:

```
   INTRINSIC name₁, name₂, . . .
```

where
   $name_1$, $name_2$, . . . are the specific (not generic) names of intrinsic library
      functions.

Purpose:
Specifies that intrinsic library functions $name_1$, $name_2$, . . . may be used as arguments in a subprogram reference. This statement must appear in the specification part of the program unit in which $name_1$, $name_2$, . . . are being used as actual arguments.

Of the functions listed in Appendix D, LGE, LGT, LLE, LLT, INT, REAL, DBLE, CMPLX, ICHAR, CHAR, MAX, and MIN may not be used as actual arguments of a subprogram.

CHAPTER REVIEW

Summary

Modular programming and top-down design are important problem-solving techniques, and most programming languages provide subprograms to support these approaches. In FORTRAN, subprograms may be functions or subroutines, and this chapter considers functions. It begins by giving a complete list of the standard FORTRAN numeric library (or predefined) functions (see Table 6.1). It then describes how programmers can design and use their own functions using function subprograms and statement functions. These techniques are illustrated with several examples. The examples in Section 6.3 demonstrate the use of functions in programs for doing numeric processing such as root finding, approximating integrals, and solving differential equations. The chapter closes with a discussion of how functions can be passed as arguments to other subprograms.

FORTRAN SUMMARY

Function Subprogram

function heading

specification part　　(same as for a program)

execution part　　(same as for a program)

Function Heading

```
type-identifier FUNCTION name(formal-argument-list)
```

where the function *name* may be any legal FORTRAN identifier, *formal-argument-list* is a list of identifiers, and *type-identifier* is optional.

Example:

```
REAL FUNCTION V(T)
```

Purpose:
Names the function and declares its arguments and the type of the value returned by the function.

Statement Function

```
name(formal-argument-list) = expression
```

Example:

```
REAL T, V
V(T) = (T + 0.1) * EXP(SQRT(T))
```

Purpose:
Defines the function with the specified name and arguments.

EXTERNAL **Statement**

```
EXTERNAL name₁, name₂, . . .
```

where $name_1$, $name_2$, ... are the names of *programmer-written* subprograms (not statement functions).

Example:

```
EXTERNAL F, FPRIME
```

Purpose:
Specifies that $name_1$, $name_2$, ... may be used as arguments to other subprograms. This statement must appear in the specification part of the program unit in which $name_1$, $name_2$, ... are being used as actual arguments.

INTRINSIC **Statement**

```
INTRINSIC name₁, name₂, . . .
```

where $name_1$, $name_2$, ... are the specific (not generic) names of intrinsic library functions.

Example:

```
INTRINSIC SIN, DEXP
```

Purpose:
Specifies that intrinsic library functions $name_1$, $name_2$, ... may be used as arguments to other subprograms. This statement must appear in the specification part of the program unit in which $name_1$, $name_2$, ... are being used as actual arguments.

PROGRAMMING POINTERS

Program Style and Design

1. *Subprograms should be documented in the same way that the main program is.* The documentation should include a brief description of the processing carried out by the subprograms, the values passed to them, the values returned by them, and what the arguments and local variables represent.

2. *Subprograms are separate program units, and the program format should reflect this fact.* In this text, we

   ▪ insert a blank comment line before and after each subprogram to set it off from other program units

   ▪ follow the stylistic standards described in earlier chapters when writing subprograms

3. *Programs for solving complex problems should be designed in a modular fashion.* The problem should be divided into simpler subproblems so that subprograms can be written to solve each of them.

Potential Problems

1. *When a function is referenced, the number of actual arguments must be the same as the number of formal arguments, and the type of each actual argument must agree with the type of the corresponding formal argument.* For example, consider the declarations

   ```
   INTEGER NUM1, NUM2, PYTHAG, K, L, M
   PYTHAG(NUM1, NUM2) = NUM1 ** 2 + NUM2 ** 2
   ```

   The function references

   ```
   PYTHAG(K, L, M)
   ```

   and

   ```
   PYTHAG(K, 3.5)
   ```

   are then incorrect. In the first case, the number of actual arguments does not agree with the number of formal arguments; in the second, the real value 3.5 cannot be associated with the integer argument NUM2.

2. *The type of a function must be declared both in the function subprogram and in the program unit that references the function.*

3. *Corresponding actual arguments and formal arguments are associated with the same memory locations. Therefore, if the value of one of the formal arguments is changed in a subprogram, the value of the corresponding actual argument also changes.* For example, if the function F is defined by the function subprogram

   ```
   FUNCTION F(X, Y)
   REAL F, X, Y

   F = X ** 2 — 2.5 * Y + 3.7 * Y ** 2
   X = 0

   END
   ```

then when the function is referenced in the main program by a statement such as

```
ALPHA = F(BETA, GAMMA)
```

where ALPHA, BETA, and GAMMA are real variables, the value of the function is assigned to ALPHA, but BETA is set equal to zero, since it corresponds to the formal argument X, whose value is changed in the subprogram. The value of a constant cannot be changed in this manner, however. For example, the function reference

```
F(2.0, GAMMA)
```

does not change the value of the constant 2.0 to zero. Values of constants and expressions that are used as actual arguments in a subprogram reference are placed in temporary memory locations, and it is the contents of these memory locations that are changed. If a variable name is enclosed in parentheses in the actual argument list, then this argument is treated as an expression, and thus the value of that variable cannot be changed by a subprogram reference. For example, the function reference

```
F((BETA), GAMMA)
```

does not change the value of BETA.

4. *User-defined functions used as actual arguments in a subprogram reference must be defined by function subprograms, not statement functions, and must be listed in an* EXTERNAL *statement in the program unit that contains that reference.*

5. *Specific names, but not generic names, of library functions may be used as actual arguments in a subprogram reference, provided that they are listed in an* INTRINSIC *statement in the program unit that contains that reference.*

PROGRAMMING PROBLEMS

Section 6.1

1. Write a program that inputs several pairs of integers, calls the function RANGE in Exercise 1 of Section 6.1 to calculate the range between each pair, and displays this range.

2. Write a program that inputs several real numbers and integers NUM, calls the function ROUND in Exercise 2 of Section 6.1 to round each real value to NUM places, and displays the rounded value.

3. Write a program that reads values for an initial population of bacteria, a rate constant, and a time (e.g., 1000, 0.15, 100), calls the function from Exercise 3 of Section 6.1 to calculate the number of bacteria at that time, and displays this value.

4. Write a program that accepts both a temperature and the letter C or F, indicating that the temperature is measured in degrees Celsius or Fahrenheit, respectively, and

then uses an appropriate function to convert the temperature to the other scale. (One of the conversion formulas is $F = (9/5)C + 32$.)

5. Write a logical-valued function that determines whether a character is one of the digits 0 through 9. Use it in a program that reads several characters and checks to see whether each is a digit.

6. Write a program that reads the coordinates of several triples of points and determines whether they can be the vertices of a triangle. (The sum of the lengths of each pair of sides must be greater than the length of the third side.) Use the function from Exercise 5 of Section 6.1 to calculate distances between points.

7. If an amount of A dollars is borrowed at an annual interest rate r (expressed as a decimal) for y years, and n is the number of payments to be made per year, then the amount of each payment is given by

$$\frac{r \cdot A/n}{1 - \left(1 + \dfrac{r}{n}\right)^{-n \cdot y}}$$

Define a statement function to calculate these payments. Use it in a program that reads several values for the amount borrowed, the interest rate, the number of years, and the number of payments per year and displays the corresponding payment for each set of values.

8. Write a program that reads several test scores and displays for each the corresponding letter grade and the numeric value of that grade. Use the functions NGRADE and LGRADE from Exercises 6 and 7 of Section 6.1.

9. Write a program that reads several pairs of integers NUM1 and NUM2 and for each pair calls the function from Exercise 8 of Section 6.1 to calculate the sum of the integers from NUM1 through NUM2 and displays this sum.

10. Write a program to calculate *binomial coefficients*

$$\binom{n}{k} = \frac{n!}{k!(n - k)!}$$

using a function subprogram to calculate factorials. Let n run from 1 through 10, and for each such n, let k run from 0 through n.

11. Suppose that in an experiment the probability that a certain outcome will occur is p; then $1 - p$ is the probability that it will not occur. The probability that in n independent trials the desired outcome will occur exactly k times is given by

$$\binom{n}{k} p^k (1 - p)^{n-k}$$

Write a program to calculate this probability for several values of n and k, using a function subprogram to calculate factorials.

12. The *power series*

$$1 + x + \frac{x^2}{2!} + \frac{x^3}{3!} + \cdots = \sum_{k=0}^{\infty} \frac{x^k}{k!}$$

converges to e^x for all values of x. Write a function subprogram that uses this series to calculate values for e^x to five-decimal-place accuracy (i.e., using terms up to the first one that is less than 10^{-5} in absolute value) and that uses a function subprogram to calculate factorials. Use these subprograms in a main program to calculate and print a table of values for the function

$$\cosh(x) = \frac{e^x + e^{-x}}{2}$$

and also the corresponding values of the library function COSH for $x = -1$ to 1 in increments of 0.1.

13. A more efficient procedure for evaluating the power series in Problem 12 is to observe that if $a_n = x^n/n!$ and $a_{n+1} = x^{n+1}/(n + 1)!$ are two consecutive terms of the series, then

$$a_{n+1} = \frac{x}{n + 1} a_n$$

Write a function subprogram to calculate e^x using the series of Problem 12 and using this relationship between consecutive terms. Then use this in a main program to print a table of values for the function

$$\sinh(x) = \frac{e^x - e^{-x}}{2}$$

and the corresponding values of the library function SINH for $x = -2$ to 2 in increments of 0.1.

14. Write a program that reads several integers and, for each, displays a message indicating whether it is a perfect square. Use the function from Exercise 10 of Section 6.1 to determine if a number is a perfect square.

15. The Euclidean algorithm for finding the greatest common divisor of two integers was described in Exercise 11 of Section 6.1. Use the function developed there in a program that calculates the GCD of any finite set of integers using the following:

$$\text{If } d = \text{GCD}(a_1, \ldots, a_n), \text{ then}$$
$$\text{GCD}(a_1, \ldots, a_n, a_{n+1}) = \text{GCD}(d, a_{n+1})$$

For example:

$$\text{GCD}(1260, 198) = 18$$

$$\text{GCD}(1260, 198, 585) = \text{GCD}(18, 585) = 9$$

$$\text{GCD}(1260, 198, 585, 138) = \text{GCD}(9, 138) = 3$$

16. Write a program that reads several integers, uses the function from Exercise 12 of Section 6.1 to determine whether each is a prime, and displays each number with the appropriate label `'IS PRIME'` or `'IS NOT PRIME'`.

17. (a) Write a function `NDAYS` that returns the number of days between two given dates. Use the function from Exercise 9 of Section 6.1 to calculate the number of days in that month, and display this number.

    (b) A person's biorhythm index on a given day is the sum of the values of his or her physical, intellectual, and emotional cycles. Each of these cycles begins at birth and forms a sine curve having an amplitude of 1 and periods of 23, 33, and 28 days, respectively. Write a program that accepts the current date, a person's name, and his or her birthdate and then calculates the biorhythm index for that person. (See Exercise 10 of Section 3.5 regarding leap years.)

Section 6.2

18. Write a menu-driven program that allows the user to convert measurements either from miles to kilometers (1 mile = 1.60935 kilometers), from feet to meters (1 foot = 0.3048 meter), or from degrees Fahrenheit to degrees Celsius ($C = (5/9)(F - 32)$). Use functions to carry out the various conversions. A sample run of the program should proceed somewhat as follows:

```
Available options are:
0. Display this menu.
1. Convert miles to kilometers.
2. Convert feet to meters.
3. Convert degrees Fahrenheit to degrees Celsius.
4. Quit.

Enter an option (0 to see menu):
3
Enter degrees Fahrenheit:
212
This is equivalent to   100.000 degrees Celsius

Enter an option (0 to see menu):
0
Available options are:
0. Display this menu.
1. Convert miles to kilometers.
2. Convert feet to meters.
3. Convert degrees Fahrenheit to degrees Celsius.
4. Quit.
```

```
Enter an option (0 to see menu):
1
Enter miles:
10
This is equivalent to      16.0935 kilometers

Enter an option (0 to see menu):
2
Enter number of feet:
1
This is equivalent to     0.3048 meters.

Enter an option (0 to see menu):
4
```

Sections 6.3 and 6.4

Root Finding

19. Another method for finding an approximate zero of a function is the *bisection method.* In this method, we begin with two numbers a and b where the function values $f(a)$ and $f(b)$ have opposite signs. If f is continuous between $x = a$ and $x = b$—that is, if there is no break in the graph of $y = f(x)$ between these two values—then the graph of f must cross the x-axis at least once between $x = a$ and $x = b$, and thus there must be at least one solution of the equation $f(x) = 0$ between a and b. To locate one of these solutions, we first bisect the interval $[a, b]$ and determine in which half f changes sign, thereby locating a smaller subinterval containing a solution of the equation. We bisect this subinterval and determine in which half f changes sign; this gives a still smaller subinterval containing a solution.

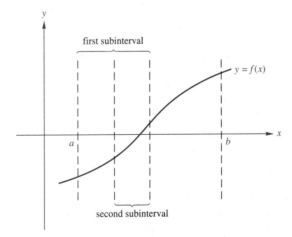

Repeating this process gives a sequence of subintervals, each of which contains a solution of the equation and has a length one-half that of the preceding interval.

Note that at each step, the midpoint of a subinterval of length L is within $L/2$ of the exact solution:

Write a program to implement the bisection method, and use it to find a solution of the equation $x^3 + x - 5 = 0$.

20. Proceed as in Exercise 1 of Section 6.4, but use the bisection method.

21. Proceed as in Exercise 2 of Section 6.4, but use the bisection method.

22. Proceed as in Exercise 3 of Section 6.4, but use the bisection method.

23. Proceed as in Exercise 4 of Section 6.4, but use the bisection method.

24. Proceed as in Exercise 5 of Section 6.4, but use the bisection method.

25. Proceed as in Exercise 6 of Section 6.4, but use the bisection method.

26. Proceed as in Exercise 7 of Section 6.4, but use the bisection method.

Numerical Integration

27. The familiar equation *work = force × distance* can be used to compute the work done by a force whose line of action is in the direction of displacement. However, if the force is applied at some angle θ to the direction of motion, the equation becomes

$$\text{work} = \text{force} \times \cos \theta \times \text{distance}$$

Write a program in which the user enters the force (newtons), the angle θ (radians), and the distance (meters) and returns the work done (joules). Run your program using a force of 9.32 N, an angle of 0.52 radians. and a path length of 30 m.

28. In Problem 27, if the angle between the force and the path of motion changes during the displacement, the work done by a force F (newtons) in moving an object from $s = a$ to $s = b$ (meters) along the line is given by

$$W = F \int_a^b \cos(\theta(s))ds \qquad \text{(joules)}$$

where $\theta(s)$ is the angle at a distance s from the initial point a. Write a program that asks the user to enter values for a, b, and F, that reads a value for n and the value of $\theta(s)$ at n equally spaced points along the path of motion from a data file, and that then uses the trapezoidal method to approximate this integral. The program should then compute and display the work done. Run your program using a force of 10.38

N, $a = 0.0$ m, $b = 30.0$ m, and the following angles at points a, $a + \Delta s$, $a + 2\Delta s$,
..., b: 0.5, 1.4, 0.75, 0.9, 1.3, 1.48, 1.5, 1.6 (all in radians).

29. Proceed as in Problem 28, but suppose that the angle θ is fixed and the force varies. In this case, the work done is given by

$$W = \cos \theta \int_a^b F(s)ds$$

where $F(s)$ is the angle at a distance s from the initial point a. Write a program that asks the user to enter values for a, b, and θ, that reads a value for n and the value of $F(s)$ at n equally spaced points along the path of motion from a data file, and that then uses the trapezoidal method to approximate this integral. The program should then compute and display the work done. Run your program using an angle of $\theta = 0.35$ radians, $a = 10.0$ m, $b = 40.0$ m, and the following forces at points a, $a + \Delta s$, $a + 2\Delta s$, ..., b: 0.0, 4.5, 9.0, 13.0, 14.0, 10.5, 12.0, 7.8, 5.0 (all in newtons).

30. Proceed as in Problems 27 and 28, but suppose that both the angle and the force vary. In this case, the work done is given by

$$W = \int_a^b F(s)\cos(\theta(s))ds$$

where $F(s)$ is the angle at a distance s from the initial point a. Write a program that asks the user to enter values for a and b, that reads a value for n and the values of $F(s)$ and $\theta(s)$ at n equally spaced points along the path of motion from a data file, and that then uses the trapezoidal method to approximate this integral. The program should then compute and display the work done. Run your program using $a = 20.0$ m, $b = 50.0$ m, and the following pairs of values for $F(s)$ and $\theta(s)$ at points a, $a + \Delta s$, $a + 2\Delta s$, ..., b (all in newtons and radians):

$F(s)$	$\theta(s)$
0.0	0.60
4.3	0.87
7.8	1.02
9.9	0.99
12.5	1.20
16.3	0.98
18.4	0.86
21.7	0.43
25.4	0.23
22.3	0.14
20.9	0.15
18.7	0.08

31. Another method of numerical integration that generally produces better approximations than the trapezoidal method is based on the use of parabolas and is known

as *Simpson's rule*. In this method, the interval $[a, b]$ is divided into an even number n of subintervals, each of length Δx, and the sum

$$\frac{\Delta x}{3}[f(x_0) + 4f(x_1) + 2f(x_2) + 4f(x_3)$$
$$+ 2f(x_4) + \cdots + 2f(x_{n-2}) + 4f(x_{n-1}) + f(x_n)]$$

is used to approximate the integral of f over the interval $[a, b]$. Write a program to approximate an integral using Simpson's rule.

32. Proceed as in Figure 6.7, but use Simpson's rule. Compare the results.

33. Proceed as in Problem 28, but use Simpson's rule.

34. Proceed as in Problem 29, but use Simpson's rule.

35. Proceed as in Problem 30, but use Simpson's rule.

36. Proceed as in Exercise 8 of Section 6.4, but use Simpson's rule with $n = 50$.

37. Proceed as in Exercise 9 of Section 6.4, but use Simpson's rule with $n = 20$.

38. Proceed as in Exercise 10 of Section 6.4, but use Simpson's rule with $n = 10, 20, 30,$ and 40. Compare the results.

39. Proceed as in Exercise 11 of Section 6.4, but use Simpson's rule with $n = 100$ and compare your result with the true answer:

$$T = \int_{7.5}^{15} 20v^{-3/2}\, dv = \frac{-40}{\sqrt{v}}\Big|_{7.5}^{15} \approx 4.27797$$

40. Proceed as in Exercise 12 of Section 6.4, but use Simpson's rule with $n = 50$.

Numerical Solutions of Differential Equations

41. Write a program to implement the Runge-Kutta method for solving differential equations. Run the program using the differential equation given in the description of Euler's method:

$$y' = 2xy$$
$$y(0) = 1$$

42. Suppose that an object at a certain temperature T_0 is dropped into a liquid at a lower temperature T_s. If the amount of liquid is quite large and is stirred, we can assume that the object's heat will spread quickly enough through the liquid so that the temperature of the liquid will not change appreciably. We can then assume that the object loses heat at a rate proportional to the difference between its temperature and the temperature of the liquid. Thus, the differential equation that models this problem is

$$T' = k(T - T_s)$$

where $T(t)$ is the temperature of the object at time t, k is the constant of proportionality, and

$$T(0) = T_0$$

is the initial condition. The exact solution of this differential equation can be shown to be

$$T = T_s + (T_0 - T_s)e^{-kt}$$

Write a program that uses the Runge-Kutta method to obtain an approximate solution. Run the program with $T_s = 70$, $T_0 = 300$, and $k = .19$ for $t = 0$ to $t = 20$ with various t increments. Print a table of approximate T-values, exact T-values, and the differences between them.

43. Proceed as in Exercise 13 of Section 6.4, but use the Runge-Kutta formula.

44. Proceed as in Exercise 14 of Section 6.4, but use the Runge-Kutta method.

45. Proceed as in Exercise 15 of Section 6.4, but use the Runge-Kutta method.

46. Proceed as in Exercise 16 of Section 6.4, but use the Runge-Kutta method.

47. Proceed as in Exercise 17 of Section 6.4, but use the Runge-Kutta method.

Section 6.5

48. Design a subprogram whose arguments are a function f and the endpoints of an interval known to contain a zero of the function and that uses the bisection method described in Problem 19 to find an approximation to this zero. Use this subprogram in a program to find a zero of the function $f(x) = x - \cos x$ in the interval $[0, \pi/2]$.

49. Proceed as in Exercise 48, but use Newton's method (see Section 6.3) instead of the bisection method. Both the function and its derivative should be passed as arguments to the root-finding subprogram.

Fortran 90

Features

Fortran 90 has added a number of new features that facilitate modular programming, including the following:

- A number of new intrinsic functions have been added. Among the predefined numeric functions are

  CEILING: CEILING(X) is the least integer greater than or equal to the real value X

  FLOOR: FLOOR(X) is the greatest integer less than or equal to the real value X

- Subprograms may be specified to be recursive by attaching the word RECURSIVE as a prefix to the subprogram heading. For a recursive function, a RESULT clause must also be attached to the function heading to specify that an identifier other than the function name will be used for the function result. To illustrate, the following recursive function can be used to calculate N factorial $= 1 \times 2 \times \cdots \times N$, usually denoted by $N!$:

```
RECURSIVE FUNCTION Factorial(N) RESULT (Fact)

    INTEGER Fact, N

    IF (N<2) THEN
       Fact = 1
    ELSE
       Fact = N * Factorial(N - 1)
    END IF
END
```

The program in Figure 6.13 uses a recursive function Number_Of_Paths to count the number of paths from one point to another in a network of streets.

- Program units may contain internal procedures. These have the same forms as function subprograms except that they may not contain other internal procedures. A CONTAINS statement in a program unit signals that internal procedure definitions follow. These must be placed at the end of the execution part of that program unit. Internal procedures may be referenced in the same manner as (external) subprograms, but only within the program unit that contains them.

- Explicit interfaces with a subprogram may be provided by means of an interface block of the form

```
INTERFACE
   interface-body
END INTERFACE
```

where *interface-body* is a copy of the heading and specification part of the subprogram followed by an END statement. The function INTEGRAL of Figure 6.12 illustrates the use of an interface block.

- Any formal argument of a subprogram may be declared to be optional by including an OPTIONAL attribute in the type statement that specifies the type of that argument; for example,

```
FUNCTION Fun(First, Second, Third, Fourth)

    INTEGER, OPTIONAL :: Second, Fourth
    INTEGER :: Fun, First, Third
```

This function can then be referenced in a statement of the form

```
Number = Fun(A, B, C, D)
```

or

```
Number = Fun(A, B, C)
```

if the fourth argument is not needed. If, however, we wish to use actual arguments corresponding to First, Third, and Fourth, we must use keyword forms for the actual argument corresponding to Third and Fourth:

```
Number = Fun(A, Third = C, Fourth = D)
```

and we can, in fact, use keyword forms for all the arguments, and these can be in any order; for example,

```
Number = Fun(First = A, Fourth = D, Third = C)
```

If optional or keyword arguments are used, then an explicit interface to the subprogram must also be provided by means of an interface block.

- An interface block of the form

```
INTERFACE OPERATOR (operator)
   interface-block for function₁
   interface-block for function₂
         .
         .
         .
END INTERFACE
```

may be used to define or overload the specified *operator*, which must be an intrinsic operator (+, −, *, /, <, .LT.,...) or a period followed by one of more letters followed by another period (e.g., .IN. and .NEGATIVE.). The specified functions implement the operation being defined. For binary operations they must have two arguments, whereas unary operations require one argument. For example, suppose that Exclusive_OR is an external function subprogram and that the specification part of some other program unit contains the interface block

```
INTERFACE OPERATOR (.XOR.)
   FUNCTION Exclusive_OR(P, Q)
     LOGICAL Exclusive_OR, P, Q
   END FUNCTION Exclusive_OR
END INTERFACE
```

If, A, B, and C are logical variables in this program unit, the statement

```
C = A .XOR. B
```

is equivalent to the statement

```
C = Exclusive_OR(A, B)
```

If two or more functions are used to implement the operator, their formal argument lists must be sufficiently dissimilar that an application of *operator* to actual operands determines exactly one of the functions for execution.

- An interface block of the form

```
INTERFACE generic-name
    interface-block for subprogram₁
    interface-block for subprogram₂
            ⋮
END INTERFACE
```

may be used to define a subprogram name *generic-name* that may be used to reference any of *subprogram₁*, *subprogram₂*, ... (all functions or all subroutines). The formal argument lists of these subprograms must be sufficiently dissimilar in number and/or type that a reference to *generic-name* with a list of actual arguments determines exactly one of *subprogram₁*, *subprogram₂*, ... for execution.

- A third kind of program unit, a *module*, is provided for packaging definitions and declarations of parameters, variables, types, and subprograms so that they can be used by other program units.

Examples

Figure 6.12 Trapezoidal approximation of an integral—Fortran 90 version.

```
    PROGRAM Definite_Integral
!-------------------------------------------------------------------
! Program to approximate the integral of a function over the interval
! [A,B] using the trapezoidal method.  This approximation is calculated
! by the function subprogram Integral; the integrand, the interval of
! integration, and the # of subintervals are passed as arguments to
! Integral.  Identifiers used are:
!   A, B      : endpoints of interval of integration
!   Integral  : approximates integral of F on [A, B]
!   Integrand : the integrand
!   Number_of_subintervals : # of subintervals into which [A, B] is cut
!
! Input:  A, B, and Number_of_subintervals
! Output: Approximation to integral of F on [A, B]
!-------------------------------------------------------------------

  IMPLICIT NONE
  REAL :: A. B
```

Figure 6.12 *(cont.)*

```
   INTERFACE
      FUNCTION Integrand(X)
         REAL :: Integrand
         REAL, INTENT(IN) :: X
      END FUNCTION Integrand
   END INTERFACE

   INTEGER :: Number_of_subintervals

   PRINT *, "Enter the interval endpoints and the # of subintervals:"
   READ *, A, B, Number_of_subintervals

   PRINT 10, Number_of_subintervals, &
            Integral(Integrand, A, B, Number_of_subintervals)
   10 FORMAT (1X, "Trapezoidal approximate value using", I4, &
             " subintervals is", F10.5)

END PROGRAM Definite_Integral

! Integral -------------------------------------------------------------
! Function to calculate the trapezoidal approximation of the integral
! of the function F over the interval [A,B] using N subintervals.
! Local variables used are:
!     I        : counter
!     Delta_X  : the length of the subintervals
!     X        : a point of subdivision
!     Y        : the value of the function at X
! Accepts: Function F, endpoints A and B, and number N of subintervals
! Returns: Approximate value of integral of F over [A, B]
!-----------------------------------------------------------------------

REAL FUNCTION Integral(F, A, B, N)

   IMPLICIT NONE

   REAL, INTENT(IN) :: A, B
   INTEGER, INTENT(IN) :: N
   REAL :: F, Delta_X, X, Y
   INTEGER :: I
```

Figure 6.12 *(cont.)*

```
! Calculate subinterval length
! and initialize the approximating sum and X

   Delta_X = (B - A) / REAL(N)
   X = A
   Integral = 0.0

! Now calculate the approximating sum
   DO I = 1, N - 1
      X = X + Delta_X
      Y = F(X)
      Integral = Integral + Y
   END DO
   Integral = Delta_X * ((F(A) + F(B)) / 2.0 + Integral)

END FUNCTION Integral

! Integrand --------------------------------------------------------------
!                           The integrand
!-------------------------------------------------------------------------


REAL FUNCTION Integrand(X)

   REAL, INTENT(IN) :: X
   Integrand = X ** 2 + 1.

END FUNCTION Integrand
```

 Figure 6.13 Counting paths in a street network— Fortran 90 version.

```
    PROGRAM Path_Counter
!-------------------------------------------------------------------------
! Program to count "northeasterly" paths from a given starting point
! in a network of streets to a specified ending point.
!   StartRow, StartColumn : coordinates of starting point
!   EndRow, EndColumn     : coordinates of ending point
!   Number_of_Paths       : recursive function to count paths
!
! Input:  StartRow, StartColumn, EndRow, EndColumn
! Output: Number of northeast paths
!-------------------------------------------------------------------------
```

Figure 6.13 *(cont.)*

```fortran
  IMPLICIT NONE
  INTEGER :: StartRow, StartColumn, EndRow, EndColumn, Number_of_Paths

  PRINT *, "Enter the starting coordinates (row then column):"
  READ *, StartRow, StartColumn
  PRINT *, "Enter the ending coordinates (row then column):"
  READ *, EndRow, EndColumn

  PRINT *, "There are", &
          Number_of_Paths(EndRow - StartRow, &
                           EndColumn - StartColumn), " paths"

END PROGRAM Path_Counter

! Number_of_Paths--------------------------------------------------------
! A recursive function to calculate the number of northeasterly paths
! in a network of streets. Identifiers used are:
!   Number_of_Rows, Number_of_Columns : number of rows and
!                 columns from starting postion to ending position
!   Num_Paths : number of paths
!
! Accepts: Number_of_Rows, Number_of_Columns
! Returns: Num_Paths
!-----------------------------------------------------------------------

RECURSIVE FUNCTION Number_of_Paths(Number_of_Rows, Number_of_Columns) &
                  RESULT (Num_Paths)

  IMPLICIT NONE
  INTEGER :: Number_of_Rows, Number_of_Columns, Num_Paths

  IF ((Number_of_Rows == 0) .OR. (Number_of_Columns == 0)) THEN
     Num_Paths = 1
  ELSE
     Num_Paths = &
         Number_of_Paths(Number_of_Rows - 1, Number_of_Columns) &
       + Number_of_Paths(Number_of_Rows, Number_of_Columns - 1)
  END IF

END FUNCTION Number_of_Paths
```

7

Programming with Subroutines

Anyone who considers arithmetical methods of producing random digits is, of course, in a state of sin.

JOHN VON NEUMANN

Great things can be reduced to small things, and small things can be reduced to nothing.

CHINESE PROVERB

From a little distance one can perceive an order in what at the time seemed confusion.

F. SCOTT FITZGERALD

There are two ways of constructing a software design: One way is to make it so simple that there are obviously no deficiencies, and the other way is to make it so complicated that there are no obvious deficiencies. The first method is far more difficult.

C.A.R. HOARE

C H A P T E R   C O N T E N T S

7.1   Subroutine Subprograms

7.2   Application: Designing a Coin Dispenser

7.3   Random Numbers and Simulation

7.4   Application: Shielding a Nuclear Reactor

7.5   Application: Checking Academic Standing

*7.6   The COMMON Statement

Chapter Review

Programming Pointers

Programming Problems

Fortran 90

*S*ubprograms in FORTRAN can be either functions or subroutines, and in the preceding chapter we considered only function subprograms. In this chapter we consider subroutine subprograms, whose execution, like function subprograms, is controlled by some other program unit, either the main program or some other subprogram.

As we also noted in Chapter 6, complex problems are best solved by dividing them into simpler subproblems and designing subprograms to solve these subproblems. In some cases it may be necessary to divide the subproblems still further until the resulting subproblems are simple enough that algorithms for their solution can be easily designed. This **top-down** approach that uses a **divide-and-conquer** strategy is also described and illustrated in this chapter.

7.1 SUBROUTINE SUBPROGRAMS

Subroutine subprograms, like function subprograms, are program units designed to perform a particular task. They differ from function subprograms, however, in the following respects:

1. Functions are designed to return a single value to the program unit that references them. Subroutines often return more than one value, or they may return no value at all but simply perform some task such as displaying a list of instructions to the user.

2. Functions return values via function names; subroutines return values via arguments.

3. A function is referenced by using its name in an expression, whereas a subroutine is referenced by a CALL statement.

The syntax of subroutine subprograms is similar to that of function subprograms and thus to that of FORTRAN (main) programs:

Subroutine Subprogram

subroutine heading
specification part
execution part

The **subroutine heading** is a SUBROUTINE **statement** of the following form.

Subroutine Heading

Form:

        SUBROUTINE name(formal-argument-list)

where
    name is the name of the subroutine and may be any legal FORTRAN identifier;
    formal-argument-list is an identifier or a list (possibly empty) of identifiers separated by commas. If there are no formal arguments, the parentheses may be omitted.

Purpose:
Names the subroutine and declares its arguments. The variables in the formal-argument-list are called **formal** or **dummy arguments** and are used to pass information to and from the subroutine.

A subroutine is referenced by a CALL **statement** of the form:

CALL *Statement*

Form:

        CALL name(actual-argument-list)

where

    name is the name of the subroutine being called;

    actual-argument-list contains the variables, constants, or expressions that are the actual arguments. The number of actual arguments must equal the number of formal arguments, and each actual argument must agree in type with the corresponding formal argument. If there are no actual arguments, the parentheses in the subroutine reference may be omitted.

Purpose:

Calls the named subroutine. Execution of the current program unit is suspended; values of the actual arguments (if any) are passed to the corresponding formal arguments; and execution of the subroutine begins. When execution of the subroutine is completed, execution of the original program unit resumes with the statement following the CALL statement.

Example: Displaying an Angle in Degrees

As a simple illustration, suppose we wish to develop a subroutine that accepts from the main program an angular measurement in degrees, minutes, and seconds and displays it as an equivalent number of degrees. For example, the value 100° 30' 36" is to be displayed as

```
100 DEGREES, 30 MINUTES, 36 SECONDS
IS EQUIVALENT TO
100.510 DEGREES
```

This subroutine will have three formal arguments, all of type INTEGER, the first representing the number of degrees, the second the number of minutes, and the third the number of seconds. Thus, an appropriate heading for this subroutine is

```
SUBROUTINE PRNDEG(DEG, MIN, SEC)
```

where DEG, MIN, and SEC must be declared of type INTEGER in the specification part of this subroutine. The complete subroutine subprogram is

```
** PRNDEG *********************************************
* Subroutine to display a measurement of DEG degrees, *
* MIN minutes and SEC seconds as the equivalent       *
* degree measure.                                     *
* Accepts:  DEG, MIN, SEC                             *
* Output:   Values of DEG, MIN, and SEC and the       *
*           equivalent degree measure                 *
******************************************************
```

```
                    SUBROUTINE PRNDEG(DEG, MIN, SEC)

                    INTEGER DEG, MIN, SEC

                    PRINT 10, DEG, MIN, SEC,
               +                 DEG + REAL(MIN)/60.0 + REAL(SEC)/3600.0
            10      FORMAT (1X, I3, ' DEGREES', I3, ' MINUTES', I3, 'SECONDS' /
               +            1X, 'IS EQUIVALENT TO' /
               +            1X, F7.3, 'DEGREES')

                    END
```

This subprogram is referenced in the program in Figure 7.1 by the CALL statement

```
        CALL PRNDEG(DEGS, MINUTS, SECONS)
```

This statement causes the values of the actual arguments DEGS, MINUTS, and SECONS to be passed to the formal arguments DEG, MIN, and SEC, respectively, and initiates execution of the subroutine. When the end of the subroutine is reached, execution resumes with the statement following this CALL statement in the main program.

Figure 7.1   Displaying an angle in degrees.

```
      PROGRAM ANGLE1
*****************************************************************
* Program demonstrating the use of a subroutine subprogram PRNDEG to  *
* display an angle in degrees.  Variables used are:                   *
*     DEGS   : degrees in the angle measurement                       *
*     MINUTS : minutes in the angle measurement                       *
*     SECONS : seconds in the angle measurement                       *
*     RESPON : user response to more-data question                    *
*                                                                     *
* Input:  DEGS, MINUTS, SECONS, RESPON                                *
* Output: Equivalent measure in degrees (displayed by PRNDEG)         *
*****************************************************************

      INTEGER DEGS, MINUTS, SECONS
      CHARACTER*1 RESPON
```

Figure 7.1 *(cont.)*

```
* Read and convert angles until user signals no more data

10      CONTINUE
            PRINT *, 'ENTER DEGREES, MINUTES, AND SECONDS'
            READ *, DEGS, MINUTS, SECONS
            CALL PRNDEG(DEGS, MINUTS, SECONS)
            PRINT *
            PRINT *, 'MORE ANGLES (Y OR N)?'
            READ '(A)', RESPON
        IF (RESPON .EQ. 'Y') GO TO 10
        END


** PRNDEG **********************************************
* Subroutine to display a measurement of DEG degrees,  *
* MIN minutes and SEC seconds as the equivalent        *
* degree measure.                                      *
* Accepts:  DEG, MIN, SEC                              *
* Output:   Values of DEG, MIN, and SEC and the        *
*           equivalent degree measure                  *
*******************************************************

        SUBROUTINE PRNDEG(DEG, MIN, SEC)

        INTEGER DEG, MIN, SEC

        PRINT 10, DEG, MIN,SEC,
     +            DEG + REAL(MIN)/60.0 + REAL(SEC)/3600.0
10      FORMAT (1X, I3, ' DEGREES', I3, ' MINUTES', I3, 'SECONDS' /
     +          1X, 'IS EQUIVALENT TO' /
     +          1X, F7.3, ' DEGREES')

        END
```

Sample run:

```
ENTER DEGREES, MINUTES, AND SECONDS
100, 30, 36
100 DEGREES 30 MINUTES 36 SECONDS
IS EQUIVALENT TO
100.510 DEGREES

MORE ANGLES (Y OR N)?
Y
```

Figure 7.1 *(cont.)*

```
ENTER DEGREES, MINUTES, AND SECONDS
360, 0, 0
360 DEGREES  0 MINUTES  0 SECONDS
IS EQUIVALENT TO
360.000 DEGREES


MORE ANGLES (Y OR N)?
Y
ENTER DEGREES, MINUTES, AND SECONDS
1, 1, 1
  1 DEGREES  1 MINUTES  1 SECONDS
IS EQUIVALENT TO
  1.017 DEGREES


MORE ANGLES (Y OR N)?
N
```

Example: Displaying an Angle in Degrees–Minutes–Seconds Format

The specification part of subroutine PRNDEG contains only type statements that specify the types of the formal arguments. In general, however, a subroutine subprogram's specification part has the same structure as the specification part of a FORTRAN program and thus may include other declarations. For example, suppose we wish to develop a subroutine DEGPRN to accept the measure of an angle in either radians or degrees and then display it in a degrees–minutes–seconds format. This subroutine will have two formal arguments: a real argument that is the measure of the angle and a logical argument that indicates whether or not radian measure has been used. An appropriate subroutine heading is

```
SUBROUTINE DEGPRN(ANGLE, RADIAN)
```

where ANGLE will be declared to be of type REAL and RADIAN of type LOGICAL in the subroutine's specification part. If ANGLE is measured in radians, it will be necessary to find its degree equivalent by multiplying ANGLE by $180/\pi$. Thus we define a real parameter PI within the subroutine and declare a real local variable DANGLE to store this angle. The integer variables DEGS, MINUTS, and SECONS are used to store degrees, minutes, and seconds, respectively. Thus the opening documentation, heading, and specification part of this subroutine are as follows; the comments indicate what processing must be done in the body of the subroutine:

```
** DEGPRN **************************************************
* Subroutine to display an angular measurement ANGLE in   *
* either radians or degrees in a degrees-minutes-seconds  *
* format.  RADIAN is true or false according to whether   *
* ANGLE is given in radians or degrees.  Local            *
* identifiers used are:                                   *
*     PI     : the constant pi                            *
*     DANGLE : the degree equivalent of ANGLE             *
*     DEGS   : the number of degrees                      *
*     MINUTS : the number of minutes                      *
*     SECONS : the number of seconds                      *
*                                                         *
* Accepts:  ANGLE and RADIAN                              *
* Output:   Value of ANGLE in degrees-minutes-seconds     *
*           format                                        *
***********************************************************

      SUBROUTINE DEGPRN(ANGLE, RADIAN)

      REAL ANGLE, PI, DANGLE
      LOGICAL RADIAN
      INTEGER DEGS, MINUTS, SECONS
      PARAMETER (PI = 3.14159)

* First get the degree equivalent of the angle

* Now determine the number of degrees, minutes, and seconds

      END
```

The complete subroutine DEGPRN is shown in Figure 7.2. The main program reads values for ANGLE and RADIAN and then passes these values to the formal arguments having the same names in subroutine DEGPRN by means of the CALL statement

```
CALL DEGPRN(ANGLE, RADIAN)
```

Note that although in the preceding example we used different names for the actual arguments and the corresponding formal arguments, this is not necessary, as this example illustrates.

Figure 7.2 Displaying an angle in degrees–minutes–seconds format.

```
      PROGRAM ANGLE2
*******************************************************************
* Program demonstrating the use of a subroutine subprogram DEGPRN to  *
* display an angle measured in radians or degrees in degrees-minutes- *
* seconds format.  Variables used are:                                *
*     ANGLE  : angle measurement                                      *
*     RADIAN : true if radian measure, else false                     *
*     RESPON : user response to more-data question                    *
*                                                                     *
* Input:  ANGLE, RADIAN, and RESPON                                   *
* Output: Value in ANGLE in degrees-minutes-seconds format (displayed *
*         by DEGPRN)                                                  *
*******************************************************************

      REAL ANGLE
      LOGICAL RADIAN
      CHARACTER*1 RESPON

* Read and convert angles until user signals no more data

10    CONTINUE
          PRINT *, 'ENTER ANGLE AND T IF IN RADIANS, F IF NOT'
          READ *, ANGLE, RADIAN
          CALL DEGPRN(ANGLE, RADIAN)
          PRINT *
          PRINT *, 'MORE ANGLES (Y OR N)?'
          READ '(A)', RESPON
      IF (RESPON .EQ. 'Y') GO TO 10

      END
```

Figure 7.2 *(cont.)*

```
** DEGPRN ***************************************************
* Subroutine to display an angular measurement ANGLE in    *
* either radians or degrees in a degrees-minutes-seconds   *
* format.  RADIAN is true or false according to whether    *
* ANGLE is given in radians or degrees.  Local             *
* identifiers used are:                                     *
*     PI     : the constant pi                             *
*     DANGLE : the degree equivalent of ANGLE             *
*     DEGS   : the number of degrees                      *
*     MINUTS : the number of minutes                      *
*     SECONS : the number of seconds                      *
* Accepts:  ANGLE and RADIAN                               *
* Output:   Value of ANGLE in degrees-minutes-seconds      *
*           format                                         *
********************************************************

      SUBROUTINE DEGPRN(ANGLE, RADIAN)

      REAL ANGLE, PI, DANGLE
      LOGICAL RADIAN
      INTEGER DEGS, MINUTS, SECONS
      PARAMETER (PI = 3.14159)

* First get the degree equivalent of the angle

      IF (RADIAN) THEN
         PRINT 10, ANGLE, 'RADIANS'
         DANGLE = (180.0 / PI) * ANGLE
      ELSE
         PRINT 10, ANGLE, 'DEGREES'
         DANGLE = ANGLE
      END IF
10    FORMAT (1X, F10.5, 1X, A / 1X, ' IS EQUIVALENT TO')

* Now determine the number of degrees, minutes, and seconds

      DEGS = INT(DANGLE)
      DANGLE = DANGLE - REAL(DEGS)
      DEGS = MOD(DEGS, 360)
      DANGLE = 60.0 * DANGLE
      MINUTS = INT(DANGLE)
      DANGLE = DANGLE - REAL(MINUTS)
      SECONS = INT(DANGLE * 60.0)
```

Figure 7.2 *(cont.)*

```
      PRINT 20, DEGS, MINUTS, SECONS
20    FORMAT (1X, I4, ' DEGREES,', I3, ' MINUTES,', I3, ' SECONDS')

      END
```

Sample run:

```
ENTER ANGLE AND T IF IN RADIANS, F IF NOT
3.14159 T
 3.14159 RADIANS
 IS EQUIVALENT TO
 180 DEGREES,   0 MINUTES,    0 SECONDS

MORE ANGLES (Y OR N)?
Y

ENTER ANGLE AND T IF IN RADIANS, F IF NOT
555.55 F
 555.55000 DEGREES
 IS EQUIVALENT TO
 195 DEGREES, 32 MINUTES, 59 SECONDS

MORE ANGLES (Y OR N)?
Y

ENTER ANGLE AND T IF IN RADIANS, F IF NOT
1 T
    1.00000 RADIANS
 IS EQUIVALENT TO
  57 DEGREES, 17 MINUTES, 44 SECONDS

MORE ANGLES (Y OR N)?
N
```

Example of a Subroutine That Returns Values: Converting Coordinates

The subroutine subprograms in the preceding examples do not return values to the main program; they only display the information passed to them. As an illustration of a subroutine that does return values to the main program, consider the problem of converting the polar coordinates (r, θ) of a point P to rectangular coordinates (x, y). The first polar coordinate r is the distance from the origin to P, and the second polar coordinate θ is the angle from the positive x-axis to the ray joining the origin with P.

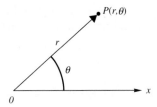

The formulas that relate the polar coordinates to the rectangular coordinates for a point are

$$x = r \cos \theta$$

$$y = r \sin \theta$$

Because the subprogram that performs this conversion must return *two* values (*x* and *y*), it is natural to use a subroutine subprogram like the following:

```
** CONVER **********************************************
* Subroutine to convert polar coordinates (R,THETA)  *
* to rectangular coordinates (X, Y).                  *
* Accepts:  Polar coordinates R and THETA             *
* Returns:  Rectangular coordinates X and Y           *
********************************************************

      SUBROUTINE CONVER(R, THETA, X, Y)

      REAL R, THETA, X, Y

      X = R * COS(THETA)
      Y = R * SIN(THETA)
      END
```

This subroutine can be referenced by the CALL statement

```
CALL CONVER(RCOORD, TCOORD, XCOORD, YCOORD)
```

where RCOORD, TCOORD, XCOORD, and YCOORD are real variables. When this CALL statement is executed, the actual arguments RCOORD, TCOORD, XCOORD, and YCO-ORD are associated with the formal arguments R, THETA, X, and Y, respectively, so that the corresponding arguments have the same values:

Actual Arguments				Formal Arguments
RCOORD	⟷	1.000000	⟷	R
TCOORD	⟷	1.570000	⟷	THETA
XCOORD	⟷	????????	⟷	X
YCOORD	⟷	????????	⟷	Y

These values are used to calculate the rectangular coordinates X and Y, and these values are then the values of the corresponding actual arguments XCOORD and YCOORD.

Actual Arguments				Formal Arguments
RCOORD	⟷	1.000000	⟷	R
TCOORD	⟷	1.570000	⟷	THETA
XCOORD	⟷	7.96274E–04	⟷	X
YCOORD	⟷	1.000000	⟷	Y

The program in Figure 7.3 reads values for RCOORD and TCOORD, calls the subroutine CONVER to calculate the corresponding rectangular coordinates, and displays these co-ordinates.

Figure 7.3 Converting polar coordinates to rectangular coordinates—version 1.

```
      PROGRAM POLAR
* * * * * * * * * * * * * * * * * * * * * * * * * * * * * * * * * * * * * * * * * * * * * * * * * * * * * * * * * * * * * *
* This program accepts the polar coordinates of a point & displays    *
* the corresponding rectangular coordinates.  The subroutine CONVER is *
* used to effect the conversion.  Variables used are:                  *
*     RCOORD, TCOORD : polar coordinates of a point                    *
*     XCOORD, YCOORD : rectangular coordinates of a point              *
*     RESPON : user response to more-data question                     *
*                                                                      *
* Input:  RCOORD, TCOORD, and RESPON                                   *
* Output: XCOORD and YCOORD                                            *
* * * * * * * * * * * * * * * * * * * * * * * * * * * * * * * * * * * * * * * * * * * * * * * * * * * * * * * * * * * * * *

      REAL RCOORD, TCOORD, XCOORD, YCOORD
      CHARACTER*1 RESPON

* Read and convert coordinates until user signals no more data
10    CONTINUE
          PRINT *, 'ENTER POLAR COORDINATES (IN RADIANS)'
          READ *, RCOORD, TCOORD
          CALL CONVER(RCOORD, TCOORD, XCOORD, YCOORD)
          PRINT *, 'RECTANGULAR COORDINATES:'
          PRINT *, XCOORD, YCOORD
          PRINT *
          PRINT *, 'MORE POINTS TO CONVERT (Y OR N)?'
          READ '(A)', RESPON
      IF (RESPON .EQ. 'Y') GO TO 10

      END
```

Figure 7.3 *(cont.)*

```
**CONVER**************************************************************
* Subroutine to convert polar coordinates (R,THETA) to rectangular   *
* coordinates (X,Y).                                                  *
* Accepts:  Polar coordinates R and THETA                            *
* Returns:  Rectangular coordinates X and Y                          *
**********************************************************************

      SUBROUTINE CONVER(R, THETA, X, Y)

      REAL R, THETA, X, Y

      X = R * COS(THETA)
      Y = R * SIN(THETA)

      END
```

Sample run:

```
ENTER POLAR COORDINATES (IN RADIANS)
1.0, 0
RECTANGULAR COORDINATES:
    1.00000  0.

MORE POINTS TO CONVERT (Y OR N)?
Y
ENTER POLAR COORDINATES (IN RADIANS)
0, 1.0
RECTANGULAR COORDINATES:
  0.  0.

MORE POINTS TO CONVERT (Y OR N)?
Y
ENTER POLAR COORDINATES (IN RADIANS)
1.0, 1.57
RECTANGULAR COORDINATES:
    7.96274E-04    1.000000

MORE POINTS TO CONVERT (Y OR N)?
Y
ENTER POLAR COORDINATES (IN RADIANS)
4.0, 3.14159
RECTANGULAR COORDINATES:
   -4.00000    1.01407E-05

MORE POINTS TO CONVERT (Y OR N)?
N
```

Argument Association

The linkage of actual arguments with formal arguments illustrated in the preceding example is accomplished by associating corresponding arguments with the same memory locations. In the preceding program, the type statement

```
REAL RCOORD, TCOORD, XCOORD, YCOORD
```

associates memory locations with the four variables RCOORD, TCOORD, XCOORD, and YCOORD.

When the READ statement is executed, values are stored in the memory locations associated with RCOORD and TCOORD; the variables XCOORD and YCOORD are undefined, as indicated by the question marks in the following diagram:

When the CALL statement

```
CALL CONVER(RCOORD, TCOORD, XCOORD, YCOORD)
```

is executed, the formal arguments R, THETA, X, and Y of subroutine CONVER are associated with the existing memory locations of the corresponding actual arguments RCOORD, TCOORD, XCOORD, and YCOORD:

The formal arguments R, THETA, X, and Y are thus *aliases* (alternative names) used in the subprogram CONVER to reference the corresponding actual arguments RCOORD, TCOORD, XCOORD, and YCOORD in the main program. When the subroutine CONVER is executed, values are calculated for X and Y, and because XCOORD and YCOORD are associated with the same memory locations as X and Y, these values are also the values of XCOORD and YCOORD:

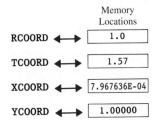

Actual Arguments	Memory Locations	Formal Arguments
RCOORD	1.0	R
TCOORD	1.57	THETA
XCOORD ⟷	7.967636E-04 ⟷	X
YCOORD ⟷	1.00000 ⟷	Y

When execution of the subroutine is completed, the association of memory locations with the formal arguments R, THETA, X, and Y is terminated, and these formal arguments become undefined. The values of the corresponding actual arguments RCOORD, TCOORD, XCOORD, and YCOORD are retained, of course, in the memory locations associated with them by the type statement when the program was compiled.

	Memory Locations
RCOORD ⟷	1.0
TCOORD ⟷	1.57
XCOORD ⟷	7.967636E-04
YCOORD ⟷	1.00000

     This method of linking together the actual and formal arguments so that information can be transmitted between them is accomplished by making available to the subprogram the *addresses* of the memory locations in which the values of the actual arguments are stored. It is thus appropriately named **call by address** (or **call by reference**). If both the actual argument and the formal argument are variables, then as we have seen, this call-by-address technique causes both of these variables to refer to the same memory location. Because *corresponding actual and formal arguments are associated with the same memory locations,* changing the value of the formal argument in the subprogram also changes the value of the corresponding actual argument.

     If the actual argument in a subroutine call is an expression, its value is placed in a temporary memory location by the processor, and the address of this location is made available to the subprogram. The values of the variables and constants that comprise the expression are not changed by any processing that takes place in the subprogram, even though the value of the formal argument corresponding to the expression may change. *Enclosing in parentheses an actual argument that is a variable protects it from being modified because it is then treated as an expression and its value is not changed by a subprogram.*

The association of arguments for function subprograms is the same as for subroutine subprograms. Ordinarily, however, we do not use arguments of a function to return values to another program unit but, rather, use the function name. Nevertheless, *it is important to remember that changing the values of formal arguments within a subprogram, whether it is a subroutine or a function, does, in fact, change the values of the corresponding actual arguments that are variables.*

Subprograms as Arguments

In Section 6.5 we showed how names of function subprograms can be used as arguments for other subprograms. Programmer-written subroutine subprograms may also be used as arguments in subprogram references. Like function subprograms, their names must be listed in an EXTERNAL statement in the program unit in which their names are used as actual arguments.

Quick Quiz 7.1

1. What are the two kinds of FORTRAN subprograms?
2. List the three parts of a subroutine subprogram.
3. In the subroutine heading PRINT(A, B), A and B are called _____ .
4. (True or false) Subroutine subprograms must always be placed after the main program.
5. (True or false) Subroutine subprograms and the main program may use the same identifiers.
6. List three differences between subroutine subprograms and function subprograms.
7. The method of linking together actual and formal arguments is termed call by _____ or call by _____.
8. An actual argument that is a variable can be protected from being modified in a subroutine by enclosing it in _____.

Questions 9–15 refer to a subroutine CALC:

```
SUBROUTINE CALC(ALPHA, NUM1, NUM2)
REAL ALPHA
INTEGER NUM1, NUM2
     :
     :
END
```

Also, assume that the following declarations have been made in the main program:

```
INTEGER CODE, IDENT
REAL RATE
```

Tell if the given statement can be used in the main program to reference CALC.

9. `Y = CALC(2.45, CODE, IDENT)`

10. `CALL CALC(RATE + 0.5, 0, CODE - IDENT)`

11. `CALL CALC(RATE, L)`

12. `GO TO CALC(4.5, 1, 2)`

13. `CALL CALC(RATE, CODE, IDENT)`

14. `CALL CALC`

15. `CALL CALC(RATE, RATE, RATE)`

16. What output would the following program produce?

```
PROGRAM QUES16

CHARACTER*3 STR1, STR2, STR3
DATA STR1, STR2, STR3 /'CAT', 'DOG', 'ELK'/

CALL CHANGE(STR1, STR2, STR3, 2)
PRINT *, 'STRING =', STR1, STR2, STR3
END


SUBROUTINE CHANGE(A, B, C, NUM)

CHARACTER*3 A, B, C, BAT
INTEGER NUM
DATA BAT /'BAT'/

IF (NUM .LT. 3) THEN
    A = BAT
    B = BAT
ELSE
    C = BAT
END IF

END
```

Exercises 7.1

1. Write a subroutine subprogram that displays the name of a month whose number (1–12) is passed to it.

2. Write a subroutine subprogram SWITCH that interchanges the values of two integer variables. For example, if A has the value 3 and B has the value 4, then the

statement CALL SWITCH(A, B) causes A to have the value 4 and B the value 3.

3. Write a subroutine subprogram that accepts a measurement in centimeters and returns the corresponding measurement in yards, feet, and inches (1 cm = 0.3937 in).

4. Write a subroutine subprogram that accepts a weight in grams and returns the corresponding weight in pounds and ounces (1 g = 0.35274 oz).

5. Write a subroutine subprogram that accepts a time in military format and returns the corresponding time in the usual representation in hours, minutes, and A.M./P.M. For example, a time of 100 should be returned as 1 hour, 0 minutes, and AM; a time of 1545 should be returned as 3 hours, 45 minutes, and PM.

6. Write a subroutine subprogram that accepts a time in the usual representation in hours, minutes, and one of the strings AM or PM, and returns the corresponding military time. (See Exercise 5.)

7.2 APPLICATION: DESIGNING A COIN DISPENSER

Problem

An automated cash register accept two inputs: the amount of a purchase and the amount given as payment. It then computes the number of dollars, quarters, dimes, nickels, and pennies to be given in change. The cashier returns the dollars to the customer but the coins are returned by an automatic coin dispenser. A subprogram to compute the number of dollars to be returned by the cashier and the number of coins of each denomination to be returned by the coin dispenser must be developed and tested.

Solution

Specification. The subprogram to be developed will accept the purchase amount and the amount paid by the customer and must return the number of dollars and the number of coins of each denomination. Thus a specification for this subprogram is

Accepts: The amount of the purchase
            The amount of the payment

Returns: The number of dollars in change
            The number of quarters in change
            The number of dimes in change
            The number of nickels in change
            The number of pennies in change

Since the subprogram must return more than one item, we will design it as a subroutine rather than as a function.

Design. To determine what sequence of operations is needed to make change, consider a specific example. Suppose the amount of a purchase is $8.49 and the customer pays with a $10 bill. We clearly must begin by subtracting the purchase amount from the payment to get the total amount of change ($1.51). This is a real value, but our return values are integers, and so at some point we must convert this real value to an integer value. Because real values are not stored exactly (e.g., 1.51 might be stored as 1.50999 . . .), it is best to convert the real amount of change (1.51) into an integer value (151) at the outset, ensuring that no significant digits are lost. An initial algorithm for this subroutine follows:

1. Compute the change to be returned in cents.
2. If the change is positive then

     Compute the number of dollars and the number of coins of each denomination to be returned.

   Else do the following:

   a. Display an appropriate message.
   b. Set the number of dollars and the number of coins of each denomination to zero.

Here only the first part of step 2 needs to be refined to give a final version of the algorithm. We will use the following variables in our description:

VARIABLES FOR COIN-DISPENSER PROBLEM

AMOUNT	Amount of purchase
PAY	Amount of payment
CHANGE	Change to be returned (in cents)
DOLLAR	Number of dollars to be returned
QUARTR	Number of quarters to be returned
DIMES	Number of dimes to be returned
NICKEL	Number of nickels to be returned
CENTS	Number of pennies to be returned

Once CHANGE has been computed as the change in cents, the number of dollars of change can be computed using integer division, dividing the value of CHANGE by 100:

$$DOLLAR = CHANGE / 100$$

The remaining change is the remainder that results from this division:

$$\text{CHANGE} = \text{remainder when CHANGE is divided by 100}$$

The number of quarters remaining in CHANGE can then be computed in a similar manner by dividing CHANGE by 25:

$$\text{QUARTR} = \text{CHANGE} / 25$$

The remainder of this division is then the amount of change remaining to be dispensed as dimes, nickels, and pennies.

$$\text{CHANGE} = \text{remainder when CHANGE is divided by 25}$$

Similar calculations are used to determine the number of dimes, nickels, and pennies.
    A complete algorithm for this problem is

ALGORITHM FOR COIN-DISPENSER PROBLEM

```
*  This algorithm computes the number of dollars, quarters, dimes, nickels, and pennies  *
*  needed to make change for a given purchase amount and a given amount paid.            *
*                                                                                         *
*  Receive:  AMOUNT, the (real) amount of the purchase                                   *
*            PAY, the (real) amount of the payment                                       *
*  Return:   DOLLAR, QUARTR, DIMES, NICKEL, CENTS                                        *
```

1. Calculate CHANGE = PAY − AMOUNT in cents.
2. If CHANGE ≥ 0 do the following:
    a. Calculate DOLLAR = CHANGE / 100.
    b. Calculate CHANGE = remainder when CHANGE is divided by 100.
    c. Calculate QUARTR = CHANGE / 25.
    d. Calculate CHANGE = remainder when CHANGE is divided by 25.
    e. Calculate DIMES = CHANGE / 10.
    f. Calculate CHANGE = remainder when CHANGE is divided by 10.
    g. Calculate NICKEL = CHANGE / 5.
    h. Calculate CENTS = remainder when CHANGE is divided by 5.
    Else do the following:
    a. Display an appropriate message.
    b. Return 0 for each of DOLLAR, QUARTR, DIMES, NICKEL, and CENTS.

Coding, Execution, and Testing. The subroutine DISPEN in Figure 7.4 implements this algorithm.

Figure 7.4 Computing change.

```
**DISPEN****************************************************************
* Subroutine to compute the dollars, quarters, dimes, nickels, and    *
* pennies in change given the amount of a purchase and the amount paid *
* by the customer. Local variable used:                               *
*     CHANGE : the amount to be returned in change (in cents)         *
*                                                                     *
* Accepts: AMOUNT of purchase and amount paid by customer (PAY)       *
* Returns: DOLLAR, QUARTR, DIMES, NICKEL, CENTS, the number of        *
*          dollars, quarters, dimes, nickels, and pennies to be       *
*          returned in change.                                        *
***********************************************************************

      SUBROUTINE DISPEN(AMOUNT, PAY,
     +                  DOLLAR, QUARTR, DIMES, NICKEL, CENTS)

      REAL AMOUNT, PAY
      INTEGER DOLLAR, QUARTR, DIMES, NICKEL, CENTS, CHANGE

*     Calculate amount of change in cents
      CHANGE = ANINT(100 * (PAY - AMOUNT))

      IF (CHANGE .GT. 0) THEN
*        Compute number of dollars
         DOLLAR = CHANGE / 100
         CHANGE = MOD(CHANGE, 100)

*        Compute number of quarters
         QUARTR = CHANGE / 25
         CHANGE = MOD(CHANGE, 25)

*        Compute number of dimes
         DIMES = CHANGE / 10
         CHANGE = MOD(CHANGE, 10)

*        Compute number of nickels and pennies
         NICKEL = CHANGE / 5
         CENTS = MOD(CHANGE, 5)
```

Figure 7.4   *(cont.)*

```
          ELSE
*             Insufficient payment
              PRINT *, '*** PAYMENT TOO SMALL BY ', -CHANGE, ' CENTS ***'
              DOLLAR = 0
              QUARTR = 0
              DIMES = 0
              NICKEL = 0
              CENTS = 0

          END IF

          END
```

To test this function we might write a **driver program** that simply reads two amounts, calls the subroutine DISPEN to calculate the change that must be given, and then displays the amounts returned by DISPEN. Figure 7.5 shows such a driver program and a sample run with several test values.

 Figure 7.5 Making change—driver program.

```
          PROGRAM DRIVER
*******************************************************************
* This is a driver program to test subroutine DISPEN.  Variables used: *
*      COST   : cost of item                                     *
*      PAID   : amount paid by customer                          *
*      NUM100 : number of dollars,                               *
*      NUM25  :    quarters,                                     *
*      NUM10  :    dimes,                                        *
*      NUM5   :    nickels,                                      *
*      NUM1   :    pennies  to be returned in change             *
*      RESPON : user response to More data? query                *
*                                                                *
* Input:  COST of item and amount PAID by customer               *
* Output: Change in dollars, quarters, dimes, nickels, and pennies *
*******************************************************************

          REAL COST, PAID
          INTEGER NUM100, NUM25, NUM10, NUM5, NUM1
          CHARACTER*1, RESPON

          PRINT *, 'THIS PROGRAM TESTS A CHANGE-DISPENSING SUBROUTINE.'
          PRINT *
```

Figure 7.5   *(cont.)*

```
*      Do the following until user indicates no more data
10     CONTINUE
         PRINT *, 'ENTER COST OF ITEM AND AMOUNT PAID BY CUSTOMER:'
         READ *, COST, PAID
         CALL DISPEN(COST, PAID, NUM100, NUM25, NUM10, NUM5, NUM1)

         PRINT 20, NUM100, 'DOLLARS', NUM25, 'QUARTERS',
     +            NUM10, 'DIMES', NUM5, 'NICKELS', NUM1, 'PENNIES'
20       FORMAT(1X, 'THE CHANGE FROM THIS PURCHASE IS:' /
     +          6(1X, I4, 1X, A /))
         PRINT *
         PRINT *, 'MORE DATA (Y OR N)?'
         READ '(A)', RESPON
       IF (RESPON .EQ. 'Y') GO TO 10

       END


************************************************************
* Insert subroutine DISPEN from Figure 7.4 here           *
************************************************************
```

Sample run:

```
THIS PROGRAM TESTS A CHANGE-DISPENSING SUBROUTINE.

ENTER COST OF ITEM AND AMOUNT PAID BY CUSTOMER:
1.01, 2.00
THE CHANGE FROM THIS PURCHASE IS:
    0 DOLLARS
    3 QUARTERS
    2 DIMES
    0 NICKELS
    4 PENNIES

MORE DATA (Y OR N)?
Y
ENTER COST OF ITEM AND AMOUNT PAID BY CUSTOMER:
1.59 3.00
THE CHANGE FROM THIS PURCHASE IS:
    1 DOLLARS
    1 QUARTERS
    1 DIMES
    1 NICKELS
    1 PENNIES
```

Figure 7.5   *(cont.)*

```
MORE DATA (Y OR N)?
Y
ENTER COST OF ITEM AND AMOUNT PAID BY CUSTOMER:
1.20, 1.00
*** PAYMENT TOO SMALL BY   20 CENTS ***
THE CHANGE FROM THIS PURCHASE IS:
    0 DOLLARS
    0 QUARTERS
    0 DIMES
    0 NICKELS
    0 PENNIES

MORE DATA (Y OR N)?
Y
ENTER COST OF ITEM AND AMOUNT PAID BY CUSTOMER:
.99, 1.00
THE CHANGE FROM THIS PURCHASE IS:
    0 DOLLARS
    0 QUARTERS
    0 DIMES
    0 NICKELS
    1 PENNIES

MORE DATA (Y OR N)?
N
```

7.3 RANDOM NUMBERS AND SIMULATION

The term **simulation** refers to modeling a dynamic process and using this model to study the behavior of the process. The behavior of some **deterministic** processes can be modeled with an equation or a set of equations. For example, an equation of the form $A(t) = A_0(.5)^{t/h}$ was used in Section 1.3 to model the radioactive decay of polonium, and linear systems are used in Section 9.6 to model an electrical network. In many problems, the process being studied involves **randomness**, for example, Brownian motion, the arrival of airplanes at an airport, and the number of defective parts a machine manufactures. Computer programs that simulate such processes use random number generators to introduce randomness into the values produced during execution.

Random Number Generators

A **random number generator** is a subprogram that produces a number selected "at random" from some fixed range in such a way that a sequence of these numbers tends to be uniformly distributed over the given range. Although it is not possible to develop an algorithm that produces truly random numbers, there are some methods that produce sequences of **pseudorandom numbers** that are adequate for most purposes. Most of these algorithms have two properties:

1. Some initial value called a **seed** is required to begin the process of generating random numbers. Different seeds will produce different sequences of random numbers.
2. Each random number produced is used in the computation of the next random number.

Many system libraries provide a random number generator, which is a subprogram that produces random real numbers uniformly distributed over the range 0 to 1.[1] The numbers produced by such a generator can be used to generate random real numbers in other ranges or to generate random integers. For example, if RANNUM is a random number in the range 0 to 1, the value of the expression

```
A + (B − A) * RANNUM
```

will be a random real number in the range A to B, and the value of the expression

```
M + INT(K * RANNUM)
```

will be a random integer in the range M through $M + K - 1$.

Example: Dice Tossing

To illustrate, suppose we wish to model the random process of tossing a pair of dice. Using the preceding expression for generating random integers, we might use the statements

```
DIE1 = 1 + INT(6*R1)
DIE2 = 1 + INT(6*R2)
PAIR = DIE1 + DIE2
```

to simulate one roll of two dice, where R1 and R2 are random real numbers in the range 0 to 1. The value of PAIR is the total number of dots showing, and the relative frequency of each value from 2 through 12 for PAIR should correspond to the probability

---

[1] Fortran 90 provides two subroutines for random number generation: RANDOM_NUMBER and RANDOM_SEED. The statement CALL RANDOM_SEED initializes the random number generator. The statement CALL RANDOM_NUMBER(X) will return a random real number X in the interval (0,1).

of that number occurring on one throw of a pair of dice. These probabilities (rounded to three decimal places) are given in the following table:

Outcome	Probability
2	0.028
3	0.056
4	0.083
5	0.111
6	0.139
7	0.167
8	0.139
9	0.111
10	0.083
11	0.056
12	0.028

The program in Figure 7.6 reads an integer indicating the number of times that two dice are to be tossed and then repeatedly asks the user to enter a possible outcome of a roll of the dice and displays the relative frequency of this outcome. For each outcome, a DO loop is used to produce the required number of dice rolls. The subroutine RANDOM is used to generate random real numbers in the range 0 to 1. For best results, the initial argument for this subroutine RANDOM should be an odd integer.[2]

Figure 7.6 Dice-roll simulation.

```
      PROGRAM DICE
* * * * * * * * * * * * * * * * * * * * * * * * * * * * * * * * * * * * * * * * * * * * * * * * * * * * * * * * * * * * * * * * * *
*  This program uses a random number generator to simulate rolling a        *
*  pair of dice several times, counting the number of times a specified     *
*  number of spots occurs. Identifiers used are:                            *
*      SPOTS  : number of spots to be counted                               *
*      COUNT  : number of times SPOTS occurred                              *
*      NROLLS : number of rolls of dice                                     *
*      R1, R2 : two random real numbers in the range 0 to 1                 *
*      DIE1,                                                                 *
*      DIE2   : number of spots on die #1, #2, respectively                 *
*      PAIR   : sum of DIE1 and DIE2 = total # of spots on the dice         *
```

---

[2] For details of the *congruential method* of generating random numbers and other techniques, see Donald Knuth, *The Art of Computer Programming, Seminumerical Algorithms*, vol. 2 (Reading, Mass.: Addison-Wesley, 1981).

Figure 7.6   *(cont.)*

```
*      ROLL   : counts dice rolls                                        *
*      RESPON : user response                                            *
*      RANDOM : random number generator (subroutine)                    *
*                                                                        *
* Input:  NROLLS, SPOTS, RESPON, seed for random number generator       *
* Output: User prompts, and the relative frequency of the number of     *
*         spots                                                          *
**************************************************************************

      INTEGER SPOTS, COUNT, NROLLS, DIE1, DIE2, PAIR, ROLL
      REAL R1, R2
      CHARACTER*1 RESPON

      PRINT *, 'ENTER NUMBER OF TIMES TO ROLL THE DICE:'
      READ *, NROLLS
      PRINT *, 'ENTER A SEED FOR THE RANDOM NUMBER GENERATOR:'
      READ *, R1


* Begin the simulation

 10   CONTINUE
         PRINT *, 'ENTER NUMBER OF SPOTS TO COUNT:'
         READ *, SPOTS
         COUNT = 0

         DO 20 ROLL = 1, NROLLS
            CALL RANDOM(R1)
            CALL RANDOM(R2)
            DIE1 = 1 + INT(6*R1)
            DIE2 = 1 + INT(6*R2)
            PAIR = DIE1 + DIE2
            IF (PAIR .EQ. SPOTS) COUNT = COUNT + 1
 20      CONTINUE

         PRINT 30, SPOTS, REAL(COUNT) / REAL(NROLLS)
 30      FORMAT (1X, 'RELATIVE FREQUENCY OF', I2, ' WAS', F6.3 /)

         PRINT *, 'MORE ROLLS (Y OR N)?'
         READ '(A)', RESPON
      IF (RESPON .EQ. 'Y') GO TO 10

      END
```

Figure 7.6 *(cont.)*

```
**RANDOM**********************************************************
* This subroutine generates a random real number in the interval from  *
* 0 to 1. The variable M is initially the seed supplied by the         *
* user; thereafter, it is the random integer generated on the pre-     *
* ceding call to the function and saved using the SAVE statement.      *
* NOTE: The constants 2147483647 and .4656613E-9 used in this sub-     *
* program are appropriate when it is executed on a machine having      *
* 32-bit memory words. For a machine having M-bit words, these two     *
* constants should be replaced by the values of 2**M — 1 and           *
* 1/(2**M — 1), respectively.                                          *
*****************************************************************


        SUBROUTINE RANDOM(RANNUM)

        INTEGER M, CONST1
        REAL RANNUM, CONST2
        PARAMETER (CONST1 = 2147483647, CONST2 = .4656613E-9)
        SAVE
        DATA M /0/

        IF (M .EQ. 0) M = INT(RANNUM)
        M = M * 65539
        IF (M .LT. 0) M = (M + 1) + CONST1
        RANNUM = M * CONST2

        END
```

Sample run:

```
ENTER NUMBER OF TIMES TO ROLL THE DICE:
1000
ENTER A SEED FOR THE RANDOM NUMBER GENERATOR:
1139
ENTER NUMBER OF SPOTS TO COUNT:
6
RELATIVE FREQUENCY OF 6 WAS 0.136

MORE ROLLS (Y OR N)?
Y
ENTER NUMBER OF SPOTS TO COUNT:
7
RELATIVE FREQUENCY OF 7 WAS 0.176
```

Figure 7.6 *(cont.)*

```
MORE ROLLS (Y OR N)?
Y
ENTER NUMBER OF SPOTS TO COUNT:
11
RELATIVE FREQUENCY OF 11 WAS 0.056

MORE ROLLS (Y OR N)?
N
```

The SAVE Statement

Normally when control returns from a subprogram, all **local variables** in the subprogram, that is, variables declared within the subprogram that are not arguments, become undefined. (Exceptions include variables initialized by a DATA statement within that subprogram that are not redefined and variables in common blocks, as described in Section 7.6.) In particular, this means that the values of such variables are not available in subsequent references to the subprogram.

In some cases it may be necessary to save values of a local variable from one execution of the subprogram to the next. For example, in the subroutine RANDOM, the value of the formal argument RANNUM must be saved from one call to the next because it is needed to generate the next random number. This can be accomplished by using a SAVE **statement** of the form

```
SAVE list
```

If *list* is omitted, all variables in the subprogram will be saved.

Normal Distributions

Most random number generators generate random numbers having a **uniform distribution,** but they can also be used to generate random numbers having other distributions. **Normal distributions** are especially important because they model many physical processes. For example, the heights and weights of people, the lifetime of light bulbs, the tensile strength of steel produced by a machine, and, in general, the variations in parts produced in almost any manufacturing process have normal distributions. Normal distributions have the familiar bell-shaped curve,

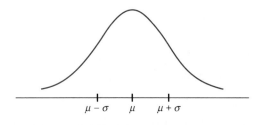

where μ is the mean of the distribution, σ is the standard deviation, and approximately two-thirds of the area under the curve lies between $\mu - \sigma$ and $\mu + \sigma$.

A normal distribution having $\mu = 0$ and $\sigma = 1$ is called a **standard normal distribution,** and random numbers having approximately this distribution can be generated quite easily from a uniform distribution with the following algorithm.

ALGORITHM FOR THE STANDARD NORMAL DISTRIBUTION

```
*   Algorithm to generate random numbers having an approximate standard normal dis-   *
*   tribution from a uniform distribution.                                            *
```

1. Set SUM equal to 0.

2. Do the following 12 times:
    a. Generate a random number X from a uniform distribution.
    b. Add X to SUM.

3. Calculate Z = SUM − 6.

The numbers Z generated by this algorithm have an approximate standard normal distribution. To generate random numbers Y having a normal distribution with mean μ and standard deviation σ, we simply add the following step to the algorithm:

4. Calculate Y = $\mu + \sigma * Z$.

Implementing this algorithm as a program is left as an exercise.

7.4 APPLICATION: SHIELDING A NUCLEAR REACTOR

Problem

When the enriched uranium fuel of a nuclear reactor is burned, high-energy neutrons are produced. Some of these are retained in the reactor core, but most of them escape. Since this radiation is dangerous, the reactor must be shielded with a slab of concrete or other material. The problem is to simulate neutrons entering this shield and to determine what percentage of them get through it.

Solution

Specification. To model the shielding in such a way that we can simulate the paths of neutrons that enter it, we will make the simplifying assumption that neutrons entering the shield follow random paths by moving forward, backward, left, or right with

(a)   (b)

Nuclear power plant at Three Mile Island. (Photos courtesy of (a) Tony Stone Images, (b) Stock Boston.)

equal likelihood, in jumps of one unit. We will also assume that losses of energy occur only when there is a change of direction, and that after a certain number of such direction changes, the neutron's energy is dissipated and it dies within the shield, provided that it has not already passed back inside the reactor core or outside through the shield.

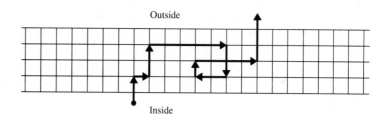

Making these simplifying assumptions, we can specify the problem as follows:

Input: Thickness of the shield
         Limit on the number of direction changes
         Number of neutrons
         Seed for the random number generator

Output: Percentage of neutrons that reach the outside

Design. To simulate the paths the neutrons take, we will generate random integers with values 1, 2, 3, or 4, corresponding to movement forward, backward, to the left, or to the right, respectively. If the net movement in the forward direction equals the thickness of the shield, the neutron escapes. If it becomes negative, the neutron returns back inside the reactor. If the number of direction changes reaches a specified limit, the neutron dies within the shield. We repeat this some given number of times and calculate what percentage of neutrons escape.

The following algorithm describes this simulation more precisely. It uses the following identifiers:

IDENTIFIERS FOR SHIELDING PROBLEM

THICK	Thickness of shield
LIMDIR	Limit on number of direction changes (before energy is dissipated)
NEWDIR	A random integer 1, 2, 3, or 4 representing direction
OLDDIR	Previous direction of neutron
NDIRS	Number of changes of direction
FORW	Net units traveled in the forward direction
N	Number of neutrons simulated
COUNT	Number of neutrons escaping through the shield
SEED	Seed for random number generator
I	Control variable for a loop

ALGORITHM FOR SHIELDING PROBLEM

```
*  Algorithm to simulate neutrons entering a shield and to determine how many reach the  *
*  outside. The neutrons are assumed to move forward, backward, left, and right with      *
*  equal likelihood and to die within the shield if a certain number of direction changes *
*  occur. A random number generator is assumed.                                           *
*  Input:     Thickness of the shield, limit on the number of direction changes, number   *
*             of particles, and a seed for the random number generator                    *
*  Output:    Percentage of particles that reach the outside                              *
```

1. Read THICK, LIMDIR, and N.

2. Read a seed for the random number generator.

3. Initialize COUNT to 0.

4. Do the following for I = 1 to N:
   a. Initialize FORW to 0, OLDDIR to 0, and NDIRS to 0.
   b. Repeat the following until particle reaches the outside of the shield (FORW ≥ THICK), returns inside the reactor (FORW < 0), or dies within the shield (NDIRS ≥ LIMDIR):
      i. Generate a random integer 1, 2, 3, or 4 for the direction NEWDIR.
      ii. If NEWDIR ≠ OLDDIR, increment NUMDIR by 1 and set OLDDIR equal to NEWDIR.
      iii. If NEWDIR = 1, increment FORW by 1.
         Else if NEWDIR = 2, decrement FORW by 1.
   c. If FORW = THICK, increment COUNT by 1.

5. Display 100 * COUNT / N.

Coding. The program in Figure 7.7 implements this algorithm. It uses the subroutine RANDOM to generate random real numbers in the range 0 to 1, which are then transformed into random integers 1, 2, 3, or 4, corresponding to the four directions forward, backward, left, and right, respectively.

Figure 7.7 Simulate shielding of nuclear reactor.

```
      PROGRAM SHIELD
*************************************************************************
* This program uses the random number generator RAND to simulate       *
* neutrons entering a shield and to determine what percentage reaches   *
* the outside.  The neutrons are assumed to move forward, backward,     *
* left, and right with equal likelihood and to die within the shield    *
* if a certain number of changes of direction have occurred.            *
* Identifiers used are:                                                 *
*     THICK  : thickness of shield                                      *
*     LIMDIR : limit on # of direction changes before energy dissipated *
*     RANNUM : a random real number in the range 0 to 1                 *
*     NEWDIR : a random integer 1, 2, 3, or 4 representing direction    *
*     OLDDIR : previous direction of neutron                            *
*     NDIRS  : number of changes of direction                           *
*     FORW   : net units forward traveled                               *
*     N      : number of neutrons simulated                             *
*     COUNT  : number of neutrons reaching outside of shield            *
*     RANDOM : random number generator (subroutine)                     *
*     I      : subscript                                                 *
*                                                                       *
* Input:   THICK, LIMDIR, N, and seed for random number generator       *
* Output:  Percentage of neutrons that reach the outside                *
*************************************************************************

      INTEGER THICK, LIMDIR, NEWDIR, OLDDIR, NDIRS, FORW, N, COUNT, I
      REAL RANNUM

      PRINT *, 'ENTER THICKNESS OF SHIELD, LIMIT ON # OF DIRECTION'
      PRINT *, 'CHANGES, AND THE NUMBER OF NEUTRONS TO SIMULATE'
      READ *, THICK, LIMDIR, N
      PRINT *, 'SEED FOR RANDOM NUMBER GENERATOR'
      READ *, RANNUM
      COUNT = 0
```

Figure 7.7   *(cont.)*

```
* Begin the simulation

      DO 20 I = 1, N
         FORW = 0
         OLDDIR = 0
         NDIRS = 0

* Repeat the following until neutron reaches outside of
* shield, returns inside reactor, or dies within shield

10        CONTINUE
             CALL RANDOM(RANNUM)
             NEWDIR = 1 + INT(4 * RANNUM)
             IF (NEWDIR.NE. OLDDIR) THEN
                NDIRS = NDIRS + 1
                OLDDIR = NEWDIR
             END IF
             IF (NEWDIR .EQ. 1) THEN
                FORW = FORW + 1
             ELSE IF (NEWDIR .EQ. 2) THEN
                FORW = FORW - 1
             END IF
          IF ((FORW .LT. THICK) .AND. (FORW .GE. 0) .AND.
     +        (NDIRS .LT. LIMDIR)) GO TO 10

          IF (FORW .EQ. THICK) THEN
             COUNT = COUNT + 1
          END IF
20     CONTINUE

      PRINT 30, 100 * COUNT / REAL(N)
30    FORMAT (1X, F5.2, '% OF THE NEUTRONS ESCAPED')

      END

****************************************************************************
*              Insert subroutine RAND (see Figure 7.6) here               *
****************************************************************************
```

Execution and Testing. The following are four sample runs of the program. The first two are test runs. In the first test case, the neutron will move only once, since each first move is interpreted as a change of direction and the limit on the number of direction changes is 1. Since each of the four possible moves is equally likely, we would expect 25 percent of the neutrons to escape, and the result produced by the program is consistent with this value. In the second test case, the shielding is 100 units thick and the limit on the number of direction changes is small. Thus we expect almost none of the neutrons to escape through the shield.

Sample run # 1:

```
ENTER THICKNESS OF SHIELD, LIMIT ON # OF DIRECTION
CHANGES, AND THE NUMBER OF NEUTRONS TO SIMULATE
1 1 1000
SEED FOR RANDOM NUMBER GENERATOR
5773
 24.80% OF THE NEUTRONS ESCAPED
```

Sample run # 2:

```
ENTER THICKNESS OF SHIELD, LIMIT ON # OF DIRECTION
CHANGES, AND THE NUMBER OF NEUTRONS TO SIMULATE
100 5 1000
SEED FOR RANDOM NUMBER GENERATOR
5823
 0.00% OF THE NEUTRONS ESCAPED
```

Sample run # 3:

```
ENTER THICKNESS OF SHIELD, LIMIT ON # OF DIRECTION
CHANGES, AND THE NUMBER OF NEUTRONS TO SIMULATE
4, 5, 100
SEED FOR RANDOM NUMBER GENERATOR
3773
 7.00% OF THE NEUTRONS ESCAPED
```

Sample run # 4:

```
ENTER THICKNESS OF SHIELD, LIMIT ON # OF DIRECTION
CHANGES, AND THE NUMBER OF NEUTRONS TO SIMULATE
8, 10, 500
SEED FOR RANDOM NUMBER GENERATOR
34793
 0.20% OF THE NEUTRONS ESCAPED
```

7.5 APPLICATION: CHECKING ACADEMIC STANDING

Top-Down Design

At several places in this text we have indicated that large and complex problems can best be solved using **top-down design.** In this approach, a **divide-and-conquer strategy** is used to divide the original problem into a number of simpler subproblems. Each of these subproblems can then be solved independently, perhaps using this same divide-and-conquer strategy to divide them into still simpler subproblems. This refinement process continues until the subproblems are simple enough that algorithms can be easily developed to solve them. Subprograms are then written to implement these algorithms, and these subprograms are combined with a main program into a complete program that solves the original problem. Because this software engineering technique is so important and because we have now considered subprograms in some detail, it is appropriate to illustrate this technique by solving a relatively complex problem.

Problem

Suppose that the engineering department at a certain university wants a program to determine the academic standing of its students. The academic standing of each student is to be checked at the end of each of the first three years of the student's academic career and is based on two criteria: the number of hours that the student has successfully completed and his or her cumulative grade point average (GPA). To be in good standing, the student must have completed at least 25 hours with a minimum GPA of 1.7 by the end of the first year. At the end of the second year, 50 hours must have been completed with a cumulative GPA of 1.85 or higher, and at the end of the third year, 85 hours must have been completed with a minimum cumulative GPA of 1.95.

Solution

The program should display the student's ID number, class level, cumulative hours, GPA for the current year, and cumulative GPA, as well as an indication of his or her academic standing. At the end of this report, the program should also display the total number of students processed, the number who are in good standing, and the average current GPA for all students. The information to be supplied to the program is the student's ID number, class level, hours accumulated, cumulative GPA, and hours and grades for courses taken during the current year. Thus, we have the following input and output specifications for this problem:

Input: Student's ID number
           Class level (1, 2, or 3)
           Cumulative hours
           Cumulative GPA
           Hours and grade for each course completed in the current year

Output: Student's ID number
Current GPA
Updated cumulative hours and cumulative GPA
Indication of academic standing
Number of students processed
Number of students in good standing
Average of all current GPAs

Using top-down design to develop this program, we begin by identifying three main tasks needed to solve it, describing them in fairly general terms:

1. INFORM. Since the program will be used by personnel who are generally not regular users of a computer system, some instructions must be displayed each time the program is used.
2. PROCES. The second task is to accept the given information for each student, calculate the relevant statistics, and determine eligibility.
3. WRAPUP. The final task is to generate and display the desired summary statistics after all the student information has been processed.

It is helpful to display these tasks and their relationship to one another in a **structure diagram** like the following:

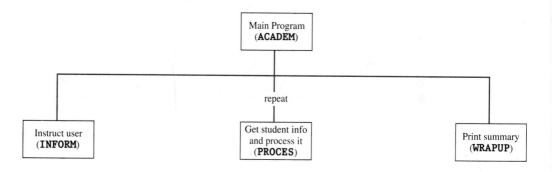

Typically, one or more of these first-level tasks are still quite complex and so must be divided into subtasks. In this example, the tasks INFORM and WRAPUP are straightforward, but the task PROCES, which is central to the entire program, is more complicated and requires further analysis. We can identify three main subtasks in PROCESS:

1. CALCUL. Read information about a student and calculate relevant statistics.
2. CHECK. Determine a student's eligibility based on the statistics calculated in CALCUL.
3. REPORT. Report information about a student, including eligibility status.

The following refinement of the earlier structure diagram summarizes this analysis:

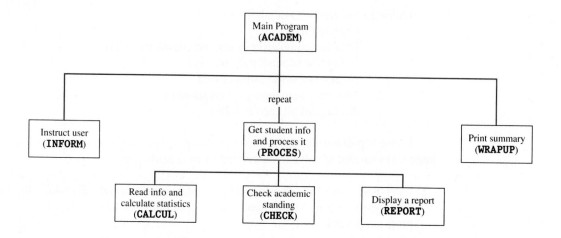

A student's eligibility is based on two criteria: an hours condition and a GPA condition. This means that two subtasks of CHECK can be identified:

1. HRSCHK. Check if a student's cumulative hours satisfies the hours condition.
2. GPACHK. Check if a student's cumulative GPA satisfies the GPA condition.

The final refinement of the structure diagram for the program thus is

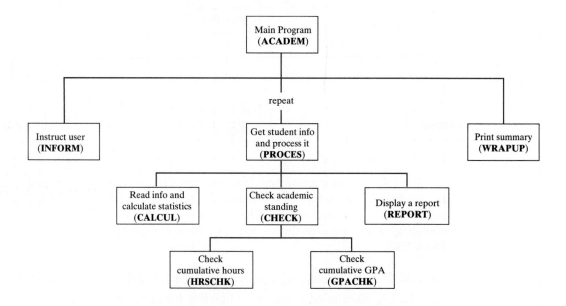

The next step is to develop algorithms for each of these tasks and subtasks. We begin with an algorithm for the main program.

VARIABLES FOR MAIN PROGRAM

NUMSTU   Total number of students

NUMGS   Number in good standing

RESPON   User response to more-data query

GPASUM   Sum of all current GPAs

ALGORITHM FOR MAIN PROGRAM

* Determine academic eligibility of individual students according to two criteria— *
* cumulative hours and cumulative GPA—and display several summary statistics for *
* all students processed. *
* Input: For each of several students, the student's number, class level, cumulative *
*   hours, cumulative GPA, hours and grades for current courses; also, user *
*   responses to "More data?" query *
* Output: For each student, the student's number, class level, current GPA, updated *
*   cumulative hours and cumulative GPA, and an indication of eligibility; *
*   also, a summary report showing the number of students processed, number *
*   who are eligible, and average of all current GPAs *

1. Call subalgorithm INFORM.

2. Initialize NUMSTU, NUMGS, and GPASUM to 0.

3. Repeat the following until user indicates no more data:
   a. Call subalgorithm PROCES.
   b. Ask user if there is more data.

4. Call WRAPUP.

The three tasks we have identified can be implemented as three subroutines, IN-FORM, PROCES, and WRAPUP. Since the procedure INFORM simply displays instructions to the user, it requires no information from other program units and thus has no formal arguments. The subroutine WRAPUP, which prints the summary, requires the total number of students (NUMSTU), the total number who are in good standing (NUMGS), and the sum of all the current GPAs (GPASUM). These values must be calculated by the subroutine PROCES and shared with WRAPUP. Thus, the main program has the form

```
PROGRAM ACADEM

INTEGER NUMSTU, NUMGS, RESPON
REAL GPASUM
DATA NUMSTU, NUMGS, GPASUM /0, 0, 0.0/

CALL INFORM
```

```
*       Repeat the following until no more data
10      CONTINUE
            CALL PROCES(NUMSTU, NUMGS, GPASUM)
            PRINT *
            PRINT *
            PRINT *, 'MORE (Y OR N)?'
            READ '(A)', RESPON
        IF (RESPON .EQ. 'Y') GO TO 10

        CALL WRAPUP(NUMSTU, NUMGS, GPASUM)

        END
```

Next we must develop the three subroutines INFORM, PROCES, and WRAPUP. Since PROCES is central to the entire program, we will consider it first:

VARIABLES FOR PROCES

NUMSTU, NUMGS, and GPASUM as in main algorithm.

SNUMB, CLASS, CUMHRS, CUMGPA, CURGPA: student's number, class, cumulative hours, cumulative GPA, and current GPA

GOODST: Indicates whether student is in good standing

ALGORITHM FOR PROCES

```
*  Read student information, determine eligibility, and maintain counts of the number of  *
*  students processed and the number eligible, and a sum of current GPAs.                 *
*  Accepts:  NUMSTU, NUMGS, and GPASUM                                                     *
*  Returns:   Updated values of NUMSTU, NUMGS, and GPASUM                                  *
```

1. Call subalgorithm CALCUL to get values for SNUMB, CLASS, CUMHRS, CUMGPA, and CURGPA.
2. Call subalgorithm CHECK to get value for GOODST.
3. Call subalgorithm REPORT to display information about student.

The three second-level subtasks of PROCES can be implemented as subroutines CALCUL, CHECK, and REPORT. An algorithm for CALCUL is as follows:

VARIABLES FOR CALCUL

NUMSTU, GPASUM as in main algorithm.

SNUMB, CLASS, CUMHRS, CUMGPA, CURGPA as in PROCES

HOURS, GRADE:	Students hours and grade for a current course
NEWHRS:	Total hours earned in current year
NEWPTS:	Honor points earned in current year
OLDPTS:	Honor points earned in past years

ALGORITHM FOR CALCUL

```
* Reads information about a student, and calculates current GPA, updated cumulative   *
* hours, cumulative GPA, count of students processed, and sum of cumulative GPAs for  *
* all students.                                                                       *
* Accepts:  NUMSTU and GPASUM                                                         *
* Input:    SNUMB, CLASS, CUMHRS, CUMGPA                                              *
*           HOURS and GRADE for each current course                                   *
* Returns:  SNUMB, CLASS, CUMHRS, CUMGPA, CURGPA, updated values of                   *
*           NUMSTU and GPASUM                                                          *
```

1. Read SNUMB, CLASS, CUMHRS, and CUMGPA for student.

2. Calculate the number of honor points the student already has earned:

$$OLDPTS = CUMHRS * CUMGPA$$

3. Initialize NEWHRS and NEWPTS to 0.

4. Read HOURS of credit and numeric GRADE for first course taken by student.

5. While the end-of-data flag has not been read, do the following:
   a. Add HOURS to NEWHRS.
   b. Add HOURS * GRADE to NEWPTS.
   c. Read HOURS of credit and numeric GRADE for next course.

6. Calculate student's current GPA (CURGPA): 0 if student took no new courses; else

$$CURGPA = \frac{NEWPTS}{NEWHRS}$$

7. Update cumulative hours for student by adding NEWHRS to CUMHRS.

8. Calculate student's cumulative GPA:

$$CUMGPA = \frac{OLDPTS + NEWPTS}{CUMHRS}$$

9. Increment NUMSTU by 1 and add CURGPA to GPASUM.

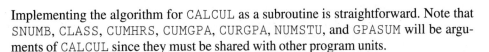

Implementing the algorithm for CALCUL as a subroutine is straightforward. Note that SNUMB, CLASS, CUMHRS, CUMGPA, CURGPA, NUMSTU, and GPASUM will be arguments of CALCUL since they must be shared with other program units.

Once the subroutine CALCUL has been written, it can be incorporated into the total program and tested before the other subprograms are developed, as shown in Figure 7.8.

We simply insert output statements in the undeveloped subprograms to signal when they are called. In this program, the execution parts of subroutines INFORM, WRAPUP, and PROCES contain **program stubs** to signal their execution, and REPORT produces a temporary printout to enable us to verify the correctness of CALCUL. The subroutine CALCUL is in its final form, as is the main program.

Figure 7.8 Academic standing—version 1.

```
      PROGRAM ACADEM
**************************************************************
* Program to determine academic standing of engineering students   *
* according to two criteria: cumulative hours and cumulative gpa.   *
* It also counts the total # of students checked and the # found to *
* be in good standing, and calculates the average current gpa for all *
* students.  Variables used are:                                    *
*     NUMSTU : total number of students                             *
*     NUMGS  : number in good standing                              *
*     RESPON : user response to more-data inquiry                   *
*     GPASUM : sum of all current GPAs                              *
*                                                                   *
* Input:  RESPON; also several items of student information in      *
*         subroutine CALCUL                                         *
* Output: Student report by subroutine REPORT and summary statistics *
*         by subroutine WRAPUP                                      *
**************************************************************

      INTEGER NUMSTU, NUMGS
      CHARACTER*1 RESPON
      REAL GPASUM
      DATA NUMSTU, NUMGS, GPASUM /3*0/

      CALL INFORM

*     Repeat the following until no more data
10    CONTINUE
          CALL PROCES(NUMSTU, NUMGS, GPASUM)
          PRINT *
          PRINT *, 'MORE (Y OR N)?'
          READ '(A)', RESPON
      IF (RESPON .EQ. 'Y') GO TO 10
      CALL WRAPUP(NUMSTU, NUMGS, GPASUM)
      END
```

Figure 7.8 *(cont.)*

```
**  INFORM  ***********************************************************************
      SUBROUTINE INFORM

      PRINT *, '*********** INFORM CALLED ***********'
      END


**  PROCES  ***********************************************************************
*  Accepts student information, determines academic standing, and            *
*  maintains counts of # processed and # in good standing, and a sum         *
*  of current GPAs.  Variables used are:                                     *
*     NUMSTU : total number of students                                      *
*     NUMGS  : number in good standing                                       *
*     GPASUM : sum of all current GPAs                                       *
*     SNUMB  : student's number                                              *
*     CLASS  : student's class                                               *
*     CUMHRS : student's cumulative hours                                    *
*     CUMGPA : student's cumulative GPA                                      *
*     CURGPA : student's current GPA                                         *
*     GOODST : indicates whether student is in good standing                 *
*  Accepts:  NUMSTU, NUMGS, and GPASUM                                       *
*  Returns:  Updated values of NUMSTU, NUMGS, and GPASUM                     *
   *****************************************************************************

      SUBROUTINE PROCES(NUMSTU, NUMGS, GPASUM)

      INTEGER NUMSTU, NUMGS, SNUMB, CLASS
      REAL GPASUM, CUMHRS, CUMGPA, CURGPA
      LOGICAL GOODST

      CALL CALCUL(SNUMB, CLASS, NUMSTU, CUMHRS, CUMGPA, CURGPA,
     +            GPASUM)
      CALL CHECK
      CALL REPORT(SNUMB, CLASS, CUMHRS, CURGPA, CUMGPA)

      END


**  WRAPUP  ***********************************************************************
      SUBROUTINE WRAPUP(NUMSTU, NUMGS, GPASUM)

      PRINT *, '*********** WRAPUP CALLED ***********'
      END
```

Figure 7.8 *(cont.)*

```
** CALCUL *******************************************************************
* Subroutine to read a student's number (SNUMB), CLASS, cumulative        *
* hours (CUMHRS), and cumulative gpa (CUMGPA); then read HOURS and        *
* GRADE for courses taken during the current year, and calculate          *
* current GPA (CURGPA), update cumulative hours, cumulative GPA, and       *
* count (NUMSTU) of students processed.  HOURS = 0 and GRADE = 0 are       *
* used to signal the end of data for a student.  Other local variables     *
* used are:                                                                *
*     NEWHRS : total hours earned during current year                      *
*     NEWPTS : honor points earned in current year                         *
*     OLDPTS : honor points earned in past years                           *
* Accepts:  NUMSTU and GPASUM                                              *
* Input:    SNUMB, CLASS, CUMHRS, CUMGPA; also HOURS and GRADE for         *
*           each of several courses                                        *
* Returns:  SNUMB, CLASS, CUMHRS, CUMGPA, CURGPA and updated values of     *
*           NUMSTU and GPASUM                                              *
****************************************************************************

      SUBROUTINE CALCUL(SNUMB, CLASS, NUMSTU, CUMHRS, CUMGPA,
     +                  CURGPA, GPASUM)

      INTEGER SNUMB, NUMSTU, CLASS
      REAL CUMHRS, CUMGPA, CURGPA, GPASUM, HOURS, GRADE, NEWHRS,
     +     NEWPTS, OLDPTS

      PRINT *,'ENTER STUDENT NUMBER, CLASS, CUM. HOURS, CUM. GPA:'
      READ *, SNUMB, CLASS, CUMHRS, CUMGPA
      OLDPTS = CUMHRS * CUMGPA
      NEWHRS = 0.0
      NEWPTS = 0.0
      PRINT *, 'HOURS AND GRADE?'
      READ *, HOURS, GRADE

* While HOURS > 0.0 do the following
10    IF (HOURS .GT. 0.0) THEN
         NEWHRS = NEWHRS + HOURS
         NEWPTS = NEWPTS + HOURS * GRADE
         PRINT *, 'HOURS AND GRADE?'
         READ *, HOURS, GRADE
      GO TO 10
      END IF
```

Figure 7.8 *(cont.)*

```
      IF (NEWHRS .EQ. 0.0) THEN
         CURGPA = 0.0
      ELSE
         CURGPA = NEWPTS / NEWHRS
      END IF
      CUMHRS = CUMHRS + NEWHRS
      CUMGPA = (OLDPTS + NEWPTS) / CUMHRS
      GPASUM = GPASUM + CURGPA
      NUMSTU = NUMSTU + 1

      END

** CHECK ***********************************************************
      SUBROUTINE CHECK

      PRINT *, '*********** CHECK CALLED ***********'
      END

** REPORT **********************************************************
      SUBROUTINE REPORT(SNUMB, CLASS, CUMHRS, CURGPA, CUMGPA)

      INTEGER SNUMB, CLASS
      REAL CUMHRS, CURGPA, CUMGPA

      PRINT *, '*********** REPORT CALLED ***********'
***** Temporary printout *****
      PRINT *, 'SNUMB: ', SNUMB
      PRINT *, 'CLASS: ', CLASS
      PRINT *, 'CUM. HOURS: ', CUMHRS
      PRINT *, 'CURR. GPA: ', CURGPA
      PRINT *, 'CUM. GPA:  ', CUMGPA
      END
```

Sample run:

```
*********** INFORM CALLED ***********
ENTER STUDENT NUMBER, CLASS, CUM. HOURS, CUM. GPA:
1234 1 0 0
HOURS AND GRADE?
5 3.0
HOURS AND GRADE?
4 3.0
HOURS AND GRADE?
3.5 3.0
```

Figure 7.8 *(cont.)*

```
HOURS AND GRADE?
4 3.0
HOURS AND GRADE?
3 3.0
HOURS AND GRADE?
2 3.0
HOURS AND GRADE?
0 0
********** CHECK CALLED **********
********** REPORT CALLED **********
SNUMB:   1234
CLASS:   1
CUM. HOURS:     21.5000
CURR. GPA:      3.00000
CUM. GPA:       3.00000

MORE (Y OR N)?
N
********** WRAPUP CALLED **********
```

The sample run in the preceding figure is a part of the testing that must be done to ensure that the procedure CALCUL is correct. Such **unit testing** should be performed on each subprogram as it is developed and added to the program. When a subprogram has been thoroughly tested, we can proceed to develop and test other subprograms. This process continues until all of the algorithms in the design plan have been coded, tested, and added to the program.

In this example, once we are convinced of the correctness of CALCUL, we may turn to developing the other subprograms. An algorithm for CHECK is as follows:

VARIABLES FOR CHECK

GOODST and NUMGS as in main algorithm

CLASS, CUMHRS, CUMGPA, CURGPA as in PROCES

SUBALGORITHM CHECK

* Check if student's cumulative hours and cumulative GPA satisfy the hours and GPA   *
* conditions for good academic standing.   *
* Accepts: A student's CLASS, CUMHRS, CUMGPA   *
*   NUMGS   *
* Returns: Student's eligibility status (GOODST)   *
*   Updated value of NUMGS   *

If CLASS is not one of 1, 2, or 3 then
   Display an illegal-class-code message
Else do the following:
   1. Call subalgorithm HRSCHK to determine whether student satisfies the hours condition for good standing.
   2. Call subalgorithm GPACHK to determine whether student satisfies the GPA condition for good standing.
   3. If student is in good standing, increment NUMGS by 1.

The subtasks HRSCHK and GPACHK can be conveniently implemented as logical-valued functions HRSCHK and GPACHK that return the value .TRUE. or .FALSE., depending on whether the student satisfies the corresponding criteria to be in good standing. Algorithms for these functions are as follows:

VARIABLES FOR HRSCHK

CLASS and CUMHRS as in PROCES

ALGORITHM FOR HRSCHK

* Check if student satisfies the hours condition for good standing.   *
* Accepts: A student's CLASS and CUMHRS   *
* Returns: True if student meets the hours criterion and false otherwise   *

If CLASS = 1 then
   Set HRSCHK to true if CUMHRS ≥ hours required for freshman good standing.
Else if CLASS = 2 then
   Set HRSCHK to true if CUMHRS ≥ hours required for sophomore good standing.
Else if CLASS = 3 then
   Set HRSCHK to true if CUMHRS ≥ hours required for junior good standing.

VARIABLES FOR GPACHK

CLASS and CUMGPA as in PROCES

ALGORITHM FOR GPACHK

*   Check if student satisfies the GPA condition for good standing.   *
*   Accepts: A student's CLASS and CUMGPA   *
*   Returns: True if student meets the hours criterion and false otherwise   *

If CLASS = 1 then
    Set GPACHK to true if CUMGPA ≥ GPA required for freshman good standing.
Else if CLASS = 2 then
    Set GPACHK to true if CUMGPA ≥ GPA required for sophomore good standing.
Else if CLASS = 3 then
    Set GPACHK to true if CUMGPA ≥ GPA required for junior good standing.

Replacing the temporary version of CHECK in the preceding program and adding the functions HRSCHK and GPACHK produces the refined program in Figure 7.9. Note that we have also modified the temporary version of REPORT and the reference to it in order to display the value of GOODST, the number of students in good standing.

Figure 7.9 Academic standing—version 2.

```
PROGRAM ACADEM
            .
            .
            .
** INFORM ****************************************************************

            .
            .
            .
    SUBROUTINE PROCES(NUMSTU, NUMGS, GPASUM)
            .
            .
            .
    CALL CALCUL(SNUMB, CLASS, NUMSTU, CUMHRS, CUMGPA, CURGPA,
   +            GPASUM)
    CALL CHECK(CLASS, CUMHRS, CUMGPA, GOODST, NUMGS)
    CALL REPORT(SNUMB, CLASS, CUMHRS, CURGPA, CUMGPA, GOODST)
            .
            .
            .
** WRAPUP ****************************************************************

            .
            .
            .
```

Figure 7.9   *(cont.)*

```
**  CALCUL  *********************************************************************
           .
           .
           .
**  CHECK  *********************************************************************
*  Subroutine to check academic standing. Two criteria are used:     *
*  cumulative hours and cumulative GPA.  Functions HRSCHK and GPACHK  *
*  are used to check these.  CLASS, CUMHRS, and CUMGPA are the class, *
*  cumulative hours, and cumulative GPA for the student being checked. *
*  GOODST is true or false according to whether or not the student is *
*  found to be in good standing, and NUMGS is the count of students who *
*  are in good standing.                                             *
*  Accepts: CLASS, CUMHRS, CUMGPA, and NUMGS                         *
*  Returns: GOODST and updated value of NUMGS                        *
*  Output:  Message indicating an illegal class code                 *
*******************************************************************************

      SUBROUTINE CHECK(CLASS, CUMHRS, CUMGPA, GOODST, NUMGS)

      INTEGER CLASS, NUMGS
      REAL CUMHRS, CUMGPA
      LOGICAL GOODST, HRSCHK, GPACHK

      IF ((CLASS .LT. 1) .OR. (CLASS .GT. 3)) THEN
         PRINT *, '*** ILLEGAL CLASS CODE ***'
         GOODST = .FALSE.
      ELSE
         GOODST = HRSCHK(CLASS, CUMHRS) .AND. GPACHK(CLASS, CUMGPA)
      END IF

      IF (GOODST) THEN
         NUMGS = NUMGS + 1
      END IF

      END

**  REPORT  ********************************************************************
           .
           .
           .
      LOGICAL GOODST
           .
           .
           .
      PRINT *, 'GOOD STANDING: ', GOODST
      END
```

Figure 7.9   *(cont.)*

```
** HRSCHK ************************************************************
* Check cumulative hours (CUMHRS) of student in CLASS.  Local       *
* parameters FRESH, SOPH, and JUNIOR give the minimum number of hours *
* required of freshmen, sophomores, and juniors, respectively.      *
* Accepts: CLASS and CUMHRS                                         *
* Returns: True or false according to whether student has accumulated *
*          enough hours                                             *
********************************************************************

      LOGICAL FUNCTION HRSCHK(CLASS, CUMHRS)

      INTEGER CLASS
      REAL CUMHRS, FRESH, SOPH, JUNIOR
      PARAMETER (FRESH = 25.0, SOPH = 50.0, JUNIOR = 85.0)

      IF (CLASS .EQ. 1) THEN
         HRSCHK = (CUMHRS .GE. FRESH)
      ELSE IF (CLASS .EQ. 2) THEN
         HRSCHK = (CUMHRS .GE. SOPH)
      ELSE
         HRSCHK = (CUMHRS .GE. JUNIOR)
      END IF

      END


** GPACHK ************************************************************
* Check cumulative GPA (CUMGPA) of student in CLASS. Local parameters *
* GPA1, GPA2, and GPA3 give the minimum GPA required of freshmen,    *
* sophomores, and juniors, respectively.                            *
* Accepts: CLASS and CUMGPA                                         *
* Returns: True or false according to whether student's GPA is high  *
*          enough                                                   *
********************************************************************

      LOGICAL FUNCTION GPACHK(CLASS, CUMGPA)

      INTEGER CLASS
      REAL CUMGPA, GPA1, GPA2, GPA3
      PARAMETER (GPA1 = 1.7, GPA2 = 1.85, GPA3 = 1.95)
```

Figure 7.9   *(cont.)*

```
        IF (CLASS .EQ. 1) THEN
            GPACHK = (CUMGPA .GE. GPA1)
        ELSE IF (CLASS .EQ. 2) THEN
            GPACHK = (CUMGPA .GE. GPA2)
        ELSE
            GPACHK = (CUMGPA .GE. GPA3)
        END IF

        END
```

Sample run:

```
* * * * * * * * * * INFORM CALLED * * * * * * * * * *
ENTER STUDENT NUMBER, CLASS, CUM. HOURS, CUM. GPA:
1234 1 0 0
HOURS AND GRADE?
5 3.0
HOURS AND GRADE?
4 3.0
HOURS AND GRADE?
3.5 3.0
HOURS AND GRADE?
4 3.0
HOURS AND GRADE?
3 3.0
HOURS AND GRADE?
2 3.0
HOURS AND GRADE?
0 0
* * * * * * * * * * REPORT CALLED * * * * * * * * * *
SNUMB:    1234
CLASS:    1
CUM. HOURS:      21.5000
CURR. GPA:       3.00000
CUM. GPA:        3.00000
GOOD STANDING:    F

MORE (Y or N)?
Y
ENTER STUDENT NUMBER, CLASS, CUM. HOURS, CUM. GPA:
55555 5 10 0
HOURS AND GRADE?
3 3.0
```

Figure 7.9 *(cont.)*

```
HOURS AND GRADE?
0 0
*** ILLEGAL CLASS CODE ***
********** REPORT CALLED **********
SNUMB:   55555
CLASS:    5
CUM. HOURS:     13.0000
CURR. GPA:      3.00000
CUM. GPA:      0.692308
GOOD STANDING:   F


MORE (Y or N)?
N
********** WRAPUP CALLED **********
```

Testing of the newly added subprograms indicates that they are correct. Thus we can proceed to develop algorithms for the remaining subtasks REPORT, INFORM, and WRAPUP:

VARIABLES FOR REPORT

SNUMB, CLASS, CUMHRS, CUMGPA, GOODST as in PROCES

ALGORITHM FOR REPORT

```
*  Displays statistics and eligibility status for a given student.           *
*  Accepts:  Student's SNUMB, CLASS, CUMHRS, CURGPA, CUMGPA, and  *
*            GOODST                                                          *
*  Output:   SNUMB, CLASS, CUMHRS, CURGPA, CUMGPA, and a message indi-  *
*            cating whether student is in good standing                      *
```

A series of output statements to display the required information in an acceptable format.

ALGORITHM FOR INFORM

```
*  Displays instructions to the user.                                        *
*  Output:   User instructions                                               *
```

A series of output statements that inform the user of the purpose of the program and provide instructions for entering the data.

VARIABLES FOR WRAPUP

NUMSTU, NUMGS, GPASUM as in main algorithm

ALGORITHM FOR WRAPUP

```
*  Displays summary statistics.                                               *
*  Accepts:  NUMSTU, NUMGS, and GPASUM                                        *
*  Output:   Number of students processed, average current GPA for all students, and  *
*            the number found to be eligible                                  *
```

1. Display NUMSTU.
2. If NUMSTU is not zero

    a. Calculate and display the average current GPA for all students.

    b. Display NUMGS.

We write and test each of these subprograms and add them to the program, producing the final version of the program shown in Figure 7.10. Each of the subprograms was tested as it was developed and added to the program. Although each was tested individually, it must also be verified that these subprograms were integrated into the program correctly, that is, that they interact with one another correctly, passing the required information to and from one another. This type of testing is called **integration testing.**

When all of the subprograms have been developed and integrated into the program, the complete program should be tested to determine that the overall system functions correctly. This is known as **system testing.**

Figure 7.10 Academic standing—version 3.

```
PROGRAM ACADEM
         .
         .
         .


** INFORM ****************************************************************
*  Subroutine to display instructions to the user.                       *
*  Output:  Several lines of instructions                                *
   **********************************************************************


   SUBROUTINE INFORM

   PRINT *, 'YOU WILL FIRST BE ASKED TO ENTER THE STUDENT''S'
   PRINT *, 'NUMBER, CLASS, CUMULATIVE HOURS, AND CUMULATIVE GPA.'
   PRINT *, 'ENTER THESE WITH AT LEAST ONE SPACE OR COMMA',
  +         ' SEPARATING THEM.'
   PRINT *
```

Figure 7.10   *(cont.)*

```
      PRINT *, 'YOU WILL THEN BE ASKED TO ENTER THE NUMBER OF HOURS AND'
      PRINT *, 'THE NUMERIC GRADE EARNED FOR EACH OF THE COURSES THE'
      PRINT *, 'STUDENT TOOK DURING THE CURRENT YEAR.  SEPARATE THE'
      PRINT *, 'NUMBER OF HOURS FROM THE GRADE BY AT LEAST ONE SPACE'
      PRINT *, 'OR BY A COMMA.  ENTER 0 FOR HOURS AND 0 FOR GRADES WHEN'
      PRINT *, 'YOU ARE FINISHED ENTERING THE INFORMATION FOR EACH',
     +            ' STUDENT.'
      PRINT *
      PRINT *
      PRINT *

      END
          .
          .
          .


      SUBROUTINE PROCES(NUMSTU, NUMGS, GPASUM)
          .
          .

      CALL CALCUL(SNUMB, CLASS, NUMSTU, CUMHRS, CUMGPA, CURGPA,
     +            GPASUM)
      CALL CHECK(CLASS, CUMHRS, CUMGPA, GOODST, NUMGS)
      CALL REPORT(SNUMB, CLASS, CUMHRS, CURGPA, CUMGPA, GOODST)
          .
          .
          .

** WRAPUP *******************************************************************
* Subroutine to print some summary statistics.                             *
* Accepts:  Number of students (NUMSTU), number in good standing           *
*           (NUMGS), and sum of all GPAs (GPASUM)                          *
* Output:   Report containing values of NUMSTU, NUMGS, and average          *
*           GPA                                                             *
****************************************************************************

      SUBROUTINE WRAPUP(NUMSTU, NUMGS, GPASUM)

      INTEGER NUMSTU, NUMGS
      REAL GRASUM

      PRINT *
      PRINT *
      PRINT *, '**********************************************************'
      PRINT *, '*                 SUMMARY STATISTICS                     *'
      PRINT *, '**********************************************************'
      PRINT *
```

Figure 7.10   *(cont.)*

```
      PRINT 10, 'NUMBER OF STUDENTS PROCESSED:   ', NUMSTU
      IF (NUMSTU .NE. 0) THEN
         PRINT 20, 'AVERAGE CURRENT GPA OF STUDENTS:',
                 GPASUM/REAL (NUMSTU)
    +    PRINT 10, 'NUMBER IN GOOD STANDING:         ', NUMGS
10       FORMAT (1X, A, I5)
20       FORMAT (1X, A, F5.2)
      END IF

      END
           .
           .
           .
** CALCUL *************************************************************
           .
           .
           .
** CHECK  *************************************************************
           .
           .
           .
**REPORT**************************************************************
* Subroutine to display the statistics for a given student.         *
* Accepts:  Student's number (SNUMB), CLASS, cumulative hours (CUMHRS),*
*           current GPA (CURGPA), cumulative GPA (CUMGPA), and       *
*           indicator (GOODST) whether student is in good standing   *
* Output:   SNUMB, CLASS, CUMHRS, CURGPA, and a message indicating   *
*           whether student is in good standing                      *
*********************************************************************

      SUBROUTINE REPORT(SNUMB, CLASS, CUMHRS, CURGPA, CUMGPA, GOODST)

      INTEGER SNUMB, CLASS
      REAL CUMHRS, CURGPA, CUMGPA
      LOGICAL GOODST

      PRINT *
      PRINT 10, SNUMB
10    FORMAT (1X, '***** REPORT FOR STUDENT', I6, ' *****')
      PRINT 20, 'CLASS:            ', CLASS
20    FORMAT(1X, A, I6)
      PRINT 30, 'CUMULATIVE HOURS:', CUMHRS
      PRINT 30, 'CURRENT GPA:      ', CURGPA
      PRINT 30, 'CUMULATIVE GPA:  ', CUMGPA
30    FORMAT(1X, A, F6.2)
```

Figure 7.10   *(cont.)*

```
      IF (GOODST) THEN
          PRINT 40, 'IN GOOD STANDING'
      ELSE
          PRINT 40, '*** NOT IN GOOD STANDING ***'
      END IF
40    FORMAT(1X, A / 1X, 35('*'))

      END
          .
          .
          .
** HRSCHK *********************************************************************
          .
          .
          .
** GPACHK *********************************************************************
          .
          .
          .
```

Sample run:

```
YOU WILL FIRST BE ASKED TO ENTER THE STUDENT'S
NUMBER, CLASS, CUMULATIVE HOURS, AND CUMULATIVE GPA.
ENTER THESE WITH AT LEAST ONE SPACE OR COMMA SEPARATING THEM.

YOU WILL THEN BE ASKED TO ENTER THE NUMBER OF HOURS AND
THE NUMERIC GRADE EARNED FOR EACH OF THE COURSES THE
STUDENT TOOK DURING THE CURRENT YEAR. SEPARATE THE
NUMBER OF HOURS FROM THE GRADE BY AT LEAST ONE SPACE
OR BY A COMMA. ENTER 0 FOR HOURS AND 0 FOR GRADES WHEN
YOU ARE FINISHED ENTERING THE INFORMATION FOR EACH STUDENT.

ENTER STUDENT NUMBER, CLASS, CUM. HOURS, CUM. GPA:
1234 1 0 0
HOURS AND GRADE?
5 3.0
HOURS AND GRADE?
4 3.0
HOURS AND GRADE?
3.5 3.0
HOURS AND GRADE?
4 3.0
HOURS AND GRADE?
3 3.0
HOURS AND GRADE?
2 3.0
```

Figure 7.10 *(cont.)*

```
HOURS AND GRADE?
0 0

***** REPORT FOR STUDENT 1234 *****
CLASS:               1
CUMULATIVE HOURS: 21.50
CURRENT GPA:      3.00
CUMULATIVE GPA:    3.00
*** NOT IN GOOD STANDING ***
*********************************

MORE (Y or N)?
Y
ENTER STUDENT NUMBER, CLASS, CUM. HOURS, CUM. GPA:
3333 2 30 3.3
HOURS AND GRADE?
5 3.3
HOURS AND GRADE?
5 4.0
HOURS AND GRADE?
5 2.7
HOURS AND GRADE?
5 3.0
HOURS AND GRADE?
3 3.7
HOURS AND GRADE?
0 0

***** REPORT FOR STUDENT 3333 *****
CLASS:               2
CUMULATIVE HOURS: 53.00
CURRENT GPA:      3.31
CUMULATIVE GPA:    3.30
IN GOOD STANDING
*********************************

MORE (Y or N)?
Y
ENTER STUDENT NUMBER, CLASS, CUM. HOURS, CUM. GPA:
4444 3 60 2.0
HOURS AND GRADE?
5 1.0
HOURS AND GRADE?
5 1.3
```

Figure 7.10   *(cont.)*

```
HOURS AND GRADE?
4 0.7
HOURS AND GRADE?
3 0.7
HOURS AND GRADE?
5 1.0
HOURS AND GRADE?
0
0


***** REPORT FOR STUDENT 4444 *****
CLASS:               3
CUMULATIVE HOURS: 82.00
CURRENT GPA:       0.97
CUMULATIVE GPA:    1.72
*** NOT IN GOOD STANDING ***
*********************************


MORE (Y or N)?
N



***********************************************************
*                   SUMMARY STATISTICS                    *
***********************************************************

NUMBER OF STUDENTS PROCESSED:      3
AVERAGE CURRENT GPA OF STUDENTS: 2.43
NUMBER IN GOOD STANDING:           1
```

7.6 THE COMMON STATEMENT

As illustrated in Section 7.5, large programming projects are usually developed as a collection of program units, each of which is designed to perform a particular part of the total processing required. Usually each of these program units must access a common set of data. Although *sharing this information via argument lists is preferred* (as we have done in the preceding sections), it is also possible to establish certain common memory areas in which this data can be stored and accessed *directly* by each of the program units. These common regions are established using the COMMON statement introduced in this section. Additional details regarding the COMMON statement are found in Chapter 12.

It must be emphasized, however, that *although common regions can be used to share data among program units, it is usually unwise to do so,* because this practice destroys the independence of these program units and thus makes modular programming more difficult. If several program units share a common area and one of these program units changes the value of a variable that has been allocated memory in this common region, the value of that variable is changed in all of the other program units. Consequently, it is difficult to determine the value of that variable at any particular point in the program.

Blank Common

One form of the COMMON **statement** establishes a common region to which no name is assigned. This region is thus called **blank** or **unnamed common.** The form of the COMMON statement for this is

---

Blank COMMON *Statement*

Form:

```
COMMON list
```

where
    list is a list of variables separated by commas.

Purpose:
Allocates memory locations in blank common to the variables in *list* in the order in which they are listed. The COMMON statement must appear in the specification part of a program unit.

When COMMON statements are used in different program units, the first item in each list is allocated the first memory location in blank common. These items are thus **associated,** because they refer to the same memory location. Successive items in the list are similarly associated because they are allocated successive memory locations in the common region.

The following restrictions apply to items that are allocated memory locations in blank common:

1. Associated items must be of the same type.
2. If they are of character type, they should be of the same length.
3. They may not be initialized in DATA statements (a BLOCK DATA subprogram, as described in Section 12.5, can be used for this purpose).
4. They may not be used as formal arguments in the subprogram in which the COMMON statement appears.
5. Numeric and character variables (or arrays) may not both be allocated memory locations from blank common.

To illustrate, suppose that one program unit contains the statements

```
REAL A, B
INTEGER M, N
COMMON A, B, M, N
```

These four variables are allocated memory locations in the common region in the following order:

Variable	Blank Common Location
A	#1
B	#2
M	#3
N	#4

If another program unit contains the statements

```
REAL W, X
INTEGER I, J
COMMON W, X, I, J
```

then W, X, I, and J are also allocated the first four memory locations in the common region:

Variable	Blank Common Location
W	#1
X	#2
I	#3
J	#4

It follows that these eight variables are then associated in the following manner:

Variable	Blank Common Location	Variable
A	#1	W
B	#2	X
M	#3	I
N	#4	J

As a simple illustration of the use of COMMON, the program in Figure 7.3 can be written as shown in Figure 7.11. Notice that no arguments are listed in the CALL statement or in the subroutine heading. The COMMON statements associate the variables RCOORD, TCOORD, XCOORD, and YCOORD in the main program with the variables R, THETA, X, and Y, respectively, in the subprogram CONVER.

Figure 7.11 Converting polar coordinates to rectangular coordinates—version 2.

```
      PROGRAM POLAR
************************************************************************
* This program accepts the polar coordinates of a point and displays  *
* the corresponding rectangular coordinates.  The subroutine CONVER is *
* used to effect the conversion; a COMMON statement is used to        *
* associate variables in the main program with variables in CONVER.   *
* Variables used are:                                                 *
*     RCOORD, TCOORD : polar coordinates of a point                   *
*     XCOORD, YCOORD : rectangular coordinates of a point             *
*     RESPON         : user response to more-data question            *
*                                                                     *
* Input:  RCOORD, TCOORD, and RESPON                                  *
* Output: XCOORD and YCOORD                                           *
************************************************************************

      CHARACTER*1 RESPON
      REAL RCOORD, TCOORD, XCOORD, YCOORD
      COMMON RCOORD, TCOORD, XCOORD, YCOORD

* Read and convert coordinates until user signals no more data

10    CONTINUE
          PRINT *, 'ENTER POLAR COORDINATES (IN RADIANS)'
          READ *, RCOORD, TCOORD
          CALL CONVER
          PRINT *, 'RECTANGULAR COORDINATES:'
          PRINT *, XCOORD, YCOORD
          PRINT *
          PRINT *, 'MORE POINTS TO CONVERT (Y OR N)?'
          READ '(A)', RESPON
      IF (RESPON .NE. 'N') GO TO 10

      END
```

Figure 7.11   *(cont.)*

```
**CONVER**************************************************************
* Subroutine to convert polar coordinates (R,THETA) to rectangular   *
* coordinates (X,Y).                                                 *
* Accepts: Polar coordinates R and THETA (in blank common)           *
* Returns: Rectangular coordinates X and Y (in blank common)         *
*********************************************************************

      SUBROUTINE CONVER

      REAL R, THETA, X, Y
      COMMON R, THETA, X, Y

      X = R * COS(THETA)
      Y = R * SIN(THETA)

      END
```

In the preceding examples we used different names for the same common locations. Although this is legal, the association between elements in different program units is much clearer if the same names are used in each program unit. This is especially important if there are a large number of program units and/or a large number of shared variables.

Named Common

In some situations it may be preferable to share one set of variables among some program units and to share another set among other program units. But this sharing is not possible using the form of COMMON statement considered thus far, because it establishes a single common region. It is possible, however, using a form of the COMMON statement that establishes common regions that are **named.** This form is as follows.

Named COMMON *Statement*

Form:

> COMMON /$name_1$/ $list_1$ /$name_2$/ $list_2$ . . .

where

> each of $name_1$, $name_2$, . . . is the name of a list of items (namely, those in $list_1$, $list_2$,..., respectively) that are to be associated with the items in a block having the same name in another program unit.

> **Purpose:**
> Establishes named common regions with the specified names and allocates memory locations in region *name*$_i$ to the variables in *list*$_i$ in the order in which they are listed. This association must be complete; that is, there must be a one-to-one correspondence between the items in associated blocks. The COMMON statement must appear in the specification part of a program unit.

For example, suppose that the variables A, B, L, and M are to be shared by the main program and a subroutine GAMMA, and the variables A, B, N1, N2, N3 shared by the main program and the subroutine BETA. The following program scheme would be appropriate:

```
REAL A, B
INTEGER L, M, N1, N2, N3
COMMON /FIRST/ A, B /SECOND/ L, M /THIRD/ N1, N2, N3
        .
        .
        .

END

SUBROUTINE GAMMA
REAL A, B
INTEGER L, M
COMMON /FIRST/ A, B /SECOND/ L, M
        .
        .
        .

END

SUBROUTINE BETA
REAL A, B
INTEGER N1, N2, N3
COMMON /FIRST/ A, B /THIRD/ N1, N2, N3
        .
        .
        .

END
```

It is possible to use a single COMMON statement to establish both named and unnamed common regions. In this case, the unnamed region is "named" by a blank (or no space at all) between the slashes (thus the name "blank" COMMON). In the preceding example, therefore, we could also have used

```
REAL A, B
INTEGER L, M, N1, N2, N3
COMMON // A,B /SECOND/ L, M /THIRD/ N1, N2, N3
        .
        .
        .

END
```

```
SUBROUTINE GAMMA
REAL A, B
INTEGER L, M
COMMON // A, B /SECOND/ L, M

      .
      .
      .

END

SUBROUTINE BETA
REAL A, B
INTEGER N1, N2, N3
COMMON // A, B /THIRD/ N1, N2, N3

      .
      .
      .

END
```

CHAPTER REVIEW

Summary

FORTRAN, like most programming languages, provides two kinds of subprograms, functions and subroutines, and this chapter considers subroutines. It begins by describing and illustrating with several examples how subroutines are written and how the CALL statement is used to reference them. Simulation, an important tool in solving problems that involve randomness, is discussed in Sections 7.3 and 7.4. Top-down design using a divide-and-conquer strategy is illustrated in Section 7.5 by developing a large program for a fairly complex software engineering project. The chapter closes with a discussion of the COMMON statement.

FORTRAN SUMMARY

Subroutine Subprogram

subroutine heading
specification part
execution part

Subroutine Heading

```
SUBROUTINE name(formal-argument-list)
```

where the subroutine *name* may be any legal FORTRAN identifier and *formal-argument-list* is a list of identifiers.

Example:

```
SUBROUTINE DEGPRN(ANGLE, RADIAN)
```

Purpose:
Names the subroutine and lists its arguments.

CALL **Statement**

```
CALL name(actual-argument-list)
```

where *name* is the name of the subroutine being called and *actual-argument-list* contains the variables, constants, or expressions that are the actual arguments.

Example:

```
CALL DEGPRN(ALPHA, BETA)
```

Purpose:
Calls the named subroutine. Execution of the current program unit is suspended and execution of the subroutine begins. When execution of the subroutine is completed, execution of the original program unit resumes with the statement following the CALL statement.

SAVE **Statement**

```
SAVE list-of-variables
```

where the list of variables may be omitted.

Examples:

```
SAVE ALPHA, BETA, GAMMA
SAVE
```

Purpose:
Saves the values of local variables from one subprogram reference to the next. If the list of variables is omitted, all local variables will be saved.

Blank COMMON **Statement**

```
COMMON list-of-variables
```

Example:

```
COMMON ALPHA, BETA
COMMON ANGLE, RADIAN
```

Purpose:
Allocates memory locations in blank common to the variables in *list-of-variables* in the order in which they are listed.

Named COMMON Statement

```
COMMON /name₁/ list₁ /name₂/ list₂ . . .
```

where each *list*$_i$ is a list of variables.

Example:

```
COMMON /FIRST/ A, B /SECOND/ L, M /THIRD/ N1, N2, N3
```

Purpose:
Establishes named common regions with the specified names and allocates memory locations in region *name*$_i$ to the variables in *list*$_i$ in the order in which they are listed.

PROGRAMMING POINTERS

Program Style and Design

1. *Subprograms should be documented in the same manner as the main program is.* The documentation should include a brief description of the processing carried out by the subprograms, the values passed to them, the values returned by them, and what the arguments and local variables represent.

2. *Subprograms are separate program units, and the program format should reflect this fact.* In this text, we

   - Insert a blank comment line before and after each subprogram to set it off from other program units.
   - Follow the stylistic standards described in earlier chapters when writing subprograms.

3. *In the formal argument list of a subroutine, it is usually considered good practice to list arguments whose values are passed to the subroutine (input arguments) before arguments whose values are returned by the subroutine (output arguments).*

4. *Programs for solving complex problems should be designed in a top-down fashion.* The problem should be divided into simpler subproblems, perhaps several times, so that subprograms can be written to solve each of them.

5. *Information should be shared among program units by using argument lists rather than common regions.* The use of common regions destroys the independence of program units and thus hinders modular design.

Potential Problems

1. *When a subprogram is referenced, the number of actual arguments must be the same as the number of formal arguments, and the type of each actual argument must agree with the type of the corresponding formal argument.* For example, consider the declarations

```
SUBROUTINE SUB(NUM1, NUM2)
INTEGER NUM1, NUM2
        .
        .
        .
```

If K, L, and M are integer variables, the subroutine references

```
CALL SUB(K, L, M)
```

and

```
CALL SUB(K, 3.5)
```

are incorrect. In the first case, the number of actual arguments does not agree with the number of formal arguments, and in the second, the real value 3.5 cannot be associated with the integer argument NUM2.

2. *Information is shared among different program units only via the arguments and the function name for function subprograms (or via common regions).* Thus, if the value of a variable in one program unit is needed by another program unit, it must be passed as an argument (or by using a common region), as this variable is not otherwise accessible to the other program unit. One consequence is that *local variables*—those not used as arguments or listed in COMMON statements—as well as statement labels in one program unit may be used in another program unit without conflict.

3. *When control returns from a subprogram, all local variables in that subprogram become undefined unless a SAVE statement is used.*

4. *Corresponding actual arguments and formal arguments are associated with the same memory locations. Therefore, if the value of one of the formal arguments is changed in a subprogram, the value of the corresponding actual argument also changes.* For example, if a subroutine is defined by

```
SUBROUTINE SUBBER(I, SUM)
INTEGER I, SUM

SUM = 0
DO 10 I = 1, 10
   SUM = SUM + I
10 CONTINUE
END
```

then when it is called by a statement such as

```
CALL SUBBER(COUNT, TOTAL)
```

where COUNT and TOTAL are integer variables, the value of TOTAL will change to the value of SUM. However, the value of COUNT will also be changed (to 10), since it corresponds to the formal argument I, whose value is changed in the subprogram; and this was probably not intended. The value of a constant cannot be changed in this manner, however. For example, the subroutine call

```
CALL SUBBER(2, TOTAL)
```

does not change the value of the constant 2 to 10. Values of constants and expressions that are used as actual arguments in a subprogram reference are placed in temporary memory locations, and it is the contents of these memory locations that are changed. If a variable name is enclosed in parentheses in the actual argument list, then this argument is treated as an expression, and thus the value of that variable cannot be changed by a subprogram reference. For example, the subroutine reference

```
CALL SUBBER((COUNT), TOTAL)
```

does not change the value of COUNT.

5. *User-defined subprograms used as actual arguments in a subprogram reference must be listed in an* EXTERNAL *statement in the program unit that contains that reference.*

6. *Items that are allocated memory locations in a common region are subject to the following restrictions:*

   - Associated items must be of the same type.
   - Associated items of character type should have the same length.
   - Numeric items and character items cannot be allocated memory locations in the same common region.
   - They may not be initialized in DATA statements.
   - They may not be used as formal arguments in the subprogram in which the COMMON statement appears.

PROGRAMMING PROBLEMS

Section 7.1

1. Write a program that reads the number of a month and calls the subprogram of Exercise 1 of Section 7.1 to display the name of the month.

2. Write a program that reads several pairs of integers and for each pair calls the subprogram SWITCH in Exercise 2 of Section 7.1 to interchange their values, and then displays their values.

3. Write a program that reads several measurements in centimeters and for each measurement calls the subprogram of Exercise 3 of Section 7.1 to find the corresponding measurement in yards, feet, and inches and then displays this converted measurement.

4. Write a program that reads several weights in grams and for each measurement calls the subprogram of Exercise 4 of Section 7.1 to find the corresponding weight in pounds and ounces and then displays this converted weight.

5. Write a program that reads several times in military format and for each time calls the subprogram of Exercise 5 of Section 7.1 to find the corresponding hours–minutes–A.M./P.M. representation and then displays this representation.

6. Write a program that reads several times in hours–minutes–A.M./P.M. format and for each time calls the subprogram of Exercise 6 of Section 7.1 to find the corresponding military representation and then displays this representation.

7. Write a program that reads the diameters and heights of several right circular cylinders and displays the circumference, total surface area (including the ends), and the volume of each. The circumference should be calculated by a statement function, the surface area by a function subprogram, and the volume in a subroutine subprogram.

8. Consider a simply supported beam to which a single concentrated load is applied:

For $a \geq b$, the maximum deflection is given by

$$\text{MAX} = \frac{-Pb(L^2 - b^2)^{3/2}}{9\sqrt{3}\ EIL}$$

the deflection at the load by

$$\text{LDEF} = \frac{-Pa^2b^2}{3EIL}$$

and the deflection at the center of the beam by

$$\text{CEN} = \frac{-Pb(3L^2 - 4b^2)}{48EI}$$

where P is the load, E is the modulus of elasticity, and I is the moment of inertia. For $a \leq b$, simply replace b with a and a with b in the preceding equations.

Write a program that produces a table of values for MAX, LDEF, and CEN as the load position is moved along the beam in 6-inch increments. It should use a subroutine to calculate these values. Run your program with the following values: $L = 360$ inches, $P = 24,000$ pounds, $E = 30 \times 10^6$ psi, and $I = 795.5$ in^4.

9. The *greatest common divisor* GCD(A, B) of two integers A and B, not both of which are zero, can be calculated by the Euclidean Algorithm described in Exercise 11 of Section 6.1. The *least common multiple* of A and B, LCM(A, B), is the smallest nonnegative integer that is a multiple of both A and B and can be calculated using

$$\text{LCM}(A,B) = \frac{|A * B|}{\text{GCD}(A,B)}$$

Write a program that reads two integers, calls a subroutine that calculates and returns their greatest common divisor and least common multiple, and displays these two values.

10. Write a program that reads a positive integer and then calls a subprogram that displays its prime factorization, that is, a subprogram that expresses a positive integer as a product of primes or indicates that it is a prime (see Exercise 12 of Section 6.1 for the definition of a prime number).

11. One simple method of calculating depreciation is the *straight-line* method described in Section 4.2. Write a subprogram that calculates and displays annual depreciation using this method for a given amount and a given number of years. Test your subprogram with a program that reads the current year, the amount to be depreciated, and the number of years, and then calls the subprogram to calculate and display the annual depreciation.

12. Another method of depreciation described in Section 4.2 is the *sum-of-the-years'-digits* method. Write a subroutine that receives the amount to be depreciated using this method and the number of years and then displays a depreciation table that shows each year number and the amount to be depreciated for that year, beginning with the current year and continuing for the specified number of years. Test your subprogram with a program that reads the current year, an amount to be depreciated, and the number of years over which it is to be depreciated, and then calls this subprogram to generate a depreciation table.

   A possible addition to your program: To find how much is saved in taxes, assume a fixed tax rate over these years, and assume that the amounts saved in taxes by claiming the depreciation as a deduction are invested and earn interest at some fixed annual rate.

13. Another method of calculating depreciation is the *double-declining balance* method as described in Programming Problem 9 of Chapter 4. Write a subroutine that receives the amount to be depreciated using this method, the number of years, and the year in which to switch to the straight-line method (Problem 11); it then dis-

plays a depreciation table that shows each year number and the amount to be depreciated for that year, beginning with the current year and continuing for the specified number of years. Test your subprogram with a program that reads the current year, an amount to be depreciated, the number of years over which it is to be depreciated, and the year in which to switch to the straight-line method, and then calls this subprogram to generate a depreciation table.

A possible addition to your program: Calculate the tax savings as described in the previous problem.

14. Proceed as in Problem 13, but print one table giving the amount to be depreciated each year, assuming that we switch in year 1 (use the straight-line method for all years), and another table giving the amount to be depreciated each year, assuming that we switch in year 2, and so on.

15. Write a subroutine that calculates the amount of city income tax and the amount of federal income tax to be withheld from an employee's pay for one pay period. Assume that the city income tax withheld is computed by taking 1.15 percent of gross pay on the first $15,000 earned per year and that the federal income tax withheld is computed by taking the gross pay less $15 for each dependent claimed and multiplying it by 20 percent.

Use this subroutine in a program that for each of several employees reads his or her employee number, number of dependents, hourly pay rate, city income tax withheld to date, federal income tax withheld to date, and hours worked for this pay period and that calculates and prints the employee number, gross pay and net pay for this pay period, the amount of city income tax and the amount of federal income tax withheld for this pay period, and the total amounts withheld through this pay period.

Section 7.4

16. The tensile strength of a certain metal component has an approximate normal distribution with a mean of 10,000 pounds per square inch and a standard deviation of 100 pounds per square inch. Specifications require that all components have a tensile strength greater than 9800; all others must be scrapped. Write a program that uses the algorithm described in Section 7.4 to generate 1000 normally distributed random numbers representing the tensile strength of these components, and determine how many must be rejected.

17. Modify the shield program in Figure 7.7 to allow the particle to travel in any direction rather than simply left, right, forward, or backward. Choose a direction (angle) at random, and let the particle travel a fixed (or perhaps random) distance in that direction.

18. Write a program to simulate the random path of a particle in a box. A direction (angle) is chosen at random, and the particle travels a fixed (or random) distance in that direction. This procedure is repeated until the particle either passes out through the top of the box or collides with one of the sides or the bottom and stops. Calculate

the average number of times the particle escapes from the box and the average number of jumps needed for it to get out.

Some modifications are as follows: Use a two-dimensional box if a three-dimensional one seems too challenging. Let the particle bounce off the sides or the bottom of the box at the same angle with which it hits rather than stop when it collides with these boundaries.

19. The classic *drunkard's walk problem:* Over an eight-block line, the home of an intoxicated chap is at block eight, and a pub is at block one. Our poor friend starts at block n, $1 \leq n \leq 8$, and wanders at random, one block at a time, either toward or away from home. At any intersection, he moves toward the pub with a certain probability, say 2/3, and toward home with a certain probability, say 1/3. Having gotten either home or to the pub, he remains there. Write a program to simulate 500 trips in which he starts at block two, another 500 in which he starts at block three, and so forth up to block seven. For each starting point, calculate and print the percentage of the time he ends up at home and the average number of blocks he walked on each trip.

20. The famous *Buffon Needle problem* is as follows: A board is ruled with equidistant parallel lines, and a needle whose length is equal to the distance between these lines is dropped at random on the board. What is the probability that it crosses one of these lines? The answer to this problem is $2/\pi$. Write a program to simulate this experiment and obtain an estimate for π.

21. Consider a quarter circle inscribed in a square whose sides have length 1:

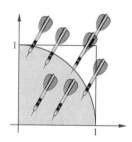

Imagine throwing q darts at this square and counting the total number p that hit within the quarter circle. For a large number of throws, we would expect

$$\frac{p}{q} \approx \frac{\text{area of quarter circle}}{\text{area of square}} = \frac{\pi}{4}$$

Write a program to approximate π using this method. To simulate throwing the darts, generate two random numbers X and Y and consider point (X, Y) as being where the dart hits.

22. A method of approximating π by throwing darts at a quarter circle inscribed in a square is described in Problem 21. This method can be generalized to find the area under the graph of any function and is known as a *Monte Carlo* method of approx-

imating integrals. To illustrate it, consider a rectangle that has base $[a, b]$ and height m, where $m \geq f(x)$ for all x in $[a, b]$:

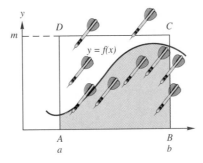

Imagine throwing q darts at rectangle $ABCD$ and counting the total number p that hit the shaded region. For a large number of throws, we would expect

$$\frac{p}{q} \approx \frac{\text{area of shaded region}}{\text{area of rectangle } ABCD}$$

Write a program to calculate areas using this Monte Carlo method. To simulate throwing the darts, generate two random numbers, X from $[a, b]$ and Y from $[0, m]$, and consider the point (X, Y) as being where the dart hits. Use your program to compute the current passing through a capacitor as described in Exercise 8 of Section 6.4.

23. Use Monte Carlo integration (see Problem 22) to find the fraction of fission neutrons with energies above a certain threshold as described in Exercise 10 of Section 6.4.

24. Use Monte Carlo integration (see Problem 22) to find the absorbed energy for the spring described in Exercise 12 of Section 6.4.

Section 7.6

25. Write a menu-driven program that allows the user to select one of the following methods of depreciation:

   1. Straight-line (see Problem 11)
   2. Sum-of-the-years'-digits (see Problem 12)
   3. Double-declining balance (see Problem 13)

   Design the program to be modular, using subprograms to implement the various options.

26. (Project) Many everyday situations involve *queues* (waiting lines): at supermarket checkout lanes, at ticket counters, at bank windows, and so on. Consider the fol-

lowing example: An airport has one runway. Each airplane takes three minutes to land and two minutes to take off. On the average, in one hour, eight planes land and eight take off. Assume that the planes arrive randomly. (Delays make the assumption of randomness quite reasonable.) There are two types of queues: airplanes waiting to land and airplanes waiting to take off. Because it is more expensive to keep a plane airborne than to have one waiting on the ground, we assume that an airplane waiting to land has priority over one waiting to take off.

Write a computer simulation of this airport's operation. To simulate landing arrivals, generate a random number corresponding to a one-minute interval; if it is less than 8/60, then a "landing arrival" occurs and joins the queue of planes waiting to land. Generate another random number to determine whether a "takeoff" arrival occurs; if so, it joins the takeoff queue. Next, check to determine whether the runway is free. If so, first check the landing queue, and if planes are waiting, allow the first airplane in the landing queue to land; otherwise, consider the queue of planes waiting to take off. Have the program calculate the average queue lengths and the average time an airplane spends in a queue. For this problem, you might simulate a 24-hour day. You might also investigate the effect of varying arrival and departure rates to simulate prime and slack times of the day, or what happens if the amount of time it takes to land or take off is increased or decreased.

Fortran 90

Features

Fortran 90 has added a number of new features that facilitate modular programming, including the following:

- A number of new intrinsic functions and subroutines have been added. Among the predefined subroutines are:

  RANDOM_NUMBER: CALL RANDOM_NUMBER(X) returns a random real number X in the interval (0, 1)

  RANDOM-SEED: CALL RANDOM-SEED initializes the random number generator

- Function and subroutine subprograms may be specified to be recursive by attaching the word RECURSIVE as a prefix to the subprogram heading. The program in Figure 6.13 illustrates the use of a recursive function.

- Program units may contain internal procedures. These have the same forms as subprograms except that they may not contain other internal procedures. A CONTAINS statement in a program unit signals that internal procedure definitions follow. These must be placed at the end of the execution part of that program unit. Internal procedures may be referenced in the same manner as (external) subprograms, but only within the program unit that contains them.

- A formal argument of a subprogram may be declared to be an IN argument, an OUT argument, or an INOUT argument by using an INTENT clause in a modified form of the type statement that specifies the type of that argument; for example, the program `Polar_to_Rectangular` in Figure 7.12 uses the following type statements to specify that the polar coordinates `R` and `Theta` passed to subroutine `Convert` are `IN` arguments and that the rectangular `X` and `Y` computed and returned by `Convert` are `OUT` arguments:

```
REAL, INTENT(IN) :: R, Theta
REAL, INTENT(OUT) :: X, Y
```

`IN` arguments may not be modified within the subprogram; `OUT` arguments are intended to return values to the corresponding actual arguments, which must therefore be variables; `INOUT` arguments are intended both to receive and to return values.

- Explicit interfaces with a subprogram may be provided by means of an interface block of the form

```
INTERFACE
    interface-body
END INTERFACE
```

where `interface-body` is a copy of the heading and specification part of the subprogram followed by an `END` statement. Figure 6.12 illustrates the use of an interface block.

- Any formal argument of a subprogram may be declared to be optional by including an `OPTIONAL` attribute in the type statement that specifies the type of that argument. See the Fortran 90 section at the end of Chapter 6 for examples.

- An interface block of the form

```
INTERFACE OPERATOR ASSIGN (=)
    interface-block for subroutine₁
    interface-block for subroutine₂
       .
       .
       .
END INTERFACE
```

may be used to extend the assignment operator (=) to other data types. The specified subroutines, each of which must have two arguments, implement assignment statements of the form

```
argument₁ = argument₂
```

If two or more subroutines are used to extend =, their formal argument lists must be sufficiently dissimilar in type that exactly one of them will be selected for execution.

- An interface block of the form

```
INTERFACE generic-name
   interface-block for subprogram₁
   interface-block for subprogram₂

           ⋮

END INTERFACE
```

may be used to define a subprogram name *generic-name* that may be used to reference any of *subprogram₁, subprogram₂, . . .* (all functions or all subroutines). The formal argument lists of these subprograms must be sufficiently dissimilar in number and/or type that a reference to *generic-name* with a list of actual arguments determines exactly one of *subprogram₁, subprogram₂, . . .* for execution.

- A third kind of program unit, a *module*, is provided for packaging definitions and declarations of parameters, variables, types, and subprograms so that they can be used by other program units. Modules are described in Section 13.1.

Example

Figure 7.12 Converting polar coordinates to rectangular coordinates—Fortran 90 version.

```fortran
PROGRAM Polar_to_Rectangular
!----------------------------------------------------------------------------
! This program accepts the polar coordinates of a point & displays
! the corresponding rectangular coordinates.  The subroutine Convert is
! used to effect the conversion.  Variables used are:
!   R_Coord, T_Coord : polar coordinates
!   X_Coord, Y_Coord : rectangular coordinates
!   Response         : user response to more-data query
!
! Input:  R_Coord, T_Coord, and Response
! Output: X_Coord and Y_Coord
!----------------------------------------------------------------------------

  IMPLICIT NONE
  REAL :: R_Coord, T_Coord, X_Coord, Y_Coord
  CHARACTER(LEN = 1) :: Response
```

Figure 7.12 *(cont.)*

```fortran
! Read and convert coordinates until user signals no more data

  DO
     PRINT *, "Enter polar coordinates (in radians):"
     READ *, R_Coord, T_Coord
     CALL Convert(R_Coord, T_Coord, X_Coord, Y_Coord)
     PRINT *, "Rectangular coordinates:"    PRINT *, X_Coord, Y_Coord
     PRINT *
     PRINT *, "More points to convert (Y or N)?"
     READ '(A)', Response
     IF (Response == "N" .OR. Response == "n") EXIT
  END DO

END PROGRAM Polar_to_Rectangular

! Convert ---------------------------------------------------------------
! Subroutine to convert polar coordinates (R,Theta) to rectangular
! coordinates (X,Y).
! Accepts: Polar coordinates R and Theta
! Returns: Rectangular coordinates X and Y
!-----------------------------------------------------------------------

SUBROUTINE Convert(R, Theta, X, Y)

  REAL, INTENT(IN) :: R, Theta
  REAL, INTENT(OUT) :: X, Y

  X = R * COS(Theta)
  Y = R * SIN(Theta)

END SUBROUTINE Convert
```

8

One-Dimensional Arrays

With silver bells, and cockle shells
And pretty maids all in a row.

MOTHER GOOSE

I've got a little list, I've got a little list.

GILBERT AND SULLIVAN, The Mikado

There is nothing more difficult to take in hand, more perilous to
conduct, or more uncertain in its success, than to take the lead in the
introduction of a new order of things.

NICCOLO MACHIAVELLI, The Prince

CHAPTER CONTENTS

8.1   Introduction to Arrays and Subscripted Variables

8.2   Input/Output of Arrays

8.3   Example: Processing a List of Failure Times

8.4   Application: Average Corn Yields

8.5   Array Processing

8.6   Application: Quality Control

8.7   Example: Vector Processing

8.8   Sorting

8.9   Application: Analyzing Construction Costs

8.10 Searching

8.11 Application: Searching a Chemistry Database

Chapter Review

Programming Pointers

Programming Problems

Fortran 90

*I*n Chapter 2 we introduced the six predefined FORTRAN data types, four for processing numeric data—integer, real, double precision, and complex—one for processing character data and one for processing logical data. These data types are called **simple** types because a data value of one of these types consists of a single item that cannot be subdivided. In many situations, however, it is necessary to process a collection of values that are related in some way, for example, a list of test scores, a collection of measurements resulting from some experiment, or a matrix. Processing collections using only simple data types can be extremely cumbersome, and for this reason, most high-level languages include special features for structuring such data. FORTRAN 77 provides one **structured** data type, the array, and in this chapter we consider one-dimensional arrays.

8.1 INTRODUCTION TO ARRAYS AND SUBSCRIPTED VARIABLES

In many of our examples, we processed a collection of data values by reading the data values one at a time and processing each value individually, for example, reading a failure time and assigning it to a variable, counting it, and adding it to a running sum. When the value was no longer needed, a new value was read for the same variable, counted, and added to the running sum. This process was repeated again and again. For many problems, however, the collection of data items must be processed several times. The following example illustrates.

Problem

Consider again the mean-time-to-failure problem from Section 4.5. Recall that in this problem a number of components in a circuit had been tested and the time at which each component failed was recorded. As a measure of the reliability of a component, the mean of these failure times was calculated. This computation required processing the list of failure times only once. Suppose now that we wish to analyze these failure times using a program to

1. Find the mean time to failure
2. Print a list of failure times greater than the mean
3. Sort the failure times so that they are in ascending order

Clearly, this will require processing the list several times. The following are two possible solutions.

Solution 1: Use One Variable for Each Failure Time. Suppose, for example, that there are 50 failure times. We might use 50 different variables, `FAIL1`, `FAIL2`, ..., `FAIL50`, thus creating 50 different memory locations to store the failure times:

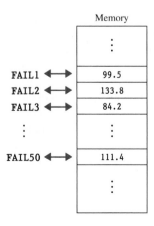

Although this approach might be practical if we have only a few data values to process, it is obviously cumbersome and awkward for large data sets, as the following program skeleton vividly demonstrates:

```
      PROGRAM FAILS

      REAL FAIL1, FAIL2, FAIL3, FAIL4, FAIL5,
     +     FAIL6, FAIL7, FAIL8, FAIL9, FAIL10,
              .
              .
              .
     +     FAIL46, FAIL47, FAIL48, FAIL49, FAIL50,
     +     MEANFT

* Read the failure times

      READ *, FAIL1, FAIL2, FAIL3, FAIL4, FAIL5,
     +        FAIL6, FAIL7, FAIL8, FAIL9, FAIL10,
                .
                .
                .
     +        FAIL46, FAIL47, FAIL48, FAIL49, FAIL50

* Calculate the mean time to failure

      MEANFT = (FAIL1 + FAIL2 + FAIL3 + FAIL4 + FAIL5
     +          + FAIL6 + FAIL7 + FAIL8 + FAIL9 + FAIL10
                .
                .
                .
     +          + FAIL46 + FAIL47 + FAIL48 + FAIL49
     +          + FAIL50) / 50.0
      PRINT *, 'MEAN TIME TO FAILURE = ', MEANFT

* Display failure times above the mean

      IF (FAIL1 .GT. MEANFT) THEN
         PRINT *, FAIL1
      END IF
      IF (FAIL2 .GT. MEANFT) THEN
         PRINT *, FAIL2
      END IF
```

```
        IF (FAIL3 .GT. MEANFT) THEN
            PRINT *, FAIL3
        END IF
                .

                .

                .
        IF (FAIL50 .GT. MEANFT) THEN
            PRINT *, FAIL50
        END IF
*  After about 200 lines of code, sort them?
*  There must be a better way!

        END
```

Solution 2: Use a Data File. If we do not use 50 different memory locations to store all of the failure times, then we are forced to read the values several times. Reentering them again and again so that the required processing can be carried out is obviously not practical. Instead, we can prepare a data file containing the failure times and read the values from it, as described in Chapter 5, rewinding the file each time we need to read through the list of failure times.

```
        PROGRAM FAILS

        REAL FAILTM, SUM, MEANFT
        INTEGER NTIMES, I, EOF

*  Read and count the failure times

        OPEN (UNIT = 10, FILE = 'TIMESFILE', STATUS = 'OLD')
        NTIMES = 0
        READ (10, *, IOSTAT = EOF) FAILTM
10      IF (EOF .GE. 0) THEN
            NTIMES = NTIMES + 1
            READ (10, *, IOSTAT = EOF) FAILTM
        GO TO 10
        END IF

*  Calculate the mean time to failure

        REWIND (UNIT = 10)
        SUM = 0
        DO 20 I = 1, NTIMES
            READ (10, *) FAILTM
            SUM = SUM + FAILTM
20      CONTINUE
        MEANFT = SUM / NTIMES
        PRINT *, 'MEAN TIME TO FAILURE =', MEANFT
```

```
* Display failure times above the mean

        REWIND (UNIT = 10)
        DO 30 I = 1, NTIMES
           READ (10, *) FAILTM
           IF (FAILTM .GT. MEANFT) THEN
              PRINT *, FAILTM
           END IF
30      CONTINUE

* Sort them???  Hm-m-m-m

        END
```

Although this program is more manageable than that in Solution 1, it is not a good solution to the problem because files are usually stored in secondary memory, from which data retrieval is slow.

Arrays

To solve this problem efficiently, we need a **data structure** to store and organize the entire collection of failure times, as in Solution 2. However, because of the slowness of file input/output, we need the values stored in main memory, as in Solution 1. Also, many kinds of list processing, such as sorting, cannot be done efficiently if the data values can be retrieved only **sequentially**, that is, when a value can be accessed only by searching from the beginning of the list. What is needed instead is a **direct access** structure that allows a data value to be stored or retrieved directly by specifying its location in the structure, so that it takes no longer to access the value in location 50 than to access that in location 5. And we prefer that the structure be stored in main memory so that storage and retrieval are fast. One such data structure is an **array** in which a fixed number of data values, all of the same type, are organized in a sequence and direct access to each value is possible by specifying its position in this sequence.

If an array is to be used in a FORTRAN program to solve the mean-time-to-failure problem, the computer must first be instructed to reserve a sequence of 50 memory locations for the failure times. For example, the specification statements

```
DIMENSION FAILTM(50)
REAL FAILTM
```

or

```
DIMENSION FAILTM(1:50)
REAL FAILTM
```

instruct the compiler to establish an array with name FAILTM consisting of 50 memory locations in which values of type REAL can be stored:

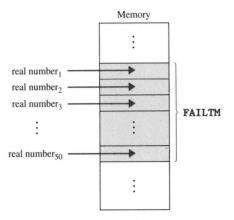

In the program we can then refer to this entire array of real numbers by using the **array variable** FAILTM, but we can also access each individual **element** of the array by means of a **subscripted variable** formed by appending a **subscript** (or **index**) enclosed in parentheses to the array variable. This subscript specifies the position of an array element. Thus, FAILTM(1) refers to the first element of the array FAILTM, FAILTM(2) to the second element, and so on. The preceding specification statements thus not only reserve a block of memory locations in which to store the elements of the array FAILTM, but they also associate the subscripted variables FAILTM(1), FAILTM(2), FAILTM(3),..., FAILTM(50) with these locations:

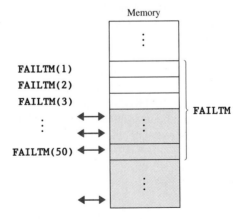

This same array could be declared by including the dimensioning information in the type statement itself,

```
REAL FAILTM(50)
```

or

```
REAL FAILTM(1:50)
```

Each subscripted variable `FAILTM(1)`, `FAILTM(2)`,..., `FAILTM(50)` names an individual memory location and hence can be used in much the same way as a simple variable can. For example, the assignment statement

```
FAILTM(4) = 177.8
```

stores the value 177.8 in the fourth location of the array `FAILTM`, and the output statement

```
PRINT *, FAILTM(10)
```

displays the value stored in the tenth location of the array `FAILTM`.

An important feature of the notation used for arrays is that the subscript attached to the array name may be an integer variable or expression. For example, the statements

```
IF (FAILTM(N) .LT. 100.0) THEN
    PRINT *, FAILTM(N), ' EARLY FAILURE'
END IF
```

retrieves the Nth item of the array `FAILTM`, compares it with 100.0, and prints it with the message `'EARLY FAILURE'` if it is less than 100.0. The statements

```
IF (FAILTM(I) .GT. FAILTM(I + 1)) THEN
    TEMP = FAILTM(I)
    FAILTM(I) = FAILTM(I + 1)
    FAILTM(I + 1) = TEMP
END IF
```

interchange the values of `FAILTM(I)` and `FAILTM(I + 1)` if the first is greater than the second.

Using an array reference in which the subscript is a variable or an expression within a loop that changes the value of the subscript on each pass through the loop is a convenient way to process each item in the array. Thus,

```
DO 10 I = 1, 50
    IF (FAILTM(I) .LT. 100.0) THEN
        PRINT *, FAILTM(I), ' EARLY FAILURE'
    END IF
10 CONTINUE
```

retrieves each item of the array `FAILTM` in sequence, beginning with `FAILTM(1)`, compares it with 100.0, and prints it with the message `'EARLY FAILURE'` if it is less than 100.0. The effect, therefore, is the same as if we write a sequence of 50 IF constructs, comparing each element of the array FAILTM with 100.0:

```
IF (FAILTM(1) .LT. 100.0) THEN
    PRINT *, FAILTM(1), ' EARLY FAILURE'
END IF
IF (FAILTM(2) .LT. 100.0) THEN
   PRINT *, FAILTM(2), ' EARLY FAILURE'
END IF
IF (FAILTM(3) .LT. 100.0) THEN
    PRINT *, FAILTM(3), ' EARLY FAILURE'
END IF

            .
            .
            .

IF (FAILTM(50) .LT. 100.0) THEN
    PRINT *, FAILTM(50), ' EARLY FAILURE'
END IF
```

The following diagram illustrates the output produced for a particular array FAILTM:

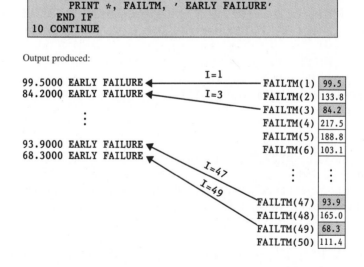

Arrays such as FAILTM involve only a single subscript and are called **one-dimensional arrays.** FORTRAN programs, however, may process arrays of more than one dimension, in which case each element of the array is designated by attaching the appropriate number of subscripts to the array name. In this chapter we consider only one-dimensional arrays; in the next chapter we discuss multidimensional arrays.

Array Declarations

The name and the range of the subscript of each one-dimensional array in a program may be declared in a DIMENSION statement of the form:

DIMENSION *Statement*

Form:

    DIMENSION *list*

where
   list is a list of **array declarations** of the form

       array-name(l:u)

       separated by commas;
   the pair *l*:*u* must be a pair of integer constants or parameters.

Purpose:
Declares that each of the identifiers *array-name* in the *list* is an array for which the range of values of the subscript will be from the lower limit *l* through the upper limit *u*; for example, the pair −2:5 declares that a certain subscript may be any of the integers −2, −1, 0, 1, 2, 3, 4, 5. If the minimum value of the subscript for an array is 1, then only the maximum subscript need be specified.

Thus, as we noted earlier, the integer array FAILTM that has a subscript ranging from 1 through 50 may be declared by the statements

```
DIMENSION FAILTM(50)
REAL FAILTM
```

or

```
DIMENSION FAILTM(1:50)
REAL FAILTM
```

Similarly, either

```
DIMENSION COUNT(20)
INTEGER COUNT
```

or

```
DIMENSION COUNT(1:20)
INTEGER COUNT
```

declares COUNT to be a one-dimensional integer array with a subscript ranging from 1 through 20. A single DIMENSION statement can be used to declare both arrays:

```
DIMENSION FAILTM(50), COUNT(20)
REAL FAILTM
INTEGER COUNT
```

As we have noted, the dimension information may also be given in a type statement. Thus,

```
REAL FAILTM(50)
INTEGER COUNT(20)
```

or

```
REAL FAILTM(1:50)
INTEGER COUNT(1:20)
```

can be used in place of the preceding statements. Similarly,

```
REAL ALPHA(20), BETA(20)
```

is acceptable in place of

```
DIMENSION ALPHA(20), BETA(20)
REAL ALPHA, BETA
```

The dimensions in array declarations can also be specified by parameters. For example, the array FAILTM can be declared by

```
INTEGER LLIM, ULIM
PARAMETER (LLIM = 1, ULIM = 50)
REAL FAILTM(LLIM:ULIM)
```

or

```
INTEGER ULIM
PARAMETER (ULIM = 50)
REAL FAILTM(ULIM)
```

Similarly, the arrays COUNT, ALPHA, and BETA can be declared by

```
INTEGER LIMIT
PARAMETER (LIMIT = 20)
INTEGER COUNT(LIMIT)
REAL ALPHA(LIMIT), BETA(LIMIT)
```

This is, in fact, the preferred method for declaring arrays because it makes programs more flexible; to modify a program to process arrays of some other size, only the PARAMETER statement need be changed.

The subscripts used in our examples of arrays have been positive valued, ranging from 1 through some upper limit. This is the most common subscript range, but as we noted earlier, FORTRAN does allow a subscript to be any integer value, positive, negative, or zero, provided that it does not fall outside the range specified in the array declaration. For example, the array declarations

```
INTEGER LLIM1, ULIM1, LLIM2, ULIM2
PARAMETER (LLIM1 = −1, ULIM1 = 3, LLIM2 = 0, ULIM2 = 5)
INTEGER GAMMA(LLIM1:ULIM1)
REAL DELTA(LLIM2:ULIM2)
```

establish two one-dimensional arrays. The integer array GAMMA may have subscript values ranging from -1 through 3; thus, the following subscripted variables may be used: GAMMA(−1), GAMMA(0), GAMMA(1), GAMMA(2), GAMMA(3). The real array DELTA has subscript values ranging from 0 through 5 so that any of the subscripted variables DELTA(0), DELTA(1), ..., DELTA(5) may be used.

8.2 INPUT/OUTPUT OF ARRAYS

There are three ways in which the elements of a one-dimensional array can be read or displayed:

1. Use a DO loop containing an input/output statement
2. Use only the array name in an input/output statement
3. Use an implied DO loop in an input/output statement

In this section we describe each of these methods.

Input/Output Using a DO Loop

As we noted in the preceding section, one way to process each item in a one-dimensional array is to use an array reference in which the subscript is a variable within a loop that changes the value of the subscript on each pass through the loop. To read or display the elements of an array, therefore, one might simply place an input or output statement containing an array reference with a variable subscript within a DO loop. For example, if we wish to read 10 velocity readings into a one-dimensional array VELOC, the following statements might be used:

```
    INTEGER LIMIT, I
    PARAMETER (LIMIT = 10)
    REAL VELOC(LIMIT)

    DO 10 I = 1, LIMIT
       READ *, VELOC(I)
10 CONTINUE
```

The DO loop containing the READ statement is equivalent to the following sequence of 10 READ statements:

```
READ *, VELOC(1)
READ *, VELOC(2)
READ *, VELOC(3)
READ *, VELOC(4)
READ *, VELOC(5)
READ *, VELOC(6)
READ *, VELOC(7)
READ *, VELOC(8)
READ *, VELOC(9)
READ *, VELOC(10)
```

Recall that each execution of a READ statement requires a new line of input data. Consequently, the 10 values to be read into the array VELOC must be entered on 10 separate lines, one value per line.

If we wish to declare a larger array and use only part of it, the statements

```
INTEGER LIMIT, NUMVEL, I
PARAMETER (LIMIT = 50)
REAL VELOC(LIMIT)

PRINT *, 'ENTER NUMBER OF VELOCITIES'
READ *, NUMVEL
DO 10 I = 1, NUMVEL
    READ *, VELOC(I)
10 CONTINUE
```

might be used. The DO loop here has the same effect as the sequence of statements

```
READ *, VELOC(1)
READ *, VELOC(2)
      .
      .
      .
READ *, VELOC(NUMVEL)
```

Arrays can be displayed in a similar manner by using a PRINT statement within a DO loop. Thus, the first 10 elements of the array VELOC can be displayed with the statements

```
DO 20 I = 1, 10
    PRINT *, VELOC(I)
20 CONTINUE
```

This is equivalent to the following sequence of 10 PRINT statements:

```
PRINT *, VELOC(1)
PRINT *, VELOC(2)
PRINT *, VELOC(3)
PRINT *, VELOC(4)
PRINT *, VELOC(5)
PRINT *, VELOC(6)
PRINT *, VELOC(7)
PRINT *, VELOC(8)
PRINT *, VELOC(9)
PRINT *, VELOC(10)
```

Because each execution of a PRINT statement causes output to begin on a new line, the 10 elements of the array VELOC are displayed on 10 lines, one value per line.

The program in Figure 8.1 illustrates this method of reading and displaying the elements of a one-dimensional array. The array declaration specifies that VELOC is a real array whose subscript may range from 1 through 50; thus, VELOC may have at most 50 elements. A value is then read for the number NUMVEL of velocities to be processed, and a DO loop is used to read this number of values into the array VELOC. These velocities are then displayed by using a PRINT statement within a DO loop.

In the sample run of the program, the value 10 is entered for NUMVEL. The READ statement in the first DO loop is thus executed 10 times, and as we have noted, this requires that the constants to be read appear on 10 lines, one per line. Similarly, because the PRINT statement in the second DO loop is executed 10 times, the elements of VELOC are displayed on 10 lines, one per line. This requirement that data values must be entered on separate lines and are printed on separate lines is one of the disadvantages of using a DO loop for input/output of lists.

Figure 8.1 List of velocities—version 1.

```
      PROGRAM VLIST1
**************************************************************************
* Sample program illustrating the use of DO loops to read and display  *
* a list of velocities. Identifiers used are:                          *
*      LIMIT  : (parameter) limit on the number of velocities          *
*      VELOC  : array to store the list of velocities                  *
*      NUMVEL : number of values read into the array VELOC             *
*      I      : subscript                                              *
*                                                                      *
* Input:  NUMVEL and a list of NUMVEL velocities                       *
* Output: The list of velocities                                       *
**************************************************************************
```

Figure 8.1   *(cont.)*

```
      INTEGER LIMIT, NUMVEL, I
      PARAMETER (LIMIT = 50)
      REAL VELOC(LIMIT)

* Read the list of velocities

      PRINT *, 'ENTER THE NUMBER OF VELOCITIES:'
      READ *, NUMVEL
      PRINT *, 'ENTER THE VELOCITY VALUES, ONE PER LINE:'
      DO 10 I = 1, NUMVEL
         READ *, VELOC(I)
10    CONTINUE

* Print the list of velocities

      PRINT 20
20    FORMAT(/1X, 'LIST OF VELOCITIES:' / 1X, 18('='))
      DO 40 I = 1, NUMVEL
         PRINT 30, I, VELOC(I)
30       FORMAT(1X, I3, '  :', F10.1)
40    CONTINUE

      END
```

Sample run:

```
ENTER THE NUMBER OF VELOCITIES:
10
ENTER THE VELOCITY VALUES, ONE PER LINE:
100.0
 98.5
 99.7
120.6
125.8
 88.7
 99.6
115.0
103.4
 98.6
```

Figure 8.1 *(cont.)*

```
LIST OF VELOCITIES:
===================
 1  :      100.0
 2  :       98.5
 3  :       99.7
 4  :      120.6
 5  :      125.8
 6  :       88.7
 7  :       99.6
 8  :      115.0
 9  :      103.4
10  :       98.6
```

Input/Output Using the Array Name

An alternative method of reading or displaying an array is to use an input or output statement containing the array name without a subscript. The effect is the same as listing all of the array elements in the input/output statement. For example, if the array VELOC is declared by

```
INTEGER LIMIT
PARAMETER (LIMIT = 10)
REAL VELOC(LIMIT)
```

the statement

```
READ *, VELOC
```

is equivalent to

```
READ *, VELOC(1), VELOC(2), VELOC(3), VELOC(4), VELOC(5),
+       VELOC(6), VELOC(7), VELOC(8), VELOC(9), VELOC(10)
```

Because the READ statement is executed only once, the values for VELOC need not be read from separate lines. All of the values may be on one line, or seven values may be on the first line with three on the next, or two values may be on each of five lines, and so on.

This method can also be used with a formatted READ statement. The number of values to be read from each line of input is then determined by the corresponding format identifier. For example, the statements

```
    READ 20, VELOC
20  FORMAT(5F6.1)
```

read the values for VELOC(1),...,VELOC(5) from the first line of data and the values for VELOC(6),...,VELOC(10) from a second line.

An array can be displayed in a similar manner. For example, the statements

```
      PRINT 30, VELOC
30 FORMAT(1X, 5F10.1)
```

are equivalent to

```
      PRINT 30, VELOC(1), VELOC(2), VELOC(3), VELOC(4),
     +          VELOC(5), VELOC(6), VELOC(7), VELOC(8),
     +          VELOC(9), VELOC(10)
30 FORMAT(1X, 5F10.1)
```

and display the elements of the array VELOC on two lines, five values per line, right justified in fields of width 10 with one digit to the right of the decimal point.

The program in Figure 8.2 illustrates this method of reading and displaying the elements of an array. Note that the array declaration

```
INTEGER LIMIT
PARAMETER (LIMIT = 10)
REAL VELOC(LIMIT)
```

specifies that VELOC is to have 10 elements. One disadvantage of this method of array input/output is that the entire array must be used; that is, the total number of elements specified in the array declaration must be read or displayed. Thus it is not possible to read or display only part of an array; for example, if the dimension of VELOC is 50, this method cannot be used to read or display values for only VELOC(1),..., VELOC(10).

Figure 8.2   List of velocities—version 2.

```
      PROGRAM VLIST2
************************************************************************
* Sample program illustrating input/output of a list of velocities  *
* by using the array name VELOC. Identifiers used are:               *
*     LIMIT  : (parameter) limit on the number of velocities         *
*     VELOC  : array to store the list of velocities                 *
*     I      : subscript                                             *
*                                                                    *
* Input:  A list of velocities                                       *
* Output: The list of velocities                                     *
************************************************************************

      INTEGER LIMIT
      PARAMETER (LIMIT = 10)
      REAL VELOC(LIMIT)
```

Figure 8.2 *(cont.)*

```
* Read the list of velocities

      PRINT *, 'ENTER THE VELOCITY VALUES AS MANY PER LINE AS DESIRED:'
      READ *, VELOC

* Print the list of velocities

      PRINT 20
20    FORMAT(/1X, 'LIST OF VELOCITIES:' / 1X, 18('=')/)
      PRINT 30, VELOC
30    FORMAT(1X, 5F10.1)

      END
```

Sample run:

```
ENTER THE VELOCITY VALUES AS MANY PER LINE AS DESIRED:
100.0   98.5   99.7 120.6 125.8
 88.7   99.6 115.0 103.4   98.6

LIST OF VELOCITIES:
===================

     100.0      98.5      99.7     120.6     125.8
      88.7      99.6     115.0     103.4      98.6
```

Input/Output Using Implied DO Loops

An implied DO loop in an input/output statement provides the most flexible method for reading or displaying the elements of an array. It allows the programmer to specify that only a portion of the array be transmitted and to specify the arrangement of the values to be read or displayed.

An **implied DO loop** has the form:

Implied DO Loop

Form:

```
(i/o-list, control-var = init-value, limit)
```

   or

```
(i/o-list, control-var = init-value, limit, step)
```

where
> *i/o-list* may, in general, be a list of variables (subscripted or simple), constants, arithmetic expressions, or other implied DO loops, separated by commas, with a comma at the end of the list; the control variable *control-var*, initial value *init-value*, *limit*, and *step* size are the same as for a DO loop.

Purpose:
An implied DO loop may be used in a READ, PRINT, or WRITE statement, or in a DATA statement (see Section 8.5). The effect of an implied DO loop is exactly that of a DO loop—as if the left parenthesis were a DO, with indexing information immediately before the matching right parenthesis and the *i/o-list* constituting the body of the DO loop.

For example, if the array VELOC is declared by

```
INTEGER LIMIT
PARAMETER (LIMIT = 50)
REAL VELOC(LIMIT)
```

and values for the first 10 elements are to be read, we can use the statement

```
READ *, (VELOC(I), I = 1, 10)
```

which is equivalent to

```
  READ *, VELOC(1), VELOC(2), VELOC(3), VELOC(4), VELOC(5),
+         VELOC(6), VELOC(7), VELOC(8), VELOC(9), VELOC(10)
```

or if we also want to read the number NUMVEL of array elements,

```
READ *, NUMVEL, (VELOC(I), I = 1, NUMVEL)
```

which has the same effect as

```
READ *, NUMVEL, VELOC(1), VELOC(2),..., VELOC(NUMVEL)
```

In a similar manner, we can display the elements:

```
PRINT *, (VELOC(I), I = 1, NUMVEL)
```

This has the same effect as

```
PRINT *, VELOC(1), VELOC(2),..., VELOC(NUMVEL)
```

The program in Figure 8.3 illustrates the use of implied DO loops to read and display the elements of a list.

Figure 8.3 List of velocities—version 3.

```
      PROGRAM VLIST3
*******************************************************************
* Sample program illustrating the use of an implied DO loop to read    *
* and display a list of velocities.  Identifiers used are:             *
*      LIMIT  : (parameter) limit on the number of velocities          *
*      VELOC  : array to store the list of velocities                  *
*      NUMVEL : number of values read into the array VELOC             *
*      I      : subscript                                              *
*                                                                      *
* Input:  NUMVEL and a list of NUMVEL velocities                       *
* Output: The list of velocities                                       *
*******************************************************************

      INTEGER LIMIT, NUMVEL, I
      PARAMETER (LIMIT = 50)
      REAL VELOC(LIMIT)

* Read the list of velocities

      PRINT *, 'ENTER THE NUMBER OF VELOCITIES:'
      READ *, NUMVEL
      PRINT *, 'ENTER THE VELOCITY VALUES AS MANY PER LINE AS DESIRED:'
      READ *, (VELOC(I), I = 1, NUMVEL)

* Print the list of velocities

      PRINT 20, NUMVEL
20    FORMAT(/1X, 'LIST OF', I3, ' VELOCITIES:' / 1X, 21('='))
      PRINT 30, (VELOC(I), I = 1, NUMVEL)
30    FORMAT(1X, 5F10.1)

      END
```

Sample run:

```
ENTER THE NUMBER OF VELOCITIES:
10
ENTER THE VELOCITY VALUES AS MANY PER LINE AS DESIRED:
100.0 98.5  99.7 120.6 125.8
88. 7 99.6 115.0 103.4  98.6

LIST OF 10 VELOCITIES:
=====================
     100.0      98.5      99.7     120.6     125.8
      88.7      99.6     115.0     103.4      98.6
```

Quick Quiz 8.2

1. An array is a _direct_ _____ access structure.

2. Each individual element of an array is accessed by using a _subscripted_ _____ variable.

3. In the array reference X(I), I is called a(n) _subscript_ _____.

4. Arrays that involve only a single subscript are called _one-dimensional_ _____ arrays. .

5. (True or false) REAL X(5) declares an array identical to the one declared by REAL X(1:5). _True_

6. (True or false) INTEGER CODE(0:10) is a legal array declaration.

7. (True or false) INTEGER CODE(1:10) declares a multidimensional array. _False_

8. (True or false) Given the declaration REAL X(10), the statement READ *, X is equivalent to the statement READ *, (X(I), I = 1, 10).

9. (True or false) Given the declaration REAL X(10), the statement PRINT *, X is equivalent to the DO loop

```
      DO 5 I = 1, 10
         PRINT *, X(I)
    5 CONTINUE
```

10. (True or false) For the statement READ *, X, the values to be stored in X must be entered one per line.

Which of the statements in Questions 11–14 are in correct form?

11. READ *, (X(I), I = 1, 5)

12. READ (X(I), I = 1, 5)

13. READ (*, *) X(I), I = 1, 5

14. X(I) (READ, I = 1, 5)

Exercises 8.2

1. Write a declaration for an array whose subscript values are integers from 0 through 10 and in which each element is a real value.

2. Write a declaration for an array whose subscript values are integers from −5 through 5 and in which each element is an integer.

3. Write a declaration for an array whose subscript values are integers from 1 through 20 and in which each element is a character string of length 10.

4. Write a declaration for an array whose subscript values are integers from 1 through 100 and in which each element is either .TRUE. or .FALSE..

Exercises 5–10 assume the following declarations:

```
INTEGER NUMBER(5)
CHARACTER*2 CODE(5)
```

For each exercise assume that the data is entered as indicated (beginning in column 1).
Tell what values will be assigned to each array element.

5. READ *, NUMBER

   Data-line: 12, 34, 56, 78, 90

6. READ *, NUMBER

   Data-line-1: 12, 34
   Data-line-2: 56, 78
   Data-line-3: 90

7.   READ 5, NUMBER
     5 FORMAT (2I2)

   Data-line-1: 12345678
   Data-line-2: 23456789
   Data-line-3: 34567890

8.   DO 10 I = 1, 5
             READ *, NUMBER(I)
       10 CONTINUE

   Data-line-1: 12 23 34
   Data-line-2: 23 34 45
   Data-line-3: 34 45 56
   Data-line-4: 45 56 67
   Data-line-5: 56 67 78

9.   READ 5, CODE
     5 FORMAT (A2)

   Data-line-1: ABCD
   Data-line-2: BCDE
   Data-line-3: CDEF
   Data-line-4: DEFG
   Data-line-5: EFGH

10.   READ 5, (NUMBER(I), I = 1, 5)
       5 FORMAT(2I3)

   Data-line-1: 123
   Data-line-2: 345678
   Data-line-3: 567890123
   Data-line-4: 789

For Exercises 11–16, assume that the following declarations have been made:

```
INTEGER NUMBER(10), I
REAL POINT(-4:5)
CHARACTER*1 SYMBOL(5)
```

Assume also that the following format statements are given,

```
100 FORMAT(10(1X, I1))
110 FORMAT(10(1X, F1.0))
120 FORMAT(5(A1, 1X))
130 FORMAT(5A1)
200 FORMAT(1X, 5I2)
210 FORMAT(1X, 5F4.0)
220 FORMAT(1X, 5A2)
```

and that the following data is entered:

```
A1B2C3D4E5F6G7H8I9J0
```

Tell what output will be produced, or explain why an error occurs.

11.
```
    READ 100, NUMBER
    DO 20 I = 1, 10
       PRINT 200, NUMBER(I)
 20 CONTINUE
```

12.
```
    READ 100, (NUMBER(I), I = 1, 10)
    PRINT 200, (NUMBER(I), I = 1, 10)
```

13.
```
    READ 110, (POINT(I), I = -4, 5)
    DO 30 I = -4, 5
       PRINT 210, POINT(I)
 30 CONTINUE
```

14.
```
    READ 110, POINT
    PRINT 210, (POINT(I), I = -4, 5)
```

15.
```
    READ 120, SYMBOL
    PRINT 220, SYMBOL
```

16.
```
    READ 130, (SYMBOL(I), I = 1, 5)
    PRINT 220, (SYMBOL(I), I = 1, 5)
```

8.3 EXAMPLE: PROCESSING A LIST OF FAILURE TIMES

Many problems involve processing lists, a list of test scores, a list of temperature readings, a list of employee records, and so on. Such processing includes displaying all the items in the list, inserting new items, deleting items, searching the list for a specified item, and sorting the list so that the items are in a certain order. Because most programming languages do not provide a predefined list type (LISP, an acronym for LISt Processing, is one exception), lists must be processed using some other structure. This is commonly done using an array to store the list, storing the *I*th list item in the *I*th position of the array.

To illustrate, suppose we wish to process a list of failure times using an array, as described in the example of Section 8.1. First we must read the failure times and store them in an array. For this, we can use any of the methods described in the preceding section. To make the program flexible, we might declare the array FAILTM by

```
INTEGER LIMIT, NTIMES, I
PARAMETER (LIMIT = 50)
REAL FAILTM(LIMIT)
```

read the number of failure times to be processed, and use an implied DO loop to read these values:

```
READ *, NTIMES
READ *, (FAILTM(I), I = 1, NTIMES)
```

Next we want to calculate the mean time to failure. For this, we must first sum the values stored in the first NTIMES locations of the array FAILTM, which is easily done by varying a subscript I from 1 to NTIMES in a DO loop, and adding the Ith element of the array to a running sum:

```
   SUM = 0
   DO 10 I = 1, NTIMES
      SUM = SUM + FAILTM(I)
10 CONTINUE
   MEANFT = SUM / REAL(NTIMES)
```

A list of failure times greater than the mean can then be displayed by using another DO loop to examine each element of the array FAILTM, comparing it with the mean MEANFT, and printing it if it is greater than MEANFT:

```
   DO 20 I = 1, NTIMES
      IF (FAILTM(I) .GT. MEANFT) THEN
         PRINT *, FAILTM(I)
      END IF
20 CONTINUE
```

The program in Figure 8.4 does this much of the processing of a collection of failure times. The last part of the problem posed in Section 8.1, that of sorting this collection, is considered in Section 8.8.

Figure 8.4 Processing a list of failure times.

```
      PROGRAM FAIL
*********************************************************************
* Program to read a list of failure times, calculate the mean time to   *
* failure, and then print a list of failure times that are greater      *
* than the mean.   Identifiers used are:                                 *
*     FAILTM  : one-dimensional array of failure times                   *
*     LIMIT   : parameter:  size of the array                            *
*     NTIMES  : number of failure times to be processed                  *
*     I       : subscript                                                 *
*     SUM     : sum of failure times                                     *
*     MEANFT  : mean time to failure                                     *
*                                                                        *
* Input:  NTIMES and a list of NTIMES failure times                      *
* Output: MEANFT and a list of failure times greater than MEANFT         *
*********************************************************************

      INTEGER LIMIT, NTIMES, I
      PARAMETER (LIMIT = 50)
      REAL FAILTM(LIMIT), SUM, MEANFT
      INTEGER NTIMES, I

* Read the failure times and store them in array FAILTM

      PRINT *, 'HOW MANY FAILURE TIMES ARE TO BE PROCESSED?'
      READ *, NTIMES
      PRINT *, 'ENTER THE FAILURE TIMES, AS MANY PER LINE AS DESIRED'
      READ *, (FAILTM(I), I = 1, NTIMES)

* Calculate the mean time to failure

      SUM = 0
      DO 10 I = 1, NTIMES
         SUM = SUM + FAILTM(I)
10    CONTINUE
      MEANFT = SUM / REAL(NTIMES)
      PRINT 100, NTIMES, MEANFT
100   FORMAT(// 1X, I3, ' FAILURE TIMES WITH MEAN =', F6.1)
```

Figure 8.4   *(cont.)*

```
* Print list of failure times greater than the mean

      PRINT 101
101   FORMAT(// 1X, 'LIST OF FAILURE TIMES GREATER THAN THE MEAN:')
      DO 20 I = 1, NTIMES
         IF (FAILTM(I) .GT. MEANFT) THEN
            PRINT 102, FAILTM(I)
102         FORMAT(1X, F9.1)
         END IF
20    CONTINUE

      END
```

Sample run:

```
HOW MANY FAILURE TIMES ARE TO BE PROCESSED?
10
ENTER THE FAILURE TIMES, AS MANY PER LINE AS DESIRED
 99.5, 133.8, 84.2, 217.5, 188.8
103.1, 93.9, 165.0, 68.3, 111.4

10 FAILURE TIMES WITH MEAN = 126.6

LIST OF FAILURE TIMES GREATER THAN THE MEAN:
     133.8
     217.5
     188.8
     165.0
```

8.4 APPLICATION: AVERAGE CORN YIELDS

Problem

Four hybrids of corn are being tested in a large number of ten-acre test plots. A collection of data pairs consisting of hybrid codes and yields in bushels from these test plots have been recorded in a data file. The average yield for each of the hybrids is to be calculated.

Solution

Specification. The input and output specifications of this problem are clear:

Input:　Pairs of hybrid codes and yields

Output:　For each hybrid, the average yield or a message indicating that no test results were reported for that particular hybrid

Design. In solving this problem, we will use the following identifiers:

IDENTIFIERS FOR THE CORN YIELD PROBLEM

LIMHYB	Limit on the number of hybrids
NUMHYB	Number of hybrids of corn being tested
HYBRID	A code (1, 2, . . . , NUMHYB) for a hybrid
COUNT	A one-dimensional array; COUNT(HYBRID) is the number of plots planted with a particular HYBRID
TYIELD	A one-dimensional array; TYIELD(HYBRID) is the total yield for a particular HYBRID

An appropriate algorithm is the following:

ALGORITHM FOR THE CORN YIELD PROBLEM

```
* Algorithm to find the average yields for each of several hybrids of corn.          *
* Input:     Hybrid codes and yields                                                 *
* Output:    For each hybrid, the average yield or a message indicating there were no *
*            results to report for that particular hybrid                            *
```

1. Open for input the file containing the corn-yield data.
2. Initialize the arrays COUNT and TYIELD to 0.
3. Read the first HYBRID code and YIELD.
4. While there is more data, do the following:
   a. Add 1 to COUNT(HYBRID).
   b. Add YIELD to TYIELD(HYBRID).
   c. Read the next HYBRID code and YIELD.
5. Do the following for HYBRID ranging from 1 through NUMHYB:

   If COUNT(HYBRID) > 0 then

   　　Display TYIELD(HYBRID) / COUNT(HYBRID).

   Else

   　　Display a message that no test results were reported for this hybrid.

Coding and Execution. The program in Figure 8.5 implements this algorithm. Note the use of PARAMETER and DATA statements to declare and initialize arrays COUNT and TYIELD.

Figure 8.5 Average corn yields.

```
      PROGRAM CORN
*********************************************************************
* Program to find the average yield for each of several hybrids of   *
* corn, using data consisting of a hybrid code and yield obtained from*
* tests of these hybrids on several test plots.  Identifiers used are:*
*     FNAME  : name of data file containing the corn-yield data       *
*     LIMHYB : parameter specifying limit on types of hybrids         *
*     NUMHYB : number of hybrids being tested                         *
*     COUNT  : COUNT(I) = number of tests of hybrid I                 *
*     TYIELD : TYIELD(I) = sum of yields for hybrid I                 *
*     HYBRID : current hybrid code                                    *
*     YIELD  : current yield being processed                          *
*                                                                     *
* Input:  Pairs of hybrid codes and yields (stored in HYBRID and YIELD)*
* Output: For each hybrid, the average yield or a message that no test *
*         results were reported for that particular hybrid            *
*********************************************************************

      CHARACTER*10 FNAME
      INTEGER LIMHYB
      PARAMETER (LIMHYB = 4)
      INTEGER COUNT(LIMHYB), HYBRID
      REAL TYIELD(LIMHYB), YIELD
      DATA COUNT, TYIELD/LIMHYB*0, LIMHYB*0.0/

*     Get the name of the the file containing the corn-yield data
*     and open it for input

      PRINT *, 'THIS PROGRAM READS PAIRS OF HYBRID CODES AND YIELDS'
      PRINT *, 'FROM A DATA FILE.  THE FIRST LINE OF THE FILE CONTAINS'
      PRINT *, 'THE NUMBER OF HYBRIDS.  EACH SUBSEQUENT LINE CONTAINS'
      PRINT *, 'A HYBRID CODE AND A YIELD.  THE LAST LINE OF THE FILE'
      PRINT *, 'CONTAINS THE PAIR 0, 0 TO SIGNAL THE END OF DATA.'
      PRINT *
      PRINT *, 'ENTER THE NAME OF THE DATA FILE TO BE USED: '
      READ '(A)', FNAME
      OPEN (UNIT = 10, FILE = FNAME, STATUS = 'OLD')
```

Figure 8.5   *(cont.)*

```
*       Read number of hybrids from the first line of the file
*       and the first hybrid code and yield from the next line

        READ (10, *) NUMHYB                      .
        READ (10, *), HYBRID, YIELD

* While there is more data, read a hybrid code and yield,
* increment the appropriate counter, and add the yield to the
* appropriate sum

20      IF (YIELD .GT. 0) THEN
           IF (HYBRID .LE. NUMHYB) THEN
              COUNT(HYBRID) = COUNT(HYBRID) + 1
              TYIELD(HYBRID) = TYIELD(HYBRID) + YIELD
           ELSE
              PRINT *, '*** ILLEGAL HYBRID CODE:', HYBRID
           END IF
           READ (10, *), HYBRID, YIELD
        GO TO 20
        END IF


* Calculate and print average yields

        PRINT 100
100     FORMAT(//1X, 'FOR HYBRID')
        DO 30 HYBRID = 1, NUMHYB
           IF (COUNT(HYBRID) .GT. 0) THEN
              PRINT 101, HYBRID, T YIELD(HYBRID) / REAL(COUNT(HYBRID))
101           FORMAT(1X, I10, ':   AVERAGE YIELD IS', F6.2)
           ELSE
              PRINT 102, HYBRID
102           FORMAT(1X, I10, ':   THERE WERE NO TEST RESULTS REPORTED')
           END IF
30      CONTINUE

        END
```

Figure 8.5   *(cont.)*

Listing of data file `FIL8-5.DAT` **used in sample run:**

```
4
1  34.0
1  32.7
2  30.1
5  29.8
3  29.8
2  32.8
1  32.0
3  28.1
1  29.4
2  28.9
3  27.4
0  0
```

Sample run:

```
THIS PROGRAM READS PAIRS OF HYBRID CODES AND YIELDS
FROM A DATA FILE.  THE FIRST LINE OF THE FILE CONTAINS
THE NUMBER OF HYBRIDS.  EACH SUBSEQUENT LINE CONTAINS
A HYBRID CODE AND A YIELD.  THE LAST LINE OF THE FILE
CONTAINS THE PAIR 0, 0 TO SIGNAL THE END OF DATA.

ENTER THE NAME OF THE DATA FILE TO BE USED:
FIL8-5.DAT

*** ILLEGAL HYBRID CODE: 5

FOR HYBRID
         1: AVERAGE YIELD IS 32.02
         2: AVERAGE YIELD IS 30.60
         3: AVERAGE YIELD IS 28.43
         4: THERE WERE NO TEST RESULTS REPORTED
```

8.5 ARRAY PROCESSING

In the preceding sections we considered array declarations, input/output of arrays, and some simple processing of lists using arrays. In this section we describe how other kinds of array processing are carried out in FORTRAN: assignment of arrays, use of arrays as arguments, and arrays in common.

Assigning Values to Arrays

As we know, a value can be assigned to a simple variable by an assignment statement of the form *variable* = *expression*. The value of an array, however, is a collection of values, and in FORTRAN, each array element must be assigned a value by a separate assignment statement. For example, if the array NUMBER is declared by

```
INTEGER NUMBER(10)
```

and we wish to assign it the sequence consisting of the squares of the first 10 positive integers, 1, 4, 9, 16, 25, 36, 49, 64, 81, 100, we can use a DO loop:

```
    DO 10 I = 1, 10
        NUMBER(I) = I**2
10 CONTINUE
```

Another way to assign a value to an array is to use a DATA statement to initialize the array during compilation. If all the elements of the array are to be assigned values, the array name together with the set of values may appear in the DATA statement. In this case the number of constants must be equal to the size of the array. For example, if ALPHA is a one-dimensional real array having 10 elements, the statements

```
REAL ALPHA(10)
DATA ALPHA /5*0.0, 4*1.0, 2.0/
```

initialize ALPHA(1), . . . , ALPHA(5) with the value 0.0, ALPHA(6), . . . , ALPHA (9) with the value 1.0, and ALPHA(10) with the value 2.0. Also, since parameters may be used as values and/or repetition indicators in DATA statements, a parameter used to declare the dimension of an array may also be used in the list of values used to initialize that array. For example, the statements

```
INTEGER LIMIT
PARAMETER (LIMIT = 10)
REAL ALPHA(LIMIT)
DATA ALPHA /LIMIT*0.0/
```

initialize each of the 10 elements of ALPHA to 0.0.

Several variables and arrays may appear in a single DATA statement, as the following example illustrates:

```
INTEGER N
REAL X, ALPHA(10), BETA(25)
DATA N, X, ALPHA, BETA /10, 3.14, 5*1.0, 30*0.0/
```

Here N is assigned the value 10; X is assigned the value 3.14; the value 1.0 is assigned to ALPHA(1),..., ALPHA(5); and the value of each of ALPHA(6),..., ALPHA(10), BETA(1),..., BETA(25) is 0.0.

Implied DO loops may also appear in the list of a DATA statement. For example, to assign 10 to N and 0.0 to the first five elements of the one-dimensional array ALPHA, the following statements can be used:

```
INTEGER N, I
REAL ALPHA(10)
DATA N, (ALPHA(I), I = 1, 5) /10, 5*0.0/
```

Arrays as Arguments

Arrays may also be used as arguments in functions and subroutine subprograms. In this case, *the actual array argument must be declared in the calling program unit, and the corresponding formal array argument must be declared in the subprogram.* When the subprogram is referenced, the first element of the actual array argument is associated with the first element of the corresponding formal array argument. Successive actual array elements are then associated with the corresponding formal array elements.

The program in Figure 8.6 illustrates the use of array arguments. It reads a list of numbers and then calls a function to calculate the mean of the numbers.

Figure 8.6 Calculating the mean of a list—version 1.

```
      PROGRAM AVE1
*****************************************************************************
* Program to read a list of numbers ITEM(1), ITEM(2), ... , ITEM(NUM)  *
* and to calculate their mean using the function subprogram MEAN.      *
* Identifiers used are:                                                *
*      ITEM   : one-dimensional array of numbers                       *
*      LIMIT  : size of array ITEM (parameter)                         *
*      I      : subscript                                              *
*      NUM    : number of items                                        *
*      MEAN   : function that finds the mean of a set of numbers       *
*                                                                      *
* Input:  NUM and a list of NUM real numbers                          *
* Output: The mean of the numbers                                     *
*****************************************************************************

      INTEGER LIMIT
      PARAMETER (LIMIT = 50)
      REAL ITEM(LIMIT), MEAN
      INTEGER NUM, I

      PRINT *, 'ENTER NUMBER OF ITEMS AND THE ITEMS'
      READ *, NUM, (ITEM(I), I = 1, NUM)
      PRINT 100, NUM, MEAN(ITEM, NUM)
100   FORMAT(1X, 'MEAN OF THE ', I3, ' NUMBERS IS ', F6.2)

      END
```

Figure 8.6 *(cont.)*

```
**MEAN*************************************************************
* Function to find the mean of the first N elements of the array X of   *
* dimension XLIMIT. Local variables used are:                           *
*      SUM : sum of the numbers                                         *
*      I   : subscript                                                  *
*                                                                       *
* Accepts:  Array X and integer N                                       *
* Returns:  The mean of the N numbers stored in X                       *
******************************************************************

      FUNCTION MEAN(X, N)

      INTEGER XLIMIT
      PARAMETER (XLIMIT = 50)
      REAL MEAN, X(XLIMIT), SUM
      INTEGER N, I

      SUM = 0
      DO 10 I = 1, N
          SUM = SUM + X(I)
10    CONTINUE
      MEAN = SUM / REAL(N)
      END
```

Sample run:

```
ENTER NUMBER OF ITEMS AND THE ITEMS
10
55, 88.5, 90, 71.5, 100, 66.5, 70.3, 81.2, 93.7, 41
MEAN OF THE  10 NUMBERS IS   75.77
```

Execution of this program associates the actual array ITEM with the formal array X so that corresponding pairs of elements refer to the same memory locations:

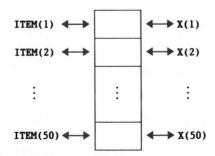

Thus if any of the array elements $X(1),\ldots,X(50)$ are assigned a value in the subprogram, the corresponding elements of the array ITEM also will be changed.

If the array X in the subprogram were dimensioned by

```
REAL X(-5:44)
```

then the first element ITEM(1) of the actual array ITEM and the first element $X(-5)$ of the formal array X would be associated; that is, they would refer to the same memory location. The successive elements of the array ITEM would then be associated in order with the elements in the array X:

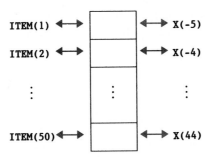

As we noted earlier, when an array is used as a formal argument, it must be declared in the subprogram, and the corresponding actual array argument must be declared in the calling program unit. To make it possible to design subprograms that can be used to process arrays of various sizes, FORTRAN allows both the array and its dimension to be passed to the subprogram. Such arrays are said to have **adjustable dimensions.** For example, the program in Figure 8.6 that uses the function subprogram MEAN to calculate the mean of a list of numbers can be rewritten as shown in Figure 8.7. Note that the formal argument XLIM is used to specify the dimension of the formal array X in this subprogram. The actual dimension 50 and the actual array ITEM are passed to the subprogram from the main program when the function is referenced.

Figure 8.7 Calculating the mean of a list—version 2.

```
      PROGRAM AVE2
* * * * * * * * * * * * * * * * * * * * * * * * * * * * * * * * * * * * * * * * * * * * * * * * * * * * * * * * * *
* Program to read a list of numbers ITEM(1), ITEM(2), ... , ITEM(NUM)  *
* and to calculate their mean using the function subprogram MEAN.       *
* Identifiers used are:                                                 *
*      ITEM    : one-dimensional array of numbers                       *
*      LIMIT   : size of array ITEM (parameter)                         *
*      I       : subscript                                              *
*      NUM     : number of items                                       *
*      MEAN    : function that finds the mean of a set of numbers       *
*                                                                       *
* Input:  NUM and a list of NUM real numbers                           *
* Output: The mean of the numbers                                      *
* * * * * * * * * * * * * * * * * * * * * * * * * * * * * * * * * * * * * * * * * * * * * * * * * * * * * * * * * *
```

Figure 8.7 *(cont.)*

```
      INTEGER LIMIT
      PARAMETER (LIMIT = 50)
      REAL ITEM(LIMIT), MEAN
      INTEGER NUM, I

      PRINT *, 'ENTER NUMBER OF ITEMS AND THE ITEMS'
      READ *, NUM, (ITEM(I), I = 1, NUM)
      PRINT 100, NUM, MEAN(ITEM, LIMIT, NUM)
100   FORMAT(1X, 'MEAN OF THE ', I3, ' NUMBERS IS ', F6.2)

      END


**MEAN*************************************************************
* Function to find the mean of first N elements of the array X of  *
* dimension XLIM.  The actual dimension is passed to the subprogram *
* by the actual argument corresonding to XLIM.   Local variables    *
* used are:                                                         *
*     SUM : sum of the numbers                                      *
*     I   : subscript                                               *
*                                                                   *
* Accepts:  Array X and integers XLIM and N                         *
* Returns:  The mean of the N numbers stored in X                   *
********************************************************************

      FUNCTION MEAN(X, XLIM, N)

      INTEGER XLIM, N, I
      REAL MEAN, X(XLIM), SUM

      SUM = 0
      DO 10 I = 1, N
         SUM = SUM + X(I)
10    CONTINUE
      MEAN = SUM / REAL(N)

      END
```

In a subprogram, it is also possible to specify that a one-dimensional formal array have the same size as the corresponding actual array by using an asterisk (*) to specify the dimension. In this case, it is not permissible to use the array name in any statement that requires information about the array size. Thus, one would not be allowed to give only the array name in an input/output statement.

Arrays in Common

To illustrate the use of arrays in COMMON statements, suppose that the statements

```
REAL A(5)
COMMON A
```

appear in one program unit and that the statements

```
REAL ALPHA(5)
COMMON ALPHA
```

appear in another program unit. These COMMON statements allocate the first five memory locations of blank common to both of the arrays A and ALPHA so that the array elements are associated in the following manner:

Array Element	Blank Common Location	Array Element
A(1)	#1	ALPHA(1)
A(2)	#2	ALPHA(2)
A(3)	#3	ALPHA(3)
A(4)	#4	ALPHA(4)
A(5)	#5	ALPHA(5)

Quick Quiz 8.5

1. (True or false) If A and B are arrays declared by REAL A(5), B(5), the statement A = B can be used to copy the values stored in B into A.
2. (True or false)

```
    SUBROUTINE PRINT(ARRAY, SIZE)

    INTEGER SIZE, ARRAY(SIZE), I

    DO 10 I = 1, SIZE
        PRINT *, ARRAY(I)
 10 CONTINUE
    END
```

is a legal FORTRAN subroutine.

For Questions 3–6, assume the declarations

```
        INTEGER NUMBER(5)
        REAL XVAL(5)
```

What values will be assigned to the array elements by the given statements?

3.
```
        DO 10 I = 1, 5
           IF (MOD(I,2) .EQ. 0 ) THEN
              NUMBER(I) = 2 * I
           ELSE
              NUMBER(I) = 2 * I + 1
           END IF
     10 CONTINUE
```

4.
```
        NUMBER(1) = 2
        DO 10 I = 2, 5
           NUMBER(I) = 2 * NUMBER(I - 1)
     10 CONTINUE
```

5.
```
        DO 10 I = 1, 5
           XVAL(I) = REAL(I) / 2.0
     10 CONTINUE
```

6.
```
        I = 0
     10 CONTINUE
           I = I + 1
           NUMBER(I) = MIN(I, 3)
        IF (I .LT. 6) GO TO 10
```

7. What output will the following program produce?

```
        PROGRAM DEMO1

        CHARACTER*3 ANIM(3)
        DATA ANIM /'APE', 'BAT', 'CAT'/

        CALL CHANGE(ANIM, 2)
        PRINT '(1X, A, 3A4)', 'ANIM =', ANIM
        END

        SUBROUTINE CHANGE(ARRAY, INDEX)

        CHARACTER*3 ARRAY(3), DIRTY
        INTEGER INDEX
        DATA DIRTY /'RAT'/

        ARRAY(INDEX) = DIRTY
        END
```

Exercises 8.5

For each of Exercises 1–4, write appropriate declarations and statements to create the specified array.

1. An array whose subscript values are integers from 0 through 5 and in which each element is the same as the subscript value.

2. An array whose subscript values are integers from 0 through 5 and in which each element is the square of the subscript value.

3. An array whose subscript values are the integers from 1 through 20 and in which an array element has the value true if the corresponding subscript is even, and false otherwise.

4. An array whose subscript values are the integers from 0 through 359 and whose elements are the values of the sine function at the angles $0°, 1°, \ldots, 359°$.

In Exercises 5–13, assume that the following declarations have been made:

```
INTEGER NUMBER(10), I
REAL POINT(-4:5)
```

and that the following data is entered:

```
1, 2, 3, 4, 5, 6, 7, 8, 9, 0
```

Tell what value (if any) is assigned to each array element or explain why an error occurs:

```
5.    DO 10 I = 1, 10
          NUMBER(I) = I / 2
   10 CONTINUE
6.    DO 10 I = 1, 6
          NUMBER(I) = I * I
   10 CONTINUE
      DO 20 I = 7, 10
          NUMBER(I) = NUMBER(I - 5)
   20 CONTINUE
7.    I = 1
   10 IF (I .NE. 10) THEN
          IF (MOD(I,3) .EQ. 0) THEN
              NUMBER(I) = 0
          ELSE
              NUMBER(I) = I
          END IF
          I = I + 1
      GO TO 10
      END IF
```

8.
```
    NUMBER(1) = 1
    I = 2
10 CONTINUE
    NUMBER(I) = NUMBER(I - 1)
    I = I + 1
    IF (I .LT. 10) GO TO 10
```

9.
```
    DO 10 I = 1, 10
    READ *, NUMBER(I)
10 CONTINUE
```

10. `READ *, NUMBER`

11. `READ *, (NUMBER(I), I = 1, 10)`

12. `READ *, (POINT(I), I = -4, 5)`

13.
```
    READ *, NUMBER
    DO 10 I = 1, 5
    IF (NUMBER(I) .LT. 5) THEN
        POINT(I - 5) = -1.1 * I
        POINT(I) = 1.1 * I
    ELSE
        POINT(I - 5) = 0
        POINT(I) = 0
    END IF
10 CONTINUE
```

Direct access to the elements in an array is accomplished by means of **address translation.** The address of the first byte (or word) in the memory block reserved for an array is called the **base address** of the array, and the address of any other element is calculated in terms of this base address. For example, if the base address for the array CODE is B and each failure time can be stored in one byte, then the address of CODE(1) is B, the address of CODE(2) is $B + 1$, the address of CODE(3) is $B + 2$, and in general, the address of CODE(I) is $B + I - 1$:

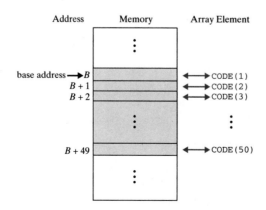

If *W* bytes are required for each element, then CODE(1) is stored in *W* consecutive bytes, beginning at the byte with address *B*, CODE(2) in a block beginning at address *B* + *W*, and in general, CODE(I) in a block of size *W* beginning at address *B* + (I − 1)**W. Each time an array element is accessed using a subscripted variable, this address translation must be performed by the system software and/or hardware to determine the location of that element in memory.

In Exercises 14–21, assume that character and logical values require one byte of storage, integers require 4 bytes, and real values require 8 bytes. Indicate with a diagram like that for CODE, where each element of an array A as declared would be stored if the base address of A is *B*. Also, give the general address translation formula for A(I).

14. INTEGER A(5)

15. REAL A(5)

16. LOGICAL A(5)

17. CHARACTER*8 A(5)

18. INTEGER A(−5:5)

19. REAL A(5:15)

20. LOGICAL A(0:9)

21. CHARACTER A(0:9)

8.6 APPLICATION: QUALITY CONTROL

Problem

A quality control engineer monitors a machine by recording the number of defective parts that machine produces each hour. This information is to be summarized in a *frequency distribution* that shows the number of one-hour periods in which there were no defective parts, one defective part, two defective parts, ..., five or more defective parts.

Solution

Specification. The input/output specifications for this problem are clear:

Input: Integers representing counts of defective parts
Output: A frequency distribution

Testing Motorola pagers. (Photo courtesy of Hewlett-Packard.)

Design. To solve this problem, we will use the following variables:

VARIABLES FOR QUALITY CONTROL PROBLEM

DEFECT: Number of defective parts counted in a one-hour period

FNAME: The name of a data file that contains these counts

COUNT: An array: COUNT(I) is the number of one-hour periods during
            which I defective parts were produced, I = 0, 1, . . . , 5

An appropriate algorithm is

ALGORITHM FOR QUALITY CONTROL PROBLEM

```
*   Algorithm to read several values for DEFECT, the number of defective parts produced   *
*   by a machine in a given one-hour period, and to determine COUNT(I) = the number       *
*   of periods in which there were I defective parts.                                      *
*   Input:    Name of data file, and values stored in this file                           *
*   Output:   Values stored in array COUNT                                                 *
```

1. Get the name of the data file and open it for input.

2. Initialize array COUNT to all zeros.

3. Read first value for DEFECT.

4. While there is more data, do the following:
   a. If DEFECT > 5, set DEFECT to 5.
   b. Increment COUNT(DEFECT) by 1.
   c. Read next value for DEFECT.

5. Display the values stored in array COUNT.

Coding, Testing, and Execution. The program in Figure 8.8 implements this algorithm. Also shown is a listing of a data file of test values and the frequency distribution produced by the program.

Figure 8.8 Generating a frequency distribution.

```
      PROGRAM FREQ1
************************************************************************
* Program to generate a frequency distribution of the number of 1-hour *
* periods in which there were 0, 1, 2, ... defective parts produced by *
* a machine.  The data is read from a file.  Identifiers used are:     *
*     MAXDEF  :   parameter representing maximum # of defective parts   *
*     COUNT   :   COUNT(I) = # of 1-hour periods with I defective parts*
*     DEFECT  :   # of defective parts read from file                  *
*     FNAME   :   name of the data file                                *
*     EOF     :   end-of-file indicator                                *
*     I       :   subscript                                            *
*                                                                      *
* Input (keyboard): File name FNAME                                    *
* Input (file):     Number of defects per hour                         *
* Output:           Frequency distribution -- elements of array COUNT  *
************************************************************************

      INTEGER MAXDEF
      PARAMETER (MAXDEF = 5)
      INTEGER DEFECT, COUNT(0:MAXDEF), I, EOF
      CHARACTER*20 FNAME
      DATA COUNT/0, MAXDEF*0/

* Get file name, open the file as unit 15

      PRINT *, 'ENTER NAME OF DATA FILE'
      READ '(A)', FNAME
      OPEN (UNIT = 15, FILE = FNAME, STATUS = 'OLD')
```

Figure 8.8 *(cont.)*

```
* While there is more data, read # of defective parts and
* increment appropriate counter
      READ (15, *, IOSTAT = EOF) DEFECT
10    IF (EOF .GE. 0) THEN
          DEFECT = MIN(DEFECT, MAXDEF)
          COUNT(DEFECT) = COUNT(DEFECT) + 1
          READ (15, *, IOSTAT = EOF) DEFECT
      GO TO 10
      END IF


* Print the frequency distribution

      PRINT 101
      PRINT 102
101   FORMAT(1X, '# OF DEFECTIVES  # OF HOURS')
102   FORMAT(1X, '================  ==========')
      DO 20 I = 0, MAXDEF
          PRINT 103, I, COUNT(I)
103       FORMAT(1X, I9, I15)
20    CONTINUE

      CLOSE (15)
      END
```

Listing of `FIL8-8.DAT` **used in sample run:**

```
0
1
0
2
2
0
1
6
3
0
3
1
2
0
1
2
0
```

Figure 8.8 *(cont.)*

Sample run:

```
ENTER NAME OF DATA FILE
FIL8-8.DAT
# OF DEFECTIVES    # OF HOURS
===============    ==========
        0               6
        1               4
        2               4
        3               2
        4               0
        5               1
```

A Graphical Solution

A **bar graph** or **histogram** is often used to display frequency distributions graphically. Each of the categories is represented by a bar whose length corresponds to the number of items in that category. Thus the frequency distribution produced by the sample run in Figure 8.8 could be represented by the following bar graph.

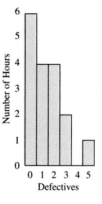

The program in Figure 8.9 is a modification of the preceding program that displays a similar bar graph.

Figure 8.9 Generating a bar graph.

```
      PROGRAM FREQ2
*************************************************************************
* Program to plot a bar graph of the number of 1-hour periods in which *
* there were 0, 1, 2, ... defective parts produced by a machine.       *
* The data is read from a file.  Identifiers used are:                 *
*     MAXDEF  :  parameter representing maximum # of defective parts    *
*     COUNT   :  COUNT(I) = # of 1-hour periods with I defective parts  *
*     DEFECT  :  # of defective parts read from file                    *
*     FNAME   :  name of the data file                                  *
*     EOF     :  end-of-file indicator                                  *
*     BGRAPH  :  subroutine to plot a bar graph                         *
*                                                                       *
* Input (keyboard): File name FNAME                                     *
* Input (file):     Number of defects per hour                          *
* Output:           Bar graph displaying elements of array COUNT        *
*************************************************************************

      INTEGER MAXDEF
      PARAMETER (MAXDEF = 5)
      INTEGER DEFECT, COUNT(0:MAXDEF), EOF
      CHARACTER*20 FNAME
      DATA COUNT /0, MAXDEF*0/

* Get file name, open the file as unit 15

      PRINT *, 'ENTER NAME OF DATA FILE'
      READ '(A)', FNAME
      OPEN (UNIT = 15, FILE = FNAME, STATUS = 'OLD')

* While there is more data, read # of defective parts and
* increment appropriate counter

      READ (15, *, IOSTAT = EOF) DEFECT
10    IF (EOF .GE. 0) THEN
          DEFECT = MIN(DEFECT, MAXDEF)
          COUNT(DEFECT) = COUNT(DEFECT) + 1
          READ (15, *, IOSTAT = EOF) DEFECT
      GO TO 10
      END IF
```

Figure 8.9   *(cont.)*

```
      CALL BGRAPH(COUNT, MAXDEF, 'DEFECTIVES', 'NUMBER OF HOURS')

      CLOSE (15)
      END


**BGRAPH********************************************************************
* Subroutine to plot a bar graph representation of a frequency         *
* distribution.  Variables used are:                                   *
*     FREQ    :  array of frequencies                                  *
*     NFREQ   :  number of frequencies                                 *
*     VLABEL  :  label for vertical axis                               *
*     HLABEL  :  label for horizontal axis                             *
*     LIMBAR  :  parameter giving the size of the array BAR            *
*     BAR     :  character array used to print one bar of bar graph    *
*     LARGE   :  largest of FREQ(0), FREQ(1), ...                      *
*     I, J    :  subscripts                                            *
*                                                                      *
* Accepts: Array FREQ, integer NFREQ, and character strings VLABEL     *
*          and HLABEL                                                  *
* Output:  A bar graph of the elements of FREQ                         *
***************************************************************************

      SUBROUTINE BGRAPH(FREQ, NFREQ, VLABEL, HLABEL)

      INTEGER NFREQ, FREQ(0:NFREQ), LIMBAR, LARGE, I, J
      PARAMETER (LIMBAR = 20)
      CHARACTER*(*), VLABEL, HLABEL
      CHARACTER*3 BAR(LIMBAR)

* Find largest count

      LARGE = FREQ(0)
      DO 10 I = 1, NFREQ
         LARGE = MAX(LARGE, FREQ(I))
10    CONTINUE

* Print the bar graph
      PRINT 100, VLABEL
100   FORMAT(//1X, A)
```

Figure 8.9 *(cont.)*

```
        DO 40 I = 0, NFREQ
           DO 20 J = 1, LIMBAR
              BAR(J) = ' '
20         CONTINUE
           DO 30 J = 1, FREQ(I)
              BAR(J) = '***'
30         CONTINUE
           PRINT 101, I, ':', BAR
101        FORMAT(1X, I10, 21A)
40      CONTINUE
        PRINT 102, ('...', I = 0, LARGE)
        PRINT 103, (I, I = 0, LARGE)
        PRINT 104, HLABEL
102     FORMAT(11X, 80A)
103     FORMAT(9X, 20I3)
104     FORMAT(11X, A)

        END
```

Sample run:

```
ENTER NAME OF DATA FILE
FIL8-9.DAT

DEFECTIVES
        0:******************
        1:***********
        2:***********
        3:******
        4:
        5:***

         .................
         0  1  2  3  4  5  6
         NUMBER OF HOURS
```

8.7 EXAMPLE: VECTOR PROCESSING

Vectors are quantities that have two attributes: magnitude and direction. They are used in science and engineering to model forces, velocities, accelerations, and many other physical quantities.

A vector in the plane or in three-dimensional space can be represented by a directed line segment whose length represents the magnitude of the vector and whose orientation specifies its direction. Two vectors are equal if they have the same magnitude and direction. Thus all the vectors in the following diagram are equal:

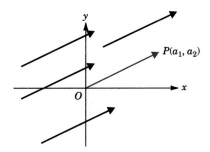

A vector like $\overrightarrow{OP}$, whose initial point is the origin, is called a *position vector*. This position vector (and all vectors equal to it) can be represented algebraically by the coordinates (a_1, a_2) of the terminal point P. The x- and y-coordinates a_1 and a_2 are called the *components* of the vector.

Similarly, vectors in three-dimensional space can be represented algebraically by ordered triples (a_1, a_2, a_3). And in general, *n-dimensional vectors* can be represented algebraically by ordered *n*-tuples $(a_1, a_2, \ldots, a_n)$. This algebraic representation is convenient for computation because the components of a vector can be stored in an array and the basic vector operations can be easily implemented using this array representation.

To illustrate, the *norm* of a vector **a** is its magnitude and is usually denoted by $|\mathbf{a}|$. For a vector in two and three dimensions, the norm is the length of the line segment that represents the vector and can be computed using the formula for the distance between two points. For example, in the preceding diagram, if **a** is the vector $\overrightarrow{OP}$ (or any of the vectors equal to it), the norm of **a** is given by

$$|\mathbf{a}| = \sqrt{(a_1 - 0)^2 + (a_2 - 0)^2} = \sqrt{a_1^2 + a_2^2}$$

In general, the norm of an *n*-dimensional vector $\mathbf{a} = (a_1, a_2, \ldots, a_n)$ is given by

$$|\mathbf{a}| = \sqrt{a_1^2 + a_2^2 + \cdots + a_n^2}$$

Writing a function subprogram to compute the norm of a vector using this formula is straightforward:

```
** NORM ***************************************************************
* Function to calculate the norm of a vector.   Identifiers used:  *
*      A      : array that stores the vector                       *
*      ARRDIM : dimension of the array                             *
*      N      : number of components in the vector (its dimension) *
*      SUM    : sum of the squares of the components               *
*      I      : subscript                                          *
*                                                                  *
* Accepts:  A, ARRDIM, and N                                       *
* Returns: Norm of the N-dimensional vector stored in A            *
********************************************************************
```

```
      FUNCTION NORM(A, ARRDIM, N)

      INTEGER ARRDIM, N, I
      REAL NORM, SUM, A(ARRDIM)

      SUM = 0.0
      DO 10 I = 1, N
          SUM = SUM + A(I)**2
10    CONTINUE
      NORM = SQRT(SUM)

      END
```

The *sum* of two vectors can be computed algebraically by simply adding corresponding components. For example, if **a** = (3, 5) and **b** = (−2, 7), then

$$\mathbf{a} + \mathbf{b} = (1, 12)$$

In general, if $\mathbf{a} = (a_1, a_2, \ldots, a_n)$ and $\mathbf{b} = (b_1, b_2, \ldots, b_n)$, then

$$\mathbf{a} + \mathbf{b} = (a_1 + b_1, a_2 + b_2, \ldots, a_n + b_n)$$

The following subroutine implements vector addition. (A subroutine is used rather than a function because a function cannot return an array.)

```
** VECSUM ****************************************************
* Subroutine to calculate the sum of two vectors.  Identifiers  *
* used are:                                                     *
*     A, B    : arrays that store the vectors                   *
*     ARRDIM  : dimension of the arrays                         *
*     N       : number of components in vectors (their dimension) *
*     VSUM    : array storing the sum of the vectors            *
*     I       : subscript                                       *
*                                                               *
* Accepts: A, B, ARRDIM, N                                      *
* Returns: VSUM                                                 *
****************************************************************

      SUBROUTINE VECSUM(A, B, N, VSUM, ARRDIM)

      INTEGER ARRDIM, N, I
      REAL A(ARRDIM), B(ARRDIM), VSUM(ARRDIM)

      DO 10 I = 1, N
          VSUM(I) = A(I) + B(I)
10    CONTINUE

      END
```

Subprograms for other vector operations are similar. Several of these operations are described in the exercises.

Exercises 8.7

In the definitions of vector operations in the following exercises, $\mathbf{a} = (a_1, a_2, \ldots, a_n)$ and $\mathbf{b} = (b_1, b_2, \ldots, b_n)$.

1. The *difference* of two vectors can be computed by subtracting corresponding components.

$$\mathbf{a} - \mathbf{b} = (a_1 - b_1, a_2 - b_2, \ldots, a_n - b_n)$$

   Write a subroutine to compute the difference of two vectors.

2. Like addition and subtraction, *multiplication of a vector by a scalar* is performed componentwise:

$$c\mathbf{a} = (ca_1, ca_2, \ldots, ca_n)$$

   Write a subroutine that multiplies a vector by a scalar.

3. The *dot* (or *scalar*) *product* $\mathbf{a} \cdot \mathbf{b}$ of two vectors is the scalar (i.e., number) obtained by adding the products of corresponding components:

$$\mathbf{a} \cdot \mathbf{b} = \sum_{i=1}^{n} a_i b_i = a_1 b_1 + a_2 b_2 + \cdots + a_n b_n$$

   Write a function subprogram to compute the dot product of two vectors.

4. The *cross* (or *vector*) *product* $\mathbf{a} \times \mathbf{b}$ of two vectors is a vector. This product is defined only for three-dimensional vectors: if $\mathbf{a} = (a_1, a_2, a_3)$ and $\mathbf{b} = (b_1, b_2, b_3)$, then

$$\mathbf{a} \times \mathbf{b} = (a_2 b_3 - a_3 b_2, a_3 b_1 - a_1 b_3, a_1 b_2 - a_2 b_1)$$

   Write a subroutine subprogram that accepts a value for n and two n-dimensional vectors and that returns the cross product of the vectors if $n = 3$ or displays an error message otherwise. Write a program to test your subprogram.

5. Write a subroutine that finds a unit vector (a vector of length 1) having the same direction as a given vector.

6. A formula that can be used to find the angle between two vectors is

$$\cos \theta = \frac{\mathbf{a} \cdot \mathbf{b}}{|\mathbf{a}| \, |\mathbf{b}|}$$

Write a function subprogram to compute the angle between two vectors.

8.8 SORTING

A common programming problem is **sorting,** that is, arranging the items in a list so that they are in either ascending or descending order. There are many sorting methods, most of which assume that arrays are used to store the items to be sorted. In this section we describe two of the simpler sorting methods: simple selection sort and bubble sort. Although they are not efficient sorting methods for large lists, they do perform reasonably well for small lists, and they are easy to understand. More efficient sorting schemes are described in the programming problems at the end of this chapter.

Simple Selection Sort

The basic idea of a selection sort of a list is to make a number of passes through the list or a part of the list, and on each pass to select one item to be correctly positioned. For example, on each pass through a sublist, the smallest item in this sublist might be found and then moved to its proper position.

As an illustration, suppose that the following list is to be sorted into ascending order:

$$67, 33, 21, 84, 49, 50, 75$$

We scan the list to locate the smallest item and find it in position 3:

67 , 33 , 21 , 84 , 49 , 50 , 75

We interchange this item with the first item and thus properly position the smallest item at the beginning of the list:

21 , 33 , 67 , 84 , 49 , 50 , 75

We now scan the sublist consisting of the items from position 2 on,

21 , 33 , 67 , 84 , 49 , 50 , 75

to find the smallest item and exchange it with the second item (itself in this case) and thus properly position the next-to-smallest item in position 2:

21 , 33 , 67 , 84 , 49 , 50 , 75

We continue in this manner, locating the smallest item in the sublist of items from position 3 on and interchanging it with the third item, then properly positioning the smallest item in the sublist of items from position 4 on, and so on until we eventually do this for the sublist consisting of the last two items:

21 , 33 , 49 , 84 , 67 , 50 , 75

21 , 33 , 49 , 50 , 67 , 84 , 75

21 , 33 , 49 , 50 , 67 , 84 , 75

21 , 33 , 49 , 50 , 67 , 75 , 84

Positioning the smallest item in this last sublist obviously also positions the last item correctly and thus completes the sort.

An algorithm for this simple selection sort is as follows.

SIMPLE SELECTION SORT ALGORITHM

* Algorithm to sort the list of items X(1), X(2), . . . , X(N) so they are in ascending order. *
* To sort them into descending order, change > to < in the comparison of X(J) with *
* SMALL in step 3. *
* Accepts: List X(1), X(2), . . . , X(N) *
* Returns: Modified list X(1), X(2), . . . , X(N); elements are sorted into ascending *
*   order *

For I ranging from 1 to N − 1, do the following:

    * On the Ith pass, first find the smallest item in the sublist X(I), . . . , X(N). *

    1. Set LOCSM equal to I.
    2. Set SMALL equal to X(LOCSM).
    3. For J ranging from I + 1 to N, do the following:
        If X(J) < SMALL then
           * Smaller item found *
           a. Set SMALL equal to X(J).
           b. Set LOCSM equal to J.

    * Now interchange this smallest item with the item at the beginning of this sublist. *

    4. Set X(LOCSM) equal to X(I).
    5. Set X(I) equal to SMALL.

The following subroutine uses this algorithm to sort a list of integers.

```
**SELSOR*******************************************************
* Subroutine to sort ITEM(1), ..., ITEM(N) into ascending order using  *
* the simple selection sort algorithm.  LIM is the upper limit on the  *
* size of the array ITEM.  For descending order change .LT. to .GT. in *
* the logical expression ITEM(I) .LT. SMALL.  Local variables used:    *
*     SMALL : smallest item in current sublist                         *
*     LOCSM : location of SMALL                                        *
*     I, J  : subscripts                                               *
*                                                                      *
* Accepts: Array ITEM and integers LIM and N                           *
* Returns: Array ITEM (modified) with first N elements in ascending    *
*          order                                                       *
**************************************************************


      SUBROUTINE SELSOR(ITEM, LIM, N)

      INTEGER LIM, ITEM(LIM), N, I

      DO 20 I = 1, N - 1

*         Find smallest item in sublist ITEM(I), ..., ITEM(N)

          SMALL = ITEM(I)
          LOCSM = I
          DO 10 J = I + 1, N
             IF (ITEM(J) .LT. SMALL) THEN
*               Smaller item found
                SMALL = ITEM(J)
                LOCSM = J
             END IF
10        CONTINUE

*         Interchange smallest item with ITEM(I) at
*         beginning of sublist

          ITEM(LOCSM) = ITEM(I)
          ITEM(I) = SMALL

20    CONTINUE

      END
```

Bubble Sort

Although simple selection sort performs reasonably well for random lists, it does not take advantage of any ordering that may be present in the list initially. Bubble sort is one sorting method that does. Although it is not efficient for random lists, it is a reasonably good method to use for partially ordered lists.

The basic approach of bubble sort is to scan the list repeatedly, comparing consecutive items and interchanging them if they are in the wrong order. If no interchanges occur on a scan, then no elements are out of order, that is, the list is sorted. To illustrate, suppose that the following list is to be sorted into ascending order:

$$67, 33, 21, 84, 49, 50, 75$$

We first compare 67 and 33 and interchange them because they are out of order:

$$33, 67, 21, 84, 49, 50, 75$$

Now we compare 67 and 21 and interchange them, giving

$$33, 21, 67, 84, 49, 50, 75$$

Next we compare 67 and 84 but do not interchange them since they are already in the correct order. Next, 84 and 49 are compared and interchanged, giving

$$33, 21, 67, 49, 84, 50, 75$$

The next elements 84 and 50 are in the wrong order and thus are interchanged:

$$33, 21, 67, 49, 50, 84, 75$$

Finally, 84 and 75 are compared and interchanged, giving

$$33, 21, 67, 49, 50, 75, 84$$

This completes the first pass through the list. Note that the largest item in the list "sinks" to the end of the list and some of the smaller items have "bubbled up" toward the front of the list. We scan the list again, comparing consecutive items and interchanging them when they are out of order, but this time we leave the last item out of the scan, since it is already in its proper position. This second scan of the list produces

$$21, 33, 49, 50, 67, 75, 84$$

On this scan, the last interchange occurred with the numbers 67 and 50, which means that the items beyond 67 are in their proper positions and hence can be omitted in the next scan. On the third scan no interchanges take place and the list has thus been sorted.

An algorithm for this bubble sort method is as follows:

BUBBLE SORT ALGORITHM

```
* Algorithm to sort the list of items X(1), X(2), ..., X(N) so they are in ascending order.  *
* To sort them into descending order, change > to < in the comparison of X(I) with  *
* X (I + 1) in step 2b.                                                          *
* Accepts:  List X(1), X(2), ..., X(N)                                           *
* Returns:  Modified list X(1), X(2), ..., X(N); elements are sorted into ascending  *
* order                                                                          *
```

1. Initialize PAIRS to N − 1; this is the number of pairs in the current sublist.
2. While PAIRS > 0 do the following:
   a. Set LAST to 1; this is the position at which the last interchange occurs.
   b. For I ranging 1 through PAIRS:
      If X(I) > X(I + 1) do the following:
         i. Interchange X(I) and X(I + 1).
         ii. Set LAST equal to I
   c. Set PAIRS equal to LAST − 1.

The following subroutine uses this algorithm to sort a list of integers.

```
**BUBBLE***************************************************************
* Subroutine to sort ITEM(1), ..., ITEM(N) into ascending order using  *
* the bubble sort algorithm. LIM is the upper limit on the size of     *
* the array ITEM. For descending order change .GT. to .LT. in the      *
* logical expression ITEM(I) .GT. ITEM(I + 1). Local variables used:   *
*     PAIRS  : number of pairs in the current sublist                  *
*     LAST   : position at which the last interchange occurs           *
*     I      : subscript                                               *
*     TEMP   : used to interchange two items in the list               *
*                                                                      *
* Accepts:  Array ITEM and integers LIM and N                          *
* Returns:  Array ITEM (modified) with first N elements in ascending   *
*           order                                                      *
************************************************************************

      SUBROUTINE BUBBLE(ITEM, LIM, N)

      INTEGER LIM, ITEM(LIM), N, PAIRS, LAST, I, TEMP
```

```
            PAIRS = N - 1

10      IF (PAIRS .GT. 0) THEN

            LAST = 1

*           Scan the sublist of the first PAIRS pairs in the list,
*           interchanging items that are out of order

            DO 20 I = 1, PAIRS
                IF (ITEM(I) .GT. ITEM(I+1)) THEN
*                   Items out of order -- interchange them
                    TEMP = ITEM(I)
                    ITEM(I) = ITEM(I+1)
                    ITEM(I+1) = TEMP

*                   Record position of last swap
                    LAST = I
                END IF
20          CONTINUE

            PAIRS = LAST - 1

            GO TO 10
        END IF

        END
```

8.9 APPLICATION: ANALYZING CONSTRUCTION COSTS

Problem

A company is planning to build a new manufacturing facility. One of the factors in selecting the site is the cost of labor in the various cities under consideration. To help analyze this data, the labor costs for these cities must be sorted so that they can be displayed in order and so that the median labor cost can be found.

Solution

Specification

Input: A list of labor costs
Output: Sorted list of labor costs
            Median labor cost

Design. The following variables will be used:

VARIABLES USED IN MEDIAN-CALCULATION PROBLEM

COST   Array that stores the labor costs

N   Number of labor costs

The **median** of a set of numbers $X_1, \ldots, X_n$ is the middle value when these numbers have been arranged in ascending order. One-half of the numbers are greater than or equal to this median value and one-half are smaller. After the list of numbers has been sorted, the median value is in position $(n + 1)/2$ if n is odd and is the average of the numbers in positions $n/2$ and $n/2 + 1$ if n is even. The following algorithm reads and stores the labor costs, sorts these costs, and then finds the median cost using this approach.

ALGORITHM FOR MEDIAN-CALCULATION PROBLEM

```
*  Algorithm to sort a list of labor costs COST(1), COST(2), . . . , COST(N) so they are in    *
*  ascending order and then find the median cost.                                              *
*  Input:     A list of labor costs                                                            *
*  Output:    Sorted list of labor costs and the median cost                                   *
```

1. Read the labor costs and store them in array COST.

2. Sort the array COST.

3. Display the sorted list of costs.

4. Calculate and display the median cost as follows:

    If N is odd

        Display COST$((N + 1)/2)$

    Else

        Display $\dfrac{\text{COST}(N/2) + \text{COST}(N/2 + 1)}{2}$

Coding, Execution, and Testing. The program in Figure 8.10 implements the preceding algorithm. It calls subroutine RDCOST to read the list of costs, calls subroutine SELSOR to sort them using the selection sort algorithm, and then calls subroutine OUTPUT to display the sorted list and the median cost. Also shown is one of the test runs with a small set of test data.

Figure 8.10 Sorting labor costs and finding median cost.

```
      PROGRAM SORTER
*****************************************************************************
* This program reads and counts a list of labor costs, sorts them in      *
* ascending order, and finds the median cost. For more costs, change      *
* the value of the parameter LIMIT. Identifiers used are:                 *
*     LIMIT   :  parameter representing maximum # of costs                *
*     COST    :  list of labor costs (in millions)                        *
*     N       :  number of labor costs                                    *
*                                                                         *
* Input:  Elements of COST -- using subroutine RDCOST                     *
* Output: Sorted elements of COST -- using subroutine OUTPUT              *
*****************************************************************************

      INTEGER LIMIT
      PARAMETER (LIMIT = 100)
      INTEGER COST(LIMIT), N

      CALL RDCOST(COST, LIMIT, N)
      CALL SELSOR(COST, LIMIT, N)
      CALL OUTPUT(COST, LIMIT, N)

      END


**RDCOST*******************************************************************
* Subroutine to read a list of up to LIMIT costs, store them in array     *
* COST, return this list and a count N of the number of values read.      *
* Local variable:                                                         *
*     INDATA  :  data value read (an actual cost or end-of-data signal)   *
*                                                                         *
* Accepts:  Array COST (undefined) and integer LIMIT                      *
* Input:    Elements of COST                                              *
* Returns:  Array COST (modified) and integer N                           *
*****************************************************************************

      SUBROUTINE RDCOST(COST, LIMIT, N)

      INTEGER LIMIT, COST(LIMIT), N, INDATA

      PRINT *, 'ENTER LABOR COSTS IN MILLIONS (0 OR NEGATIVE TO STOP).'
      N = 0
      READ *, INDATA
```

Figure 8.10 *(cont.)*

```
* While there is another data value, count it, store it in
* the next location of array COST, and read another value.

10      IF (INDATA .GT. 0) THEN
            N = N + 1
            COST(N) = INDATA
            READ *, INDATA
        GO TO 10
        END IF

        END


* * * * * * * * * * * * * * * * * * * * * * * * * * * * * * * * * * * * * * * * * * * * * * * * * * * * * * *
* Insert subroutine SELSOR here, or if bubble sort is preferred,         *
* insert subroutine BUBBLE and change CALL SELSOR(COST, LIMIT, N) in     *
* the main program to CALL BUBBLE(COST, LIMIT, N)                        *
* * * * * * * * * * * * * * * * * * * * * * * * * * * * * * * * * * * * * * * * * * * * * * * * * * * * * * *


* *OUTPUT* * * * * * * * * * * * * * * * * * * * * * * * * * * * * * * * * * * * * * * * * * * * * * * * * *
* Subroutine to display the sorted list of N COSTs and the median        *
* cost.  LIMIT is the upper limit on the array COST. Local variable:     *
*     I  : subscript                                                     *
*                                                                        *
* Accepts:  Array COST and integers LIMIT and N                          *
* Output:   First N elements of COST and the median cost                 *
* * * * * * * * * * * * * * * * * * * * * * * * * * * * * * * * * * * * * * * * * * * * * * * * * * * * * * *


        SUBROUTINE OUTPUT(COST, LIMIT, N)

        INTEGER LIMIT, COST(LIMIT), N, I

        PRINT 100, 'SORTED LIST', '====== ===='
100     FORMAT(2(/, 1X, A))
        DO 10 I = 1, N
            PRINT 101, COST(I)
101         FORMAT(1X, I6)
10      CONTINUE
        IF (MOD(N,2) .NE. 0) THEN
            PRINT 102, REAL (COST((N + 1)/2))
        ELSE
            PRINT 102, REAL ((COST(N/2) + COST(N/2 + 1))) / 2.0
        END IF
102     FORMAT(/1X, 'MEDIAN = ', F7.1, ' MILLION DOLLARS')

        END
```

Figure 8.10 *(cont.)*

Sample run:

```
ENTER LABOR COSTS IN MILLIONS (0 OR NEGATIVE TO STOP).
870
778
655
640
956
538
1050
529
689
0

SORTED LIST
====== ====
    529
    538
    640
    655
    689
    778
    870
    956
   1050

MEDIAN =    689.0 MILLION DOLLARS
```

Exercises 8.9

For each of the arrays X in Exercises 1–4, show X after each pass of simple selection sort.

1.
i	1	2	3	4	5	6	7	8
$X(i)$	30	50	80	10	60	20	70	40

2.
i	1	2	3	4	5	6	7	8
$X(i)$	20	40	70	60	80	50	30	10

3.
i	1	2	3	4	5	6	7	8
$X(i)$	80	70	60	50	40	30	20	10

4.
i	1	2	3	4	5	6	7	8
$X(i)$	10	20	30	40	50	60	70	80

For each of the arrays *X* in Exercises 5–8, show *X* after each pass of bubble sort.

   5. The list in Exercise 1.
   6. The list in Exercise 2.
   7. The list in Exercise 3.
   8. The list in Exercise 4.
   9. One variation of simple selection sort for a list stored in an array $X(1), \ldots, X(n)$ is to locate both the smallest and the largest elements while scanning the list and to position them at the beginning and the end of the list, respectively. On the next scan, this process is repeated for the sublist $X(2), \ldots, X(n-1)$, and so on. Write an algorithm to implement this double-ended selection sort.

For each of the arrays *X* in Exercises 10–13, show *X* after each pass of the double-ended selection sort described in Exercise 9.

   10. The list in Exercise 1.
   11. The list in Exercise 2.
   12. The list in Exercise 3.
   13. The list in Exercise 4.

8.10 SEARCHING

Another important problem is **searching** a collection of data for a specified item and retrieving some information associated with that item. For example, one searches a telephone directory for a specific name in order to retrieve the phone number listed with that name. We consider two kinds of searches, linear search and binary search.

Linear Search

A **linear search** begins with the first item in a list and searches sequentially until either the desired item is found or the end of the list is reached. The following algorithm describes this method of searching:

LINEAR SEARCH ALGORITHM

```
* Algorithm to linear search a list X(1), X(2), . . ., X(N) for a specified ITEM. The logi-  *
* cal variable FOUND is set to true and LOC is set to the position of ITEM if the search  *
* is successful; otherwise, FOUND is set to false.                                        *
* Accepts:  List X(1), X(2), . . . , X(N) and ITEM.                                       *
* Returns:  If ITEM is found in the list:                                                 *
*                   FOUND = true and LOC = position of ITEM.                              *
*             If ITEM is not found in the list:                                           *
*                   FOUND = false (and LOC = N + 1).                                      *
```

   1. Initialize LOC to 1 and FOUND to false.

2. While LOC ≤ N and not FOUND, do the following:
       If ITEM = X(LOC), then
              Set FOUND to true.
       Else
              Increment LOC by 1.

The following subroutine uses this algorithm to search a list of character strings.

```
**LINSCH**********************************************************
* Subroutine to search the list ITEM for UITEM using linear search.  *
* If UITEM is found in the list, FOUND is returned as true and the   *
* LOCation of the item is returned; otherwise FOUND is false. LIM is *
* the limit on the size of ITEM.                                     *
*                                                                    *
* Accepts:  Array ITEM, integers LIM and N, and UITEM               *
* Returns:  If UITEM is found:                                      *
*              FOUND = true and LOC = its position in the list ITEM *
*           Otherwise:                                              *
*              FOUND = false (and LOC = last position examined)     *
******************************************************************


      SUBROUTINE LINSCH(ITEM, LIM, N, UITEM, FOUND, LOC)

      INTEGER LIM, N, LOC
      CHARACTER*(*) ITEM(LIM), UITEM
      LOGICAL FOUND

      LOC = 1
      FOUND = .FALSE.

*     While LOC less than or equal to N and not FOUND do

10    IF ((LOC .LE. N) .AND. .NOT. FOUND) THEN
         IF (UITEM .EQ. ITEM(LOC)) THEN
            FOUND = .TRUE.
         ELSE
            LOC = LOC + 1
         END IF
      GO TO 10
      END IF

      END
```

Binary Search

   If a list has been sorted, **binary search** can be used to search for an item more efficiently than linear search. Whereas linear search may require n comparisons to locate a particular item, binary search will require at most $\log_2 n$ comparisons. For example, for a list of 1024 (= 2^{10}) items, binary search will locate an item using at most 10 comparisons whereas linear search may require 1024 comparisons.

In the binary search method, we first examine the middle element in the list, and if this is the desired element, the search is successful. Otherwise we determine whether the item being sought is in the first half or the second half of the list and then repeat this process, using the middle element of that list.

To illustrate, suppose the list to be searched is

1279
1331
1373
1555
1824
1898
1995
2002
2335
2665
3103

and we are looking for 1995. We first examine the middle number 1898 in the sixth position. Because 1995 is greater than 1898, we can disregard the first half of the list and concentrate on the second half.

1995
2002
2335
2665
3103

The middle number in this sublist is 2335, and the desired item 1995 is less than 2335, so we discard the second half of this sublist and concentrate on the first half.

1995
2002

Because there is no middle number in this sublist, we examine the number immediately preceding the middle position; that is the number 1995.

In general, the algorithm for binary search is as follows:

BINARY SEARCH ALGORITHM

* Algorithm to binary search a list X(1), X(2), . . . , X(N) that has been ordered so the *
* elements are in ascending order. The logical variable FOUND is set to true and LOC *
* is set to the position of the ITEM being sought if the search is successful; otherwise, *

```
*   FOUND is set to false.                                              *
*   Accepts:  List X(1), X(2), . . . , X(N) and ITEM.                   *
*   Returns:  If ITEM is found in the list:                            *
*                 FOUND = true and LOC = position of ITEM.             *
*             If ITEM is not found in the list:                        *
*                 FOUND = false.                                        *
```

1. Initialize FIRST to 1 and LAST to N. These values represent the positions of the first and last items of the list or sublist being searched.

2. Initialize the logical variable FOUND to false.

3. While FIRST ≤ LAST and not FOUND, do the following:
   a. Find the middle position in the sublist by setting MIDDLE equal to the integer quotient $(FIRST + LAST) / 2$.
   b. Compare the ITEM being searched for with X(MIDDLE). There are three possibilities:
      i. ITEM < X(MIDDLE): ITEM is in the first half of the sublist; set LAST equal to MIDDLE − 1.
      ii. ITEM > X(MIDDLE): ITEM is in the second half of the sublist; set FIRST equal to MIDDLE + 1.
      iii. ITEM = X(MIDDLE): ITEM has been found; set LOC equal to MIDDLE and FOUND to true.

The following subroutine uses this algorithm to search a list of character strings.

```
**BINSCH*****************************************************************
* Subroutine to search the list ITEM for UITEM using binary search.    *
* If UITEM is found in the list, FOUND is returned as true and the     *
* LOCation of the item is returned; otherwise FOUND is false. LIM is   *
* the limit on the size of ITEM. In this version of binary search,     *
* UITEM and the elements of ITEM are character strings.  Local         *
* variables used are:                                                   *
*      FIRST   :  first item in (sub)list being searched               *
*      LAST    :  last   "    "      "       "      "                    *
*      MIDDLE  :  middle "    "      "       "      "                    *
*                                                                       *
* Accepts:  Array ITEM, integers LIM and N, and UITEM                  *
* Returns:  If UITEM is found:                                         *
*               FOUND = true and LOC = its position in the list ITEM   *
*           Otherwise:                                                  *
*               FOUND = false (and LOC = last position examined)       *
************************************************************************
```

```
        SUBROUTINE BINSCH(ITEM, LIM, N, UITEM, FOUND, LOC)

        INTEGER LIM, N, LOC, FIRST, LAST, MIDDLE
        CHARACTER*(*) ITEM(LIM), UITEM
        LOGICAL FOUND

        FIRST = 1
        LAST = N
        FOUND = .FALSE.              _____

*       While FIRST less than or equal to LAST and not FOUND do

10      IF ((FIRST .LE. LAST) .AND. .NOT. FOUND) THEN
           MIDDLE = (FIRST + LAST) / 2
           IF (UITEM .LT. ITEM(MIDDLE)) THEN
              LAST = MIDDLE - 1
           ELSE IF (UITEM .GT. ITEM(MIDDLE)) THEN
              FIRST = MIDDLE + 1
           ELSE
              FOUND = .TRUE.
              LOC = MIDDLE
           END IF
        GO TO 10
        END IF

        END
```

8.11 APPLICATION: SEARCHING A CHEMISTRY DATABASE

Problem

Each line of a data file contains the chemical formula and name of an inorganic compound and its specific heat (the ratio of the amount of heat required to raise the temperature of a body 1°C to that required to raise an equal mass of water 1°C). The file has been sorted so that the chemical formulas are in alphabetical order. A table-lookup program is to be developed that will allow the user to enter a formula and that will then search the list of formulas and display the name and specific heat corresponding to that formula.

Solution

Specification. From the statement of the problem, we see that part of the input for this problem is a list of chemical formulas, names, and specific heats stored in a file and arranged so that the formulas are in alphabetical order. After these have been read in and stored, the user will input various formulas from the keyboard. The output will be the corresponding names and specific heats or a message indicating that none could be found. In summary, we have the following input/output specifications:

Input: A list of chemical formulas, names, and specific heats (data file)
          User-entered chemical formulas (keyboard)

Output: Names and specific heats for formulas entered or a message
          indicating that the formula could not be found

Design. We will use the following variables for this problem:

VARIABLES FOR TABLE-LOOKUP PROBLEM

FORMUL	Array that stores the chemical formulas
NAME	Array that stores the names
SPHEAT	Array that stores the specific heats
UFORM	A formula entered by the user
LOC	Location of UFORM in the array FORMUL

The following algorithm uses binary search to search the array FORMUL for the formulas entered by the user:

ALGORITHM FOR TABLE-LOOKUP PROBLEM

```
* Algorithm to read a list of chemical formulas, names, and specific heats, store these in  *
* arrays, and then search this list for specific formulas and retrieve the corresponding      *
* names and specific heats.                                                                    *
* Input:     A list of chemical formulas, names, and specific heats                           *
* Output:    Names and specific heats for specific formulas or a                              *
*            message indicating that a formula could not be found                             *
```

1. Read the formulas, names, and specific heats and store them in arrays
   FORMUL, NAME, and SPHEAT, respectively.

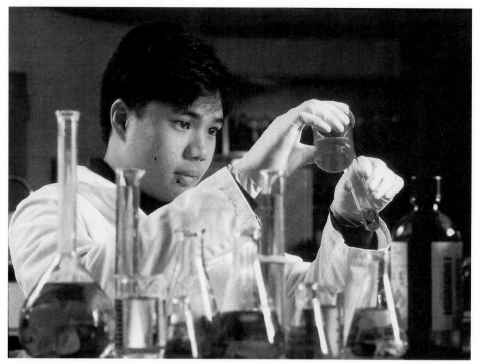

Experimentation in a chemistry lab. (Photo courtesy of Uniphoto Picture Agency.)

2. Enter the first formula UFORM ("QUIT" to stop).
3. While UFORM ≠ "QUIT" do the following:
    a. Use binary search to find the location LOC of UFORM in the array FORMUL or to determine that it is not present.
    b. If UFORM is found,
        Display NAME(LOC) and SPHEAT(LOC).
      Else
        Display a "Not Found" message.
    c. Enter the next formula UFORM.

Coding, Execution, and Testing. The program in Figure 8.11 implements the preceding algorithm. It calls subroutine RDDATA to read and store the chemical formulas, names, and specific heats and then calls subroutine LOOKUP to read formulas entered by the user and call subroutine SEARCH to search the array FORMUL for each formula. The program was tested with various data files, and a sample run with a small file is included.

Figure 8.11 Searching a list of chemical formulas.

```
      PROGRAM CHEM
****************************************************************
* Program to read a file containing the chemical formula, name, and   *
* specific heat for various inorganic compounds and store these in    *
* parallel arrays. File is sorted so that the formulas are in         *
* alphabetical order. The user enters a formula; the list of formulas *
* is searched using the binary search algorithm; and if the formula is*
* found, its name and specific heat are displayed. Identifiers used    *
* are:                                                                 *
*     LIMIT   :  parameter specifying maximum # of array elements      *
*     LENGTH  :  parameter specifying length of character strings      *
*     FORMUL  :  array of formulas                                     *
*     NAME    :  array of names                                        *
*     SPHEAT  :  array of specific heats                               *
*     N       :  number of records in the file                         *
*                                                                      *
* Input:  Arrays FORMUL, NAME, and SPHEAT (from RDDATA)               *
* Output: Names and specific heats for certain formulas (by LOOKUP)   *
****************************************************************


      INTEGER LIMIT, LENGTH, N
      PARAMETER (LIMIT = 100, LENGTH = 10)
      CHARACTER*(LENGTH) FORMUL(LIMIT), NAME(LIMIT)*(2*LENGTH)
      REAL SPHEAT(LIMIT)

      CALL RDDATA(FORMUL, NAME, SPHEAT, LIMIT, N)
      CALL LOOKUP(FORMUL, NAME, SPHEAT, LIMIT, N)

      END


**RDDATA********************************************************
* Subroutine to read a list of up to LIM chemical formulas, names,     *
* and specific heats, store them in parallel arrays FORMUL, NAME, and  *
* SPHEAT, and count (N) how many are stored. Local variables used:     *
*     FNAME : name of file from which data is read                     *
*     EOF   : end-of-file indicator                                    *
*                                                                      *
* Accepts:          Arrays FORMUL, NAME, SPHEAT, N (undefined) and     *
*                   integer LIM                                        *
* Input (keyboard): File name FNAME                                    *
* Input (file):     Elements of FORMUL, NAME, SPHEAT                   *
* Returns:          Arrays FORMUL, NAME, SPHEAT(modified) and integer N*
****************************************************************
```

Figure 8.11 *(cont.)*

```
      SUBROUTINE RDDATA(FORMUL, NAME, SPHEAT, LIM, N)

      INTEGER LIM, N, EOF
      CHARACTER*(*) FORMUL(LIM), NAME(LIM)
      REAL SPHEAT(LIM)
      CHARACTER*20 FNAME

* Open the file, then read, count, and store the items

      PRINT *, 'ENTER NAME OF FILE'
      READ '(A)', FNAME
      OPEN (UNIT = 15, FILE = FNAME, STATUS = 'OLD')
      N = 1

*     While there is more data in the file, read it and
*     store it in the parallel arrays

      READ (UNIT = 15, FMT = 100, IOSTAT = EOF)
     +      FORMUL(N), NAME(N), SPHEAT(N)
100   FORMAT(2A, F5.0)
10    IF (EOF .GE. 0) THEN
         N = N + 1
         READ (UNIT = 15, FMT = 100, IOSTAT = EOF)
     +         FORMUL(N), NAME(N), SPHEAT(N)
         GO TO 10
      ELSE
         N = N - 1
      END IF

      CLOSE(15)

      END


**LOOKUP*******************************************************
* Subroutine that allows user to enter formulas. The array FORMUL    *
* having N chemical formulas is then searched for this formula, and  *
* if found, the corresponding elements of the parallel arrays NAME   *
* and SPHEAT are displayed. User enters QUIT to stop searching. LIM   *
* dimensions the arrays. Local variables used are:                    *
*     UFORM   :  formula entered by the user                          *
*     FOUND   :  signals if UFORM found in array FORMUL               *
*     LOC     :  location of UFORM in FORMUL if found                 *
*     LENGTH  :  parameter used to specify length of UFORM            *
```

Figure 8.11 *(cont.)*

```
*                                                                      *
* Accepts:          Arrays FORMUL, NAME, SPHEAT, and                   *
*                   integers LIM and N                                 *
* Input (keyboard): Several values of UFORM or a 'QUIT' signal         *
* Output:           For each formula that is found, its specific       *
*                   heat; otherwise a 'NOT FOUND' message              *
***********************************************************************

      SUBROUTINE LOOKUP(FORMUL, NAME, SPHEAT, LIM, N)

      INTEGER LIM, N, LOC, LENGTH
      PARAMETER (LENGTH = 10)
      CHARACTER*(*) FORMUL(LIM), NAME(LIM)
      CHARACTER*(LENGTH) UFORM
      REAL SPHEAT(LIM)
      LOGICAL FOUND

      PRINT *
      PRINT *, 'ENTER FORMULA TO SEARCH FOR, (QUIT TO STOP)'
      READ '(A)', UFORM

* While UFORM not equal to 'QUIT', search FORMUL array for it,
* display information found, and read next UFORM

10    IF (UFORM. NE. 'QUIT') THEN
         CALL BINSCH(FORMUL, LIMIT, N, UFORM, FOUND, LOC)
         IF (FOUND) THEN
            PRINT 100, 'HAS SPECIFIC HEAT', SPHEAT(LOC)
100         FORMAT(6X, A, F7.4)
         ELSE
            PRINT 100, ' NOT FOUND'
         END IF
         PRINT *
         PRINT *, 'ENTER FORMULA TO SEARCH FOR, (QUIT TO STOP)'
         READ '(A)', UFORM
      GO TO 10
      END IF

      END


***********************************************************
*              Insert subroutine BINSCH here             *
***********************************************************
```

Figure 8.11 *(cont.)*

Listing of `FIL8-11.DAT` used in sample run:

```
AGCL      SILVER CHLORIDE     0.0804
ALCL3     ALUMINUM CHLORIDE   0.188
AUI       OLD IODIDE          0.0404
BACO3     BARIUM CARBONATE    0.0999
CACL2     CALCIUM CHLORIDE    0.164
CACO3     CALCIUM CARBONATE   0.203
FE2O3     FERRIC OXIDE        0.182
H2O2      HYDROGEN PEROXIDE   0.471
KCL       POTASSIUM CHLORIDE  0.162
LIF       LITHIUM FLOURIDE    0.373
NABR      SODIUM BROMIDE      0.118
NACL      SODIUM CHLORIDE     0.204
PBBR2     LEAD BROMIDE        0.0502
SIC       SILICON CARBIDE     0.143
SNCL2     STANNOUS CHLORIDE   0.162
ZNSO4     ZINC SULFATE        0.174
```

Sample run:

```
ENTER NAME OF FILE
FIL8-11.DAT

ENTER FORMULA TO SEARCH FOR, (QUIT TO STOP)
AGCL
      HAS SPECIFIC HEAT 0.0804

ENTER FORMULA
NACL
      HAS SPECIFIC HEAT 0.2040

ENTER FORMULA
FECO3
          NOT FOUND

ENTER FORMULA
FE2O3
      HAS SPECIFIC HEAT 0.1820
```

Figure 8.11 *(cont.)*

```
ENTER FORMULA
ZNSO4
      HAS SPECIFIC HEAT 0.1740

ENTER FORMULA
QUIT
```

CHAPTER REVIEW

Summary

In this chapter we described arrays and subscripted variables. We began by describing how arrays are declared and how subscripts can be used to provide direct access to the elements in an array. We described three methods of input/output of array elements: (1) using a DO loop, (2) using the array name, and (3) using an implied DO loop. We also described array assignment and how arrays can be used as arguments of subprograms. The important problem of sorting was considered in Section 8.8. Two sorting methods were described and illustrated with examples: simple selection sort and bubble sort. In Section 8.10 we considered another important list-processing problem—searching. We described two search methods: linear search, which may be used with any list, and binary search, which may be used for sorted lists.

FORTRAN SUMMARY

DIMENSION Statement

```
DIMENSION list-of-array-declarations
```

where each array declaration has the form

```
array-name(l:u)
```

Here l is the minimum value of a subscript and u is the maximum value. If the minimum subscript value is 1, only the maximum subscript need be specified.

Examples:

```
DIMENSION FAILTM(50), COUNT(1:20)
REAL FAILTM
INTEGER COUNT
```

```
INTEGER LIMIT
PARAMETER (LIMIT = 50)
DIMENSION FAILTM(LIMIT)
REAL FAILTM
```

Purpose:

Declares that each identifier *array-name* in the list of array declarations is an array for which the range of values of the subscript will be from the lower limit *l* through the upper limit *u*.

Declaration of Arrays in Type Statements

Array declarations may appear in type statements.

Examples:

```
REAL FAILTM(50), TEMP(1:20)
INTEGER COUNT(20)

INTEGER LIMIT
PARAMETER (LIMIT = 50)
REAL FAILTM(LIMIT)
```

PROGRAMMING POINTERS

Program Style and Design

1. *Arrays can be used to store lists of values.* If the data values must be processed more than once in a program, it is appropriate to store them in an array. Otherwise, it is usually better to use simple variables.

2. *Use a reasonable size when declaring an array.* The dimension of an array is determined by the number of data values to be stored. Do not needlessly overdimension an array, because this wastes memory.

3. *Use parameters to dimension an array.* If it is necessary to change the size of an array, only the parameter needs to be changed.

Potential Problems

1. *All arrays in a FORTRAN program must be dimensioned.* If, for example, ALPHA has been declared by

```
REAL ALPHA
```

but has not been dimensioned, the compiler may interpret a reference to an element of ALPHA, as in

```
X = ALPHA(1)
```

as a reference to a function named ALPHA, which is an error.

2. *Arrays must be declared in each program unit in which they are used.* The dimension can be specified by constants or parameters, and in subprograms adjustable dimensions are allowed.

3. *Subscripts must be integer valued and must stay within the range specified in the array declarations.* Related to this requirement are two kinds of errors that can easily occur when using arrays. The first error results from forgetting to declare a subscript to be of integer type. For example, consider the program segment

```
INTEGER ALPHA(10)

DO 10 ELM = 1, 10
    ALPHA(ELM) = 0
10 CONTINUE
    .
    .
    .
```

Because the type of ELM has not been declared, the FORTRAN naming convention implies that it is of real type. Consequently, an error results when the array ALPHA is referenced by the statement

```
ALPHA(ELM) = 0
```

because the subscript is not of integer type.

Another error results from allowing a subscript to get "out of bounds," that is, to have a value less than the lower bound or greater than the upper bound specified in the array declaration. The result of an out-of-range subscript is compiler-dependent. If a compiler does range checking, an error will result, and execution is usually terminated. For some compilers, however, no such range checking is done, and the memory location that is accessed is determined simply by counting forward or backward from the base address of the array. This is illustrated by the program in Figure 8.12. Here A, B, and C are arrays declared by

```
INTEGER A(4), B(4), C(4)
```

and the illegal array references B(-2) and B(7) access the memory locations associated with A(2) and C(3):

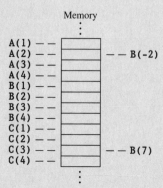

Thus modifying $B(-2)$ and $B(7)$ changes $A(2)$ and $C(3)$, respectively. This change is obviously undesirable. An array reference such as $B(500)$ that is very much out of range may even cause a program instruction to be modified! Consequently, *it is important to ensure that subscripts do not get out of range.*

Figure 8.12 Why array subscripts must stay in bound.

```
      PROGRAM ARRAYS
***************************************************************
* Program to demonstrate what may result when subscripts get out of   *
* bounds.  Variables used are                                  *
*     A, B, C : one-dimensional arrays of integers             *
*                                                              *
* Output:  Arrays A, B, and C before and after subscripts get out of  *
*          range                                               *
***************************************************************

      INTEGER A(4), B(4), C(4)
      DATA A /1,2,3,4/, B /5,6,7,8/, C /9,10,11,12/

* Display the original arrays

      PRINT 100, 'A =', A
      PRINT 100, 'B =', B
      PRINT 100, 'C =', C
100   FORMAT(1X, A, 4I5)

* Reference array B with a subscript that is out of bounds

      B(-2) = -999
      B(7) = 999

* Print each of the arrays again

      PRINT *
      PRINT 100, 'A =', A
      PRINT 100, 'B =', B
      PRINT 100, 'C =', C

      END
```

Figure 8.12 *(cont.)*

Sample run:

```
A =     1     2     3     4
B =     5     6     7     8
C =     9    10    11    12

A =     1  -999    3     4
B =     5     6     7     8
C =     9    10   999    12
```

PROGRAMMING PROBLEMS

Section 8.2

1. The Cawker City Candy Company records the number of cases of candy produced each day over a four-week period. Write a program that reads these production numbers and stores them in an array. The program should then accept from the user a week number and a day number and display the production level for that day. Assume that each week consists of five workdays.

2. The Cawker City Candy Company maintains two warehouses, one in Chicago and one in Detroit, each of which stocks at most 25 different items. Write a program that first reads the product numbers of the items stored in the Chicago warehouse and stores them in an array and then repeats this for the items stored in the Detroit warehouse, storing these product numbers in another array. The program should then find and display the *intersection* of these two lists of numbers, that is, the collection of product numbers common to both lists. The lists should not be assumed to have the same number of elements.

3. Repeat Exercise 2, but find and display the *union* of the two lists, that is, the collection of product numbers that are elements of at least one of the lists.

4. A hardware store sells lawn sprinklers. Past experience has indicated that the selling season is only six months long, lasting from April 1 through September 30. The sales division has forecast the following sales for next year:

Month	Demand
April	40
May	20
June	30
July	40
August	30
September	20

All sprinklers are purchased from an outside source at a cost of $8.00 per sprinkler. However, the supplier sells them only in lots of 10, 20, 30, 40, or 50; monthly orders for fewer than 10 sprinklers or more than 50 are not accepted. Discounts based on the size of the lot ordered are as follows:

Lot Size	Discount (percent)
10	5
20	5
30	10
40	20
50	25

For each order placed, the store is charged a fixed cost of $15.00 to cover shipping costs, insurance, packaging, and so on, regardless of the number ordered (except that there is no charge for a month when none is ordered). Assume that orders are placed on the first of the month and are received immediately. The store also incurs a carrying charge of $1.80 for each sprinkler remaining in stock at the end of any one month.

Write a program to calculate the total seasonal cost, the price that must be charged per sprinkler in order for the hardware store to break even, and the price that must be charged to realize a profit of 30 percent. Run your program with each of the following six ordering policies and determine which is the best:

Policy Number	Number Ordered/Month					
	April	May	June	July	August	September
1	40	20	30	40	30	20
2	50	50	50	30	0	0
3	40	50	0	40	50	0
4	50	50	40	40	0	0
5	50	10	50	20	50	0
6	50	50	0	50	30	0

5. Suppose that a row of mailboxes is numbered 1 through 150 and that beginning with mailbox 2, we open the doors of all the even-numbered mailboxes. Next, beginning with mailbox 3, we go to every third mailbox, opening its door if it is closed and closing it if it is open. We repeat this procedure with every fourth mailbox, then every fifth mailbox, and so on. Write a program to determine which mailboxes will be closed when this procedure is completed.

6. A *prime number* is an integer greater than 1 whose only positive divisors are 1 and the integer itself. One method for finding all the prime numbers in the range 2 through n is known as the *Sieve of Eratosthenes*. Consider the list of numbers

from 2 through n. Here 2 is the first prime number, but the multiples of 2 (4, 6, 8, ...) are not, and so they are "crossed out" in the list. The first number after 2 that was not crossed out is 3, the next prime. We then cross out all higher multiples of 3 (6, 9, 12, ...) from the list. The next number not crossed out is 5, the next prime; we cross out all higher multiples of 5 (10, 15, 20, ...). We repeat this procedure until we reach the first number in the list that has not been crossed out and whose square is greater than n. Then all the numbers that remain in the list are the primes from 2 through n. Write a program that uses this sieve method to find all the prime numbers from 2 through n. Run it for $n = 50$ and for $n = 500$.

7. Write a program to investigate the *birthday problem*: If there are n persons in a room, what is the probability that two or more of them have the same birthday? You might consider values of n, say from 10 through 40, and for each value of n, generate n random birthdays, and then scan the list to see whether two of them are the same. To obtain some approximate probabilities, you might do this 100 times for each value of n.

Section 8.5

8. Write a program that calls subprograms to read and count a list of numbers and to calculate their mean, variance, and standard deviation. Print how many numbers there are and their mean, variance, and standard deviation with appropriate labels. If $\bar{x}$ denotes the mean of the numbers $x_1, \ldots, x_n$, the *variance* is the average of the squares of the deviations of the numbers from the mean:

$$\text{variance} = \frac{1}{n}\sum_{i=1}^{n}(x_i - \bar{x})^2$$

and the *standard deviation* is the square root of the variance.

9. Letter grades are sometimes assigned to numeric scores by using the grading scheme commonly called *grading on the curve*. In this scheme, a letter grade is assigned to a numeric score, according to the following table:

x = Numeric Score	Letter Grade
$x < m - \frac{3}{2}\sigma$	F
$m - \frac{3}{2}\sigma \leq x < m - \frac{1}{2}\sigma$	D
$m - \frac{1}{2}\sigma \leq x < m + \frac{1}{2}\sigma$	C
$m + \frac{1}{2}\sigma \leq x < m + \frac{3}{2}\sigma$	B
$m + \frac{3}{2}\sigma \leq x$	A

where m is the mean score and σ is the standard deviation. Extend the program of Exercise 8 to read a list of real numbers representing numeric scores, calculate their mean and standard deviation, and then find and display the letter grade corresponding to each numeric score.

10. Write a subprogram to evaluate a polynomial $a_0 + a_1x + a_2x^2 + \cdots + a_nx^n$ for any degree n, coefficients $a_0, a_1, \ldots, a_n$, and values of x that are supplied to it as arguments. Then write a program that reads a value of n, the coefficients, and various values of x and then uses this subprogram to evaluate the polynomial at these values.

11. A more efficient way of evaluating polynomials is *Horner's method* (also known as *nested multiplication*) in which a polynomial $a_0 + a_1x + a_2x^2 + \cdots + a_nx^n$ is rewritten as

$$a_0 + (a_1 + (a_2 + \cdots + (a_{n-1} + a_nx)x) \cdots x)x$$

For example:

$$7 + 6x + 5x^2 + 4x^3 + 3x^4 = 7 + (6 + (5 + (4 + 3x)x)x)x$$

Proceed as in Exercise 10, but use Horner's method to evaluate the polynomial.

12. Write a program to read the files STUDENT.DAT and STUPDATE.DAT (see Appendix B) and produce an updated grade report. This grade report should show

(a) the current date

(b) the student's name and student number

(c) a list of the names, grades and credits for each of the current courses under the headings COURSE, GRADE, and CREDITS

(d) current GPA (multiply the credits by the numeric grade—A = 4.0, A− = 3.7, B+ = 3.3, B = 3.0, . . . , D− = 0.7, F = 0.0—for each course to find honor points earned for that course; sum these to find the total new honor points, then divide the total new honor points by the total new credits to give the current GPA, rounded to two decimal places)

(e) total credits earned (old credits from STUDENT.DAT plus total new credits)

(f) new cumulative GPA (first, calculate old honor points = old credits times old cumulative GPA, then new cumulative GPA = sum of old honor points and new honor points divided by updated total credits)

13. Write a subroutine to add two large integers of any length, say up to 300 digits. A suggested approach is as follows: Treat each number as a list, each of whose elements is a block of digits of that number. For example, the integer 179,534,672,198 might be stored with N(1) = 198, N(2) = 672, N(3) = 534, N(4) = 179. Then add the two integers (lists) element by element, carrying from one element to the next when necessary. Test your subroutine with a program that reads two large integers and calls the subroutine to find their sum.

14. Proceed as in Exercise 13, but write a subroutine to multiply two large integers, say of length up to 300 digits.

15. A data structure that is sometimes implemented using an array is a *stack*. A stack is a list in which elements may be inserted or deleted at only one end of the list, called the *top* of the stack. Because the last element added to a stack will be the first one removed, a stack is called a *Last-In-First-Out (LIFO)* structure. A stack can be implemented as an array STACK, with STACK(1) representing the bottom of the stack and STACK(TOP) the top, where TOP is the position of the top element of the stack. Write subprograms PUSH and POP to implement insertion and deletion operations for a stack. Use these subprograms in a program that reads a command I (Insert) or D (Delete); for I, an integer is then read and inserted into ("pushed onto") the stack; for D, an integer is deleted ("popped") from the stack and displayed.

16. Another data structure that can be implemented using an array is a *queue*. A queue is a list in which elements may be inserted at one end, called the *rear*, and removed at the other end, called the *front*. Because the first element added is the first to be removed, a queue is called a *First-In-First-Out (FIFO)* structure. Write subprograms to implement insertion and deletion operations for a queue. Use these subprograms in a program like that in Exercise 15 to insert integers into or delete integers from a queue. (*Note:* The most efficient representation of a queue as an array is obtained by thinking of the array as being circular, with the first array element immediately following the last array element.)

17. (Project) A problem from the area of *artificial intelligence:* The game of *Nim* is played by two players. There are three piles of objects, and each player is allowed to take any number (at least one) of objects from any pile on his or her turn. The player taking the last object wins. Write a program in which the computer "learns" to play Nim. One way to "teach" the computer is to have the program assign a value to each possible move based on experience gained from playing games. The value of each possible move is stored in some array, and each value is set to 0. The program then keeps track of each move the computer makes as it plays the game. At the end of each game that the computer wins, the value of each move the computer made is increased by 1. At the end of any game that the computer loses, the value of each move the computer made is decreased by 1. The computer plays by selecting, from all legal moves, the one that has the largest value. When there are several possible moves having this same largest value, some strategy must be chosen. (One possibility is to have it select a move randomly.)

18. (Project) The spread of a contagious disease and the propagation of a rumor have a great deal in common. Write a program to simulate the spread of a disease or a rumor. You might proceed as follows: establish a population of N individuals, and assign to each individual four parameters (perhaps different numbers to various individuals):

   (a) a "resistance" parameter: the probability that the individual will be infected by the disease (rumor) upon transmission from a carrier;

   (b) a "recovery" (or "forgetting") parameter: the probability that the infected individual will recover from the disease (forget the rumor) before transmitting it to others in the population;

(c) an "activity" parameter: the probability that the individual will contact another person;

(d) a "transmission" parameter: the probability that the individual will in fact transmit the disease (rumor) to another person he or she contacts.

A person who comes in contact with an infected person either becomes infected or does not; a random number can be compared with his or her resistance parameter to determine the result.

Once a person is infected, that is, becomes a carrier, another random number can be compared with his or her recovery (forgetting) parameter to determine whether or not he or she will recover from the disease (forget the rumor) before contacting other persons.

The activity parameter of a person who does not recover from the disease (forget the rumor) before contacting other persons determines how many persons he or she will contact, and the transmission parameter determines the actual number of persons to whom the disease (rumor) will be transmitted. The specific individuals can then be selected at random from the population and the disease (rumor) transmitted to them.

Select one individual to initiate the process. You might keep track of the number of persons infected in each stage; the "degrees of exposure (credibility)," that is, the number of persons exposed once, twice, and so on; the effect of using certain percentages to indicate the decreased chances of reinfection; and so on.

Section 8.8

19. Write a program that reads a list of numbers, calls a double-ended selection sort subroutine (see Exercise 9 of Section 8.9) to sort the list, and then displays the sorted list.

20. Write a program that reads two lists of integers that have been sorted so that they are in ascending order and then calls a subroutine to *merge* these lists into a third list in which the integers are also in ascending order. Run the program for at least the following lists:

    (a) List-1: 1, 3, 5, 7, 9
        List-2: 2, 4, 6, 8, 10

    (b) List-1: 1, 4, 5, 6, 9, 10
        List-2: 2, 3, 7, 8

    (c) List-1: 1, 2, 3, 4, 5, 6, 7
        List-2: 8, 9, 10

    (d) List-1: 10
        List-2: 1, 2, 3, 4, 5, 6, 7, 8, 9

21. *Insertion sort* is an efficient sorting method for small data sets. It consists of beginning with the first item $X(1)$, then inserting $X(2)$ into this one-item list in the correct position to form a sorted two-element list, then inserting $X(3)$ into this two-element

list in the correct position, and so on. For example, to sort the list 7, 1, 5, 2, 3, 4, 6, 0, the steps are as follows (the element being inserted is highlighted):

List

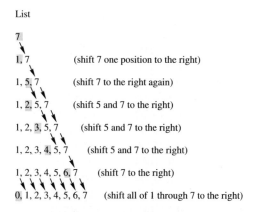

7

1, 7   (shift 7 one position to the right)

1, 5, 7   (shift 7 to the right again)

1, 2, 5, 7   (shift 5 and 7 to the right)

1, 2, 3, 5, 7   (shift 5 and 7 to the right)

1, 2, 3, 4, 5, 7   (shift 5 and 7 to the right)

1, 2, 3, 4, 5, 6, 7   (shift 7 to the right)

0, 1, 2, 3, 4, 5, 6, 7   (shift all of 1 through 7 to the right)

Write a subroutine to sort a list of items using this insertion sort method and then write a main program that reads a set of values and calls this subroutine to sort them.

22. Insertion sort (see Exercise 21) performs best for small lists and for partially sorted lists. *Shell sort* (named after Donald Shell) uses insertion sort to sort small sublists to produce larger, partially ordered sublists. Specifically, one begins with a "gap" of a certain size g and then uses insertion sort to sort sublists of elements that are g apart, first, $X(1)$, $X(1 + g)$, $X(1 + 2g)$, . . . , then the sublist $X(2)$, $X(2 + g)$, $X(2 + 2g)$, . . . , then $X(3)$, $X(3 + g)$, $X(3 + 2g)$, . . . , and so on. Next the size of the gap g is reduced, and the process repeated. This continues until the gap g is 1, and the final insertion sort results in the sorted list.

Write a subroutine to sort a list of items using this Shell sort method, beginning with a gap g of the form $(3^k - 1)/2$ for some integer k, and dividing it by 3 at each stage. Then write a main program that reads a set of values and calls this subroutine to sort them.

23. The investment firm of Pikum and Loozum has been recording the trading price of a particular stock over a 15-day period. Write a program that reads these prices and sorts them into increasing order, using the insertion sort scheme described in Problem 21. The program should display the trading range, that is, the lowest and highest prices recorded, and also the median price.

Section 8.10

24. In general, one need not linearly search an entire list to determine that it does not contain a given item if the list has been previously sorted. Write a modified linear search algorithm for such an ordered list. Then implement this algorithm as a subroutine and write a program that reads a list of real values, stores them in an array LIST, and then calls the subroutine to search the list for a given real number entered during execution.

25. The following data was collected by a company and represents discrete values of a function for which an explicit formula is not known:

x	f(x)
1.123400	167.5600
2.246800	137.6441
3.370200	110.2523
4.493600	85.38444
5.617000	63.04068
6.740400	43.22099
7.863800	25.92535
8.987200	11.15376
10.11060	−1.093781
11.23400	−10.81726
12.35740	−18.01665
13.48080	−22.69202
14.60420	−24.84334
15.72760	−24.47060
16.85100	−21.57379
17.97440	−16.15295
19.09780	−8.208008
20.22120	2.260895
21.34460	15.25394
22.46800	30.77100
23.59140	48.81213
24.71480	69.37738
25.83820	92.46655
26.96160	118.0799
28.08500	146.2172

One can, however, use *linear interpolation* to approximate the $f(x)$-value for any given x-value between the smallest and the largest x-values. First, find the two x-values x_i and x_{i+1} in the list that bracket the given x-value, using a modified linear search procedure similar to that in Problem 24, and then interpolate to find the approximate corresponding $f(x)$-value:

$$f(x) = f(x_i) + \frac{f(x_{i+1}) - f(x_i)}{x_{i+1} - x_i}(x - x_i)$$

(If the x-value is out of range, print a message.) Test your program with the following x-values: $-7.8, 1.1234, 13.65, 22.5, 23.5914, 25, 25.085,$ and 33.8.

26. The Cawker City Candy Company manufactures different kinds of candy, each identified by a product number. Write a program that reads two arrays, NUMBER and PRICE, in which NUMBER(1) and PRICE(1) are the product number and the unit price for the first item, NUMBER(2) and PRICE(2) are the product num-

ber and the unit price for the second item, and so on. The program should then allow the user to select one of the following options:

1. Retrieve and display the price of a product whose number is entered by the user.
2. Print a table displaying the product number and the price of each item.

Make the program modular by using subprograms to perform the various tasks.

Fortran 90

Features

- Assignment of one array to another is permitted, provided that the arrays have the same number of elements.
- Array constants of the form

```
(/ value₁, value₂, ..., valueₖ /)
```

are allowed, where each $value_i$ is a constant expression or an *implied-do constructor* of the form

```
(value-list, implied-do-control)
```

For example, if A is declared by

```
INTEGER, DIMENSION(10) :: A
```

it can be assigned the sequence $1, 2, 3, \ldots, 10$ by any of the following statements:

```
A = (/ 1, 2, 3, 4, 5, 6, 7, 8, 9, 10 /)
A = (/ (I, I = 1, 10) /)
A = (/ 1, (I, I = 2, 9), 10 /)
```

- Operators and functions normally applied to simple expressions may also be applied to arrays having the same number of elements. In this case, operations applied to an array are carried out elementwise. To illustrate, consider the following declarations:

```
INTEGER, DIMENSION(4)   :: A, B
INTEGER, DIMENSION(0:3) :: C
INTEGER, DIMENSION(6:9) :: D
LOGICAL, DIMENSION(4)   :: P
```

If A and B are assigned values

```
A = (/ 1, 2, 3, 4 /)
B = (/ 5, 6, 7, 8 /)
```

the statement

```
A = A + B
```

assigns A the sequence 6, 8, 10, 12. If C is assigned a value

```
C = (/ -1, 3, -5, 7 /)
```

the statement

```
D = 2 * ABS(C) + 1
```

assigns to D the sequence 3, 7, 11, 15. Logical operations are also allowed. For example, the statement

```
P = (C > 0) .AND. (MOD(B, 3) = 0)
```

assigns to P the sequence of truth values .FALSE., .TRUE., .FALSE., .FALSE.

- Array sections, which are arrays consisting of selected elements from a parent array, are allowed. Such array sections are defined by specifications of the form

```
array-name(subscript-triplet)
```

or

```
array-name(vector-subscript)
```

A subscript triplet has the form

```
lower : upper : stride
```

and specifies the elements in positions *lower, lower* + *stride, lower* + *2* ** stride,* . . . going as far as possible without going beyond *upper,* if *stride* > 0, or below *upper* if *stride* < 0. If *stride* is omitted, it is taken to be 1. For example, if A, B, and I are arrays dimensioned by

```
INTEGER, DIMENSION(10):: A
INTEGER, DIMENSION(5):: B
INTEGER :: I, J
```

and A is assigned a value by

```
A = (/ 11, 22, 33, 44, 55, 66, 77, 88, 99, 110 /)
```

then the statement

```
B = A(2:10:2)
```

assigns to B the section of array A consisting of the elements 22, 44, 66, 88, 110. The statement

```
A(1:10:2) = (/ J**2, J = 1, 5 /)
```

changes the elements in the odd positions of A to be 1, 4, 9, 16, 25.

A vector subscript is a sequence of subscripts of the parent array. For example, if A is the array considered earlier,

```
A = (/ 11, 22, 33, 44, 55, 66, 77, 88, 99, 110 /)
```

and I is the subscript vector

```
I = (/ 6, 5, 3, 9, 1 /)
```

then the assignment statement

```
B = A(I)
```

assigns B the section of array A consisting of the elements 66, 55, 33, 99, and 11, whereas the assignment statement

```
B = A((/ 5, 3, 3, 4, 3/))
```

assigns to B the sequence of elements 55, 33, 33, 44, and 33.

- A WHERE construct of the form

```
WHERE (logical-array-expression)
    sequence₁ of array-assignment-statements
ELSEWHERE
    sequence₂ of array-assignment-statements
END WHERE
```

(where the ELSEWHERE part is optional) may be used to assign values to arrays depending on the value of a logical array expression. For example, if arrays A and B are declared by

```
INTEGER, DIMENSION(5) :: A
REAL, DIMENSION(5) :: B
```

and A is assigned the value

```
A = (/ 0, 2, 5, 0, 10 /)
```

the WHERE construct

```
WHERE (A > 0)
    B = 1.0 / REAL(A)
ELSEWHERE
    B = -1.0
END WHERE
```

assigns to B the sequence −1.0, 0.5, 0.2, −1.0, 0.1.

- Formal array arguments in subprograms may be *assumed-shape arrays* in which the dimension of the array is taken to be the dimension of the corresponding actual array argument. In this case the declaration of the formal array in the subprogram has the form

```
type, DIMENSION(lower:) :: array-name
```

or

```
type, DIMENSION(:) :: array-name
```

In the second case, the lowest subscript is taken to be 1. Any program unit that calls the subprogram must have an explicit interface (see the Fortran 90 section of Chapter 6).

- The dimension of local arrays in subprograms may be specified by formal arguments or by the values of the array inquiry functions SIZE, LBOUND, and UBOUND for the corresponding actual array argument. For example, the subroutine

```
SUBROUTINE Swap(A, B)
! Subroutine to interchange elements of A and B

  REAL, DIMENSION(:) :: A, B        !assumed-size arrays
  REAL, DIMENSION(SIZE(A)) :: Temp !local array

  Temp = A
  A = B
  B = Temp
END SUBROUTINE Swap
```

- The value returned by a function may be an array.
- Several new predefined functions for processing arrays have been added, including:

DOT_PRODUCT(A, B):	Returns the dot product of A and B
MAXVAL(A):	Returns the maximum value in array A
MAXLOC(A):	Returns a one-dimensional array containing one element whose value is the position of the first occurrence of the maximum value in A
MINVAL(A):	Returns the minimum value in array A
MINLOC(A):	Returns a one-dimensional array containing one element whose value is the position of the first occurrence of the minimum value in A
PRODUCT(A):	Returns the product of the elements of A
SUM(A):	Returns the sum of the elements of A

- Arrays may be *allocatable arrays*, which means that space is not allocated to them at compile time but, rather, by an ALLOCATE statement during execution; their bounds are also specified at that time. Such arrays are useful in applications in which their sizes are known only after some data has been read or some calculation performed.

An array is declared to be allocatable by including the ALLOCATABLE attribute in its type declaration. For example, the type specification statement

```
REAL, DIMENSION(:), ALLOCATABLE :: A, B
```

declares A and B to be one-dimensional allocatable arrays. The actual bounds are determined by an ALLOCATE statement, for example,

```
ALLOCATE (A(N), B(1:N+1))
```

where N is an integer variable. When this statement is executed, sufficient memory is allocated for the arrays A and B.

Examples

The following programs and subprograms illustrate several of the new array features in Fortran 90. The program in Figure 8.13 illustrates the use of an allocatable array, and the function MEAN declares the formal argument X as an assumed-shape array and uses the array functions SUM and SIZE to compute the mean of the elements of X.

Figure 8.13 Calculating the mean of a list—Fortran 90 version.

```fortran
    PROGRAM Mean_of_a_List
!------------------------------------------------------------------
! Program to read a list of numbers Item(1), Item(2), ...,
! Item(NumItems) and calculate their mean using the function
! subprogram Mean.  Identifiers used are:
!   NumItems : number of items
!   Item     : one-dimensional array of items
!   Mean     : function to find the mean
!
! Input:  NumItems and a list of NumItems real numbers
! Output: The mean of the numbers
!------------------------------------------------------------------

  IMPLICIT NONE
  REAL, DIMENSION (:), ALLOCATABLE :: Item
  INTEGER :: NumItems

  INTERFACE
    REAL FUNCTION Mean(X)
      REAL X(:)
    END FUNCTION Mean
  END INTERFACE
```

Figure 8.13   *(cont.)*

```
  PRINT *, "Enter number of items:"
  READ *, NumItems

  ALLOCATE (Item(NumItems))

  PRINT *, "Enter the items:"
  READ *, Item

  PRINT 100, NumItems, Mean(Item)
  100 FORMAT(1X, "Mean of the ", I3, " numbers is ", F6.2)

END PROGRAM Mean_of_a_List

! Mean---------------------------------------------------------
! Function to find the mean of elements of the array X.
!
! Accepts: Array X
! Returns: The mean of the numbers stored in X
!-------------------------------------------------------------

REAL FUNCTION Mean(X)

  REAL, DIMENSION(:) :: X

  Mean = SUM(X) / REAL(SIZE(X))

END FUNCTION Mean
```

Most of the vector operations described in Section 8.6 can be implemented very easily in Fortran 90. For example, the function DOT_PRODUCT can be used to find the dot product of two vectors A and B,

```
    A_dot_B = DOT_PRODUCT(A, B)
```

and the sum of A and B can be computed simply as

```
    Sum_of_A_and_B = A + B
```

The norm of a vector A is also easy to compute:

```
    Norm_of_A = SQRT(SUM(A * A))
```

Array sections and the array functions MINVAL and MINLOC can be used to simplify array operations. Figure 8.14 illustrates this for the subroutine for selection sort in
Section 8.7.

Figure 8.14 Selection sort — Fortran 90 version.

```fortran
! Selection_Sort ----------------------------------------------------
! Subroutine to sort Item(1), ..., Item(N) into ascending order using
! the simple selection sort algorithm. Variables used are:
!   Item                : array of integers to be sorted
!   NumItems            : number of items
!   I                   : subscript
!   TempLoc             : stores location of minimum value
!   SmallestItem        : smallest item in current sublist
!   Location_Smallest   : location of SmallestItem
!
! Accepts: Array Item
! Returns: Array Item (modified) with first NumItems elements in
!          ascending order
!-------------------------------------------------------------------

SUBROUTINE Selection_Sort(Item)

  INTEGER :: Item(:), TempLoc(1)
  INTEGER :: NumItems, I, SmallestItem, Location_Smallest

  NumItems = SIZE(Item)

  DO I = 1, NumItems - 1

!   Find smallest item in sublist Item(I), ..., Item(NumItems)

    SmallestItem = MINVAL(Item(I:NumItems))
    TempLoc = MINLOC(Item(I:NumItems))
    Location_Smallest = (I - 1) + TempLoc(1)

!   Interchange smallest item with Item(I) at
!   beginning of sublist

    Item(Location_Smallest) = Item(I)
    Item(I) = SmallestItem
  END DO

END SUBROUTINE Selection_Sort
```

9

Multidimensional Arrays

Everyone knows how laborious the usual Method is of attaining to Arts and Sciences; whereas by his Contrivance, the most ignorant Person at a reasonable Charge, and with a little bodily Labour, may write Books in Philosophy, Poetry, Politicks, Law, Mathematicks, and Theology, without the least Assistance from Genius or Study. He then led me to the Frame, about the sides whereof all his Pupils stood in Ranks. It was Twenty Foot square . . . linked by slender Wires. These Bits . . . were covered on every Square with Paper pasted upon them; and on These Papers were written all the Words of their Language. . . .

The Professor then desired me to observe, for he was going to set his Engine at work. The Pupils at this Command took each of them hold of an Iron Handle, whereof there were Forty fixed round the Edges of the Frame; and giving them a sudden Turn, the whole Disposition of the Words was entirely changed. . . .

JONATHAN SWIFT, *Gulliver's Travels*

CHAPTER CONTENTS

9.1 Introduction to Multidimensional Arrays and Multiply Subscripted Variables

9.2 Processing Multidimensional Arrays

9.3 Application: Pollution Tables

9.4 Application: Oceanographic Data Analysis

9.5 Example: Matrix Processing

9.6 Application: Electrical Networks

Chapter Review

Programming Pointers

Programming Problems

Fortran 90

*I*n the preceding chapter we considered one-dimensional arrays and used them to process lists of data. We also observed that FORTRAN provides arrays of more than one dimension and that two-dimensional arrays are useful when the data being processed can be arranged in rows and columns. Similarly, a three-dimensional array is appropriate when the data can be arranged in rows, columns, and ranks. When there are several characteristics associated with the data, still higher dimensions may be appropriate, with each dimension corresponding to one of these characteristics. In this chapter we consider how such multidimensional arrays are processed in FORTRAN programs.

9.1 INTRODUCTION TO MULTIDIMENSIONAL ARRAYS AND MULTIPLY SUBSCRIPTED VARIABLES

There are many problems in which the data being processed can be naturally organized as a table. For example, suppose that water temperatures are recorded four times each day at each of three locations near the discharge outlet of a nuclear power plant's cooling system. These temperature readings can be arranged in a table having four rows and three columns:

Time	Location 1	Location 2	3
1	65.5	68.7	62.0
2	68.8	68.9	64.5
3	70.4	69.4	66.3
4	68.5	69.1	65.8

In this table, the three temperature readings at time 1 are in the first row, the three temperatures at time 2 are in the second row, and so on.

These 12 data items can be conveniently stored in a two-dimensional array. The array declaration

```
DIMENSION TEMTAB(4, 3)
REAL TEMTAB
```

or

```
DIMENSION TEMTAB(1:4, 1:3)
REAL TEMTAB
```

reserves 12 memory locations for these data items. This dimensioning information can also be included in the type statement:

```
REAL TEMTAB(4, 3)
```

or

```
REAL TEMTAB(1:4, 1:3)
```

The doubly subscripted variable

```
TEMTAB(2,3)
```

then refers to the entry in the second row and third column of the table, that is, to the temperature 64.5 recorded at time 2 at location 3. In general

```
TEMTAB(I,J)
```

refers to the entry in the Ith row and Jth column, that is, to the temperature recorded at time I at location J.

To illustrate the use of an array with more than two dimensions, suppose that the temperature readings are made for one week so that seven temperature tables are collected:

Time	Location 1	2	3	
1	66. 5	69. 4	68.4	
2	68. 4	71. 2	69. 3	Day 7
3	70. 1	71. 9	70. 2	
4	69. 5	70. 0	69. 4	

Time	Location 1	2	3	
1	63. 7	66. 2	64. 3	
2	64. 0	68. 8	64. 9	Day 2
			66. 3	
			65. 8	

Time	Location 1	2	3	
1	65. 5	68. 7	62. 0	
2	68. 8	68. 9	64. 5	Day 1
3	70. 4	69. 4	66. 3	
4	68. 5	69. 1	65. 8	

A three-dimensional array TEMP declared by

```
DIMENSION TEMP(4,3,7)
REAL TEMP
```

or

```
DIMENSION TEMP(1:4, 1:3, 1:7)
REAL TEMP
```

or

```
REAL TEMP(4,3,7)
```

or

```
REAL TEMP(1:4, 1:3, 1:7)
```

can be used to store these 84 temperature readings. The value of the triply subscripted variable

```
TEMP(1,3,2)
```

is the temperature recorded at time 1 at location 3 on day 2, that is, the value 64.3 in the first row, third column, second rank. In general,

```
TEMP(TIME,LOC,DAY)
```

is the temperature recorded at time TIME at location LOC on day DAY.

The general form of an **array declaration** is

Array Declaration

Form:

$$array\text{-}name(l_1:u_1, \quad l_2:u_2, \quad \ldots \ldots, \quad l_k:u_k)$$

where
the number k of dimensions is at most seven; and each pair $l_i:u_i$ must be a pair of integer constants or parameters specifying the range of values for the ith subscript to be from l_i through u_i.

Purpose:
Declare a k-dimensional array.

There must be one such array declaration for each array used in a program, and these declarations may appear in DIMENSION or type statements. For example, the statements

```
      DIMENSION GAMMA(1:2, -1:3), KAPPA(5:12),
     +          BETA(0:2, 0:3, 1:2)
      REAL GAMMA, BETA
      INTEGER KAPPA
```

or

```
      REAL GAMMA(1:2, -1:3), BETA(0:2, 0:3, 1:2)
      INTEGER KAPPA(5:12)
```

establish three arrays. The array GAMMA is a two-dimensional 2×5 real array, with the first subscript either 1 or 2 and the second subscript ranging from -1 through 3. Thus, the doubly subscripted variables GAMMA(1,−1), GAMMA(1,0), GAMMA(1,1), GAMMA(1,2), GAMMA(1,3), GAMMA(2,−1), GAMMA(2,0), GAMMA(2,1), GAMMA(2,2), and GAMMA(2,3) may be used. The first subscript in the three-dimensional $3 \times 4 \times 2$ real array BETA is equal to 0, 1, or 2; the second subscript ranges from 0 through 3; and the third subscript is equal to 1 or 2. The one-dimensional integer array KAPPA has subscripts ranging from 5 through 12.

9.2 PROCESSING MULTIDIMENSIONAL ARRAYS

In the preceding section we gave several examples of multidimensional arrays and showed how such arrays are declared in a FORTRAN program. We also noted that each element of an array can be accessed directly by using a multiply subscripted variable consisting of the array name followed by the subscripts that specify the location of that element in the array. In this section we consider the processing of multidimensional arrays, including the input and output of arrays or parts of arrays.

As we observed in the preceding chapter, the most natural order for processing the elements of a one-dimensional array is the usual sequential order, from first item to last. For multidimensional arrays, however, there are several orders in which the subscripts may be varied when processing the array elements.

Two-dimensional arrays are often used when the data can be organized as a table consisting of rows and columns. This suggests two natural orders for processing the elements of a two-dimensional array: **rowwise** and **columnwise**. Rowwise processing means that the array elements in the first row are processed first, then those in the second row are processed next; and so on, as shown in Figure 9.1a for the 3×4 array A, which has three rows and four columns. In columnwise processing, the elements in the first column are processed first; then those in the second column are processed next; and so on, as illustrated in Figure 9.1b. In most cases, the user can select one of these orderings by controlling the way the subscripts vary. *If this is not done, the FORTRAN convention is that two-dimensional arrays will be processed columnwise.*

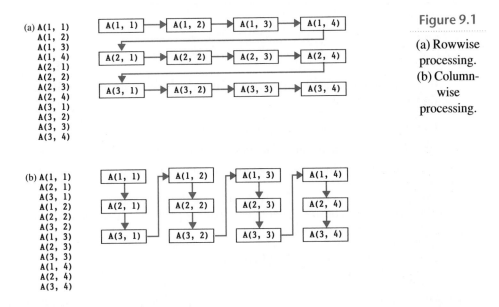

Figure 9.1

(a) Rowwise processing.
(b) Columnwise processing.

In the list of array elements shown in Figure 9.1a, we observe that in rowwise processing of a two-dimensional array, the second subscript varies first and the first subscript varies second; that is, the second subscript must vary over its entire range before the first subscript changes. It is just the opposite for columnwise processing, as we see from Figure 9.1b: the first subscript varies first and the second subscript second; that is, the first subscript must vary over its entire range before the second subscript changes.

For arrays of three or more dimensions, the elements can be processed in many ways. One of the common orders is the analogue of columnwise processing for the two-dimensional case; that is, the first subscript varies first, followed by the second subscript, then by the third, and so on. This method is illustrated in Figure 9.2 for the $2 \times 4 \times 3$ array B, which has two rows, four columns, and three ranks.

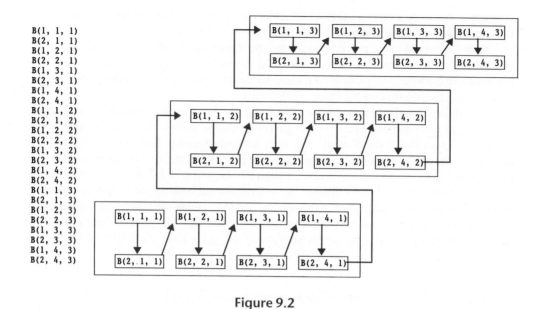

B(1, 1, 1)
B(2, 1, 1)
B(1, 2, 1)
B(2, 2, 1)
B(1, 3, 1)
B(2, 3, 1)
B(1, 4, 1)
B(2, 4, 1)
B(1, 1, 2)
B(2, 1, 2)
B(1, 2, 2)
B(2, 2, 2)
B(1, 3, 2)
B(2, 3, 2)
B(1, 4, 2)
B(2, 4, 2)
B(1, 1, 3)
B(2, 1, 3)
B(1, 2, 3)
B(2, 2, 3)
B(1, 3, 3)
B(2, 3, 3)
B(1, 4, 3)
B(2, 4, 3)

Figure 9.2

Processing a three-dimensional array.

In Section 8.2 we considered three ways in which data could be input or output for one-dimensional arrays:

1. Use a DO loop containing an input/output statement.
2. Use only the array name in an input/output statement.
3. Use an implied DO loop in an input/output statement.

Each of these three techniques can also be used for the input and output of multidimensional arrays, and we consider each in turn, paying particular attention to the order in which the elements are processed.

Input/Output Using D O Loops

When DO loops are used to read or display a multidimensional array, the input/output statement is placed within a set of nested DO loops, each of which controls one of the array's subscripts. For example, reconsider the problem of reading temperature values into the 4 × 3 real array TEMTAB declared by

```
REAL  TEMTAB(4,3)
```

so that it has the value

$$\begin{bmatrix} 65.5 & 68.7 & 62.0 \\ 68.8 & 68.9 & 64.5 \\ 70.4 & 69.4 & 66.3 \\ 68.5 & 69.1 & 65.8 \end{bmatrix}$$

Suppose we use the following statements:

```
    DO 20 TIME = 1, 4
        DO 10 LOC = 1, 3
            READ *, TEMTAB(TIME,LOC)
10      CONTINUE
20 CONTINUE
```

Here the outer DO loop sets the value of the control variable TIME to 1, and the inner DO loop is then executed using 1 as the value for TIME. The effect is the same as executing

```
    DO 10 LOC = 1, 3
        READ *, TEMTAB(1,LOC)
10 CONTINUE
```

which is equivalent to the three READ statements:

```
READ *, TEMTAB(1,1)
READ *, TEMTAB(1,2)
READ *, TEMTAB(1,3)
```

The first pass through the outer DO loop thus reads values for the first row of TEMTAB, so that the first three values entered must be

```
65.5
68.7
62.0
```

Note that they must be entered on separate lines, one per line, because the READ statement is executed three times and each execution requires a new line of input.

Now the outer DO loop sets the value of TIME to 2, and the inner DO loop is executed again,

```
    DO 10 LOC = 1, 3
        READ *, TEMTAB(2,LOC)
10      CONTINUE
```

which is equivalent to the three READ statements

```
READ *, TEMTAB(2,1)
READ *, TEMTAB(2,2)
READ *, TEMTAB(2,3)
```

so that the next three values entered must be

```
68.8
68.9
64.5
```

again on separate lines. The outer DO loop then causes the inner DO loop to be executed again, with TIME set equal to 3,

```
      DO 10 LOC = 1, 3
            READ *, TEMTAB(3,LOC)
   10  CONTINUE
```

which is equivalent to

```
   READ *, TEMTAB(3,1)
   READ *, TEMTAB(3,2)
   READ *, TEMTAB(3,3)
```

so that the values for the third row of TEMTAB must be entered on separate lines:

```
   70.4
   69.4
   66.3
```

Finally, the value of TIME is set to 4, and the inner DO loop is executed again,

```
      DO 10 LOC = 1, 3
            READ *, TEMTAB(4,LOC)
   10  CONTINUE
```

which has the same effect as

```
   READ *, TEMTAB(4,1)
   READ *, TEMTAB(4,2)
   READ *, TEMTAB(4,3)
```

for which the values for the fourth row of TEMTAB must be entered:

```
   68.5
   69.1
   65.8
```

Columnwise input is also possible; we need only reverse the order of the two DO loops:

```
      DO 20 LOC = 1, 3
         DO 10 TIME = 1, 4
            READ *, TEMTAB(TIME,LOC)
   10      CONTINUE
   20  CONTINUE
```

These statements are equivalent to the following sequence of 12 READ statements:

```
READ *, TEMTAB(1,1)
READ *, TEMTAB(2,1)
READ *, TEMTAB(3,1)
READ *, TEMTAB(4,1)
READ *, TEMTAB(1,2)
READ *, TEMTAB(2,2)
READ *, TEMTAB(3,2)
READ *, TEMTAB(4,2)
READ *, TEMTAB(1,3)
READ *, TEMTAB(2,3)
READ *, TEMTAB(3,3)
READ *, TEMTAB(4,3)
```

Because the READ statement is executed 12 times, the data values must be entered on 12 separate lines, 1 per line:

```
65.5
68.8
70.4
68.5
68.7
68.9
69.4
69.1
62.0
64.5
66.3
65.8
```

Because the data values must appear on separate lines, one value per line, this method is cumbersome for large arrays. A similar problem also occurs with output, since each execution of a PRINT or WRITE statement within nested DO loops such as

```
      DO 20 TIME = 1, 4
         DO 10 LOC = 1, 3
            PRINT *, TEMTAB(TIME,LOC)
10       CONTINUE
20    CONTINUE
```

causes output to begin on a new line. Thus, the elements of the array are displayed on separate lines, one value per line, rather than in a tabular format.

Input/Output Using the Array Name

In this method of reading or displaying an array, the array name without subscripts appears in the input/output statement. As we observed for one-dimensional arrays, this is equivalent to listing a *complete* set of array elements in the input/output list. The total number of elements specified in the array declaration must be read or displayed, and it is therefore not possible to read or display only part of an array using this method.

Another disadvantage of this method is the order in which multidimensional arrays are read or displayed. Because the order in which the subscripts vary is not specified by the programmer, the standard columnwise order (or its analogue for arrays of more than two dimensions) is used. For example, the statements

```
INTEGER TABLE(3,4)
READ *, TABLE
```

cause values to be read columnwise into the array TABLE. Thus, for the input data

```
77, 56, 32, 25, 99, 10
100, 46, 48, 89, 77, 33
```

the value assigned to TABLE is

$$\begin{bmatrix} 77 & 25 & 100 & 89 \\ 56 & 99 & 46 & 77 \\ 32 & 10 & 48 & 33 \end{bmatrix}$$

The output statement

```
PRINT '(1X, 4I5/)', TABLE
```

displays the elements in columnwise order and so produces the output

```
    77    56    32    25

    99    10   100    46

    48    89    77    33
```

We note that in contrast with the first method for input/output of arrays, the format in which the data is input or displayed may be specified. The number of items on each line of input or output is determined by the programmer.

Input/Output Using Implied DO Loops

An implied DO loop, introduced in Section 8.2, has the form

```
(i/o-list, control-variable = initial-value, limit)
```

or

```
(i/o-list, control-variable = initial-value, limit, step-size)
```

The fact that the input/output list may contain other implied DO loops makes it possible to use implied DO loops to read or display multidimensional arrays. For example, the statement

```
READ *, ((TABLE(ROW,COL), COL = 1, 4), ROW = 1, 3)
```

is equivalent to the statement

```
 READ *, (TABLE(ROW,1), TABLE(ROW,2),
+           TABLE(ROW,3), TABLE(ROW,4), ROW = 1, 3)
```

which has the same effect as

```
 READ *, TABLE(1,1), TABLE(1,2), TABLE(1,3), TABLE(1,4),
+           TABLE(2,1), TABLE(2,2), TABLE(2,3), TABLE(2,4),
+           TABLE(3,1), TABLE(3,2), TABLE(3,3), TABLE(3,4)
```

and thus reads the elements of the array TABLE in rowwise order. Note that because the READ statement is executed only once, all the data values to be read can be entered on the same line, or with four values on each of three lines, or with seven values on one line, four on the next, and one on another line, and so on.

Columnwise input is possible by interchanging the indexing information in the nested implied DO loops. Thus, the statement

```
READ *, ((TABLE(ROW,COL), ROW = 1, 3), COL = 1, 4)
```

which is equivalent to

```
READ *, (TABLE(1,COL), TABLE(2,COL), TABLE(3,COL), COL = 1, 4)
```

or

```
 READ *, TABLE(1,1), TABLE(2,1), TABLE(3,1),
+           TABLE(1,2), TABLE(2,2), TABLE(3,2),
+           TABLE(1,3), TABLE(2,3), TABLE(3,3),
+           TABLE(1,4), TABLE(2,4), TABLE(3,4)
```

may be used if the elements of TABLE are to be entered in columnwise order. Similarly, the statement

```
READ *, (((B(I,J,K), I = 1, 2), J = 1, 4), K = 1, 3)
```

reads values into the three-dimensional array B in the order indicated in Figure 9.2.

Note the use of parentheses and commas in these statements. They should be used exactly as indicated. Each implied DO loop must be enclosed in parentheses, and a comma must separate the list from the indexing information in the implied DO loop.

In contrast with the two preceding methods of array input/output, using an implied

DO loop in an input/output list permits the programmer to determine the format of the input/output data and to read or display only part of an array. For example, if ALPHA is a 3 × 10 real array, the statements

```
      PRINT 50, ((ALPHA(K,L), L = 4, 10, 3), K = 1, 3, 2)
  50 FORMAT(1X, 3F12.4)
```

will display the values of ALPHA(1,4), ALPHA(1,7), ALPHA(1,10), ALPHA(3,4), ALPHA(3,7), and ALPHA(3,10) in this order, with three numbers per line. The same output would also be produced by the statements

```
      DO 60 K = 1, 3, 2
         PRINT 50, (ALPHA(K,L), L = 4, 10, 3)
  50     FORMAT(1X, 3F12.4)
  60 CONTINUE
```

The program in Figure 9.3 illustrates the flexibility of implied DO loops. It reads the number of times NTIMES at which temperatures are recorded and the number of locations NLOCS at which these readings are made, and then uses implied DO loops to read NTIMES * NLOCS values into the two-dimensional array TEMTAB declared by

```
      REAL TEMTAB(MAXTIM,MAXLOC)
```

where MAXTIM and MAXLOC are integer parameters with the values 24 and 10, respectively, and to display these temperatures in tabular format.

Figure 9.3 I/O of two-dimensional arrays.

```
      PROGRAM TEMPS
*********************************************************************
* Program illustrating the use of nested implied DO loops to read and  *
* print the elements of a two-dimensional array. Identifiers used are: *
*     TEMTAB : two-dimensional array of temperatures                   *
*     MAXTIM : parameter specifying maximum # of times                 *
*     MAXLOC : parameter specifying maximum # of locations             *
*     NTIMES : # of times temperatures are recorded                    *
*     NLOCS  : # of locations at which temperatures are recorded       *
*     TIME   : row subscript for the table                             *
*     LOC    : column subscript for the table                          *
*                                                                      *
* Input:  NTIMES, NLOCS, and elements of TEMTAB                        *
* Output: The array TEMTAB in table format                            *
*********************************************************************

      INTEGER MAXTIM, MAXLOC, NTIMES, NLOCS, TIME, LOC
      PARAMETER (MAXTIM = 24, MAXLOC = 10)
      REAL TEMTAB(MAXTIM,MAXLOC)
```

Figure 9.3   *(cont.)*

```
      PRINT *, 'ENTER # OF TIMES TEMPERATURES ARE RECORDED'
      PRINT *, 'AND # OF LOCATIONS WHERE RECORDED:'
      READ *, NTIMES, NLOCS

      PRINT *, 'ENTER THE TEMPERATURES AT THE FIRST LOCATION,'
      PRINT *, 'THEN THOSE AT THE SECOND LOCATION, AND SO ON:'

      READ *, ((TEMTAB(TIME,LOC), LOC = 1, NLOCS), TIME = 1, NTIMES)

      PRINT *
      PRINT 100, (LOC, LOC = 1, NLOCS)
100   FORMAT(1X, T13, 'LOCATION' / 1X, 'TIME', 10I6)
      DO 130 TIME = 1, NTIMES
          PRINT 110, TIME, (TEMTAB(TIME,LOC), LOC = 1, NLOCS)
110       FORMAT(/1X, I3, 2X, 10F6.1/)
130   CONTINUE

      END
```

Sample run:

```
ENTER # OF TIMES TEMPERATURES ARE RECORDED
AND # OF LOCATIONS WHERE RECORDED:
4, 3
ENTER THE TEMPERATURES AT THE FIRST LOCATION,
THEN THOSE AT THE SECOND LOCATION, AND SO ON:
65.5, 68.7, 62.0
68.8, 68.9, 64.5
70.4, 69.4, 66.3
68.5, 69.1, 65.8

            LOCATION
TIME     1     2     3

  1     65.5  68.7  62.0

  2     68.8  68.9  64.5

  3     70.4  69.4  66.3

  4     68.5  69.1  65.8
```

The following examples exhibit some of the additional flexibility provided by implied DO loops. In these examples the integer variable NTOT has the value 152; NUM is the one-dimensional integer array containing the four numbers 16, 37, 76, and 23; and RATE is a 3 × 4 real array

$$\begin{bmatrix} 16.1 & 7.3 & 18.4 & 6.5 \\ 0.0 & 1.0 & 1.0 & 3.5 \\ 18.2 & 16.9 & 0.0 & 0.0 \end{bmatrix}$$

Input/output statement:

```
    READ *, N, (NUM(I), I = 1, N), M,
   +          ((RATE(I,J), J = 1, N), I = 1, M)
```

Possible lines of input data:

```
    4
    16, 37, 76, 23
    3
    16.1, 7.3, 18.4, 6.5
    0.0, 1.0, 1.0, 3.5
    18.2, 16.9, 0.0, 0.0
```

Input/output statement:

```
    PRINT 5, ('ROW', I, (RATE(I,J), J = 1, 4), I = 1, 3)
  5 FORMAT(1X, A, I2, '--', 4F6.1/)
```

Output produced:

```
ROW  1--   16.1    7.3   18.4    6.5

ROW  2--    0.0    1.0    1.0    3.5

ROW  3--   18.2   16.9    0.0    0.0

```

Input/output statement:

```
    PRINT 6, (J, (RATE(I,J), I = 1,3), NUM(J), J = 1,4),
   +          'TOTAL', NTOT
  6 FORMAT (4(1X, I4, 5X, 3F6.1, I10/), 1X, A, T35, I3)
```

Output produced:

```
    1       16.1   0.0  18.2        16
    2        7.3   1.0  16.9        37
    3       18.4   1.0   0.0        76
    4        6.5   3.5   0.0        23
TOTAL                               152
```

Multidimensional Arrays as Arguments

In the preceding chapter we noted that one-dimensional arrays may be used as arguments in function and subroutine subprograms. Much of the discussion there also applies to multidimensional arrays. In particular, an actual multidimensional array argument must be declared in the calling program unit, and the corresponding formal array argument must be declared in the subprogram.

When higher-dimensional arrays are used as arguments, the elements are associated in the standard columnwise order. Suppose, for example, that the array ALPHA declared by

```
REAL ALPHA(3,4)
```

is used as the actual argument and that the corresponding formal argument is declared in the subprogram by

```
REAL TABLE(3,4)
```

Then the first elements of the arrays ALPHA and TABLE are associated, and successive elements are associated in columnwise order, as follows:

```
ALPHA(1, 1) ←→  ┌───┐  ←→ TABLE(1, 1)
ALPHA(2, 1) ←→  │   │  ←→ TABLE(2, 1)
ALPHA(3, 1) ←→  │   │  ←→ TABLE(3, 1)
     ⋮          │ ⋮ │       ⋮
ALPHA(3, 4) ←→  └───┘  ←→ TABLE(3, 4)
```

The same method of establishing the correspondence between the elements of two arrays is used even if they have different dimensions. For example, if the array ALPHA is associated with the one-dimensional array Y declared by

```
REAL Y(12)
```

then the array elements are associated as follows:

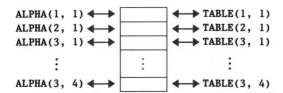

```
ALPHA(1, 1) ←→  ┌───┐  ←→ Y(1)
ALPHA(2, 1) ←→  │   │  ←→ Y(2)
ALPHA(3, 1) ←→  │   │  ←→ Y(3)
ALPHA(1, 2) ←→  │   │  ←→ Y(4)
ALPHA(2, 2) ←→  │   │  ←→ Y(5)
ALPHA(3, 2) ←→  │   │  ←→ Y(6)
     ⋮          │ ⋮ │       ⋮
ALPHA(3, 4) ←→  └───┘  ←→ Y(12)
```

Normally, when two arrays are associated as arguments, the first element of the actual array is associated with the first element of the formal array. It is possible, however, to specify that some other element of the actual array be matched with the first element of the formal array. This is accomplished by using that array element name as the actual argument. For example, a subroutine call of the form

```
CALL SUB(ALPHA(1,4))
```

would associate the array elements ALPHA(1,4), ALPHA(2,4), ALPHA(3,4) with the first three elements of the corresponding formal array argument.

Like one-dimensional arrays, multidimensional arrays may have adjustable dimensions; that is, the dimensions used to declare the formal array argument in a subprogram may be arguments of the subprogram whose values are passed from the calling program unit. However, *it is important to ensure that the dimensions of the formal arrays match those of the corresponding actual arrays since otherwise the array values will not be associated correctly.* See Potential Problem 4 in the Programming Pointers at the end of this chapter for an illustration of what may happen if the dimensions do not match. The desired association can be achieved by *passing the declared dimensions of an actual array to the subprogram and using them to dimension the corresponding formal array;* for example:

```
      INTEGER GRID(ROWLIM, COLLIM), NROWS, NCOLS
                   .
                   .
                   .
      CALL PRNTAB(GRID, ROWLIM, COLLIM, NROWS, NCOLS)
                   .
                   .
                   .
      SUBROUTINE PRNTAB(G, RLIM, CLIM, M, N)

      INTEGER RLIM, CLIM, G(RLIM,CLIM), M, N, I, J

      DO 10 I = 1, M
         PRINT '(10I5)', (G(I,J), J = 1, N)
  10  CONTINUE
      END
```

Multidimensional Arrays in Common

To illustrate the use of multidimensional arrays in COMMON statements, suppose that the statements

```
REAL B(2,3)
COMMON B
```

appear in one program unit and that the statements

```
REAL BETA(2,3)
COMMON BETA
```

appear in another program unit. These COMMON statements allocate the first nine memory locations of blank common to both of the arrays B and BETA in a columnwise order
so that the array elements are associated in the following manner:

Array Element	Blank Common Location	Array Element
B(1,1)	#1	BETA(1,1)
B(2,1)	#2	BETA(2,1)
B(1,2)	#3	BETA(1,2)
B(2,2)	#4	BETA(2,2)
B(1,3)	#5	BETA(1,3)
B(2,3)	#6	BETA(2,3)

Quick Quiz 9.2

1. (True or false) The statement INTEGER NUMTAB(1:2, 1:2) is equivalent to the
   statement INTEGER NUMTAB(2, 2).

2. The following is an example of _____ processing (rowwise or columnwise):

```
      DO 20 J = 1,10
          DO 10 I = 1, 10
              READ *, NUMTAB(I, J)
  10      CONTINUE
  20 CONTINUE
```

3. Unless specified otherwise, two-dimensional arrays in FORTRAN are processed in a
   _____ (rowwise or columnwise) manner.

For Questions 4–6, assume that NUMTAB is the integer array declared in Question 1
and that the following values are entered: 1, 2, 3, 4. Tell what value (if any) will be
assigned to NUMTAB(1, 2) by the given statements.

4.   READ *, NUMTAB

5.   READ *, (NUMTAB(I,J), J = 1, 2), I = 1, 2)

6.   READ *, (NUMTAB(J, I), J = 1, 2), I = 1, 2)

7.   DO 2 I = 1, 2
         DO 1 J = 1, 2
             READ *, NUMTAB(I, J)
  1   CONTINUE
  2 CONTINUE

8. Given the declaration `INTEGER T(2,2,2)` and that the values entered in response to the statement
   ```
   READ *, (((T(I,J,K), I = 1,2), J = 1,2), K = 1,2)
   ```
   are `1, 2, 3, 4, 5, 6, 7, 8,` what value will be assigned to `T(1,2,1)`?

9. (True or false) The array `T` in Question 8 has six elements.

10. (True or false) Input/output using implied `DO` loops is the most flexible method of array I/O.

11. How many lines of output will be produced if the `READ` statement in Question 7 is replaced by `PRINT *, NUMTAB(I, J)`?

For Questions 12–14, assume the declarations

```
INTEGER MAT(3,3)
DATA MAT/9*0/
```

What values will be assigned to the array `MAT` by the given statements?

12.
```
    DO 10 I = 1, 3
       MAT(I,I) = 1
10 CONTINUE
```

13.
```
    DO 10 I = 1, 3
       DO 5 J = I, 3
          MAT(I,J) = 1
  5    CONTINUE
10 CONTINUE
```

14.
```
    DO 10 I = 1, 3
       DO 5 J = 1, 3
          MAT(I,J) = I * J
  5    CONTINUE
10 CONTINUE
```

Which of the statements in Questions 15-20 will reserve 200 storage locations?

15. `DIMENSION TABLE(100:100)`   16. `INTEGER ARRAY(10,20)`

17. `DIMENSION TABLE(4:50)`   18. `DIMENSION XRAY(-50:49, 0:1)`

19. `DIMENSION DIM(2,2,2,5,5)`   20. `REAL TEN(100:299)`

Exercises 9.2

1. Write a declaration for a two-dimensional array whose rows are numbered from 1 through 5, whose columns are numbered from 1 through 10, and in which each element is a real value.

2. Write a declaration for a two-dimensional array whose rows are numbered from 0 through 4, whose columns are numbered from 1900 through 1910, and in which each element is a character string of length 5.

3. Write statements to set each element in the array of Exercise 1 to the sum of the row number and the column number in which that element appears.

4. Write statements to set each element in the array of Exercise 2 to a string of blanks.

For Exercises 5–16, assume that the following declarations have been made

```
INTEGER ARRAY(3,3), NUM(6), I, J
```

and that the following data is entered for those of the statements that involve input:

```
1, 2, 3, 4, 5, 6, 7, 8, 9
```

Tell what value (if any) is assigned to each array element, or explain why an error results:

```
5.     DO 20 I = 1, 3
            DO 10 J = 1, 3
                ARRAY(I,J) = I + J
   10      CONTINUE
   20 CONTINUE

6.     DO 20 I = 1, 3
            DO 10 J = 3, 1, -1
                IF (I .EQ. J) THEN
                    ARRAY(I,J) = 0
                ELSE
                    ARRAY(I,J) = 1
                END IF
   10      CONTINUE
   20 CONTINUE

7.     DO 20 I = 1, 3
            DO 10 J = 1, 3
                IF (I .LT. J) THEN
                    ARRAY(I,J) = -1
                ELSE IF (I .EQ. J) THEN
                    ARRAY(I,J) = 0
                ELSE
                    ARRAY(I,J) = 1
                END IF
   10      CONTINUE
   20 CONTINUE
```

8.     ```
       DO 30 I = 1, 3
          DO 10 J = 1, I
             ARRAY(I,J) = 0
   10   CONTINUE
          DO 20 J = I + 1, 3
             ARRAY(I,J) = 2
   20   CONTINUE
   30 CONTINUE
       ```

9.     ```
       DO 20 I = 1, 3
          DO 10 J = 1, 3
             READ *, ARRAY(I,J)
   10     CONTINUE
   20 CONTINUE
       ```

10.   `READ *, ARRAY`

11.   `READ *, ((ARRAY(I,J), J = 1, 3), I = 1, 3)`

12.   `READ *, ((ARRAY(J,I), I = 1, 3), J = 1, 3)`

13.   `READ *, ((ARRAY(I,J), I = 1, 3), J = 1, 3)`

14.    ```
       DO 10 I = 1, 3
          READ *, (ARRAY(I,J), J = 1, 3)
   10 CONTINUE
       ```

15.    ```
       READ *, NUM
       DO 20 I = 1, 3
          DO 10 J = 1, 3
             ARRAY(I,J) = NUM(I) + NUM(J)
   10     CONTINUE
   20 CONTINUE
       ```

16.    ```
       READ *, NUM, (ARRAY(1,J), J = 1, 3)
       DO 20 I = 1, 2
          DO 10 J = 1, 3
             ARRAY(NUM(I + 1), NUM(J)) = NUM(I + J)
   10   CONTINUE
   20 CONTINUE
       ```

For Exercises 17–20, assume that the following declaration has been made

```
REAL TABLE(5,5)
```

and that the following lines of data are entered:

data-line-1:	123456789876543
data-line-2:	564738291928374
data-line-3:	135798642123456
data-line-4:	123454321567896
data-line-5:	498376251427485
```

Tell what values (if any) will be assigned to array TABLE, or explain why an error results:

17.   READ 5, TABLE
```
     5 FORMAT (5F3.2)
```

18.   READ 5, ((TABLE(I, J), J = 1, 5), I = 1, 5)
```
     5 FORMAT (5F3.0)
```

19.   READ 5, ((TABLE(J, I), J = 1, 5), I = 1, 5)
```
     5 FORMAT (5F3.0)
```

20.   DO 10 I = 1, 5
```
          READ 5, (TABLE(I,J), J = 1, 5)
     5    FORMAT (5F2.1)
    10 CONTINUE
```

9.3 APPLICATION: POLLUTION TABLE

Problem

In a certain city, the air pollution is measured at two-hour intervals, beginning at midnight. These measurements are recorded for a one-week period and stored in a file, the first line of which contains the pollution levels for day 1, the second line for day 2, and so on. For example, the pollution file for a certain week contains the following data:

```
30 30 31 32 35 40 43 44 47 45 40 38
33 32 30 34 40 48 46 49 53 49 45 40
38 35 34 37 44 50 51 54 60 58 51 49
49 48 47 53 60 70 73 75 80 .75 73 60
55 54 53 65 70 80 90 93 95 94 88 62
73 70 65 66 71 78 74 78 83 75 66 58
50 47 43 35 30 33 37 43 45 52 39 31
```

A program must be written to produce a weekly report that displays the pollution levels in a table of the form

```
                                  TIME
      DAY:   1    2    3    4    5    6    7    8    9   10   11   12
      ---------------------------------------------------------------
        1 :  30   30   31   32   35   40   43   44   47   45   40   38
        2 :  33   32   30   34   40   48   46   49   53   49   45   40
        3 :  38   35   34   37   44   50   51   54   60   58   51   49
        4 :  49   48   47   53   60   70   73   75   80   75   73   60
        5 :  55   54   53   65   70   80   90   93   95   94   88   62
        6 :  73   70   65   66   71   78   74   78   83   75   66   58
        7 :  50   47   43   35   30   33   37   43   45   52   39   31
```

and that also displays the average pollution level for each day and the average pollution level for each sampling time.

Solution

Specification.

Input: Air pollution levels (from a file)

Output: A table of pollution levels
         Average pollution level for each day
         Average pollution level for each sampling time

Design. The following variables will be used:

▼

VARIABLES FOR POLLUTION REPORT PROBLEM

POLTAB	A two-dimensional array containing pollution levels
SUM	Used to add the rows/columns of POLTAB
NTIMES	Number of sampling times
NDAYS	Number of days
DAY, TIME	Subscripts

▲

The required algorithm is as follows:

▼

ALGORITHM FOR POLLUTION REPORT PROBLEM

```
*  Algorithm to read a two-dimensional array POLTAB from a file containing pollution  *
*  levels measured at selected times for several days. These measurements are displayed  *
*  in tabular form. The average pollution level for each day and the average pollution  *
*  level for each sampling time are then calculated.                                 *
*  Input:     Pollution levels                                                       *
*  Output:    A table of pollution levels, the average pollution level               *
*             for each day (row averages), and the average pollution                 *
*             level for each sampling time (column averages)                         *
```

1. Read the contents of the pollution file into the array POLTAB so that each row contains the pollution measurements for a given day and each column contains the pollution measurements for a given time.

2. Print the array POLTAB with appropriate headings.

3. Calculate the average pollution level for each day, that is, the average of each of the rows, as follows:
   a. For DAY ranging from 1 through the number NDAYS of days, do the following:
      i. Set SUM equal to 0.

Monitoring air pollution. (Photo courtesy of Photo Researchers, Inc.)

    ii. For TIME ranging from 1 through the number NTIMES of sampling times:
        Add POLTAB(DAY, TIME) to SUM.
    iii. Display SUM/NTIMES.

4. Calculate the average pollution level for each sampling time, that is, the average of each of the columns, as follows:
    a. For TIME ranging from 1 through NTIMES, do the following:
      i. Set SUM equal to 0.
      ii. For DAY ranging from 1 through NDAYS:
        Add POLTAB(DAY,TIME) to SUM.
      iii. Display SUM/NDAYS.

Coding, Execution and Testing. The program in Figure 9.4 implements this algorithm. Also included is a sample run with the data file described previously. The program was tested with several small data files to check its correctness, but sample runs with these files are not shown here.[1]

Figure 9.4 Pollution report.

```
      PROGRAM POLLUT
************************************************************
* This program reads the elements of the two-dimensional array POLTAB  *
* from a file and produces a report showing a table of pollution       *
* levels, the average pollution level for each day, and the average    *
* pollution level for each sampling time. Identifiers used are:        *
*     NDAYS   : parameter giving the number of rows (days)             *
*     NTIMES  : parameter giving the number of columns (times)         *
*     POLTAB  : an NDAYS X NTIMES array of pollution levels            *
*     DAY,TIME: row, column subscripts                                 *
*     SUM     : variable used in accumulating row & column sums        *
*                                                                      *
* Input (file):    The pollution levels                                *
* Output (screen): The array POLTAB in table format, the average       *
*                  pollution level for each day, and the average       *
*                  pollution level for each sampling time              *
************************************************************

      INTEGER NDAYS, NTIMES
      PARAMETER (NDAYS = 7, NTIMES = 12)
      INTEGER POLTAB(NDAYS,NTIMES), DAY, TIME
      REAL SUM

* Read the pollution levels and display them in a table
* of the required form

      OPEN (UNIT = 15, FILE = 'FIL9-4.DAT', STATUS = 'OLD')
      READ (15,*) ((POLTAB(DAY,TIME), TIME = 1, NTIMES), DAY = 1, NDAYS)
      PRINT 100, (TIME, TIME = 1, NTIMES)
100   FORMAT(T30, 'TIME' / 1X, 'DAY:', 12I4 / 1X, 53('-'))
      PRINT 110,
     +    (DAY, (POLTAB(DAY,TIME), TIME = 1, NTIMES), DAY = 1, NDAYS)
110   FORMAT(1X, I2, ' :', 12I4)
```

Figure 9.4 *(cont.)*

```
* Calculate average pollution level for each day (row averages)

      PRINT *
      DO 20 DAY = 1, NDAYS
         SUM = 0
         DO 10 TIME = 1, NTIMES
            SUM = SUM + POLTAB(DAY,TIME)
10       CONTINUE
         PRINT 120, 'FOR DAY', DAY, SUM / REAL(NTIMES)
120      FORMAT(1X, 'AVERAGE POLLUTION LEVEL ', A7, I3, ':', F6.1)
20    CONTINUE

* Calculate average pollution level for each time (column averages)

      PRINT *
      DO 40 TIME = 1, NTIMES
         SUM = 0
         DO 30 DAY = 1, NDAYS
            SUM = SUM + POLTAB(DAY,TIME)
30       CONTINUE
         PRINT 120, 'AT TIME', TIME, SUM / REAL(NDAYS)
40    CONTINUE

      CLOSE (15)
      END
```

Sample run:

```
                           TIME
DAY:    1    2    3    4    5    6    7    8    9   10   11   12
------------------------------------------------------------
 1 :   30   30   31   32   35   40   43   44   47   45   40   38
 2 :   33   32   30   34   40   48   46   49   53   49   45   40
 3 :   38   35   34   37   44   50   51   54   60   58   51   49
 4 :   49   48   47   53   60   70   73   75   80   75   73   60
 5 :   55   54   53   65   70   80   90   93   95   94   88   62
 6 :   73   70   65   66   71   78   74   78   83   75   66   58
 7 :   50   47   43   35   30   33   37   43   45   52   39   31
```

Figure 9.4 *(cont.)*

```
AVERAGE POLLUTION LEVEL FOR DAY  1:   37.9
AVERAGE POLLUTION LEVEL FOR DAY  2:   41.6
AVERAGE POLLUTION LEVEL FOR DAY  3:   46.8
AVERAGE POLLUTION LEVEL FOR DAY  4:   63.6
AVERAGE POLLUTION LEVEL FOR DAY  5:   74.9
AVERAGE POLLUTION LEVEL FOR DAY  6:   71.4
AVERAGE POLLUTION LEVEL FOR DAY  7:   40.4

AVERAGE POLLUTION LEVEL AT TIME  1:   46.9
AVERAGE POLLUTION LEVEL AT TIME  2:   45.1
AVERAGE POLLUTION LEVEL AT TIME  3:   43.3
AVERAGE POLLUTION LEVEL AT TIME  4:   46.0
AVERAGE POLLUTION LEVEL AT TIME  5:   50.0
AVERAGE POLLUTION LEVEL AT TIME  6:   57.0
AVERAGE POLLUTION LEVEL AT TIME  7:   59.1
AVERAGE POLLUTION LEVEL AT TIME  8:   62.3
AVERAGE POLLUTION LEVEL AT TIME  9:   66.1
AVERAGE POLLUTION LEVEL AT TIME 10:   64.0
AVERAGE POLLUTION LEVEL AT TIME 11:   57.4
AVERAGE POLLUTION LEVEL AT TIME 12:   48.3
```

9.4 APPLICATION: OCEANOGRAPHIC DATA ANALYSIS

Problem

A petroleum exploration company has collected some depth readings for a square section of the ocean. The diagonal of this square is parallel to the equator. The company has divided the square into a grid with each intersection point (node) of the grid separated by five miles. The entire square is fifty miles on each side. Two separate crews did exploratory drilling in this area, one in the northern half (above the diagonal) and the other in the southern half. A program is to be written to find the approximate average ocean depth for each crew and the overall average for the entire square. The following depth data (in feet) was collected by the crews.

301.3	304.5	312.6	312.0	325.6	302.0	299.8	297.6	304.6	314.7	326.8
287.6	294.5	302.4	315.6	320.9	315.7	300.2	312.7	308.7	324.5	322.8
320.8	342.5	342.5	323.5	333.7	341.6	350.5	367.7	354.2	342.8	330.9
312.6	312.0	325.6	301.3	304.5	302.0	314.7	326.8	299.8	297.6	304.6
302.4	308.7	324.5	315.6	287.6	294.5	320.9	315.7	300.2	312.7	322.8
320.8	333.7	341.6	350.5	367.7	354.2	342.8	342.5	342.5	323.5	330.9
312.0	325.6	326.8	302.0	299.8	297.6	304.6	314.7	301.3	304.5	312.6
294.5	302.4	315.6	320.9	315.7	300.2	312.7	308.7	324.5	287.6	322.8
320.8	342.5	323.5	333.7	341.6	350.5	367.7	342.5	354.2	342.8	330.9
312.0	304.6	314.7	326.8	301.3	304.5	312.6	325.6	302.0	299.8	297.6
312.7	308.7	324.5	322.8	287.6	294.5	302.4	315.6	320.9	315.7	300.2

NORTH

Solution

Specification. From the description of the problem, we have the following input/output specifications:

Input: A collection of depth readings

Output: The average of the readings in the northern half of the grid
The average of the readings in the southern half of the grid
The average of all the readings

Design. We will use the following variables for this problem:

VARIABLES FOR OCEANOGRAPHIC DATA ANALYSIS

DEPTH	A two-dimensional array of depth readings
N	The size of the grid ($N \times N$)

HALF	Number of readings in each half of the grid
NSUM	Sum of the northern readings
SSUM	Sum of the southern readings
OSUM	Sum of all readings
NAVE	Average of the northern readings
SAVE	Average of the southern readings
OAVE	Average of all readings
I, J	Subscripts

An algorithm for solving this problem is as follows:

ALGORITHM FOR OCEANOGRAPHIC DATA ANALYSIS

*
*   Algorithm to find the average ocean depth in each half (separated by the diagonal) of   *
*   a square section of the ocean and the overall average. The depth readings are stored in   *
*   the $N \times N$ two-dimensional array DEPTH.   *
*   Input: The size N and the depth readings   *
*   Output: The average of elements above the diagonal, the average of elements below   *
*   the diagonal, and the average of all the elements   *

1. Get the name of the data file and open the file for reading.

2. Read N and the depth readings from the file, storing in the array DEPTH.

3. Initialize NSUM, SSUM, and OSUM to 0.

4. Do the following for I ranging from 1 to N:
   Do the following for J ranging from 1 to N:
      a. If $I < J$ then
          Add DEPTH(I, J) to NSUM
        Else if $I > J$ then
          Add DEPTH(I, J) to SSUM.
      b. Add DEPTH(I, J) to OSUM.

5. Calculate $HALF = \dfrac{N^2 - N}{2}$.

6. Calculate the north, south, and overall average depths by

$$NAVE = \frac{NSUM}{HALF}, SAVE = \frac{SSUM}{HALF}, \text{ and } OAVE = \frac{OSUM}{N^2}.$$

7. Display DEPTH, NAVE, SAVE, and OAVE.

Figure 9.5 shows the structure of this algorithm in flowchart form.

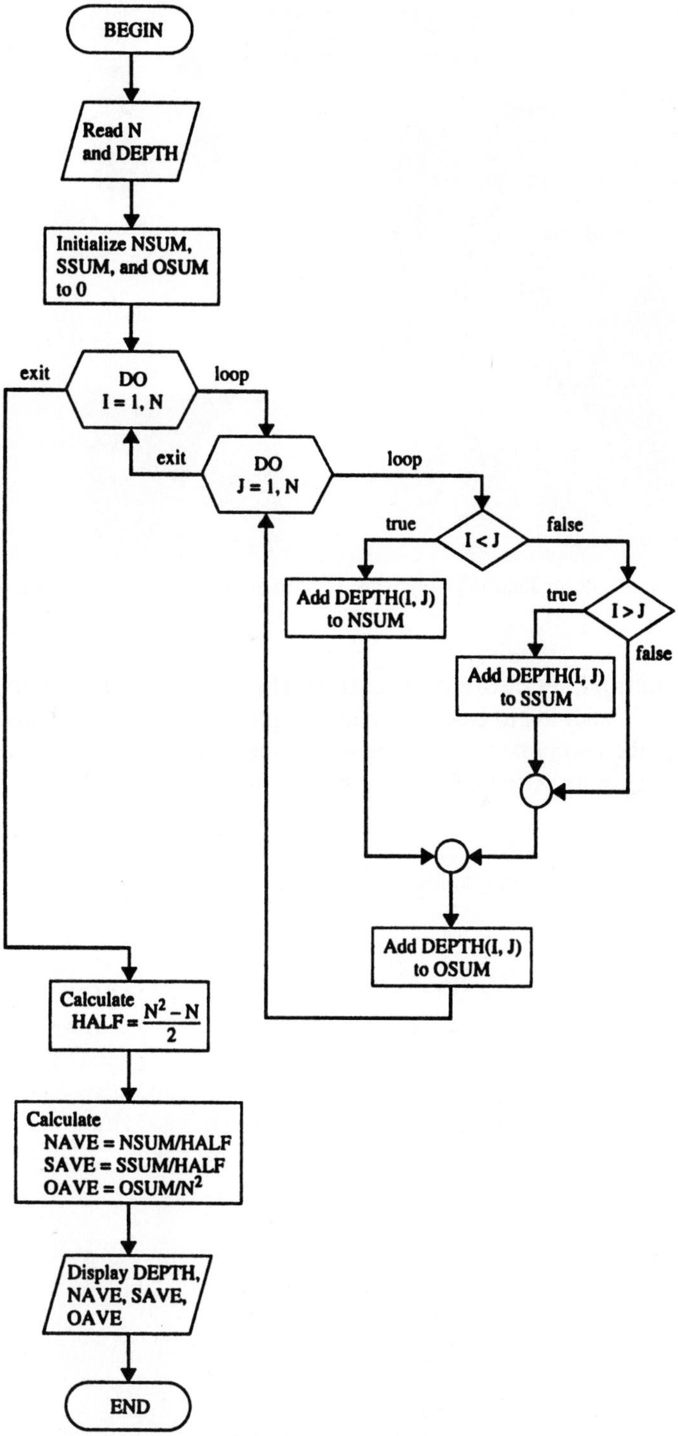

Figure 9.5

Flowchart for oceanographic data analysis.

Famed sea explorer Jacques Cousteau. (Photo courtesy of Uniphoto Picture Agency.)

Coding, Execution, and Testing. The program in Figure 9.6 implements the algorithm. In addition to calculating and displaying the three required averages, it also displays the grid of depth readings so that the input data is echoed and can be used to check the results. Also included is a sample run using the given data file.

Figure 9.6 Oceanographic data analysis.

```
     PROGRAM OCEAN
* * * * * * * * * * * * * * * * * * * * * * * * * * * * * * * * * * * * * * * * * * * * * * * * * * * * * * * * * * * * * * * * * * * * * *
* Program to find the average ocean depth in each half (separated by     *
* the diagonal) of a square section of the ocean.  Identifiers used:     *
*     DEPTH  : a two-dimensional array of depth readings                 *
*     FNAME  : name of the file containing depth readings                *
*     LIMIT  : limit on the size of DEPTH (parameter)                    *
*     N      : the number of rows (or columns)                           *
*     I, J   : subscripts                                                *
*     NSUM   : the sum of the northern depths                            *
*     NAVE   : the average of the northern depths                        *
*     SSUM   : the sum of the southern depths                            *
*     SAVE   : the average of the southern depths                        *
*     OSUM   : the overall sum                                           *
*     OAVE   : the overall average                                       *
*     HALF   : number of elements in each half                           *
```

Figure 9.6 *(cont.)*

```
* Note: It is assumed that the elements on the diagonal are        *
*        included in the overall average but not in either half.   *
*                                                                  *
* Input:  The elements of array DEPTH                              *
* Output: The array DEPTH in table format, NAVE, SAVE, and OAVE    *
*******************************************************************

      INTEGER LIMIT
      PARAMETER (LIMIT = 11)
      CHARACTER*20 FNAME
      INTEGER N, I, J, HALF
      REAL DEPTH(LIMIT,LIMIT), NSUM, NAVE, SSUM, SAVE, OSUM, OAVE

* Get the name of the input file, open it for input
      PRINT *, 'ENTER NAME OF DATA FILE:'
      READ '(A)', FNAME
      OPEN (UNIT = 10, FILE = FNAME, STATUS = 'OLD')

* Read N and the array DEPTH from the file; initialize sums to 0
      READ (10,*) N, ((DEPTH(I,J), J = 1, N), I = 1, N)
      NSUM = 0.0
      SSUM = 0.0
      OSUM = 0.0

* Calculate the north, south, and overall sums
      DO 20 I = 1,N
         DO 10 J = 1, N
            IF (I .LT. J) THEN
               NSUM = NSUM + DEPTH(I,J)
            ELSE IF (I .GT. J) THEN
               SSUM = SSUM + DEPTH(I,J)
            END IF
            OSUM = OSUM + DEPTH(I,J)
10       CONTINUE
20    CONTINUE

* Calculate the north, south, and overall average depths
      HALF = (N**2 - N) / 2
      NAVE = NSUM / REAL(HALF)
      SAVE = SSUM / REAL(HALF)
      OAVE = OSUM / REAL(N**2)
```

Figure 9.6 *(cont.)*

```
* Display the DEPTH array and the average depths
      PRINT 100
      PRINT 110, ((DEPTH(I,J), J = 1, N), I = 1, N)
100   FORMAT(1X, T29, 'OCEAN DEPTHS')
110   FORMAT(/1X, 11F6.1)

      PRINT 120, NAVE, SAVE, OAVE
120   FORMAT(// 1X, 'NORTHERN HALF AVERAGE DEPTH', T30, F6.2, ' FEET',
     +         // 1X, 'SOUTHERN HALF AVERAGE DEPTH', T30, F6.2, ' FEET',
     +         // 1X, 'OVERALL AVERAGE DEPTH', T30, F6.2, ' FEET')

      END
```

Sample run:

```
ENTER NAME OF DATA FILE:
FIL9-6.DAT
                         OCEAN DEPTHS

 301.3 304.5 312.6 312.0 325.6 302.0 299.8 297.6 304.6 314.7 326.8

 287.6 294.5 302.4 315.6 320.9 315.7 300.2 312.7 308.7 324.5 322.8

 320.8 342.5 342.5 323.5 333.7 341.6 350.5 367.7 354.2 342.8 330.9

 312.6 312.0 325.6 301.3 304.5 302.0 314.7 326.8 299.8 297.6 304.6

 302.4 308.7 324.5 315.6 287.6 294.5 320.9 315.7 300.2 312.7 322.8

 320.8 333.7 341.6 350.5 367.7 354.2 342.8 342.5 342.5 323.5 330.9

 312.0 325.6 326.8 302.0 299.8 297.6 304.6 314.7 301.3 304.5 312.6

 294.5 302.4 315.6 320.9 315.7 300.2 312.7 308.7 324.5 287.6 322.8

 320.8 342.5 323.5 333.7 341.6 350.5 367.7 342.5 354.2 342.8 330.9

 312.0 304.6 314.7 326.8 301.3 304.5 312.6 325.6 302.0 299.8 297.6

 312.7 308.7 324.5 322.8 287.6 294.5 302.4 315.6 320.9 315.7 300.2

NORTHERN HALF AVERAGE DEPTH 318.31 FEET

SOUTHERN HALF AVERAGE DEPTH 318.63 FEET

OVERALL AVERAGE DEPTH        318.02 FEET
```

9.5 EXAMPLE: MATRIX PROCESSING

A two-dimensional array with numeric entries having m rows and n columns is called an $m \times n$ **matrix**. Matrices arise naturally in many problems in engineering and applied mathematics, and in this section we descibe some of the basic matrix operations that are useful in these applications.

Several matrix operations such as addition and subtraction are defined element-wise; that is, two matrices of the same size are added or subtracted by adding and subtracting corresponding elements. For example,

$$\begin{bmatrix} 1 & 0 & 2 \\ -1 & 3 & 5 \end{bmatrix} + \begin{bmatrix} 4 & 2 & 1 \\ 7 & 0 & 3 \end{bmatrix} = \begin{bmatrix} 5 & 2 & 3 \\ 6 & 3 & 8 \end{bmatrix}$$

$$\begin{bmatrix} 1 & 0 & 2 \\ -1 & 3 & 5 \end{bmatrix} - \begin{bmatrix} 4 & 2 & 1 \\ 7 & 0 & 3 \end{bmatrix} = \begin{bmatrix} -3 & -2 & 1 \\ -8 & 3 & 2 \end{bmatrix}$$

One important matrix operation that is not defined elementwise is matrix multiplication. Suppose that A is an $m \times n$ matrix and B is an $n \times p$ matrix. The **product AB** is the $m \times p$ matrix for which

the entry in row i and column j

= the sum of the products of the entries in row i of A with
   the entries in column j of B

$= A_{i1}B_{1j} + A_{i2}B_{2j} + \cdots + A_{in}B_{nj}$

$= \displaystyle\sum_{k=1}^{n} A_{ik}B_{kj}$

Note that the number of columns (n) in A is equal to the number of rows in B, which must be the case for the product of A with B to be defined.

For example, suppose that A is the 2×3 matrix

$$A = \begin{bmatrix} 1 & 0 & 2 \\ 3 & 0 & 4 \end{bmatrix}$$

and B is the 3×4 matrix

$$B = \begin{bmatrix} 4 & 2 & 5 & 3 \\ 6 & 4 & 1 & 8 \\ 9 & 0 & 0 & 2 \end{bmatrix}$$

Because the number of columns (3) in A equals the number of rows in B, the product matrix AB is defined. The entry in the first row and the first column, A_{11}, is

$$1 \times 4 + 0 \times 6 + 2 \times 9 = 22$$

Similarly, the entry A_{12} in the first row and the second column is

$$1 \times 2 + 0 \times 4 + 2 \times 0 = 2$$

The complete product matrix AB is the 2×4 matrix given by

$$AB = \begin{bmatrix} 22 & 2 & 5 & 7 \\ 48 & 6 & 15 & 17 \end{bmatrix}$$

An algorithm for multiplying matrices is as follows:

MATRIX MULTIPLICATION ALGORITHM

```
*  Algorithm to calculate the matrix product PROD of the ROWSA × COLSA matrix A  *
*  with the ROWSB × COLSB matrix B. COLSA must equal ROWSB for the product  *
*  to be defined.                                                            *
```

1. If COLSA does not equal ROWSB, the number of columns in A is not equal to the number of rows in B, and their product is not defined; terminate the algorithm. Otherwise proceed with the following steps:

2. For I ranging from 1 to the number of rows ROWSA of A, do the following:
   For J ranging from 1 to the number of columns COLSB of B, do the following:
   a. Set SUM equal to 0.
   b. For K ranging from 1 to the number of columns COLSA of A (which is equal to the number of rows ROWSB of B):
      Add A(I, K) * B(K, J) to SUM.
   c. Set PROD(I, J) equal to SUM.

The following subroutine implements this algorithm:

```
**MATMUL*****************************************************************
* Subroutine to calculate the product of a ROWSA X COLSA matrix A     *
* with a ROWSB X COLSB matrix B; LIMIT is a limit on the dimensions   *
* of these matrices. COLSA must equal ROWSB for the product to be     *
* defined (PRODOK = .TRUE.), and the product PROD is then a           *
* ROWSA X COLSB  matrix. Local variables used are:                    *
*     I, J, K :  subscripts                                           *
*                                                                     *
* Accepts:  Arrays A and B, integers LIMIT, ROWSA, COLSA, ROWSB,      *
*           and COLSB                                                 *
* Returns:  Array PROD and logical variable PRODOK                    *
* ********************************************************************
```

```
      SUBROUTINE MATMUL(A, B, PROD, LIMIT, ROWSA, COLSA,
     +                    ROWSB, COLSB, PRODOK)

      INTEGER LIMIT, ROWSA, COLSA, ROWSB, COLSB, I, J, K
      REAL A(LIMIT, LIMIT), B(LIMIT, LIMIT), PROD(LIMIT, LIMIT), SUM

      LOGICAL PRODOK
      PRODOK = (COLSA .EQ. ROWSB)

      IF (.NOT. PRODOK) RETURN

*     Else product is defined -- compute it
      DO 30 I = 1, ROWSA
         DO 20 J = 1, COLSB
            SUM = 0
            DO 10 K = 1, COLSA
               SUM = SUM + A(I,K) * B(K, J)
10          CONTINUE
            PROD (I,J) = SUM
20       CONTINUE
30    CONTINUE
      END
```

There are many other important operations on matrices. Several of these are described in the exercises.

Exercises 9.5

1. If A_{ij} and B_{ij} are the entries in the ith row and jth column of $m \times n$ matrices A and B, respectively, then the **sum $A + B$** is the $m \times n$ matrix for which the entry in the ith row and jth column is $A_{ij} + B_{ij}$. Design an algorithm to compute the sum of two matrices.

2. Write a subprogram to implement the algorithm in Exercise 1.

3. Modify the following program so that when the square array A is displayed, it has been changed into its transpose. The *transpose* of an $m \times n$ matrix A is the $n \times m$ matrix whose rows are the columns of A.

```
      PROGRAM MAT3
*************************************************
* Program to read matrix A, replace it by its   *
* transpose, and display it.                     *
*************************************************

      INTEGER N, I, J
      REAL A(10,10)
```

```
                      PRINT *, 'ENTER THE # OF ROWS (= # of COLUMNS)'
                      READ *, N

                      READ 100, ((A(I,J), J = 1, N), I = 1, N)
          100   FORMAT(10F10.3)

          *

          * Place your statements to replace A by its transpose here

          *

                      PRINT 110
          110   FORMAT(///, T30, 'THE TRANSPOSE OF A' //)
                      PRINT 120, ((A(I,J), J = 1, N), I = 1, N)
          120   FORMAT(1X, 10F10.3)
                      END
```

4. Given the following program,

   (a) Write declarations for all the arrays and other variables used in the program.

   (b) Calculate (by hand) the values stored in arrays A, B, and C.

   (c) Add statements to create array D = A * B + C.

   (d) Add statements to create array E, the transpose of array D (see Exercise 3).

```
                      PROGRAM MAT4
          * * * * * * * * * * * * * * * * * * * * * * * * * * * * * * * * * * * * * * * * * *
          * Program to do various matrix calculations. *
          * * * * * * * * * * * * * * * * * * * * * * * * * * * * * * * * * * * * * * * * * *

          *

          * Place your declaration statements here

          *

                      DO 20 I = 1, 3
                          DO 10 J = 1, 3
                              A(J,I) = I + J
                              B(I,J) = I - J
          10        CONTINUE
          20    CONTINUE
                      DO 40 I = 1, 3
                          DO 30 J = 1, 3
                              C(I,J) = 5
          30        CONTINUE
          40    CONTINUE

          *

          * Place your statements to calculate D here

          *
```

```
       DO 50 I = 1, 3
          PRINT 60, (D(I, J), J = 1, 3)
60          FORMAT (1X, 3I7)
50     CONTINUE
*
* Place your statements to find E here
*
       PRINT *
       DO 70 I = 1, 3
          PRINT 60, (E(I,J), J = 1, 3)
70     CONTINUE
       END
```

9.6 APPLICATION: ELECTRICAL NETWORKS

Problem

Consider the following electrical network containing six resistors and a battery:

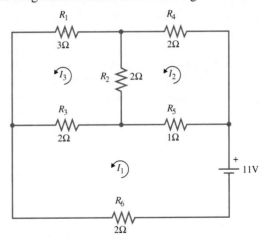

We wish to find the currents I_1, I_2, and I_3 in the three loops (where current is considered positive when the flow is in the direction indicated by the arrows).

Solution

Specification. The input information for this problem is the circuit pictured in the diagram; in particular, the six resistances $R_1, R_2, \ldots, R_6$ will be needed to solve the problem. The output consists of the currents I_1, I_2, and I_3 in the three loops.

Design. The current through resistor R_1 is I_3, the current through resistor R_2 is $I_2 - I_3$, and so on. Ohm's law states that the voltage drop across a resistor is $R * I$, where R is the resistance in ohms and I is the current in amperes. One of Kirchhoff's laws states that the algebraic sum of the voltage drops around any loop is equal to the applied voltage. These laws give rise to the following system of linear equations for the loop currents I_1, I_2, and I_3:

$$2I_1 + 1(I_1 - I_2) + 2(I_1 - I_3) = 11$$
$$2I_2 + 2(I_2 - I_3) + 1(I_2 - I_1) = 0$$
$$3I_3 + 2(I_3 - I_1) + 2(I_3 - I_2) = 0$$

Collecting terms gives the simplified linear system

$$5I_1 - 1I_2 - 2I_3 = 11$$
$$-1I_1 + 5I_2 - 2I_3 = 0$$
$$-2I_1 - 2I_2 + 7I_3 = 0$$

To find the loop currents, we must solve this **linear system**; that is, we must find the values for I_1, I_2, and I_3 that satisfy these equations simultaneously.

Linear systems arise in many areas of mathematics, science, and engineering, such as solving differential equations, electrical circuit problems, statical systems, and dynamical systems. Several methods for solving them have been developed, including the method called **Gaussian elimination**. To use this method to solve the preceding system, we first eliminate I_1 from the second equation by adding 1/5 times the first equation to the second equation. Similarly, we eliminate I_1 from the third equation by adding 2/5 times the first equation to the third equation. This yields the linear system

$$5I_1 - 1I_2 - 2I_3 = 11$$
$$4.8I_2 - 2.4I_3 = 2.2$$
$$-2.4I_2 + 6.2I_3 = 4.4$$

which is equivalent to the original system in that they have the same solution. We then eliminate I_2 from the third equation by adding $2.4/4.8 = 1/2$ times the second equation to the third, yielding the new equivalent linear system

$$5I_1 - 1I_2 - 2I_3 = 11$$
$$4.8I_2 - 2.4I_3 = 2.2$$
$$5I_3 = 5.5$$

Once the original system has been reduced to such a *triangular* form, it is easy to find the solution. It is clear from the last equation that the value of I_3 is

$$I_3 = \frac{5.5}{5} = 1.100$$

Substituting this value for I_3 in the second equation and solving for I_2 gives

$$I_2 = \frac{2.2 + 2.4(1.1)}{4.8} = 1.008$$

and substituting these values for I_2 and I_3 in the first equation gives

$$I_1 = \frac{11 + 1.008 + 2(1.100)}{5} = 2.842$$

Refining the Method. The computations required to solve a linear system can be carried out more conveniently if the coefficients and constants of the linear system are stored in a matrix. For the preceding linear system, this gives the following 3×4 matrix:

$$LIN = \begin{bmatrix} 5 & -1 & -2 & 11 \\ -1 & 5 & -2 & 0 \\ -2 & -2 & 7 & 0 \end{bmatrix}$$

The first step in the reduction process was to eliminate I_1 from the second and third equations by adding multiples of the first equation to these equations. This corresponds to adding multiples of the first row of the matrix LIN to the second and third rows so that all entries in the first column except LIN(1, 1) are zero. Thus, we add $-LIN(2, 1)/LIN(1, 1) = 1/5$ times the first row of LIN to the second row and $-LIN(3, 1)/LIN(1, 1) = 2/5$ times the first row of LIN to the third row to obtain the new matrix:

$$LIN = \begin{bmatrix} 5 & -1 & -2 & 11 \\ 0 & 4.8 & -2.4 & 2.2 \\ 0 & -2.4 & 6.2 & 4.4 \end{bmatrix}$$

The variable I_2 was then eliminated from the third equation. The corresponding operation on the rows of the preceding matrix is to add $-LIN(3, 2)/LIN(2, 2) = 1/2$ times the second row to the third row. The resulting matrix, which corresponds to the final triangular system, thus is

$$LIN = \begin{bmatrix} 5 & -1 & -2 & 11 \\ 0 & 4.8 & -2.4 & 2.2 \\ 0 & 0 & 5 & 5.5 \end{bmatrix}$$

From this example, we see that the basic row operation performed at the ith step of the reduction process is

$$\text{For } k = i + 1, i + 2, \ldots, n,$$

$$\text{Replace row}_k \text{ by row}_k - \frac{\text{LIN } (k, i)}{\text{LIN } (i, i)} \times \text{row}_i$$

Clearly, for this to be possible, the element LIN(i, i), called a **pivot element**, must be nonzero. If it is not, we must interchange the ith row with a later row to produce a nonzero pivot. In fact, to minimize the effect of roundoff error in the computations, it is best to rearrange the rows to obtain a pivot element that is largest in absolute value.

The following algorithm, which summarizes the Gaussian elimination method for solving a linear system, uses this pivoting strategy. Note that if it is not possible to find a nonzero pivot element at some stage, the linear system is said to be a **singular** system and it does not have a unique solution.

▼

```
*    GAUSSIAN ELIMINATION ALGORITHM                                          *
*                                                                            *
*    Algorithm to solve a linear system of N equations with N unknowns using Gaussian *
*    elimination. LIN is the N × (N + 1) matrix that stores the coefficients and constants *
*    of the linear system.                                                   *
*    Input:     Coefficients and constants of the linear system              *
*    Output:    Solution of the linear system or a message indicating that the system *
*               is singular                                                  *
```

1. Enter the coefficients and constants of the linear system and store them in the matrix LIN.

2. For I ranging from 1 to N, do the following:
   a. Find the entry LIN(K, I), K = I, I+1, ..., N that has the largest absolute value to use as a pivot.
   b. If the pivot is zero, display a message that the system is singular and terminate the algorithm. Otherwise proceed.
   c. Interchange row I and row K.
   d. For J ranging from I + 1 to N, do the following:

   $$\text{Add} \frac{-\text{LIN } (J, I)}{\text{LIN}(I, I)} \text{ times the Ith row of LIN to the Jth row of}$$

   LIN to eliminate X(I) from the Jth equation.

3. Set X(N) equal to $\dfrac{\text{LIN } (N, N + 1)}{\text{LIN } (N, N)}$.

4. For J ranging from N − 1 to 1 in steps of −1, do the following:
   Substitute the values of X(J + 1), ..., X(N) in the Jth equation and solve for X(J).

Coding and Execution. The program in Figure 9.7 implements this algorithm for Gaussian elimination. Because real numbers cannot be stored exactly, the statement implementing step 2c checks if ABS(LIN(I,I)) is less than some small positive number EPSIL rather than if LIN(I,I) is exactly 0.

Figure 9.7 Gaussian elimination.

```
      PROGRAM LINSYS
*********************************************************************
* Program to solve a linear system using Gaussian elimination.      *
* Identifiers used are:                                             *
*     LIMROW : maximum number of rows in the matrix                 *
*     LIMCOL : maximum number of columns (LIMROW + 1) in the matrix *
*     N      : number of equations and unknowns                     *
*     I, J   : subscripts                                           *
*     LIN    : matrix for the linear system                         *
*     X      : solution                                             *
*     SINGUL : indicates if system is (nearly) singular             *
*                                                                   *
* Input:   The number of equations, the coefficients, and the       *
*          constants of the linear system                           *
* Output:  The solution of the linear system or a message indicating*
*          that the system is (nearly) singular                     *
*********************************************************************

      INTEGER LIMROW, LIMCOL
      PARAMETER (LIMROW = 10, LIMCOL = LIMROW + 1)
      REAL LIN(LIMROW, LIMCOL), X(LIMROW)
      INTEGER N, I, J
      LOGICAL SINGUL

* Read coefficients and constants

      PRINT *, 'ENTER NUMBER OF EQUATIONS'
      READ *, N
      DO 10 I = 1, N
         PRINT *, 'ENTER COEFFICIENTS AND CONSTANT OF EQUATION ',
     +             I, ': '
         READ *, (LIN(I,J), J = 1, N + 1)
10    CONTINUE
```

Figure 9.7 *(cont.)*

```
* Use subroutine GAUSS to find the solution,
* and then display the solution

      CALL GAUSS(LIN, LIMROW, LIMCOL, N, X, SINGUL)
      IF (.NOT. SINGUL) THEN
         PRINT *, 'SOLUTION IS'
         DO 20 I = 1, N
            PRINT 100, I, X(I)
100         FORMAT(1X, 'X(', I2, ') =', F8.3)
20       CONTINUE
      ELSE
         PRINT *, 'MATRIX IS (NEARLY) SINGULAR'
      END IF

      END


**GAUSS*************************************************************
* Subroutine to find solution of a linear system of N equations in N  *
* unknowns using Gaussian elimination, provided a unique solution     *
* exists.  The coefficients and constants of the linear system are    *
* stored in the matrix LIN, which has LIMROW rows and LIMCOL columns.  *
* If the system is singular, SINGUL is returned as true, and the      *
* solution X is undefined. Local identifiers used are:                *
*     I,J,K  : subscripts                                             *
*     MULT   : multiplier used to eliminate an unknown                *
*     ABSPIV : absolute value of pivot element                        *
*     PIVROW : row containing pivot element                           *
*     EPSIL  : a small positive real value ("almost zero")           *
*     TEMP   : used to interchange rows of matrix                     *
*                                                                     *
* Accepts: Two-dimensional array LIN, integers LIMROW, LIMCOL, and N   *
* Returns: One-dimensional array X and logical value SINGUL           *
**********************************************************************

      SUBROUTINE GAUSS(LIN, LIMROW, LIMCOL, N, X, SINGUL)

      REAL LIN(LIMROW, LIMCOL), X(LIMROW), TEMP, MULT, EPSIL
      PARAMETER (EPSIL = 1E-7)
      INTEGER N, PIVROW
      LOGICAL SINGUL

      SINGUL = .FALSE.
      DO 50 I = 1, N
```

Figure 9.7 *(cont.)*

```
*          Locate pivot element

           ABSPIV = ABS(LIN(I,I))
           PIVROW = I
           DO 10 K = I + 1, N
              IF (ABS(LIN(K,I)) .GT. ABSPIV) THEN
                 ABSPIV = ABS(LIN(K,I))
                 PIVROW = K
              END IF
10         CONTINUE

*          Check if matrix is (nearly) singular

           IF (ABSPIV .LT. EPSIL) THEN
              SINGUL = .TRUE.
              RETURN
           END IF

*          It isn't, so interchange rows PIVROW and I if necessary

           IF (PIVROW .NE. I) THEN
              DO 20 J = 1, N + 1
                 TEMP = LIN(I,J)
                 LIN(I,J) = LIN(PIVROW,J)
                 LIN(PIVROW,J) = TEMP
20            CONTINUE
           END IF

*          Eliminate Ith unknown from equations I + 1, ..., N

           DO 40 J = I + 1, N
              MULT = -LIN(J,I) / LIN(I,I)
              DO 30 K = I, N + 1
                 LIN(J,K) = LIN(J,K) + MULT * LIN(I,K)
30            CONTINUE
40         CONTINUE

50      CONTINUE
```

Figure 9.7 *(cont.)*

```
* Find the solutions by back substitution

        X(N) = LIN(N, N + 1) / LIN(N,N)
        DO 70 J = N - 1, 1, -1
           X(J) = LIN(J, N + 1)
           DO 60 K = J + 1, N
              X(J) = X(J) - LIN(J,K) * X(K)
60         CONTINUE
           X(J) = X(J) / LIN(J,J)
70      CONTINUE

        END
```

Sample runs:

```
ENTER NUMBER OF EQUATIONS
3
ENTER COEFFICIENTS AND CONSTANT OF EQUATION 1:
 5 -1 -2 11
ENTER COEFFICIENTS AND CONSTANT OF EQUATION 2:
-1  5 -2 0
ENTER COEFFICIENTS AND CONSTANT OF EQUATION 3:
-2 -2  7 0
SOLUTION IS
X( 1) =  2.842
X( 2) =  1.008
X( 3) =  1.100


ENTER NUMBER OF EQUATIONS
3
ENTER COEFFICIENTS AND CONSTANT OF EQUATION 1:
1 1 1  1
ENTER COEFFICIENTS AND CONSTANT OF EQUATION 2:
2 3 4  2
ENTER COEFFICIENTS AND CONSTANT OF EQUATION 3:
3 4 5  3
MATRIX IS (NEARLY) SINGULAR
```

Exercises 9.6

1. Write the system of linear equations for the loop currents I_1, I_2, and I_3 in the following simple resistor and battery circuit. Then use Gaussian elimination to find these currents.

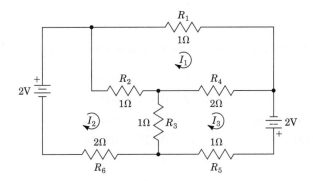

2. Consider the following electrical network:

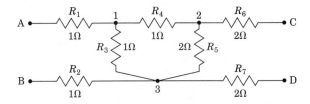

If the voltages at the endpoints are $V_A = V_B = V_C = V_D = 1$ V, then applying Kirchoff's law of currents at the nodes 1, 2, and 3 yields (after some simplification) the following system of linear equations for the voltages V_1, V_2, and V_3 at these nodes:

$$\frac{5}{2}V_1 - \frac{1}{2}V_2 - V_3 = 1$$

$$\frac{-1}{2}V_1 + \frac{3}{2}V_2 - \frac{1}{2}V_3 = \frac{1}{2}$$

$$-V_1 - \frac{1}{2}V_2 + 3V_3 = \frac{3}{2}$$

Use Gaussian elimination to find these voltages.

3. Consider the following material balance problem: A solution that is 80 percent oil, 15 percent usable by-products, and 5 percent impurities enters a refinery. One output is 92 percent oil and 6 percent usable by-products. The other output is 60 percent oil and flows at the rate of 1000 L/h.

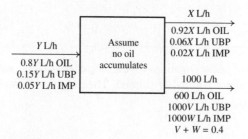

We thus have the following system of material balance equations:

Total: $Y = \quad X + 1000$

Oil: $0.8Y = 0.92X + 600$

Usable by-products: $0.15Y = 0.06X + 1000V$

Impurities: $0.05Y = 0.02X + 1000W$

Also: $V + W = 0.4$

Use Gaussian elimination to solve this linear system. Check that your solution also satisfies the last equation.

4. Consider the following statical system:

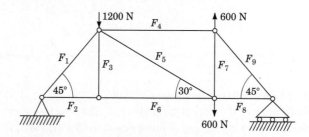

Since the sum of all forces acting horizontally or vertically at each pin is zero, the following system of linear equations can be used to obtain the tensions $F_1, F_2, \ldots, F_9$:

$$
\begin{bmatrix}
\sqrt{2}/2 & 0 & 0 & -1 & -\sqrt{3}/2 & 0 & 0 & 0 & 0 \\
\sqrt{2}/2 & 0 & 1 & 0 & 1/2 & 0 & 0 & 0 & 0 \\
0 & 1 & 0 & 0 & 0 & -1 & 0 & 0 & 0 \\
0 & 0 & -1 & 0 & 0 & 0 & 0 & 0 & 0 \\
0 & 0 & 0 & 0 & 0 & 0 & 1 & 0 & \sqrt{2}/2 \\
0 & 0 & 0 & 1 & 0 & 0 & 0 & 0 & -\sqrt{2}/2 \\
0 & 0 & 0 & 0 & 3/2 & 1 & 0 & -1 & 0 \\
0 & 0 & 0 & 0 & -1/2 & 0 & -1 & 0 & 0 \\
0 & 0 & 0 & 0 & 0 & 0 & 0 & 1 & \sqrt{2}/2
\end{bmatrix}
\begin{bmatrix}
F_1 \\ F_2 \\ F_3 \\ F_4 \\ F_5 \\ F_6 \\ F_7 \\ F_8 \\ F_9
\end{bmatrix}
=
\begin{bmatrix}
0 \\ -1200 \\ 0 \\ 0 \\ 600 \\ 0 \\ 0 \\ -600 \\ 0
\end{bmatrix}
$$

Use Gaussian elimination to find these tensions.

5. The population of a country (or of a region) is divided into age groups. If n is the number of age groups and $P_i(t)$ is the number of individuals in age group i at time t, the dynamic model describing the populations of the different age groups is given by

$$P_1(t + 1) = b_1 P_1(t) + b_2 P_2(t) + \cdots + b_n P_n(t) + c_1$$
$$P_{i+1}(t + 1) = a_i P_i(t) + c_i, \text{ for } i = 1, \ldots, n - 1$$

Here, each a_i is the percentage of persons in age group i who move into age group $i + 1$ at the next time period; each b_i is the birthrate for age group i; and each c_i is the number of persons belonging to age group i that move into the region.

If this dynamic system reaches equilibrium at a certain time period t so that for each age group i, $P_i(t) = P_i(t + 1) = P_i(t + 2) = \cdots =$ some constant value p_i, then the preceding system of difference equations can be rewritten as the following system of steady-state equations:

$$p_1 = b_1 p_1 + b_2 p_2 + \cdots + b_n p_n + c_1$$
$$p_2 = a_1 p_1 + c_2$$
$$p_3 = a_2 p_2 + c_3$$
$$\vdots$$
$$p_n = a_{n-1} p_{n-1} + c_n$$

Use Gaussian elimination to solve this linear system for $n = 4$, $a_1 = 0.8$, $a_2 = 0.7$, $a_3 = 0.6$, $b_1 = 0$, $b_2 = 0.05$, $b_3 = 0.15$, $b_4 = 0.1$, and each $c_i = 100$.

6. In Section 4.8 we described the method of least squares for finding the equation of a line that best fits a set of data points. This method can also be used to find best-fitting curves of higher degree. For example, to find the equation of the parabola

$$y = A + Bx + Cx^2$$

that best fits a set of n data points, the values of A, B, and C must be determined for which the sum of the squares of the deviations of the observed y-values from the predicted y-values (using the equation) is as small as possible. These values are found by solving the linear system

$$nA + (\Sigma x)B + (\Sigma x^2)C = \Sigma y$$
$$(\Sigma x)A + (\Sigma x^2)B + (\Sigma x^3)C = \Sigma xy$$
$$(\Sigma^2)A + (\Sigma x^3)B + (\Sigma x^4)C = \Sigma x^2 y$$

Find the equation of the least-squares parabola for the following set of data points:

x	y
0.05	0.957
0.12	0.851
0.15	0.832
0.30	0.720
0.45	0.583
0.70	0.378
0.84	0.295
1.05	0.156

7. Linear systems similar to those in Exercise 6 must be solved to find least-squares curves of higher degrees. For example, for a least-squares cubic

$$y = A + Bx + Cx^2 + Dx^3$$

the coefficients A, B, C, and D can be found by solving the following system of equations:

$$nA + (\Sigma x)B + (\Sigma x^2)C + (\Sigma x^3)D = \Sigma y$$

$$(\Sigma x)A + (\Sigma x^2)B + (\Sigma x^3)C + (\Sigma x^4)D = \Sigma xy$$

$$(\Sigma x^2)A + (\Sigma x^3)B + (\Sigma x^4)C + (\Sigma x^5)D = \Sigma x^2 y$$

$$(\Sigma x^3)A + (\Sigma x^4)B + (\Sigma x^5)C + (\Sigma x^6)D = \Sigma x^3 y$$

Find the equation of the least-squares cubic for the set of data points in Exercise 6.

CHAPTER REVIEW

Summary

In this chapter we described multidimensional arrays and multiply subscripted variables. We began by describing how such arrays are declared and how multiple subscripts are used to access the elements of the array. Section 9.2 describes several techniques for processing multidimensional arrays and describes various orders in which array elements can be processed, such as rowwise and columnwise. The three methods of array input/output described in Chapter 8 for one-dimensional arrays—using DO loops, using the array name, and using implied DO loops—are described for multidimensional arrays together with the use of arrays as arguments. Several applications of two-dimensional arrays are given, including their use in processing matrices.

FORTRAN SUMMARY

Array Declarations

$array\text{-}name(l_1:u_1, \quad l_2:u_2, \quad . \quad . \quad . \quad , \quad l_k:u_k)$

where

the number k of dimensions is at most seven; and each pair $l_i : u_i$ must be a pair of integer constants or parameters specifying the range of values for the ith subscript to be from l_i through u_i.

These array declarations may appear in DIMENSION statements,

DIMENSION *list-of-array-declarations*

or in type statements.

Examples:

```
DIMENSION ALPHA(5,10), BETA(5,5,2)
DIMENSION GAMMA(1:2, -1:3), DELTA(5:12), COUNT (0:2, 0:3, 1:2)
REAL ALPHA, BETA, GAMMA, DELTA
INTEGER KAPPA
```

or

```
REAL ALPHA(5,10), BETA(5,5,2), GAMMA(1:2, -1:3), DELTA(5:12)
INTEGER COUNT(0:2, 0:3, 1:2)
```

Purpose:

Declares that the identifier $array\text{-}name$ is an array for which the range of values of the first subscript will be from the lower limit l_1 through the upper limit u_1, the range of values of the second subscript will be from the lower limit l_2 through the upper limit u_2, and so on.

PROGRAMMING POINTERS

Program Style and Design

1. *Two-dimensional arays are especially useful for storing tables of values.* If the data values can be viewed as arranged in rows and columns and they must be processed more than once in a program, it is convenient to store them in a two-dimensional array.

2. *Use a reasonable size when declaring an array.* The dimensions of an array are determined by the number of data values to be stored. Especially for higher-dimensional arrays, one should not needlessly overdimension an array, as this can require a large amount of memory.

3. *Use parameters to dimension an array.* If it is necessary to change the size of an array, only the parameters need to be changed.

Potential Problems

The difficulties encountered in using multidimensional arrays are similar to those for one-dimensional arrays, considered in the preceding chapter. The first three potential problems listed here are simply restatements of some of the programming pointers in Chapter 8, and the reader should refer to those pointers for an expanded discussion.

1. *All arrays in a FORTRAN program must be dimensioned.*
2. *Arrays must be declared using constants or parameters to specify the dimensions.*
3. *Subscripts must be integer valued and must stay within the range specified in the array declarations.*
4. *Unless some other order is specified, two-dimensional arrays are processed columnwise.* In general, the FORTRAN convention for processing multidimensional arrays is to vary each subscript over its entire range before varying the subscript that follows it. Any other processing order must be established by the programmer.

To illustrate, suppose that the two-dimensional array TABLE is declared by

```
INTEGER TABLE(3,4)
```

and the following data is to be read into the array:

```
11, 22, 27, 35, 39, 40, 48, 51, 57, 66, 67, 92
```

If these values are to be read and assigned in a rowwise manner so that the value of TABLE is

$$
\begin{bmatrix}
11 & 22 & 27 & 35 \\
39 & 40 & 48 & 51 \\
57 & 66 & 67 & 92
\end{bmatrix}
$$

the following READ statement is appropriate:

```
READ *, ((TABLE(I,J), J = 1, 4), I = 1, 3)
```

If the values are to be read and assigned in a columnwise manner so that the value of TABLE is

$$\begin{bmatrix} 11 & 35 & 48 & 66 \\ 22 & 39 & 51 & 67 \\ 27 & 40 & 57 & 92 \end{bmatrix}$$

the statements should be

```
READ *, ((TABLE(I,J), I = 1, 3), J = 1, 4)
```

or

```
READ *, TABLE
```

Like one-dimensional arrays, multidimensional arrays may have adjustable dimensions; that is, the dimensions used to declare the formal array argument in a subprogram may be arguments of the subprogram whose values are passed from the calling program unit. However, *some care must be exercised to ensure that the dimensions of the formal arrays match those of the corresponding actual arrays.* To illustrate, suppose that GRID is a 10 × 10 array declared by

```
INTEGER ROWLIM, COLLIM
PARAMETER (ROWLIM = 10, COLLIM = 10)
INTEGER GRID(ROWLIM,COLLIM), NROWS, NCOLS
```

but that the actual number of rows and columns are NROWS = 3 and NCOLS = 4, respectively, and that the value of GRID is

$$GRID = \begin{bmatrix} 90 & 80 & 0 & 40 \\ 60 & 55 & 95 & 83 \\ 72 & 71 & 93 & 89 \end{bmatrix}$$

Suppose also that a subroutine PRNTAB to print this array uses adjustable dimensions for the corresponding formal array argument:

```
      SUBROUTINE PRNTAB(G, M, N)

      INTEGER M, N, G(M,N), I, J

      DO 10 I = 1, M
         PRINT '(10I5)', (G(I,J), J = 1, N)
   10 CONTINUE
      END
```

If the subroutine is called with the statement

```
CALL PRNTAB(GRID, NROWS, NCOLS)
```

the formal array G is considered to be a 3×4 array, since it is dimensioned as an M $\times$ N array and the values passed to M and N are NROWS = 3 and NCOLS = 4, respectively. And since actual arrays and formal arrays are associated in a column-wise manner, the elements of GRID and G are associated as follows:

GRID(1, 1)	⟷	90	⟷	G(1, 1)
GRID(2, 1)	⟷	60	⟷	G(2, 1)
GRID(3, 1)	⟷	72	⟷	G(3, 1)
GRID(4, 1)	⟷	??	⟷	G(1, 2)
GRID(5, 1)	⟷	??	⟷	G(2, 2)
GRID(6, 1)	⟷	??	⟷	G(3, 2)
GRID(7, 1)	⟷	??	⟷	G(1, 3)
GRID(8, 1)	⟷	??	⟷	G(2, 3)
GRID(9, 1)	⟷	??	⟷	G(3, 3)
GRID(10, 1)	⟷	??	⟷	G(1, 4)
GRID(1, 2)	⟷	80	⟷	G(2, 4)
GRID(2, 2)	⟷	55	⟷	G(3, 4)

Thus, the 3×4 array displayed by the subroutine is

$$\begin{bmatrix} 90 & ?? & ?? & ?? \\ 60 & ?? & ?? & 80 \\ 72 & ?? & ?? & 55 \end{bmatrix}$$

where ?? denotes an undefined value, which undoubtedly is not what was intended.

The desired association can be achieved by *passing the declared dimensions of an actual array to the subprogram and using them to dimension the corresponding formal array*:

```
CALL PRNTAB(GRID, ROWLIM, COLLIM, NROWS, NCOLS)
          .
          .
          .
SUBROUTINE PRNTAB(G, RLIM, CLIM, M, N)

INTEGER RLIM, CLIM, G(RLIM,CLIM), M, N, I, J

DO 10 I = 1, M
   PRINT '(10I5)', (G(I,J), J = 1, N)
10 CONTINUE
END
```

PROGRAMMING PROBLEMS

Section 9.2

1. A car manufacturer has collected data on the noise level (measured in decibels) produced by six different models of cars at seven different speeds. This data is summarized in the following table:

Car	Speed (mph) 20	30	40	50	60	70	80
1	88	90	94	102	111	122	134
2	75	77	80	86	94	103	113
3	80	83	85	94	100	111	121
4	68	71	76	85	96	110	125
5	77	84	91	98	105	112	119
6	81	85	90	96	102	109	120

Write a program that will display this table in a nice format and that will calculate and display the average noise level for each car model, the average noise level at each speed, and the overall average noise level.

2. A number of students from three different engineering sections, 1, 2, and 3, performed the same experiment to determine the tensile strength of sheets made from two different alloys. Each of these strength measurements is a real number in the range 0 through 10. Write a program to read several lines of data, each consisting of a section number and the tensile strength of the two types of sheets recorded by a student in that section, and calculate
   (a) for each section, the average of the tensile strengths for each type of alloy,
   (b) the number of persons in a given section who recorded strength measures of 5 or higher,
   (c) the average of the tensile strengths recorded for alloy 2 by students who recorded a tensile strength lower than 3 for alloy 1.

3. A certain company manufactures four electronic devices using five different components that cost $10.95, $6.30, $14.75, $11.25, and $5.00, respectively. The number of components used in each device is given in the following table:

Device Number	Component Number 1	2	3	4	5
1	10	4	5	6	7
2	7	0	12	1	3
3	4	9	5	0	8
4	3	2	1	5	6

Write a program to
(a) calculate the total cost of each device,
(b) calculate the total cost of producing each device if the estimated labor cost for each device is 10 percent of the cost in part (a).

4. An electronics firm manufactures four types of radios. The number of capacitors, resistors, and transistors (denoted by C, R, and T, respectively) in each of these is given in the following table:

Radio Type	C	R	T
1	2	6	3
2	6	11	5
3	13	29	10
4	8	14	7

Each capacitor costs $0.35, a resistor costs $0.20, and a transistor costs $1.40. Write a program to find the total cost of the components for each of the types of radios.

5. A company produces three different products. They are processed through four different departments, A, B, C, and D, and the following table gives the number of hours that each department spends on each product:

Product	A	B	C	D
1	20	10	15	13
2	18	11	11	10
3	28	0	16	17

The cost per hour of operation in each of the departments is as follows:

Department	A	B	C	D
Cost per hour	$140	$295	$225	$95

Write a program to find the total cost of each of the products.

6. Write a program to calculate and print the first ten rows of *Pascal's triangle*. The first part of the triangle has the form

```
            1
          1   1
        1   2   1
      1   3   3   1
    1   4   6   4   1
```

in which each row begins and ends with ones and every other entry in a row is the sum of the two entries just above it. If displaying the triangle in this form seems too challenging, you might display it in the form

```
1
1   1
1   2   1
1   3   3   1
1   4   6   4   1
```

7. A *magic square* is an $n \times n$ array in which all of the integers $1, 2, 3, \ldots, n^2$ appear exactly once, and all the column sums, row sums, and diagonal sums are equal. For example, the following is a 5×5 magic square in which all rows, columns, and diagonals sum to 65:

17	24	1	8	15
23	5	7	14	16
4	6	13	20	22
10	12	19	21	3
11	18	25	2	9

The following is a procedure for constructing an $n \times n$ magic square for any odd integer n. Place 1 in the middle of the top row. Then after placing integer k, move up one row and one column to the right to place the next integer $k + 1$, unless one of the following occurs:

(a) If a move takes you above the top row in the jth column, move to the bottom of the jth column and place the integer there.

(b) If a move takes you outside to the right of the square in the ith row, place the integer in the ith row at the left side.

(c) If a move takes you to an already filled square or if you move out of the square at the upper right corner, place $k + 1$ immediately below k.

Write a program to construct a magic square for any odd value of n.

8. Suppose that each of the four edges of a thin square metal plate is maintained at a constant temperature and that we wish to determine the steady-state temperature at each interior point of the plate. To do this, we divide the plate into squares (the corners of which are called *nodes*) and find the temperature at each interior node by averaging the four neighboring temperatures; that is, if T_{ij} denotes the old temperature at the node in row i and column j, then

$$\frac{T_{i-1,j} + T_{i,j-1} + T_{i,j+1} + T_{i+1,j}}{4}$$

will be the new temperature.

To model the plate, we can use a two-dimensional array, with each array element representing the temperature at one of the nodes. Write a program that first reads the four constant temperatures (possibly different) along the edges of the plate, and some estimate of the temperature at the interior points, and uses these values to initialize the elements of the array. Then determine the steady-state temperature at each interior node by repeatedly averaging the temperatures at its four neighbors, as just described. Repeat this procedure until the new temperature at each interior node differs from the old temperature by no more than some specified small amount. Then print the array and the number of iterations used to produce the final result. (It may also be of interest to print the array at each stage of the iteration.)

9. Write a program similar to that in Problem 8 to find steady-state temperatures in a fireplace, a diagram of which follows. The north, west, and east wall temperatures are held constant, and the south wall is insulated. The steady-state temperatures at each interior node are to be calculated using the averaging process described in Problem 8, but those for the nodes along the south wall are to be calculated using the formula

$$\frac{2T_{i-1,j} + T_{i,j-1} + T_{i,j+1}}{4}$$

Your program should read the constant north, west, and east temperatures and a constant fire wall temperature (e.g., 10, 50, 40, 1500), the number of rows and columns in the grid (e.g., 4, 7), the numbers of the fire's first and last rows and the first and last columns (e.g., 3, 4, and 3, 6), a small value to be used as a termination criterion (e.g., .0001), and an initial guess for the interior temperatures (e.g., 500).

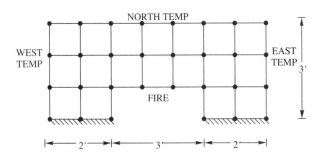

10. The game of *Life*, invented by the mathematician John H. Conway, is intended to model life in a society of organisms. Consider a rectangular array of cells, each of which may contain an organism. If the array is assumed to extend indefinitely in both directions, each cell will have eight neighbors, the eight cells surrounding it. Births and deaths occur according to the following rules:
    (a) An organism is born in an empty cell that has exactly three neighbors.
    (b) An organism dies from isolation if it has fewer than two neighbors.
    (c) An organism dies from overcrowding if it has more than three neighbors.

The following display shows the first five generations of a particular configuration of organisms:

Write a program to play the game of Life and investigate the patterns produced by various initial configurations. Some configurations die off rather quickly; others repeat after a certain number of generations; others change shape and size and may move across the array; and still others may produce "gliders" that detach themselves from the society and sail off into space.

Section 9.5

11. Proceed as in Problem 3, but use the subroutine MATMUL to compute the required matrix products.

12. Proceed as in Problem 4, but use the subroutine MATMUL to find the total cost of the components for each of the types of radios.

13. Proceed as in Problem 5, but use the subroutine MATMUL to find the total cost of each of the products.

14. The vector–matrix equation

$$
\begin{bmatrix} N \\ E \\ D \end{bmatrix} = \begin{bmatrix} \cos\alpha & -\sin\alpha & 0 \\ \sin\alpha & \cos\alpha & 0 \\ 0 & 0 & 1 \end{bmatrix} \begin{bmatrix} \cos\beta & 0 & \sin\beta \\ 0 & 1 & 0 \\ -\sin\beta & 0 & \cos\beta \end{bmatrix} \begin{bmatrix} 1 & 0 & 0 \\ 0 & \cos\gamma & -\sin\gamma \\ 0 & \sin\gamma & \cos\gamma \end{bmatrix} \begin{bmatrix} I \\ J \\ K \end{bmatrix}
$$

is used to transform local coordinates (I, J, K) for a space vehicle to inertial coordinates (N, E, D). Write a program that reads values for α, β, and γ and a set of local coordinates (I, J, K) and then uses the subroutine MATMUL to determine the corresponding inertial coordinates.

15. A *Markov chain* is a system that moves through a discrete set of states in such a way that when the system is in state i, there is probability P_{ij} that it will next move to state j. These probabilities are given by a *transition matrix P*, whose (i, j) entry is P_{ij}. It is easy to show that the (i, j) entry of P^n gives the probability of starting in state i and ending in state j after n steps.

One model of gas diffusion is known as the *Ehrenfest urn model*. In this model, there are two urns A and B containing a given number of balls (molecules). At each instant, a ball is chosen at random and is transferred to the other urn. This is a Markov chain if we take as a state the number of balls in urn A and let P_{ij} be the probability that a ball is transferred from A to B if there are i balls in urn A. For example, for four balls, the transition matrix P is given by

$$\begin{bmatrix} 0 & 1 & 0 & 0 & 0 \\ 1/4 & 0 & 3/4 & 0 & 0 \\ 0 & 1/2 & 0 & 1/2 & 0 \\ 0 & 0 & 3/4 & 0 & 1/4 \\ 0 & 0 & 0 & 1 & 0 \end{bmatrix}$$

Write a program that reads a transition matrix P for such a Markov chain and calculates and displays the value of n and P^n for several values of n.

16. A *directed graph*, or *digraph*, consists of a set of *vertices* and a set of *directed arcs* joining certain of these vertices. For example, the following diagram pictures a directed graph having five vertices numbered 1, 2, 3, 4, and 5 and seven directed arcs joining vertices 1 to 2, 1 to 4, 1 to 5, 3 to 1, 3 to itself, 4 to 3, and 5 to 1:

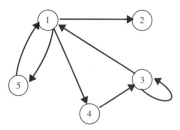

A directed graph having n vertices can be represented by its *adjacency matrix*, which is an $n \times n$ matrix, with the entry in the ith row and jth column a 1 if vertex i is joined to vertex j, and 0 otherwise. The adjacency matrix for this graph is

$$\begin{bmatrix} 0 & 1 & 0 & 1 & 1 \\ 0 & 0 & 0 & 0 & 0 \\ 1 & 0 & 1 & 0 & 0 \\ 0 & 0 & 1 & 0 & 0 \\ 1 & 0 & 0 & 0 & 0 \end{bmatrix}$$

If A is the adjacency matrix for a directed graph, the entry in the ith row and jth column of A^k gives the number of ways that vertex j can be reached from the vertex i by following k edges. Write a program to read the number of vertices in a directed graph and a collection of ordered pairs of vertices representing directed arcs, construct the adjacency matrix, and then find the number of ways that each vertex can be reached from every other vertex by following k edges for some value of k.

Section 9.6

17. The *inverse* of an $n \times n$ matrix A is a matrix A^{-1} for which both the products $A * A^{-1}$ and $A^{-1} * A$ are equal to the *identity matrix*, which is a square matrix with 1s on the diagonal from the upper left to the lower right and 0s elsewhere. The inverse of a matrix A can be calculated by solving the linear systems $A\mathbf{x} = \mathbf{b}$ for each of the following constant vectors $\mathbf{b}$:

$$\begin{bmatrix} 1 \\ 0 \\ 0 \\ \vdots \\ 0 \end{bmatrix} \begin{bmatrix} 0 \\ 1 \\ 0 \\ \vdots \\ 0 \end{bmatrix} \begin{bmatrix} 0 \\ 0 \\ 1 \\ \vdots \\ 0 \end{bmatrix} \cdots \begin{bmatrix} 0 \\ 0 \\ 0 \\ \vdots \\ 1 \end{bmatrix}$$

These solutions give the first, second, third, $\ldots$, nth column of A^{-1}. Write a program that uses Gaussian elimination to solve these linear systems and thus calculate the inverse of a matrix.

18. A general three-term equation for fitting a curve is

$$y = A + Bf(x) + Cg(x)$$

where f and g can be any functions of x. The least-squares curve of this type can be found by solving the linear system

$$\begin{aligned} nA + (\Sigma f(x))B + (\Sigma g(x))C &= \Sigma y \\ (\Sigma f(x))A + (\Sigma f(x)^2)A + (\Sigma f(x)g(x))C &= \Sigma f(x)y \\ (\Sigma g(x))A + (\Sigma f(x)g(x))B + (\Sigma g(x)^2)C &= \Sigma g(x)y \end{aligned}$$

for A, B, and C. Write a subprogram whose arguments are the functions f and g and a set of data points and that finds the coefficients A, B, and C, for this least-squares curve.

Fortran 90

Features

The Fortran 90 features described at the end of the preceding chapter for one-dimensional arrays apply to multidimensional arrays as well. In particular:

- Assignment of one array to another is permitted, provided that the arrays have the same dimension and the same extent (number of subscripts) in each dimension.
- A reference to the intrinsic function RESHAPE of the form

```
RESHAPE(source-array, shape, pad-array, order)
```

returns an array with values obtained from the specified *source-array*, with the specified *shape*, followed by elements of the array *pad-array*; and order is a one-dimensional array that specifies the order in which the subscripts are to be varied when filling in the resulting array. The arguments *pad-array* and order are optional. For example, if A and B are declared by

```
INTEGER, DIMENSION(2,3) :: A
INTEGER, DIMENSION(6) :: B
```

and B has been assigned a value by

```
B = (/ 11, 22, 33, 44, 55, 66 /)
```

then the statement

```
A = RESHAPE(B, (/ 2, 3 /))
```

assigns to A the array

$$\begin{bmatrix} 11 & 33 & 55 \\ 22 & 44 & 66 \end{bmatrix}$$

The statement

```
A = RESHAPE((/11, 22, 33, 44/), (/2, 3/), &
            (/0, 0/), (/2, 1/))
```

assigns to A the array

$$\begin{bmatrix} 11 & 22 & 33 \\ 44 & 0 & 0 \end{bmatrix}$$

- Operators and functions normally applied to simple expressions may also be applied to arrays having the same number of elements and to arrays and simple expressions. In this case, operations applied to an array are carried out elementwise. To illustrate, consider the following declarations:

```
INTEGER, DIMENSION(2,2) :: A, B
DATA A /11, 22, 33, 44/
```

so that A is initialized as the 2×2 array

$$A = \begin{bmatrix} 11 & 33 \\ 22 & 44 \end{bmatrix}$$

The statement

```
B = 2*A + 1
```

assigns to B the array

$$B = \begin{bmatrix} 23 & 67 \\ 45 & 89 \end{bmatrix}$$

and the statement

```
B = A * A
```

assigns to B the array

$$B = \begin{bmatrix} 121 & 1089 \\ 484 & 1936 \end{bmatrix}$$

Note that this is the elementwise product of A with itself, and not the usual matrix product as described in Section 9.6.

- Array sections, which are arrays consisting of selected elements from a parent array, are allowed. Such array sections are defined by specifications of the form

```
array-name(section-subscript-list)
```

where each item in the `section-subscript-list` is a subscript, or a subscript triplet, or a vector subscript. (See the Fortran 90 features of Chapter 8 for a description of subscript triplet and vector subscripts.) For example, if A is an array declared by

```
INTEGER, DIMENSION(2,3) :: A
```

with value

$$A = \begin{bmatrix} 11 & 22 & 33 \\ 44 & 55 & 66 \end{bmatrix}$$

the array section A(1:2:1, 2:3:1), or simply A(:, 2:3), is the 2×2 subarray

$$\begin{bmatrix} 22 & 33 \\ 55 & 66 \end{bmatrix}$$

and the value of the array section A(2, 1:3:1), or simply, A(2, :), is the one-dimensional array consisting of the last row of the array:

$$[44 \quad 55 \quad 66]$$

The value of the array section A((/ 2, 1 /), 2:3), in which the first item in the section subscript list is the subscript vector (/2, 1/) and the second item is the subscript triplet $2:3$ with stride 1, is the 2×2 array

$$\begin{bmatrix} 55 & 66 \\ 22 & 33 \end{bmatrix}$$

- The WHERE construct described in the Fortran 90 section of Chapter 8 for one-dimensional arrays may also be used with multidimensional arrays.

- Formal array arguments in subprograms may be *assumed-shape arrays* in which the dimension of the array is taken to be the dimension of the corresponding actual array argument. In this case the declaration of the formal array in the subprogram has the form

      array-name(lower₁:, lower₂:, ...)

or

      array-name(:, :, ...)

In the second case, the lowest subscript in each dimension is taken to be 1. Any program unit that calls this subprogram must have an explicit interface (see the Fortran 90 section of Chapter 6).

- The dimensions of local arrays in subprograms may be specified by formal arguments or by the values of the array inquiry functions SIZE, LBOUND, and UBOUND for the corresponding actual array argument. When used with a single array argument, the functions LBOUND and UBOUND return vectors specifying the array's lower bounds and upper bounds, respectively. They may also be used with a second argument specifying a given dimension for which the lower or upper bound is desired. For example, if array TEMP is declared by

      REAL, DIMENSION(0:9, 1:5, 2:2) :: TEMP

the value of LBOUND(TEMP) is the one-dimensional integer array (/ 0, 1, −2 /), and the value of LBOUND(TEMP, 3) is −2. Similarly, SIZE may be called with a single array argument and returns the number of elements in the array, or with a second argument to find the size along a single dimension. Thus SIZE(TEMP) returns the value 250, and SIZE(TEMP, 1) returns the value 10.

- As several examples have indicated, the value returned by a function may be an array.
- Several new predefined functions for processing arrays have been added, including

MAXVAL(A, D): Returns an array of one less dimension than A containing the maximum values in array A along dimension D. If D is omitted, the maximum value in the entire array is returned.

MAXLOC(A): Returns a one-dimensional array containing one element whose value is the position of the first occurrence of the maximum value in A.

MINVAL(A, D): Returns an array of one less dimension than A containing the minimum values in array A along dimension D. If D is omitted, the minimum value in the entire array is returned.

MINLOC(A): Returns a one-dimensional array containing one element whose value is the position of the first occurrence of the minimum value in A.

PRODUCT(A, D): Returns an array of one less dimension than A containing the products of the elements of A along dimension D. If D is omitted, the elementwise product of the elements in the entire array is returned.

SUM(A, D):   Returns an array of one less dimension than A containing the sums of the elements of A along dimension D. If D is omitted, the sum of the elements in the entire array is returned.

SPREAD(A, D, N): Returns an array of dimension one more than the dimension of A obtained by broadcasting N copies of A along dimension D. For example, SPREAD((/ 11, 22, 33 /), 1, 2) returns the array

$$\begin{bmatrix} 11 & 22 & 33 \\ 11 & 22 & 33 \end{bmatrix}$$

and SPREAD((/ 11, 22, 33 /), 2, 2) returns the array

$$\begin{bmatrix} 11 & 11 \\ 22 & 22 \\ 33 & 33 \end{bmatrix}$$

MATMUL(A, B):   Returns the matrix product of A and B.
TRANSPOSE(A):   Returns the transpose of the two-dimensional array A.

- Arrays may be *allocatable arrays*, for which space is not allocated at compile time but, rather, by an ALLOCATE statement during execution; their bounds are also specified at that time. An array is declared to be allocatable by including the ALLOCATABLE attribute in its type declaration, which must also specify the number of dimensions in the array, but not the bounds in each dimension. For example, the type specification statement

```
REAL, DIMENSION(:, :), ALLOCATABLE :: A, B
```

declares A and B to be two-dimensional allocatable arrays. The actual bounds in each dimension are determined by an ALLOCATE statement, for example,

```
ALLOCATE (A(N, N), B(N, 1:N+1))
```

where N is an integer variable. When this statement is executed, sufficient memory is allocated for the $N \times N$ real array A and the $N \times (N + 1)$ real array B.

The memory allocated to an array can be released by using a DEALLOCATE statement; for example

```
DEALLOCATE (A, B)
```

Examples

The new array operations provided in Fortran 90 can be used to simplify implementing several of the basic matrix operations. For example, the sum of two matrices A and B (of matching sizes) can be computed simply by writing

```
Sum_of_A_and_B = A + B
```

Similarly, subtraction of matrices and multiplication of a matrix by a scalar are easy to do:

```
Difference_of_A_and_B = A - B
Scalar_Mult_of_A = Scalar * A
```

The new predefined function MATMUL can be used to multiply matrices,

```
Product_of_A_and_B = MATMUL(A, B)
```

rendering the subroutine MATMUL of Section 9.5 unnecessary.

The program in Figure 9.8 shows how the new SUM function can be used to compute row and column averages in a table. These averages are stored in an allocatable one-dimensional array Average_Level. This program is a modification of the pollution report program in Figure 9.4.

Figure 9.8 Pollution report—Fortran 90 version.

```
PROGRAM Pollution_Report
!------------------------------------------------------------------------
! This program reads the elements of the two-dimensional array
! Pollution_Table from a file and produces a report showing a table
! of pollution levels, the average pollution level for each day,
! and the average pollution level for each sampling time.
! Identifiers used are:
!   NumDays           : parameter giving the number of rows (days)
!   NumTimes          : parameter giving the number of columns (times)
!   Pollution_Table : an NumDays X NumTimes array of pollution levels
!   Day, Time         : row, column subscripts
!   Average_Level   : row/column average pollution levels
!
! Input (file):    The pollution levels
! Output (screen): The array Pollution_Table in table format, the
!                  average pollution level for each day, and the
!                  average pollution level for each sampling time
!------------------------------------------------------------------------

   IMPLICIT NONE

   INTEGER, PARAMETER :: NumDays = 7, NumTimes = 12
   INTEGER, DIMENSION(NumDays, NumTimes) :: Pollution_Table
   INTEGER :: Day, Time
   REAL, DIMENSION(:), ALLOCATABLE :: Average_Level
```

Figure 9.8 *(cont.)*

```fortran
! Read the pollution levels and display them in a table
! of the required form

  OPEN (UNIT = 15, FILE = "FIL9-4.DAT", STATUS = "OLD")
  READ (15,*) &
     ((Pollution_Table(Day,Time), Time = 1, NumTimes), &
                                Day = 1, NumDays)
  PRINT 100, (Time, Time = 1, NumTimes)
  100 FORMAT(T30, "Time" / 1X, "Day:", 12I4 / 1X, 53("-"))

  PRINT 110, &
     (Day, (Pollution_Table(Day,Time), Time = 1, NumTimes), &
                                Day = 1, NumDays)
  110 FORMAT(1X, I2, " :", 12I4)

! Calculate average pollution level for each day (row averages)

  ALLOCATE (Average_Level(NumDays))

  Average_Level = REAL(SUM(Pollution_Table, 2)) / REAL(NumTimes)

  PRINT *
  DO Day = 1, NumDays
     PRINT 120, "for day", Day, Average_Level(Day)
     120 FORMAT(1X, "Average pollution level ", A7, I3, ":", F6.1)
  END DO

! Calculate average pollution level for each time (column averages)

  DEALLOCATE(Average_Level)
  ALLOCATE(Average_Level(NumTimes))

  Average_Level = REAL(SUM(Pollution_Table, 1)) / REAL(NumDays)

  PRINT *
  DO Time = 1, NumTimes
     PRINT 120, "at time", Time, Average_Level(Time)
  END DO

  CLOSE (15)

END PROGRAM Pollution_Report
```

10

Other Data Types

Ten decimals are sufficient to give the circumference of the earth to the fraction of an inch.

S. NEWCOMB

All such expressions as , $\sqrt{-1}$, $\sqrt{-2}$, . . . are neither nothing, nor greater than nothing, nor less than nothing, which necessarily constitutes them imaginary or impossible.

L. EULER

An average English word is four letters and a half. By hard, honest labor I've dug all the large words out of my vocabulary and shaved it down till the average is three and a half. . . .

MARK TWAIN

CHAPTER CONTENTS

10.1 The `DOUBLE PRECISION` Data Type

10.2 Application: Ill-Conditioned Linear Systems

10.3 The `COMPLEX` Data Type

10.4 Application: A-C Circuits

10.5 The `CHARACTER` Data Type

10.6 Application: Finite-State Machines

10.7 Character Functions

10.8 Application: Data Security

10.9 Application: Computer Graphics

Chapter Review

Programming Pointers

Programming Problems

Fortran 90

*T*he internal representation used for real data values, also called **single-precision** values, usually provides approximately seven significant digits.[1] In many computations, however, particularly those involving iteration or long sequences of calculations, single precision is not adequate to express the precision required. To overcome this limitation, FORTRAN provides the **double-precision** data type, which provides twice as many significant digits. This is one of the new data types considered in this chapter.

The second data type considered in this chapter is the complex type. A **complex number** is a number of the form

$$a + bi$$

---

[1] As noted in Section 2.11, many machines use 32 bits for a single-precision value, with 24 bits for the mantissa and 8 for the exponent. For double-precision values, 64 bits are used—48 for the mantisa and 16 for the exponent.

where *a* and *b* are real numbers and

$$i^2 = -1$$

The first real number, *a*, is called the **real part** of the complex number, and the second real number, *b*, is called the **imaginary part.** In FORTRAN a complex number is represented as a pair of (single-precision) real numbers.

The character data type is also considered in this chapter. In earlier chapters we described character constants, character variables and their declarations, assignment of values to character variables, input and output of character data, and comparison of character values in a logical expression. In this chapter we consider some of the more advanced character-processing capabilities of FORTRAN.

10.1   THE DOUBLE PRECISION DATA TYPE

In Section 2.11 we considered the internal representation of data and noted that because of the finite length of memory words, most real numbers cannot be stored exactly. Even such "nice" decimal fractions as 0.1 do not have terminating binary representations and thus cannot be represented exactly in the computer's memory. In this connection, we observed in Section 3.2 that because of this approximate representation, logical expressions formed by comparing two real quantities with .EQ. often are evaluated as false, even though the quantities are algebraically equal. In particular, we observed in Figure 3.3 that even though

```
X * (1.0 / X)
```

is algebraically equal to 1 for all nonzero values of X, the logical expression

```
X * (1.0 / X) .EQ. 1
```

is false for most real values of X. We also observed that many other familiar algebraic equalities fail to hold for real data values.

As another example of the effect of approximate representation, consider again the following program, used in Section 2.11 to illustrate the effect of roundoff error:

```
PROGRAM DEMO1

REAL A, B, C

READ *, A, B
C = ((A + B) ** 2 - 2 * A * B - B ** 2) / A ** 2
PRINT *, C
END
```

The output produced by one computer system for various values of A and B is shown in the following table:

A	B	C
0.5	888.0	1.00000
0.1	888.0	−12.5000
0.05	888.0	−50.0000
0.003	888.0	−13888.9
0.001	888.0	−125000.0

Except for the first value, the values of C are completely inaccurate. They should all be 1.0, since the expression

$$\frac{(A + B)^2 - 2AB - B^2}{A^2}$$

used to compute C simplifies to

$$\frac{A^2}{A^2}$$

and thus is identically 1 (provided $A \neq 0$).

For computations in which more precision is needed than is available using the real data type, FORTRAN provides the double-precision data type. When the preceding program with A, B, and C declared to be double precision was executed with the given values for A and B, the value displayed for C in each case differed from 1 by less than 0.017.

The DOUBLE PRECISION Type Statement

The names of variables, arrays, or functions that are double precision may be any legal FORTRAN names, but their types must be declared using the DOUBLE PRECISION **type statement.** For example, the statement

```
DOUBLE PRECISION Z, BETA(5,5)
```

declares the variable Z and the 5 × 5 array BETA to be double precision. The statements

```
DOUBLE PRECISION FUNCTION F(X, Y)
DOUBLE PRECISION X, Y
```

or

```
FUNCTION F(X, Y)
DOUBLE PRECISION F, X, Y
```

declare F to be a double-precision–valued function of two double-precision arguments X and Y.

Double-Precision Values

Double-precision constants are written in scientific notation with a D used to indicate the exponent. Thus,

```
3.1415926535898D0
1D-3
0.2345678D+05
```

are double-precision constants.

All variables, arrays, and functions that are to have double-precision values must be declared to be double precision. If R is a double-precision variable and A has not been declared to be double precision, the computation in the statement

```
A = 3.1415926535898D0 * R ** 2
```

will be carried out in double precision, but the resulting value will then be assigned to the single-precision variable A, thus losing approximately half of the significant digits.

Similarly, values assigned to double-precision variables should be double-precision values. For example, consider the following program:

```
PROGRAM DEMO2

REAL X
DOUBLE PRECISION A, B

X = 0.1
B = 0.1D0
A = X
PRINT *, A
A = B
PRINT *, A
END
```

On some systems the values displayed for A by the first two PRINT statements resemble the following:

```
0.99999994039536D-01
0.10000000000000D+00
```

The value 0.1D0 of the double-precision variable B is stored with more precision than the value 0.1 of the single-precision variable X. This accounts for the discrepancy between the two values displayed for A.

Although mixed-mode expressions involving double-precision, real, and integer constants and variables are permitted and are evaluated to produce double-precision values, accuracy may be lost because of the use of single-precision constants or variables. For example, consider the following statements:

```
DOUBLE PRECISION A, B
      .
      .
      .
A = (B + 3.7) ** 2
```

Because of the presence of the single-precision constant 3.7, the value for A is limited to single-precision accuracy. To ensure double-precision accuracy for the value of A, the assignment statement

```
A = (B + 3.7D0) ** 2
```

should be used.

Double-precision variables and arrays may be assigned initial values in a DATA statement. In this case, a double-precision form for the constants being assigned must be used.

Double Precision I/O—The D Descriptor

Formatted input and output of double-precision data can be accomplished with a D descriptor of the form

```
rDw.d
```

where

- D indicates that the data is to be input or output in D form
- w is an integer constant indicating the total width of the field from which the data is to be read in the case of input, or displayed in the case of output
- d is an integer constant indicating the number of digits to the right of the decimal point
- r is an integer constant indicating the number of times the field is to be repeated

For example, the statements

```
      DOUBLE PRECISION A, B, C

      READ 10, A, B, C
   10 FORMAT(2D15.0, D7.0)
```

can be used to read values from the input data line

```
1.66932506172D0   -.7325379D-02   1.1D0
```

When double-precision values are displayed using a D descriptor, they usually appear in a *normalized form:* a negative sign, if necessary, followed by one leading zero; then the decimal point followed by the specified number of digits to the right of the decimal point; and finally D with the appropriate exponent displayed in the next four spaces. The F, G, and E descriptors may also be used for the input and output of double-precision values. For example, for the variables A, B, and C assigned values by the preceding READ statement, the statements

```
    PRINT 20, A, B, C
    PRINT 30, A, B, C
    PRINT 40, A, B, C
20 FORMAT(1X, D20.12, 2D20.6)
30 FORMAT(1X, F20.12, 2F20.6)
40 FORMAT(1X, E20.12, 2E20.6)
```

produce output resembling the following:

```
  0.166932506172D+01        -0.732538D-02        0.110000D+01
          1.669325061720        -0.007325          1.100000
  0.166932506172E+01        -0.732538E-02        0.110000E+01
```

Double-Precision Functions

Most of the library functions listed in Table 6.1, such as ABS, COS, and LOG, may also be used with double-precision arguments. Three other library functions are especially useful for processing double-precision data:

DBLE(x)	Transforms the value of the integer or real argument x or the real part of the complex argument x to double-precision form
DPROD(x_1, x_2)	Calculates the double-precision product of the real arguments x_1, x_2
REAL(x)	Converts the double-precision argument x to a single-precision number

10.2 APPLICATION: ILL-CONDITIONED LINEAR SYSTEMS

Problem

In Section 9.6 we considered the problem of solving systems of linear equations. Such systems arise in the analysis of electrical networks, in analyzing statical systems, in finding least-squares approximations, in solving differential equations, and in many other problems in science and engineering.

Some linear systems, called *ill-conditioned systems*, are very difficult to solve accurately. One characteristic of such systems is that they are very sensitive to perturbations of the coefficients and constant terms. Small changes in one or more of these coefficients or constants may produce large changes in the solution. For example, consider the linear system

$$\text{(I)} \quad \begin{aligned} 2x + 6y &= 8 \\ 2x + 6.0000003y &= 8.0000003 \end{aligned}$$

for which the solution is

$$x = 1$$
$$y = 1$$

If this linear system is changed to

$$\text{(II)} \quad \begin{aligned} 2x + 6y &= 8 \\ 2x + 6.0000003y &= 7.9999994 \end{aligned}$$

the solution becomes

$$x = 10$$
$$y = -2$$

The change in the solution is on the order of 10^7 times the change in the constant term.

Solution

When these linear systems were solved using the program in Figure 9.7 for solving linear systems with Gaussian elimination, the results were

$$x = 4.000$$
$$y = 0.000$$

for system (I) and

$$x = 7.000$$
$$y = -1.000$$

for system (II).

     The program in Figure 10.1 uses double-precision arithmetic to carry out the computations involved in Gaussian elimination. Note that in the sample runs, the correct solutions to these linear systems are obtained.

Figure 10.1 Gaussian elimination with double precision.

```
      PROGRAM LINSYS
************************************************************************
* Program to solve a linear system using Gaussian elimination.      *
* Identifiers used are:                                             *
*     LIMROW : maximum number of rows in the matrix                 *
*     LIMCOL : maximum number of columns (LIMROW + 1) in the matrix *
*     N      : number of equations and unknowns                     *
*     I, J   : subscripts                                           *
*     LIN    : matrix for the linear system                         *
*     X      : solution                                             *
*     SINGUL : indicates if system is (nearly) singular             *
*                                                                   *
* Input:  The number of equations, the coefficients, and the        *
*         constants of the linear system                            *
* Output: The solution of the linear system or a message indicating *
*         that the system is (nearly) singular                      *
************************************************************************

      INTEGER LIMROW, LIMCOL
      PARAMETER (LIMROW = 10, LIMCOL = LIMROW + 1)
      DOUBLE PRECISION LIN(LIMROW, LIMCOL), X(LIMROW)
      INTEGER N, I, J
      LOGICAL SINGUL

* Read coefficients and constants

      PRINT *, 'ENTER NUMBER OF EQUATIONS'
      READ *, N
      DO 10 I = 1, N
         PRINT *, 'ENTER COEFFICIENTS AND CONSTANT OF EQUATION ',
     +             I, ': '
         READ *, (LIN(I,J), J = 1, N + 1)
10    CONTINUE

* Use subroutine GAUSS to find the solution,
* and then display the solution
```

Figure 10.1 *(cont.)*

```
      CALL GAUSS(LIN, LIMROW, LIMCOL, N, X, SINGUL)
      IF (.NOT. SINGUL) THEN
         PRINT *, 'SOLUTION IS'
         DO 20 I = 1, N
            PRINT 100, I, X(I)
100         FORMAT(1X, 'X(', I2, ') =', F8.3)
20       CONTINUE
      ELSE
         PRINT *, 'MATRIX IS (NEARLY) SINGULAR'
      END IF

      END


**GAUSS*********************************************************************
* Subroutine to find solution of a linear system of N equations in N    *
* unknowns using Gaussian elimination, provided a unique solution       *
* exists. The coefficients and constants of the linear system are       *
* stored in the matrix LIN, which has LIMROW rows and LIMCOL columns.   *
* If the system is singular, SINGUL is returned as true, and the        *
* solution X is undefined. Local identifiers used are:                  *
*     I,J,K  : subscripts                                               *
*     MULT   : multiplier used to eliminate an unknown                  *
*     ASBPIV : absolute value of pivot element                          *
*     PIVROW : row containing pivot element                             *
*     EPSIL  : a small positive real value ("almost zero")              *
*     TEMP   : used to interchange rows of matrix                       *
*                                                                       *
* Accepts: Two-dimensional array LIM, integers LIMROW, LIMCOL, and N    *
* Returns: One-dimensional array X and logical value SINGUL             *
**************************************************************************

      SUBROUTINE GAUSS(LIN, LIMROW, LIMCOL, N, X, SINGUL)

      DOUBLE PRECISION LIN(LIMROW, LIMCOL), X(LIMROW), TEMP, MULT, EPSIL
      PARAMETER (EPSIL = 1D-15)
      INTEGER N, PIVROW
      LOGICAL SINGUL
```

Figure 10.1 *(cont.)*

```
        SINGUL = .FALSE.
        DO 50 I = 1, N

*       Locate pivot element

        ABSPIV = ABS(LIN(I,I))
        PIVROW = I
        DO 10 K = I + 1, N
           IF (ABS(LIN(K,I)) .GT. ABSPIV) THEN
              ABSPIV = ABS(LIN(K,I))
              PIVROW = K
           END IF
10      CONTINUE

*       Check if matrix is (nearly) singular

        IF (ABSPIV .LT. EPSIL) THEN
           SINGUL = .TRUE.
           RETURN
        END IF

*       It isn't, so interchange rows PIVROW and I if necessary

        IF (PIVROW .NE. I) THEN
           DO 20 J = 1, N + 1
              TEMP = LIN(I,J)
              LIN(I,J) = LIN(PIVROW,J)
              LIN(PIVROW,J) = TEMP
20         CONTINUE
        END IF

*       Eliminate Ith unknown from equations I + 1, ..., N

        DO 40 J = I + 1, N
           MULT = -LIN(J,I) / LIN(I,I)
           DO 30 K = I, N + 1
              LIN(J,K) = LIN(J,K) + MULT * LIN(I,K)
30         CONTINUE
40      CONTINUE

50   CONTINUE
```

Figure 10.1 *(cont.)*

```
* Find the solutions by back substitution

      X(N) = LIN(N, N + 1) / LIN(N,N)
      DO 70 J = N - 1, 1, -1
         X(J) = LIN(J, N + 1)
         DO 60 K = J + 1, N
            X(J) = X(J) - LIN(J,K) * X(K)
60       CONTINUE
         X(J) = X(J) / LIN(J,J)
70    CONTINUE

      END
```

Sample runs:

```
ENTER NUMBER OF EQUATIONS
2
ENTER COEFFICIENTS AND CONSTANT OF EQUATION 1:
2 6 8
ENTER COEFFICIENTS AND CONSTANT OF EQUATION 2:
2 6.0000003 8.0000003
SOLUTION IS
 X( 1) =   1.000
 X( 2) =   1.000


ENTER NUMBER OF EQUATIONS
2
ENTER COEFFICIENTS AND CONSTANT OF EQUATION 1:
2 6 8
ENTER COEFFICIENTS AND CONSTANT OF EQUATION 2:
2 6.0000003 7.9999994
SOLUTION IS
 X( 1) =   10.000
 X( 2) =  -2.000
```

It should be noted that although double precision reduces the effects of limited precision, it is not a panacea. Simply declaring everything in the program to be double precision does not avoid all of the problems caused by single precision, because double-precision representations of most real numbers still are only approximate.

10.3 THE COMPLEX DATA TYPE

Although the complex number system has many important applications, it is perhaps not as familiar as the real number system. Thus in this section we review the basic properties of and operations on complex numbers and describe how they are represented and used in FORTRAN programs.

Representation of Complex Numbers

Since complex numbers have two parts, a real part and an imaginary part, they can be plotted in a coordinatized plane by taking the horizontal axis to be the real axis and the vertical axis to be the imaginary axis, so that the complex number $a + bi$ is represented as the point $P(a, b)$:

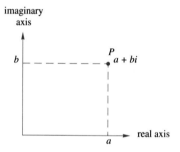

An alternative geometric representation is to associate the complex number $z = a + bi$ with the vector $\overrightarrow{OP}$ from the origin to the point $P(a, b)$:

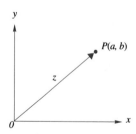

In FORTRAN, a complex constant is represented as a pair of real constants

$$(a, b)$$

where a and b are single-precision constants representing the real part and the imaginary part of the complex number, respectively. For example,

```
(1.0, 1.0)
(-6.0, 7.2)
(-5.432, -1.4142)
```

are complex constants equivalent to

$$1.0 + 1.0i$$
$$-6.0 + 7.2i$$
$$-5.432 - 1.4142i$$

respectively.

The COMPLEX Type Statement

The names of variables, arrays, or functions that are complex may be any legal FORTRAN names, but their types must be declared using the COMPLEX **type statement.** For example, the statement

```
COMPLEX A, RHO(10,10)
```

declares the variable A and the 10×10 array RHO to be complex. The statements

```
COMPLEX FUNCTION GAMMA(Z, W)
COMPLEX Z, W
```

or

```
FUNCTION GAMMA(Z, W)
COMPLEX GAMMA, Z, W
```

declare GAMMA to be a complex-valued function of two complex arguments Z and W.

Operations on Complex Numbers

The **sum** of two complex numbers $z = a + bi$ and $w = c + di$ is

$$z + w = (a + c) + (b + d)i$$

If vector representation is used for complex numbers, this corresponds to the usual sum of vectors; that is, the vector representing $z + w$ is the sum of the vectors representing z and w:

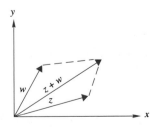

Similarly, the **difference** of z and w defined by

$$z - w = (a - c) + (b - d)i$$

corresponds to vector subtraction:

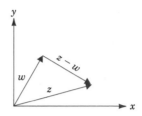

The **product** of two complex numbers $z = a + bi$ and $w = c + di$ is

$$z \cdot w = (ac - bd) + (ad + bc)i$$

This complex number is represented by a vector whose magnitude is the product of the magnitudes of the vectors representing z and w and whose angle of inclination is the sum $\theta_1 + \theta_2$ of the angles of inclination of the vectors:

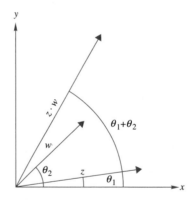

To see why this geometric representation of the product of two complex numbers is correct, it is helpful to consider the **polar representation** of complex numbers. To describe this representation, consider a vector $\overrightarrow{OP}$ from the origin to point P, and suppose that r is the length of $\overrightarrow{OP}$ and that θ is the angle from the positive x-axis to OP, so that the polar coordinates of point P are (r, θ):

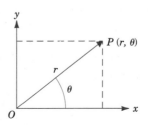

It is clear from this diagram that the relation between the rectangular coordinates (a, b) of point P and its polar coordinates (r, θ) is

$$a = r \cos \theta$$
$$b = r \sin \theta$$

It follows that the complex number represented by $\overrightarrow{OP}$ can be written in polar form as

$$r \cos \theta + ir \sin \theta = r(\cos \theta + i \sin \theta)$$

A basic property of complex numbers is that

$$e^{i\theta} = \cos \theta + i \sin \theta$$

and thus an alternative form of the polar representation of a complex number is

$$re^{i\theta}$$

Now consider two complex numbers:

$$z = r_1 e^{i\theta_1}$$
$$w = r_2 e^{i\theta_2}$$

The familiar properties of exponents then give

$$z \cdot w = (r_1 e^{i\theta_1})(r_2 e^{i\theta_2}) = r_1 r_2 e^{i(\theta_1 + \theta_2)}$$

which agrees with the geometric representation of the product of two complex numbers described earlier.

The **quotient** of two complex numbers z and w is

$$\frac{z}{w} = \frac{ac + bd}{c^2 + d^2} + \frac{bc - ad}{c^2 + d^2} i \quad (\text{provided } c^2 + d^2 \neq 0)$$

In the same manner as for multiplication, we can use polar representation and properties of exponents to show that this quotient corresponds to a vector whose magnitude is the quotient of the magnitudes of the vectors representing z and w and whose angle of inclination is the difference $\theta_1 - \theta_2$ of the vectors' angles of inclination.

These four basic arithmetic operations for complex numbers are denoted in FORTRAN by the usual operators $+, -, *,$ and $/$. The exponentiation operation $**$ is defined for a complex number only when the exponent is an integer.

Mixed-mode expressions and assignments involving integer, real, and complex values are allowed, but *double-precision values may not be combined with complex values; nor may a double-precision value be assigned to a complex variable or a complex value to a double-precision variable.* For example, suppose that C and Z are complex variables with the value of C given by

```
C = (6.2, 2.4)
```

Then the assignment statement

```
Z = 4.0 * C / 2
```

assigns the complex value $(12.4, 4.8)$ to Z. If this same expression is assigned to the real variable X

```
X = 4.0 * C / 2
```

only the real part of the expression's value is assigned to X; thus, X has the value 12.4. Similarly, if N is an integer variable, the statement

```
N = 4.0 * C / 2
```

assigns the integer part of this value to N, so that N has the value 12.

The only relational operators that may be used with complex values are .EQ. and .NE.. Two complex values are **equal** if, and only if, their real parts are equal and their imaginary parts are equal.

Complex Functions

Some of the mathematical functions commonly used with complex numbers are the absolute value, conjugate, and complex exponential functions. For the complex number $z = a + bi$, these functions are defined as follows:

Absolute value:	$\|z\| = \sqrt{a^2 + b^2}$
Conjugate:	$\bar{z} = a - bi$
Complex exponential:	$e^z = e^a(\cos b + i \sin b)$

If vector representation is used for complex numbers, $|z|$ is the magnitude of the vector representing z; $\bar{z}$ is represented by the vector obtained by reflecting the vector representing z in the x-axis; and the complex exponential e^z is associated with the polar representations of z (see Programming Problem 6 at the end of this chapter).

These three functions are implemented in FORTRAN by the library functions ABS, CONJG, and EXP, respectively. Several of the other library functions listed in Table 6.1, such as SIN, COS, and LOG, may also be used with complex arguments. Three library functions that are useful in converting from real type to complex type, and vice versa, are

AIMAG(z)	Gives the imaginary part of the complex argument z as a single-precision number
CMPLX(x, y) or CMPLX(x)	Converts the two integer, real, or double-precision arguments x and y into a complex number. The first argument x becomes the real part of the complex number, and the second argument y becomes the imaginary part. The second form is equivalent to CMPLX(x, 0).
REAL(z)	Gives the real part of the complex argument z

Complex I/O

Complex values may be read using a list-directed READ statement, with the complex numbers entered as a pair of real numbers enclosed in parentheses. They may also be read using a formatted READ statement. In this case, a pair of F, E, or G descriptors may be used for each complex value to be read, and parentheses are not used to enclose the parts of the complex number when it is entered. Complex values displayed using a list-directed output statement appear as a pair of real values separated by a comma and enclosed within parentheses. For formatted output of complex values, a pair of F, E, or G descriptors is used for each complex value.

The following program illustrates the input and output of complex numbers and complex arithmetic:

```
      PROGRAM DEMO3

      COMPLEX X, Y, W, Z, A

      READ *, X, Y
      READ 5, W
5     FORMAT(2F2.0)
      PRINT *, X, Y, W
      PRINT 10, X, Y, W
10    FORMAT(1X, F6.2, ' +', F8.2, 'I')
      Z = (X + Y) / (1.0,2.2)
      A = X * Y
      PRINT 10, Z, A
      END
```

If the following data is entered,

```
(3,4), (.75,-2.23)
 5 7
```

the output produced will be

```
(3.00000,4.00000)   (0.750000,-2.23000)   (5.00000,7.00000)
    3.00 +     4.00I
    0.75 +    -2.23I
    5.00 +     7.00I
    1.31 +    -1.11I
   11.17 +    -3.69I
```

Example: Solving Equations

Quadratic Equations. In Section 3.2 we considered the problem of solving quadratic equations

$$Ax^2 + Bx + C = 0$$

and noted that if the discriminant $B^2 - 4AC$ is negative, there are no real roots. In this case, the quadratic equation has two complex solutions, which can be found by using the quadratic formula. For example, for the equation

$$x^2 + 2x + 5 = 0$$

the discriminant is

$$2^2 - 4 \cdot 1 \cdot 5 = -16$$

so the roots are complex. The quadratic formula gives the roots

$$\frac{-2 \pm \sqrt{-16}}{2} = \frac{-2 \pm 4i}{2} = -1 \pm 2i$$

The program in Figure 10.2 reads the complex coefficients A, B, and C of a quadratic equation, uses the quadratic formula to calculate the roots, and displays them as complex numbers.

Figure 10.2 Quadratic equations—complex roots.

```
      PROGRAM CQUAD
*****************************************************************
*  Program to solve a quadratic equation having complex coefficients   *
*  using the quadratic formula. Variables used are:                    *
*       A, B, C      : the coefficients of the quadratic equation      *
*       DISC         : the discriminant, B ** 2 - 4 * A * C            *
*       ROOT1, ROOT2 : the two roots of the equation                  *
*                                                                      *
*  Input:   A, B, and C                                                *
*  Output: ROOT1 and ROOT2                                            *
*****************************************************************
```

Figure 10.2 *(cont.)*

```
        COMPLEX A, B, C, DISC, ROOT1, ROOT2

* Get the coefficients

        PRINT *, 'ENTER THE COEFFICIENTS OF THE QUADRATIC EQUATION'
        READ *, A, B, C

* Calculate and display the roots

        DISC = SQRT(B ** 2 - 4.0 * A * C)
        ROOT1 = (-B + DISC) / (2.0 * A)
        ROOT2 = (-B - DISC) / (2.0 * A)
        PRINT *, 'THE ROOTS ARE:'
        PRINT 10, ROOT1, ROOT2
10      FORMAT (5X, F7.3, ' +', F7.3, 'I')

        END
```

Sample runs:

```
ENTER THE COEFFICIENTS OF THE QUADRATIC EQUATION
(1,0), (-5,0), (6,0)
THE ROOTS ARE:
     3.000 +   0.000I
     2.000 +   0.000I

ENTER THE COEFFICIENTS OF THE QUADRATIC EQUATION
(1,0), (2,0), (5,0)
THE ROOTS ARE:
    -1.000 +   2.000I
    -1.000 + -2.000I

ENTER THE COEFFICIENTS OF THE QUADRATIC EQUATION
(1,0), (0,0), (1,0)
THE ROOTS ARE:
     0.000 +   1.000I
     0.000 + -1.000I
```

Polynomial Equations.   For higher-degree polynomials there is no general formula analogous to the quadratic formula for finding roots. For such polynomials, we can use Newton's method, as described in Section 6.3, to approximate a real root if there is one. As the preceding example with quadratic equations demonstrates, however, a polynomial equation may have no real roots. Newton's method can still be used in this case to find a complex root. Modifying the program in Figure 6.6 to use Newton's method to find complex roots of polynomials is left as an exercise (see Programming Problem 8).

Linear Systems.   In Section 9.6, we considered the problem of determining the loop currents in a direct-current (d-c) circuit and found these currents by solving a system of linear equations. Whereas the current, voltage, and resistance of a d-c circuit can be represented by real numbers, these same quantities are represented by complex numbers for alternating-current (a-c) circuits. Consequently, the equations in a linear system for finding loop currents in an a-c circuit have coefficients that are complex numbers. Such a system can be solved using the Gaussian elimination method if the real operations are replaced by complex operations.

10.4 APPLICATION: AC CIRCUITS

Problem

An a-c circuit contains a capacitor, an inductor, and a resistor in series:

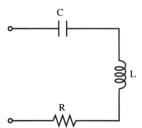

A program must be written to calculate the current in this circuit for several frequencies and voltages.

Solution

Specification.   The input to the problem will be the resistance, the inductance, the capacitance, the frequency of the a-c source, and the voltage. The output will be the current in the circuit. Thus a specification for the problem is as follows:

Input: Resistance (ohms)

Inductance (henrys)

Capacitance (farads)

Frequency (radians/second)

Voltage (volts)

Output: Current (amperes)

Design.   The impedance Z_R for a resistor is simply the resistance R, but for inductors and capacitors, it is a function of the frequency. The impedance Z_L of an inductor is the complex value given by

$$Z_L = \omega L i$$

where ω is the frequency (in radians per second) of the a-c source and L is the self-inductance (in henrys).[2] For a capacitor, the impedance is

$$Z_C = \frac{-i}{\omega C}$$

where C is the capacitance (in farads). The total impedance Z is then given by

$$Z = Z_R + Z_L + Z_C$$

and the instantaneous current I by

$$I = \frac{V}{Z}$$

An algorithm for this problem is straightforward:

ALGORITHM FOR AC CIRCUIT PROBLEM

```
*   Algorithm to compute the current in an a-c circuit containing a capacitor, an inductor,   *
*   and a resistor in series.                                                                 *
*   Input:     Resistance (R), inductance (L), capacitance (C), frequency (OMEGA)             *
*   Output:    Current (I)                                                                    *
```

1. Enter R, L, C
2. Enter OMEGA.
3. Enter the voltage V as a complex number.
4. Compute the impedance Z.
5. Compute the current I.
6. Display I.

Coding, Execution and Testing. The program in Figure 10.3 implements this algorithm. Also shown is a sample run with a set of test data.

---

[2] It is customary in electrical engineering to use j instead of i to denote the complex number $\sqrt{-1}$. This helps to avoid confusion with I or i used to denote current.

Figure 10.3 AC circuit.

```
      PROGRAM ACCIRC
****************************************************************
* Program to compute the current in an a-c circuit containing a  *
* capacitor, an inductor, and a resistor in series. Variables    *
* used are:                                                      *
*    R    : resistance (ohms)                                    *
*    L    : inductance (henrys)                                  *
*    C    : capacitance (farads)                                 *
*    OMEGA : frequency (radians/second)                          *
*    V    : voltage (volts)                                      *
*    Z    : total impedance                                      *
*    I    : current (amperes)                                    *
*                                                                *
* Input:  R, L, C, OMEGA, and V                                  *
* Output: I                                                      *
****************************************************************


      REAL R, L, C, OMEGA
      COMPLEX V, Z, I

      PRINT *, 'ENTER RESISTANCE (OHMS), INDUCTANCE (HENRIES), ',
     +         'AND CAPACITANCE (FARADS):'
      READ *, R, L, C

      PRINT *, 'ENTER FREQUENCY (RADIANS/SECOND):'
      READ *, OMEGA
      PRINT *, 'ENTER VOLTAGE AS A COMPLEX NUMBER IN THE FORM (X, Y):'
      READ *, V

* Calculate resistance using complex arithmetic
      Z = R + OMEGA * L * (0.0, 1.0) - (0.0, 1.0) / (OMEGA * C)

* Calculate and display current using complex arithmetic
      I = V / Z
      PRINT *
      PRINT 100, I, ABS(I)
100   FORMAT(1X, 'INSTANTANEOUS CURRENT = ', F10.4, ' + ',
     +          F10.4, 'I' / 1X, 'WITH MAGNITUDE = ', F10.4)

      END
```

Figure 10.3 *(cont.)*

Sample run:

```
ENTER RESISTANCE (OHMS), INDUCTANCE (HENRIES), AND CAPACITANCE (FARADS):
5000, .03, .02
ENTER FREQUENCY (RADIANS/SECOND):
377
ENTER VOLTAGE AS A COMPLEX NUMBER IN THE FORM (X, Y):
(60000, 134)

INSTANTANEOUS CURRENT =    12.0000 +      0.0000I
WITH MAGNITUDE =     12.0000
```

Quick Quiz 10.4

1. (True or false) The double-precision data type makes it possible to store the exact representation of any real number.

2. (True or false) If Z is a complex variable, then the statement Z = (2.0, 3.0) is a valid assignment statement.

3. (True or false) If Z is a complex variable and X and Y are real variables, then the statement Z = (X, Y) is a valid assignment statement.

4. (True or false) The statement COMPLEX FUNCTION F(X, Y) declares that the function F is a function of two complex arguments.

5. (True or false) The formatted output of a complex value is accomplished using a Cw.d format descriptor.

6. (True or false) Double-precision values displayed with a D descriptor usually appear in normalized form.

7. (True or false) The library function DPROD is used to calculate the product of two double-precision numbers.

8. (True or false) In the complex number $a + bi$, a and b are termed the real parts and i the imaginary part.

9. (True or false) Double-precision values may not be combined with complex values.

10. (True or false) Double-precision values may be assigned to complex variables.

11. (True or false) If Z is a complex variable, Z .GT. (0, 0) is a valid logical expression.

For Questions 12–16, assume that $z = 8 + 3i$ and $w = 7 + 2i$.

12. Compute $z + w$.

13. Compute $z - w$.

14. Compute $z \cdot w$.

15. Compute z / w.

16. Calculate $|z|$.

Questions 17–21 assume the following declarations and assignments:

```
REAL R1, R2, R3
COMPLEX C1, C2, C3

R1 = 1.5
R2 = 2.1
C1 = (1.0, 3.0)
C2 = (2.0, 1.0)
```

What values will be assigned to the given variable in each of the assignment statements?

17. `C3 = C1 * C2`

18. `C3 = CONJG(C2)`

19. `C3 = CMPLX(R1, R2)`

20. `R3 = C2`

21. `C3 = R1`

For Questions 22 and 23, tell how the data must be entered for the given READ statement so that the value assigned to C1 is the complex constant $1.5 + 2.5i$.

22.   `READ *, C1`

23.   `READ 5, C1`
      `5 FORMAT (2F4.2)`

Exercises 10.4

For Exercises 1–12, calculate the given expression given that $z = 1 + 2i$ and $w = 3 - 4i$.

1. $z + w$ 2. $z - w$ 3. $z \cdot w$ 4. $\dfrac{z}{w}$

5. z^2 6. $\bar{z}$ 7. $\bar{w}$ 8. $\dfrac{z + \bar{z}}{2}$

9. $\dfrac{z - \bar{z}}{2i}$ 10. $z \cdot \bar{z}$ 11. $\dfrac{1}{z}$ 12. $\dfrac{z + w}{z - w}$

13–24. Repeat Exercises 1–12 for $z = 6 - 5i$ and $w = 5 + 12i$.

25–36. Repeat Exercises 1–12 for $z = 1 + i$ and $w = 1 - i$.

For Exercises 37–54, assume the declarations

```
INTEGER N1, N2
REAL R1, R2
DOUBLE PRECISION D1, D2
COMPLEX C1, C2
```

and the assignment statements

```
N1 = 2
R1 = 0.5
D1 = .1D0
C1 = (6.0,8.0)
```

Find the value assigned to the specified variable by the given assignment statement, or indicate why there is an error.

37. R2 = D1
38. N2 = D1
39. R2 = C1
40. N2 = C1
41. D2 = C1
42. D2 = N1
43. R2 = REAL(C1)
44. R2 = AIMAG(C1)
45. C2 = C1 * (0,1)
46. C2 = 1 / C1
47. R2 = ABS(C1)
48. N2 = CONJG(C1)
49. C2 = C1 ** N1
50. C2 = C1 ** R1
51. C2 = CMPLX(N1, R1)
52. C2 = N1 + R1 * D1 + C1
53. C2 = REAL(C1) + AIMAG(C1)
54. C2 = EXP((0,0))

10.5 THE CHARACTER DATA TYPE

Recall that a character constant is a string of characters from the FORTRAN character set enclosed in apostrophes (single quotes) and that the number of characters enclosed is the length of the constant.

As we have seen, character variables may be declared using a type statement of the form

```
CHARACTER*n, list
```

where *list* is a list of variables being typed as character and *n* is the length of their values. The comma preceding the list may be omitted; the length specification *n* also may be omitted, in which case it is assumed to be 1.

For example, the statement

```
CHARACTER*10 STREET, CITY, STATE
```

declares STREET, CITY, and STATE to be of character type with string values of length 10. The length specification may be overridden for any variable in the list by appending a length descriptor of the form *m* to its name; thus

```
CHARACTER*10 STREET*20, CITY, STATE
```

declares CITY and STATE to have values of length 10 and STREET to have values of length 20. In Chapter 6 we also noted that when a formal argument of character type is being declared in a function or subroutine subprogram, a declaration of the form

```
CHARACTER*(*) list-of-identifiers
```

which contains the **assumed length specifier** *, may be used. In this case, the formal argument will have the same length as the corresponding actual argument.

Character Operations

Concatenation.   For character data there is one binary operation that can be used to combine two character values. This operation is **concatenation** and is denoted by //. Thus

```
'CENTI' // 'METERS'
```

produces the string

```
'CENTIMETERS'
```

and if SQUNIT is a variable declared by

```
CHARACTER*7 SQUNIT
```

and is assigned a value by

```
SQUNIT = 'SQUARE '
```

then

```
SQUNIT // 'CENTI' // 'METERS'
```

yields the string

```
'SQUARE CENTIMETERS'
```

Substring.   Another operation commonly performed on character strings is accessing a sequence of consecutive characters from a string. Such a sequence is called a **substring** of the given string. For example, the substring consisting of the fourth through seventh characters of the character constant

```
'CENTIMETERS'
```

is the string

```
'TIME'
```

In FORTRAN, a substring can be extracted from the value of a character variable by specifying the name of the variable followed by the positions of the first and last characters of the substring, separated by a colon (:) and enclosed in parentheses. For example, if character variable UNITS has the value

```
'CENTIMETERS'
```

then

```
UNITS(4:7)
```

has the value

```
'TIME'
```

The initial and final positions of the substring may be specified by any integer constants, variables, or expressions. If the initial position is not specified, it is assumed to be 1, and if the final position is not specified, it is assumed to be the last position in the value of the character variable. To illustrate, consider the following statements:

```
CHARACTER*15 COURSE, NAME*20
COURSE = 'ENGINEERING'
```

Then

```
COURSE(:6)
```

has the value

```
'ENGINE'
```

and the value of

```
COURSE(8:)
```

is

```
'RING♭♭♭♭'
```

where ♭ denotes a blank. If N has the value 3, then

```
COURSE(N:N + 2)
```

has the value

```
'GIN'
```

Care must be taken to ensure that the first position specified for a substring is positive and that the last position is greater than or equal to the first position but not greater than the length of the given string.

Substring references may be used to form character expressions just as character variables are used. For example, they may be concatenated with other character values, as in

```
COURSE(:3) // COURSE(8:8) // ' 141'
```

the value of which is the string

```
'ENGR 141'
```

An assignment statement or an input statement may also be used to modify part of a string by using a substring reference. Only the character positions specified in the substring name are assigned values; the other positions are not changed. To illustrate, consider the statements

```
CHARACTER*8 COURSE
```

```
COURSE = 'CPSC 141'
```

The assignment statement

```
COURSE(1:4) = 'ENGR'
```

or

```
COURSE(:4) = 'ENGR'
```

changes the value of COURSE to

```
'ENGR 141'
```

Positions to which new values are being assigned may not be referenced, however, in the character expression on the right side of such assignment statements. Thus

```
COURSE(2:4) = COURSE(5:7)
```

is valid, whereas

```
COURSE(2:4) = COURSE (3:5)
```

is not because the substring being modified overlaps the substring being referenced.

Character Input/Output

Output.   Character values can be displayed using either list-directed or formatted output. List-directed output of a character value consists of the string of characters in that value, displayed in a field whose width is equal to the length of that value. For example, if STRA and STRB are declared by

```
CHARACTER*8 STRA, STRB
```

and are assigned values by

```
STRA = 'SQUARE'
STRB = 'CENTIMETERS'
```

the statement

```
PRINT *, '***', STRA, '***', STRB, '***'
```

produces the output

```
***SQUARE  ***CENTIMET***
```

Note the two trailing blanks in the value of STRA that result from the padding that occurs when a string of length 6 is assigned to a character variable of length 8. Note also that the last three characters in the string 'CENTIMETERS' are not displayed because they were truncated in the assignment of the value to STRB.

Character expressions may also appear in the output list of a PRINT statement. For example,

```
PRINT *, STRA(:2) // '. ' // STRB(:1) // STRB(6:6) // '.'
```

produces as output

```
SQ. CM.
```

An A descriptor is used for formatted output of character values. To illustrate, consider the following program segment:

```
      CHARACTER*15 ITEM, COLOR*5

      ITEM = 'MM CAMERA'
      COLOR = 'BLACK'
      PRINT 5, COLOR, 'RED'
5     FORMAT(1X, A, A4)
      PRINT 10, COLOR
10    FORMAT(1X, A1)
      PRINT 15, 'MOVIE-' // ITEM(4:9)
15    FORMAT(1X, A)
      PRINT 20, 35, ITEM
20    FORMAT(1X, I2, A)
```

These statements produce the following output:

```
BLACK RED
B
MOVIE-CAMERA
35MM CAMERA
```

Input.   Character values can be read using either list-directed or formatted input. For list-directed input, character values must be enclosed in single quotes. For formatted input, when a value is read for a character variable, *all* characters in the field associated with the corresponding A descriptor are read. For example, if the line of data

```
SCIENTIFIC FORTRAN
```

is read by the statements

```
      CHARACTER*8 STRA, STRB

      READ 20, STRA, STRB
20    FORMAT(2A)
```

the value

```
SCIENTIF
```

is assigned to STRA and

```
IC FORTR
```

to STRB.

A substring reference may also appear in an input list. For example, if COURSE has the value

```
'CPSC141'
```

and the input for the statement

```
READ '(A)', COURSE(2:6)
```

is

```
LAS 3
```

the value of COURSE is changed to

```
'CLAS 341'
```

10.6 APPLICATION: FINITE-STATE MACHINES

In our discussion of system software in Chapter 1, we mentioned **compilers**, which are programs whose function is to translate a source program written in some high-level language such as FORTRAN into an object program written in machine code. This object program is then executed by the computer.

The basic phases of the compiler are summarized in the following diagram:

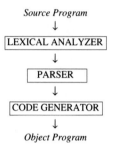

The input to a compiler is a stream of characters that comprise the source program. Before the translation can actually be carried out, this stream of characters must be broken up into meaningful groups, such as identifiers, key words, constants, and operators. For example, for the assignment statement

```
ALPHA = 200*BETA + 5
```

or as a "stream" of characters

```
ALPHA♭=♭200*BETA♭+♭5
```

(where ♭ is a blank), the following units must be identified:

ALPHA	identifier
=	assignment operator
200	integer constant
*	arithmetic operator
BETA	identifier
+	arithmetic operator
5	integer constant

These units are called **tokens**, and the part of the compiler that recognizes these tokens is called the **lexical analyzer.**

It is the task of the **parser** to group these tokens together to form the basic **syntactic structures** of the language as determined by the syntax rules. For example, it must recognize that the three consecutive tokens

integer-constant   arithmetic-operator   identifier
↓   ↓   ↓
200   *   BETA

can be grouped together to form a valid arithmetic expression; that

arithmetic-expression   arithmetic-operator   integer-constant
↓   ↓
+   500

constitutes a valid arithmetic expression; and then that

identifier   assignment-operator   arithmetic-expression
↓   ↓
ALPHA   =

forms a valid assignment statement. The complete **parse tree** constructed during compilation of the preceding statement is

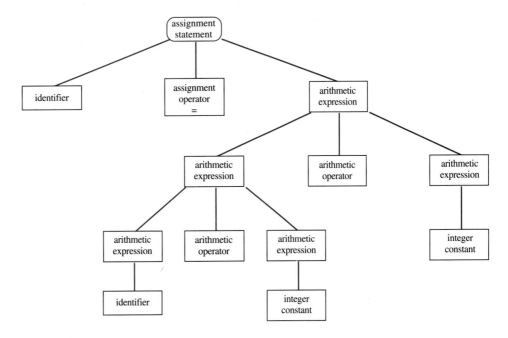

Later phases of the compiling process generate the machine code for this assignment statement.

A tool that is useful in designing lexical analyzers and in modeling many other processes made up of a finite sequence of events is the **finite-state machine** (also called a **finite automaton**), which has a finite number of states with transitions from one state to another that depend on the current state of the machine and an input. If the machine is in one of certain states called *accepting states* after an input string is processed, then that string is said to be *recognized* or *accepted* by the machine. For example, a finite-state machine to recognize bit strings that contain 01 is

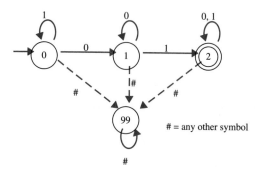

Here, the arrow pointing to state 0 indicates that this is the initial state. The machine begins processing input symbols in this state and makes transitions from one state to another or remains in the current state as specified by the labels on the arrows.

To illustrate, consider the input string 0011. The finite-state machine begins in state 0, and because the first input symbol is 0, it transfers to state 1. Since the next input symbol is a 0, the machine remains in state 1. However, the third symbol is a 1, which causes a transition to state 2. The final symbol is a 1 and causes no state change. The end of the input string has now been reached, and because the finite-state machine is in an accept state as indicated by the double circle, it has accepted the string 0011. It is easy to see that any bit string containing 01 will be processed in a similar manner and lead to the accept state, and that only such strings will cause the machine to terminate in state 2. For example, the string 11000 is not accepted because the machine will be in state 1 after processing this string, and state 1 is not an accept state. Neither is the bit string 100201 accepted, since the "illegal" symbol 2 causes a transition from state 1 to state 99, which is not an accept state.

State 99 is a "reject" or "dead" state: once it is entered, it is never exited. The transitions to this state are shown as dashed lines, since the existence of such a state is usually assumed and transitions are not drawn in the diagram; for any state and any input symbol for which no transition is specified, it is assumed that the transition is to such a reject state. Thus, the finite-state machine is usually drawn as

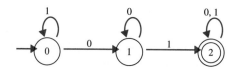

As another example, consider the following finite-state machine:

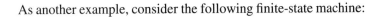

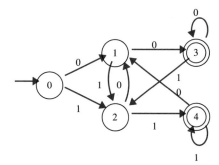

After some analysis and experimentation it should become clear that to terminate processing in one of the accept states 3 or 4, the last two input symbols must both be 0s or both be 1s. This finite-state machine thus recognizes bit strings ending in 00 or 11.

To show how a finite-state machine can be used to advantage in the design of lexical analyzers, we consider the problem of recognizing FORTRAN integer constants. A finite-state machine that does this is

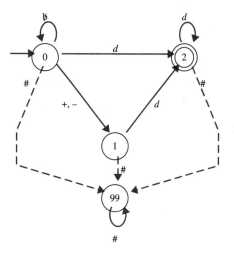

where d denotes one of the digits 0, 1, ... , 9; ƀ denotes a blank; and state 2 is the only accepting state. The machine begins in state 0, and if the first input symbol is a blank, it stays in state 0, "gobbling up" leading blanks; if it is a + or −, it goes to state 1; if it is a digit, it goes to state 2; otherwise, the input character is not valid, and thus the string does not represent a valid integer.

Writing program statements corresponding to such a finite-state machine is then straightforward. The program in Figure10.4 illustrates this. It reads a string of characters and determines whether it represents a valid FORTRAN integer. The part of the program highlighted in color implements the preceding finite-state machine.

Figure 10.4 Lexical analysis.

```
        PROGRAM LEX
* * * * * * * * * * * * * * * * * * * * * * * * * * * * * * * * * * * * * * * * * * * * * * * * * * * * * * * * * * * * * * * * * * *
* This program implements a simple lexical analyzer for FORTRAN        *
* integer constants. A finite-state machine that recognizes integer    *
* constants was used in designing the program.  Identifiers used:       *
*      DEAD   : dead state                                              *
*      STATE  : current state                                           *
*      I      : index                                                   *
*      STRING : input string to be checked                             *
*      SYMBOL : a character in STRING                                   *
*      MARK   : end-of-string mark                                      *
*      RESPON : user response                                           *
*                                                                       *
* Input:  STRING, RESPON                                                *
* Output: User prompt, message indicating if string is a valid          *
*         integer                                                       *
* * * * * * * * * * * * * * * * * * * * * * * * * * * * * * * * * * * * * * * * * * * * * * * * * * * * * * * * * * * * * * * * * * *

        INTEGER DEAD
        PARAMETER (DEAD = 99)
        INTEGER STATE, I
        CHARACTER*1 SYMBOL, MARK, RESPON, STRING*80
        DATA MARK /';'/

* Repeat the following until no more strings to check

10      CONTINUE
        PRINT *, 'Enter the string to be checked (end with ', MARK, ')'
        READ '(A)', STRING
        I = 1

*       Begin in initial state
        STATE = 0
```

Figure 10.4 *(cont.)*

```
*          While Ith symbol in STRING is not the end-of-string mark do
20         IF (STRING(I:I) .NE. MARK) THEN

               SYMBOL = STRING(I:I)
               IF (STATE .EQ. 0) THEN
                   IF (SYMBOL .EQ. ' ') THEN
                       STATE = 0
                   ELSE IF (SYMBOL .EQ. '+' .OR. SYMBOL .EQ. '−') THEN
                       STATE = 1
                   ELSE IF (SYMBOL .GE. '0' .AND. SYMBOL .LE. '9') THEN
                       STATE = 2
                   ELSE
                       STATE = DEAD
                   END IF

               ELSE IF (STATE .EQ. 1 .OR. STATE .EQ. 2) THEN
                   IF (SYMBOL .GE. '0' .AND. SYMBOL .LE. '9') THEN
                       STATE = 2
                   ELSE
                       STATE = DEAD
                   END IF
               END IF

               I = I + 1
           GO TO 20
           END IF

           IF (STATE .EQ. 2) THEN
               PRINT *, 'VALID INTEGER'
           ELSE
               PRINT *, 'NOT A VALID INTEGER'
           END IF

           PRINT *
           PRINT *, 'MORE DATA (Y OR N)'
           READ '(A)', RESPON
       IF (RESPON .EQ. 'Y') GO TO 10

       END
```

Figure 10.4 *(cont.)*

Sample run:

```
Enter the string to be checked (end with ;)
1234;
VALID INTEGER

MORE DATA (Y OR N)
Y
Enter the string to be checked (end with ;)
+9999;
VALID INTEGER

MORE DATA (Y OR N)
Y
Enter the string to be checked (end with ;)
—1;
VALID INTEGER

MORE DATA (Y OR N)
Y
Enter the string to be checked (end with ;)
123+4;
NOT A VALID INTEGER

MORE DATA (Y OR N)
Y
Enter the string to be checked (end with ;)
ABCDEF;
NOT A VALID INTEGER

MORE DATA (Y OR N)
N
```

Exercises 10.6

1. ASCII is a coding scheme that uses seven bits to represent characters. An extra bit is commonly added for error detection. In an *even-parity* error-detecting scheme, this extra bit is set to 1 if the number of 1s in the ASCII code is odd and 0 otherwise. Design a finite-state machine to recognize bit strings containing an odd number of 1s.

2. Design a finite-state machine to recognize bit strings containing 00 or 11.

3. Design a finite-state machine to recognize bit strings containing an even number of zeros and an even number of ones.

4. Design a finite-state machine to recognize bit strings in which the remainder when n is divided by 3 is 1, where n is the number of ones.

10.7 CHARACTER FUNCTIONS

In Section 10.5 we described the CHARACTER data type and some of the basic character operations. FORTRAN also provides several functions for processing characters strings and in this section we describe these functions. We also continue the description of character comparison begun in Section 3.1.

The INDEX and LEN Functions

INDEX. When extracting or modifying substrings, it is often convenient to locate a given pattern within a string. For example, we might wish to search the string

```
'ATOMIC WEIGHT OF KRYPTON'
```

to find the location of the substring

```
'WEIGHT'
```

This can be done using the FORTRAN library function INDEX of the form

```
INDEX(string₁, string₂)
```

where $string_1$ and $string_2$ are any expressions of character type. The first argument is the string being searched, and the second is the substring whose location is to be determined. The value of the function is the integer value corresponding to the character position at which the first occurrence of that substring begins, or 0 if the substring does not appear in the given string. Thus the value of

```
INDEX('ATOMIC WEIGHT OF KRYPTON', 'WEIGHT')
```

is 8, whereas the value of

```
INDEX('ATOMIC WEIGHT OF KRYPTON', 'NUMBER')
```

is 0.

The following table gives more examples of the index function. In these examples, UNITS and DIST are assumed to be declared by

```
CHARACTER UNITS*15, DIST*6
```

and to have the values

```
UNITS = 'FEET PER SECOND'
DIST = 'METERS'
```

Expression	Value
INDEX(UNITS, DIST)	0
INDEX(UNITS, 'PER')	6
INDEX(UNITS, DIST(4:5))	7
INDEX(UNITS, 'E')	2
UNITS(INDEX(UNITS, 'S'):)	'SECOND'
DIST(3:INDEX(UNITS, ' '))	'TER'
DIST // UNITS(INDEX(UNITS, ' '):)	'METERS PER SECOND'

LEN. Another FORTRAN library function that may be used with character data is the LEN function of the form

```
LEN(string)
```

where *string* is any character expression. The value of this function is the length of the specified string.

Suppose that NAME has been declared to be of character type by the statement

```
CHARACTER*20 NAME
```

and consider the assignment statement

```
NAME = 'JOHN DOE'
```

The following table shows the results of several uses of the LEN function:

Function	Result
PRINT *, LEN('JOHN DOE')	8 is displayed
PRINT *, LEN(NAME)	20 is displayed
N = LEN('MR. '//NAME)	24 is assigned to N
PRINT *, LEN(NAME(9:))	12 is displayed
DO 10 I = 1, LEN(NAME)	Loop is repeated 20 times

As the preceding examples show, for a character constant, the value of the LEN function is simply the number of characters in that constant, and for a character variable, it is the declared length of that variable. Consequently, this function has a rather limited use. However, a statement such as

```
DO 10 I = 1, LEN(NAME)
```

is preferred to

```
DO 10 I = 1, 20
```

because it does not have to be changed if the program is modified by changing the declared length of NAME. The LEN function is also useful in subprograms in which an assumed length specifier is used to declare arguments of character type.

Example: Text Editing

The preparation of textual material such as research papers, books, and computer programs often involves the insertion, deletion, and replacement of parts of the text. The software of most computers systems includes an **editing** package that makes it easy to carry out these operations. As an example showing the text-processing capabilities of FORTRAN, we consider the editing problem of replacing a specified substring in a given line of text with another string. A solution to this problem is given in the program in Figure 10.5. The sample run shows that in addition to string replacements, the program can be used to make insertions and deletions. For example, changing the substring

```
A N
```

in the line of text

```
A NATION CONCEIVED IN LIBERTY AND AND DEDICATED
```

to

```
A NEW N
```

yields the edited line

```
A NEW NATION CONCEIVED IN LIBERTY AND AND DEDICATED
```

Entering the edit change

```
AND //
```

changes the substring

```
AND⌷
```

(where ♭ denotes a blank) in the line of text to an *empty* or *null* string containing no characters, and so the edited result is

```
A NEW NATION CONCEIVED IN LIBERTY AND DEDICATED
```

Figure 10.5 Text editor.

```
       PROGRAM EDITOR
* * * * * * * * * * * * * * * * * * * * * * * * * * * * * * * * * * * * * * * * * * * * * * * * * * * * * * * * *
* Program to perform some basic text-editing functions on lines of    *
* text.  The basic operation is replacing a substring of the text     *
* with another string.  This replacement is accomplished by a command *
* of the form                                                         *
*                       oldstring/newstring/                          *
* where oldstring specifies the substring in the text to be replaced  *
* with newstring; newstring may be an empty string, which then causes *
* oldstring (if found) to be deleted.  The text lines are read from a *
* file, and after editing, the edited lines are written to another    *
* file.  Identifiers used are:                                        *
*     OLDFIL : name of the input file                                 *
*     NEWFIL : name of the output file                                *
*     EOF    : end-of-file indicator                                  *
*     TEXT   : a character string representing a line of text         *
*     LENGTH : length of text line                                    *
*     CHANGE : a character string specifying the edit operation       *
*              Value is of the form:                                  *
*                       'oldstring/newstring/'                        *
*     RESPON : user response (Y or N)                                 *
*                                                                     *
* Input (keyboard): OLDFIL, NEWFIL, TEXT, CHANGE, RESPON              *
* Output (screen):  User prompts, TEXT                                *
* Input (file):     Lines of text                                     *
* Output (file):    Edited lines of text                              *
* * * * * * * * * * * * * * * * * * * * * * * * * * * * * * * * * * * * * * * * * * * * * * * * * * * * * * * * *

       INTEGER LENGTH, EOF
       PARAMETER (LENGTH = 80)
       CHARACTER*(LENGTH) TEXT, CHANGE, OLDFIL*20, NEWFIL*20, RESPON*1

       PRINT *, 'ENTER THE NAME OF THE INPUT FILE'
       READ '(A)', OLDFIL
       PRINT *, 'ENTER THE NAME OF THE OUTPUT FILE'
       READ '(A)', NEWFIL
       OPEN (UNIT = 15, FILE = OLDFIL, STATUS = 'OLD')
       OPEN (UNIT = 16, FILE = NEWFIL, STATUS = 'NEW')
```

Figure 10.5 *(cont.)*

```
* While there is more data, read a line of text and edit it
      READ (15, '(A)', IOSTAT = EOF) TEXT
10    IF (EOF .GE. 0) THEN
         PRINT *, TEXT
         PRINT *, 'EDIT THIS LINE (Y OR N)?'
         READ '(A)', RESPON

*        While RESPON <> 'N', get editing change, modify the
*        line of text, and display the edited line
20       IF (RESPON .NE. 'N') THEN
            PRINT *, 'ENTER EDIT CHANGE'
            READ '(A)', CHANGE
            CALL EDIT(TEXT, CHANGE)
            PRINT *, TEXT
            PRINT *, 'MORE EDITING (Y OR N)'
            READ '(A)', RESPON
         GO TO 20
         END IF

         WRITE (16, '(A)') TEXT
         PRINT *
         READ (15, '(A)', IOSTAT = EOF) TEXT
      GO TO 10
      END IF

      CLOSE(15)
      CLOSE(16)
      END

**EDIT**************************************************************************
* Subroutine to edit a line of TEXT by replacing a substring of the    *
* text by another string as specified by the command CHANGE, which has *
* the form                                                             *
*                      oldstring/newstring/                            *
* newstring (which may be empty) replaces the first occurrence of      *
* oldstring in TEXT.  Local identifiers used are:                      *
*     TXTEND : last part of edited text                                *
*     SLASH1 : position of first slash (/) in CHANGE                   *
*     SLASH2 : position of second slash (/) in CHANGE                  *
```

Figure 10.5 *(cont.)*

```
*      OLDSTR : old string -- to be replaced              *
*      OLDLEN : actual length of OLDSTR                   *
*      NEWSTR : new replacement string                   *
*      NEWLEN : actual length of NEWSTR                   *
*      INDOLD : index of old string in TEXT              *
*                                                        *
* Accepts: TEXT, CHANGE                                  *
* Returns: TEXT (modified)                               *
*********************************************************

      SUBROUTINE EDIT(TEXT, CHANGE)

      INTEGER LENGTH, SLASH1, SLASH2, OLDLEN, NEWLEN, INDOLD
      PARAMETER (LENGTH = 80)
      CHARACTER*(LENGTH) TEXT, CHANGE, OLDSTR, NEWSTR, TXTEND

* Attempt to locate slash delimiters in CHANGE
      SLASH1 = INDEX(CHANGE, '/')
      SLASH2 = SLASH1 + INDEX(CHANGE(SLASH1 + 1 : ), '/')
      IF (SLASH1 .EQ. 0 .OR. SLASH2 .EQ. SLASH1) THEN
          PRINT *, 'MISSING SLASH'
          RETURN
      END IF

* Slashes were found, so continue with editing
* First extract OLDSTR and NEWSTR from CHANGE, and locate
* OLDSTR in TEXT

      OLDLEN = SLASH1 - 1
      OLDSTR = CHANGE( : OLDLEN)
      NEWLEN = SLASH2 - SLASH1 - 1
      NEWSTR = CHANGE(SLASH1 + 1: SLASH2 - 1)
      INDOLD = INDEX(TEXT, OLDSTR( : OLDLEN))
```

Figure 10.5 *(cont.)*

```
      IF (INDOLD .GT. 0) THEN
*         Append text following OLDSTR to NEWSTR
          TXTEND = NEWSTR( :NEWLEN) // TEXT(INDOLD + OLDLEN : )

*         Prepend text preceding OLDSTR (if any) to form edited TEXT
          IF (INDOLD .EQ. 1) THEN
              TEXT = TXTEND
          ELSE
              TEXT = TEXT( : INDOLD - 1) // TXTEND
          END IF
      END IF

      END
```

Listing of `FIL10-5.DAT` **used in sample run:**

```
FOURSCORE AND FIVE YEARS AGO, OUR MOTHERS
BROUGHT FORTH ON CONTINENT
A NATION CONCEIVED IN LIBERTY AND AND DEDICATED
TO THE PREPOSITION THAT ALL MEN
ARE CREATED EQUAL.
```

Sample run:

```
ENTER THE NAME OF THE INPUT FILE
FIL10-5.DAT
ENTER THE NAME OF THE OUTPUT FILE
FIL10-5.OUT
FOURSCORE AND FIVE YEARS AGO, OUR MOTHERS
EDIT THIS LINE (Y OR N)?
Y
ENTER EDIT CHANGE
FIVE/SEVEN/
FOURSCORE AND SEVEN YEARS AGO, OUR MOTHERS
MORE EDITING (Y OR N)
Y
ENTER EDIT CHANGE
MO/FA/
FOURSCORE AND SEVEN YEARS AGO, OUR FATHERS
MORE EDITING (Y OR N)
N
```

Figure 10.5 *(cont.)*

```
BROUGHT FORTH ON CONTINENT
EDIT THIS LINE (Y OR N)?
Y
ENTER EDIT CHANGE
ON/ON THIS
MISSING SLASH
BROUGHT FORTH ON CONTINENT
MORE EDITING (Y OR N)
Y
ENTER EDIT CHANGE
ON/ON THIS/
BROUGHT FORTH ON THIS CONTINENT
MORE EDITING (Y OR N)
N

A NATION CONCEIVED IN LIBERTY AND AND DEDICATED
EDIT THIS LINE (Y OR N)?
Y
ENTER EDIT CHANGE
A N/A NEW N/
A NEW NATION CONCEIVED IN LIBERTY AND AND DEDICATED
MORE EDITING (Y OR N)
Y
ENTER EDIT CHANGE
AND //
A NEW NATION CONCEIVED IN LIBERTY AND DEDICATED
MORE EDITING (Y OR N)
N

TO THE PREPOSITION THAT ALL MEN
EDIT THIS LINE (Y OR N)?
Y
ENTER EDIT CHANGE
PRE/PRO/
TO THE PROPOSITION THAT ALL MEN
MORE EDITING (Y OR N)
N

ARE CREATED EQUAL.
EDIT THIS LINE (Y OR N)?
N
```

Figure 10.5 *(cont.)*

Listing of *FIL10-5.OUT* **produced by sample run:**

```
FOURSCORE AND SEVEN YEARS AGO, OUR FATHERS
BROUGHT FORTH ON THIS CONTINENT
A NEW NATION CONCEIVED IN LIBERTY AND DEDICATED
TO THE PROPOSITION THAT ALL MEN
ARE CREATED EQUAL.
```

Character Comparison

In Section 3.1 we stated that character strings are compared using the encoding schemes (such as ASCII and EBCDIC) that represent character information in a computer. Each such encoding scheme assigns a unique integer to each character that the machine can process. These characters can then be arranged in an order in which one character precedes another if its numeric code is less than the numeric code of the other. This ordering of characters based on their numeric codes is called a **collating sequence** and varies from one computer to another. The ANSI FORTRAN 77 standard, however, partially specifies this sequence. It requires that the uppercase letters A through Z and the digits 0 through 9 be ordered in the usual way and that the letters and digits not overlap. The blank character must precede both A and 0 in the ordering. The standard does not, however, specify any particular order for special characters or their relation to other characters.

When characters are compared in a logical expression, this collating sequence is used. Thus,

```
'C' .LT. 'D'
'Z' .GT. 'W'
```

are true logical expressions since C must precede D and Z must follow W in every collating sequence. However, the truth or falsity of the logical expressions

```
'1' .LT. 'A'
'*' .GT. ')'
```

depends on the encoding scheme used in a particular computer. Both logical expressions are true for ASCII but false for EBCDIC.

Similarly, the logical expressions

```
'HCL' .LT. 'NACL'
'CO2' .GT. 'C'
```

are true, since strings are compared character by character using the collating sequence and in the first case, H must precede N, and in the second case, O must follow a blank character. (Recall that strings of different lengths are compared as though the shorter string is blank-padded so that two strings of equal length are compared.) However, the truth or falsity of such logical expressions as

```
'3' .LT. 'B'
'PDQ+123' .GT. 'PDQ*123'
```

depends on the collating sequence used in a particular computer.

The LLT, LLE, LGT, and LGE Functions

The variation in collating sequences may cause the same program to execute differently on different machines. This difficulty can be circumvented, however, by using the special functions LLT, LLE, LGT, and LGE. The LLT function has the form

```
LLT(string₁, string₂)
```

where $string_1$ and $string_2$ are character expressions. The value of this function is true if $string_1$ precedes $string_2$ using the collating sequence *determined by ASCII encoding* and is false otherwise. Thus

```
LLT('1', 'A')
```

is true *regardless* of which collating sequence is in effect.

Similarly,

```
LLE(string₁, string₂)
```

is true if $string_1$ precedes or is equal to $string_2$ using the ASCII collating sequence;

```
LGT(string₁, string₂)
```

is true if $string_1$ follows $string_2$; and

```
LGE(string₁, string₂)
```

is true if $string_1$ follows or is equal to $string_2$ using the ASCII collating sequence.

The ICHAR and CHAR Functions

The position of a character in the collating sequence can be obtained by using the ICHAR function of the form

```
ICHAR(char)
```

where *char* is an expression whose value is a single character. The value of this function is the integer that corresponds to the character's position in the computer's collating sequence.

The inverse function CHAR has the form

```
CHAR(integer)
```

and produces a single character whose position in the collating sequence is the specified integer, provided, of course, that this integer is in the appropriate range. Thus, if X has a single character as its value,

```
CHAR(ICHAR(X))
```

is equal to X, and if K is an integer variable whose value is in the appropriate range,

```
ICHAR(CHAR(K))
```

is equal to K.

Quick Quiz 10.7

1. (True or false) The default length of a character variable is 6 .
2. (True or false) Given the variable declaration CHARACTER*4 COURSE, the statement COURSE = 'MATHEMATICS' assigns COURSE the value 'MATH'.
3. (True or false) If STR is a character variable of length 5, then the assignment STR = 'ABC' assigns the value ' ♭♭ ABC' to STR.
4. (True or false) Given the declaration CHARACTER*6 C1, C2, C3 , the following statements

   ```
   C1 = 'SHELL'
   C2 = 'SEASHORE'
   C3 = C1(2:) // C2(6:6)
   ```

   assign C3 the value 'HELLO'.
5. (True or false) The logical expression 'HUMAN' .GT. 'HELIUM' has the value .TRUE..
6. (True or false) The logical expression 'HUMAN' .GT. 'HUM' has the value .TRUE..
7. (True or false) Character constants must be enclosed in single quotation marks for both list-directed and formatted input.
8. (True or false) The value of INDEX('SHE SELLS SEASHELLS', 'HE') is 2.
9. The value of LLT('A', 'B') is _____ .
10. The value of (CHAR(ICHAR('A'))) .EQ. ('A') is _____ .

For Questions 11–14, assume the following statements:

```
CHARACTER*5 BETA, ANIMAL, ROBOT, R2D2*8, STAR
ROBOT = 'THREE'
STAR = 'WARS'
```

Find the value (if any) assigned to the character variable (indicate each blank with a ƀ).

11. `BETA = 'B'`

12. `ANIMAL = 'KANGAROO'`

13. `R2D2 = ROBOT//'CPO'`

14. `STAR(4:5) = ROBOT(:1)//'S'`

Exercises 10.7

For Exercises 1–17, assume the declarations

```
CHARACTER*10 ALPHA, BETA*5, GAMMA*1, LABEL1*4,
+            LABEL2*3, STR1*3, STR2*4
```

have been made and that `STR1 = 'FOR'`, `STR2 = 'TRAN'`, `LABEL1 = 'FOOT'`, `LABEL2 = 'LBS'`. Find the value assigned to the given variable, or indicate why the statement is not valid.

1. `GAMMA = 123`

2. `GAMMA = '123'`

3. `ALPHA = 'ONE' // 'TWO'`

4. `ALPHA = '1' // '2'`

5. `BETA = 'ANTIDISESTABLISHMENTARIANISM'`

6. `BETA = '1,000,000,000'`

7. `BETA = 'ONE' // 23`

8. `ALPHA = STR1 // STR2 // '-77'`

9. `BETA = STR1 // STR2 // '-77'`

10. `ALPHA = LABEL1 // LABEL2`

11. `GAMMA = LABEL1`

12. `ALPHA = LABEL1 // '-' // LABEL2`

13. `BETA = STR1 // STR2(:1)`

14. `ALPHA = STR2(2:3) // 'NDOM'`

15. `STR2(2:3) = 'UR'`

16. `STR2(:2) = STR2(3:)`
17. `STR1(:2) = STR1(2:)`

For Exercises 18–22, assume that `FIRST`, `LAST`, and `NAME` are character variables with lengths 5, 5, and 14, respectively. Find the value assigned to the specified variable.

18. `FIRST = 'BILL'`
19. `LAST = 'SMITH'`
20. `NAME = 'MR. ' // FIRST // LAST`
21. `NAME = 'THE HONORABLE ' // FIRST // LAST`
22. `NAME = LAST // ', ' // FIRST(1:1)`

For Exercises 23–27, assume that `NAME` is assigned a value by

```
CHARACTER*7 NAME
NAME = 'FORTRAN'
```

Find the value assigned to `NAME`, or indicate why an error occurs.

23. `NAME(4:6) = 'LOR'`
24. `NAME(4: ) = 'EST'`
25. `NAME( :3) = 'FOR'`
26. `NAME(5: ) = NAME( :3)`
27. `NAME(3: ) = NAME( :5)`

For Exercises 28–33, assume the declarations

```
INTEGER N
REAL A
CHARACTER*40 FORM, S1*10, S2*6
```

Show how the data should be entered so that the `READ` statement will assign N, A, S1, and S2 the values 1, 1.1, MODEL-XL11, and CAMERA, respectively.

28. `READ *, N, A, S1, S2`
29. `READ 10, N, A, S1, S2`
    `10 FORMAT (I2, F4.1, 2A)`
30. `READ '(I1, A, F2. A)', N, S1, A, S2`
31. `FORM = '(25X, I3, T1, F5.0, 1X, A, T18, A)'`
    `READ FORM, N, A, S1, S2`
32. `FORM = '(I5, F5.0, 2A15)'`
    `READ FORM, N, A, S1, S2`
33. `READ 20, N, A, S1, S2`
    `20 FORMAT (T9, I1, TL1, F2.1, T1, 2A)`

For each of Exercises 34–36, fill in the blank so the resulting statement(s) will produce the indicated output, or explain why it isn't possible or why an error occurs. Assume that X and Y are real variables with values 2.5341, 3.1619, respectively; Z is an integer variable with value 20; and FORM is a character variable with length 40. *Assume that printer controls are in effect. Note*: ƀ denotes a blank.

34.   PRINT 20, 'Xƀ=', X, 'Yƀ=', Y
        20 FORMAT _____

Output
Xƀ = ƀ2.53ƀƀYƀ = ƀ0.316E+01

35.   FORM = _____
        PRINT FORM, Z, 'CUBEƀOFƀZƀ=ƀ', Z**3

Output
(blank line)
Z'Sƀ VALUEƀISƀ20
CUBEƀOFƀZƀ=ƀ***

36.   PRINT 20, 'F', 'ABCD', 'ABCD', '2', 2
        20 FORMAT _____

Output
ƀƀF
ABCABCDƀƀ22

37. Write a statement to assign the first five characters of the value of the character variable STRING to the character variable SUB.

38. Assume that NAME = 'SMITH, BILL', and that FIRST and LAST are character variables of length 5. Write a statement to extract the first and last names from NAME and then combine them so that the value 'BILL SMITH' is assigned to the variable STRING. (STRING is a character variable of length 10.)

10.8 APPLICATION: DATA SECURITY

Problem

It is often necessary to code information in order to keep it secure, for example, computer passwords, electronic mail, data transmitted when funds are transmitted electronically, and information stored in databases. The string of characters comprising the information is transformed into another string that is an encrypted form of the information, which may be safely stored or transmitted. At a later time it can be decrypted by reversing the encrypting process to recover the original information. The problem considered here is how to encrypt and decrypt information. We will describe several solutions to this problem.

Solution

Caesar Cipher. Data encryption has been used to send secret military and political messages from the days of Julius Caesar to the present. The Caesar cipher scheme consists of replacing each character by the character that appears k positions later in the character set for some integer k. In the original Caesar cipher, k was 3, so that each occurrence of A in the message was replaced by D, each B by E, each C by F, and so on, with "wrap around" at the end of the character set. For example, we would encrypt the string "IDESOFMARCH" as follows:

Original string:	I	D	E	S	O	F	M	A	R	C	H
	↓	↓	↓	↓	↓	↓	↓	↓	↓	↓	↓
Encrypted string:	L	G	H	V	R	I	P	D	U	F	K

The program in Figure 10.6 uses the character functions of the preceding section to implement the Caesar cipher encryption scheme. Its basic approach is to examine each character in the character string, and if it is a *printable* character (i.e., its ASCII value is in the range 32 through 126), then it is shifted KEY positions. This shifting is accomplished by converting each character to its numeric representation (ASCII) using the function ICHAR and then adding the offset KEY to the numeric code of the character. For example, suppose that KEY is 3 and the character being examined is 'A'. The ASCII code of 'A' is 65, and adding 3 gives 68, which is the ASCII code of 'D', the coded value of 'A'.

The shifting is complicated by the wrap around required for values near the end of the character set. For example, suppose that KEY is 10 and the character being examined is 'z', whose ASCII code is 122. If we simply add 10 to 122, we get 132, which is not the ASCII code of a printable character. Instead, the values must wrap around to the beginning of the printable characters,

ASCII Value:	32,	33,	34,	⋯,	115,	116,	117,	118,	⋯,	126
KEY = 10	↓	↓	↓	↓	↓	↓	↓	↓	↓	↓
Shifted Value:	42,	43,	44,	⋯,	125,	126,	32,	33,	⋯,	41

so that the value that is 10 positions from 'z' is 39, the ASCII value of the single-quote character ('). This wrap around can be accomplished by processing a character as follows:

1. Scale the value from the range 32 through 126 into the range 0 through 94 by subtracting 32.

2. Add the offset.

3. Since the resulting value may be outside the range 0 through 94, wrap it around by using the MOD function to find the remainder when the value is divided by 95, the number of printable chars.

4. Scale the resulting value from the range 0 through 94 back into the range 32 through 126 by adding 32.

The statement

```
CODE = MOD((ICHAR(SYMBOL) - 32 + KEY), 95) + 32
```

in the program carries out this translation. The CHAR function is then used to convert this numerical value back to a character:

```
MESS(I:I) = CHAR(CODE)
```

Figure 10.6 Caesar cipher encryption.

```
      PROGRAM CODER
*****************************************************************
* This program encrypts a character string using the Caesar cipher  *
* scheme.  Variables used are the following:                        *
*      STRING  : string to be encrypted                             *
*      KEY     : integer to be added in encrypting the string       *
*      SYMBOL  : an individual character of the string              *
*      CODE    : numeric code for SYMBOL (ASCII is assumed)         *
*      I       : counter                                            *
*                                                                   *
* Input:  STRING and KEY                                            *
* Output: User prompts and STRING (encrypted)                       *
*****************************************************************

      CHARACTER*80 STRING, SYMBOL*1
      INTEGER KEY, CODE, I

* Get the string to be encrypted and the key
      PRINT *, 'ENTER STRING TO BE ENCRYPTED (END WITH !):'
      READ '(A)', STRING
      PRINT *, 'ENTER KEY:'
      READ *, KEY

* Extract the first character in the string
      I = 1
      SYMBOL = STRING(1:1)
```

Figure 10.6 *(cont.)*

```
* While not the end of the string do

10    IF (I .LT. LEN(STRING) .AND. SYMBOL .NE. '!') THEN

*         Encrypt the I-th character of the string
          CODE = MOD((ICHAR(SYMBOL) − 32 + KEY), 95) + 32
          STRING(I:I) = CHAR(CODE)

*         Get the next character in the string
          I = I + 1
          SYMBOL = SYMBOL(I:I)

      GO TO 10
      END IF

* String has now been encrypted -- display it
      PRINT *, 'ENCRYPTED STRING:'
      PRINT *, STRING
      END
```

Sample runs (assuming ASCII):

```
ENTER STRING TO BE ENCRYPTED (END WITH !):
IDESOFMARCH!
ENTER KEY:
3
ENCRYPTED STRING:
LGHVRIPDUFK!

ENTER STRING TO BE ENCRYPTED (END WITH !):
THE REDCOATS ARE COMING!
ENTER KEY:
5
ENCRYPTED STRING:
YMJ%WJIHTFYX%FWJ%HTRNSL!

ENTER STRING TO BE ENCRYPTED (END WITH !):
LGHVRIPDUFK!
ENTER KEY:
−3
ENCRYPTED STRING:
IDESOFMARCH!
```

Note that, as the last sample run demonstrates, the offset KEY may be negative, which permits this program to be used both to encrypt and to decrypt strings. The negative offset KEY = −3 is used to decrypt the string encrypted earlier with an offset of 3:

Cryptogram:	L	G	H	V	R	I	P	D	U	F	K
	↓	↓	↓	↓	↓	↓	↓	↓	↓	↓	↓
Message:	I	D	E	S	O	F	M	A	R	C	H

Vignère Cipher. The Caesar cipher is obviously not a very secure scheme, since it is easy to "break the code" by simply trying the 26 possible values for the key k. An improved substitution operation is to use a *keyword* to specify several different displacements of letters rather than the single offset k of the Caesar cipher. In this **Vignère cipher** scheme, a keyword is added character by character to the string, where each letter is represented by its position in the character set and wrap around occurs as with the Caesar cipher scheme. For example, if the positions of A, B, C, . . . , Z are given by 0, 1, 2, . . . , 25, respectively, and the keyword is DAGGER, the string "IDESOF-MARCH" is encrypted as follows:

Original string:	I	D	E	S	O	F	M	A	R	C	H
	↓	↓	↓	↓	↓	↓	↓	↓	↓	↓	↓
Repeated keyword:	D	A	G	G	E	R	D	A	G	G	E
	↓	↓	↓	↓	↓	↓	↓	↓	↓	↓	↓
Encrypted string:	L	D	K	Y	S	W	P	A	X	I	L

The original string can be recovered by subtracting the characters in this keyword from those in the encrypted string.

Substitution Tables. A different encryption method is to use a **substitution table**, for example:

Original string:	A	B	C	D	E	F	G	H	I	J	K	L	M
Substitute string:	Q	W	E	R	T	Y	U	I	O	P	A	S	D

	N	O	P	Q	R	S	T	U	V	W	X	Y	Z
	F	G	H	J	K	L	Z	X	C	V	B	N	M

The string "IDESOFMARCH" would then be encrypted using this substitution table as follows:

Original string:	I	D	E	S	O	F	M	A	R	C	H
	↓	↓	↓	↓	↓	↓	↓	↓	↓	↓	↓
Encrypted string:	O	R	T	L	G	Y	D	Q	K	E	I

To decrypt, one simply uses the substitution table in reverse.

Since there are 95! (approximately 10^{148}) possible substitution tables, this scheme is considerably more secure than the simple Caesar cipher scheme. Experienced cryptographers can easily break the code, however, by analyzing frequency counts of certain letters and combinations of letters.

Permutation Operations. Another basic operation in some encryption schemes is **permutation**, in which characters or blocks of characters are rearranged. For example, we might divide a string into blocks (substrings) of size 3 and permute the characters in each block as follows:

Original position:	1	2	3
Permuted position:	3	1	2

Thus the string "IDESOFMARCH" would be encrypted (after the addition of a randomly selected character X so that the string length is a multiple of the block length) as

Original string: I D E S O F M A R C H X

Encrypted string: D E I O F S A R M H X C

To decrypt a string, one must know the key permutation and its inverse:

Original position:	1	2	3
Permuted position:	2	3	1

DES. Many modern encryption schemes combine several substitution and permutation operations. Perhaps the best known is the **Data Encryption Standard (DES)** developed in the early 1970s by researchers at the IBM Corporation. The scheme is described in *Federal Information Processing Standards Publication* 46 (FIPS Pub 46).[3] It consists essentially of a permutation followed by a sequence of 16 substitutions and a final permutation. The substitution operations are similar to those in earlier examples. Some are obtained by the addition of keywords (16 different ones), and others use substitution tables.

DES was adopted in 1977 by the National Institute of Standards and Technology (formerly the National Bureau of Standards) as the standard encryption scheme for sensitive federal documents. It has been the subject of some controversy, however, because of questions about its security. In fact, two Israeli scientists, E. Biham and A. Shamir (one of the developers of the popular public key encrpytion scheme described later) recently announced a mathematical technique that makes it possible to break the DES code under certain circumstances.

Public Key Encryption. Each of the preceding encryption schemes requires that both the sender and the receiver know the encryption key or keys. This means that although an encrypted message may be transmitted through some public channel such as

---

[3] Copies of this publication can be obtained from the National Institute of Standards and Technology of the U.S. Department of Commerce.

a telephone line that is not secure, the keys must be transmitted in some secure manner, for example, by a courier. This problem of maintaining secrecy of the key is compounded when it must be shared by several persons.

Some encryption schemes eliminate this problem by using two keys, one for encryption and one for decryption. These schemes are called **public key encryption schemes** because the encryption key is made public by the receiver to all those who will transmit messages to him or her; the decryption key, however, is known only to the receiver. The security of these schemes depends on it being nearly impossible to determine the decryption key if one knows only the encryption key.

In 1978, R. L. Rivest, A. Shamir, and L. Adelman proposed one method of implementing a public key encryption scheme.[4] The public key is a pair (e, n) of integers, and one encrypts a message string M by first dividing M into blocks $M_1, M_2, \ldots, M_k$ and converting each block M_i of characters to an integer P_i in the range 0 through $n - 1$ (for example, by concatenating the ASCII codes of the characters). M is then encrypted by raising each block to the power e and reducing modulo n:

$$\text{Message:} \quad M = M_1 M_2 \cdots M_k \rightarrow P_1 P_2 \cdots P_k$$
$$\text{Cryptogram:} \quad C = C_1 C_2 \cdots C_k, \ C_i = P_i^e \text{ modulo } n$$

(Here x modulo n is the remainder when x is divided by n.) The cryptogram C is decrypted by raising each block C_i to the power d and reducing modulo n, where d is a secret decryption key.

To illustrate, suppose that characters are converted to numeric values using the codes $0, 1, 2, \ldots, 25$ for the letters A, B, C, . . . , Z, respectively, and that $(17, 2773)$ is the public encryption key. To encrypt the string $M =$ "IDESOFMARCH" using the RSA (Rivest-Shamir-Adelman) algorithm, we divide M into two-character blocks M_1, $M_2, \ldots, M_6$ (after appending a randomly selected character X) and represent each block M_i as an integer P_i in the range 0 through $2773 - 1 = 2772$ by concatenating the numeric codes of the characters that comprise the block:

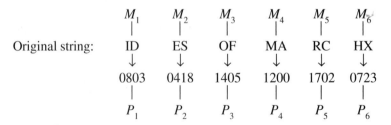

Each of these blocks P_i is then encrypted by calculating $C_i = P_i^{17}$ modulo 2773:

	Encrypted codes:	0779	1983	2641	1444	0052	0802
		C_1	C_2	C_3	C_4	C_5	C_6

[4] R. L. Rivest, A. Shamir, and L. Adelman, "A Method for Obtaining Digital Signatures and Public-Key Cryptosystems," *Communications of the ACM*, February 1978, pp. 120–126.

For this encryption key, the corresponding decrypting key is $d = 157$. Thus, we decrypt by calculating C_i^{157} modulo 2773 for each block C_i. For the preceding encrypted string this gives

Decrypted codes: 0803   0418   1405   1200   1702   0723

which is the numeric form of the original string.

The number n is the product of two large "random" primes p and q,

$$n = p \cdot q$$

In the preceding example, we used the small primes 47 and 59 to simplify the computations, but Rivest, Shamir, and Adelman suggest that p and q have several hundred digits. The decrypting key d is then selected to be some large integer that is relatively prime to both $p - 1$ and $q - 1$; that is, one that has no factors in common with either number. In our example, $d = 157$ has this property. The number e is then selected to have the property that

$$e \cdot d \text{ modulo } ((p - 1) \cdot (q - 1)) \text{ is equal to } 1$$

To break this code, one must be able to determine the value of d from the values of n and e. Because of the manner in which d and e are selected, this is possible if n can be factored into a product of primes. Thus, the security of the RSA encryption scheme is based on the difficulty of determining the prime factors of a large integer. Even with the best factorization algorithms known today, this is a prohibitively time-consuming task. A study a few years ago gave the following table displaying some estimated times, assuming that each operation required one microsecond:

Number of Digits in Number Being Factored	Time
50	4 hours
75	104 days
100	74 years
200	4 billion years
300	5×10^{15} years
500	4×10^{25} years

Although research on factorization continues, no efficient algorithms have been found that significantly reduce the times in the preceding table. Improved algorithms and the use of high-speed computers have made factorization possible in less time than the table shows, but not significantly less for large numbers. This public key encryption scheme thus appears (so far) to be quite secure and is being endorsed by a growing number of major computer vendors; and the adoption of a public key encryption standard is being considered by the National Institute of Standards and Technology.

Exercises 10.8

1. A pure permutation encryption scheme is very insecure. Explain why by describing how an encryption scheme that merely permutes the bits in an n-bit string can easily be cracked by studying how certain basic bit strings are encrypted. Show this for $n = 4$.

For Exercises 2–7, use the character codes 0, 1, . . . , 25 given in the text.

2. Encrypt the string "PUBLIC" using the Caesar cipher scheme with key = 3.

3. Encrypt the string "PUBLIC" using the Vignère cipher scheme with keyword "AND".

4. Encrypt the string "PUBLIC" using the substitution table given in the text.

5. Encrypt the string "PUBLIC" using the permutation given in the text:

Original position: 1   2   3

Permuted position: 3   1   2

6. Encrypt the string "PUBLIC" using the RSA scheme with encryption key $(e, n) = (5, 2881)$.

7. One decrypting key for the RSA scheme in Exercise 6 is $d = 1109$. Use it to decrypt the codes obtained in Exercise 6.

10.9 APPLICATION: COMPUTER GRAPHICS

The number and quality of software packages and even hand-held calculators that can be used to generate high-resolution graphs of functions is increasing rapidly. For example, Figure 10.7 a shows the graph of $y = x * \cos(x)$ for $-8 \leq x \leq 8$ as plotted on a Texas Instruments TI-85 calculator, and Figure 10.7 b shows the same graph as produced by the powerful software package Mathematica™.

The window containing each of the plots shown in Figure 10.7 is simply a two-dimensional array of points (called *pixels*) on the screen, some of which (those corresponding to points on the graph of the function) are "on" (black) and the rest of which are "off" (white). Figure 10.8 shows an enlarged view of the portion of the graphics window near the origin in Figure 10.7; the grid structure of this part of the window is evident.

Figure 10.7

(a) Plot of $y = x * \cos(x)$ on a Texas Instruments TI-85 calculator (Photo by Randal Nyhof, Nyhof School Pictures).
(b) Plot of $y = x * \cos(x)$ produced by Mathematica.

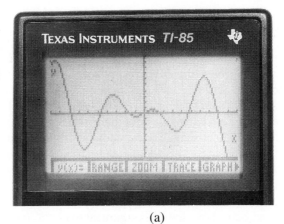

(a)

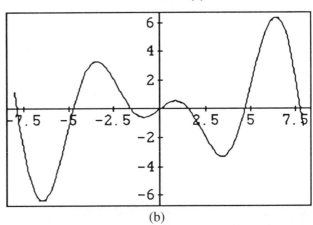

(b)

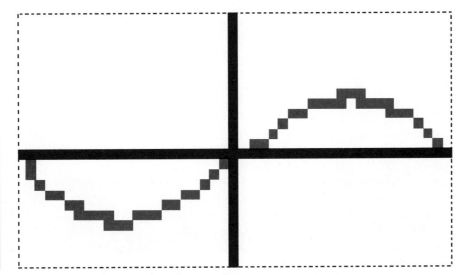

Blow-up of graphics window.

Figure 10.8

Blow-up of graphics window.

Example 1: Scatter Plots

The subroutine PLOT in the program of Figure 10.9 uses this same approach to produce a **scatter plot** of a collection of data points. For example, Figure 10.10 shows a scatter plot of cutting times (in minutes) using an oxyacetylene torch versus metal thicknesses (in inches—see Exercise 3 of Section 4.8). A listing of a file containing these (thickness, time) pairs is given in Figure 10.9. Such plots are used in exploratory data analysis. For example, as in Figure 10.10, they might suggest that the data points are clustered about some line (or about some other curve). The least-squares method described in Section 4.8 could then be used to find the equation of the line that best fits these data points, and this equation could then be used to predict cutting times for other metal thicknesses.

Subroutine PLOT in Figure 10.9 produces a scatter plot of data points stored in a file whose name is passed as an argument to PLOT. It uses a VLIMIT $\times$ HLIMIT character array WINDOW, each element of which is a single character corresponding to a point in a graphics window. The first line of the data file contains values for XMIN and XMAX, the minimum and maximum X values, and for YMIN and YMAX, the minimum and maximum Y values. The rows of the two-dimensional array WINDOW correspond to X values ranging from XMIN to XMAX in increments of DELX = (XMAX − XMIN) / HLIMIT, and the rows correspond to Y values ranging from YMIN to YMAX in steps of DELY = (YMAX − YMIN, / VERT. For each X value, the Y value nearest the actual Y data value is determined, and the point WINDOW(X, Y) is set to some plotting character such as '*' ("on"); all other elements of WINDOW are blank ("off").

A Hewlett Packard Deskjet 600 Plotter.

Figure 10.9 Scatter plot.

```
      PROGRAM SPLOT
*****************************************************************
* Program to produce a scatter plot of a data set stored in a file.  *
* The name of the file is passed to subroutine PLOT.  Identifiers     *
* used are:                                                           *
*     FNAME : name of file containing data set to be plotted          *
*     PLOT  : subroutine called to produce scatter plot               *
*                                                                     *
* Input:  FNAME                                                       *
* Output: User prompts and the scatter plot                           *
*****************************************************************

      CHARACTER*20 FNAME

      PRINT *, 'THIS PROGRAM PRODUCES A SCATTER PLOT OF DATA POINTS'
      PRINT *, 'STORED IN A DATA FILE. THE FIRST LINE OF THIS FILE'
      PRINT *, 'MUST CONTAIN THE MINIMUM AND MAXIMUM X VALUES AND'
      PRINT *, 'THE MINIMUM AND MAXIMUM Y VALUES, IN THIS ORDER.'
      PRINT *
      PRINT *, 'ENTER THE NAME OF THE DATA FILE:'
      READ '(A)', FNAME
      CALL PLOT(FNAME)

      END


**PLOT***********************************************************
* Subroutine to produce a scatter plot of data points stored in a file,*
* the first line of which contains values for XMIN, XMAX, YMIN, and    *
* YMAX, in this order. Local identifiers used are:                     *
*     FNAME  : name of file containing the data points                 *
*     HLIMIT,                                                          *
*     VLIMIT : parameters: limits on the size of the graphics WINDOW   *
*     WINDOW : two-dimensional character array -- the graphics window  *
*     SYMBOL : plotting character -- represents a point on the graph   *
*     XMIN, XMAX : minimum and maximum X values                        *
*     YMIN, YMAX : minimum and maximum Y values                        *
*     DELX, DELY : X and Y increments                                  *
```

Figure 10.9 *(cont.)*

```
*      X, Y   : a point on the graph                              *
*      XLOC, YLOC : location of a point in the window             *
*      COUNT  : counts units on Y-axis for labeling purposes      *
*      EOF    : end-of-file indicator                             *
*                                                                 *
* Accepts:          FNAME                                         *
* Output (screen):  The graphics WINDOW                           *
*******************************************************************

       SUBROUTINE PLOT(FNAME)

       CHARACTER*(*) FNAME
       REAL XMIN, XMAX, YMIN, YMAX, DELX, DELY, X, Y
       INTEGER HLIMIT, VLIMIT, XLOC, YLOC, EOF, COUNT
       PARAMETER (HLIMIT = 65, VLIMIT = 20)
       CHARACTER*1 WINDOW(0: HLIMIT, 0:VLIMIT), SYMBOL
       PARAMETER (SYMBOL = '*')

       OPEN (UNIT = 20, FILE = FNAME, STATUS = 'OLD')

       READ (20, *) XMIN, XMAX, YMIN, YMAX
       DELX = (XMAX - XMIN) / REAL(HLIMIT)
       DELY = (YMAX - YMIN) / REAL(VLIMIT)

       DO 20 YLOC = 0, VLIMIT
           DO 10 XLOC = 0, HLIMIT
               WINDOW(XLOC, YLOC) = ' '
10         CONTINUE
20     CONTINUE

* Read data pairs and turn on points in WINDOW corresponding to pairs

       READ (20, *, IOSTAT = EOF) X, Y
30     IF (EOF .GE. 0) THEN
           XLOC = NINT((X - XMIN)/ DELX)
           YLOC = NINT((Y - YMIN)/ DELY)
           WINDOW(XLOC, YLOC) = SYMBOL
           READ (20, *, IOSTAT = EOF) X, Y
       GO TO 30
       END IF
```

Figure 10.9 *(cont.)*

```
* Draw the WINDOW together with labeled Y-axis

        Y = YMAX
        COUNT = 5 * (VLIMIT / 5)
        DO 40 YLOC = VLIMIT, 0, -1
            IF (MOD(COUNT, 5) .EQ. 0) THEN
                PRINT 100, Y, (WINDOW(XLOC,YLOC), XLOC = 0, HLIMIT)
100             FORMAT(1X, F8.2, ':', 200A)
            ELSE
                PRINT 101, (WINDOW(XLOC,YLOC), XLOC = 0, HLIMIT)
101             FORMAT(9X, ':', 200A)
            END IF
            COUNT = COUNT - 1
            Y = Y - DELY
40      CONTINUE


* Draw a labeled X-axis

        PRINT 102, ('.', XLOC = 0, HLIMIT)
102     FORMAT(9X, 200A)
        PRINT 103, (XMIN + XLOC*DELX, XLOC = 0, HLIMIT, 10)
103     FORMAT(3X, 50F10.3)

        END
```

Listing of file `FIL10-9.DAT` **that produced Figure 10.10:**

```
0.25, 5.0, 0.030, 0.102
0.25   0.036
0.5    0.039
0.375  0.037
3.5    0.078
2.0    0.058
1.0    0.046
5.0    0.102
0.75   0.042
1.25   0.050
4.5    0.093
1.5    0.053
3.0    0.073
```

Figure 10.9 *(cont.)*

```
2.5    0.065
4.0    0.085
0.5    0.044
1.25   0.044
3.5    0.084
0.5    0.030
```

```
0.10:
     :
     :
     :                                                                    *
     :                                                          *         *
0.08:                                                           *
     :
     :
     :                                              *
     :
0.07:                                       *
     :
     :                                *
     :                         *
     :                      *
0.05:                  *
     :      *    *         *
     :      *
     : * *
     :    *
0.03:
     . . . . . . . . . . . . . . . . . . . . . . . . . . . . . . . . . . . . . . . . . . .
     0.250        0.929      1.607       2.286       2.964       3.643       4.321       5.000
```

Figure 10.10

Scatter plot produced by program in Figure 10.9

Example 2: Density Plots and Level Curves

In the introduction to this section and in Example 1 we described how two-dimensional graphs of functions $y = f(x)$ of a single variable x and scatter plots of data sets can be displayed. Graphs of functions $z = f(x, y)$ of two variables x and y are surfaces in three dimensions and are considerably more difficult to display on a two-dimensional screen. Some software packages are able to generate good two-dimensional representations of many three-dimensional surfaces. For example, Figure 10.11 shows a graph produced by Mathematica of the surface defined by the function

$$z = e^{-(x^2 + y^2)}$$

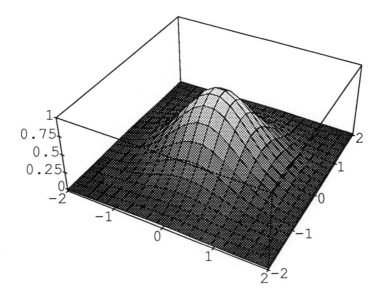

Figure 10.11

Mathematica plot of $z = e^{-(x^2 + y^2)}$.

Note that in this representation, shading is used to represent the height of the function, with lighter shades for larger values and darker shades for smaller values. This shading, together with the curved grid lines and the enclosing box, produces a visual illusion of a three-dimensional surface. Another representation of a surface that also uses shading but not perspective is a **density plot** obtained by projecting a representation like that in Figure 10.11 onto a plane. Figure 10.12 shows the density plot generated by Mathematica for this surface. The various densities of gray again indicate different heights of the function.

The program in Figure 10.13 produces a density plot for a function F. It uses a character array WINDOW of 10 different characters, with WINDOW(X, Y) representing the height of the function at point (X, Y). The order of the characters in the DATA statement

Figure 10.12

Density plot of
$$z = e^{-(x^2 + y^2)}$$
in
Mathematica.

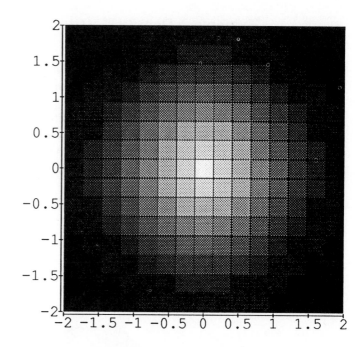

corresponds to increasing Z values, beginning with ZMIN, the minimum Z value. The sample run shows the output produced for the function $f(x, y) = e^{-(x^2+y^2)}$ with ZMIN = 0 and ZMAX = 1, using the characters '0', '1', . . . , '9'.

Figure 10.13 Density plot.

```
     PROGRAM DENSTY
*****************************************************************************
* Program to produce a density plot of a function Z = F(X, Y). F is       *
* defined by a function subprogram and is passed to subroutine DNPLOT.    *
* Identifiers used are:                                                    *
*      F            : function to be plotted                               *
*      XMIN, XMAX : minimum and maximum X values                           *
*      YMIN, YMAX : minimum and maximum Y values                           *
*      ZMIN, ZMAX : minimum and maximum Z values                           *
*                                                                          *
* Input:   XMIN, XMAX, YMIN, YMAX                                          *
* Output: User prompts and plot of Z = F(X, Y)                            *
*****************************************************************************
```

Figure 10.13 *(cont.)*

```
      REAL F, XMIN, XMAX, YMIN, YMAX, ZMIN, ZMAX
      EXTERNAL F

      PRINT *, 'ENTER MINIMUM AND MAXIMUM X VALUES, THEN Y VALUES'
      READ *, XMIN, XMAX, YMIN, YMAX
      PRINT *, 'ENTER MINIMUM AND MAXIMUM VALUES OF FUNCTION'
      READ *, ZMIN, ZMAX
      CALL DNPLOT(F, XMIN, XMAX, YMIN, YMAX, ZMIN, ZMAX)

      END


**F*******************************************************************
*                 Function whose graph is to be plotted            *
*********************************************************************


      FUNCTION F(X,Y)

      REAL F, X, Y

      F = EXP(-(X**2 + Y**2))
      END


**DNPLOT************************************************************
* Subroutine to generate a density plot of a function Z = F(X, Y) for *
* X ranging from XMIN to XMAX and Y ranging from YMIN to YMAX; Z is    *
* allowed to range from ZMIN to ZMAX.  Local identifiers used are:     *
*      FNAME  : name of file containing the output                    *
*      HLIMIT,                                                         *
*      VLIMIT : parameters: limits on the size of the graphics WINDOW *
*      WINDOW : two-dimensional character array -- the graphics window *
*      LGRAY  : parameter: largest index in array GRAY                *
*      GRAY   : array of symbols representing shades of gray          *
*      DELX   : X increment                                           *
*      DELY   : Y increment                                           *
*      DELZ   : Z increment                                           *
*      X, Y, Z: a point on the graph                                  *
*      XLOC,                                                          *
*      YLOC   : location of a point in the window                    *
*      ZSHADE : shade of gray used to represent height Z             *
```

Figure 10.13 *(cont.)*

```
*                                                                         *
* Accepts:          F, XMIN, XMAX, YMIN, YMAX, ZMIN, ZMAX                 *
* Input (keyboard): FNAME                                                 *
* Output (screen):  User prompt                                           *
* Output (file):    The graphics WINDOW                                   *
***************************************************************************

       SUBROUTINE DNPLOT (F, XMIN, XMAX, YMIN, YMAX, ZMIN, ZMAX)

       REAL F, XMIN, XMAX, YMIN, YMAX, ZMIN, ZMAX, DELX, DELY, DELZ
       INTEGER HLIMIT, VLIMIT, XLOC, YLOC, LGRAY, ZSHADE
       PARAMETER (HLIMIT = 75, VLIMIT = 45, LGRAY = 9)
       CHARACTER*1 WINDOW(0:HLIMIT, 0:VLIMIT), GRAY(0:LGRAY), FNAME*20

*   Initialize array of characters to indicate "densities of gray"
*   that in turn represent heights of function F

       DATA GRAY /'0','1','2','3','4','5','6','7','8','9'/


       PRINT *, 'ENTER NAME OF FILE TO CONTAIN THE DENSITY PLOT'
       READ '(A)', FNAME
       OPEN (UNIT = 20, FILE = FNAME, STATUS = 'NEW')

       DELX = (XMAX - XMIN) / REAL(HLIMIT)
       DELY = (YMAX - YMIN) / REAL(VLIMIT)
       DELZ = (ZMAX - ZMIN) / REAL(LGRAY)

* "Shade" each element of WINDOW with appropriate gray

       Y = YMIN
       DO 20 YLOC = 0, VLIMIT
          X = XMIN
          DO 10 XLOC = 0, HLIMIT
             Z = F(X, Y)
```

Figure 10.13 *(cont.)*

```
*               Find gray shade corresponding to Z value

                IF (Z .GE. ZMAX) THEN
                    ZSHADE = LGRAYS
                ELSE
                    ZSHADE = NINT((Z - ZMIN) / DELZ)
                END IF

                WINDOW(XLOC, YLOC) = GRAY(ZSHADE)
                X = X + DELX
10         CONTINUE

           Y = Y + DELY
20      CONTINUE

* Draw the WINDOW in the file

        DO 30 YLOC = VLIMIT, 0, -1
            WRITE(20, *)(WINDOW(XLOC,YLOC), XLOC = 0, HLIMIT)
30      CONTINUE

        END
```

Sample run:

```
ENTER MINIMUM AND MAXIMUM X VALUES, THEN Y VALUES
-2 2 -2 2
ENTER MINIMUM AND MAXIMUM VALUES OF FUNCTION
0 1
ENTER NAME OF FILE TO CONTAIN THE DENSITY PLOT
FIL10-13.OUT
```

Figure 10.13 *(cont.)*

Listing of `FIL10-13.OUT` (reduced:)

```
000000000000000000000000000000000000000000000000000000000000000000000000000
000000000000000000000000000000000000000000000000000000000000000000000000000
000000000000000000000000000000000000000000000000000000000000000000000000000
000000000000000000000000000011111111111111111111100000000000000000000000000
000000000000000000000000011111111111111111111111111111000000000000000000000
000000000000000000000001111111111111111111111111111111110000000000000000000
000000000000000000011111111111111222222222221111111111111110000000000000000
000000000000000001111111111112222222222222222222211111111111100000000000000
000000000000001111111111222222222333333333332222222221111111111000000000000
000000000001111111112222222333333333333333333332222222211111111110000000000
000000000011111112222223333333444444444444443333332222222111111110000000000
00000000011111112222233333444444455555555444444333332222221111111100000000
0000000001111111222233334444455555556665555555544444333322221111111110000000
00000000111111122223333444555566666666666666655554443333222211111111000000
000000011111112222333444556666777777777666655554444333222211111110000000
0000000111111122223334445556667777788888777766655544433322221111111100000000
00000011111112222333445556667778888888888887776665554433322221111111100000000
00000011111112222333445556677788888999988887776665544433322221111111000000
00000011111112222333444556677788889999999988887776655444333222211111110000000
00000011111112222333444556677788889999999988887776655444333222211111110000000
00000011111112222333444556677788889999999988887776655444333222211111110000000
00000011111112222333444556667778888899998888777666554443332222111111110000000
0000001111111222233344455666777888888888888777666555444333222211111110000000
00000011111112222333445556667777888887777766655544433322221111111100000000
000000011111112222333444555666667777776666655554444333222211111110000000
00000001111111222233334444555566666666666666655554443333222211111111000000
0000000011111112222333344444555555566655555555544444333322221111111110000000
00000000011111112222233333444444455555555444444333332222221111111100000000
000000000011111112222223333333444444444444443333332222222111111110000000000
000000000001111111112222222333333333333333333332222222211111111110000000000
000000000000001111111111222222222333333333332222222221111111111000000000000
000000000000000001111111111112222222222222222222211111111111100000000000000
000000000000000000011111111111111222222222221111111111111110000000000000000
000000000000000000000001111111111111111111111111111111110000000000000000000
000000000000000000000000011111111111111111111111111111000000000000000000000
000000000000000000000000000011111111111111111111100000000000000000000000000
000000000000000000000000000000000000000000000000000000000000000000000000000
000000000000000000000000000000000000000000000000000000000000000000000000000
000000000000000000000000000000000000000000000000000000000000000000000000000
000000000000000000000000000000000000000000000000000000000000000000000000000
```

Characters other than '0', '1', . . . , '9' can be used simply by changing the DATA statement in this program. For example, if "gray-scale characters" were available, a density plot similar to that in Figure 10.12 could be generated. Figure 10.14 shows the result obtained when ordinary characters such as '#', '@', and '+' are used to achieve various densities and the output is reduced still more than that in Figure 10.14.

Another common two-dimensional representation of a three-dimensional surface $z = f(x, y)$ is obtained by displaying its **level curves** or **contour maps**. A level curve consists of all points (x, y) where the function has a particular constant value. For example, if $f(x, y)$ represents the temperature at point (x, y), the level curve $f(x, y) = 30$ is an isothermal curve consisting of all points where the temperature is 30.

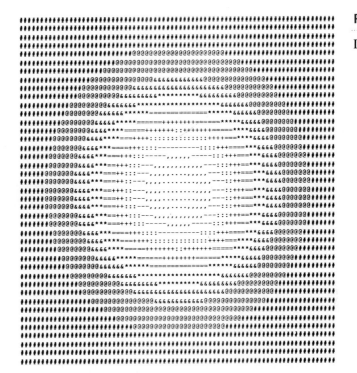

Figure 10.14

Density plot of $e^{-(x^2+y^2)}$.

The level curves for $f(x, y) = e^{-(x^2+y^2)}$ can be seen in the density plots produced by the program in Figure 10.13 as the circles that separate one level from another. Figure 10.15 shows the level curves for this function as produced by Mathematica. The largest

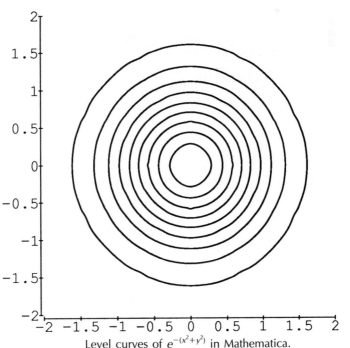

Figure 10.15

Level curves of $e^{-(x^2+y^2)}$ in Mathematica.

Level curves of $e^{-(x^2+y^2)}$ in Mathematica.

circle is the level curve $e^{-(x^2+y^2)} = 0.1$, or equivalently $x^2 + y^2 = |\ln(0.1)|$; the smallest circle is the level curve $e^{-(x^2+y^2)} = 0.9$, which can also be written $x^2 + y^2 = |\ln(0.9)|$; the other circles are level curves corresponding to $0.8, 0.7, \ldots, 0.2$.

The ideas in this example can be modified to display an image that is represented in digitized form and then enhance this image. This digitized representation might be a table of light intensities transmitted from a remote sensor such as a television camera in a satellite. This problem of visual image processing and enhancement is described in the exercises.

CHAPTER REVIEW

Summary

In this chapter we considered the DOUBLE PRECISION and COMPLEX data types and extended the discussion of the CHARACTER data type begun in Chapter 3. We described double-precision constants, declarations of double-precision variables, input/output of double-precision values, and several double-precision library functions. We illustrated how double precision may be helpful in solving ill-conditioned linear systems. We described complex numbers, variables, and operations, input/output of complex values, and several complex library functions. We used the COMPLEX data type in a program for analyzing an ac circuit. We reviewed character constants and variables and character input/output. We also described the concatenation and substring operations, the INDEX and LEN functions, functions for comparing characters, and the CHAR and ICHAR functions. Applications using these character-processing features included text processing, lexical analysis, cryptography, and computer graphics.

FORTRAN SUMMARY

Type Statements

```
DOUBLE PRECISION list-of-variable-names
COMPLEX list-of-variable-names
CHARACTER*n list-of-variable-names
```

Examples:

```
DOUBLE PRECISION Z, BETA(5,5)
COMPLEX A, RHO(10,10)
CHARACTER *10 FNAME, LNAME, INIT*1
```

Purpose:
Type statements declare the type of values that variables will have.

Operations

Concatenation: *char-expression₁* // *char-expression₂*

Examples:
Given the declarations and assignment

```
CHARACTER*7 SQUNIT
SQUNIT = 'SQUARE '
```

the expression

```
SQUNIT // 'CENTI' // 'METERS'
```

produces the string

```
'SQUARE CENTIMETERS'
```

Substring: *char-variable(init-position : final-position)*

Examples:
Given the declarations and assignment

```
CHARACTER*12 UNITS
UNITS = 'CENTIMETERS'
```

the values of

```
UNITS(:4), UNITS(4:7), and UNITS(6:)
```

are

```
'CENT', 'TIME', and 'METERS'
```

respectively.

Functions

Function	Description
DBLE(x)	Transforms x to double-precision form
DPROD(x, y)	Double-precision product of x and y
REAL(x)	Converts x to single precision
AIMAG(z)	Imaginary part of z

Function	Description
`REAL(z)`	Real part of z
`CMPLX(x, y)`	Converts x, y into a complex number
`CMPLX(x)`	Converts x into a complex number
`CONJG(z)`	Conjugate of z
`INDEX(s_1, s_2)`	Index of string s_2 in string s_1
`LEN(s)`	Length of string s
`LLT(s_1, s_2)`	Determines if string $s_1 <$ string s_2 (in ASCII)
`LLE(s_1, s_2)`	Determines if string $s_1 \leq s_2$ (in ASCII)
`LGT(s_1, s_2)`	Determines if string $s_1 >$ string s_2 (in ASCII)
`LGE(s_1, s_2)`	Determines if string $s_1 \geq$ string s_2 (in ASCII)
`ICHAR(c)`	Numeric code of c
`CHAR(i)`	Character whose numeric code is i

PROGRAMMING POINTERS

Program Style and Design

1. *The* REAL *data type provides approximately seven significant digits. The* DOUBLE PRECISION *data type should be used for computations that require extended precision.*

2. *The* COMPLEX *data type should be used for computations that require complex numbers and operations.*

3. *Formatted output of complex values requires two real descriptors.*

4. *For formatted input of complex data, complex values are not enclosed in parentheses.*

5. *For formatted input of character data, string values are not enclosed in quotes.*

Potential Problems

1. *Precision may be lost in double-precision expressions and assignments because of the presence of single-precision constants and/or variables.*

   To illustrate, consider the declarations

   ```
   REAL X
   DOUBLE PRECISION A, B
   ```

   In the assignment statement

   ```
   B = 0.1 * A ** 2
   ```

precision may be lost because of the single-precision constant 0.1. This statement should be written as

```
B = 0.1D0 * A ** 2
```

Similarly, in the assignment statement

```
X = (A + B) * (A - B)
```

the expression on the right side is evaluated in double precision, but the resulting value is then assigned to the single-precision variable X. Remember, however, that simply declaring everything to be double precision does not solve all of the problems arising from limited precision. For example, the logical expression

```
A * (1.0D0 / A) .EQ. 1.0D0
```

is still false for most double-precision values of A.

2. *Double-precision and complex values may not both be used in an expression, nor may a double-precision (complex) value be assigned to a complex (double-precision) variable.*

3. *A pair of real constants representing a complex data value is enclosed in parentheses for list-directed input but not for formatted input.*

4. *Formatted output of complex values requires two real descriptors.*

5. *Complex values may be compared only with the relational operators .EQ. and .NE..*

The character data type was introduced in earlier chapters and was described in more detail in this chapter. Some of the following programming pointers are summaries of earlier programming pointers, and the reader should refer to those for an expanded discussion.

6. *The first position specified in a substring reference should be no greater than the last position; also, both positions should be positive and no greater than the length of the string.* For a substring consisting of the leftmost characters of a string, the position need not be specified. Thus, if STRING is declared by

```
CHARACTER*10 STRING
```

then the substring reference

```
STRING( :4)
```

is equivalent to

```
STRING(1:4)
```

Similarly, for a substring consisting of the rightmost characters, the last position need not be specified. Thus,

```
STRING(6: )
```

is equivalent to

```
STRING(6:10)
```

7. *In an assignment to a substring, the value being assigned may not be a character expression that references any of the same positions to which values are being assigned.* Thus, for the character variable declared by

```
CHARACTER*10 STRING
```

the following assignment statement is not allowed:

```
STRING(3:7) = STRING(6:10)
```

8. *The collating sequence used to compare characters depends on the numeric codes used to represent characters.* For example,

```
'123' .LT. 'A23'
```

is true if ASCII coding is used, but it is false for EBCDIC.

9. *Character constants must be enclosed in single quotation marks for list-directed input but not for formatted input.*

10. *In assignment statements and in list-directed input, if the value being assigned or read has a length greater than that specified for the character variable (or substring), the rightmost characters are truncated. If the value has a length less than that of the variable (or substring), blanks are added at the right.* An acronym sometimes used to remember this is

   - **APT:** for **A**ssignment (and list-directed input), blank **P**adding and **T**runcation both occur on the right.

   See Potential Problem 13 in the Programming Pointers section of Chapter 2 for more details.

11. *For formatted input/output, characters are truncated or blanks are added according to whether the field width is too small or too large. For input, truncation occurs on the left and blank padding on the right; for output, truncation occurs on the right and blank padding on the left.* The acronyms similar to that in Potential Problem 10 are

   - **POT:** **P**adding on the left with blanks occurs for formatted **O**utput, or **T**runcation of rightmost characters occurs.

   - **TIP:** **T**runcation of leftmost characters occurs for formatted **I**nput, or **P**adding with blanks on the right occurs.

See Potential Problem 3 in the Programming Pointers section of Chapter 5 for more details.

PROGRAMMING PROBLEMS

Sections 10.1 and 10.2

1. For the sequence of numbers $a_0, a_1, a_2, \ldots$ defined by

$$a_0 = e^1 - 1$$

and

$$a_{n+1} = (n + 1)a_n - 1 \qquad \text{for } n = 0, 1, 2, \ldots$$

it can be shown that for each n,

$$a_n = n!\left[e^1 - \left(1 + 1 + \frac{1}{2!} + \cdots + \frac{1}{n!}\right)\right]$$

so that this sequence converges to 0. Write a program that prints a table of values of a_n for $n = 0, 1, 2, \ldots, 15$, calculated first in single precision and then in double precision.

2. Write a program to find a double-precision approximation to the zero of a function using Newton's method (see Section 6.3).

3. Write a program to find a double-precision approximation to an integral using the trapezoidal method or Simpson's rule (see Section 6.3 and Programming Problem 31 in Chapter 6).

4. Repeat Programming Problem 13 in Chapter 6 for calculating values of the hyperbolic sine function sinh by using a subprogram to calculate e^x, but perform all calculations in double precision. In particular, use the series to calculate values for e^x using double-precision arithmetic to achieve ten-decimal-place accuracy.

Sections 10.3 and 10.4

5. Write a program that reads three complex numbers P, Q, and R and then determines whether the triangle whose vertices are the points corresponding to P, Q, and R in the complex plane is a right triangle.

6. The exponentiation operator ** is defined for complex values only when the exponent is an integer. To calculate z^a when z is complex and a is real or complex, we can use

$$z^a = e^{a \log z}$$

Write a function that calculates z^a. Use the function in a program that reads values for z and a and then calls the function to calculate the value of z^a.

7. Write a subroutine that converts a complex number from its usual representation to its polar representation. Use the subroutine in a program that reads a complex number z and a positive integer n and finds the *nth roots of z* as given by

$$z^{1/n} = r^{1/n} \left[\cos \left(\frac{\theta + 2k\pi}{n} \right) + i \sin \left(\frac{\theta + 2k\pi}{n} \right) \right]$$

$$k = 0, 1, \ldots, n - 1$$

8. Modify the program in Figure 6.6 to use Newton's method to find complex roots of polynomials. Use Horner's method (i.e., nested multiplication) as described in Programming Problem 10 of Chapter 8 to evaluate the polynomials efficiently.

9. In a circuit containing a resistor and an inductor in series, the voltage is given by

$$V = (R + i\omega L)I$$

where V is the voltage in volts, R is the resistance in ohms, L is the inductance in henrys, and ω is the angular velocity in radians per second. Write a program that can be used to compute the voltage (complex) given the current (complex), or to find the current given the voltage. Use $R = 1.3\Omega$, $L = 0.55$ mH, and $\omega = 365.0$ rad/s.

Sections 10.5 – 10.7

10. Write a program that reads a character string and prints it in reverse order, beginning with the last nonblank character.

11. Write a program to determine whether a specified string occurs in a given string, and if so, print an asterisk ($*$) under the first position of each occurrence.

12. Write a program to count the occurrences of a specified character in several lines of text.

13. Write a program to count the occurrences of a specified string in several lines of text.

14. Write a program that permits the input of a name consisting of a first name, a middle name or initial, and a last name, in that order, and then prints the last name followed by a comma and then the first and middle initials, each followed by a period. For example, the input `JOHN HENRY DOE` should produce `DOE, J. H.`

15. Write a program to read `STUDENT.DAT` and display the name and cumulative GPA of all students with a given major that is entered during execution.

16. A file contains grade records for students in a freshman engineering class. Each record consists of several lines of information. The first line contains the student's name in columns 1 through 30 and the letter T or F in column 31 to indicate whether a letter grade is to be assigned (T) or the course is to be graded on a pass/fail basis (F). The next ten lines contain the test scores for this student, one integer score per

line in columns 1 through 3. Write a program to read these records and, for each student, display on a single line his or her name, term average (in the form xxx.x), and final grade. If the student has selected the pass/fail option, the final grade is `'PASS'` for a term average of 70.0 or above and `'FAIL'` otherwise. If the student has selected the letter grade option, the final grade is `'A'` for a term average of 90.0 or above, `'B'` for a term average of 80.0 through 89.9, `'C'` for a term average of 70.0 through 79.9, `'D'` for a term average of 60.0 through 69.9, and `'F'` otherwise.

17. The following data file contains for each of several objects its shape (cube or sphere), its critical dimension (edge or radius), its density, and the material from which it is made:

```
sphere    2.0     .00264    aluminum
cube      3.0     .00857       brass
cub       1.5     .0113         lead
sphere    1.85    .0088       nickel
CUBE      13.7    .00035       cedar
SPHERE    2.85    .00075         oak
```

Write a program to read these records and produce a table displaying the following information for each object:

(a) Shape
(b) Critical dimension
(c) Material
(d) Volume
(e) Mass
(f) Whether the object will float when immersed in an oil bath
(g) Mass of oil displaced by the object

An object will float if its density is less than or equal to the density of oil, .00088 kg/cm^3. Your program should check that each object's shape is one of the strings `'cube'`, `'CUBE'`, `'sphere'`, or `'SPHERE'`.

18. Rev. Zeller developed a formula for computing the day of the week on which a given date fell or will fall. Suppose that we let a, b, c, and d be integers defined as follows:

$a =$ The month of the year, with March $= 1$, April $= 2$, and so on, with January and February being counted as months 11 and 12 of the preceding year

$b =$ The day of the month

$c =$ The year of the century

$d =$ The century

For example, July 31, 1929, gives $a = 5$, $b = 31$, $c = 29$, $d = 19$; January 3, 1988, gives $a = 11$, $b = 3$, $c = 87$, $d = 19$. Now calculate the following integer quantities:

$w =$ The integer quotient $(13a - 1)/5$
$x =$ The integer quotient $c/4$

$y =$ The integer quotient $d / 4$

$z =$ $w + x + y + b + c - 2d$

$r =$ z reduced modulo 7; that is, r is the remainder of z divided by 7, $r = 0$ represents Sunday; $r = 1$ represents Monday, and so on

Write a program to accept a date as input and then calculate on what day of the week that date fell or will fall.

(a) Verify that December 12, 1960, fell on a Monday and that January 1, 1995, fell on a Sunday.

(b) On what day of the week did January 25, 1963, fall?

(c) On what day of the week did June 2, 1964, fall?

(d) On what day of the week did July 4, 1776, fall?

(e) On what day of the week were you born?

19. Write a program that will convert ordinary Hindu-Arabic numerals into Roman numerals and/or vice versa. (I = 1, V = 5, X = 10, L = 50, C = 100, D = 500, and M = 1000. Roman numeration also uses a subtraction principle: IV = 5 − 1 = 4, IX = 10 − 1 = 9, XL = 50 − 10 = 40, XC = 100 − 10 = 90, CD = 500 − 100 = 400, CM = 1000 − 100 = 900, but no other cases of a smaller number preceding a larger are allowed.)

20. A string is said to be a *palindrome* if it does not change when the order of the characters in the string is reversed. For example,

```
MADAM
463364
ABLE WAS I ERE I SAW ELBA
```

are palindromes. Write a program to read a string and then determine whether it is a palindrome.

21. Write a simple *text-formatting* program that reads a file of text and produces another file in which blank lines are removed, multiple blanks are replaced with a single blank, and no lines are longer than some given length. Put as many words as possible on the same line. You will have to break some lines of the given file, but do not break any words or put punctuation marks at the beginning of a new line.

22. Extend the text-formatting program of Problem 21 to right justify each line except the last in the new file by adding evenly distributed blanks in lines where necessary.

23. A real number in FORTRAN has one of the forms $m \, . \, n$, $+ \, m \, . \, n$, or $- \, m \, . \, n$, where m and n are nonnegative integers and either (but not both) may be omitted; or it may be expressed in scientific form $x E e$, $x E + e$, or $x E − e$, where x is an integer or a real number not in scientific form and e is a nonnegative integer. Write a program that reads a string of characters and then checks to see if it represents a valid real constant.

24. (Project) A *rational number* is of the form a/b, where a and b are integers with $b \neq 0$. Write a program to do rational-number arithmetic. The program should read and display each rational number in the format a/b, or simply a if the denominator

is 1. The following examples illustrate the menu of commands that the user should be allowed to enter:

Input	Output	Comments
3/8 + 1/6	13/24	$a/b + c/d = (ad + bc)/bd$ reduced to lowest terms
3/8 − 1/6	5/24	$a/b - c/d = (ad - bc)/bd$ reduced to lowest terms
3/8 * 1/6	1/16	$a/b * c/d = ac/bd$ reduced to lowest terms
3/8 / 1/6	9/4	$a/b / c/d = ad/bc$ reduced to lowest terms
3/8 I	8/3	Invert a/b
8/3 M	2 + 2/3	Write a/b as a mixed fraction
6/8 R	3/4	Reduce a/b to lowest terms
6/8 G	2	Greatest common divisor of numerator and denominator
1/6 L 3/8	24	Lowest common denominator of a/b and c/d
1/6 < 3/8	true	$a/b < c/d$?
1/6 <= 3/8	true	$a/b \le c/d$?
1/6 > 3/8	false	$a/b > c/d$?
1/6 >= 3/8	false	$a/b \ge c/d$?
3/8 = 9/24	true	$a/b = c/d$?
2/3 X + 2 = 4/5	X = −9/5	Solution of linear equation $(a/b)X + c/d = e/f$

25. Write a program for a lexical analyzer to recognize assignment statements of the form

    ```
    variable = constant
    ```

    where `constant` is an integer constant or a real constant.

26. Write a program for a lexical analyzer to recognize assignment statements of the form

    ```
    variable = string constant
    ```

27. Extend the program of Problem 26 to allow substrings and the concatenation operator.

28. Write a program for a lexical analyzer to process assignment statements of the form

    ```
    logical-variable = logical-value
    ```

    Have it recognize the following tokens: variable, logical constant, assignment operator, and logical operator (.NOT., .AND., .OR., .EQV., and .NEQV.).

Section 10.8

29. Write a program to encrypt and decrypt a message using the Vignère cipher scheme.
30. Write a program to encrypt and decrypt a message using a substitution table.
31. Write a program to encrypt and decrypt a message using a permutation scheme.
32. Write a program that implements the RSA scheme.
33. The *Morse code* is a standard encoding scheme that uses substitutions similar to those in the scheme described in this section. The substitutions used in this case are shown in the following table. Write a program to read a message and encode it using Morse code or to read a message in Morse code and decode it.

A · −	M − −	Y − · − −
B − · · ·	N − ·	Z − − · ·
C − · − ·	O − − −	1 · − − − −
D − · ·	P · − − ·	2 · · − − −
E ·	Q − − · −	3 · · · − −
F · · − ·	R · − ·	4 · · · · −
G − − ·	S · · ·	5 · · · · ·
H · · · ·	T −	6 − · · · ·
I · ·	U · · −	7 − − · · ·
J · − − −	V · · · −	8 − − − · ·
K − · −	W · − −	9 − − − − ·
L · − · ·	X − · · −	0 − − − − −

Section 10.9

34. Modify the program in Figure 10.9 to plot the graph of a function $y = f(x)$.
35. Modify the program in Figure 10.9 to plot the graph of parametric equations of the form

$$x = x(t), \quad y = y(t), \quad a \le t \le b$$

36. In Example 2, we noted that the ideas in that example can be modified to carry out *visual image processing* and *enhancement*. Make a file that represents light intensities of an image in digitized form, say, with intensities from 0 through 9. Write a program that reads these intensities from the file and then reconstructs and displays them using a different character for each intensity. This image might then be en-

hanced to sharpen the contrast. For example, "gray" areas might be removed by replacing all intensities in the range 0 through some value by 0 (light) and intensities greater than this value by 9 (dark). Design your program to accept a threshold value that distinguishes light from dark and then enhances the image in the manner described.

37. An alternative method for enhancing an image (see Problem 36) is to accept three successive images of the same object and, if two or more of the intensities agree, to use that value; otherwise, use the average of the three values. Modify the program of Problem 36 to use this technique for enhancement.

Fortran 90

Features

The DOUBLE PRECISON and COMPLEX data types described in this chapter are also supported in Fortran 90. The main variations and extensions include the following:

- The precision of a real, double-precision, or complex constant or variable may be specified by using KIND type parameters. Every processor must provide at least two kinds of precision, one corresponding to single-precision real type and one corresponding to double-precision type. A KIND = clause is used in the declaration of parameters and variables to specify their precision:

  ```
  REAL (KIND = kind-type-parameter) list-of-identifiers
  ```

  Two intrinsic functions, SELECTED_REAL_KIND and KIND, are used to determine the kind type parameters. A reference to SELECTED_REAL_KIND has the form

  ```
  SELECTED_REAL_KIND(N)
  ```

  where N is an integer, and returns the kind type parameter that will provide at least N decimal digits of precision. For example, the statements

  ```
  INTEGER, PARAMETER :: PREC10 = SELECTED_REAL_KIND(10)
  REAL (KIND = PREC10) V, W
  ```

  declare that V and W are real variables whose values are to have at least 10 decimal digits of precision. A reference to the KIND function has the form

  ```
  KIND(X)
  ```

  and returns the kind type parameter of X. For example, the declaration

  ```
  REAL (KIND = KIND(1.0D0)) A, B
  ```

  is equivalent to

  ```
  DOUBLE PRECISION A, B
  ```

- The intrinsic function PRECISION can be used to determine the precision of a real or complex value (which may be an array). Thus for the variable W just declared, PRECISION(W) would return the value 10.

- The REAL function can be referenced with a second argument,

```
REAL(x, kind-type-parameter)
```

to convert x of integer, real, or complex type to a real value whose precision is specified by the kind type parameter. Similarly, the CMPLX function can be referenced with a kind type parameter

```
CMPLX(x, y, kind-type-parameter)
CMPLX(x, kind-type-parameter)
```

to form the complex number $x + yi$ in the first case, and $x + 0i$ in the second, whose components have the precision specified by the kind type parameter.

- The components of a complex value may have any precision. In particular, they may be double-precision values.

Fortran 90 adds some new features to the character data type, including the following:

- Character strings may be enclosed either in apostrophes ('string') or in quotation marks ("string"). A string that is enclosed in apostrophes may contain quotation marks, and a string that is enclosed in quotation marks may contain apostophes.

- A string may be empty, thus having length 0. A character constant consisting of two consecutive apostrophes or two consecutive quotation marks denotes an empty string.

- A substring specification may be attached to a string constant.

- Character strings to be read by a list-directed input statement need not be enclosed in apostrophes or within quotation marks unless

  1. They contain blanks, commas, or slashes.
  2. They extend over more than one line.
  3. The leading nonblank character is a quotation mark or an apostrophe.
  4. A repetition indicator is used.

  In this case the input value is terminated by the first blank, comma, or end of line that is encountered.

- The OPEN statement may contain a DELIM = 'APOSTROPHE', 'QUOTE', or 'NONE' clause to specify the delimiter used for character strings written with list-directed or NAMELIST formatting.

- Several new instrinsic string-processing functions are provided:

ACHAR(I):	The character whose ASCII code is I
ADJUSTL(STR):	Returns string obtained from STR by moving leading blanks to the right end

ADJUSTR(STR):   Returns string obtained from STR by moving trailing blanks to the left end

IACHAR(CH):   The ASCII code of character CH

LEN_TRIM(STR):   Length of string STR, ignoring trailing blanks

REPEAT(STR, N):   Returns string formed by concatenating N copies of STR

SCAN(STR1, STR2) or SCAN(STR1, STR2, BACK): Returns position of leftmost character of STR1 that appears in STR2 (or rightmost if the second form is used with BACK = .TRUE.), 0 if none appears in STR2

TRIM(STR):   Returns initial substring of STR with trailing blanks removed

VERIFY(STR1, STR2) or VERIFY(STR1, STR2, BACK): Returns position of leftmost character of STR1 that is not in STR2 (or rightmost if the second form is used with BACK = .TRUE.), 0 if all appear in STR2

Examples:
The program in Figure 10.16 is a Fortran-90 version of that in Figure 10.2.

Figure 10.16 Quadratic equations—complex roots (Fortran 90 version).

```
PROGRAM Complex_Quadratic_Equations
!-----------------------------------------------------------------------
! Program to solve a quadratic equation having complex coefficients:
! using the quadratic formula. Identifiers used are:
!
!    A, B, C          : the coefficients of the quadratic equation
!    Discriminant     : the discriminant, B ** 2 - 4 * A * C
!    Root_1, Root_2   : the two complex roots of the equation
!
! Input:  A, B, and C
! Output: Root_1 and Root_2
!-----------------------------------------------------------------------

   IMPLICIT NONE

   COMPLEX :: A, B, C, Discriminant, Root_1, Root_2

! Get the coefficients

   PRINT *, "Enter the coefficients of the quadratic equation"
   READ 5, A, B, C
 5 FORMAT (6F3.1)
```

Figure 10.16 *(cont.)*

```
! Calculate and display the roots

  Discriminant = SQRT(B ** 2 - 4.0 * A * C)
  Root_1 = (-B + Discriminant) / (2.0 * A)
  Root_2 = (-B - Discriminant) / (2.0 * A)
  PRINT *, "The roots are:"
  PRINT 10, Root_1, Root_2
  10 FORMAT (5X, F7.3, " +", F7.3, "i")

END PROGRAM Complex_Quadratic_Equations
```

The program in Figure 10.17 is a Fortran 90 version of the program in Figure 10.6 for encrypting a message using the Caesar cipher method.

Figure 10.17 Caesar cipher encryption — Fortran 90 version.

```
PROGRAM Caesar_Cipher
!----------------------------------------------------------------------
! This program encrypts a character string using the Caesar cipher
! scheme. Variables used are the following:
!   String     : string to be encrypted
!   Symbol     : an individual character of the string
!   Key        : integer to be added in encrypting the string
!   ASCII_Code : ASCII code for Symbol
!   I          : counter
!
! Input:  String and Key
! Output: User prompts and String (encrypted)
!----------------------------------------------------------------------

  IMPLICIT NONE

  CHARACTER(LEN = 80):: String, Symbol*1
  INTEGER :: Key, ASCII_Code, I

! Get the string to be encrypted and the key
  PRINT *, "'Enter string to be encrypted (end with !);"
  READ "(A)", String
  PRINT *, "Enter Key:"
  READ *, Key
```

Figure 10.17 *(cont.)*

```fortran
! Extract the first character in the string
  I = 1
  SYMBOL =  String(1:1)

! Do the following
  DO
    IF (I == LEN)String) .OR. Symbol == "!") EXIT
    ! If end of string, terminate repetition
    ! otherwise continue with the following

    ! Encrypt the I-th character of the string
    ASCII_Code = MOD((IACHAR(Symbol) - 32 + Key), 95) + 32
    String(I:I) = ACHAR(ASCII_Code)

    ! Get the next character in the string
    I = I + 1
    Symbol = String(I:I)
  END DO

! String has now been encrypted -- display it
  PRINT*, "Encrypted string:"
  PRINT*, String

END PROGRAM Caesar_Cipher
```

11

File Processing

*T*he goal is information at your fingertips.

BILL GATES

*T*he next best thing to knowing something is knowing where to find it.

SAMUEL JOHNSON

... it became increasingly apparent to me that, over the years, Federal agencies have amassed vast amounts of information about virtually every American citizen. This fact, coupled with technological advances in data collection and dissemination, raised the possibility that information about individuals conceivably could be used for other than legitimate purposes and without the prior knowledge or consent of the individuals involved.

PRESIDENT GERALD R. FORD

C H A P T E R C O N T E N T S

11.1 The OPEN, CLOSE, and INQUIRE Statements

11.2 File Input/Output and Positioning

11.3 Application: Pharmacy Inventory

Chapter Review

Programming Pointers

Programming Problems

Fortran 90

*I*n Section 2.10 and in Chapter 5 we introduced file processing for those applications involving large data sets that can be processed more conveniently if stored on disk or some other form of external (secondary) memory. We considered simple forms of several FORTRAN statements that are used to process files. In this chapter we review these statements, give their complete forms, and introduce some additional file concepts.

The files we have considered thus far are called **sequential files**. These are files in which the lines of data or **records** are written in sequence and must be read in that same order. This means that to read a particular record in a sequential file, all of the preceding records must first be read. In contrast, **direct-access files** are files in which each record may be accessed directly, usually by referring to a record number. This means that a particular record may be accessed without reading (or writing) those records that precede it. All records in a direct-access file must have the same fixed length, whereas records in a sequential file may be of varying lengths.

Another distinction between files is that they may be **formatted** or **unformatted.** All the files we have considered thus far have been formatted, which means that they consist of records in which information is represented in external character form. In contrast, unformatted files are those in which the information is represented in internal binary form. Thus, the precise form of the records in an unformatted file is machine-dependent, as it depends on the way in which values are stored internally in a particular system. For this reason, unformatted files are discussed only briefly in this chapter. We focus our attention instead on formatted files.

11.1 THE OPEN, CLOSE, AND INQUIRE STATEMENTS

A file must be connected to a unit number using the OPEN statement introduced in Sections 2.10 and 5.5 before input from or output to that file can take place. When such input/output is completed, the file should be disconnected from its unit number using the CLOSE statement, also introduced in Section 5.5. In some situations, it may also be convenient to inquire about certain properties of a file, and the INQUIRE statement may be used for this purpose.

Opening Files

The OPEN **statement** has the general form

```
OPEN (open-list)
```

where *open-list* must include

1. A unit specifier indicating a unit number to be connected to the file being opened.

In most cases, it also includes

2. A FILE = clause giving the name of the file being opened.
3. A STATUS = clause specifying whether the file is new, old, or scratch or has an unknown status.

It may also include other specifiers selected from the following list:

4. An IOSTAT = clause indicating whether the file has been successfully opened.
5. An ERR = clause specifying a statement to be executed if an error occurs while attempting to open the file.
6. An ACCESS = clause specifying the type of access as sequential or direct.
7. A FORM = clause specifying whether the file is formatted or unformatted.
8. A RECL = clause specifying the record length for a direct-access file.
9. A BLANK = clause specifying whether blanks in a numeric field are to be interpreted as zeros or are to be ignored.

Unit Specifier. The unit specifier has the form

```
UNIT = integer-expression
```

or simply

```
integer-expression
```

where the value of *integer-expression* is a nonnegative integer that is the unit number to be connected to this file. Reference to this file by subsequent READ or WRITE statements is by means of this unit number. If the second form of the unit specifier is used, it must be the first item in the open list.

FILE = Clause. The FILE = clause has the form

FILE = *character-expression*

where the value of *character-expression* (ignoring trailing blanks) is the name of the file to be connected to the specified unit number.

STATUS = Clause. The STATUS = clause has the form

STATUS = *character-expression*

where the value of *character-expression* (ignoring trailing blanks) is one of the following:

OLD
NEW
SCRATCH
UNKNOWN

If the value is OLD or NEW, the name of the file must have been given in the FILE = clause. OLD means that the file already exists in the system, and NEW means that the file does not yet exist and is being created by the program. The OPEN statement creates an empty file with the specified name and changes its status to OLD. If the status is SCRATCH, the file must not be named in a FILE = clause. The OPEN statement creates a work file that is used during execution of this program but that is deleted by a CLOSE statement or by normal termination of the program. A status of UNKNOWN means that none of the preceding applies. In this case, the status of the file depends on the particular system being used. If the STATUS = clause is omitted, the file is assumed to have an UNKNOWN status.

IOSTAT = Clause. The IOSTAT = clause is of the form

IOSTAT = *status-variable*

where *status-variable* is an integer variable to which the value zero is assigned if the file is opened successfully and a positive value is assigned otherwise. A positive value usually represents the number of an appropriate error message in a list found in system manuals.

ERR = Clause. The ERR = clause has the form

ERR = *n*

where n is the label of an executable statement that is the next statement executed if an error occurs in attempting to open the file.

ACCESS = **Clause.** The ACCESS = clause is of the form

```
ACCESS = access-method
```

where `access-method` is a character expression whose value (ignoring trailing blanks) is

```
SEQUENTIAL    or    DIRECT
```

If this clause is omitted, the file is assumed to be sequential.

FORM = **Clause.** The FORM = clause is of the form

```
FORM = form-specifier
```

where `form-specifier` is a character expression whose value (ignoring trailing blanks) is either

```
FORMATTED    or    UNFORMATTED
```

If this clause is omitted, the file being opened is assumed to be formatted if it is a sequential file or to be unformatted if it is a direct-access file.

RECL = **Clause.** The RECL = clause has the form

```
RECL = record-length
```

where `record-length` is an integer expression whose value must be positive. This clause is used only for direct-access files and specifies the length of the records in the file. For a formatted file, the record length is the number of characters in each record of that file. For an unformatted file, it is a processor-dependent measure of the record length.

BLANK = **Clause.** The BLANK = clause has the form

```
BLANK = blank-specifier
```

where `blank-specifier` is a character expression whose value (ignoring trailing blanks) is either

```
ZERO    or    NULL
```

The first specification causes blanks in the numeric fields of records in the file being opened to be interpreted as zeros, whereas the NULL specifier causes such blanks to be ignored. In all cases, however, a numeric field consisting only of blanks is interpreted as zero.

Illustration. As an illustration, suppose that a file has been previously created and saved under the name INFO1 and that data values are to be read from this file. A unit number such as 10 must first be connected to this file by an OPEN statement such as

```
OPEN (UNIT = 10, FILE = 'INFO1', STATUS = 'OLD')
```

Alternatively, the name of the file can be read during execution:

```
CHARACTER*10 INFILE
PRINT *, 'ENTER NAME OF INPUT FILE'
READ *, INFILE
OPEN (UNIT = 10, FILE = INFILE, STATUS = 'OLD')
```

Because the ACCESS = and FORM = clauses are not used, the file is assumed to be sequential and formatted. If we wish to specify this explicitly, we can use

```
  OPEN (UNIT = 10, FILE = INFILE, STATUS = 'OLD',
+       FORM = 'FORMATTED', ACCESS = 'SEQUENTIAL')
```

The statement

```
OPEN (UNIT = 10, FILE = INFILE, STATUS = 'OLD', ERR = 50)
```

also serves the same purpose, but if an error occurs during the opening of the file, the ERR = clause will cause execution to continue with the statement labeled 50.

If the program is to create a new file named INFO2, we might attach the unit number 11 to it with the statement

```
OPEN (UNIT = 11, FILE = 'INFO2', STATUS = 'NEW')
```

Execution of this statement changes the status of this file to OLD, so that it will exist after execution of the program is completed. On the other hand, if a temporary work file is needed only during execution, we might use a statement such as

```
OPEN (UNIT = 12, STATUS = 'SCRATCH')
```

This temporary file will then be deleted if it is closed by a CLOSE statement or when execution terminates.

Closing Files

The CLOSE **statement** is used to disconnect a file from its unit number. This statement is of the form

```
CLOSE (close-list)
```

where *close-list* must include

1. A unit specifier.

It may also include items selected from the following:

2. An IOSTAT = clause.
3. An ERR = clause.
4. A STATUS = clause specifying whether the file is to be kept or deleted.

The IOSTAT = and ERR = clauses are used to detect errors that may occur when attempting to close the file and have the same form as the corresponding clauses in the OPEN statement. The STATUS = clause has the form

```
STATUS = character-expression
```

where the value of *character-expression* (ignoring trailing blanks) is

```
KEEP      or      DELETE
```

depending on whether the file is to continue to exist or not exist after the CLOSE statement is executed. KEEP may not be used for a SCRATCH file. If the STATUS = clause is omitted, scratch files are deleted, but all other types are kept. Thus, to close the file INFO2 with the unit number 11 referred to earlier so that it is saved after execution, we could use any of the following statements:

```
CLOSE (11)
CLOSE (UNIT = 11)
CLOSE (UNIT = 11, STATUS = 'KEEP')
```

A file that has been closed by a CLOSE statement may be reopened by an OPEN statement; the same unit number may be connected to it, or a different one may be used. All files that are not explicitly closed with a CLOSE statement are automatically closed when execution of the program is terminated (except when termination is caused by an error).

The INQUIRE Statement

The INQUIRE **statement** may be used to ascertain the properties of a file or of its connection to a unit number. It has the form

```
INQUIRE (inquiry-list)
```

where *inquiry-list* must include a unit specifier or a file specifier, but not both, and may include an IOSTAT = clause and/or an ERR = clause. The inquiry list may also contain a number of other clauses, each of which serves as a question concerning some property of the file. When the INQUIRE statement is executed, a value is assigned to the variable in each clause that answers the question. A complete list of the clauses and their meanings is given in Table 11.1.

Table 11.1 Clauses Allowed in an INQUIRE Statement

Clause	Variable Type	Values and Their Meanings
IOSTAT = *variable*	Integer	Zero if no error condition exists; positive if an error exists.
EXIST = *variable*	Logical	True if the file with the specified name or unit number exists; false otherwise.
OPENED = *variable*	Logical	True if the specified file or unit number has been connected to a unit number or file, respectively; false otherwise.
NUMBER = *variable*	Integer	Either the file's unit number or undefined.
NAMED = *variable*	Logical	True if the file has a name; false otherwise.
NAME = *variable*	Character	Either the name of the file or undefined if the file has no name.
ACCESS = *variable*	Character	SEQUENTIAL if the file is open for sequential access; DIRECT if it is open for direct access; undefined otherwise.
SEQUENTIAL = *variable*	Character	YES if the file can be connected for sequential access; NO if it cannot; UNKNOWN if the file's suitability for sequential access cannot be determined.
DIRECT = *variable*	Character	YES if the file can be connected for direct access; NO if it cannot; UNKNOWN if the file's suitability for direct access cannot be determined.
FORM = *variable*	Character	FORMATTED if the file is open for formatted data transfer; UNFORMATTED if the file is open for unformatted data transfer; undefined if the file is not open.
FORMATTED = *variable*	Character	YES if the file is formatted; NO if the file is unformatted; UNKNOWN if the record type cannot be determined.
UNFORMATTED = *variable*	Character	YES if the file is unformatted; NO if the file is formatted; UNKNOWN if the record type cannot be determined.
RECL = *variable*	Integer	Record length for a direct-access file; undefined if the file is not connected for direct access.

Table 11.1 *(cont.)*

Clause	Variable Type	Values and Their Meanings
NEXTREC = *variable*	Integer	One plus the number of the last record read from or written to a direct-access file; undefined if the file is not connected for direct access or the record number cannot be determined.
BLANK = *variable*	Character	ZERO if the blanks in numeric fields are to be interpreted as zeros; NULL if they are to be ignored; undefined if the file is not open.

11.2 FILE INPUT/OUTPUT AND POSITIONING

File input/output is accomplished using the general READ and WRITE statements introduced in Section 2.10 and in Chapter 5. The complete forms of these statements are considered in this section. Some file positioning is also carried out by these statements. Other positioning statements that may be used for sequential files are the REWIND, BACKSPACE, and ENDFILE statements.

File Input
Data can be read from a file using a READ **statement** of the general form

```
READ (control-list) input-list
```

The *input-list* is a list of variable names, substring names, array names, or implied DO loops, separated by commas. The *control-list* must include

1. A unit specifier indicating the unit number connected to the file.
   It may also include one or more of the following:
2. A format specifier describing the format of the information to be read.
3. An IOSTAT = clause to check the status of the input operation, in particular, to detect an end-of-file condition or an input error.
4. An END = clause specifying a statement to be executed when the end of a sequential file is reached.
5. An ERR = clause specifying a statement to be executed if an input error occurs.
6. A REC = clause indicating the number of the record to be read for a direct-access file.

The forms of the unit specifier, format specifier, the IOSTAT = clause, and the END = clause were described in detail in Chapter 5.

ERR = Clause. The ERR = clause has the form

```
ERR = n
```

where n is the label of a statement to be executed if an input error occurs. For example, suppose that NUMBER and NAME are declared by

```
INTEGER NUMBER
CHARACTER*20 NAME
```

For the READ statement

```
      READ (15, 10, ERR = 20) NUMBER, NAME
10 FORMAT(I5, A20)
```

if the following data is read from the file with unit number 15

```
123 JOHN HENRY DOE
```

an input data error occurs because the character J in the fifth column is read as part of the value for the integer variable NUMBER. The ERR = clause then causes execution to continue with the statement numbered 20, which might be a statement to print an error message such as

```
20 PRINT *, 'INPUT DATA ERROR'
```

IOSTAT = Clause. In Chapter 5 we noted that when a READ statement containing an IOSTAT = clause of the form

```
IOSTAT = integer-variable
```

is executed, the variable in this clause is assigned

1. A positive value (usually the number of an error message in a list found in system manuals) if an error occurs.
2. A negative value if the end of data is encountered but no input error occurs.
3. Zero if neither an input error nor the end of data occurs.

Up to now we have used the IOSTAT = clause only to detect the end of data. However, it also provides an alternative to the ERR = clause for detecting input errors. For example, if ERROR is an integer variable, the preceding statements could also be written as

```
      READ (15, 10, IOSTAT = ERROR) NUMBER, NAME
10 FORMAT(I5, A20)
      IF (ERROR .GT. 0) THEN
         PRINT *, 'INPUT DATA ERROR'
      END IF
```

REC = Clause. The REC = clause has the form

```
REC = integer-expression
```

where the value of the *integer-expression* is positive and indicates the number of the record to be read from a direct-access file. The clause must be used if input is to be from a file connected for direct access. The control list may not contain both a REC = clause and an END = clause.

Example 1: Direct-Access Inventory File

All the files used in the example programs in this text have thus far been sequential files. The program in Figure 11.1 uses a direct-access file to retrieve information in a parts inventory file. The name FNAME of the file is read during execution and is then opened with the statement

```
  OPEN (UNIT = 10, FILE = FNAME, STATUS = 'OLD',
+      ACCESS = 'DIRECT', FORM = 'FORMATTED',
+      RECL = RECLEN)
```

The user then enters a part number, which is used to access a record of the file:

```
  READ (10, '(A)', REC = PARTNO, IOSTAT = BADNUM), INFO
```

The information in this record INFO is then displayed to the user.

Figure 11.1 Direct-access inventory file.

```
      PROGRAM INVEN
*************************************************************************
* Program to read a part number during execution, access a record in   *
* a direct-access parts inventory file, and display this record.        *
* Identifiers used are:                                                 *
*     RECLEN : a parameter specifying record length (parameter)         *
*     PARTNO : part number                                              *
*     FNAME  : name of the file                                         *
*     INFO   : a record in the file                                     *
*     BADNUM : 0 if valid part number, otherwise nonzero                *
*                                                                       *
* Input (keyboard): FNAME, PARTNO                                       *
* Input (file):     INFO                                                *
*                                                                       *
* Output (screen):  User prompts, INFO, or error message and PARTNO     *
*                   for an invalid part number                          *
*                                                                       *
```

Figure 11.1 *(cont.)*

```
* Note: The compiler used for this program requires that the          *
* end-of-line character in a file record be counted in determining    *
* the record length; therefore, RECLEN is set at 31.                  *
***********************************************************************

      INTEGER PARTNO, RECLEN, BADNUM
      PARAMETER (RECLEN = 31)
      CHARACTER*20 FNAME, INFO*(RECLEN)

* Get the name of the file and open it for direct access

      PRINT *, 'ENTER NAME OF FILE'
      READ '(A)', FNAME
      OPEN (UNIT = 10, FILE = FNAME, STATUS = 'OLD',
     +      ACCESS = 'DIRECT', FORM = 'FORMATTED', RECL = RECLEN)

      PRINT *, 'ENTER PART NUMBER (0 TO STOP)'
      READ *, PARTNO

* While there are more part numbers to process do the following

10    IF (PARTNO .NE. 0) THEN
         READ (10, '(A)', REC = PARTNO, IOSTAT = BADNUM) INFO
         IF (BADNUM .EQ. 0) THEN
            PRINT '(1X, ''PART'', I3, '': '', A)', PARTNO, INFO
         ELSE
            PRINT '(1X, ''INVALID PART NUMBER: '', I3)', PARTNO
         END IF
         PRINT *
         PRINT *, 'PART NUMBER?'
         READ *, PARTNO
      GO TO 10
      END IF

      CLOSE(10)
      END
```

Listing of test file used in sample run:

```
CHROME-BUMPER...$152.95.....15
SPARK-PLUG........$1.25....125
DISTRIBUTOR-CAP..$39.95.....57
FAN-BELT..........$5.80.....32
DOOR-HANDLE......$18.85.....84
```

Figure 11.1 *(cont.)*

Sample run:

```
ENTER NAME OF FILE
FIL11-1.DAT
ENTER PART NUMBER (0 TO STOP)
4
PART   4: FAN-BELT..........$5.80.....32

PART NUMBER?
2
PART   2: SPARK-PLUG........$1.25....125

PART NUMBER?
10
INVALID PART NUMBER:   10

PART NUMBER?
0
```

File-Positioning Statements

There are three FORTRAN statements that may be used to position a sequential file. Each of these statements has two possible forms:

REWIND *unit*	or	REWIND (*position-list*)
BACKSPACE *unit*	or	BACKSPACE (*position-list*)
ENDFILE *unit*	or	ENDFILE (*position-list*)

In the first form, *unit* is the unit number connected to the file. In the second form, *position-list* must contain

1. A unit specifier of the form *unit* or UNIT = *unit*.

It may also contain

2. An ERR = clause specifying the number of a statement to be executed if an error occurs while positioning the file.

3. An IOSTAT = clause specifying a status variable that is assigned 0 if the file is successfully positioned or a positive value if some error occurs.

The REWIND **statement** positions the file at its initial point, that is, at the beginning of the file's first record. The BACKSPACE **statement** positions the file at the beginning of the preceding record. If the file is at its initial point, these statements have no effect.

The ENDFILE **statement** writes into the file a special record called an **end-of-file record**. When this record is encountered by a READ statement, an end-of-file condition occurs that can be detected by an IOSTAT = clause or an END = clause in the control list of the READ statement. After the execution of an ENDFILE statement, no more data can be transferred to or from this file until the file is repositioned at some record preceding the end-of-file record.

File Output

Data is written to a file using a WRITE **statement** of the general form

```
WRITE (control-list) output-list
```

The *output-list* is a list of expressions, array names, or implied DO loops separated by commas. The *control-list* must include

1. A unit specifier indicating the unit number connected to the file.

It may also include one or more of the following:

2. A format specifier describing the form of the information being output.
3. An ERR = clause specifying a statement to be executed if an output error occurs.
4. An IOSTAT = clause to check the status of the output operation.
5. A REC = clause indicating the number of the record to which the information is to be output for a direct-access file.

The form of each of these items is the same as for a READ statement.

The format of the output to a direct-access file must be supplied by the user. Also, the REC = clause may not appear when the output is list directed (indicated by an asterisk for the format specifier).

Example 2: Merging Files

An important problem in file processing is merging two files that have been previously sorted so that the resulting file is also sorted. To illustrate, suppose that FILE1 and FILE2 have been sorted and contain the following integers:

FILE1: 2 4 5 7 9 15 16 20   FILE2: 1 6 8 10 12

To merge these files to produce FILE3, we read one element from each file, say X from FILE1 and Y from FILE2:

FILE1: 2 4 5 7 9 15 16 20   FILE2: 1 6 8 10 12
    ↑   ↑
    X   Y

We write the smaller of these values, in this case Y, into FILE3

    FILE3: 1

and then read another value for Y from FILE2:

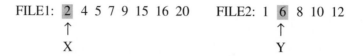

Now X is smaller than Y, and so it is written to FILE3, and a new value for X is read from FILE1:

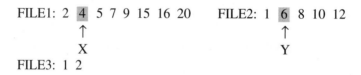

Again, X is less than Y, and so X is written to FILE3 and a new X value is read from FILE1:

    FILE1: 2 4 **5** 7 9 15 16 20   FILE2: 1 **6** 8 10 12
             ↑   ↑
             X   Y
    FILE3: 1 2 4

Continuing in this manner, we eventually reach the value 15 for X and the value 12 for Y:

    FILE1: 2 4 5 7 9 **15** 16 20   FILE2: 1 6 8 10 **12**
                ↑   ↑
               X   Y
    FILE3: 1 2 4 5 6 7 8 9 10

Because Y is smaller than X, we write Y to FILE3:

    FILE3: 1 2 4 5 6 7 8 9 10 12

Because the end of FILE2 has been reached, we simply copy the remaining values of FILE1 to FILE3 to obtain the final sorted file FILE3:

    FILE3: 1 2 4 5 6 7 8 9 10 12 15 16 20

The general algorithm to merge two sorted files is as follows:

ALGORITHM TO MERGE FILES

* Algorithm to merge sorted files FILE1 and FILE2 to produce the sorted file FILE3.   *
* Input (files):   Elements from FILE1, FILE2 and FILE3   *
* Output (files): Elements to FILE1, FILE2 and FILE3   *

1. Open FILE1, FILE2, and FILE3.

2. Read the first element X from FILE1 and the first element Y from FILE2.

3. While the end of neither FILE1 nor FILE2 has been reached, do the following:

   If $X \leq Y$ then

   a. Write X to FILE3.
   b. Read a new X value from FILE1.

   Else do the following:
   a. Write Y to FILE3.
   b. Read a new Y value from FILE2.

4. If the end of FILE1 has not been reached, copy the rest of FILE1 into FILE3. If the end of FILE2 has not been reached, copy the rest of FILE2 into FILE3.

In this algorithm, we assumed that the file components are numbers, strings, and so on that can be compared. If the files contain records that are sorted on the basis of some key field in the records, then the key field of X is compared with the key field of Y in step 3. The program in Figure 11.2 implements this modified merge algorithm. It merges two files whose records consist of a student number, student name, and cumulative GPA and that have been sorted so that the student numbers are in ascending order.

Figure 11.2 Merging files.

```
      PROGRAM MERGE
* * * * * * * * * * * * * * * * * * * * * * * * * * * * * * * * * * * * * * * * * * * * * * * * * * * * *
*  Program to read two files of records containing a student number, a    *
*  student name, and a cumulative GPA, where the files are sorted so      *
*  that student numbers are in ascending order, and merge these two       *
*  files to produce another that is also sorted. Variables used are:      *
*     FNAME1, FNAME2 : names of files to be merged                        *
*     FNAME3         : name of file produced                              *
*     SNUMB1, SNUMB2 : number of student in FILE1, FILE2                  *
*     SNAME1, SNAME2 : name of student in FILE1, FILE2                    *
*     GPA1, GPA2      : cumulative GPA of student in FILE1, FILE2         *
*     EOF1, EOF2      : indicator of end of FILE1, FILE2                  *
```

Figure 11.2 *(cont.)*

```
*                                                                        *
* Input (keyboard): FNAME1, FNAME2, FNAME3                               *
* Input (file):     SNUMB2, SNUMB2, SNAME1, SNAME2, GPA1, GPA2           *
* Output (screen):  User prompts and message that sorting has been       *
*                   completed                                            *
* Output (file):    Records sorted with student numbers in ascending     *
*                   order                                                *
*************************************************************************

      CHARACTER*20, FNAME1, FNAME2, FNAME3, SNAME1, SNAME2
      INTEGER SNUMB1, SNUMB2, EOF1, EOF2
      REAL GPA1, GPA2

* Get the names of the files and open them

      PRINT *, 'ENTER THE NAMES OF THE FILES TO BE MERGED AND THE NAME'
      PRINT *, 'OF THE FILE TO BE PRODUCED ON SEPARATE LINES:'
      READ '(A)', FNAME1, FNAME2, FNAME3
      OPEN (UNIT = 10, FILE = FNAME1, STATUS = 'OLD',
     +     ACCESS = 'SEQUENTIAL')
      OPEN (UNIT = 20, FILE = FNAME2, STATUS = 'OLD',
     +     ACCESS = 'SEQUENTIAL')
      OPEN (UNIT = 30, FILE = FNAME3, STATUS = 'NEW',
     +     ACCESS = 'SEQUENTIAL')

* Read the first two records from each file

      READ (10, 100, IOSTAT = EOF1) SNUMB1, SNAME1, GPA1
      READ (20, 100, IOSTAT = EOF2) SNUMB2, SNAME2, GPA2
100   FORMAT(I5, 1X, A, F4.2)

* While neither the end of FILE1 or FILE2 has been reached,
* do the following:

10    IF (EOF1 .EQ. 0 .AND. EOF2 .EQ. 0) THEN
         IF (SNUMB1 .LE. SNUMB2) THEN
            WRITE (30, 100) SNUMB1, SNAME1, GPA1
            READ (10, 100, IOSTAT = EOF1) SNUMB1, SNAME1, GPA1
         ELSE
            WRITE (30, 100) SNUMB2, SNAME2, GPA2
            READ (20, 100, IOSTAT = EOF2) SNUMB2, SNAME2, GPA2
         END IF
      GO TO 10
      END IF
```

Figure 11.2 *(cont.)*

```
* If more records remain in FILE1, copy them to FILE3

20    IF (EOF1 .EQ. 0) THEN
          WRITE (30, 100) SNUMB1, SNAME1, GPA1
          READ (10, 100, IOSTAT = EOF1) SNUMB1, SNAME1, GPA1
      GO TO 20
      END IF

* If more records remain in FILE2, copy them to FILE3

30    IF (EOF2 .EQ. 0) THEN
          WRITE (30, 100) SNUMB2, SNAME2, GPA2
          READ (20, 100, IOSTAT = EOF2) SNUMB2, SNAME2, GPA2
      GO TO 30
      END IF

      PRINT *
      PRINT *, 'FILE MERGING IS COMPLETE'

      END
```

Sample run:

```
ENTER THE NAMES OF THE FILES TO BE MERGED AND THE NAME
OF THE FILE TO BE PRODUCED ON SEPARATE LINES:
FIL11-2A.DAT
FIL11-2B.DAT
FIL11-2C.DAT

FILE MERGING IS COMPLETE
```

Data files used in sample run:

```
FIL11-2A.DAT:

12320 JOHN HENRY DOE      3.50
12346 FRED SAMUEL DOE     3.48
13331 MARY JANE SMITH     3.85
13345 PETER VANDER VAN    2.99
14400 ALFRED E. NEWMAN    1.00
15555 HENRY SMITHSMA      2.05
```

Figure 11.2 *(cont.)*

```
FIL11-2B.DAT:

12360 ALICE M. VAN DOE      2.15
12365 JANE E. JONES         1.89
13400 JESSE JAMES           1.66
14001 RICHARD VAN VAN       4.00
```

`FIL11-2C.DAT` **produced by the sample run:**

```
12320 JOHN HENRY DOE        3.50
12346 FRED SAMUEL DOE       3.48
12360 ALICE M. VAN DOE      2.15
12365 JANE E. JONES         1.89
13331 MARY JANE SMITH       3.85
13345 PETER VANDER VAN      2.99
13400 JESSE JAMES           1.66
14001 RICHARD VAN VAN       4.00
14400 ALFRED E. NEWMAN      1.00
15555 HENRY SMITHSMA        2.05
```

Example 3: External Sorting: Mergesort

The sorting algorithms we considered in Chapter 8 are *internal* sorting schemes; that is, the entire collection of items to be sorted must be stored in main memory. In many sorting problems, however, the data sets are too large to store in main memory and so must be stored in external memory. To sort such collections of data, an *external* sorting algorithm is required. One popular and efficient external sorting method is the **merge-sort** technique, a variation of which, called **natural mergesort,** we examine here.

As the name *mergesort* suggests, the basic operation in this sorting scheme is merging data files. To see how the merge operation can be used in sorting a file, consider the following file F containing 15 integers:

F: 75 55 15 20 80 30 35 10 70 40 50 25 45 60 65

Notice that several segments of F contain elements that are already in order:

F: | 75 | 55 | 15 20 80 | 30 35 | 10 70 | 40 50 | 25 45 60 65 |

These segments, enclosed by vertical bars, are called *subfiles* or *runs* in F and subdivide F in a natural way.

We begin by reading these subfiles of F and alternately writing them to two other files, F1 and F2,

F1: |75 |15 20 80 | 10 70 | 25 45 60 65 |
F2: |55 | 30 35 | 40 50 |

and then identifying the sorted subfiles in F1 and F2:

F1: |75 | 15 20 80 | 10 70 | 25 45 60 65 |
F2: |55 | 30 35 40 50 |

Note that although the subfiles of F1 are the same as those copied from F, two of the original subfiles written into F2 have combined to form a larger subfile.

We now merge the first subfile of F1 with the first subfile of F2, storing the elements back in F.

F: |55 75 |

Next the second subfile of F1 is merged with the second subfile of F2 and written to F.

F: |55 75 | 15 20 30 35 40 50 80 |

This merging of corresponding subfiles continues until the end of either or both of the files F1 and F2 is reached. If either file still contains subfiles, these are simply copied into F. Thus, in our example, because the end of F2 has been reached, the remaining subfiles of F1 are copied back into F.

F: |55 75 | 15 20 30 35 40 50 80 | 10 70 | 25 45 60 65 |

Now file F is again split into files F1 and F2 by copying its subfiles alternately into F1 and F2.

F1: |55 75 | 10 70 |
F2: | 15 20 30 35 40 50 80 | 25 45 60 65 |

Identifying the sorted subfiles in each of these files, we see that for this splitting, none of the original subfiles written into either F1 or F2 combine to form larger ones. Once again we merge corresponding subfiles of F1 and F2 back into F.

F: | 15 20 30 35 40 50 55 75 80 | 10 25 45 60 65 70 |

When we now split F into F1 and F2, each of the files F1 and F2 contains a single sorted subfile, and each is, therefore, completely sorted.

F1: | 15 20 30 35 40 50 55 75 80 |
F2: | 10 25 45 60 65 70 |

Thus, when we merge F1 and F2 back into F, F will also contain only one sorted subfile and hence will be sorted.

F: | 10 15 20 25 30 35 40 45 50 55 60 65 70 75 80 |

This example shows that the mergesort method has two steps: (1) splitting file F into two other files, F1 and F2, and (2) merging corresponding subfiles in these two files. These steps are repeated until each of the smaller files contains a single sorted subfile; when these are merged, the resulting file is completely sorted. Designing an algorithm to split the file and a program to implement the mergesort scheme is left as an exercise.

Unformatted Files

Information is stored in a formatted file using a standard coding scheme such as ASCII or EBCDIC, and when such a file is listed, these codes are automatically converted to the corresponding characters by the terminal, printer, or other output device. In contrast, information is stored in an **unformatted** or **binary file** using the internal representation scheme for the particular computer being used. This representation usually cannot be correctly displayed in character form by the output device, nor can it be used easily with another computer system.

There are, however, some advantages in using unformatted files. When information in a formatted file is read by a FORTRAN program, two separate processes are involved: (1) the transfer of the information from the file and (2) the conversion of this information to internal form. Similarly, the output of information to a formatted file involves two steps: (1) conversion to external form and (2) the actual transfer of this information to the file. Because such conversion is time-consuming, it may be desirable to eliminate it, especially when a file is to be read and processed only by the computer and not displayed to the user. Another advantage in using unformatted files is that data items are usually stored more compactly using their internal representation rather than their external representation in one of the standard coding schemes.

Unformatted file input/output is accomplished by using a READ or WRITE statement in which the format specification is omitted. For example, the statement

```
WRITE (UNIT = 10, ERR = 100) NUM, RATE, TIME
```

writes values of NUM, RATE, and TIME to the unformatted file having unit number 10.

The variables in the input list of a READ statement used to read information from an unformatted file should match in number and type the variables in the output lists of the WRITE statements that produced that file. Also, both formatted and unformatted input/output statements cannot be used with the same file.

Internal Files

An **internal file** is a sequence of memory locations containing information stored in character form and named by a character variable, a character array or array element, or a character substring. Such internal files are useful in converting information from character form to numeric form.

For example, suppose the character variable DATE is assigned the value

```
DATE = 'JULY 4, 1776'
```

and we wish to extract the year 1776 from this character string and convert it to a numeric form suitable for computations. To do this, we first use a substring reference to extract the substring to be converted:

```
YEAR = DATE(9:12)
```

The value of the character variable YEAR is the character string '1776', and thus YEAR can be viewed as an internal file. The information

```
1776
```

stored in this file can be read and assigned to a numeric variable NYEAR by using a READ statement in which the name YEAR of this internal file is used as the unit specifier:

```
READ (UNIT = YEAR, FMT = '(I4)') NYEAR
```

or simply

```
READ (YEAR, '(I4)') NYEAR
```

The integer 1776 can also be read and assigned to NYEAR by using the character substring name DATE(9:12) as the name of the internal file:

```
READ (DATE(9:12), '(I4)') NYEAR
```

or by considering DATE as the name of the internal file and using the appropriate positioning descriptors in the format identifier:

```
READ (DATE, '(8X, I4)') NYEAR
```

In no case, however, is list-directed input allowed.

Conversely, a numeric constant can be converted to the corresponding character string and assigned to a character variable by considering that character variable to be an internal file and writing to it. For example, suppose the integer variable N has been assigned the value

```
N = 1776
```

and we wish to concatenate the corresponding character string '1776' to the character constant 'JULY 4,'. To do this, we first convert the value of N to character form and assign the resulting string to the character variable REVOL by the statement

```
WRITE (UNIT = REVOL, FMT = '(I4)') N
```

or simply

```
WRITE (REVOL, '(I4)') N
```

in which REVOL is viewed as an internal file. The value of REVOL can then be concatenated with 'JULY 4, ' and assigned to the character variable DATE by

```
DATE = 'JULY 4, ' // REVOL
```

When a character array is viewed as an internal file, the number of records in that file is equal to the number of elements in the array, and the length of each record is equal to the declared length of the array elements. Each READ and WRITE statement using this array as an internal file begins transferring data with the first array element.

List-directed input/output is not allowed for internal files, nor may the auxiliary input/output statements

```
OPEN
CLOSE
INQUIRE
BACKSPACE
ENDFILE
REWIND
```

be used for such files.

11.3 APPLICATION: PHARMACY INVENTORY

Problem

Each day, the large pharmaceutical company Uppers and Downers receives and fills thousands of orders for the drugs and pharmaceutical supplies it manufactures. Since customers depend on these drugs for their health and well-being, it is critical that the company be able to process and fill these orders promptly. This means that an adequate inventory of the drugs and supplies must be maintained at all times. The computing services department has been requested to develop a program to manage this inventory.

Solution

Specification. The problem here is that of maintaining an inventory file. The program to be developed must accept as input an order number followed by a list of item numbers and order quantities for several items. For each of these items, the appropriate record in the inventory file must be read to determine whether there is sufficient stock to fill the order. If there is, the quantity ordered is subtracted from the number in stock, and a message is displayed indicating this fact. If the number remaining in stock is less than the reorder point for that item, an appropriate warning message must be displayed so that a production run can be scheduled. If there are not enough items to fill the order, a message indicating how much of the order can be filled at this time must be displayed.

In summary, the input/output specifications for this problem are:

Input (user):	Order numbers
	Item numbers
	Order quantities
Input (file):	Records of information about items in inventory:
	Item number
	Name
	Lot size
	Price
	Reorder point
	Number in stock
	Optimal inventory level
Output (screen):	User prompts
	Messages re the order being processed and reordering information
Output (file):	Updated records for items in inventory

Design. Because an inventory file typically contains a large number of records and because a large number of transactions is processed using this file, sequential access to

Pharmaceutical supplies.

such a file is inefficient. Consequently, the inventory file will be organized as a direct-access file, which allows one to access a specific record directly rather than to search sequentially through all the records preceding it. In order to access a specific record in a direct-access file, it is necessary to know its record number. Thus, a correspondence must be established between the item number and the number of the record in the inventory file that contains the information relevant to this item. This is accomplished by constructing an array INDEX, consisting of a list of item numbers arranged in the same order as in the file. Thus the position of a given item number in this array is the same as the number of the corresponding record in the file. When the program is executed, the elements of the array INDEX are read from a file that contains the item numbers. This file is unformatted because it is read only by the program and is not intended for display to the user.

There are two major tasks that the program must carry out. The first is the initialization task, which consists of opening the necessary files and constructing the array INDEX. The second task is the transaction processing, which consists of accepting the order information from the user, searching the index file to determine the appropriate record number, and carrying out the necessary processing using the order information and the information found in this record. The structure diagram in Figure 11.3 displays these tasks and subtasks and the relationship between them.

Figure 11.3

Structure diagram for inventory program.

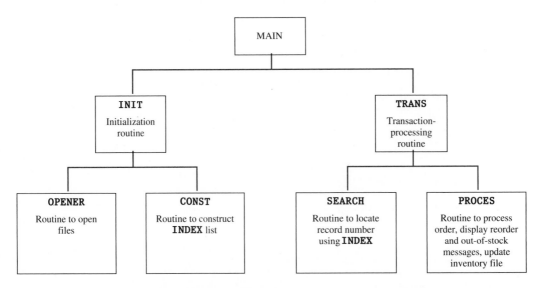

Most of these program components are quite simple and we will not give detailed algorithms for them, but instead give informal descriptions of their purposes.

Main program: Calls the subprogram INIT and then repeatedly calls the subprogram TRANS until the user indicates that there are no more transactions to process.

INIT:	Opens the inventory file and the index file by calling the subprogram OPENER. It then calls subprogram CONST to construct the array INDEX of item numbers.
TRANS:	Accepts an order for a certain item and calls subprogram SEARCH to search the array INDEX to find the position of this item in the inventory file. If the item is found, subprogram PROCES then processes the order.
OPENER:	Generates a unit number and attaches it to a specified file. It then opens this file with specified format, status, and access attributes.
CONST:	Constructs the array INDEX of item numbers.
TRANS:	Accepts an order for a certain item and calls subprogram SEARCH to search the array INDEX to find the position of this item in the inventory file.
SEARCH:	Linear searches the array INDEX for a specified item number.
PROCESS:	Processes a given order by determining if there is sufficient stock to fill the order, updates the record for that item, and checks if the in-stock level has fallen below the reorder point.

Coding, Execution, and Testing. The program in Figure 11.4 has the structure just described. The processing carried out by the subroutines INIT, TRANS, OPENER, CONST, SEARCH, and PROCESS is straightforward, and their documentation explains clearly their input/output and accepts/returns specifications. Also shown is a small test file used in a sample run and a listing of the updated test file produced by this run.

 Figure 11.4 Inventory program.

```
      PROGRAM INVEN
**MAIN*****************************************************************
* This program accepts an order from the terminal, searches an inven-  *
* tory file to see if the item ordered is in stock, updates the file,  *
* and displays an out-of-stock message and reorder message when        *
* necessary.  The search of the inventory file uses an index of item   *
* numbers.  This index is read into main memory from an unformatted    *
* file.  Identifiers used are:                                         *
*    LIMIT  : upper limit on the number of items in inventory file     *
*    LREC   : length of records in inventory file                      *
*    INUNIT : unit number of INFILE                                    *
*    INDEX  : array of item numbers (INDEX(0) = # of items)            *
*    RESPON : response from user (Y or N) re more orders to process    *
*                                                                      *
* Input (keyboard): RESPON, file names, and order information          *
* Input (file):     The array INDEX and items in inventory records     *
* Output (screen):  Messages and user prompts                          *
* Output (file):    Updated inventory records                          *
*    *******************************************************************
```

Figure 11.4 *(cont.)*

```
      INTEGER LREC, LIMIT
      PARAMETER (LIMIT = 1000, LREC = 58)
      CHARACTER*1 RESPON
      INTEGER INUNIT, INDEX(0:LIMIT)

      CALL INIT (INUNIT, INDEX, LIMIT, LREC)

* Repeat the following until there are no more transactions

10    CONTINUE
          CALL TRANS(INUNIT, INDEX, LIMIT)
          PRINT *, 'MORE TRANSACTIONS (Y OR N)'
          READ '(A)', RESPON
      IF (RESPON .EQ. 'Y') GO TO 10

      END


**INIT***********************************************************************
* This subroutine opens the inventory file and the index file and con- *
* structs the array INDEX of item numbers.  Variables used are:        *
*     INUNIT, INDEX, LIMIT, LREC as in MAIN                            *
*     INFILE           : name of inventory file                       *
*     IXFILE, IXUNIT : name and unit number of index file             *
*                                                                      *
* Accepts: INDEX, LIMIT, LREC                                          *
* Input:   INFILE, IXFILE                                              *
* Returns: INUNIT, INDEX                                               *
* Output:  User prompts                                                *
***************************************************************************


      SUBROUTINE INIT(INUNIT, INDEX, LIMIT, LREC)

      CHARACTER*20 INFILE, IXFILE
      INTEGER INUNIT, LIMIT, INDEX(0:LIMIT), IXUNIT, LREC

* Get name of inventory file and open it as a direct access file
      PRINT *, 'ENTER NAME OF INVENTORY FILE:'
      READ '(A)', INFILE
      CALL OPENER(INFILE, INUNIT, 'FORMATTED', 'OLD', 'DA', LREC)

* Get name of index file and open it as an unformatted file
      PRINT *, 'ENTER NAME OF INDEX FILE:'
      READ '(A)', IXFILE
      CALL OPENER(IXFILE, IXUNIT, 'UNFORMATTED', 'OLD', 'SE', 0)
```

Figure 11.4 *(cont.)*

```
* Construct the array INDEX
      CALL CONST(IXUNIT, INDEX, LIMIT)

      END


**OPENER************************************************************
* Subroutine to open a file and assign it a unit number. Successive  *
* calls to this subroutine assign unit numbers 10, 11, 12, ... A call *
* to OPENER with TYPE = 'SE' opens a sequential file, and a call with *
* TYPE = 'DA' opens a direct-access file. Variables used are:         *
*     FNAME  : name of file to be opened                              *
*     NUNIT  : unit number to be connected to file (integer)          *
*     N      : last unit number assigned by subroutine                *
*     FORMSP : 'FORMATTED' or 'UNFORMATTED' depending on whether file *
*            : is formatted or unformatted                            *
*     STAT   : status of file ('OLD', 'NEW', 'SCRATCH', etc.)         *
*     TYPE   : indicates if file is sequential or direct access       *
*     LREC   : length of records for direct-access files             *
*                                                                     *
* Accepts: FNAME, FORMSP, STAT, TYPE, LREC                            *
* Returns: NUNIT                                                      *
* Output:  Messages re opening of files                               *
***********************************************************************

      SUBROUTINE OPENER(FNAME, NUNIT, FORMSP, STAT, TYPE, LREC)

      CHARACTER*(*) FNAME, FORMSP, STAT, TYPE
      INTEGER LREC, NUNIT, N
      SAVE N
      DATA N/10/

      IF(TYPE .EQ. 'SE') THEN
*        Open FNAME as a sequential file
         OPEN(UNIT = N, FILE = FNAME, FORM = FORMSP, STATUS = STAT,
     +        ERR = 10)
      ELSE

*        Open FNAME as a direct-access file
         OPEN(UNIT = N, FILE = FNAME, FORM = FORMSP, STATUS = STAT,
     +        ACCESS = 'DIRECT', RECL = LREC, ERR = 10)
      END IF

* Assign a unit number and increment counter for unit numbers
      NUNIT = N
      N = N + 1
```

Figure 11.4 *(cont.)*

```
* Do the following if error occurs in attempt to open files
10    PRINT *, FNAME, ' CANNOT BE OPENED'
      RETURN

      END


**CONST**************************************************************
* This subroutine constructs the array INDEX of item numbers from an *
* (unformatted) index file. IXUNIT, INDEX, and LIMIT are as          *
* in MAIN. Other variables used are:                                 *
*     I     : count of records in inventory file (stored in          *
*             INDEX(0) before return)                                *
*     ITNUM : item number                                            *
*                                                                    *
* Accepts:      IXUNIT, INDEX, LIMIT                                 *
* Input (file): Elements of the array INDEX                          *
* Returns:      INDEX                                                *
********************************************************************

      SUBROUTINE CONST(IXUNIT, INDEX, LIMIT)

      INTEGER LIMIT, INDEX(0:LIMIT), IXUNIT, I, ITNUM

      I = 0

* While there is more data, do the following:

10    CONTINUE
          READ (IXUNIT, END = 20) ITNUM
          I = I + 1
          INDEX(I) = ITNUM
      GO TO 10
20    CONTINUE

* Store the count in INDEX(0)
      INDEX(0) = I

      END
```

Figure 11.4 *(cont.)*

```
**TRANS*****************************************************************
* This subroutine processes a transaction.  It accepts an order for a  *
* certain item from the keyboard, searches the array INDEX to find the *
* number of the record in the inventory file describing this item, and *
* then updates this record (displaying out-of-stock and/or reorder     *
* messages on the screen when necessary). Variables used are:          *
*     INUNIT, INDEX, LIMIT as in MAIN and INIT                         *
*     NUMORD : order number                                            *
*     ITNUM  : item number                                             *
*     QUANT  : number of items ordered                                 *
*     NUMREC : number of record containing information re ITNUM        *
*              (value 0 indicates item not found)                      *
*                                                                      *
* Accepts: INUNIT, INDEX, LIMIT                                        *
* Input :  NUMORD, ITNUM, QUANT                                        *
* Accepts: INUNIT, INDEX, LIMIT                                        *
* Output : User prompts                                                *
***********************************************************************

      SUBROUTINE TRANS(INUNIT, INDEX, LIMIT)

      INTEGER LIMIT, INDEX (0:LIMIT), INUNIT, NUMORD, ITNUM, QUANT,
     +         NUMREC

* Get first order
      PRINT *, 'ENTER ORDER #'
      READ *, NUMORD
      PRINT *, '(ENTER 0/ FOR ITEM # TO TERMINATE ORDER)'
      PRINT *, 'ITEM #, QUANTITY'
      READ *, ITNUM, QUANT
```

Figure 11.4 *(cont.)*

```
* While ITNUM not equal to 0, process orders:

10    IF (ITNUM .NE. 0) THEN

*        Search the array INDEX for the item number
         CALL SEARCH(ITNUM, INDEX, LIMIT, NUMREC)

*        If item found, process the order
         IF (NUMREC .NE. 0)
    +        CALL PROCES(NUMREC, QUANT, NUMORD, INUNIT)

*        Get next order
         PRINT *, 'ITEM #, QUANTITY'
         READ *, ITNUM, QUANT
      GO TO 10
      END IF

      END

**SEARCH***********************************************************
* This subroutine searches the array INDEX of item numbers to locate   *
* the number NUMREC of the record in the inventory file containing     *
* information re the item with item number ITNUM. LIMIT is as in MAIN  *
* and FOUND is a logical variable indicating whether the item has been *
* found.                                                               *
*                                                                      *
* Accepts: INDEX, ITNUM, LIMIT                                         *
* Returns: NUMREC                                                      *
***********************************************************************

      SUBROUTINE SEARCH(ITNUM, INDEX, LIMIT, NUMREC)

      INTEGER LIMIT, INDEX(0:LIMIT), ITNUM, NUMREC, I
      LOGICAL FOUND

      I = 1
      FOUND = .FALSE.
```

Figure 11.4 *(cont.)*

```
* While FOUND is false and I is less than or equal to the
* number of items in the array INDEX do the following:

10    IF ((.NOT. FOUND) .AND. (I .LE. INDEX(0))) THEN
          IF (ITNUM .EQ. INDEX(I)) THEN
              NUMREC = I
              FOUND = .TRUE.
          ELSE
              I = I + 1
          END IF
      GO TO 10
      END IF


      IF (.NOT. FOUND) THEN
          PRINT *, 'BAD ITEM NUMBER'
          NUMREC = 0
      END IF


      END


**PROCES**************************************************************
* This subroutine processes an order (order # NUMORD) for QUANT items. *
* The NUMREC-th record of the inventory file (unit number INUNIT) is   *
* examined to determine whether the number in stock is sufficient to   *
* fill the order. If not, an out-of-stock message will be displayed    *
* at the terminal. In either case, this record will be updated.        *
* Also, if the new number in stock is below the reorder point, a        *
* reorder message will be displayed at the terminal. New variables      *
* used are:                                                             *
*      INFO    :   unused information in a record                       *
*      REORD   :   reorder point                                        *
*      INSTOK  :   number of items in stock                             *
*      INLEV   :   desired inventory level                              *
*      STOCK   :   INSTOK - QUANT (# remaining in stock)                *
*      FORM    :   an i/o format                                        *
*                                                                       *
* Accepts:        NUMREC, QUANT, NUMORD, INUNIT                         *
* Input file) :   ITNUM, INFO, REORD, INSTOK, INLEV                     *
* Output(screen): Messages re the order being processed and reordering  *
*                 information                                           *
* Output(file):   ITNUM, INFO, REORD, INSTOK (updated), INLEV           *
  *********************************************************************
```

Figure 11.4 *(cont.)*

```
      SUBROUTINE PROCES(NUMREC, QUANT, NUMORD, INUNIT)

      CHARACTER*36 INFO, FORM
      INTEGER NUMREC, QUANT, NUMORD, INUNIT, REORD, INSTOK, INLEV, STOCK
      SAVE FORM
      DATA FORM / '(I4, A35, 3I6)' /

* Read record from inventory file and how many are left stock
      READ (INUNIT, FORM, REC = NUMREC) ITNUM, INFO, REORD, INSTOK,
     +     INLEV
      STOCK = INSTOK - QUANT

*Check if enough in stock to fill order
      IF (STOCK .LT. 0) THEN
         PRINT *, 'OUT OF STOCK ON ITEM #', ITNUM
         PRINT *, 'BACK ORDER', -STOCK, ' FOR ORDER #', NUMORD
         PRINT *, 'ONLY', INSTOK,' UNITS CAN BE SHIPPED AT THIS TIME'
         PRINT *, 'THE DESIRED INVENTORY LEVEL IS', INLEV
         INSTOK = 0
      ELSE
         INSTOK = STOCK
         PRINT *, 'DONE'
      END IF

* Update the inventory file
      WRITE (INUNIT, FORM, REC = NUMREC) ITNUM, INFO, REORD, INSTOK,
     +     INLEV

*Check if item should be reordered
      IF ((STOCK .GE. 0) .AND. (STOCK .LE. REORD)) THEN
         PRINT *, 'ONLY',INSTOK,' UNITS OF',ITNUM,' REMAIN IN STOCK'
         PRINT *, 'REORDER POINT IS', REORD
         PRINT *, 'DESIRED INVENTORY LEVEL IS', INLEV
      END IF

      END
```

Figure 11.4 *(cont.)*

Sample run:

```
ENTER NAME OF INVENTORY FILE:
FIL11-4A.DAT
ENTER NAME OF INDEX FILE:
FIL11-4B.DAT
ENTER ORDER #
11111
(ENTER 0/ FOR ITEM # TO TERMINATE ORDER)
ITEM #, QUANTITY
1011, 1200
DONE
ITEM #, QUANTITY
1021, 700
DONE
ITEM #, QUANTITY
1040, 80
DONE
ITEM #, QUANTITY
0/
MORE TRANSACTIONS (Y OR N)
Y
ENTER ORDER #
11119
(ENTER 0/ FOR ITEM # TO TERMINATE ORDER)
ITEM #, QUANTITY
1021, 95
DONE
ONLY  1962 UNITS OF  1021 REMAIN IN STOCK
REORDER POINT IS  2000
DESIRED INVENTORY LEVEL IS  3000
ITEM #, QUANTITY
1022, 945
DONE
ONLY  2000 UNITS OF  1022 REMAIN IN STOCK
REORDER POINT IS  2000
DESIRED INVENTORY LEVEL IS  3000
ITEM #, QUANTITY
1040, 100
DONE
ITEM #, QUANTITY
0/
MORE TRANSACTIONS (Y OR N)
N
```

Figure 11.4 *(cont.)*

Contents of test file `FIL11-4A.DAT` **used in sample run:**

```
1011IBUPROFEN-600mg           500   2398 15000 21773 25000
1012CARBAMAZEPINE-200mg       500   7155  2500  2528  3500
1021LEVOTHYROXINE-0.2mg      1000   3900  2000  2757  3000
1022SULFAMEETHOXAZOLE DS      500   6775  2000  2945  3000
1023TERFENADINE-60mg          500  37953  2500  3302  3500
1031AMOXICILLIN-500mg         500   4773 10000 10175 15000
1033CIPROFLAXIN-500mg         100  30248  2000  2155  3000
1037HYDROCHLOROTHIAZIDE-50mg 5000   2565  1500  1770  2500
1040CYCLOBENZAPRINE-10mg      100   7925  2000  2188  2500
```

Contents of updated file produced by sample run:

```
1011IBUPROFEN-600mg           500   2398 15000 20573 25000
1012CARBAMAZEPINE-200mg       500   7155  2500  2528  3500
1021LEVOTHYROXINE-0.2mg      1000   3900  2000  1962  3000
1022SULFAMEETHOXAZOLE DS      500   6775  2000  2000  3000
1023TERFENADINE-60mg          500  37953  2500  3302  3500
1031AMOXICILLIN-500mg         500   4773 10000 10175 15000
1033CIPROFLAXIN-500mg         100  30248  2000  2155  3000
1037HYDROCHLOROTHIAZIDE-50mg 5000   2565  1500  1770  2500
1040CYCLOBENZAPRINE-10mg      100   7925  2000  2008  2500
```

Quick Quiz 11.3

1. What are the major differences between sequential files and direct-access files?
2. Write a statement that will associate an existing sequential file named TESTDATA with unit number 12.
3. Write a statement that will associate unit number 10 with a direct-access file to be created by the program with record length 30 and named NEWDATA.
4. Write a READ statement that will read an integer value for the variable ITEMNO from the first 5 character positions of record 100 of the file associated with unit number 10.
5. What is an unformatted file, and when is it appropriate to use such a file?
6. Describe how natural mergesort sorts the list 4, 1, 7, 3, 6, 2, 5.

Exercises 11.3

Following the example of the text, show the various splitting–merging stages of mergesort for the following lists of numbers:

1. 1, 5, 3, 8, 7, 2, 6, 4
2. 1, 8, 2, 7, 3, 6, 5, 4
3. 1, 2, 3, 4, 5, 6, 7, 8
4. 8, 7, 6, 5, 4, 3, 2, 1

CHAPTER REVIEW

Summary

This chapter takes a detailed look at files. It describes both sequential and direct-access files as well as formatted and unformatted files. Section 11.1 completes the description of the OPEN and CLOSE statements begun in Chapter 5 and also describes the INQUIRE statement. Section 11.2 describes file input/output in detail, together with the file-positioning statements BACKSPACE, REWIND, and ENDFILE. It illustrates the use of direct-access files with an information retrieval example using a direct-access inventory file. The problems of merging and sorting files are also considered and programs given for their solutions. The application to a pharmacy inventory problem in the last section illustrates most of FORTRAN's file-processing capabilities.

FORTRAN SUMMARY

OPEN Statement

```
OPEN (open-list)
```

where open-list includes:

1. A unit specifier indicating a unit number to be connected to the file being opened:

```
UNIT = integer-expression
```

or simply

```
integer-expression
```

2. A clause of the form

```
FILE = character-expression
```

indicating the name of the file being opened.

3. A

```
STATUS = character-expression
```

clause specifying whether the file is `'NEW'`, `'OLD'`, `'SCRATCH'`, or `'UNKNOWN'`.

and may also include:

4. An

```
IOSTAT = integer-variable
```

clause that assigns 0 to the integer variable if the file was opened successfully and a positive value otherwise.

5. An

```
ERR = statement-label
```

clause specifying a statement label to be executed if an error occurs while attempting to open the file.

6. A clause of the form

```
ACCESS = access-method
```

specifying the type of access as SEQUENTIAL or DIRECT.

7. A

```
FORM = form-specifier
```

clause specifying whether the file is FORMATTED or UNFORMATTED.

8. A

```
RECL = record-length
```

clause specifying the record length for a direct-access file.

9. A clause of the form

```
BLANK = blank-specifier
```

specifying whether blanks in a numeric field are to be interpreted as ZERO or are to be ignored (NULL).

Examples:

```
 OPEN (UNIT = 10, FILE = 'INFO1', STATUS = 'OLD')
 OPEN (UNIT = 10, FILE = INFILE, STATUS = 'OLD',
+     FORM = 'FORMATTED', ACCESS = 'SEQUENTIAL')
```

Purpose:
The OPEN statement opens a file with the specifed unit number and makes it available for input and output.

CLOSE **Statement**

```
CLOSE (close-list)
```

where *close-list* must include a unit specifier and may also include an IOSTAT = clause and an ERR = clause as described earlier together with a STATUS = clause specifying whether the file is to be kept (KEEP) or deleted (DELETE).

Examples:

```
CLOSE(12)
CLOSE(UNIT = 12)
CLOSE (UNIT = 12, STATUS = 'KEEP')
```

Purpose:
The CLOSE statement closes the file associated with the specifed unit number.

INQUIRE **Statement**

```
INQUIRE (UNIT = unit number, inquiry-list)
INQUIRE (FILE = file number, inquiry-list)
```

where "UNIT =" and "FILE =" are optional, and *inquiry-list* may include a number of different clauses as described in Table 11.1:

```
ACCESS = variable
ERR = label
EXIST = variable
```

```
FORM = variable
FORMATTED = variable
IOSTAT = variable
NAME = variable
NAMED = variable
NEXTREC = variable
NUMBER = variable
OPENED = variable
RECL = variable
SEQUENTIAL = variable
```

Examples:

```
LOGICAL FILEEX
CHARACTER*10 ACTYPE
INTEGER UNUMB

INQUIRE (UNIT = 12, EXISTS = FILEEX, ACCESS = ACTYPE)

INQUIRE (FILE = 'FILXY.DAT', EXISTS = FILEEX,
+        NUMBER = UNUMB)
```

Purpose:
Each of the clauses (except the ERR = clause) in the inquiry list acts as a question concerning some property of the file; a value that answers the question is assigned to the variable in each clause.

READ **Statement**

```
READ format-specifier, input-list
```

or

```
READ (control-list) input-list
```

where *input-list* is a list of variables, substring names, array names, or implied DO loops; and *control-list* must include

  1. A unit specifier (as described earlier) indicating the unit number connected to the file.

It may also include one or more of the following:

  2. A format specifier describing the format of the information to be read:

```
FMT = format-specifier
```

or simply

```
format-specifier
```

where *format-specifier* is one of the following:

1. * (an asterisk);
2. a character constant or a character variable (or expression or array) whose value specifies the format for the output;
3. the label of a FORMAT statement.

3. An

```
IOSTAT = integer-variable
```

clause that assigns a positive value to the integer variable if an input error occurs, a negative value if the end of data occurs, and zero if neither occurs.

4. An

```
END = statement-number
```

clause specifying a statement to be executed when the end of the file is reached.

5. An ERR = clause (described earlier) specifying a statement to be executed if an input error occurs.

6. A clause of the form

```
REC = integer-expression
```

indicating the number of the record to be read for a direct-access file.

Example:

```
READ (10, '(A)', REC = PARTNO, IOSTAT = BADNUM), INFO
READ (12, *, END = 20) CODE, TEMP, PRESS
```

Purpose:
The READ statement reads values for the variables in the input list from the specified input device, using the format specified by the format specifier.

WRITE Statement

```
WRITE (control-list) output-list
```

where *output-list* has the same syntax as in the PRINT statement; and *control-list* must include a unit specifier (as described earlier) indicating the unit number connected to the file. It may also include one or more of the following (described earlier):

1. A format specifier describing the form of the information being output.
2. An ERR = clause specifying a statement to be executed if an output error occurs.
3. An IOSTAT = clause to check the status of the output operation.
4. A REC = clause indicating the number of the record to which the information is to be output for a direct-access file.

Examples:

```
      WRITE (*, *) 'AT TIME ', TIME, ' VELOCITY IS ', VELOC
      WRITE (20, 10), TIME, VELOC
   10 FORMAT(1X, 'AT TIME', F6.2, ' VELOCITY IS ', F6.3)
```

Purpose:
The WRITE statement writes the values of the expressions in the output list to the specified output file, using the format determined by the format specifier.

File-Positioning Statements

```
      REWIND unit          or    REWIND (position-list)
      BACKSPACE unit       or    BACKSPACE (position-list)
      ENDFILE unit         or    ENDFILE (position-list)
```

where *unit* is the unit number connected to a file. In the second form, *position-list* must contain a unit specifier. It may also contain any of the following (defined earlier):

1. An ERR = clause specifying the number of a statement to be executed if an error occurs while positioning the file.
2. An IOSTAT = clause specifying a status variable that is assigned 0 if the file is successfully positioned or a positive value if some error occurs.

Example:

```
   REWIND 12
   BACKSPACE 12
   ENDFILE 12
```

Purpose:
The REWIND statement positions the file at its beginning. The BACKSPACE statement positions the file at the beginning of the preceding record. The ENDFILE statement writes a special end-of-file record into the file.

PROGRAMMING PROBLEMS

1. Write a program to concatenate two files, that is, to append one file to the end of the other.

2. (a) Design an algorithm to perform the file splitting required by mergesort.

   (b) Write a program to read records from USERS.DAT (described in Appendix B) and sort them using mergesort so that the resources used to date are in increasing order.

3. Information about computer terminals in a computer network is maintained in a direct-access file. The terminals are numbered 1 through 100, and information about the nth terminal is stored in the nth record of the file. This information consists of a terminal type (string), the building in which it is located (string), the transmission rate (integer), an access code (character), and the date of last service (month, day, year). Write a program to read a terminal number, retrieve and display the information about that terminal, and modify the date of last service for that terminal.

4. (Project) Some text formatters allow command lines to be placed in the file of unformatted text. These command lines might have forms such as the following:

   .P m n Insert m blank lines before each paragraph and indent each paragraph n spaces.

   .W n Page width (line length) is n.

   .L n Page length (number of lines per page) is n.

   .I n Indent by n spaces all lines following this command line.

   .U   Undent all following lines, and reset to the previous left margin.

   Write a program to read a file containing lines of text and some of these command lines throughout, and produce a new file in which these formatting commands have been implemented.

5. (Project) Modify and extend the text editor program of Section 10.7 so that other editing operations can be performed. Include commands of the following forms in the menu of options:

   Fn Find and display the nth line of the file.

   Pn Print n consecutive lines, beginning with the current line.

   Mn Move ahead n lines from the current line.

   T   Move to the top line of the file.

   C/$string_1$/$string_2$/   Change the current line by replacing $string_1$ with $string_2$.

L *string*	Search the file starting from the current line to find a line containing *string*.
D*n*	Delete *n* consecutive lines, beginning with the current line.
I *line*	Insert the given *line* after the current line.

6. (Project) A *pretty printer* is a special kind of text formatter that reads a file containing a source program and then prints it in a "pretty" format. For example, a pretty printer for FORTRAN might insert blank lines between subprograms, indent and align statements within other statements such as block IF statements and DO loops, and so on, to produce a format similar to that used in the sample programs in this text. Write a pretty print program for FORTRAN programs to indent and align statements in a pleasing format.

7. (Project) Write a menu-driven program that uses STUDENT.DAT and STUP-DATE.DAT (see Appendix B) and allows (some of) the following options. For each option, write a separate subprogram so that options and corresponding subprograms can be easily added or removed.

(1) Locate a student's permanent record when given his or her student number and print it in a nicer format than that in which it is stored.

(2) Same as option 1, but locate the record when given the student's name.

(3) Print a list of all student names and numbers in a given class (1, 2, 3, 4, 5).

(4) Same as option 3 but for a given major.

(5) Same as option 3 but for a given range of cumulative GPAs.

(6) Find the average cumulative GPAs for (a) all females, (b) all males, (c) all students with a specified major, and (d) all students.

(7) Produce updated grade reports with the following format (where *xx* is the current year):

```
            GRADE REPORT — SEMESTER 2   5/29/xx

                  DISPATCH UNIVERSITY

      10103      JAMES L. JOHNSON

                  GRADE          CREDITS
                  =====          =======
      ENGL 176     C                4
      EDUC 268     B                4
      EDUC 330     B+               3
      P E 281      C                3
      ENGR 317     D                4

      CUMULATIVE CREDITS:          28
      CURRENT GPA:                 2.22
      CUMULATIVE GPA:              2.64
```

Here, letter grades are assigned according to the following scheme: A = 4.0, A− = 3.7, B+ = 3.3, B = 3.0, B− = 2.7, C+ = 2.3, C = 2.0, C− = 1.7, D+ = 1.3, D = 1.0, D− = 0.7, and F = 0.0. (See Programming Problem 20 in Chapter 2 for details on the calculation of GPAs.)

(8) Same as option 7, but instead of producing grade reports, produce a new file containing the updated total credits and new cumulative GPAs.

(9) Produce an updated file when a student (a) drops or (b) adds a course.

(10) Produce an updated file when a student (a) transfers into or (b) withdraws from the university.

Fortran 90

Features

The new file-processing features added in Fortran 90 consist mainly of new clauses that may be included in the OPEN, INQUIRE, READ, and WRITE statements.

- New clauses that may be used in an OPEN statement are

  POSITION = 'REWIND' or 'APPEND', or 'ASIS': Positions the file at its initial point, at the end of the file, or leaves its position unchanged, respectively.

  ACTION = 'READ' or 'WRITE', or 'READWRITE': Opens the file for reading only, for writing only, or both, respectively.

  DELIM = 'APOSTROPHE', 'QUOTE', or 'NONE': Character strings to be written to the file by list-directed output or by name-list formatting are enclosed in apostrophes or quotation marks or with no enclosing delimiters, respectively.

  PAD = 'YES' or 'NO': Specifies whether or not an input character value is to be padded with blanks.

- New clauses that may be used in READ and WRITE statements are

  NML = name-list-group-name: See the Fortran 90 section in Chapter 5 for a description of NAMELIST input/output.

  ADVANCE = 'NO' or 'YES': Enables or disables nonadvancing input/output.

  SIZE = integer-variable: Used in nonadvancing input statements to count characters read.

  EOR = label: Transfers control to the specified statement if an end-of-record condition is encountered in a nonadvancing input/output statement.

- New clauses that may be used in the INQUIRE statement are

  POSITION = character-variable: Assigns 'REWIND', 'APPEND', or 'ASIS' to the specified character variable, according to the file position specified in the OPEN statement for that file.

  ACTION = character-variable: Assigns 'READ', 'WRITE', or 'READWRITE' to the specified character variable, according to the action specified in the OPEN statement for that file.

READ = *character-variable*: Assigns 'YES', 'NO', or 'UNKNOWN' to the specified character variable, according to whether READ is allowed, not allowed, or undetermined for the specified file.

WRITE = *character-variable*: Assigns 'YES', 'NO', or 'UN-KNOWN' to the specified character variable, according to whether WRITE is allowed, not allowed, or undetermined for the specified file.

READWRITE = *character-variable*: Assigns 'YES', 'NO', or 'UN-KNOWN' to the specified character variable, according to whether READ-WRITE is allowed, not allowed, or undetermined for the specified file.

DELIM = *character-variable*: Assigns 'APOSTROPHE', 'QUOTE', or 'NONE' to the specified character variable, according to the delimiter specified in the OPEN statement for that file.

PAD = *character-variable*: Assigns 'YES' or 'NO' to the specified character variable, according to whether or not padding is specified in the OPEN statement for that file.

IOLENGTH = *integer-variable*: Assigns to the specified integer variable the length of an unformatted output list in processor-dependent units. This value may be used in a RECL = clause in an OPEN statement for unformatted direct-access files.

Example

The program in Figure 11.5 is a Fortran 90 version of the program in Figure 11.1 for processing a direct-access inventory file.

Figure 11.5 Direct-access inventory file — Fortran 90 version.

```
PROGRAM Direct_Access_File_Demo
!-------------------------------------------------------------------------------
! Program to read a part number during execution, access a record in
! a direct-access parts inventory file, and display this record.
! Variables used are:
!   RecordLength  : length of records in the file (parameter)
!   PartNumber    : a part number, 0 if invalid part number;
!                       otherwise nonzero
!   BadNumber     : indicates if record number was bad
!   FileName      : name of the file
!   PartsRecord   : a record in the file
!
! Input (keyboard): FileName, PartNumber
! Input (file):     PartsRecord
! Output (screen):  User prompts, PartsRecord, or error message and
!                   PartsNumber for an invalid part number
!-------------------------------------------------------------------------------
```

Figure 11.5 *(cont.)*

```fortran
  IMPLICIT NONE

  INTEGER, PARAMETER :: RecordLength = 31
  INTEGER :: PartNumber, BadNumber

  CHARACTER*20 :: FileName, PartsRecord*(RecordLength)

! Get the name of the file and open it for direct access

  PRINT *, "Enter name of file: "
  READ *, Filename
  OPEN (UNIT = 10, FILE = FileName, STATUS = "OLD", &
        ACCESS = "DIRECT", FORM = "FORMATTED", &
        RECL = RecordLength)

! Repeat the following so long as there are more
! part numbers to process:

  DO
     PRINT *
     PRINT *, "Enter part number (0 to stop): "
     READ *, PartNumber

     IF (PartNumber == 0) EXIT

     READ (10, '(A)', REC = PartNumber, IOSTAT = BadNumber) PartsRecord
     IF (BadNumber == 0) THEN
        PRINT '(1X, "Part", I3, ": ", A)', PartNumber, PartsRecord
     ELSE
        PRINT '(1X, "Invalid part number: ", I3)', PartNumber
     END IF
  END DO

  CLOSE(10)

END PROGRAM Direct_Access_File_Demo
```

12

Additional FORTRAN Features

The superfluous is very necessary.

VOLTAIRE

We have more useless information than ignorance of what is useful.

VAUVENARGUES

Ho! Ha-ha! Guard! Turn! Parry! Dodge! Spin! Ha! Thrust!

DAFFY DUCK

If builders built buildings the way programmers wrote programs, then the first woodpecker that came along would destroy civilization.

WEINBERG'S SECOND LAW

C H A P T E R C O N T E N T S

12.1 Miscellaneous Input/Output Topics

12.2 The STOP and PAUSE Statements

12.3 The IMPLICIT Statement

12.4 Other Control Statements: Arithmetic IF, Computed GO TO, Assigned GO TO

12.5 More About COMMON and Block Data Subprograms

12.6 The EQUIVALENCE Statement

12.7 Alternate Entries and Returns

Fortran 90

*T*here are a number of FORTRAN features that we have not yet discussed, because they are not commonly used and in some cases are not consistent with the principles of structured programming. But because they are part of the standard FORTRAN language, we examine these miscellaneous topics in this chapter.

12.1 MISCELLANEOUS INPUT/OUTPUT TOPICS

In Chapter 5 we described several of the more commonly used format descriptors. These descriptors are used to specify the precise format of output produced by a formatted PRINT or WRITE statement and to specify the format of values to be read by a formatted READ statement. In this section we describe a number of less commonly used format descriptors, as well as some additional features of list-directed input that were not mentioned in Chapter 2 or 5.

The G Descriptor

In addition to the E and F descriptors for the input and output of real data, a G (general) descriptor of the form

$$rGw.d \quad \text{or} \quad rGw.dEe$$

may be used, where

w is an integer constant that indicates the total width of the field in which the data is to be displayed

d is an integer constant indicating the number of significant digits to be displayed

r is the repetition indicator, an integer constant indicating the number of such fields; it is not required if there is only one field

e is the number of positions to be used in displaying the exponent

A real value that is output using a G descriptor is displayed using an F or E descriptor, depending on the magnitude (absolute value) of the real number.

Intuitively, the G descriptor functions like an F descriptor for values that are neither very large nor very small, but like an E descriptor otherwise. More precisely, suppose that a real quantity has a value that if expressed in normalized scientific notation would have the form

$$\pm 0.d_1 d_2 \ldots d_n \times 10^k$$

and this value is to be displayed using a G$w.d$ descriptor. If $0 \le k \le d$, this value is output in "F form" with a field width of $w - 4$ followed by four blanks. If, however, k is negative or greater than d, it is output using an E$w.d$ descriptor. In either case, d significant digits are displayed. The following examples illustrate:

Value	G Descriptor	Output Produced
0.123456	G12.6	0.123456 _ _ _ _
0.123456E1	G11.6	1.23456 _ _ _ _
0.123456E5	G11.6	12345.6 _ _ _ _
0.123456E6	G11.6	123456. _ _ _ _
0.123456E7	G12.6	0.123456E+07

Although the G descriptor is intended primarily for real output, it may also be used for real input in a manner similar to that of the F descriptor.

The L Descriptor

An L descriptor is used for formatted input/output of logical values. This format descriptor has the form

    rLw

where

w is an integer constant specifying the field width

r is the repetition indicator, an integer constant specifying the number of such fields. It may be omitted if there is only one field.

For output, the field consists of $w - 1$ spaces followed by a T or an F. For example, if A, B, and C are logical variables given by

```
LOGICAL A, B, C

A = .TRUE.
B = .FALSE.
C = .FALSE.
```

the statements

```
    PRINT 30, A, B, C, A .OR. C
30 FORMAT(1X, L4, L2, 2L5)
```

or

```
PRINT '(1X, L4, L2, 2L5)', A, B, C, A .OR. C
```

produce

```
   T F    F    T
------------------
```

Logical data can also be read using an L descriptor. The input value consists of optional blanks followed by an optional period followed by a T for true or an F for false; any characters following T or F are ignored. For example, if the line of data

```
 .TRUE   TWO.F FT
------------------
```

is read by the statements

```
    LOGICAL A, B, C, D, E

    READ 40, A, B, C, D, E
40 FORMAT(2L6, 3L2)
```

or

```
    READ '(2L6, 3L2)', A, B, C, D, E
```

then A, B, and E are assigned the value true, and C and D the value false.

Scale Factors

To permit more general usage of the E, F, G, and D descriptors, they may be preceded by scale factors of the form

$$nP$$

where n is an integer constant. In the case of output, a descriptor of the form

```
nPFw.d
```

causes the displayed value to be multiplied by 10^n. For the E (and D) descriptor,

```
nPEw.d      or      nPEw.dEe
```

causes the fractional part of the displayed value to be multiplied by 10^n and the exponent to be decreased by n. For the G descriptor, a scale factor has an effect only if the value being output is in a range that causes it to be displayed in E form, and in this case the effect of the scale factor is the same as that described for the E descriptor.

To illustrate the use of scale factors, suppose that the values of the integer variable N and the real variables X, Y, and Z are given by

```
N:    27
X:    −93.2094
Y:    −0.0076
Z:    55.3612
```

and consider the following statements:

```
  PRINT 1, N, X, Y, Z
  PRINT 2, N, X, Y, Z
  PRINT 3, N, X, Y, Z
1 FORMAT(1X, I2, 2F11.3, E12.4)
2 FORMAT(1X, I2, 1P2F11.3, 3PE12.4)
3 FORMAT(1X, I2, −1P2F11.3, E12.4)
```

The output produced by these statements is

```
27     −93.209     −0.008  0.5536E+02
27    −932.094     −0.076  553.61E−01
27      −9.321     −0.001  0.0554E+03
```

As the last FORMAT statement demonstrates, once a scale factor has been given in a format specifier, it holds for all E, F, G, and D descriptors that follow it in the same format specifier. If a subsequent scale factor of zero is desired in that format specifier, it must be specified by 0P.

In the case of input, scale factors may be used with the descriptors for real data in much the same manner as they were for output. The only difference is that if a real value is input in E form, the scale factor has no effect. For example, for the statements

```
   REAL A, B, C
   READ 15, A, B, C
15 FORMAT(2PF6.0, −2PF6.0, F6.0)
```

if the data

```
 _ _ 1.1_ _ _1.1_ _ _1.1
 _ _ _ _ _ _ _ _ _ _ _ _ _ _ _
```

is read, the following assignments are made:

    A: 110.0
    B: .011
    C: .011

(The scale factor -2 remains in effect for the last descriptor.) If the data was entered in the form

```
 _1.1E0_ _ _1.1_1.1E0
 _ _ _ _ _ _ _ _ _ _ _ _ _ _ _
```

the assignment would be

    A: 1.1
    B: .011
    C: 1.1

The BN and BZ Descriptors

As we observed in Section 5.3, blanks within a numeric input field may be interpreted as zeros, or they may be ignored. Which interpretation is to be used may be specified by the programmer by including a BN or BZ descriptor in the format specifier. If a BN ("Blank Null") or BZ ("Blank Zero") descriptor is encountered during a scan of the list of descriptors, all blanks in fields determined by subsequent numeric descriptors in that format specifier are ignored or interpreted as zero, respectively. In all cases, a numeric field consisting entirely of blanks is interpreted as the value 0.

To illustrate, consider the following data line:

```
 537_ _6.258E3_
 _ _ _ _ _ _ _ _ _ _ _ _
```

If NUM is an integer variable and ALPHA is a real variable, the statements

```
      READ 40, NUM, ALPHA
 40 FORMAT(BZ, I5, F8.0)
```

assign the following values to NUM and ALPHA:

    NUM: 53700
    ALPHA: 6.258E30

since the BZ descriptor causes the two blanks in the field corresponding to the I5 descriptor and the single blank in the field corresponding to the F8.0 descriptor to be interpreted as zeros. On the other hand,

```
    READ 41, NUM, ALPHA
41 FORMAT(BN, I5, F8.0)
```

assign the values

```
NUM:    537
ALPHA:  6.258E3
```

since the BN descriptor causes these same blanks to be ignored. The statements

```
    READ 42, NUM, ALPHA
42 FORMAT(BZ, I5, BN, F8.0)
```

assign the values

```
NUM:    53700
ALPHA:  6.258E3
```

The S, SP, and SS Descriptors

The S, SP, and SS descriptors may be used to control the output of plus (+) signs in a numeric output field. If the SP ("Sign Positive") descriptor appears in a format specifier, all positive numeric values output by the statement are preceded by a + sign. On the other hand, the SS ("Sign Suppress") descriptor suppresses the output of all such + signs. An S descriptor may be used to restore control to the computer system, which has the option of displaying or suppressing a + sign.

The H Descriptor

We have seen that character constants may be displayed by including them in the list of descriptors of a format specifier; for example,

```
(1X, 'FOR', I5, ' SAMPLES, THE AVERAGE IS', F8.2)
```

Strings may also be displayed by using a Hollerith descriptor of the form

```
nHstring
```

where n is the number of characters in *string*. Thus, the preceding format specifier can also be written

```
(1X, 3HFOR, I5, 24H SAMPLES, THE AVERAGE IS, F8.2)
```

The TL and TR Descriptors

The TL and TR descriptors are positional descriptors of the form

```
TLn     and     TRn
```

where n is a positive integer constant. They indicate that input or output of the next data value is to occur n positions to the left or right, respectively, of the current position. Thus a descriptor of the form TLn causes a backspace of n positions. In the case of input, this makes it possible to read the same input value several times. For example, for the data line

```
123
```

the statements

```
      INTEGER NUM
      REAL ALPHA, BETA

      READ 50, NUM, ALPHA, BETA
50 FORMAT(I3, TL3, F3.1, TL3, F3.2)
```

assign the integer value 123 to NUM, the real value 12.3 to ALPHA, and the real value 1.23 to BETA:

```
NUM:    123
ALPHA:  12.3
BETA:   1.23
```

In the case of output, a descriptor of the form TLn causes a backspace of n positions on the current output line. However, subsequent descriptors may cause characters in these n positions to be replaced rather than overprinted. For both input and output, a descriptor of the form TRn functions in exactly the same manner as does nX.

List-Directed Input

In a data line, consecutive commas with no intervening characters except blanks represent **null values,** which leave unchanged the corresponding variables in the input list of a list-directed READ statement. If the variables have previously been assigned values, the values are not changed; if they have not been assigned values, the variables remain undefined. A slash in a data line terminates the input and leaves unchanged the values of the remaining variables in the input list.

If the same value is to be read for r consecutive variables in the input list, this common value may be entered in the corresponding data line in the form

```
r*value
```

A repeated null value may be indicated by

    r*

In this case, the corresponding *r* consecutive items in the input list are unchanged.

The following examples illustrate these conventions for list-directed input. They are not used in list-directed output, except that a given processor has the option of displaying

    r*value

for successive output items that have the same value.

Statement	Data Entered	Result
READ *, J, K, A, B	1,,,2.3	J = 1 K and A are unchanged B = 2.3
READ *, J, K, A, B,	,,,,	J, K, A, and B all are unchanged
READ *, J, K, A, B	1,2/	J = 1 K = 2 A and B are unchanged
READ *, J, K, A, B	/	J, K, A, and B all are unchanged
READ *, J, K, A, B	2*1, 2*2.3	J = 1 and K = 1 A = 2.3 and B = 2.3
READ *, J, K, A ,B	1, 2*, 2.3	J = 1 K and A are unchanged B = 2.3

In the third and fourth examples, any values following the slash would be ignored.

12.2 THE STOP AND PAUSE STATEMENTS

The END statement in a FORTRAN program serves to terminate execution of the program. In more complex programs it may be necessary to stop execution before the END statement is reached. In such cases, execution can be terminated with a STOP **statement,** which has the form

    STOP

or

    STOP constant

where *constant* is an integer constant with five or fewer digits or is a character constant. Usually the constant is displayed when execution is terminated by a STOP statement of the second form, but the precise form of the termination message depends on the compiler.

In some cases, it may be desirable to interrupt program execution and then either terminate or continue it after examining some of the results produced. A PAUSE **statement** may be used for this purpose. This statement has the form

```
PAUSE
```

or

```
PAUSE constant
```

where `constant` is an integer constant with five or fewer digits or a character constant that is usually displayed when execution is interrupted; the exact message (if any) depends on the compiler.

When the PAUSE statement is encountered, execution of the program is interrupted, but it may be resumed by means of an appropriate command. Execution resumes with the first executable statement following the PAUSE statement that caused execution to be suspended. The action required to resume execution depends on the system.

12.3 THE IMPLICIT STATEMENT

The usual FORTRAN *naming convention is that unless otherwise specified, all variable names beginning with* I, J, K, L, M, *or* N *are integers and all other variables are real.* The programmer can override this naming convention with an IMPLICIT **statement,** which has the form

```
IMPLICIT type₁ (a₁, a₂, ... ), type₂ (b₁, b₂, ... ), . . .
```

where each a_i, b_i,... is a letter or a pair of letters separated by a hyphen (-), and each $type_i$ is one of the following:

```
INTEGER
REAL
CHARACTER*n
LOGICAL
DOUBLE PRECISION
COMPLEX
```

The effect of this statement is to declare that all variables whose names begin with one of the letters a_1, a_2,... are $type_1$ variables, all those whose names begin with one of the letters b_1, b_2, ... are $type_2$ variables, and so on. For example, the statement

```
IMPLICIT INTEGER (A-F, Z), CHARACTER*10 (L, X, Y)
```

declares that all variables whose names begin with A, B C, D, E, F, or Z are of integer type and that all those whose names begin with L, X, or Y are character variables whose values are of length 10.

The IMPLICIT statement and all type statements (as well as other declaration statements considered in earlier chapters) must precede all executable statements in a program, and among these, the IMPLICIT statement must precede all others. All variables whose names begin with letters other than those listed in the IMPLICIT statement have types determined by the naming convention or by subsequent type declarations. Thus, in the following set of statements

```
IMPLICIT CHARACTER*10 (A, L-N, Z), CHARACTER*5 (D-G)
INTEGER NUMBER, ZIP
CHARACTER*20 ADDRESS, LNAME, FNAME*12
REAL ALPHA, LAMBDA
```

the last three type statements override the types specified for the indicated variables by the naming convention established by the IMPLICIT statement or by the default FORTRAN naming convention.

As we have noted, however, it is good programming practice to declare explicitly the type of each variable, because this encourages the programmer to think carefully about what each variable represents and how it is to be used. It is important that variables of a given type be used in a manner that is consistent with that data type, as the program may not execute correctly otherwise. Consequently, the programmer should not rely on the IMPLICIT statement or the default FORTRAN naming convention to determine the types of variables.

12.4 OTHER CONTROL STATEMENTS: ARITHMETIC IF, COMPUTED GO TO, ASSIGNED GO TO

In our discussion in Chapter 3 of the three basic control structures—sequential structure, selection structure, and repetition structure—the selection structure was implemented using an IF or IF-ELSE IF construct and the logical IF statement. Three other statements in FORTRAN may also be used to implement selection structures, but they are less commonly used. They are the arithmetic IF statement, the computed GO TO statement, and the assigned GO TO statement.

The Arithmetic IF Statement

The **arithmetic IF statement** has the form

```
IF (expression) n₁, n₂, n₃
```

where the expression enclosed in parentheses is an arithmetic expression and n_1, n_2, and n_3 are labels of executable statements, not necessarily distinct. When this statement is executed, the value of the expression is calculated, and execution continues with statement n_1 if this value is negative, with statement n_2 if it is zero, and with statement n_3 if it is positive. For example, consider the arithmetic IF statement

```
IF (X ** 2 - 10.5) 10, 15, 20
```

If X has the value 3.1, statement 10 will be executed next.

The program in Figure 12.1 is a modification of the program in Figure 3.2 to solve quadratic equations:

$$Ax^2 + Bx + C = 0$$

An arithmetic IF statement is used in place of an IF-ELSE IF construct to select the appropriate statements for execution, depending on whether the value of the discriminant $B^2 - 4AC$ is negative, zero, or positive.

Figure 12.1 Quadratic equations—version 4.

```
      PROGRAM QUAD4
* * * * * * * * * * * * * * * * * * * * * * * * * * * * * * * * * * * * * * * * * * * * * * * * * * * * * * * * * * * * * * *
* Program to solve a quadratic equation using the quadratic formula.   *
* It uses an arithmetic IF statement to select the appropriate action   *
* depending on whether the discriminant DISC is negative, zero, or      *
* positive.  Variables used are:                                        *
*    A, B, C      : the coefficients of the quadratic equation          *
*    DISC         : the discriminant, B ** 2 - 4 * A * C                *
*    ROOT1, ROOT2 : the two roots of the equation                       *
*                                                                       *
* Input:  The coefficients A, B, and C                                  *
* Output: The two roots or the repeated root of the equation or the     *
*         (negative) discriminant and a message indicating that there   *
*         are no real roots                                             *
* * * * * * * * * * * * * * * * * * * * * * * * * * * * * * * * * * * * * * * * * * * * * * * * * * * * * * * * * * * * * * *

      REAL A, B, C, DISC, ROOT1, ROOT2

      PRINT *, 'ENTER THE COEFFICIENTS OF THE QUADRATIC EQUATION'
      READ *, A, B, C
      DISC = B ** 2 - 4.0 * A * C
      IF (DISC) 10, 20, 30

* No real roots

10    PRINT *, 'DISCRIMINANT IS', DISC
      PRINT *, 'THERE ARE NO REAL ROOTS'
      STOP
```

Figure 12.1 *(cont.)*

```
* Repeated real root

20     ROOT1 = -B / (2.0 * A)
       PRINT *, 'REPEATED ROOT IS', ROOT1
       STOP

* Distinct real roots

30     DISC = SQRT(DISC)
       ROOT1 = (-B + DISC) / (2.0 * A)
       ROOT2 = (-B - DISC) / (2.0 * A)
       PRINT *, 'THE ROOTS ARE', ROOT1, ROOT2
       END
```

The Computed GO TO Statement

The **computed** GO TO **statement** has the form

```
GO TO (n₁, n₂, . . . , nₖ), integer-expression
```

where $n_1, n_2, \ldots, n_k$ are labels of executable statements, not necessarily distinct. The comma preceding the integer expression is optional. When this statement is executed, the value of the expression is computed. If this value is the integer i, execution will continue with the statement whose label is n_i. The computed GO TO statement can thus be used to implement a multialternative selection structure. For example, if J and K are integer variables, the statement

```
GO TO (50, 10, 5, 50, 80, 100), J - K
```

selects one of the statements $5, 10, 50, 80, 100$ for execution, depending on the value of the expression J − K. If J − K has the value 5, statement 80 is executed next.

The Assigned GO TO Statement

The **assigned** GO TO **statement** uses an integer variable to select the statement to be executed next. It has the form

```
GO TO integer-variable
```

or

```
GO TO integer-variable, (n₁, . . . , nₖ)
```

where $n_1, \ldots, n_k$ are labels of executable statements. The comma following the integer variable in the second form is optional.

Before execution of this statement, a statement label must be assigned to the integer variable by an ASSIGN **statement** of the form

```
ASSIGN statement-label TO integer-variable
```

The assigned GO TO statement then causes execution to continue with the statement whose label has been assigned to the specified integer variable.

In the second form of the assigned GO TO statement, at the time of execution a check is made to determine whether the statement label assigned to the integer variable is in the list $n_1, \ldots, n_k$. If it is not, an error message results. In the first form of the assigned GO TO statement, no such validation of the value of the integer variable takes place; if it is out of range, execution continues with the next executable statement in the program.

12.5 MORE ABOUT COMMON AND BLOCK DATA SUBPROGRAMS

Other COMMON Features

In Section 7.5 we used the COMMON statement to establish common regions for simple variables and for arrays with the same dimensions. It is also possible to use the COMMON statement to establish common regions for arrays of different dimensions. For example, the statements

```
INTEGER B(3,4)
COMMON B
```

in one program unit and the statements

```
INTEGER BETA(2,6)
COMMON BETA
```

in another allocate the first 12 memory locations of the blank common region to both B and BETA, resulting in the following associations:

Array Element	Blank Common Location	Array Element
B(1,1)	#1	BETA(1,1)
B(2,1)	#2	BETA(2,1)
B(3,1)	#3	BETA(1,2)
B(1,2)	#4	BETA(2,2)
B(2,2)	#5	BETA(1,3)
B(3,2)	#6	BETA(2,3)
B(1,3)	#7	BETA(1,4)

Array Element	Blank Common Location	Array Element
B(2,3)	#8	BETA(2,4)
B(3,3)	#9	BETA(1,5)
B(1,4)	#10	BETA(2,5)
B(2,4)	#11	BETA(1,6)
B(3,4)	#12	BETA(2,6)

A COMMON statement may be used to associate two or more arrays with a single array. If the statements

```
REAL A(3,3), CONS(3)
COMMON A, CONS
```

appear in one program unit and

```
REAL AUG(3,4)
COMMON AUG
```

appear in another, the following associations will be established:

Array Element	Blank Common Location	Array Element
A(1,1)	#1	AUG(1,1)
A(2,1)	#2	AUG(2,1)
A(3,1)	#3	AUG(3,1)
A(1,2)	#4	AUG(1,2)
A(2,2)	#5	AUG(2,2)
A(3,2)	#6	AUG(3,2)
A(1,3)	#7	AUG(1,3)
A(2,3)	#8	AUG(2,3)
A(3,3)	#9	AUG(3,3)
CONS(1)	#10	AUG(1,4)
CONS(2)	#11	AUG(2,4)
CONS(3)	#12	AUG(3,4)

It also is possible to mix both simple variables and arrays in COMMON statements. For example, if the statements

```
REAL COEFF(2,2), C, D
COMMON COEFF, C, D
```

appear in one program unit and the statements

```
REAL GAUSS(2,3)
COMMON GAUSS
```

appear in another, these variables and array elements will be associated as follows:

Array Element	Blank Common Location	Array Element
COEFF(1,1)	#1	GAUSS(1,1)
COEFF(2,1)	#2	GAUSS(2,1)
COEFF(1,2)	#3	GAUSS(1,2)
COEFF(2,2)	#4	GAUSS(2,2)
C	#5	GAUSS(1,3)
D	#6	GAUSS(2,3)

When arrays are listed in a COMMON statement, it is possible to dimension the arrays in the COMMON statement itself. For example, the preceding two pairs of statements can be written as

```
REAL COEFF, C, D
COMMON COEFF(2,2), C, D
```

and

```
REAL GAUSS
COMMON GAUSS(2,3)
```

In our examples thus far, the association established between items has been complete; that is, there is a one-to-one correspondence between the items. It also is possible to establish a partial correspondence, in which some of the items listed in one of the COMMON statements are not associated with items in the other COMMON statement. For example, the statements

```
REAL A, X(3)
COMMON A, X
```

in one program unit and

```
REAL B(6)
COMMON B
```

in another program unit establish a partial association as follows:

```
   A  ↔  B(1)
 X(1)  ↔  B(2)
 X(2)  ↔  B(3)
 X(3)  ↔  B(4)
          B(5)
          B(6)
```

Numeric and character type variables may not be allocated memory locations from the same common region. Named common regions, however, are separate regions. Consequently, numeric variables may be allocated to one named region and character variables to another, with both regions established in the same COMMON statement. Thus, the statements

```
REAL X, Y
INTEGER M, N
CHARACTER*10 A, B, C
COMMON /NUMER/ X, Y, M, N /CHARAC/ A, B, C
```

may appear in one program unit and the statements

```
REAL X, Z
INTEGER I, J
CHARACTER*10 ALPHA, BETA, GAMMA
COMMON /NUMER/ X, Z, I, J /CHARAC/ ALPHA, BETA, GAMMA
```

in another.

Block Data Subprograms

We noted in Section 7.6 that items that are allocated memory locations in blank common may not be initialized in DATA statements. However, items allocated memory locations from a named common region may be initialized in a DATA statement, provided that this initialization is done in a special kind of subprogram called a **block data subprogram.**

The first statement of a block data subprogram is

```
BLOCK DATA
```

or

```
BLOCK DATA name
```

A program may have more than one block data subprogram, but at most one of these may be unnamed. *A block data subprogram contains no executable statements.* Only comments and the following statements may appear in block data subprograms:

```
IMPLICIT
PARAMETER
DIMENSION
COMMON
SAVE
EQUIVALENCE
DATA
END
```

Type statements

The last statement of the subprogram must, of course, be an END statement.

A block data subprogram initializes items in named common regions by listing these items in COMMON statements and specifying their values in DATA statements. Suppose, for example, that variables A and B and the array character variable CODE and the character array NAME are allocated locations in common region BLOCK2. The following block data subprogram could be used to initialize A, B, LIST(1),..., LIST(5), CODE, and the entire array NAME:

```
BLOCK DATA
INTEGER M, N
PARAMETER (M = 20, N = 50)
REAL A, B
INTEGER LIST(M)
CHARACTER*10 CODE, NAME(N)
COMMON /BLOCK1/ A, B, LIST /BLOCK2/ CODE, NAME
DATA A, B, (LIST(I), I = 1, 5) /2.5, 3.5, 5*0/
DATA CODE, NAME /'&', N*' '/
END
```

12.6 THE EQUIVALENCE STATEMENT

The EQUIVALENCE **statement** makes it possible to associate variables and arrays in the *same* program unit so that they refer to the same memory locations. This statement is of the form

```
EQUIVALENCE (list₁), (list₂), ...
```

where each of $list_1$, $list_2$,... is a list of variables, arrays, array elements, or substring names separated by commas, which are to be allocated the same memory locations. Each of the sets of items that constitute one of the lists in parentheses is said to be an **equivalence class**. *The* EQUIVALENCE *statement is nonexecutable and must appear at the beginning of the program before all executable statements.*

As an illustration, consider the statements

```
INTEGER M1, M2, NUM
REAL X, Y, ALPHA(5), BETA(5)
EQUIVALENCE (X, Y), (M1, M2, NUM), (ALPHA, BETA)
```

The variables and elements of the arrays that appear in the EQUIVALENCE statement are allocated in the following manner:

```
            X  ↔ Y
          M1 ↔ M2 ↔ NUM
   ALPHA(1)  ↔ BETA(1)
   ALPHA(2)  ↔ BETA(2)
   ALPHA(3)  ↔ BETA(3)
   ALPHA(4)  ↔ BETA(4)
   ALPHA(5)  ↔ BETA(5)
```

Because associated variables refer to the same memory locations, changing the value of one of these variables also changes the value of all variables in the same equivalence class.

The following rules govern the use of EQUIVALENCE statements:

1. Two (or more) items may not be equivalenced if they *both* (or *all*) appear in a COMMON statement(s) in the same program unit.

2. Formal arguments may not be equivalenced.

3. Items of character type may be equivalenced only with other items of character type. Numeric items of different types may be equivalenced, but extreme care must be exercised because of the different internal representations used for different numeric types.

The EQUIVALENCE statement is most often used to make efficient use of memory by associating the elements of large arrays. Suppose, for example, a program processes a 100 × 100 array BIG and a 40 × 250 array TABLE. If the array BIG is no longer needed when the processing of TABLE begins, the two arrays can be equivalenced by the statement

```
EQUIVALENCE (BIG, TABLE)
```

In the preceding examples, arrays have been equivalenced by specifying the array names in the same equivalence class. This has the effect of associating the first elements in these arrays and successive elements. For example, the statements

```
REAL A(5), B(5)
EQUIVALENCE (A, B)
```

associate the elements of the arrays A and B in the following manner:

```
A(1)    A(2)    A(3)    A(4)    A(5)
 ↕       ↕       ↕       ↕       ↕
B(1)    B(2)    B(3)    B(4)    B(5)
```

The name of an array element may also be used in specifying the items of an equivalence class. The statement

```
EQUIVALENCE (A(1), B(1))
```

establishes the same associations as in the preceding example. This same association can also be established with the statement

```
EQUIVALENCE (A(3), B(3))
```

or

```
EQUIVALENCE (A(4), B(4))
```

and so on. The array elements listed in an equivalence class indicate the elements at which the association is to begin, with the remaining elements in the arrays associated in the natural way. Thus, the statement

```
EQUIVALENCE (A(2), B(3))
```

establishes the following associations:

```
A(1)    A(2)    A(3)    A(4)    A(5)
 ↕       ↕       ↕       ↕
B(1)    B(2)    B(3)    B(4)    B(5)
```

Similarly, the statements

```
REAL P, X(3), Y(5), Z(7)
EQUIVALENCE (P, X, Y(3), Z(4))
```

establish the following associations:

```
                        P
                        ↕
                       X(1)    X(2)    X(3)
                        ↕       ↕       ↕
        Y(1)    Y(2)    Y(3)    Y(4)    Y(5)
         ↕       ↕       ↕       ↕       ↕
Z(1)    Z(2)    Z(3)    Z(4)    Z(5)    Z(6)    Z(7)
```

If variables of character type are equivalenced, association begins with the first character position of each variable and continues with successive positions. If substrings are equivalenced, association begins with the first positions of the specified substrings, with the remaining character positions associated in the natural way. For example, the statements

```
CHARACTER*5 F, G, H, I, J*7, K*8
EQUIVALENCE (F, G), (H, J), (I(2: ), K(4: ))
```

establish the following associations:

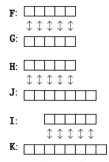

When character arrays are equivalenced using the array names, association begins with the first character position of the first elements of each array and continues with successive character positions of successive array elements. For example, the statements

```
CHARACTER*4 A(3), B(6)*2
EQUIVALENCE (A, B)
```

establish the following associations:

```
      A(1)      A(2)      A(3)
     ┌──┐      ┌──┐      ┌──┐
  ┌──┬──┬──┬──┬──┬──┬──┬──┬──┬──┬──┬──┐
  └──┴──┴──┴──┴──┴──┴──┴──┴──┴──┴──┴──┘
   ↕  ↕  ↕  ↕  ↕  ↕  ↕  ↕  ↕  ↕  ↕  ↕
  ┌──┬──┬──┬──┬──┬──┬──┬──┬──┬──┬──┬──┐
  └──┴──┴──┴──┴──┴──┴──┴──┴──┴──┴──┴──┘
   └─┬─┘└─┬─┘└─┬─┘└─┬─┘└─┬─┘└─┬─┘
  B(1) B(2) B(3) B(4) B(5) B(6)
```

Specifying an array element or a substring of an array element in an equivalence class is also possible. In this case, association begins with the first character position of the array element or substring indicated and continues in the manner described for arrays and substrings.

It is possible for a variable or an array to appear in both an EQUIVALENCE statement and a COMMON statement. To illustrate, suppose that one program unit contains the statements

```
REAL BIG(100,100), LARGE(40, 250)
EQUIVALENCE (BIG, LARGE)
COMMON BIG
```

and another program unit contains the statements

```
REAL X(10000)
COMMON X
```

Each of the following triples of array elements then refers to the same memory location:

BIG(1,1),	LARGE(1, 1),	X(1)
BIG(2,1),	LARGE(2, 1),	X(2)
⋮	⋮	⋮
BIG(100,1),	LARGE(20, 3),	X(100)
BIG(1,2),	LARGE(21, 3),	X(101)
⋮	⋮	⋮
BIG(100,100),	LARGE(40, 250),	X(10000)

Some care must be exercised, however, when using such a combination of EQUIV-ALENCE and COMMON statements. When an array appears in an EQUIVALENCE statement, it may imply an extension of a common region. For example, the statements

```
REAL X, Y, Z, A(5)
COMMON X, Y, Z
EQUIVALENCE (Y, A(2))
```

establish the following associations:

Array Element	Blank Common Location	Array Element
X	#1	A(1)
Y	#2	A(2)
Z	#3	A(3)
	#4	A(4)
	#5	A(5)

with the implied extension of blank common by the addition of memory locations #4 and #5. Such an extension "in the direction of increasing locations" is allowed, but an extension to locations preceding the first one is not. Thus, replacement of the preceding EQUIVALENCE statement by

```
EQUIVALENCE (Y, A(3))
```

is not allowed, since this statement would require the following extension:

Array Element	Blank Common Location	Array Element
		A(1)
X	#1	A(2)
Y	#2	A(3)
Z	#3	A(4)
	#4	A(5)

12.7 ALTERNATE ENTRIES AND RETURNS

The ENTRY Statement

The normal entry point of a subprogram is the first executable statement following the FUNCTION or SUBROUTINE statement. In some cases, some other entry may be convenient. For example, it may be necessary to assign values to certain variables the first time a subprogram is referenced but not on subsequent references.

Multiple entry points are introduced in subprograms by using ENTRY **statements** of the form

```
ENTRY name(argument-list)
```

where *name* is the name of the entry point and *argument-list* is similar to the argument list in a FUNCTION or SUBROUTINE statement.

ENTRY statements are *nonexecutable* and thus have no effect on the normal execution sequence in the subprogram. Entry into the subprogram can be directed to the first executable statement following an ENTRY statement.

Suppose we wish to prepare a function subprogram to evaluate $Ax^2 + Bx + C$ for various values of x. In this case, we could use the following function subprogram:

```
FUNCTION QUAD(X)
REAL QUAD, X, A, B, C, POLY

READ *, A, B, C

ENTRY POLY(X)
QUAD = A * X ** 2 + B * X + C
SAVE A, B, C
END
```

The first reference to this function in the main program would be with a statement such as

```
VAL = QUAD(Z)
```

which would cause values for A, B, and C in the subprogram to be read and the function evaluated at Z. Subsequent references to this function might be by a statement such as

```
Y = POLY(Z)
```

In such cases, entry into the subprogram would be at the first statement following the ENTRY statement; thus, the function would be evaluated at Z using the values for A, B, and C read previously.

Different entry points in a subprogram may have different argument lists. In this case, care must be taken to ensure that the actual argument list in a reference agrees with the formal argument list in the corresponding ENTRY statement.

Normally, all entry names in a function subprogram are of the same type as that of the function name. In this case, any of these names may be used to assign the function value to be returned. Thus, the statement

```
POLY = A * X ** 2 + B * X + C
```

could be used in place of the statement

```
QUAD = A * X ** 2 + B * X + C
```

in the function subprogram QUAD.

If any entry name is of character type, then all entry names, including the function name, must be of character type, and all must have the same lengths. For numeric-valued functions, entry names may be of different types, but for each reference to some entry name, there must be at least one statement that assigns a value to an entry name having the same type as the name being referenced.

Alternate Returns

In certain situations, it may be convenient to return from a subroutine at some point other than the normal return point (the first executable statement following the CALL statement). This can be accomplished as follows:

1. In the CALL statement, specify the alternate points of return by using arguments of the form

   $$* n$$

   where n denotes a statement label indicating the statement to be executed upon return from the subprogram.

2. Use asterisks (*) as the corresponding formal arguments in the SUBROUTINE statement.

3. Use a statement in the subroutine of the form

```
RETURN k
```

where k is an integer expression whose value indicates which of the alternate returns is to be used.

The following example illustrates:

Main Program:
```
      .
      .
      .
      CALL SUBR(A, B, C, *30, *40)
   20 D = A * B
      .
      .
      .
   30 D = A + B
      .
      .
      .
   40 D = A - B
      .
      .
      .
      END

      SUBROUTINE SUBR(X, Y, TERM, *, *)
      .
      .
      .
      IF (TERM .LT. 0) RETURN 1
      IF (TERM .GT. 0) RETURN 2
      END
```

The return to the main program from the subroutine SUBR is to statement 30 if the value of TERM is less than 0, to statement 40 if it is greater than zero, and to statement 20 (normal return) if it is equal to zero.

Fortran 90

For several of the FORTRAN features described in this chapter, better alternatives are already available in FORTRAN 77, and so these features have been declared to be "obsolescent" in Fortran 90, which means that they are candidates for deletion in a future Fortran language standard. These obsolescent features are

- the `PAUSE` statement
- the arithmetic `IF` statement
- the `ASSIGN` statement
- the assigned `GO TO` statement
- alternate returns

13

New Directions in Fortran 90

...the most important thing in the programming language is the name.
A language will not succeed without a good name. I have recently
invented a very good name and now I am looking for a suitable
language.

D. E. KNUTH

I dont know what the language of the year 2000 will be like, but I
know it will be called FORTRAN.

UNKNOWN

Yea, from the table of my memory
I'll wipe away all trivial fond records.

WILLIAM SHAKESPEARE, HAMLET

[Pointers] are like little jumps, leaping wildly from one part of a data
structure to another. Their introduction into high-level languages has
been a step backward from which we may never recover.

C. A. R. HOARE

C H A P T E R   C O N T E N T S

13.1   Modules

13.2   Derived Data Types

13.3   Pointers and Linked Structures

At the end of every chapter starting with Chapter 2, we have included sections entitled Fortran 90 in which we have described some of the variations of and extensions to FOR-TRAN 77 that are provided in Fortran 90, including improved source form features, new data type declarations, additional selection and repetition structures, internal procedures, additional input/output facilities, and array operations. There are also several fundamental additions to Fortran that extend the language in more modern directions by supporting important new software-engineering concepts and techniques. These include modules, which facilitate modular programming, user-defined data types, and pointer types that may be used to implement linked data structures. In this chapter we describe each of these Fortran 90 features.

13.1 MODULES

In many applications there are parameters, variables, types, and subprograms that must be shared by several program units or by separate programs. Fortran 90 provides a program unit called a **module**, which is a package of declarations and definitions that can be imported into other program units. This makes it possible to reuse these declarations and definitions in separate programs or program units without rewriting them in each unit in which they are needed.

The simplest form of a module consists only of a heading, a specification part, and an END statement:

```
MODULE module-name
   specification part
END MODULE module-name
```

where the specification part has the same form as for other program units and the word MODULE and the module name are optional in the END statement. For example, the module in Figure 13.1 defines the real parameter Pi and declares Radius to be a real variable.

Figure 13.1 Module Circle— version 1.

```
MODULE Circle
!--------------------------------------------------------------------
! Module containing definitions and declarations for
! processing circles with known radii.
!
! Exports:   parameter Pi
!            variable Radius
!--------------------------------------------------------------------

   REAL, PARAMETER :: Pi = 3.141592
   REAL :: Radius

END MODULE Circle
```

Once a module has been compiled, its parameters, variables, types, and subprograms are ready to be *exported* to programs, subprograms, and other modules. They must be *imported* into these program units by placing a USE statement of the form

```
USE module-name
```

or

```
USE module-name, ONLY : item-list
```

at the beginning of the specification part of that unit. The first form makes available all of the items in the specified module (except those that have been declared to be private items), and the second form makes available only those items specified in *item-list*. The program in Figure 13.2 with an attached external function illustrates.

Figure 13.2 Processing circles — version 1.

```fortran
PROGRAM Process_Circles_1
!--------------------------------------------------------------------
! Program to calculate and display areas of circles.
! Imports from module Circle:
!          real variable Radius
! Input:   Radius of circle
! Output:  Area of circle
!--------------------------------------------------------------------

   USE Circle, ONLY : Radius
   REAL :: Area

   DO
      PRINT *, "Enter radius of circle (negative to stop):"
      READ *, Radius
      IF (Radius < 0) EXIT
      PRINT *, "Area = ", Area(Radius)
      PRINT *
   END DO

END PROGRAM Process_Circles_1


!--------------------------------------------------------------------
! Function to calculate area of a circle.
! Imports from Circle:  Pi and Radius
! Accepts:  Radius of circle
! Returns:  Area of circle
!--------------------------------------------------------------------

REAL FUNCTION Area(R)

   USE Circle, ONLY : Pi
   REAL :: R

   Area = Pi * R**2

END FUNCTION Area
```

Figure 13.2 *(cont.)*

Sample runs:

```
Enter radius of circle (negative to stop):
1
Area =    3.1415920

Enter radius of circle (negative to stop):
2.5
Area =    19.6349506

Enter radius of circle (negative to stop):
−1
```

Besides definitions and declarations of parameters, variables, and types, modules may also contain procedures. In this case, the form of the module is

```
MODULE module-name
    specification part
CONTAINS
    module procedures
END MODULE module-name
```

For example, we could package the function Area with the declarations of Pi and Radius in the module Circle, as shown in Figure 13.3.

Figure 13.3 Module Circle — version 2.

```
MODULE Circle
!----------------------------------------------------------------
! Module containing definitions, declarations, and a function
! Area for processing circles with known radii.
!
! Exports:   parameter Pi
!            variable Radius
!            function Area
!----------------------------------------------------------------

   REAL, PARAMETER :: Pi = 3.141592
   REAL :: Radius
```

Figure 13.3 *(cont.)*

```
CONTAINS

!----- Area------------------------------------------------
! Function to calculate area of a circle.
! Accepts:  Radius of circle
! Returns:  Area of circle
!----------------------------------------------------------

   REAL FUNCTION Area(Radius)

      Area = Pi * Radius**2

   END FUNCTION Area

END MODULE Circle
```

The program `Process_Circles_1` in Figure 13.2 could now be written as shown in Figure 13.4.

 Figure 13.4 Processing circles — version 2.

```
PROGRAM Process_Circles_2
!----------------------------------------------------------
! Program to calculate and display areas of circles with
! given radii.
! Imports from module Circle:
!          real parameter Pi
!          real variable Radius
!          real-valued function Area
! Input:   Radius of circle
! Output:  Area of circle
!----------------------------------------------------------

   USE Circle
```

Figure 13.4 *(cont.)*

```
   DO
      PRINT *, "Enter radius of circle (negative to stop):"
      READ *, Radius
      IF (Radius < 0) EXIT
      PRINT *, "Area = ", Area(Radius)
   END DO

END PROGRAM Process_Circles_2
```

The USE statement imports the definitions and declarations of the real parameter Pi, the real variable Radius, and the real-valued function Area from module Circle.

In the same way, these items can be imported into and used in any other program unit in which it is necessary to find the area of a circle with a given radius. The program in Figure 13.5 reads the diameter of a circle, divides by two to get its radius, and then uses the items imported from module Circle to find the circle's area.

Figure 13.5 Processing circles — version 3.

```
PROGRAM Process_Circles_3
!-----------------------------------------------------------
! Program to calculate and display areas of circles with
! given diameters.
! Imports from module Circle:
!           real parameter Pi
!           real variable Radius
!           real-valued function Area
! Input:    Diameter of circle
! Output:   Area of circle
!-----------------------------------------------------------

   USE Circle
   REAL :: Diameter
```

Figure 13.5 *(cont.)*

```
    DO
        PRINT *, "Enter diameter of circle (negative to stop):"
        READ *, Diameter
        IF (Diameter < 0) EXIT
        Radius = Diameter / 2.0
        PRINT *, "Area = ", Area(Radius)
    END DO

END PROGRAM Process_Circles_3
```

As described in the Fortran 90 sections of Chapters 6 and 7, interface blocks may be used to specify functions used to define or overload operators, to specify subroutines used to extend the assignment operator, and to specify a collection of subprograms that may be referenced by a single generic subprogram name. When the functions or subroutines are procedures contained in a module, a special form of the interface block must be used to specify these procedures:

```
INTERFACE specifier
    MODULE PROCEDURE list-of-procedures
END INTERFACE
```

where *specifier* has one of the forms

```
OPERATOR (operator)
ASSIGNMENT (=)
generic-name
```

This is especially useful when using modules to define new data types, as described in the next section.

In the preceding examples of modules, all of the items defined and declared in a module are *public* items, which means that they all can be imported from the module into a program unit. It is also possible to specify that certain items within a module are *private* to that module; that is, they can be used only within that module and are not accessible outside it. This can be done by listing these items in a PRIVATE statement or by specifying the attribute PRIVATE in the type statements used to declare those items. For example, the parameter Pi can be declared to be private to the module Circle by inserting the statement

```
PRIVATE Pi
```

in the specification part of the module or by modifying the declaration of Pi as

```
REAL, PRIVATE, PARAMETER :: Pi = 3.141592
```

A `PUBLIC` statement and the attribute `PUBLIC` are also available for explicitly specifying those items that are exported from the module.

13.2 DERIVED DATA TYPES

FORTRAN 77 provides six simple data types — `INTEGER`, `REAL`, `DOUBLE PRECISION`, `COMPLEX`, `CHARACTER`, and `LOGICAL` — and one structured data type, the array, but it makes no provision for user-defined types. Fortran 90 refers to the aforementioned types as *intrinsic* data types, and to these can be added user-defined types that are *derived* from these intrinsic types. These new types are called **derived types,** and an item of such a type is called a **structure.**

Arrays are used to store elements of the same type. In many situations, however, we need to process items that are related in some way but that are not all of the same type. For example, a date consists of a month name (of character type), a day (of integer type), and a year (of integer type); a record of computer usage might contain, among other items, a user's name and password (character strings), identification number (integer), and resources used to date (real). In Fortran 90, a derived data type can be used to declare a structure, which can be used to store such related data items of possibly different types. The positions in the structure in which these data items are stored are called the **components** of the structure. Thus, a structure for storing computer usage information might contain a name component, a password component, an identification number component, and a resources used component.

A simple form of a derived type definition is

```
TYPE type-name
    type specification statement for component-list₁
    type specification statement for component-list₂
              .
              .
              .
END TYPE type-name
```

where `type-name` is a valid Fortran identifier that names the derived type, and each of the type specification statements declares the type of one or more components. For example, the type definition

```
TYPE Computer_User
    CHARACTER (LEN = 20) :: Name, Password
    INTEGER :: IdNumber
    REAL :: ResourcesUsed
END TYPE Computer_User
```

defines the derived type `Computer_User`. A structure of this type will have four components: `Name` and `Password`, which are of character type with values of length 20; `IdNumber` of integer type; and `ResourcesUsed` of real type.

The components of a structure need not be of different types. For example, the type definition

```
TYPE Point
   REAL :: X, Y
END TYPE Point
```

defines the derived type `Point`, and a structure of type `Point` will have two components named X and Y, each of which is of real type.

Such type definitions are placed in the specification part of a program unit. The type identifiers they define can then be used in a type specification statement of the form

```
TYPE (type-name) :: list-of-identifiers
```

to declare the types of structures. For example, the type specification statement

```
TYPE (Point) :: P, Q
```

declares structures P and Q of type `Point`;

```
TYPE (Computer_User) :: Person
```

declares a structure Person of type `Computer_User`; and

```
TYPE (Computer_User) :: User(50)
```

or

```
TYPE (Computer_User), DIMENSION(50) :: User
```

declares a one-dimensional array User, each of whose elements is a structure of type `Computer_User`.

Values of a derived type are sequences of values for the components of that derived type. Their form is

```
type-name (list of component values)
```

For example,

```
Point(2.5, 3.2)
```

is a value of type `Point` and can be assigned to variable P of type `Point`,

```
P = Point(2.5, 3.2)
```

or associated with a parameter Origin of type `Point`,

```
TYPE (Point), PARAMETER :: Origin = Point(2.5, 3.2)
```

Similarly,

```
Computer_User("John Q. Doe", "SECRET", 12345, 234.98)
```

is a value of type `Computer_User` and can be assigned to the variable `Person` or to a component of the array `User`:

```
Person = Computer_User("John Q. Doe", "SECRET", 12345, 234.98)
User(1) = Person
```

The values of the components in such *derived-type constructors* may also be variables or expressions. For example, if A is a real variable with value 1.1, the assignment statement

```
P = Point(A, 2*A)
```

assigns the structure having real components 1.1 and 2.2 to the variable P.

A reference to an individual component of a structure has the form

```
structure-name%component-name
```

For example, `P%X` is the first component of the structure `P` of type `Point`, and `P%Y` is the second component; `User(1)%Name`, `User(1)%Password`, `User(1)%IdNumber`, and `User(1)%ResourcesUsed` refer to the four components of the structure `User(1)`.

The components of a structure may be of any type; in particular, they may be other structures. For example, the declarations

```
TYPE Point
    REAL :: X, Y
END TYPE Point

TYPE Circle
    TYPE (Point) :: Center
    REAL :: Radius
END TYPE Circle

TYPE (Circle) :: C
```

declare C to be a structure whose values are of type `Circle`. Such a structure has two components: The first component `Center` is of type `Point` and is itself a structure having two real components named X and Y; the second component `Radius` is of type REAL.

The components within such a **nested structure** may be accessed by simply affixing a second component identifier to the name of the larger structure. Thus, if C is assigned a value by

```
C = Circle(Point(2.5, 3.2), 10)
```

representing a circle of radius 10, centered at (2.5, 3.2), the value of `C%Center%X` is 2.5, the value of `C%Center%Y` is 3.2, and the value of `C%Radius` is 10.0.

Each component of a structure has a specified type, and any reference to that component of the form *structure-name%component-name* may be used in the same way as any item of that type. For example, since `Person%Name` is of character type, it may be assigned a value in an assignment statement

```
Person%Name = "Mary Q. Smith"
```

or by an input statement

```
READ "(A)", Person%Name
```

Its value can be displayed by using an output statement

```
PRINT *, Person%Name
```

and its value can be modified by a substring reference:

```
Person%Name(1:4) = "Joan"
```

The only intrinsic operation provided for structures is the assignment operation (=); all other processing must be carried out using the individual components. As we noted in the preceding section, however, it is possible to define new operations on any data type and, in particular, operations on derived types. For example, suppose that two circles are said to be equal if they have the same center and the same radius, and we wish to extend the relational operator == to include this meaning for structures of type `Circle`. An interface block of the following form can be used to overload ==:

```
INTERFACE OPERATOR (==)
   MODULE PROCEDURE Equal
END INTERFACE
```

A function `Equal` to implement == for structures of type `Circle` is

```
! Function to determine if two circles C1 and C2 are equal,
! which means that they have the same center and equal radii.

FUNCTION Equal(C1, C2)

   TYPE (Circle) :: C1, C2
   LOGICAL :: Equal

   Equal = C1%Center%X == C2%Center%X .AND. &
           C1%Center%Y == C2%Center%Y .AND. &
           C1%Radius == C2%Radius

END FUNCTION Equal
```

The type definitions of `Circle`, the preceding interface block, and the function `Equal` can be packaged in a module like that shown in Figure 13.6. We have also included a modified version of the function `Area` from the preceding section.

Figure 13.6 Module `Circle_Type`.

```
MODULE Circle_Type

!-------------------------------------------------------------
! Module to define the derived data type Circle for processing
! circles with given centers and radii.  It also extends the
! relational operator == to type Circle.  Two circles are
! equal if they have the same center and equal radii.
!
! Exports:  derived type Point
!           derived type Circle
!           operator ==
!           parameter Pi
!           function Area
!-------------------------------------------------------------

   TYPE Point
      REAL :: X, Y
   END TYPE Point

   TYPE Circle
      TYPE (Point) :: Center
      REAL :: Radius
   END TYPE Circle

   INTERFACE OPERATOR (==)
      MODULE PROCEDURE Equal
   END INTERFACE

   REAL, PARAMETER :: Pi = 3.141592

CONTAINS

   !------ Equal -----------------------------------------------
   ! Function to determine if two circles are equal.
   ! Accepts:  circles C1 and C2
   ! Returns:  true if C1 and C2 have the same center and
   !           the equal radii; false otherwise.
   !------------------------------------------------------------
```

Figure 13.6 *(cont.)*

```
FUNCTION Equal(C1, C2)

   TYPE (Circle), INTENT(IN) :: C1, C2
   LOGICAL :: Equal

   Equal = C1%Center%X == C2%Center%X .AND. &
           C1%Center%Y == C2%Center%Y .AND. &
           C1%Radius == C2%Radius

END FUNCTION Equal

!----- Area --------------------------------------------
! Function to calculate area of a circle.
! Accepts:  a circle C
! Returns:  area of circle
!------------------------------------------------------

REAL FUNCTION Area(C)

   TYPE (Circle) :: C

   Area = Pi * C%Radius ** 2

END FUNCTION Area

END MODULE Circle_Type
```

This new data type may then be used in any other program unit, like that shown in Figure 13.7, by simply importing it from this module:

Figure 13.7 Processing circles — version 4.

```fortran
PROGRAM Process_Circles_4
!-------------------------------------------------------------
! Program to read centers and radii of several circles
! and display the areas of those that are not the unit
! circle.
! Imports from module Circle:
!          derived type Circle
!          derived type Point
!          operator ==
!          parameter Pi
!          function Area
! Other identifiers used:
!          UnitCircle : unit circle, centered at origin,
!                       radius = 1.
!          Cir : a circle
! Input:   Circle Cir
! Output:  Area of Cir or message indicating Cir is the
!          unit circle
!-------------------------------------------------------------

   USE Circle_Type
   TYPE (Circle) :: UnitCircle = Circle(Point(0.0, 0.0), 1.0), Cir

!  Process circles
   DO
      PRINT *, "Enter radius of circle (negative to stop):"
      READ *, Cir%Radius
      IF (Cir%Radius < 0) EXIT

      PRINT *, "Enter coordinates of center of Circle:"
      READ *, Cir %Center%X, Cir %Center%Y

!     Check if Cir is the unit circle and display its
!     area if it is not
      IF (Cir == UnitCircle) THEN
         PRINT *, "Circle is the unit circle"
      ELSE
         PRINT *, "Area = ", Area(Cir)
      END IF
      PRINT *
   END DO

END PROGRAM Process_Circles_4
```

13.3 POINTERS AND LINKED STRUCTURES

Variables are symbolic addresses of memory locations. The relationship between a variable and the memory location (s) it names is a static one that is established when the program is compiled and remains fixed throughout the execution of the program (except for allocatable arrays described in the Fortran 90 section of Chapter 8). Although the contents of a memory location associated with a variable may change, variables themselves can be neither created nor destroyed during execution. Consequently, these variables are called **static variables**.

In some situations, however, the memory requirements are known only while the program is executing, so that static variables are not adequate. In such cases, a method for acquiring additional memory locations as needed during execution and for releasing them when they are no longer needed is required. Variables that are created and disposed of during execution are called **dynamic variables**. At one point during execution, there may be a particular memory location associated with a dynamic variable, and at a later time, no memory location or a different one may be associated with it.

Unlike **static data structures**, such as arrays, whose sizes and associated memory locations are fixed once they are allocated, **dynamic data structures** expand or contract as required during execution, and their associated memory locations may change. A dynamic data structure is a collection of elements called **nodes** of the structure that are linked together. This linking is established by associating with each node a pointer that points to the next node in the structure. One of the simplest linked structures is a *linked list*, which might be pictured as follows:

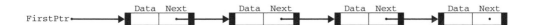

Dynamic data structures are especially useful for storing and processing data sets whose sizes change during program execution, for example, the collection of jobs that have been entered into a computer system and are awaiting execution or the collection of passenger names and seat assignments on a given airplane flight.

Construction of a dynamic data structure requires the ability to allocate memory locations as needed during program execution. Because the number of locations is not known in advance, they cannot be allocated in the usual manner using variable declarations, since such allocations are made at compile time. Instead, the ALLOCATE statement described in the Fortran 90 section of Chapter 8 is used for this purpose. When it is executed, it returns a memory location where a node of the data structure can be stored. To access this location so that data can be stored in it or retrieved from it, a special kind of variable is needed to *point to* this location. Such variables are called **pointer variables**, or simply **pointers**.

The nodes of a dynamic data structure may be of any type but are most often structures. A pointer to the memory location storing one of these nodes must be declared to have the POINTER attribute in a type statement of the form

```
TYPE (type-name), POINTER :: pointer-variable
```

where *type-name* specifies the type of the nodes. For example, the declarations

```
TYPE Inventory_Info
   INTEGER :: Number
   REAL :: Price
END TYPE Inventory_Info


TYPE (Inventory_Info), POINTER :: InvPtr
```

can be used to declare a pointer `InvPtr` to nodes of type `Inventory_Info`.

The `ALLOCATE` statement may then be used during program execution to acquire memory locations in which inventory records can be stored. A statement of the form

```
ALLOCATE (list-of-pointer-variables)
```

associates distinct memory locations with the specified pointer variables. Thus the statement

```
ALLOCATE (InvPtr)
```

associates with `InvPtr` a location in memory where a value of type `Inventory_Info` can be stored. We say that `InvPtr` "points" to this memory location and picture this by a diagram like the following:

	Number	Price
InvPtr →	?	?

The contents of boxes representing components of a structure of type `Inventory_Info` are shown here as question marks to indicate that these components are initially undefined.

Each execution of an `ALLOCATE` statement acquires new memory locations for each of the pointer variables in it. This means that any of these pointer variables are disassociated from any other memory locations to which they may have pointed and are now associated with new locations; the other memory locations are no longer accessible (unless pointed to by some other pointer variables). It also means that the `ALLOCATE` statement will never cause two different pointer variables to be associated with the same memory locations. Thus, if `TempPtr` is also a pointer of the same type as `InvPtr`, the statement

```
ALLOCATE (TempPtr)
```

will acquire a new memory location pointed to by `TempPtr`:

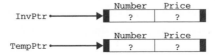

Whenever a pointer name is used in an expression or is on the left side of an assignment statement, it refers to the value stored in the memory location to which it points. Thus, for the most part, a pointer variable like `InvPtr` can be used in a program unit as though it were a structure of type `Inventory_Info`. For example, the statement

```
InvPtr = Inventory_Info(3511, 7.50)
```

is legal and copies the values 3511 and 7.50 into the memory location pointed to by `InvPtr`:

	Number	Price
InvPtr ● ————————▶	3511	7.50

Similarly, if `Item` is a static variable of type `Inventory_Info`, the assignment statement

```
Item = InvPtr
```

is legal and copies the contents of the memory location pointed to by `InvPtr` into the memory locations associated with `Item`, just as though `InvPtr` were itself a structure of type `Inventory_Info`.

One consequence of this convention is that an assignment statement involving two pointers such as

```
TempPtr = InvPtr
```

is treated as an assignment involving two structures and copies the structure pointed to by `InvPtr` into the location pointed to by `TempPtr`:

	Number	Price
InvPtr ● ————————▶	3511	7.50

	Number	Price
TempPtr ● ————————▶	3511	7.50

It does *not* assign the value of `InvPtr` (which is a memory address) to `TempPtr`. A special assignment operator (=>) is used to copy the value (memory address) of a pointer variable and assign it to another pointer variable. Thus, the statement

```
TempPtr => InvPtr
```

assigns the value of `InvPtr` to `TempPtr` so that both point to the same memory location:

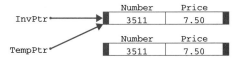

	Number	Price
InvPtr ● ————▶	3511	7.50

	Number	Price
TempPtr ●	3511	7.50

The previous location (if any) pointed to by `TempPtr` can no longer be accessed unless pointed to by some other pointer.

In some situations it is necessary to assign a value to a pointer variable that indicates that it does not point to any memory location. This can be done by using a `NULLIFY` statement of the form

```
NULLIFY (list-of-pointer-variables)
```

The intrinsic function `ASSOCIATED` can be used to test whether a pointer has been nullified. A reference of the form

```
ASSOCIATED(pointer-variable)
```

returns false if the specified pointer variable has been nullified and true otherwise; it is undefined if the pointer variable has been neither allocated nor nullified.

If the memory locations pointed to by certain pointer variables are no longer needed, they may be released and made available for later allocation by using a `DEALLOCATE` statement of the form

```
DEALLOCATE (list-of-pointer-variables)
```

This statement frees the memory locations pointed to by the specified pointers and nullifies these pointer variables.

One of the important properties of pointer variables is that they make it possible to implement dynamic data structures such as linked lists. A **linked list** consists of a collection of elements called **nodes** linked together by pointers, together with a pointer to the first node in the list. The nodes contain two different kinds of information: (1) the actual data item being stored, and (2) a **link** or pointer to the next node in the list. A linked list containing the integers 95, 47, and 83, with 95 as the first element, might thus be pictured as follows:

In this diagram, `FirstPtr` is a pointer to the first node in the list. The `Data` component of each node stores one of the integers, and the `Next` component is a pointer to the next node. The dot in the last node having no arrow emanating from it represents a nullified pointer and indicates that there is no next node.

The nodes in a linked list are represented in Fortran 90 as structures having two kinds of components, **data components** and **link components**. The data components have types that are appropriate for storing the necessary information, and the link components are pointers. For example, the type nodes in the preceding linked list may be defined by

```
TYPE List_Node
    INTEGER :: Data
    TYPE (List_Node), POINTER :: Next
END TYPE List_Node
```

Each node in this list is a structure of type `List_Node`, consisting of two components. The first component `Data` is of integer type and is used to store the data. The second component `Next` is a pointer and points to the next node in the list.

In addition to the nodes of the list in which to store the data items, a pointer to the first node is needed. Thus we declare a pointer variable `FirstPtr` by

```
TYPE (List_Node), POINTER :: FirstPtr
```

To illustrate the basic steps in the construction of a linked list, suppose that the integers 83 and 47 have already been stored in a linked list:

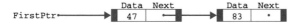

and suppose that we wish to add 95 to this list. In the construction, we use two pointers, `FirstPtr` to point to the first node in the list and `TempPtr` as a temporary pointer.

```
TYPE (List_Node), POINTER :: FirstPtr, TempPtr
```

We first acquire a new node temporarily pointed to by `TempPtr`,

```
ALLOCATE (TempPtr)
```

and store 95 in the data component of this structure:

```
TempPtr%Data = 95
```

This node can then be joined to the list by setting its link component so that it points to the first node:

```
TempPtr%Next => FirstPtr
```

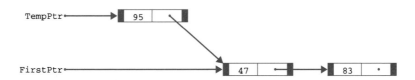

The pointer `FirstPtr` is then updated to point to this new node:

```
FirstPtr => TempPtr
```

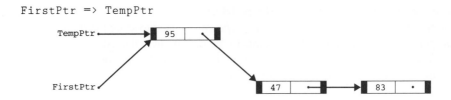

To construct the entire list, we could first initialize an empty list:

```
NULLIFY (FirstPtr)
```

and then repeat the preceding four statements three times, replacing 95 by 83 in the second assignment statement, then by 47, and finally again using the value 95. In practice, however, such linked lists are usually constructed by reading the data values rather than by assigning them by means of assignment statements. In this example, the linked list could be constructed by using the following program segment, where Item is an integer variable:

```
! Initially the list is empty
  NULLIFY (FirstPtr)

! Read the data values and construct the list
  DO
      READ *, Item
      IF (Item == End_Data_Flag) EXIT
      ALLOCATE (TempPtr)
      TempPtr%Data = Item
      TempPtr%Next => FirstPtr
      FirstPtr => TempPtr
  END DO
```

Once a linked list has been constructed, we may want to **traverse** it from beginning to end, displaying each element in it. To traverse a list stored in an array, we can easily move through the list from one element to the next by varying an array subscript in some repetition structure. To traverse a linked list, we move through the list by varying a pointer variable in a repetition structure.

To illustrate, suppose we wish to display the integers stored in the linked list:

We begin by initializing a pointer variable CurrPtr to point to the first node

```
CurrPtr => FirstPtr
```

and display the integer stored in this node:

```
PRINT *, CurrPtr%Data
```

To move to the next node, we follow the link from the current node:

```
CurrPtr => CurrPtr%Next
```

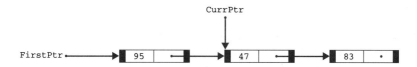

After displaying the integer in this node, we move to the next node:

```
CurrPtr => CurrPtr%Next
```

and display its data. Since we have now reached the last node, we need some way to signal this condition. But this is easy, for if we attempt to move to the next node, CurrPtr becomes nullified:

The function ASSOCIATED can be used to determine when this occurs:

```
CurrPtr => FirstPtr
DO
    IF (.NOT. ASSOCIATED(CurrPtr)) EXIT
    PRINT *, CurrPtr%Data
    CurrPtr => CurrPtr%Next
END DO
```

The program in Figure 13.8 constructs a linked list of integers and then uses these statements to traverse the list. The list is constructed by adding the integers at the beginning of the list. Thus when the list is traversed, the integers are displayed in the opposite order in which they were entered.

Figure 13.8 Linked list.

```fortran
PROGRAM Linked_List
!------------------------------------------------------------
! Program to construct a linked list of integers and then
! traverse the list.  Identifiers used are:
!   FirstPtr : pointer to first node in the list
!   Number   : integer read and inserted into the list
!   TempPtr  : pointer used in constructing the list
!   CurrPtr  : pointer used in traversing the list
!   Data     : node component that stores an integer
!   Next     : node component that points to the next node
!   Response : user response to more-data query
!
! Input:   Integers
! Output:  Integers stored in the list
!------------------------------------------------------------

   TYPE List_Node
      INTEGER :: Data
      TYPE (List_Node), POINTER :: Next
   END TYPE List_Node

   TYPE (List_Node), POINTER :: FirstPtr, TempPtr, CurrPtr

   INTEGER :: Number
   CHARACTER (LEN = 1) :: Response

   ! Initialize an empty list
   NULLIFY (FirstPtr)

   ! Read the integers and construct the list
   DO
      PRINT *, "Enter number to add to list:"
      READ *, Number
      ALLOCATE (TempPtr)
      TempPtr%Data = Number
      TempPtr%Next => FirstPtr
      FirstPtr => TempPtr

      PRINT *, "More data (Y or N)? "
      READ *, Response
      IF (Response == "N") EXIT
   END DO
```

Figure 13.8 *(cont.)*

```
    ! Traverse the list and display the integers (in reverse order)
    PRINT *
    PRINT *, "Numbers in the list are:"
    CurrPtr => FirstPtr
    DO
        IF (.NOT. ASSOCIATED(CurrPtr)) EXIT
        PRINT *, CurrPtr%Data
        CurrPtr => CurrPtr%Next
    END DO

END PROGRAM Linked_List
```

Sample run:
```
Enter number to add to list:
83
More data (Y or N)?
Y
Enter number to add to list:
47
More data (Y or N)?
Y
Enter number to add to list:
95
More data (Y or N)?
N

Numbers in the list are:
95
47
83
```

In general, linked lists are preferred over arrays for processing dynamic lists, whose sizes vary as items are added and deleted, because the number of nodes in a linked list is limited only by the available memory and because the insertion and deletion operations are easy to implement.

To insert an element into a linked list, we first obtain a new node temporarily accessed via a pointer `TempPtr`,

```
ALLOCATE (TempPtr)
```

and store the element in its data component:

```
TempPtr%Data = Element
```

There are now two cases to consider: (1) inserting the element at the beginning of the list, and (2) inserting it after some specified element in the list. The first case has already been illustrated. For the second case, suppose that the new node is to be inserted between the nodes pointed to by `PredPtr` and `CurrPtr`:

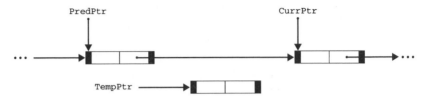

The node is inserted by setting the pointer in the link component of the new node to point to the node pointed to by `CurrPtr`,

```
TempPtr%Next => CurrPtr
```

and then resetting the pointer in the link component of the node pointed to by `PredPtr` to point to the new node:

```
PredPtr%Next => TempPtr
```

The following diagram illustrates:

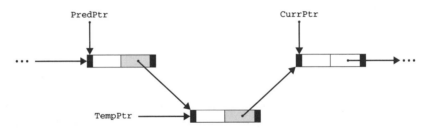

For deletion, there also are two cases to consider: (1) deleting the first element in the list, and (2) deleting an element that has a predecessor. The first case is easy and consists of the following steps, assuming that `CurrPtr` points to the node to be deleted:

1. Set `FirstPtr` to point to the second node in the list:

```
FirstPtr => CurrPtr%Next
```

2. Release the node pointed to by `CurrPtr`:

```
DEALLOCATE (CurrPtr)
```

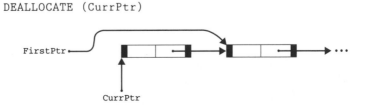

For the second case, suppose that the predecessor of the node to be deleted is pointed to by `PredPtr`:

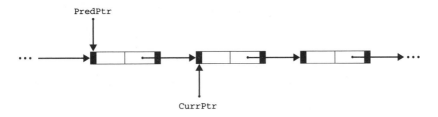

The node is deleted by setting the link component of the node pointed to by `PredPtr` so that it points to the successor of the node to be deleted,

```
PredPtr%Next => CurrPtr%Next
```

and then releasing the node pointed to by `CurrPtr`:

```
DEALLOCATE (CurrPtr)
```

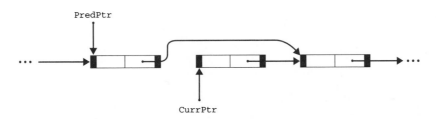

In this section we have shown how pointers and structures can be used to implement linked lists. Other useful dynamic data structures include linked stacks, linked queues, and trees, and these can also be implemented using techniques similar to those for linked lists.

"Where shall I begin, please Your Majesty?" he asked. *"Begin at the beginning,"* the King said, gravely, *"and go on till you come to the end; then stop."*

LEWIS CARROLL, *Alice's Adventures in Wonderland*

A

ASCII and EBCDIC

ASCII and EBCDIC Codes of Printable Characters

Decimal	Binary	Octal	Hexadecimal	ASCII	EBCDIC
32	00100000	040	20	SP (Space)	
33	00100001	041	21	!	
34	00100010	042	22	''	
35	00100011	043	23	#	
36	00100100	044	24	$	
37	00100101	045	25	%	
38	00100110	046	26	&	
39	00100111	047	27	' (Single quote)	
40	00101000	050	28	(	
41	00101001	051	29	)	
42	00101010	052	2A	*	
43	00101011	053	2B	+	
44	00101100	054	2C	, (Comma)	
45	00101101	055	2D	- (Hyphen)	
46	00101110	056	2E	. (Period)	
47	00101111	057	2F	/	
48	00110000	060	30	0	
49	00110001	061	31	1	
50	00110010	062	32	2	
51	00110011	063	33	3	
52	00110100	064	34	4	
53	00110101	065	35	5	
54	00110110	066	36	6	
55	00110111	067	37	7	
56	00111000	070	38	8	
57	00111001	071	39	9	
58	00111010	072	3A	:	
59	00111011	073	3B	;	
60	00111100	074	3C	<	
61	00111101	075	3D	=	
62	00111110	076	3E	>	
63	00111111	077	3F	?	
64	01000000	100	40	@	SP (Space)
65	01000001	101	41	A	
66	01000010	102	42	B	
67	01000011	103	43	C	
68	01000100	104	44	D	
69	01000101	105	45	E	
70	01000110	106	46	F	
71	01000111	107	47	G	
72	01001000	110	48	H	
73	01001001	111	49	I	

ASCII and EBCDIC Codes of Printable Characters *(cont.)*

Decimal	Binary	Octal	Hexadecimal	ASCII	EBCDIC
74	01001010	112	4A	J	¢
75	01001011	113	4B	K	. (Period)
76	01001100	114	4C	L	<
77	01001101	115	4D	M	(
78	01001110	116	4E	N	+
79	01001111	117	4F	O	|
80	01010000	120	50	P	&
81	01010001	121	51	Q	
82	01010010	122	52	R	
83	01010011	123	53	S	
84	01010100	124	54	T	
85	01010101	125	55	U	
86	01010110	126	56	V	
87	01010111	127	57	W	
88	01011000	130	58	X	
89	01011001	131	59	Y	
90	01011010	132	5A	Z	!
91	01011011	133	5B	[	$
92	01011100	134	5C	\	*
93	01011101	135	5D	]	)
94	01011110	136	5E	^	;
95	01011111	137	5F	_ (Underscore)	¬ (Negation)
96	01100000	140	60	`	- (Hyphen)
97	01100001	141	61	a	/
98	01100010	142	62	b	
99	01100011	143	63	c	
100	01100100	144	64	d	
101	01100101	145	65	e	
102	01100110	146	66	f	
103	01100111	147	67	g	
104	01101000	150	68	h	
105	01101001	151	69	i	
106	01101010	152	6A	j	^
107	01101011	153	6B	k	, (Comma)
108	01101100	154	6C	l	%
109	01101101	155	6D	m	_ (Underscore)
110	01101110	156	6E	n	>
111	01101111	157	6F	o	?
112	01110000	160	70	p	
113	01110001	161	71	q	
114	01110010	162	72	r	
115	01110011	163	73	s	
116	01110100	164	74	t	

ASCII and EBCDIC Codes of Printable Characters *(cont.)*

Decimal	Binary	Octal	Hexadecimal	ASCII	EBCDIC
117	01110101	165	75	u	
118	01110110	166	76	v	
119	01110111	167	77	w	
120	01111000	170	78	x	
121	01111001	171	79	y	
122	01111010	172	7A	z	:
123	01111011	173	7B	{	#
124	01111100	174	7C	|	@
125	01111101	175	7D	}	' (Single quote)
126	01111110	176	7E	~	=
127	01111111	177	7F		''
128	10000000	200	80		
129	10000001	201	81		a
130	10000010	202	82		b
131	10000011	203	83		c
132	10000100	204	84		d
133	10000101	205	85		e
134	10000110	206	86		f
135	10000111	207	87		g
136	10001000	210	88		h
137	10001001	211	89		i
.	.	.	.		.
.	.	.	.		.
.	.	.	.		.
145	10010001	221	91		j
146	10010010	222	92		k
147	10010011	223	93		l
148	10010100	224	94		m
149	10010101	225	95		n
150	10010110	226	96		o
151	10010111	227	97		p
152	10011000	230	98		q
153	10011001	231	99		r
.	.	.	.		.
.	.	.	.		.
.	.	.	.		.
162	10100010	242	A2		s
163	10100011	243	A3		t
164	10100100	244	A4		u
165	10100101	245	A5		v
166	10100110	246	A6		w
167	10100111	247	A7		x
168	10101000	250	A8		y

ASCII and EBCDIC Codes of Printable Characters *(cont.)*

Decimal	Binary	Octal	Hexadecimal	ASCII	EBCDIC
169	10101001	251	A9		z
.	.	.	.		.
.	.	.	.		.
.	.	.	.		.
192	11000000	300	C0		}
193	11000001	301	C1		A
194	11000010	302	C2		B
195	11000011	303	C3		C
196	11000100	304	C4		D
197	11000101	305	C5		E
198	11000110	306	C6		F
199	11000111	307	C7		G
200	11001000	310	C8		H
201	11001001	311	C9		I
.	.	.	.		.
.	.	.	.		.
.	.	.	.		.
208	11010000	320	D0		}
209	11010001	321	D1		J
210	11010010	322	D2		K
211	11010011	323	D3		L
212	11010100	324	D4		M
213	11010101	325	D5		N
214	11010110	326	D6		O
215	11010111	327	D7		P
216	11011000	330	D8		Q
217	11011001	331	D9		R
.	.	.	.		.
.	.	.	.		.
.	.	.	.		.
224	11100000	340	E0		\
225	11100001	341	E1		
226	11100010	342	E2		S
227	11100011	343	E3		T
228	11100100	344	E4		U
229	11100101	345	E5		V
230	11100110	346	E6		W
231	11100111	347	E7		X
232	11101000	350	E8		Y
233	11101001	351	E9		Z
.	.	.	.		.
.	.	.	.		.
.	.	.	.		.

ASCII and EBCDIC Codes of Printable Characters *(cont.)*

Decimal	Binary	Octal	Hexadecimal	ASCII	EBCDIC
240	11110000	360	F0		0
241	11110001	361	F1		1
242	11110010	362	F2		2
243	11110011	363	F3		3
244	11110100	364	F4		4
245	11110101	365	F5		5
246	11110110	366	F6		6
247	11110111	367	F7		7
248	11111000	370	F8		8
249	11111001	371	F9		9
.	.	.	.		.
.	.	.	.		.
.	.	.	.		.
255	11111111	377	FF		

ASCII Codes of Control Characters

Decimal	Binary	Octal	Hexadecimal	Character
0	00000000	000	00	NUL (Null)
1	00000001	001	01	SOH (Start of heading)
2	00000010	002	02	STX (End of heading and start of text)
3	00000011	003	03	ETX (End of text)
4	00000100	004	04	EOT (End of transmission)
5	00000101	005	05	ENQ (Enquiry — to request identification)
6	00000110	006	06	ACK (Acknowledge)
7	00000111	007	07	BEL (Ring bell)
8	00001000	010	08	BS (Backspace)
9	00001001	011	09	HT (Horizontal tab)
10	00001010	012	0A	LF (Line feed)
11	00001011	013	0B	VT (Vertical tab)
12	00001100	014	0C	FF (Form feed)
13	00001101	015	0D	CR (Carriage return)
14	00001110	016	0E	SO (Shift out — begin non-ASCII bit string)
15	00001111	017	0F	SI (Shift in — end non-ASCII bit string)
16	00010000	020	10	DLE (Data link escape — controls data transmission)

ASCII Codes of Control Characters *(cont.)*

Decimal	Binary	Octal	Hexadecimal	Character
17	00001001	021	11	DC1 (Device control 1)
18	00010010	022	12	DC2 (Device control 2)
19	00010011	023	13	DC3 (Device control 3)
20	00010100	024	14	DC4 (Device control 4)
21	00010101	025	15	NAK (Negative acknowledge)
22	00010110	026	16	SYN (Synchronous idle)
23	00010111	027	17	ETB (End of transmission block)
24	00011000	030	18	CAN (Cancel — ignore previous transmission)
25	00011001	031	19	EM (End of medium)
26	00011010	032	1A	SUB (Substitute a character for another)
27	00011011	033	1B	ESC (Escape)
28	00011100	034	1C	FS (File separator)
29	00011101	035	1D	GS (Group separator)
30	00011110	036	1E	RS (Record separator)
31	00011111	037	1F	US (Unit separator)

EBCDIC Codes of Control Characters

Decimal	Binary	Octal	Hexadecimal	Character
0	00000000	000	00	NUL (Null)
1	00000001	001	01	SOH (Start of heading)
2	00000010	002	02	STX (End of heading and start of text)
3	00000011	003	03	ETX (End of text)
4	00000100	004	04	PF (Punch off)
5	00000101	005	05	HT (Horizontal tab)
6	00000110	006	06	LC (Lower case)
7	00000111	007	07	DEL (Delete)
10	00001010	012	0A	SMM (Repeat)
11	00001011	013	0B	VT (Vertical tab)
12	00001100	014	0C	FF (Form feed)
13	00001101	015	0D	CR (Carriage return)
14	00001110	016	0E	SO (Shift out — begin non-ASCII bit string)
15	00001111	017	0F	SI (Shift in — end non-ASCII bit string)
16	00010000	020	10	DLE (Data link escape — controls data transmission)

EBCDIC Codes of Control Characters *(cont.)*

Decimal	Binary	Octal	Hexadecimal	Character
17	00001001	021	11	DC1 (Device control 1)
18	00010010	022	12	DC2 (Device control 2)
19	00010011	023	13	DC3 (Device control 3)
20	00010100	024	14	RES (Restore)
21	00010101	025	15	NL (Newline)
22	00010110	026	16	BS (Backspace)
23	00010111	027	17	IL (Idle)
24	00011000	030	18	CAN (Cancel — ignore previous transmission)
25	00011001	031	19	EM (End of medium)
26	00011010	032	1A	CC (Unit backspace)
28	00011100	034	1C	IFS (Interchange file separator)
29	00011101	035	1D	IGS (Interchange group separator)
30	00011110	036	1E	IRS (Interchange record separator)
31	00011111	037	1F	IUS (Interchange unit separator)
32	00100000	040	20	DS (Digit select)
33	00100001	041	21	SOS (Start of significance)
34	00100010	042	22	FS (File separator)
36	00100100	044	24	BYP (Bypass)
37	00100101	045	25	LF (Line feed)
38	00100110	046	26	ETB (End of transmission block)
39	00100111	047	27	ESC (Escape)
42	00101010	052	2A	SM (Start message)
45	00101101	055	2D	ENQ (Enquiry — to request identification)
46	00101110	056	2E	ACK (Acknowledge)
47	00101111	057	2F	BEL (Ring bell)
50	00110010	062	32	SYN (Synchronous idle)
52	00110100	064	34	PN (Punch on)
53	00110101	065	35	RS (Record separator)
54	00110110	066	36	UC (Upper case)
55	00110111	067	37	EOT (End of transmission)
60	00111100	074	3C	DC4 (Device control 4)
61	00111101	075	3D	NAK (Negative acknowledge)
63	00111111	077	3F	SUB (Substitute a character for another)

B

Sample Files

This appendix contains sample data files that may prove useful with some of the exercises in the text: INVENTOR.DAT, STUDENT.DAT, USERS.DAT, INUP-DATE.DAT, STUPDATE.DAT, USUPDATE.DAT, and LSQUARES.DAT. Descriptions of these files and sample listings follow.

An Inventory File

INVENTOR.DAT

Columns	Contents
1–4	Item number
5–28	Item name
29–33	Unit price (no decimal point, but three digits before and two after the decimal point are assumed)
34–36	Reorder point
37–39	Number currently in stock
40–42	Desired inventory level

The file is sorted so that the item numbers of the records are in increasing order.

   INVENTOR.DAT

```
1011TELEPHOTO POCKET CAMERA   5495 15 20 25
1012MINI POCKET CAMERA        2495 15 12 20
1021POL. ONE-STEP CAMERA      4995 10 20 20
1022SONAR 1-STEP CAMERA      18995 12 13 15
1023PRONTO CAMERA             7495  5 15 15
10318MM ZOOM MOVIE CAMERA    27999 10  9 15
1032SOUND/ZOOM 8MM CAMERA    31055 10 15 15
104135MM SLR XG-7 MINO. CAM.38900 12 10 20
104235MM SLR AE-1 PENT. CAM.34995 12 11 20
104335MM SLR ME CAN. CAM.   31990 12 20 20
104435MM HI-MATIC CAMERA    11995 12 13 20
104535MM COMPACT CAMERA      8999 12 20 20
1511ZOOM MOVIE PROJECTOR    12995  5  7 10
1512ZOOM-SOUND PROJECTOR    23999  5  9 15
1521AUTO CAROUSEL PROJECTOR 21999  5 10 10
1522CAR. SLIDE PROJECTOR    11495  5  4 10
2011POCKET STROBE            1495  5  4 15
2012STROBE SX-10             4855 10 12 20
```

INVENTOR.DAT   *(cont.)*

```
2013ELEC.FLASH SX-10          2899 15 10 20
3011TELE CONVERTER            3299 15 13 30
301228MM WIDE-ANGLE LENS      9799 15 14 25
3013135MM TELEPHOTO LENS      8795 15 13 25
301435-105 MM ZOOM LENS      26795  5  8 10
301580-200 MM ZOOM LENS      25795  5  7 10
3111HEAVY-DUTY TRIPOD         6750  5  4 10
3112LIGHTWEIGHT TRIPOD        1995  5 10 10
351135MM ENLARGER KIT        15999  5 10 10
401140X40 DELUXE SCREEN       3598  5  4 15
401250X50 DELUXE SCREEN       4498  5 10 10
5011120-SLIDE TRAY             429 25 17 40
5012100-SLIDE TRAY             295 25 33 40
5021SLIDE VIEWER               625 15 12 25
5031MOVIE EDITOR              5595 10 12 20
6011CONDENSER MICROPHONE      5995  5 10 10
6111AA ALKALINE BATTERY         89100 80200
7011GADGET BAG                1979 20 19 35
8011135-24 COLOR FILM          149 50 45100
8021110-12 COLOR FILM           99 50 60100
8022110-24 COLOR FILM          145 50 42100
8023110-12 B/W FILM             59 25 37 75
8024110-24 B/W FILM             95 25 43 75
8031126-12 COLOR FILM           89 50 44100
8032126-12 B/W FILM             59 25 27 50
80418MM FILM CASSETTE          689 50 39100
804216MM FILM CASETTE         1189 50 73100
9111COMBINATION CAMERA KIT   95999 10  8 15
```

An Inventory-Update File

INUPDATE.DAT

Columns	Contents
1–7	Order number (three letters followed by four digits)
8–11	Item number (same as those used in INVENTOR.DAT)
12	Transaction code (S = sold, R = returned)
13–15	Number of items sold or returned

The file is sorted so that item numbers are in increasing order. (Some items in INVENTOR.DAT may not have update records; others may have more than one.)

```
CCI75431012S    2
LTB34291012S    7
DJS67621021S    9
NQT18501022S    1
WYP64251023S    4
YOK22101023R    2
QGM31441023S    1
NPQ86851031S    5
MAP81021031S   13
JRJ63351031S    1
UWR93861032S    3
TJY19131032S   11
YHA94641041S    5
SYT74931041S    3
FHJ16571042S    7
OJQ12211043S    8
UOX77141043S    2
ERZ21471043S    7
MYW25401044S    1
UKS35871045S    2
AAN37591045S    2
WZT41711045S   12
TYR94751511S    1
FRQ41841511S    1
TAV36041512S    2
DCW93631522S    1
EXN39641522R    1
OIN55241522S    1
EOJ82181522S    1
YFK06832011S    2
PPX47432012S    4
DBR17092013S    4
JOM54082013S    3
PKN06712013S    1
LBD83913011S    9
DNL63263012S    9
BTP53963013S    1
GFL49133013S    8
EHQ75103013S    7
QQL64723013S    5
SVC65113014S    4
XJQ93913014S    4
ONO52513111S    3
CXC77803111S    1
VGT81693112S    8
IMK58613511S    2
QHR19443511S    1
```

INUPDATE.DAT   *(cont.)*

```
ZPK62114011S    2
VDZ29704012S    6
BOJ90695011S    6
MNL70295011S    9
MRG87035021S   10
DEM92895021S    1
BXL16515031S    2
VAF87336111S   65
UYI03687011S    2
VIZ68798011S   16
GXX90938011S   19
HHO56058021S   41
BOL23248021S   49
PAG92898023S   15
MDF55578023S   17
IQK33888024S   12
OTB13418024S   28
SVF56748031S   24
ZDP94848031S   15
OSY81778032S   15
GJQ01858032S    8
VHW01898041S   20
WEU92258041S    6
YJO37558041S    8
```

A Student File

STUDENT.DAT

Columns	Contents
1–5	Student number
6–19	Student's last name
20–29	Student's first name
30	Student's middle initial
31–53	Address
54–60	Phone number
61	Sex (M or F)
62	Class level (1, 2, 3, 4, or 5 for special)
63–66	Major (four-letter abbreviation)
67–69	Total credits earned to date (an integer)
70–72	Cumulative GPA (no decimal point, but one digit before and two after the decimal point are assumed)

The file is sorted so that the student numbers are in increasing order.

    STUDENT.DAT

```
10103JOHNSON          JAMES      LWAUPUN, WISCONSIN        7345229M1ENGR 15315
10104ANDREWS          PETER      JGRAND RAPIDS, MICHIGAN 9493301M2CPSC 42278
10110PETERS           ANDREW     JLYNDEN, WASHINGTON       3239550M5ART  63205
10113VANDENVANDER     VANNESSA   VFREMONT, MICHIGAN        5509237F4HIST110374
10126ARISTOTLE        ALICE      ACHINO, CALIFORNIA        3330861F3PHIL 78310
10144LUCKY            LUCY       LGRANDVILLE, MICHIGAN     7745424F5HIST 66229
10179EULER            LENNIE     LTHREE RIVERS, MICHIGAN 6290017M1MATH 15383
10191NAKAMURA         TOKY       OCHICAGO, ILLINOIS        4249665F1SOCI 12195
10226FREUD            FRED       ELYNDEN, WASHINGTON       8340115M1PSYC 15185
10272SPEARSHAKE       WILLIAM    WGRAND RAPIDS, MICHIGAN 2410744M5ENGL102295
10274TCHAIKOVSKY      WOLFGANG   ABYRON CENTER, MICHIGAN 8845115M3MUSC 79275
10284ORANGE           DUTCH      VGRAAFSCHAAP, MICHIGAN    3141660M2ENGR 42298
10297CAESAR           JULIE      SDENVER, COLORADO         4470338F4HIST117325
10298PSYCHO           PRUNELLA   EDE MOTTE, INDIANA        5384609F4PSYC120299
10301BULL             SITTING    UGALLUP, NEW MEXICO       6632997M1EDUC 14195
10302CUSTER           GENERAL    GBADLANDS, SOUTH DAKOTA 5552992M3HIST 40195
10303FAHRENHEIT       FELICIA    OSHEBOYGAN, WISCONSIN     5154997F2CHEM 40385
10304DEUTSCH          SPRECHEN   ZSPARTA, MICHIGAN         8861201F5GERM 14305
10307MENDELSSOHN      MOZART     WPEORIA, ILLINOIS         2410744M3MUSC 76287
10310AUGUSTA          ADA        BLAKEWOOD, CALIFORNIA     7172339F2CPSC 46383
10319GAUSS            CARL       FYORKTOWN, PENNSYLVANIA 3385494M2MATH 41400
10323KRONECKER        LEO        PTRAVERSE CITY, MICHIGAN6763991M3MATH 77275
10330ISSACSON         JACOB      ASILVER SPRINGS, MD       4847932M5RELI 25299
10331ISSACSON         ESAU       BSILVER SPRINGS, MD       4847932M5RELI 25298
10339DEWEY            JOHANNA    ASALT LAKE CITY, UTAH     6841129F2EDUC 41383
10348VIRUS            VERA       WSAGINAW, MICHIGAN        6634401F4CPSC115325
10355ZYLSTRA          ZELDA      ADOWNS, KANSAS            7514008F1ENGL 16195
10377PORGY            BESS       NCOLUMBUS, OHIO           4841771F2MUSC 44278
10389NEWMANN          ALFRED     ECHEYENNE, WYOMING        7712399M4EDUC115099
10395MEDES            ARCHIE     LWHITINSVILLE, MA         9294401M3ENGR 80310
10406MACDONALD        RONALD     BSEATTLE, WASHINGTON      5582911M1CPSC 15299
10415AARDVARK         ANTHONY    AGRANDVILLE, MICHIGAN     5325912M2ENGR 43279
10422GESTALT          GLORIA     GWHEATON, ILLINOIS        6631212F2PSYC 42248
10431GOTODIJKSTRA     EDGAR      GCAWKER CITY, KANSAS      6349971M1CPSC 15400
10448REMBRANDT        ROBERTA    ESIOUX CENTER, IOWA       2408113F1ART  77220
10458SHOEMAKER        IMELDA     MHONOLULU, HAWAII         9193001F1POLS 15315
10467MARX             KARL       ZHAWTHORNE, NEW JERSEY 5513915M3ECON 78275
10470SCROOGE          EBENEZER   TTROY, MICHIGAN           8134001M4SOCI118325
10482NIGHTINGALE      FLORENCE   KROCHESTER, NEW YORK      7175118F1NURS 15315
10490GAZELLE          GWENDOLYN DCHINO, CALIFORNIA         3132446F2P E  43278
```

STUDENT.DAT *(cont.)*

```
10501PASTEUR       LOUISE      AWINDOW ROCK, ARIZONA    4245170F1BIOL 16310
10519ELBA          ABLE        MBOZEMAN, MONTANA        8183226M3SPEE 77340
10511LEWIS         CLARK       NNEW ERA, MICHIGAN       6461125M4GEOG114337
10515MOUSE         MICHAEL     EBOISE, IDAHO            5132771M5EDUC 87199
10523PAVLOV        TIFFAN      TFARMINGTON, MICHIGAN    9421753F1BIOL 13177
10530CHICITA       JUANIT      AOKLAHOMA CITY, OK       3714377F5ENGL 95266
10538BUSCH         ARCH        EST LOUIS, MISSOURI      8354112M3ENGR 74275
10547FAULT         PAIGE       DPETOSKEY, MICHIGAN      4543116F5CPSC 55295
10553SANTAMARIA    NINA        PPLYMOUTH, MASSACHUSETTS2351881F1HIST 15177
10560SHYSTER       SAMUEL      DEVERGLADES, FLORIDA     4421885M1SOCI 13195
10582YEWLISS       CAL         CRUDYARD, MICHIGAN       3451220M3MATH 76299
10590ATANASOFF     ENIAC       CSPRINGFIELD, ILLINOIS   6142449F1CPSC 14188
10597ROCKNE        ROCKY       KPORTLAND, OREGON        4631744M4P E 116198
10610ROOSEVELT     ROSE        YSPRING LAKE, MICHIGAN   9491221F5E SC135295
10623XERXES        ART         ICINCINATTI, OHIO        3701228M4GREE119325
10629LEIBNIZ       GOTTFRIED   WBOULDER, COLORADO       5140228M1MATH 13195
10633VESPUCCI      VERA        DRIPON, CALIFORNIA       4341883F5GEOG 89229
10648PRINCIPAL     PAMELA      PALBANY, NEW YORK        7145513F1EDUC 14175
10652CICERO        MARSHA      MRAPID CITY, SD          3335910F3LATI 77287
10657WEERD         DEWEY       LDETROIT, MICHIGAN       4841962M4PHIL115299
10663HOCHSCHULE    HORTENSE    CLINCOLN, NEBRASKA       7120111F5EDUC100270
10668EINSTEIN      ALFRED      MNEWARK, NEW JERSEY      3710225M2ENGR 41278
10675FIBONACCI     LEONARD     ONASHVILLE, TENNESSEE    4921107M4MATH115325
10682ANGELO        MIKE        LAUSTIN, TEXAS           5132201M4ART 117374
10688PASCAL        BLAZE       RBROOKLYN, NEW YORK      7412993M1CPSC 15198
```

A Student-Update File

STUPDATE.DAT

Columns	Contents
1–5	Student number (Same as those used in STUDENT.DAT)
6–12	Name of course #1 (e.g., CPSC141)
13–14	Letter grade received for course #1 (e.g., A-, B+, C)
15	Credits received for course #1
16–22	Name of course #2
23–24	Letter grade received for course #2
25	Credits received for course #2

STUPDATE.DAT *(cont.)*

Columns	Contents
26–32	Name of course #3
33–34	Letter grade received for course #3
35	Credits received for course #3
36–42	Name of course #4
43–44	Letter grade received for course #4
45	Credits received for course #4
46–52	Name of course #5
53–54	Letter grade received for course #5
55	Credits received for course #5

The file is sorted so that the student numbers are in increasing order. There is one update record for each student in STUDENT.DAT.

 STUPDATE.DAT

```
10103ENGL176C 4EDUC268B 4EDUC330B+3P E 281C 3ENGR317D 4
10104CPSC271D+4E SC208D-3PHIL340B+2CPSC146D+4ENGL432D+4
10110ART 520D 3E SC259F 1ENGL151D+4MUSC257B 4PSYC486C 4
10113HIST498F 3P E 317C+4MUSC139B-3PHIL165D 3GEOG222C 3
10126PHIL367C-4EDUC420C-3EDUC473C 3EDUC224D-3GERM257F 4
10144HIST559C+3MATH357D 3CPSC323C-2P E 246D-4MUSC379D+4
10179MATH169C-4CHEM163C+4MUSC436A-3MATH366D-2BIOL213A-4
10191SOCI177F 4POLS106A 4EDUC495A-3ENGR418B+2ENGR355A 4
10226PSYC116B 3GERM323B-4ART 350A 4HIST269B+4EDUC214C+3
10272ENGL558A-4EDUC169D+3PSYC483B+4ENGR335B+2BIOL228B 4
10274MUSC351B 4PSYC209C-4ENGR400F 1E SC392A 4SOCI394B-3
10284ENGR292D 4PSYC172C 4EDUC140B 4MATH274F 4MUSC101D+4
10297HIST464F 1HIST205F 1ENGR444F 1MATH269F 1EDUC163F 1
10298PSYC452B 3MATH170C+4EDUC344C-2GREE138C-2SPEE303A-3
10301EDUC197A 4P E 372B 3ENGR218D 4MATH309C 4E SC405C-4
10302CHEM283F 1P E 440A 2MATH399A-3HIST455C-4MATH387C-3
10303HIST111D-3ART151 C+3ENGL100C-3PSYC151D+3PE104  A-1
10304GERM526C-2CHEM243C 4POLS331B-4EDUC398A 3ENGR479D+4
10307MUSC323B+3MATH485C 4HIST232B+4EDUC180A 3ENGL130B+4
10310CPSC264B 2POLS227D+3ENGR467D-3MATH494D-4ART 420C+4
10319MATH276B 2E SC434A 3HIST197B-4GERM489B-2ART 137C-3
10323MATH377D-4EDUC210D 4MATH385D-4ENGR433C 2HIST338A-4
```

STUPDATE.DAT *(cont.)*

```
10330HIST546C+3E SC440B+3GREE472C+3BIOL186B 4GEOG434C+2
10331HIST546C 3E SC440B+3GREE472C 3BIOL186B+4GEOG434C+2
10339EDUC283B 3CPSC150B 3ENGR120D 4CPSC122F 4ART 216B 4
10348CPSC411C-3HIST480C+4PSYC459B 4BIOL299B+4ECON276B+3
10355ENGL130C-3CPSC282C+4CPSC181A-4CPSC146C-4SOCI113F 1
10377SOCI213D+3PSYC158D 4MUSC188C 3PSYC281D-4ENGR339B+4
10389EDUC414D+4PSYC115C-2PSYC152D-4ART 366D-3ENGR366F 4
10395ENGR396B 4HIST102F 3ENGL111A 4PSYC210D-2GREE128A 4
10406CPSC160C+4CPSC233C 1LATI494C+3ENGL115C-3MATH181A 3
10415ENGR287C 4EDUC166B-4EDUC106A-3P E 190F 3MATH171B-3
10422PSYC275A-4MATH497A 4EDUC340F 1GERM403C-4MATH245D+4
10431CPSC187D-4CPSC426F 4ENGR476B-4BIOL148B+3CPSC220F 3
10448ART 171D+3CPSC239C-3SOCI499B-4HIST113D+3PSYC116C 4
10458POLS171F 1CPSC187C+4CHEM150B 2PHIL438D-4PHIL254D 4
10467ECON335D-3E SC471B+4MATH457C+3MATH207C 2BIOL429D 4
10470MUSC415C+3POLS177C 3CPSC480A 4PSYC437B 3SOCI276D 4
10482ENGL158D-4EDUC475B 3HIST172B-2P E 316F 4ENGR294A-3
10490P E 239F 4ENGL348F 3LATI246F 4CPSC350F 4MATH114F 1
10501BIOL125F 4CPSC412F 3E SC279F 4ENGR153F 2ART 293F 1
10519SPEE386B+4HIST479C 4PSYC249B-2GREE204B-4P E 421A 1
10511E SC416B 3MATH316D-4MATH287C 2MATH499A-4E SC288D 3
10515EDUC563D+3PHIL373D-3ART 318B 4HIST451F 1ART 476C+3
10523BIOL183D-2HIST296D+4HIST380B+4ENGR216C 4MATH412B-2
10530ENGL559F 1EDUC457D+4CPSC306A 3ENGR171B+1CPSC380A 4
10538ENGR328A-4ENGR336C 3EDUC418D+3PHIL437B+4CPSC475D 4
10547CPSC537A-4ART 386D 4HIST292D-4ENGR467A-4P E 464B+4
10553HIST170A-4SOCI496D-3PHIL136B+4CPSC371D-4CPSC160A-1
10560SOCI153D+3MATH438D+4CPSC378C 4BIOL266F 3EDUC278D+3
10582MATH388A-3P E 311B 3ECON143D 4MATH304C+3P E 428C+4
10590CPSC134B-3E SC114B+3CPSC492C 4ENGL121C 4ENGR403A-4
10597P E 423A-3BIOL189D+3PHIL122D-4ENGL194C-4SOCI113D+3
10610E SC594C-3PHIL344F 4CPSC189B+2ENGR411D-3MATH241A 4
10623GREE412B-4ENGL415D-3ENGL234D-4MATH275F 1SOCI124B+3
10629MATH137D 2MATH481F 3E SC445F 1MATH339D 4ART 219B+4
10633GEOG573B 4ENGL149C+4EDUC113B+4ENGR458C-2HIST446D+4
10648EDUC132D+4MUSC103D-4ENGL263C 4ENGL134B+4E SC392A 3
10652LATI363F 3BIOL425F 1CPSC267C 4EDUC127C+3MATH338B 4
10657PHIL429F 1ART 412D-4MUSC473B-4SOCI447C-4MATH237D+2
10663EDUC580B-4ENGR351B+4SOCI283D 4ART 340C 4PSYC133D+3
10668ENGR274B+4SOCI438C 1P E 327C 4BIOL158A 4EDUC457A-4
10675MATH457A 4ENGR114C 4CPSC218C 3E SC433C-3PSYC243C+1
10682ART 483D+3GERM432C 3ENGL103B+4MUSC169C-3SOCI381C-2
10688CPSC182F 1HIST371C+4PSYC408F 1MUSC214B+4MATH151C 3
```

A Users File

USERS.DAT

Columns	Contents
1–15	User's last name
16–30	User's first name
31–35	Identification number
36–40	Password
41–44	Resource limit (in dollars)
45–49	Resources used to date (no decimal point, but three digits before and two after the decimal point are assumed)

The file is sorted so that the identification numbers of the records are in increasing order.

USERS.DAT

```
MILTGEN         JOSEPH          10101MOE   75038081
SMALL           ISAAC           10102LARGE 65059884
SNYDER          SAMUEL          10103R2-D2 25019374
EDMUNDSEN       EDMUND          10104ABCDE 25017793
BRAUNSCHNEIDER  CHRISTOPHER     10105BROWN 85019191
PIZZULA         NORMA           10106PIZZA 35022395
VANDERVAN       HENRY           10107VAN   75016859
FREELOADER      FREDDIE         10108RED    450 7661
ALEXANDER       ALVIN           10109GREAT 65040504
MOUSE           MICHAEL         10110EARS    50 4257
LUKASEWICZ      ZZZYK           10111RPN    350 7350
CHRISTMAS       MARY            10112NOEL   850 3328
SINKE           CJ              10113TRAIN 75032753
NIJHOFF         LARAN           10114KKID  55038203
LIESTMA         STAN            10115SAAB   550 2882
ZWIER           APOLLOS         10116PJ    95025618
JAEGER          TIM             10117BIKE  45033701
VANZWALBERG     JORGE           10118EGYPT 35024948
JESTER          COURTNEY        10119JOKER 45028116
MCDONALD        RONALD          10120FRIES 250 3500
NEDERLANDER     BENAUT          10121DUTCH 650 3836
HAYBAILER       HOMER           10122FARM  850 3732
SPEAR           WILLIAM         10123SHAKE 25024673
ROMEO           JULIET          10124XOXOX 15010019
GREEK           JIMMY           10125WAGER 250    3
```

USERS.DAT *(cont.)*

```
VIRUS          VERA             10126WORM   750 6735
BEECH          ROCKY            10127BOAT   55039200
ENGEL          ANGEL            10128WINGS  150 1639
ABNER          LIL              10129DAISY  950 8957
TRACY          DICK             10130CRIME  85046695
MCGEE          FIBBER           10131MOLLY  75033212
BELL           ALEXANDER        10132PHONE  85033743
COBB           TYRUS            20101TIGER   50 3281
GEORGE         RUTH             20102BABE   25010934
DESCARTES      RONALD           20103HORSE  35026993
EUCLID         IAN              20104GREEK  95018393
DANIELS        EZEKIEL          20105LIONS  35012869
TARZAN         JANE             20106APES   15010031
HABBAKUK       JONAH            20107WHALE  350 6363
COLOMBUS       CHRIS            20108PINTA  85020224
BYRD           RICHARD          20109NORTH  55016849
BUNYON         PAUL             20110BABE   55033347
CHAUCER        JEFF             20111POEM   950 3702
STOTLE         ARI              20112LOGIC  75033774
HARRISON       BEN              20113PRES   55026297
JAMES          JESSE            20114GUNS   250 5881
SCOTT          FRANCINE         20115FLAG   35016811
PHILLIPS       PHYLLIS          20116GAS66  65032222
DOLL           BARBARA          20117KEN    350 2634
FINN           HUCK             20118TOM    350 2286
SAWYER         TOM              20119HUCK   95046030
NEWMANN        ALFRED           20120MAD    45011600
SIMON          SIMPLE           20121SAYS   55048605
SCHMIDT        MESSER           20122PLANE  250 3531
LUTHER         CALVIN           20124REF    77766666
YALE           HARVARD          20125IVY    15012770
```

A User-Update File

USUPDATE.DAT

Columns	Contents
1–5	Account number
6–10	Resources used (no decimal point, but three digits before and two after the decimal point are assumed)

The file is sorted so that the account numbers are in increasing order.

 USUPDATE.DAT

```
10101   732
10101  2133
11003  3502
10105   555
10105   329
10105    89
10105  1053
10109  8934
10116  1234
10116   583
10116  1563
10117  5023
10117  9823
10118  4523
10118   234
10118  8993
10120  2331
10122   345
10122   679
10122    78
10122  3402
10122   222
10122   328
10123  3409
10130    45
10130    89
10130   328
10132  4412
10132  1210
20101  1122
20101   534
20101  1001
20101   634
20111  1164
20111   154
20111  3226
20111  9923
20121  5545
20121  6423
20121  3328
```

A Least-Squares File

LSQUARES.DAT   This is a text file in which each line contains a pair of real numbers representing the *x*-coordinate and the *y*-coordinate of a point.

 LSQUARES.DAT

2.18	1.06		5.63	8.58
7.46	12.04		8.94	15.27
5.75	8.68		7.34	11.48
3.62	4.18		6.55	9.92
3.59	3.87		4.89	7.07
7.5	12.32		9.59	15.82
7.49	11.74		1.81	0.45
7.62	12.07		0.99	-0.71
7.39	12.17		4.82	6.91
1.88	0.58		9.68	16.24
6.31	10.09		1.21	-0.22
2.53	2.04		4.54	5.64
5.44	8.25		1.48	0.3
1.21	-0.76		6.58	9.8
9.07	15.5		3.05	3.56
3.95	5.0		6.19	9.62
9.63	17.01		6.47	9.83
9.75	16.91		8.13	10.75
9.99	16.67		7.31	11.73
3.61	4.69		0.33	-1.93
9.06	15.0		5.12	7.41
5.03	6.62		5.23	7.73
4.45	6.12		7.14	11.02
4.54	5.89		1.27	-0.21
0.92	-1.02		2.51	1.59
0.82	-1.5		5.26	7.86
2.62	2.1		4.74	6.19
5.66	8.53		2.1	2.12
8.05	13.05		5.27	7.73
8.99	14.85		2.85	2.63
5.12	7.03		1.99	1.09
3.85	4.43		8.91	15.03
6.08	9.21		2.19	1.21
1.42	0		1.6	-0.05
2.58	2.38		8.93	15.12
5.99	9.42		3.19	3.56
0.63	-1.63		3.37	3.64
9.98	17.25			

C

Program Composition

This diagram indicates the correct placement of the various types of FORTRAN statements in a program unit. The arrows indicate the order in which the statements may be used. For example, the arrow from the PARAMETER statements block to the DATA statements block indicates that all PARAMETER statements must precede all DATA statements in a program unit. The horizontal two-headed arrows indicate that these types of statements may be interspersed. For example, comment lines may appear anywhere in a program unit before the END statement.

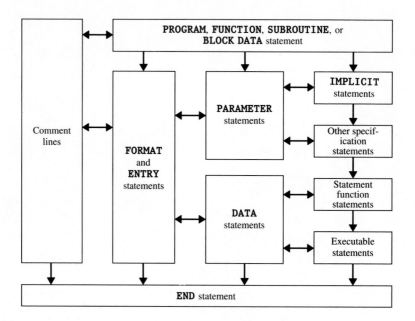

D

Generic and Specific Names of Functions

Function Description	Generic Name	Specific Name	Number of Arguments	Type of Arguments	Type of Function
Conversion of numeric to integer	INT	—	1	Integer	Integer
		INT		Real	Integer
		IFIX		Real	Integer
		IDINT		Double	Integer
		—		Complex	Integer
Conversion of numeric to real	REAL	REAL	1	Integer	Real
		FLOAT		Integer	Real
		—		Real	Real
		SNGL		Double	Real
		—		Complex	Real
Conversion of numeric to double precision	DBLE	—	1	Integer	Double
		—		Real	Double
		—		Double	Double
		—		Complex	Double
Conversion of numeric to complex	CMPLX	—	1	Integer	Complex
		—		Real	Complex
		—		Double	Complex
		—		Complex	Complex
Conversion of integer to character	—	CHAR	1	Integer	Character
Conversion of character to integer	—	ICHAR	1	Character	Integer
Truncation	AINT	AINT	1	Real	Real
		DINT		Double	Double
Rounding to nearest integer	ANINT	ANINT	1	Real	Real
		DNINT		Double	Double
Rounding to nearest integer	NINT	NINT	1	Real	Integer
		IDNINT		Double	Integer
Absolute value	ABS	IABS	1	Integer	Integer
		ABS		Real	Real
		DABS		Double	Double
		CABS		Complex	Real

Function Description	Generic Name	Specific Name	Number of Arguments	Type of Arguments	Type of Function
Remaindering	`MOD`	`MOD`	2	Integer	Integer
		`AMOD`		Real	Real
		`DMOD`		Double	Double
Transfer of sign	`SIGN`	`ISIGN`	2	Integer	Integer
		`SIGN`		Real	Real
		`DSIGN`		Double	Double
Positive difference	`DIM`	`IDIM`	2	Integer	Integer
		`DIM`		Real	Real
		`DDIM`		Double	Double
Double-precision product		`DPROD`	2	Real	Double
Maximum value	`MAX`	`MAX0`	≥ 2	Integer	Integer
		`AMAX1`		Real	Real
		`DMAX1`		Double	Double
	—	`AMAX0`		Integer	Real
	—	`MAX1`		Real	Integer
Minimum value	`MIN`	`MIN0`	≥ 2	Integer	Integer
		`AMIN1`		Real	Real
		`DMIN1`		Double	Double
	—	`AMIN0`		Integer	Real
	—	`MIN1`		Real	Integer
Length of character item	—	`LEN`	1	Character	Integer
Index of a substring	—	`INDEX`	2	Character	Integer
Imaginary part of a complex value	—	`AIMAG`	1	Complex	Real
Conjugate of a complex value	—	`CONJG`	1	Complex	Complex
Square root	`SQRT`	`SQRT`	1	Real	Real
		`DSQRT`		Double	Double
		`CSQRT`		Complex	Complex
Exponential	`EXP`	`EXP`	1	Real	Real
		`DEXP`		Double	Double
		`CEXP`		Complex	Complex
Natural logarithm	`LOG`	`ALOG`	1	Real	Real
		`DLOG`		Double	Double
		`CLOG`		Complex	Complex
Common logarithm	`LOG10`	`ALOG10`	1	Real	Real
		`DLOG10`		Double	Double

Function Description	Generic Name	Specific Name	Number of Arguments	Type of Arguments	Type of Function
Sine	SIN	SIN DSIN CSIN	1	Real Double Complex	Real Double Complex
Cosine	COS	COS DCOS CCOS	1	Real Double Complex	Real Double Complex
Tangent	TAN	TAN DTAN	1	Real Double	Real Double
Arcsine	ASIN	ASIN DASIN	1	Real Double	Real Double
Arccosine	ACOS	ACOS DACOS	1	Real Double	Real Double
Arctangent	ATAN	ATAN DATAN	1	Real Double	Real Double
	ATAN2	ATAN2 DATAN2	2	Real Double	Real Double
Hyperbolic sine	SINH	SINH DSINH	1	Real Double	Real Double
Hyperbolic cosine	COSH	COSH DCOSH	1	Real Double	Real Double
Hyperbolic tangent	TANH	TANH DTANH	1	Real Double	Real Double
Lexically greater than or equal to	—	LGE	2	Character	Logical
Lexically greater than	—	LGT	2	Character	Logical
Lexically less than or equal to	—	LLE	2	Character	Logical
Lexically less than	—	LLT	2	Character	Logical

E

Internal Representation

We noted in Section 1.2 that a binary scheme having only the two binary digits 0 and 1 is used to represent information in a computer. These binary digits, called *bits*, are organized into groups of 8 called *bytes*, and bytes in turn are grouped together into *words*. Common word sizes are 16 bits (= 2 bytes) and 32 bits (= 4 bytes). Each byte or word has an *address* that can be used to access it, making it possible to store information in and retrieve information from that byte or word. To understand how this is done, we must know something about the binary number system.

NUMBER SYSTEMS

The number system that we are accustomed to using is a **decimal** or **base-10** number system, which uses the digits 0, 1, 2, 3, 4, 5, 6, 7, 8, and 9. The significance of these digits in a numeral depends on the positions that they occupy in that numeral. For example, in the numeral

$$485$$

the digit 4 is interpreted as

$$4 \text{ hundreds}$$

and the digit 8 as

$$8 \text{ tens}$$

and the digit 5 as

$$5 \text{ ones}$$

Thus, the numeral 485 represents the number four hundred eighty-five and can be written in **expanded form** as

$$(4 \times 100) + (8 \times 10) + (5 \times 1)$$

or

$$(4 \times 10^2) + (8 \times 10^1) + (5 \times 10^0)$$

The digits that appear in the various positions of a decimal (base-10) numeral thus are coefficients of powers of 10.

Similar positional number systems can be devised using numbers other than 10 as a base. The **binary** number system uses 2 as the base and has only two digits, 0 and 1. As in a decimal system, the significance of the bits in a binary numeral is determined by their positions in that numeral. For example, the binary numeral

$$101$$

can be written in expanded form (using decimal notation) as

$$(1 \times 2^2) + (0 \times 2^1) + (1 \times 2^0)$$

that is, the binary numeral 101 has the decimal value

$$4 + 0 + 1 = 5$$

Similarly, the binary numeral 111010 has the decimal value

$$(1 \times 2^5) + (1 \times 2^4) + (1 \times 2^3) + (0 \times 2^2) + (1 \times 2^1) + (0 \times 2^0)$$
$$= 32 + 16 + 8 + 0 + 2 + 0$$
$$= 58$$

When necessary, to avoid confusion about which base is being used, it is customary to write the base as a subscript for nondecimal numerals. Using this convention, we could indicate that 5 and 58 have the binary representations just given by writing

$$5 = 101_2$$

and

$$58 = 111010_2$$

Two other nondecimal numeration systems are important in the consideration of computer systems: **octal** and **hexadecimal.** The octal system is a base-8 system and uses the eight digits 0, 1, 2, 3, 4, 5, 6, and 7. In an octal numeral such as

$$1703_8$$

the digits are coefficients of powers of 8; this numeral is therefore an abbreviation for the expanded form

$$(1 \times 8^3) + (7 \times 8^2) + (0 \times 8^1) + (3 \times 8^0)$$

and thus has the decimal value

$$512 + 448 + 0 + 3 = 963$$

A hexadecimal system uses a base of 16 and the digits 0, 1, 2, 3, 4, 5, 6, 7, 8, 9, A (10), B (11), C (12), D (13), E (14), and F (15). The hexadecimal numeral

$$5E4_{16}$$

has the expanded form

$$(5 \times 16^2) + (14 \times 16^1) + (4 \times 16^0)$$

which has the decimal value

$$1280 + 224 + 4 = 1508$$

Table E.1 shows the decimal, binary, octal, and hexadecimal representations for the first 31 nonnegative integers.

Table E.1 Numeric Representation

Decimal	Binary	Octal	Hexadecimal
0	0	0	0
1	1	1	1
2	10	2	2
3	11	3	3
4	100	4	4
5	101	5	5
6	110	6	6
7	111	7	7
8	1000	10	8
9	1001	11	9
10	1010	12	A
11	1011	13	B
12	1100	14	C
13	1101	15	D
14	1110	16	E
15	1111	17	F
16	10000	20	10
17	10001	21	11
18	10010	22	12
19	10011	23	13
20	10100	24	14
21	10101	25	15
22	10110	26	16
23	10111	27	17
24	11000	30	18
25	11001	31	19
26	11010	32	1A
27	11011	33	1B
28	11100	34	1C
29	11101	35	1D
30	11110	36	1E
31	11111	37	1F

DATA STORAGE

Integers. When an integer value must be stored in the computer's memory, the binary representation of that value is typically stored in one word of memory. To illustrate, consider a computer whose word size is sixteen, and suppose that the integer value 58 is to be stored. A memory word is selected, and a sequence of sixteen bits formed from the binary representation 111010 of 58 is stored there:

Memory

Negative integers must also be stored in a binary form in which the sign of the integer is part of the representation. There are several ways that this can be done, but one of the most common is the **two's complement** representation. In this scheme, positive integers are represented in binary form, as just described, with the leftmost bit set to 0 to indicate that the value is positive. The representation of a negative integer $-n$ is obtained by first finding the binary representation of n, complementing it—that is, changing each 0 to 1 and each 1 to 0, and then adding 1 to the result. For example, the two's complement representation of -58 using a string of sixteen bits is obtained as follows:

1. Represent 58 by a 16-bit binary numeral:

$$0000000000111010$$

2. Complement this bit string:

$$1111111111000101$$

3. Add 1:

$$1111111111000110$$

Note that the leftmost bit in this two's complement representation of a negative integer is always 1, indicating that the number is negative.

Since integers are stored in a single word of memory, the word size of a computer determines the range of the integers that can be stored internally. For example, the largest positive integer that can be stored in a 16-bit word is

$$0111111111111111_2 = 2^{15} - 1 = 32767$$

and the smallest negative integer is

$$1000000000000000_2 = -2^{15} = -32768$$

The range of integers that can be represented using a 32-bit word is

$$10000000000000000000000000000000_2 = -2^{31} = -2147483648$$

through

$$01111111111111111111111111111111_2 = 2^{31} - 1 = 2147483647$$

Representation of an integer outside the allowed range would require more bits than can be stored in a single word, a phenomenon known as **overflow.** This limitation may be partially overcome by using more than one word to store an integer. Although this enlarges the range of integers that can be stored exactly, it does not resolve the problem of overflow; the range of representable integers is still finite.

Real Numbers.   Numbers that contain decimal points are called **real numbers** or **floating-point numbers.** In the decimal representation of such numbers, each digit is the coefficient of some power of 10. Digits to the left of the decimal point are coefficients of nonnegative powers of 10, and those to the right are coefficients of negative powers of 10. For example, the decimal numeral 56.317 can be written in expanded form as

$$(5 \times 10^1) + (6 \times 10^0) + (3 \times 10^{-1}) + (1 \times 10^{-2}) + (7 \times 10^{-3})$$

or, equivalently, as

$$(5 \times 10) + (6 \times 1) + \left(3 \times \frac{1}{10}\right) + \left(1 \times \frac{1}{100}\right) + \left(7 \times \frac{1}{1000}\right)$$

Digits in the binary representation of a real number are coefficients of powers of two. Those to the left of the **binary point** are coefficients of nonnegative powers of two, and those to the right are coefficients of negative powers of two. For example, the expanded form of 110.101 is

$$(1 \times 2^2) + (1 \times 2^1) + (0 \times 2^0) + (1 \times 2^{-1}) + (0 \times 2^{-2}) + (1 \times 2^{-3})$$

and thus has the decimal value

$$4 + 2 + 0 + \frac{1}{2} + 0 + \frac{1}{8} = 6.625$$

There is some variation in the schemes used for storing real numbers in computer memory, but one common method is the following. The binary representation

$$110.101_2$$

of the real number 6.625 can also be written equivalently as

$$0.110101_2 \times 2^3$$

Typically, one part of a memory word (or words) is used to store a fixed number of bits of the **mantissa** or **fractional part,** 0.110101_2, and another part to store the **exponent,**

$3 = 11_2$. For example, if the leftmost 24 bits in a 32-bit word are used for the mantissa and the remaining eight bits for the exponent, 6.625 can be stored as

where the first bit in each part is reserved for the sign.[1]

Because the binary representation of the exponent may require more than the available number of bits, we see that the **overflow** problem discussed in connection with the integer representation will also occur in storing a real number whose exponent is too large. A negative exponent that is too small to be stored causes an **underflow.** (See Section 2.11.) Also, there obviously are some real numbers whose mantissas have more than the allotted number of bits; consequently, some of these bits will be lost when storing such numbers. In fact, most real numbers do not have finite binary representations and thus cannot be stored exactly in any computer. For example, the binary representation of the real number 0.7 is

$$(0.10110011001100110\ldots)_2$$

where the block 0110 is repeated indefinitely. If only the first 24 bits are stored and all remaining bits are truncated, the stored representation of 0.7 will be

$$(0.101100110011001100110011001)_2$$

which has the decimal value 0.6999999284744263. If the binary representation is rounded to 24 bits, the stored representation for 0.7 will be

$$(0.101100110011001100110011010)_2$$

which has the decimal value 0.7000000476837159. In either case, the stored value is not exactly 0.7. This error, called **roundoff error,** can be reduced, but not eliminated, by using a larger number of bits to store the binary representation of real numbers.

Logical and Character Values

Computers store and process not only numeric data but also logical or boolean data (false or true), character data, and other types of nonnumeric information. Storing logical values is easy: False can be encoded as 0, true as 1, and these bits stored.

The schemes used for the internal representation of character data are based on the assignment of a numeric code to each of the characters in the character set. Several standard coding schemes have been developed, such as ASCII (American Standard Code

---

[1] In most computers, exponents are stored using *biased notation* so that it is easier to compare exponents. In biased notation, a bias 2^{n-1} is added to the exponent, where n is the number of bits used to store the exponent. Thus for a 32-bit word the 8 bits for the exponent, the bias would be $2^7 = 128 = 10000000$. For the real value 6.625, the exponent would be stored as 10000011.

for Information Interchange) and EBCDIC (Extended Binary Coded Decimal Interchange Code). A complete table of ASCII and EBCDIC codes for all characters is given in Appendix A.

Characters are represented internally using these binary codes. A byte can thus store the binary representation of one character. For example, the character string HI can be stored in two bytes with the code for H in the first byte and the code for I in the second byte; with ASCII code, the result is as follows:

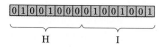

Memory words of size 32 (bits) are usually divided into four bytes and thus can store four characters. Character strings whose length exceeds the number of bytes in a word are usually stored in adjacent words of memory.

Exercises E

1. Convert each of the following binary numerals to base 10:
   (a) 1001   (b) 110010
   (c) 1000000   (d) 111111111111111 (fifteen 1s)
   (e) 1.1   (f) 1010.10101

2. Convert each of the following octal numerals to base 10:
   (a) 123   (b) 2705   (c) 10000
   (d) 77777   (e) 7.2   (f) 123.45

3. Convert each of the following hexadecimal numerals to base 10:
   (a) 12   (b) 1AB   (c) ABC
   (d) FFF   (e) 8.C   (f) AB.CD

4. Converting from octal representation to binary representation is easy, as we need only replace each octal digit with its three-bit binary equivalent. For example, to convert 617_8 to binary, replace 6 with 110, 1 with 001, and 7 with 111, to obtain 110001111_2. Convert each of the octal numerals in Exercise 2 to binary numerals.

5. Imitating the conversion scheme in Exercise 4, convert each of the hexadecimal numerals in Exercise 3 to binary numerals.

6. To convert a binary numeral to octal, place the digits in groups of three, starting from the binary point, or from the right end if there is no binary point, and replace each group with the corresponding octal digit. For example, $10101111_2 = 010\ 101\ 111_2 = 257_8$. Convert each of the binary numerals in Exercise 1 to octal numerals.

7. Imitating the conversion scheme in Exercise 6, convert each of the binary numerals in Exercise 1 to hexadecimal numerals.

8. One method for finding the **base-b** representation of a whole number given in base-10 notation is to divide the number repeatedly by b until a quotient of zero results. The successive remainders are the digits from right to left of the base-b representation. For example, the binary representation of 26 is 11010_2, as the following computation shows:

$$
\begin{array}{r}
0\ \text{R}\ 1 \\ \hline
2\,)\,\overline{1}\ \text{R}\ 1 \\ \hline
2\,)\,\overline{3}\ \text{R}\ 9 \\ \hline
2\,)\,\overline{6}\ \text{R}\ 1 \\ \hline
2\,)\,\overline{13}\ \text{R}\ 0 \\ \hline
2\,)\,\overline{26}
\end{array}
$$

Convert each of the following base-10 numerals to (i) binary, (ii) octal, and (iii) hexadecimal:

(a) 27   (b) 99   (c) 314   (d) 5280

9. To convert a decimal fraction to its base-b equivalent, repeatedly multiply the fractional part of the number by b. The integer parts are the digits from left to right of the base-b representation. For example, the decimal numeral 0.6875 corresponds to the binary numeral 0.1011_2, as the following computation shows:

$$
\begin{array}{r|l}
 & .6875 \\
 & \times\,2 \\ \hline
1 & .375 \\
 & \times\,2 \\ \hline
0 & .75 \\
 & \times\,2 \\ \hline
1 & .5 \\
 & \times\,2 \\ \hline
1 & .0
\end{array}
$$

Convert the following base-10 numerals to (i) binary, (ii) octal, (iii) hexadecimal:

(a) 0.5   (b) 0.25   (c) 0.625
(d) 16.0625   (e) 8.828125

10. Even though the base-10 representation of a fraction may terminate, its representation in some other base need not terminate. For example, the following computation shows that the binary representation of 0.7 is $(0.10110011001100110011001100110 \ldots)_2$, where the block of bits 0110 is repeated indefinitely. This representation is commonly written as $0.1\overline{0110}_2$.

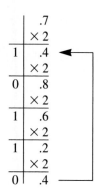

Convert the following base-10 numerals to (i) binary, (ii) octal, (iii) hexadecimal:

(a) 0.3   (b) 0.6   (c) 0.05   (d) $0.\overline{3} = 0.33333 \cdots = 1/3$

11. Find the decimal value of each of the following 16-bit integers, assuming a two's complement representation:

(a) 0000000001000000   (b) 1111111111111110
(c) 1111111110111111   (d) 0000000011111111
(e) 1111111100000000   (f) 1000000000000001

12. Find the 16-bit two's complement representation for each of the following integers:

(a) 255   (b) 1K
(c) −255   (d) −256
(e) -34567_8 (f) $-3ABC_{16}$

13. Assuming an 11-bit mantissa and a 5-bit exponent, and assuming that two's complement representation is used for each, indicate how each of the following real numbers would be stored in a 16-bit word if extra bits in the mantissa are (i) truncated or (ii) rounded:

(a) 0.375   (b) 37.375
(c) 0.03125   (d) 63.84375
(e) 0.1   (f) 0.01

14. Using the tables for ASCII and EBCDIC in Appendix A, indicate how each of the following character strings would be stored in 2-byte words using (i) ASCII or (ii) EBCDIC:

(a) TO   (b) FOUR
(c) AMOUNT   (d) ETC.
(e) J.DOE   (f) A#*4–C

F

Answers to
Quick Quizzes

Quick Quiz 1.2

1. **(a)** Mechanical devices for calculation
   (b) Stored program for automatic control of a process
2. D, E, R, O, V, Q, I, H, T, P, W, M, F, U, B, S, G, A, J, K, C, L, N

Quick Quiz 1.4

1. Problem analysis and specification
   Data organization and algorithm design
   Program coding
   Execution and testing
   Maintenance
2. Input and output
3. Sequence, selection, and repetition
4. false
5. flowchart
6. syntax
7. top-down design or divide-and-conquer strategy
8. syntax errors
   run-time errors
   logical errors
9. **(a)** Input :   temperature on Celsius scale

   Output : corresponding temperature on Fahrenheit scale

   * This algorithm converts a temperature of DEGC on the Celsius scale to the   *
   * corresponding temperature DEGF on Fahrenheit scale   *

   1. Enter DEGC
   2. Calculate   DEGF = 1.8 * DEGC + 32
   3. Display DEGF

Quick Quiz 1.4 *(cont.)*

(b)

```
              PROGRAM TEMPS
****************************************************************
*                                                              *
* Program to convert a temperature of DEGC degrees on the      *
* Celsius scale to the corresponding temperature DEGF on       *
* the Fahrenheit scale                                         *
*                                                              *
****************************************************************
      REAL DEGC, DEGF

      PRINT *, 'ENTER THE TEMPERATURE IN DEGREES CELSIUS:'
      READ *, DEGC

      DEGF = 1.8 * DEGC + 32.0
      PRINT *, FAHRENHEIT TEMPERATURE IS: 'DEGF
      END
```

Quick Quiz 2.2

1. Integer
   Real
   Double Precision
   Complex
   Logical
   Character

2. Program heading
   Specification part
   Execution part

3. single quotes (')

4. A letter

5. 6

6. Not legal: CALORIE is too long

7. Not legal: the character - is not legal in an identifier

8. Not legal: identifier must begin with a letter

9. Not legal : the character . is not legal in an identifier

Quick Quiz 2.2 *(cont.)*

10. Not legal : the character / is not legal in an identifier
11. Not legal : the character $ is not legal in an identifier
12. Integer
13. None: Comma not allowed in numeric constant
14. Real
15. Real
16. Real
17. Character
18. None: Doesn't begin with a digit or a sign and is not enclosed in quotes
19. None: Apostrophes within strings must be doubled
20. Character
21. None : $ not allowed in numeric constant
22. Real
23. None: Doesn't begin with a digit or sign and is not enclosed in quotes
24. Integer
25. None : + not allowed in numeric constant
26. Character
27. REAL MU
28. REAL TIME, DIST
29. CHARACTER*20 NAME1, NAME2, NAME3*10
30. Real
31. Neither : identifier must have at most 6 letters or digits
32. Real
33. Integer
34. Integer
35. Real
36. Real
37. Integer
38. REAL GRAV
    PARAMETER (GRAV = 32)
39. REAL MARS, EARTH
    PARAMETER (MARS = 1.2E12, EARTH = 1.5E10)
40. CHARACTER*8 COURSE
    INTEGER CNUMB
    PARAMETER (COURSE = 'CPSC 141', CNUMB = 141)

Quick Quiz 2.2 *(cont.)*

```
41. REAL RATE1, RATE2)
    DATA  RATE1, RATE2 /1.25, 2.33/
42. CHARACTER*4  DEPT
    INTEGER COURS1, COURS2
    DATA  DEPT / 'CPSC' / COURS1, COURS2 / 141, 142 /
43. INTEGER LIM1, LIM2, LIM3, LIM4, LIM5, LIM6
    DATA  LIM1, LIM2, LIM3, LIM4, LIM5, LIM6 / 3*10, 2*20, 30/
```

Quick Quiz 2.3

1. 1
2. 2.6
3. 2
4. 5
5. 11
6. 25
7. 12.25
8. 36.0
9. 2
10. 3.0
11. 11.0
12. 1
13. 12.25
14. 5.1
15. 4.0
16. 6.25
17. 3.0
18. `10 + 5 * B + 4 * A * C`
19. `SQRT(A + 3 * B ** 2)`

Quick Quiz 2.4

1. valid
2. not valid: variable must be on the left of =
3. valid
4. not valid: variable must be on the left of =
5. valid : but not recommended because it is a mixed mode assignment
6. not valid: ' 1 ' is a character constant
7. valid
8. not valid: multiple assignments are not legal
9. 12.25
10. 6.1
11. 6
12. 10
13. 5.0
14. 1
15. not valid: 1 is a numeric constant
16. '1'
17. 'ONET'
18. '12bb'　　　(where b is a blank)
19. DIST = RATE * TIME
20. C = SQRT(A**2 + B**2)
21. COUNT = COUNT + 1

Quick Quiz 2.6

1. Lines that contain only blanks or that have a C or an asterisk (*) in column 1 are comments.
2. Executable statements specify actions to be taken during execution of the program. Nonexecutable statements provide information that is used during compilation of a program.
3. true
4. false
5. false

Quick Quiz 2.6 *(cont.)*

6. false

7. true

8. A blank line.

9. `37.0  7`
   `X =  1.74  I =   29`
   `4.23`
   `15`

10. Column 1 : E
    Column 1–5 : B
    Column 6 : A
    Column 7–72 : C
    Column 73– : D

Quick Quiz 3.1

1. `.TRUE.    .FALSE.`

2. `.LT.,   .LE.,   .GT.,   .GE.,   .EQ.,   .NE.`

3. `.NOT.,  .AND.,  .OR.,  .EQV.,  .NEQV.`

4. `.FALSE.`

5. `.TRUE.`

6. `.FALSE.`

7. `.FALSE.`

8. `.TRUE.`

9. `.TRUE.`

10. `.TRUE.`

11. `.TRUE.`

12. Invalid; should be `(0 .LE. COUNT) .AND. (COUNT .LE. 5)`

13. `.TRUE.`

14. `X .NE. 0`

15. `-10 .LT. X .AND. X .LT. 10` or more simply, `ABS(X) .LT. 10`

16. `(X .GT. 0 .AND. Y .GT. 0) .OR. (X .LT. 0 .. Y .LT. 0)` or simply, `X * Y .GT. 0`

Quick Quiz 3.5

1. Legal
2. Not legal : logical expression should be enclosed in parentheses
3. Legal
4. Not legal : logical operator is `.EQ.`
5. Not legal : logical expression is not correct.
6. Not legal : logical expression is not correct.
7. 6
8. 5
9. 6
10. 10
11. 10
12. 10
13. `EXCELLENT`
14. `EXCELLENT`
15. `GOOD`
16. `FAIR`
17. `BAD`
18.
```
 IF ((NUMBER .LT. 0) .OR. (NUMBER .GT. 100))
+PRINT *, 'OUT OF RANGE'
```
19.
```
 IF (X .LT. 1.5) THEN
    N = 1
 ELSE IF (X .LT. 2.5) THEN
    N = 2
 ELSE
    N = 3
 END IF
```

Quick Quiz 3.7

1. false
2. false
3. false

Quick Quiz 3.7 *(cont.)*

4. false

5. false

6. false

7. true

8. false

9. true

10. true

11. ```
LOGICAL LARGER
   LARGER = A .GT. B
```

12. ```
LOGICAL FRESH, UPPER
   LARGER = CLASS .EQ. 1
   UPPER = .NOT. FRESH
```

Quick Quiz 4.1

1. **a.** *Repetition controlled by a counter* in which the body of the loop is executed once for each value of some control variable in a specified range of values.

   b. *Repetition controlled by a logical expression* in which the decision to continue or to terminate repetition is determined by the value of some logical expression.

2. ```
HELLO
HELLO
HELLO
HELLO
HELLO
```

3. ```
HELLO
HELLO
HELLO
```

4. ```
1 2
2 3
3 4
4 5
5 6
6 7
```
```

Quick Quiz 4.1 *(cont.)*

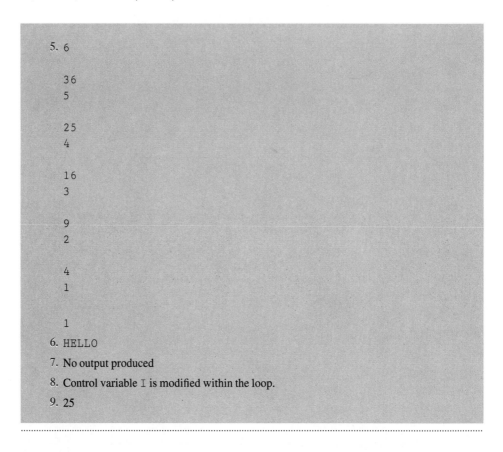

5. 6

 3 6
 5

 2 5
 4

 1 6
 3

 9
 2

 4
 1

 1

6. HELLO
7. No output produced
8. Control variable I is modified within the loop.
9. 25

Quick Quiz 4.7

1. In a pretest loop, the logical expression that controls the repetition is evaluated before the body of the loop is executed. In a posttest loop, the termination test is made after the body of the loop is executed.

2. A pretest loop

3. False

4. True

5. Syntax errors, run-time errors, and logic errors

6. run-time

7. syntax

8. logic

Quick Quiz 4.7 *(cont.)*

9. 1
    2
    4
    16
    32
    64

10. **(a)** 0   **(b)** No output is produced
        1
        2
        3
        4

11. **(a)** 0   **(b)** 0
        1
        2
        3
        4

Quick Quiz 5.3

1. False
2. True
3. False
4. False
5. False
6. False
7. True
8. Slash
9. right
10. 1
11. I =987   X = 234.560THE END
12. ￼￼987￼￼￼￼￼234.6
    ￼￼−44￼￼￼￼￼10.1
13. ￼￼￼￼￼234.
    987￼￼￼￼￼￼￼−44
14. 99, 876, 123.45, 6.0   (other answers are possible)

Quick Quiz 5.3 *(cont.)*

15. ᵇ99876123.45ᵇᵇᵇᵇᵇ6   (other answers are possible)

16. ᵇ99ᵇ123.45ᵇᵇᵇᵇ876ᵇᵇᵇᵇᵇᵇ6

17. ᵇ99876123456

18. 9912345
    87660

Quick Quiz 5.5

1. unit number
2. `FORMAT`
3. `WRITE(*, *) ANSWER`
4. False
5. `OPEN(UNIT = 15, FILE = 'QUIZ', STATUS = 'OLD')`
6. `READ (15, '(T6, I3)') SCORE`
7. True
8. True
9. False
10. `REWIND`

Quick Quiz 6.1

1. Functions and subroutines
2. Heading, specification part, and execution part
3. Formal arguments
4. `REAL`
5. function subprogram, calling program unit
6. True
7. True
8. actual
9. 6

Quick Quiz 6.1 *(cont.)*

10. False
11. True
12. ```
REAL FUNCTION F(X)
REAL X
F = X**2 * SIN(X)
END
```
13. ```
REAL F, X
F(X) = X**2 * SIN(X)
```

Quick Quiz 7.1

1. Functions and subroutines
2. Heading, specification part, and execution part
3. Formal arguments
4. True
5. True
6. 1. Functions are designed to return a single value to the program unit that references them. Subroutines often return more than one value, or they may return no value at all but simply perform some task such as displaying a list of instructions to the user.

   2. Functions return values via function names; subroutines return values via arguments.

   3. A function is referenced by using its name in an expression, whereas a subroutine is referenced by a CALL statement.
7. address, reference
8. parentheses
9. Cannot be used. CALC must be referenced with a CALL statement
10. Can be used.
11. Cannot be used. Incorrect number of arguments
12. Cannot be used. CALC must be referenced with a CALL statement
13. Can be used
14. Cannot be used. Incorrect number of arguments
15. Cannot be used. Type mismatch
16. STRING =BATBATELK

Quick Quiz 8.2

1. direct
2. subscripted
3. subscript or index
4. one-dimensional
5. True
6. True
7. False
8. True
9. False
10. False
11. Correct
12. Not correct
13. Not correct
14. Not correct

Quick Quiz 8.5

1. False
2. True
3. NUMBER(1) = 3
   NUMBER(2) = 4
   NUMBER(3) = 7
   NUMBER(4) = 8
   NUMBER(5) = 11
4. NUMBER(1) = 2
   NUMBER(2) = 4
   NUMBER(3) = 8
   NUMBER(4) = 16
   NUMBER(5) = 32
5. XVAL(1) = 0.5
   XVAL(2) = 1.0
   XVAL(3) = 1.5
   XVAL(4) = 2.0
   XVAL(5) = 2.5

Quick Quiz 8.5 *(cont.)*

```
6. NUMBER(1)  = 1
   NUMBER(2)  = 2
   NUMBER(3)  = 3
   NUMBER(4)  = 3
   NUMBER(5)  = 3
7. ANIM = APE RAT CAT
```

Quick Quiz 9.2

1. True
2. columnwise
3. columnwise
4. 3
5. 2
6. 3
7. No value assigned
8. 3
9. False
10. True
11. 4
12. $\begin{bmatrix} 1 & 0 & 0 \\ 0 & 1 & 0 \\ 0 & 0 & 1 \end{bmatrix}$
13. $\begin{bmatrix} 1 & 1 & 1 \\ 0 & 1 & 1 \\ 0 & 0 & 1 \end{bmatrix}$
14. $\begin{bmatrix} 1 & 2 & 3 \\ 2 & 4 & 6 \\ 3 & 6 & 9 \end{bmatrix}$
15. No
16. Yes
17. Yes

Quick Quiz 9.2 *(cont.)*

18. Yes
19. Yes
20. Yes

Quick Quiz 10.4

1. False
2. True
3. False
4. False
5. False
6. True
7. True
8. False
9. True
10. False
11. False
12. $15 + 5i$

13. $1 + i$
14. $50 + 37i$
15. $(62 + 5i) / 53$
16. $\sqrt{73}$
17. $(-1.0, 7.0)$
18. $(2.0, -1.0)$
19. $(1.5, 2.1)$
20. 2.0
21. $(1.5, 0)$
22. `(1.5, 2.5)`
23. `b̸1.5b̸2.5`

Quick Quiz 10.7

1. False
2. True
3. False
4. False
5. True
6. True
7. False

8. True
9. `.TRUE.`
10. `.TRUE.`
11. `Bb̸b̸b̸b̸`
12. `KANGA`
13. `THREECPO`
14. `WARTS`

Quick Quiz 11.3

1. To access a particular record in a sequential file, all of the preceding records must first be accessed. Each record in a direct-access file can be accessed directly, usually by using a record number.

2. `OPEN (UNIT = 12, FILE = 'TESTDATA', STATUS = 'OLD')`

3. `OPEN (UNIT = 10, FILE = 'NEWDATA', ACCESS = 'DIRECT',`
   `+       RECL = 30, STATUS = 'NEW')`

4. `READ(10, '(I5)', REC = 100) ITEMNO`

5. Files in which information is represented in internal binary form. They are used for files that are to be read and processed only by the computer and not displayed to the user.

6. Given file

   F: 4 1 7 3 6 2 5

   Split:

   F1: |4 | 3 6|
   F2: |1 7 | 2 5|

   Merge:

   F: |1 4 7 | 2 3 5 6|

   Split:

   F1: |1 4 7|
   F2: |2 3 5 6|

   Merge:

   F: |1 2 3 4 5 6 7|

Index of Programming Problems

Chapter 1

Circle properties (Problem 5, p. 36)
Resistance in a circuit (Problem 6, p. 36)

Chapter 2

Circuit with resistors in series (Problems 1, 2, p. 106)
Right triangle calculations (Problem 3, p. 106)
Pythagorean triples (Problem 4, p. 106)
Area and perimeter of a triangle (Problem 5, p. 107)
Current in an AC circuit (Problem 6, p. 107)
Path of a rocket (Problem 7, p. 107)
Speed of a satellite (Problem 8, p. 107)
Polar coordinates (Problem 9, p. 108)
Hanging cable (Problem 10, p. 108)
Converting units of measurement (Problem 11 p. 108)
Volume of an oblate spheroid (Problem 12, p. 108)
Shear strength of a shaft (Problem 13, p. 109)
Period of a pendulum (Problem 14, p. 109)
Minimizing cost of oil tank construction (Problem 15, p. 110)
Volume and mass of a hollow ball (Problem 16, p. 110)
Depreciation—declining balance method (Problem 17, p. 110)
Packaging problem (Problem 18, p. 111)
Equations of lines (Problem 19, p. 111)
GPA calculation (Problem 20, p. 112)

Chapter 3

Area and perimeter of geometric figures (Problem 1, p. 173)
Quadratic equations (Problem 2, p. 173)
Intersecting, parallel, perpendicular lines (Problem 3, p. 173)
Collinear points (Problem 4, p. 174)

Safe loading of a column (Problem 5, p. 174)
Gas company charges (Problem 6, p. 174)
Fluid flow in a pipe (Problem 7, p. 174)
Pesticide-spraying criteria (Problem 8, p. 174)
Classifying triangles (Problem 9, p. 175)
Binary full-adder (Problem 10, p. 175)
Binary adder (Problem 11, p. 175)

Chapter 4

Series evaluation (Exercises 24, 25, p. 227)
Grade assignment (Exercise 26, p. 228)
Average noise level (Exercise 27, p. 228)
Divide-and-average algorithm (Exercise 28, p. 228, Problem 16, p. 246)
Point of diminishing returns (Exercise 29, p. 228)
Draining a reservoir—Manning formula (Exercise 30, p. 228, Problem 19, p. 249)
Tension in a cable (Exercise 31, p. 229)
Least-squares estimate for density of water (Exercise 2, p. 235)
Least-squares estimate for cutting time for oxyacetylene torch (Exercise 3, p. 235)
Table of prices (Problem 1, p. 243)
Velocity of a ship (Problem 2, p. 243)
Motion of a rod in a machine (Problem 3, p. 243)
Genotypes (Problem 4, p. 244)
Fibonacci numbers (Problems 5, 6, p. 244; Problem 12, p. 246)
Infinite series (Problem 7, p. 245)
Amortization table (Problem 8, p. 245)
Double-declining balance method of depreciation (Problem 9, p. 245)
Range of a set of noise levels (Problem 10, p. 246)
Calculating miles per gallon (Problem 13, p. 246)
Smallest and largest numbers in a list (Problem 14, p. 246)
Bouncing ball (Problem 15, p. 246)
Mean, variance, standard deviation (Problem 17, p. 246)
Geometric mean and harmonic mean (Problem 18, p. 248)
Ladder in a hallway (Problem 20, p. 249)
Least-squares exponential fit for altitude and barometric pressure (Problem 21, p. 249)
Correlation coefficient (Problem 22, p. 250)

Chapter 5

Integer arithmetic (Problems 1, 2, 3 p. 308)
Growth of a culture of bacteria (Problem 4, p. 309)
Angle measurements (Problem 5, p. 309)
GPA calculation (Problem 6, p. 309)
File processing:
    Conversion of military time to ordinary time (Problem 7, p. 309)
    Searching USERS.DAT (Problem 8, p. 310)

Report generation from STUDENT.DAT (Problem 9, p. 310)
Searching INVENTORY.DAT (Problem 10, p. 310)
Report generation from USERS.DAT (Problem 11, p. 310)
GPA calculation from STUDENT.DAT (Problem 12, p. 310)

Chapter 6

Root-finding: steady state of a circuit (Exercise 1, p. 361, Problem 20, p. 382)
Root-finding: van der Waal's equation (Exercise 2, p. 361, Problem 21, p. 382)
Root-finding: annuity formulas (Exercise 3, p. 362, Problem 22, p. 382)
Root-finding: minimizing drag (Exercise 4, p. 362, Problem 23, p. 382)
Root-finding: frequency of a vibrating mass (Exercise 5, p. 362, Problem 24, p. 382)
Root-finding: tensions in a hanging cable (Exercise 6, p. 363, Problem 25, p. 382)
Root-finding: depth of water in a trough (Exercise 7, p. 364, Problem 26, p. 382)
Numerical integration: voltage across a capacitor (Exercise 8, p. 364, Problem 36, p. 384)
Numerical integration: area of a wall of an elliptical room (Exercise 9, p. 364, Problem 37, p. 384)
Numerical integration: energies of fission neutrons (Exercise 10, p. 365, Problem 38, p. 384)
Numerical integration: velocity of a particle moving through a fluid (Exercise 11, p. 365, Problem 39, p. 384)
Numerical integration: absorbed energy in a compressed spring (Exercise 12, p. 365, Problem 40, p. 384)
Differential equations: linear lag behavior of components in a control system (Exercise 13, p. 366, Problem 43, p. 385)
Differential equations: draining a tank (Exercise 14, p. 366, Problem 44, p. 385)
Differential equations: discharge through an outlet pipe of a gas well (Exercise 15, p. 367, Problem 45, p. 385)
Differential equations: flux in an iron core (Exercise 16, p. 368, Problem 46, p. 385)
Differential equations: population sizes (Exercise 17, p. 369, Problem 47, p. 385)
Range of a set of numbers (Problem 1, p. 377)
Rounding real numbers (Problem 2, p. 377)
Number of bacteria in a culture (Problem 3, p. 377)
Temperature conversion (Problem 4, p. 377)
Checking if characters are digits (Problem 5, p. 378)
Determining vertices of a triangle (Problem 6, p. 378)
Calculating monthly payments (Problem 7, p. 378)
Assigning grades (Problem 8, p. 378)
Sum of a range of integers (Problem 9, p. 378)
Binomial coefficients (Problem 10, p. 378)
Probability of outcome of an experiment (Problem 11, p. 378)
Calculating cosh(x) using power series (Problem 12, p. 379)
Calculating sinh(x) using power series (Problem 13, p. 379)
Checking if numbers are perfect squares (Problem 14, p. 379)
GCD calculation (Problem 15, p. 380)

Testing primality (Problem 16, p. 380)
Biorhythm index (Problem 17, p. 380)
Converting units of measurement (Problem 18, p. 380)
Root finding — bisection method (Problem 19, p. 381, Problem 48, p. 385)
Work done by a force (Problems 27–30, pp. 382–383)
Numerical integration — Simpson's method (Problems 31–35, pp. 383–384)
Differential equations: Runge–Kutta method (Problem 41, p. 384)
Differential equations: cooling problem (Problem 42, p. 384)
Root finding — Newton's method (Problem 49, p. 384)

Chapter 7

Displaying names of months (Exercise 1, p. 409, Problem 1, p. 460)
Interchanging two integer values (Exercise 2, p. 409, Problem 2, p. 461)
Converting centimeters to yards, feet, and inches (Exercise 3, p. 410, Problem 3, p. 461)
Converting grams to pounds and ounces (Exercise 4, p. 410, Problem 4, p. 461)
Converting military time to standard time (Exercise 5, p. 410, Problem 5, p. 461)
Converting standard time to military time (Exercise 6, p. 410, Problem 6, p. 461)
Circumference, surface area, and volumes of cylinders (Problem 7, p. 461)
Beam deflection (Problem 8, p. 461)
GCD and LCM (Problem 9, p. 462)
Prime factorization (Problem 10, p. 462)
Straight-line depreciation (Problem 11, p. 462)
Sum-of-the-years'-digits depreciation (Problem 12, p. 462)
Double-declining balance depreciation (Problems 13, 14, pp. 462–463)
Calculating withholding taxes (Problem 15, p. 463)
Tensile strength (Problem 16, p. 463)
Shielding a nuclear reactor (Problem 17, p. 463)
Random motion of a particle (Problem 18, p. 463)
Drunkard's walk problem (Problem 19, p. 464)
Buffon needle problem (Problem 20, p. 464)
Monte Carlo method for computing area of a circle (Problem 21, p. 464)
Numerical integration: Monte Carlo method (Problems 22–24, pp. 464–465)
Menu-driven program for calculating depreciation (Problem 25, p. 465)
Simulation of airport operation (Problem 26, p. 465)

Chapter 8

Vector processing: difference of two vectors (Exercise 1, p. 519)
Vector processing: multiplication of a vector by a scalar (Exercise 2, p. 519)
Vector processing: dot product of two vectors (Exercise 3, p. 519)
Vector processing: cross product of two vectors (Exercise 4, p. 519)
Vector processing: unit vectors (Exercise 5, p. 519)
Vector processing: angle between two vectors (Exercise 6, p. 520)
Retrieving production levels for given weeks and days (Problem 1, p. 545)

Intersection of two lists of product numbers (Problem 2, p. 545)
Union of two lists of product numbers (Problem 3, p. 545)
Evaluating ordering policies (Problem 4, p. 545)
The mailbox problem (Problem 5, p. 546)
Sieve method for finding prime numbers (Problem 6, p. 546)
Birthday problem (Problem 7, p. 547)
Mean, variance, and standard deviation (Problem 8, p. 547)
Grading on the curve (Problem 9, p. 547)
Evaluation of polynomials (Problems 10, 11, p. 548)
Producing updated grade reports from files (Problem 12, p. 548)
Large-integer arithmetic (Problems 13, 14, pp. 548–549)
Stacks (Problem 15, p. 549)
Queues (Problem 16, p. 549)
Artificial intelligence problem (Problem 17, p. 549)
Simulating the spread of a contagious disease and rumor propagation (Problem 18,
    p. 549)
Double-ended selection sort (Problem 19, p. 550)
Merging lists (Problem 20, p. 550)
Insertion sort (Problem 21, p. 550)
Shell sort (Problem 22, p. 551)
Range of a list of stock prices (Problem 23, p. 551)
Modified linear search (Problem 24, p. 551)
Linear interpolation (Problem 25, p. 552)
Search arrays of product numbers and prices (Problem 26, p. 552)

Chapter 9

Sum of two matrices (Exercises 1, 2, p. 595)
Transpose of a matrix (Exercise 3, p. 595)
Linear systems: loop currents (Exercise 1, p. 605)
Linear systems: voltages in an electrical network (Exercise 2, p. 605)
Linear systems: material balance equations (Exercise 3, p. 605)
Linear systems: tensions in a statical system (Exercise 4, p. 606)
Linear systems: populations of various age groups (Exercise 5, p. 607)
Linear systems: equation of least-squares parabola (Exercise 6, p. 607)
Linear systems: equation of least-squares cubic curve (Exercise 7, p. 607)
Averaging a table of noise levels (Problem 1, p. 613)
Tensile strength (Problem 2, p. 613)
Manufacturing costs (Problems 3, 4, 5, pp. 614–615, Problems 11, 12, 13, p. 617)
Pascal's triangle (Problem 6, p. 614)
Magic squares (Problem 7, p. 615)
Steady-state temperatures in a metal plate (Problem 8, p. 615)
Steady-state temperatures in a fireplace (Problem 9, p. 616)
Conway's game of Life (Problem 10, p. 616)
Transforming local coordinates into inertial coordinates (Problem 14, p. 617)
Markov chains—Ehrenfest urn model (Problem 15, p. 617)

Directed graphs (Problem 16, p. 618)
Inverse of a matrix (Problem 17, p. 619)
General least-squares curve fitting (Problem 18, p. 619)

Chapter 10

Comparing single- and double-precision computations (Problem 1, p. 705)
Root finding with Newton's method (Problem 2, p. 705)
Approximating integrals (Problem 3, p. 705)
Calculating values of hyperbolic sine function (Problem 4, p. 705)
Triangle properties using complex numbers (Problem 5, p. 705)
Complex exponents (Problem 6, p. 705)
Polar representation and finding nth roots of complex numbers (Problem 7, p. 706)
Finding complex roots with Newton's method (Problem 8, p. 706)
AC circuits (Problem 9, p. 706)
Reversing a string (Problem 10, p. 706)
Locating a string in a given string (Problem 11, p. 706)
Counting occurrences of characters and strings in lines of text (Problems 12, 13, p. 706)
Reversing a name (Problem 14, p. 706)
File processing using STUDENT.DAT (Problem 15, p. 706)
Processing grade information (Problem 16, p. 706)
Mass and oil displacement caused by various shapes (Problem 17, p. 707)
Rev. Zeller's method to find the day on which a date falls (Problem 18, p. 707)
Hindu-Arabic and roman numeral conversion (Problem 19, p. 708)
Palindromes (Problem 20, p. 708)
Text formatting (Problems 21, 22, p. 708)
Lexical analysis of FORTRAN real numbers (Problem 23, p. 708)
Rational number arithmetic (Problem 24, p. 708)
Lexical analysis of assignment statements (Problems 25, 26, 27, 28, pp. 709–710)
Vignère encryption and decryption (Problem 29, p. 710)
Encryption and decryption using substitution tables (Problem 30, p. 710)
Encryption and decryption using permutations (Problem 31, p. 710)
RSA public-key encryption and decryption (Problem 32, p. 710)
Morse code (Problem 33, p. 710)
Plotting the graph of a function (Problem 34, p. 710)
Plotting graphs of parametric equations (Problem 35, p. 710)
Visual image processing and enhancement (Problem 36, 37, p. 710)

Chapter 11

Concatenation of files (Problem 1, p. 757)
Mergesort (Problem 2, p. 757)
Processing a direct access file of computer network information (Problem 3, p. 757)
Text formatting (Problem 4, p. 757)
Text editing (Problem 5, p. 757)
Pretty printer (Problem 6, p. 758)
Menu-driven operations using STUDENT.DAT (Problem 7, p. 758)

Index

A

Abacus, 3
ACCESS = clause, 718, 720, 723
Actual arguments, 321, 394
Ada Augusta, 3
Adder, 167, 175
Addition, 29, 38, 54, 56, 99
Address, 12, 842
Address translation, 508
A descriptor, 264, 275
Adjustable dimensions, 503
ADVANCE = clause, 311
Aiken, Howard, 6
Algorithms, 17–20, 24, 42–43
   structured, 25
Allocatable arrays, 556, 623
ALLOCATE statement, 556–57, 623, 803, 804
Alternate returns, 785–86
ALU. *See* Arithmetic-logic unit.
American National Standards Institute. *See* ANSI.
Analytical Engine, 4, 5 fig., 10
.AND., 123–24, 168
AND gates, 162
ANSI, 9–10, 42
apostrophe, 44, 103
Apple Computer Company, 7
Approximate representation, effect of, 628–29
Argument association, 321–22, 406–08
Argument lists, sharing information via, 450
Arguments
   actual, 321, 394
   arrays as, 501–04
   dummy, 318, 331, 394
   formal, 318
   subprograms as, 369–73, 410
Arithmetic, mechanization of, 3
Arithmetic errors, 94–96

Arithmetic IF statement, 151, 772–74
Arithmetic-logic unit (ALU), 10
Arithmetic operations, 29, 38, 54–57, 125
Array constants, 553
Array declarations, 479–81, 564, 609
Array name, input/output using, 485–87, 569–79
Array processing, 499–505
Arrays, 470–559, 803
   allocatable, 556, 623
   as arguments, 501–04
   assigning values to, 500–501, 553
   assumed-shape, 556, 622
   base address of, 508
   in common, 505, 576–77
   element of, 476
   input/output of, 481–89, 566–74
   multidimensional, 560–625
   one-dimensional, 470–559
   processing multidimensional, 564–77
   three-dimensional, 563, 566
   two-dimensional, 562ff, 572–73, 609
Array sections, 554
Array variable, 476
Artificial intelligence, 549
ASCII, 122, 847
Assembler, 14
Assembly language, 13
Assigned GO TO statement, 151, 774–75
Assignment statement, 29, 38, 60–64, 99–100, 105–160
ASSIGN statement, 775
Associated items, 451
Assumed length specifier, 392, 652
Assumed-shape arrays, 556, 622
Asterisk, 21, 30, 72, 75, 97, 261, 263
   as format specifier, 256, 272
   to specify dimension, 504
Atanasoff, John, 6

Augusta, Ada, 4
Auxiliary memory, 12

B

Babbage, Charles, 4, 5, 10
BACKSPACE statement, 291, 305, 728, 756
Backus, John, 9, 41
Bar graph, 513–16
Base address, of array, 508
Base-10 number system, 842
Batch processing, 23
Berry, Clifford, 6
Binary file, 736
Binary full-adder, 166, 175
Binary half-adder, 162–164
Binary number system, 842–43
Binary point, 846
Binary search, 531–34
Binary scheme, 12
Birthday problem, 547
Bisection method, 381
Bits, 12, 842
Blank COMMON statement, 451–54, 457–58
BLANK = clause, 718, 720, 724
Blank null, 767
Blanks, within field, 273, 767–68
Blank zero, 767
Block data subprograms, 778–79
Block IF statement, 128, 169
BN descriptor, 767–68
body of a loop, 181, 183
Bubble sort, 523–25
Buffon Needle problem, 464
Bytes, 12, 842
BZ descriptor, 767–68

C

Caesar cipher, 679–81, 714–15
Call by address, 407
Call by reference, 407
CALL statement, 394–95, 457, 785
CASE construct, 177
Central processing unit (CPU), 10
Character comparison, 673–74
Character data type, 628, 651–57, 712
Character functions, 665–75
Character input, 275–76, 655–57

Character output, 263–64, 655–57
Character strings, 44–45
CHARACTER type statement, 47, 73, 98, 651–52
Character values, 847–48
CHAR function, 674–75
Clause
  ACCESS =, 718, 720, 723
  ADVANCE =, 311
  BLANK =, 718, 720, 724
  DIRECT =, 723
  END =, 290, 304
  ERR =, 718, 719, 722, 725
  EXIST =, 723
  FILE =, 719
  FORMATTED =, 723
  FORM =, 718, 720, 723
  IOSTAT =, 289, 304, 718, 719, 722, 723, 725
  NAMED =, 723
  NEXTREC =, 724
  NUMBER =, 723
  OPENED =, 723
  REC =, 726
  RECL =, 718, 720, 723
  SEQUENTIAL =, 723
  STATUS =, 719, 722
  UNFORMATTED =, 723
CLOSE statement, 288, 305, 721–22, 753
Closing files, 288
Coding, 20–22, 28–32, 78, 84, 89–90
Coin dispenser, designing, 410–16
Collating sequence, 673
Columns, 74, 100, 103
Columnwise processing, 565
Comment lines, 75
Comments, 21, 25, 30, 31, 37, 72, 75, 97, 103
COMMON statement, 450–56, 775–78
  arrays in, 505
  multidimensional arrays in, 576–77
Compilers, 9, 14, 658
Compile-time errors, 32
COMPLEX data type, 638–46, 711–15
Complex functions, 642
Complex input/output, 643
Complex number, 627, 638–42
COMPLEX type statement, 639
Components
  of structure, 796
  of vector, 517
Compound logical expressions, 123–25, 169
Compound selection structures, 141
Computed GO TO statement, 151, 774

Computers
    electronic, 6–8
    first-generation, 6
    fourth-generation, 7
    Mark I, 6
    second-generation, 6
    third-generation, 7
Computing devices, early, 3–6
Computing systems, 10–12
Concatenation, 652–53
Conjunction, 123
Constants, 43–51
    character, 44–45
    in Fortran 90, 113–15
    logical, 160
    named, 48–50
Construction costs, analyzing, 525–29
Continuation indicator, 74, 113
CONTINUE statement, 182
Contour maps, 698
Control, methods of, 25–26
Control characters, 258–59, 303
Control-list, 724, 729
Control statements, 772–75
Control variable, 183, 237, 240
Control unit, 10
Correlation coefficient, 249
Counter-controlled loops, 236
CPU. See Central processing unit.
Cross product, of two vectors, 519
CYCLE statement, 251

D

Data components, 806
Data Encryption Standard (DES), 683
Data security, 678–86
DATA statement, 50–51, 73, 97, 98, 104, 242, 836
Data structure, 475, 803
Data types, 42–51
    CHARACTER, 47, 73, 98, 651–57
    COMPLEX, 638–46
    derived, 796–802
    DOUBLE PRECISION, 628–32
    in Fortran, 42, 96
    INTEGER, 29, 37, 46, 73, 98
    intrinsic, 796
    LOGICAL, 160–61, 171
    REAL, 29, 37, 46 73, 98
D descriptor, 631–32

Debugging, 216–24
Decimal number system, 842
Decimal representation of real constant, 43
Declaration, in subprogram, 329
Density plots, 693–700
Depreciation, 191–97, 245, 462
Derived data types, 796–802
Design, 76–77, 82–83, 86–88
Desk checking, 219
Difference
    of complex numbers, 640
    of two vectors, 519
Difference Engine, 4, 5 fig.
Differential equations, numerical solutions of,
            352–56, 384–85
Digraph, 618
Dimensions, of multidimensional arrays, 611
DIMENSION statement, 479, 541–42
Direct-access files, 717
Direct-access inventory file, 726–28
Direct access structure, 475
Directed graph, 618
DIRECT = clause, 723
Disjunction, 123
Divide-and-conquer strategy, 27, 428
Division, 29, 38, 54, 56, 99
Documentation, 19, 21, 31, 43, 72
DO loops, 182–89, 236, 237, 239, 240, 250
    implied, 487–89, 570–74
    input/output using, 481–85, 566–69
DO statement, 182
Dot product, of two vectors, 519
Double-declining balance depreciation, 245, 462
Double-precision data type, 627–32
Double-precision functions, 632
Double-precision input/output, 631–32
DOUBLE PRECISION type statement, 629–30
DO WHILE statement, 204–05, 236
Driver program, 414–16
Drunkard's walk problem, 464
Dummy arguments, 318
Dynamic data structures, 803
Dynamic variables, 803

E

EBCDIC, 122, 848
Eckert, J. P., 6
E descriptor, 262–63
Ehrenfest urn model, 617

Electrical networks, 597–604
Element, of array, 476
ELSE statement, 130, 178
ELSE IF statement, 147, 178
END = clause, 290, 304
ENDFILE statement, 729, 756
END IF statement, 130
End-of-data flag, 200
End-of-file record, 729
END statement, 39, 74, 100, 319
Engineering descriptor EN, 311
ENIAC, 6
E notation, 274
ENTRY statement, 784–85
.EQ., 121, 168
equivalence, 123
EQUIVALENCE statement, 779–84
.EQV., 123–24, 168
ERR = clause, 718, 719, 722, 725
Errors
    arithmetic, 94–96
    compile-time, 32
    logic, 33, 79, 216, 223
    overflow, 94
    roundoff, 94, 95–96, 134–36, 847
    run-time, 33, 216
    syntax, 32, 216
    types of, 237
    underflow, 94
Euler's method, 353–56
Executable statements, 73, 97
Execution part, 42, 74, 97, 318
EXIST = clause, 723
EXIT statement, 251
Expanded form, 842
Exponent, 846
Exponentiation, 29, 38, 54, 56, 99
Expressions
    logical, 121–25, 169
    relational, 121
External memory, 12
External sorting, 734–36
EXTERNAL statement, 369–72, 375, 408

F

Factorial function, 324–25
.FALSE., 160, 169
F descriptor, 261–62, 273
Fibonacci numbers, 244

FILE = clause, 719
File input/output, 91–93, 288–89, 724–36
File-positioning statements, 290–91, 728–29, 756
Files
    binary, 736
    closing, 288, 721–22
    direct-access, 717, 726–28
    formatted, 717
    internal, 736–38
    merging, 729–36
    opening, 92, 286–87, 718–21
    sequential, 717
    unformatted, 717, 736
Finite-state machines, 658–64
First-generation computers, 6
First-In First-Out (FIFO) structure, 549
First-order differential equation, 352
Floating-point numbers, 846
Flowchart, 25
Flowchart symbols, 26 fig.
Flow lines, 25
Formal arguments, 318, 331, 394
Format
    program, 74
    scanning, 267–69
Format descriptors, 257–58
    repeating groups of, 265–66
Format specifier, 256–58, 283
FORMAT statement, 257, 301–02
FORMATTED = clause, 723
Formatted files, 717
Formatted input, 271–78
Formatted output, 256–69
FORM = clause, 718, 720, 723
FORTRAN, 9, 28, 41
FORTRAN 66, 42
FORTRAN 77, 9, 42
Fortran 90, 9, 42, 112–17, 176–79, 200, 250–53, 786–813
    arrays in, 553–59
    extended precision, complex, and chararacter data types in, 711–15
    file processing in, 759–61
    and input/output, 311–13
    and multidimensional arrays, 619–25
    programming with functions with, 385–91
    subroutines in, 466–69
Fourth-generation computer, 7
Fractional part, 94, 846
Frequency distribution, 509, 511–16

Function heading, 318, 374
FUNCTION statement, 318
Functions, 57–59, 99, 315–91
  as arguments, 369–73
  CHAR, 674–75
  character, 665–75
  complex, 642
  declaring type, 329–30
  double-precision, 632
  factorial, 324–25
  ICHAR, 674–75
  INDEX, 665–66
  intrinsic, 315
  LEN, 666–67
  LGE, 674
  LGT, 674
  library, 315–17
  LLE, 674
  LLT, 674
  Poisson probability, 325–30
  programmer-defined, 317
  REAL, 712
  recursive, 386, 391
  of several variables, 322–23
  statement, 330–32, 374–75
  type of, 329–30
Function subprograms, 317–19, 374

G

Gates, 162
Gates, Bill, 8
Gaussian elimination, 598, 600–604, 634–37
G descriptor, 763–64
.GE., 121, 168
Generalization, 17
General READ statement, 284–85
Golden ratio, 244
GO TO statement, 201
  assigned, 151, 774–75
Grading on the curve, 547
Graphical user interfaces (GUI), 8
Graphics, computer, 686–700
Greatest common divisor, 462
.GT., 121, 168

H

Hardware, 6
H descriptor, 768

Heading, 43
  function, 318, 374
  program, 72, 97
  subroutine, 394
Hexadecimal number system, 843
High-level languages, 8
Histogram, 513–16
Hollerith, Herman, 6
Hollerith descriptor, 768
Horner's method, 548

I

IBM, 6, 9
IBM PCs, 7
IBM System/360, 7
ICHAR function, 674–75
Identifiers, 31, 37, 45, 60, 97, 102, 115
Identity matrix, 619
I descriptor, 259–61, 272
IF construct, 128, 129–31, 176
IF-ELSE-IF construct, 146–51, 170–71
IF statement, 128–36
Ill-conditioned linear systems, 633–37
Imaginary part, of complex number, 628
IMPLICIT NONE, 48 fn
IMPLICIT statement, 47, 771–72
Implied DO loops, 487–89, 570–74
Indentation, 25
Index, 476
INDEX function, 665–66
Infinite loop, 201, 240, 241
Initialization, variable, 50–51
Initial value, of control variable, 185
Input, 16, 17, 23, 24
  character, 275–76
  file, 724–28
  formatted, 271–78
  integer, 272–73
  list-directed, 68–72, 161, 769–70
  multiple lines of, 277–78
  real, 273–74
Input characters, skipping, 276–77
Input-list, 724
Input/output, 30, 66–72, 254–313, 763–70
  of arrays, 481–89, 566–74
  character, 655–57
  complex, 643
  double-precision, 631–32
  file, 91–93, 288–89

Input/output (*cont.*)
  using array name, 485–87, 569–70
  using DO loops, 481–85, 566–69
  using implied DO loops, 570–74
Input/output devices, 12
Input statement, 38, 100
INQUIRE statement, 722–24, 753–54
Insertion sort, 550–51
Integer constant, 43
Integer input, 272–73
Integer output, 259–61
Integers, 43
  negative, 845
  storage of, 844–46
INTEGER type statement, 29, 37, 46, 73, 98
Integration testing, 445
Interactive mode, 23
Interface blocks, 387–88, 467–68, 795
Internal files, 736–38
Internal memory, 10
International Standards Organization (ISO), 9
Intrinsic data types, 796
Intrinsic functions, 315
INTRINSIC statement, 372–73, 375
Inventory file, 823–24
  maintaining, 738–50
Inventory-update file, 824–26
Inverse, of matrix **A**, 619
Inverter, 162
IOSTAT = clause, 289, 304, 718, 719, 722, 723, 725
ISO, 9

J

Jacquard, Joseph Marie, 4
Jobs, Steven, 7

K

K, 12
Kind type parameter, 114

L

Language
  assembly, 13
  high-level, 8
  machine, 9

Last-In First-Out (LIFO) structure, 549
L descriptor, 764–65
.LE., 121, 168
Least common multiple, 462
Least-squares approximation, 230–35
Least-squares file, 834
LEN function, 666–67
Length specifier, 47
Level curves, 693–700
Lexical analysis, 658, 662–64
LGE function, 674
LGT function, 674
Library functions, 315–17
Life cycle, 23
Linear interpolation, 552
Linear search, 530–31
Linear system, 598, 646
Link, 806
Linked lists, 803, 806, 808, 810–11
Linked structures, 803–13
LISP, 492
List, processing, 492–95
List-directed input, 68–72, 161, 769–70
List-directed output, 67–68, 161
LLE function, 674
LLT function, 674
Local identifiers, 324–25
Local variables, 421
Logarithm, 3, 56, 58, 99
Logical circuits, design of, 161–65
Logical constants, 160, 169
Logical data type, 160–61
Logic errors, 33, 79, 216, 223
Logical expressions, 121–25, 169
  compound, 123–25, 169
  repetition controlled by, 181
  simple, 121–23, 169
Logical IF statement, 129, 170
Logical operators, 123, 125, 168
LOGICAL type statement, 160, 171
Logical variable, 160,169
Login procedure, 22
Loop, 181ff
Loop-forever repetition structure, 251
.LT., 121, 168

M

$m \times n$ matrix, 593
Machine language, 8

Magic numbers, 49, 102
Magic square, 615
Main program, 320
Maintenance, 34
Mantissa, 846
Mark I computer, 6
Markov chain, 617
Matrix
    identity, 619
    $m \times n$, 593
    multiplication, 593–95
    transpose of, 595
Matrix processing, 593–97
Mauchly, J. W., 6
Mean, 247, 248, 501–02, 503–04
Mechanization of arithmetic, 3
Median, 526
Megabyte, 12
Memory
    auxiliary, 12
    external, 12
    nonvolatile, 10
    organization of, 12–14
    primary, 10
    random access, 10
    read-only, 10
    secondary, 12
    volatile, 10
Memory unit, 10
Menu-driven program, 334, 337
Mergesort, 734–36
Merging
    files, 729–36
    lists, 550
Method of least squares, 231
Minicomputer, 7
Mixed-mode assignment, 62, 105
Mixed-mode expressions, 55–56, 641
Modular programming, 334–44
Module, 789–96
    program, 27
Monte Carlo integration, 464
MS-DOS, 8
Multialternative selection structure, 147, 171
Multidimensional arrays, 560–625
    as arguments, 575–76
    in COMMON statements, 576–77
    processing, 564–77
Multiplication, 29, 38, 54, 56, 99
    matrix, 593–95

    of vector by scalar, 519
Multiply subscripted variables, 561–64

N

Named COMMON statement, 454–56, 458
Named constants, 48–50, 103
NAMED = clause, 723
NAMELIST feature, 311
Naming convention, 47
Natural mergesort, 734
n-dimensional vectors, 517
.NE., 121, 168
negation, 123
.NEQ., 123–24, 168
Nested DO loop, 187
Nested IF constructs, 141–46
Nested multiplication, 548
Nested structure, 798
Newton's method, 344–48, 645
NEXTREC = clause, 724
Nodes, 803, 806
Nonequivalence, 123
Nonexecutable statements, 73
Nonvolatile memory, 10
Normal distribution, 421–22
Normalized form, 263, 632
Norm, of vector, 517
Notebook computer, 7
.NOT., 123–24, 168
NOT gate, 162
Noyce, Robert, 7
NULLIFY statement, 806
NULL specifier, 720
Null values, 769–70
NUMBER = clause, 723
Numerical integration, 348–52, 370, 382–85
Numerical methods, 344

O

Object program, 9
Octal number system, 843
One-dimensional arrays, 470–559
Opcode, 12
OPENED = clause, 723
Opening documentation, 21, 43, 72
Opening files, 92, 286–87, 718–21

OPEN statement, 92, 101, 287, 304–05, 718–21, 751–53
Operand, 12
Operating systems, 8
Operations, 29, 99
  arithmetic, 29, 38, 54–57, 125
  character, 652–55
Operators
  logical, 123, 125, 168
  relational, 121, 125, 168, 176
  unary, 57
.OR., 123–24, 168
OR gate, 162
Oughtred, William, 3
Output, 16, 17, 24
  file, 729–36
  formatted, 256–69
  integer, 259–61
  list-directed, 67–68, 161
  real, 261–62
Output-list, 729
Output statement, 38–39, 100
Overflow, 846, 847
Overflow errors, 94

P

Parameters, in Fortran 90, 113
PARAMETER statement, 48–50, 73, 97, 98, 836
Parentheses, 56–57, 124, 128
Parser, 659
Parse tree, 659
Pascal, Blaise, 3, 4
Pascal's triangle, 614
PAUSE statement, 770–71
Peripheral devices, 12
Pivot element, 600
Pixels, 686
Pointers, 803–13
Pointer variables, 803
Poisson probability function, 325–30
Polar coordinates, 108, 402–05, 453–54, 468–69
Polar representation, of complex numbers, 640
Polynomial equations, solving, 645
Portable programs, 10
Positional descriptors, 264–65
Position vector, 517
Posttest loop, 213, 238, 239
Posttest repetition structure, 213–16

POT, 704
Precision, in double-precision expressions, 702–03
Pretest loop, 200
Primary memory, 10
Prime number, 546
PRINT statement, 30, 39, 67–68, 100, 256, 301
Priority rules, 56–57
Program composition, 72–73
Program heading, 72, 97
Programmer-defined functions, 317
Programs, 16, 42–43
  development of, 16–23
  object, 9
  portable, 10
PROGRAM statement, 21, 37, 72, 97
Program structure, 97
Program stubs, 434
Program testing, 32–33, 79–80, 84–85, 90–91, 216–24
Pseudocode, 24–25
Pseudorandom numbers, 417
Public key encryption, 683–86
Punched-card systems, 6
Pythagorean triples, 106

Q

Quadratic equations, 131–34, 173, 644–45, 713–14, 773–74
Query-controlled input loop, 214
Queue, 549

R

Random access memory (RAM), 10
Random number generators, 417
Random numbers, 416–22
Read-only memory (ROM), 10
READ statement, 30, 39, 68–69, 92, 271, 277, 284–85, 303–04, 724, 754–55
REAL function, 712
Real input, 273–74
Real numbers, 43–44, 846–47
Real output, 261–62
Real part, of complex number, 628
REAL type statement, 29, 37, 46, 73, 98
REC = clause, 726
RECL = clause, 718, 720, 723
Records, 717

Recursive function, 386, 391
Refinement, 18
Registers, 10
Regression coefficients, 231
Regression equation, 231
Relational expressions, 121
Relational operators, 121, 125, 168, 176
Repetition, 25, 119, 181–253
Repetition indicator, 260, 265, 311
Repetition structure, 181
RETURN statement, 319
REWIND statement, 290, 305, 728, 756
Reynold's number, 120, 152
Right justified, 260, 261
Ritchie, Dennis, 8
Root finding, 344–48, 381–82
Roundoff errors, 94, 95–96, 134–36, 847
Rowwise processing, 565
RSA (Rivest-Shamir-Adelman) algorithm, 684
Runge-Kutta method, 356
Run-time errors, 33, 216
Run-time formatting, 297–300

S

SAVE statement, 421, 457
Scale factors, 765–67
Scatter plots, 688–92
Scientific representation of real constant, 44
S descriptor, 768
Searching, 530–34
    example, 534–41
Secondary memory, 12
Second-generation computers, 6
Seed, 417
Selection, 25, 119ff, 181
Selection structures
    compound, 141–51
    simple, 128–36
Sentinel-controlled while loops, 200
Sequence, 119, 181
SEQUENTIAL = clause, 723
Sequential execution, 25
Sequential files, 717
Sequential retrieval, 475
Shell sort, 551
Sieve of Eratosthenes, 546
Sign Positive, 768
Sign Suppress, 768

Silicon chips, 7
Simple data types, 471
Simple logical expressions, 121–23, 169
Simple selection sort, 520–22
Simpson's rule, 384
Simulation, 416–22
Single-precision, 43–44, 627
Singular system, 600
Slash descriptor, 266–67, 311
Slide rule, 3
Software engineering, 23, 119
Sort
    bubble, 523–25
    insertion, 550–51
    Shell, 551
    simple selection, 520–22
Sorting, 520–25
    external, 734–36
Source program, 8
SP descriptor, 768
Specification, 16–17, 23, 76, 82, 86
Specification part, 42, 73, 97
    of functions, 318
    of subroutines, 394, 398
SS descriptor, 768
Stack, 549
Standard coding schemes, 122
Standard deviation, 247
Standard normal distribution, 422
Statement
    ALLOCATE, 556–57, 623, 803, 804
    arithmetic IF, 151, 772–74
    ASSIGN, 775
    assigned GO TO, 774–75
    assignment, 29, 38, 60–64, 99–100, 105, 160
    BACKSPACE, 291, 305, 728, 756
    blank COMMON, 451–54, 457–58
    block IF, 128, 169
    CALL, 394–95, 457, 785
    CHARACTER type statement, 47, 73, 98, 651–52
    CLOSE, 288, 305, 721–22, 753
    COMMON, 450–56, 505, 576–77, 775–78
    COMPLEX type, 639
    computed GO TO, 151, 774
    CONTINUE, 182
    control, 772–75
    correct placement of various types of, 836
    CYCLE, 251
    DATA, 50–51, 98, 836
    DIMENSION, 479, 541–42

Statement (*cont.*)
  DO, 182
  DOUBLE PRECISION type, 629–30
  DO WHILE, 204–05, 236
  ELSE, 130, 178
  ELSE IF, 147, 178
  END, 39, 74, 100, 319
  ENDFILE, 729, 756
  END IF, 130
  ENTRY, 784–85
  EQUIVALENCE, 779–84
  executable, 73
  EXIT, 251
  EXTERNAL, 369–72, 375, 408
  file-positioning, 290–91, 728–29, 756
  format, 257, 301–02
  FUNCTION, 318
  GO TO, 201
  IF, 128–36
  IMPLICIT, 47, 771–72
  input, 38, 100
  INQUIRE, 722–24, 753–54
  INTEGER type, 29, 37, 46, 73, 98
  INTRINSIC, 372–73, 375
  logical IF, 129, 170
  LOGICAL type, 160, 171
  named COMMON, 454–56, 458
  nonexecutable, 73
  NULLIFY, 806
  OPEN, 92, 101, 287, 304–05, 718–21, 751–53
  output, 38–39, 100
  PARAMETER, 48–50, 73, 97–98, 836
  PAUSE, 770–71
  PRINT, 30, 39, 67–68, 100, 256, 301
  PROGRAM, 21, 37, 72, 97
  READ, 30, 39, 68–69, 92, 271, 277, 284–85,
      303–04, 724, 754–55
  REAL type, 29, 37, 46, 73, 98
  RETURN, 319
  REWIND, 290, 305, 728, 756
  SAVE, 421, 457
  STOP, 770–71
  SUBROUTINE, 394
  type, 29, 37, 46, 73, 98, 105, 160, 171, 542,
      629–30, 639, 651–52
  USE, 790
  WRITE, 30, 34, 67–68, 92, 100, 282–84,
      302–03, 729, 755–56
Statement functions, 330–32, 374–75
Statement label, 74

Static variables, 803
STATUS = clause, 719, 722
Step size, 185
STOP statement, 770–71
Stored programs, 3, 4, 6
Straight-line depreciation, 193, 462
String constants, 104
Strings, 44–45
Structure, 796
Structured algorithms, 25–26
Structured data type, 471
Structure diagram, 27, 429
Structured program, 25, 119
Student file, 826–28
Student-update file, 828–30
Subprograms, 315
  as arguments, 408
  declaration in, 329
  function, 317–19
  subroutine, 393–408, 456
Subroutine heading, 394, 456
Subroutines 392–469
SUBROUTINE statement, 394
Subscript, 476, 543–45
Subscripted variables, 472–81
Substring, 653–55
Subtraction, 29, 38, 54, 56, 99
Successive refinement, 27
Sum
  of complex numbers, 639
  of two vectors, 518
Summation, 197–98
Sum-of-the-years'-digits method, 193, 462
Supercomputer, 7
Syntactic structures, 659
Syntax, 28
Syntax errors, 32, 216
System software, 8–10
System testing, 445

T

Tables of computed values, printing, 269–71
T descriptor, 264–65, 276
Temperature conversion application, 76–81
Test-at-the-bottom loop, 213
Test-at-the-top loop, 200
Testing, 22–23, 32–33, 79–80, 84–85, 90–91,
      216–24
Text editing, 667–73

THEN, 128
Third-generation computers, 7
Thompson, Ken, 8
TL descriptor, 769
Tokens, 658
Top-down approach, 27, 30, 393, 428
Trace tables, 219
Trapezoidal method, 349–52, 370–73, 388–89
Traversing, linked list, 808
TR descriptor, 769
.TRUE., 160, 169
Truth tables, 124
Two-dimensional arrays, 562ff, 609
    input/output of, 572–73
Two's complement representation, 845
Two-state devices, 12
Types, 29
Type statements, 29, 37, 46, 73, 98
    CHARACTER, 47, 73, 98, 651–52
    COMPLEX, 639
    DOUBLE PRECISION, 629–30
    INTEGER, 29, 37, 46, 73, 98
    LOGICAL, 160, 171
    REAL, 29, 37, 46, 73, 98

U

Unary operators, 57
Underflow, 847
Underflow errors, 94
UNFORMATTED = clause, 723
Unformatted files, 717, 736
Uniform distribution, 421
Unit specifier, 283, 718–19
Unit testing, 438
UNIVAC, 6
UNIX, 8
Unnamed common, 451–54
User-update file, 832–33
Users file, 831–32
USE statement, 790

V

Validation, 32
Variable initialization, 50–51
Variables, 29, 43–51, 60ff, 803
    control, 183, 237, 240
    dynamic, 803
    in Fortran 90, 113–15
    local, 421
    logical, 160, 169
    multiply subscripted, 561–64
    pointer, 803
    static, 803
    subscripted, 472–81, 561–64
Variance, 247
Vector processing, 516–19
Vectors, 516
    arithmetic of, 519
    components of, 517
    norm of, 517
    sum of two, 518
Verification, 32
Vignere cipher, 682
Volatile memory, 10
von Liebnitz, Gottfried Wilhelm, 3, 4
von Neumann, John, 6

W

WHERE construct, 555
While loop, 197–200, 236, 238, 239, 250
    implementing, 200–205
Word, 12, 842
Workstation, 7
Wozniak, Steve, 7
WRITE statement, 30, 39, 67–68, 92, 100 282–84,
        302–03, 729, 755–56

X

X descriptor, 264–65, 276

Examples, Applications, and Sample Programs

Chapter 1

Radioactive decay (pp. 16–23)

Chapter 2

Velocity of a projectile (pp. 66–72, 93, 115–116)
Temperature conversion (pp. 76–81, 116–117)
Circuits with parallel resistors (pp. 82–85)
Acid dilution (pp. 85–91)

Chapter 3

Quadratic equations (pp. 131–134)
Effect of roundoff error (pp. 134–136)
Pollution index classification (pp. 136–141, 148, 151, 178–179)
Pay calculation (pp. 142–146)
Fluid flow in a pipe (pp. 151–156)
Logical circuits (pp. 161–165)

Chapter 4

Calculating depreciation (pp. 181–182, 191–197)
Mean time to failure (pp. 182, 205–213, 252–253)
Damped vibration curve (pp. 185–187)
List of products of two numbers (pp. 187–189)
Summation of integers (pp. 197–200, 201–205)
Temperature conversions (pp. 213–216)
Range of noise levels (in decibels) (pp. 216–223)
Least-squares line (pp. 230–236)

Chapter 5

Table of computed values (pp. 269–271, 312–313)
Time, temperature, pressure, and volume readings (pp. 292–300)

Chapter 6

Voltages across a capacitor (pp. 319–321, 331)
Pollution index classification (pp. 323–324)
Poisson probability (pp. 325–329)
Beam deflection (pp. 334–344)
Root finding—Newton's method (pp. 344–348)
Numerical integration—trapezoidal method (pp. 348–352, 370–373, 388–390)
Differential equations—Euler's method (pp. 352–356)
Differential equations—Runge–Kutta method (p. 356)
Road construction (pp. 357–361)
Counting paths in a street network (recursively) (pp. 390–391)

Chapter 7

Displaying an angle in degrees (pp. 395–398)
Displaying an angle in degrees–minutes–seconds format (pp. 398–402)
Conversion of polar coordinates to rectangular coordinates (pp. 402–406, 453–454, 468–469)
Designing a coin dispenser (pp. 410–416)
Using random numbers in a dice-roll simulation (pp. 417–421)
Normal distribution (pp. 421–422)